ANNUAL 2012

The New York Times

THE OBITS

ANNUAL 2012

Edited and With an Introduction by
WILLIAM McDONALD

Foreword by Pete Hamill

WORKMAN PUBLISHING • NEW YORK

Published simultaneously in Canada by Thomas Allen & Son Limited.

ISBN 978-0-7611-6576-7
ISSN 2162-6839

Design by Orlando Adiao

Workman Publishing Company, Inc.
225 Varick Street
New York, NY 10014-4381

www.workman.com

Printed in the United States of America
First printing October 2011

10 9 8 7 6 5 4 3 2 1

TABLE OF CONTENTS

OCTOBER 2010

NOVEMBER 2010

DECEMBER 2010

JANUARY 2011

APRIL 2011

MAY 2011

JUNE 2011

JULY 2011

FOREWORD

by Pete Hamill

THE CAUSE OF DEATH, of course, is always life. We humans all die, a fact so unremarkable that in these tightly rendered portraits of the recently dead, the technical reason for death is almost always covered in a single sentence. What matters is the life, and how it was lived.

Obviously, the editors of The New York Times could fill every column of every page in the daily newspaper with stories of the newly dead. They narrow the choices to people whose accomplishments have mattered to others, or whose fame or notoriety might require more than a curt, cold footnote. That is, they choose people whose lives have helped shape the tale of their times. These men and women come from various small worlds within the larger society: art, politics, government, the law, sports, crime, science, media, movies, theater, music. Most eras are remembered as highlight films, with certain politicians and generals hogging center stage, and others adding soundtracks, or creating the entertainments that become part of collective memory. The individual stories are always part of a larger tale.

Most writers of obituaries (and I've written a few myself at other newspapers) know that they are not presenting the last words on their subjects. Many lives await full biographies, informed by the testimony of friends and enemies, wives, husbands and children, the secrets of correspondence, or F.B.I. files, or hard research into the assumptions of the present tense. It is always easier to describe a monster (biographies are still being written about Hitler) than a person who improved the world with laughter, intelligence or grace. Great biographies usually require the distance and objectivity that comes with the passage of time. The true value of some human beings can begin to rise while other reputations fade into obscurity, like statues in leafy corners of a public park. All obituaries are journalism, first drafts of history, but not history itself. An obit is made of knowable facts. It is not a eulogy, pasty with oratory. Nor is it an indictment. The obit says: here's why this human was important, at the moment of writing.

And yet the obituary in the daily paper can provoke true emotions in the minds of many readers. There is a sense of finality to every obit, the fall of a last curtain. No matter what the reader thought of the subject, that man, that woman no matter how remarkable cannot add another sentence to his or her role in the ongoing story of the times. It's over. If the person is admired, we mourn the death and celebrate the life. If the person is despised, we remember the reasons for our contempt. And then turn the page.

An obit is made of knowable facts. It is not a eulogy, pasty with oratory. Nor is it an indictment. The obit says: here's why this human was important, at the moment of writing.

For some readers, turning the page is not always easy. If the subject is someone we knew, reading the obit is also charged with a certain genuine sorrow. It announces a permanent interruption, often leading to absurd moments. Of the honored dead in this volume, I've wanted to call Elaine Kaufman and ask her what she thought of the Times obit. The same with Wilfrid Sheed, and Norris Church Mailer, and Jack Levine, and Burt Roberts. They were friends. And I remain filled with questions that I never asked them, or jokes I never passed on, or affection I never expressed.

And because I was a journalist for five decades, a privileged witness through possession of a press card, there are others here that I knew in more casual, glancing ways: Peter Yates and Sargent Shriver, Arthur Penn and George Shearing, Edwin Newman and David Broder, Bobby Thomson and Ted Kheel, Paul Conrad and Kevin McCarthy, Tony Curtis and Billy Taylor. I learned something from each of them. I've learned even more about them than I thought I knew, from reading these handsomely etched obituaries.

Reading them as a whole, they've also made me think about the times that produced so many of this volume's honored dead. They lived the formative years of their lives during the Great Depression, when for their parents, often immigrants, a job any job was an elusive goal. Work that you actually loved was thought to be a romantic delusion. That was a time of austerity and limits for millions of Americans, and the four years of savage war that followed Pearl Harbor added to the sense of the future deferred. Where I lived in working-class Brooklyn, none of the young men profited from the war. They fought it.

But there were advantages to those years, too. Many of the people here were young in the years before the triumph of television, a time when kids went to public libraries to find free entertainment in books (along with visions of the wider world). They couldn't afford expensive food or fancy clothes or a university. They were careful about money, and even the rich avoided presenting any image of luxury or extravagance. But there came a time, after 1945, when an optimistic sense of the American future was made real for millions by the G.I. Bill of Rights. Including some of the people in this book. Yes: obituaries are about people one at a time. But they are also part of a collective narrative.

So are all of us who lived during even a small part of their time on the stage. The obits remind us of the role of accident, chance or luck in the living of any life, along with determination and will. Most of us have learned lessons about life and its brother, death, from people who seldom make their way into the obituaries of any newspaper. One lesson is the acceptance of the inevitable. As the writer and entertainer Malachy McCourt likes to say: "I come from a long line of dead people."

As do we all.

INTRODUCTION

by William McDonald

An estimated 55.5 million people around the world die every year, a population almost the size of Italy's. The New York Times obituary pages acknowledge about 1,000 of them.

Put another way, roughly 155,000 people die between any one issue of the newspaper and the next — a daily toll large enough to fill Yankee Stadium three times over. On average, The Times will publish obits about three of them.

As The Times's obituaries editor, I spend a good part of my day huddling with my colleagues to select those scant few, and as the editor of this book, working with far less space than a year's worth of broadsheet allows — to say nothing of the boundless Internet — I've had the daunting task of whittling the roster even more, of choosing among the already chosen, of separating the extraordinary from the merely exceptional.

Of course, the wider pool of candidates from which The Times draws is hardly in the tens of millions, or even in the tens of thousands; as a news organization, we may try to keep our finger on the pulse of the world, but not to that degree. We start with an only paper-thin fraction of the total — the deaths we happen to hear about — and then get choosy. We're exclusive in the extreme. We have to be. We have only so much space, so many hands and so many hours in the day, and we have a very wide world to watch.

By necessity, then, but also by choice, we confine ourselves to writing about people who made a difference on a large stage — people, we think, who will command the broadest interest. If you made news in life, the rule of thumb goes, chances are your death is news, too. We may betray an occasional hometown bias, but we generally cast our net well beyond the Hudson River and Long Island Sound. (Besides, we find that many people far from New York want to read all about it all the same, whether out of love, hate or curiosity.)

News of a death most often arrives by e-mail — almost never by the postman these days — or someone picks up the phone. Sometimes a Web site or a wire service alerts us, or another newspaper does, having beaten us to the punch. (Even the obituary trade can be competitive.) And sometimes we hear by simple word of mouth.

Like deans of admission, we sift through the candidates, study their curriculums vitae, read their letters of reference and sort the prospects into piles: yes, no, maybe. (An entirely separate, smaller and somehow poignant batch is composed of material submitted by fully breathing obituary candidates themselves, asking us to keep it on file for that inevitable day.) We also do our own homework: we investigate, research and ask around before deciding yes, no or maybe.

Some might think our exclusivity presumptuous. Who, after all, anointed the editors of The New York Times to stand by the roadside as a parade of humanity passes and single out this one, this one and that one (but not that one) as worthy of being remembered?

We seek only to report deaths and to sum up lives, illuminating why, in our judgment, those lives were significant — why, that is, we've chosen them. The justification for the obituary is in the story it tells.

The answer is that no one did, actually, because that is not precisely what we decide. We make no judgments, moral or otherwise, about human worth. What we do try to judge, however, is newsworthiness, and that's a whole other standard.

Nor, by the way, is it our intent to honor the dead; we leave the tributes to the eulogists. We seek only to report deaths and to sum up lives, illuminating why, in our judgment, those lives were significant — why, that is, we've chosen them. The justification for the obituary is in the story it tells.

We use no formula, scoring system or checklist to determine who will make the cut. But we do hold to certain criteria, slippery as they may be. Fame, of the widespread kind, will usually get someone past the velvet ropes, no questions asked. Tony Curtis? Right this way, sir. Accomplishment, with wide impact, matters as much, and it often goes hand in hand with fame. Bob Feller left an indelible mark on the baseball record books, and he was long celebrated for it. Joan Sutherland's incomparable voice still echoes around the world.

But achievement may also speak softly. The work of Eugene Goldwasser and Baruch Blumberg, in the quiet of their biomedical research laboratories, helped preserve and even save the lives of millions, and for that they deserved to be remembered, as they were in The Times and as they are between these covers.

Still others may be chosen in part to represent a group whose contributions were forgotten or ignored. Violet Cowden, a member of the Women Airforce Service Pilots in World War II, comes to mind. Her story is included here. So is that of Barney Hajiro, one of 22 Japanese-American soldiers who, slighted by racial prejudice, waited more than half a century for their battlefield valor to be recognized with Medals of Honor. Some died waiting.

Always eager to write about such unsung heroes and heroines, we look at everyone who comes our way, never dismissing anyone out of hand, and confer:

Manfred Gans? *Who was he?* Great story. He's sent to England as a teen-ager to escape the Nazis, joins the British army, then makes his way across Europe through German-held territory to find his parents in a concentration camp. *Great story indeed. And it's been verified? Then let's do it.*

Don Van Vliet. *Oh, you mean Captain Beefheart. Absolutely.*

Robbins Barstow? *What did he do?* He documented his postwar suburban family in home movies, captured a cultural moment and inspired a home-movie revival. *That's a tale worth telling. Yes.*

What about Joanne Siegel? *Come again?* Joanne Siegel: you might call her the original Lois Lane. *Are we sure? O.K.*

But for every yes there are innumerable no's. A baseball player who lasted a season. A beloved professor who never published. An actor whose star had faded. Fame and accomplishment are relative; the public eye is easily distracted, and only a moment or two in its fickle gaze may not be enough to merit a backward look in The Times. The same might be said of a sparkling résumé. The best schools, a successful corporate climb, charitable good works and distinguished service awards are impressive and laudable, but not necessarily newsworthy to a national readership.

With rejection often comes disappointment, and sometimes vexation. One man once wrote asking how we could choose to write about a gangster while ignoring his father, who had sat on a dozen boards of directors. We might rather have had dinner with his father, to be sure, but the answer was that the gangster had made headlines — in 48-point type in the tabloids. (Which brings to mind another qualification for newsworthiness, that black-sheep sibling of fame: infamy.)

Once our decisions are made, the writers take over. Most people refer to any newspaper article as a story, but probably none deserves that description more than an obituary. These are life stories, after all, told with the urgency of journalism and the sweep of biography. They have beginnings and, unlike most newspaper stories, endings. They carry news, certainly — the fact of death — but once that has been reported, usually in the first paragraph, very little, if anything, is said about it from then on. It's the life we're interested in, and distilling it into 600, 900 or 2,000 words — the count is another measure of newsworthiness — is something of an art.

It's also something of an impossibility, for any life is too full and nuanced and complex to be compressed into a slender column of words in 8.7-point Imperial (not Times Roman, incidentally). But a good reporter, plumbing biographical sources, public documents and the memories of the living, can nevertheless offer a fair rendering. What emerges is a kind of portrait, as on a canvas stretched on a frame. The long, messy business of a life cannot all be contained there, but if the work is done well, the essential elements will be present, and the likeness, a composition of broad strokes and fine details, will be an honest one.

The obituary writers at The Times did that routinely over the course of a year, alongside critics and commentators who sometimes stood back to appraise the deceased. All had good material to work with: some of the most consequential, fascinating and colorful figures of our age. You might think of this book, then, as a gallery of their portraits, mounted cheek by jowl according to a chronology of last days, some finding themselves in agreeable company, others beside strange bedfellows, all of them bound together by the inscrutable accident of death.

They invite us to look, at who they were and what they did in their hour upon the stage, and perhaps to reflect, on the passage of a year, and on the passing of an era.

THE OBITS

AUGUST 2010
TO JULY 2011

ROBERT F. BOYLE

Behind the Scenes, a Hollywood Virtuoso

OCT. 10, 1909 - AUG. 1, 2010

ROBERT F. BOYLE, the eminent Hollywood production designer who created some of the most memorable scenes and images in cinematic history — Cary Grant clinging to Mount Rushmore in "North by Northwest," the bird's-eye view of the seagull attack in "The Birds," the colorfully ramshackle shtetl for "Fiddler on the Roof" — died on Aug. 1 in Los Angeles. He was 100.

Mr. Boyle worked on more than 80 films as art director or production designer, synonyms for a job he once defined as "being responsible for the space in which a film takes place."

As a young assistant fresh out of architecture school at the University of Southern California, he worked on the Cecil B. DeMille western "The Plainsman" (1936) and Fritz Lang's "You and Me" (1938). Over the next six decades he worked with a long list of top directors, including Douglas Sirk, Richard Brooks and Norman Jewison.

At the 2008 Academy Awards, as his list of credits was read aloud, he stepped onto the stage to tumultuous applause to receive a special Oscar for his life's work in art direction.

Mr. Boyle is best known for his work with Alfred Hitchcock, with whom he produced indelible scenes like the climactic struggle atop the Statue of Liberty in "Saboteur" and the crop-dusting sequence with Cary Grant in "North by Northwest," not to mention the seagull attack in

STUDIO MAGIC: Mr. Boyle used a toy plane for the crop-duster sequence with Cary Grant in Hitchcock's "North by Northwest." He and Hitchcock collaborated on many films, including "Shadow of a Doubt" and "The Birds."

AUG

"The Birds." He was also Hitchcock's production designer for "Marnie."

"It was a meeting of equals: the director who knew exactly what he wanted, and the art director who knew how to get it done," Mr. Boyle told Film Comment in 1978.

His art direction earned him Academy Award nominations for "North by Northwest" and "Fiddler on the Roof" as well as for "Gaily, Gaily," a period comedy set in early 20th-century Chicago, and "The Shootist," John Wayne's last film. He was also the subject of an Oscar-nominated 2000 documentary by Daniel Raim, "The Man on Lincoln's Nose."

Mr. Jewison called Mr. Boyle "the last of the great art directors."

"His films have a look, an ambience, a setting that's very real because of his scrupulous attention to detail," Mr. Jewison said in an interview for this obituary. "Every nuance he could bring to bear to make a film real, he'd do it. He was a real cinematic artist."

Robert Francis Boyle was born on Oct. 10, 1909, in Los Angeles and grew up on a ranch in the San Joaquin Valley. His degree in architecture, received in 1933, was of little use during the Depression, so he began working as a bit player for RKO Pictures. Fascinated by set design, he introduced himself to the studio's art director, who directed him to Paramount. There he was hired by the great art director Hans Dreier, and wound up doing a bit of everything.

"We were illustrators, draftsmen, we would supervise the construction on the sets," he told an interviewer for the Margaret Herrick Library of the Academy of Motion Picture Arts and Sciences in 1998. "We did almost anything that the art director thought we ought to do."

After doing second-unit work on "The Plainsman," with Gary Cooper, and "Union Pacific," both directed by Cecil B. DeMille, and "Lives of a Bengal Lancer," Mr. Boyle left Paramount to paint in Mexico but soon returned to the United States and began working for RKO and Universal. One of his first films for Universal was "The Wolf Man" (1941), with Lon Chaney Jr.

Art directors enjoyed a varied diet in those days. "We might be doing the Bengal Lancers one day and Ma and Pa Kettle the next and something else the next," he told the Herrick Library.

"Saboteur" (1942) was his first collaboration with Hitchcock and the beginning of a series of unforgettably suspenseful cinematic sequences. For the climactic battle between Robert Cummings and Norman Lloyd, Mr. Boyle and his team constructed a studio model of the hand and the torch of the Statue of Liberty. To create the illusion that Mr. Lloyd, the villain, was falling in an uncontrolled spin from a great height, Mr. Boyle twirled him on a revolving chair as a crane mounted with a camera swooped upward at dizzying speed.

Mr. Boyle worked with Hitchcock on one more film, "Shadow of a Doubt," before serving in the Army Signal Corps in France and Germany as a combat photographer during World War II. After the war they resumed their collaboration, and he married Bess Taffel, a contract writer at RKO who was blacklisted during the McCarthy era. She died in 2000. Mr. Boyle, who lived in Los Angeles, is survived by two daughters and three grandchildren.

Mr. Boyle's touch is evident in the cleverly orchestrated Mount Rushmore sequence in "North by Northwest," in which large-format still photographs were rear-projected using stereopticon slides. He also used studio mock-ups of sections of the stone heads — "just enough to put the actors on so we could get down shots, up shots, side shots, whatever we needed," Mr. Boyle said. For the famous scene in which a crop-duster strafes Cary Grant on a desolate road, Mr. Boyle combined location footage with a toy airplane and toy truck on a miniature field created in the studio.

Mr. Boyle said that the attack sequence in "The Birds" may have been his trickiest bit of work. To simulate the point of view of the swooping birds descending on Tippi Hedren in a phone booth, Mr. Boyle and his team climbed a cliff overlooking an island off Santa Barbara, Calif., and photographed seagulls as assistants threw fish into the water, encouraging the birds to dive. Only the telephone booth was real. The town of Bodega Bay, actually a composite of several towns, was reproduced on mattes.

For "Gaily, Gaily," Mr. Boyle re-created turn-of-the-century Chicago on a backlot at Universal, right down to the elevated tracks in the Loop. Notoriously finicky about locations, he traveled the length and breadth of Eastern Europe for "Fiddler on the Roof" before settling on a location in what was then Yugoslavia.

For "In Cold Blood," based on Truman Capote's book about multiple murders in Kansas, Mr. Boyle took the opposite tack, using as a set the actual farmhouse where the killings took place.

Trickery for its own sake did not interest him. "If it doesn't have any meaningful application to the story, it's never a great shot," he said.

Mr. Boyle took on projects of every description. He worked on Ma and Pa Kettle comedies and "Abbott and Costello Go to Mars." He was the art director for Sam Fuller on "The Crimson Kimono" and for J. Lee Thompson on "Cape Fear." He was the production designer for "The Shootist" and "Private Benjamin."

A movie, he said, "starts with the locale, with the environment that people live in, how they move within that environment." Sometimes that environment has to be built.

"I'm all for construction, because we're dealing with the magic of movies," he told Variety in 2008. "And I always feel that if you build it, you build it for the dream rather than the actuality. We make up our own truth."

— *By William Grimes*

LOLITA LEBRÓN

'Viva Puerto Rico!' and Shots Rang Out

NOV. 19, 1919 - AUG. 1, 2010

LOLITA LEBRÓN, who blazed her way to notoriety with a Luger pistol and patriotic shouts as she led three other Puerto Rican nationalists in an attack on the United States House of Representatives on March 1, 1954, died on Aug. 1 in San Juan, P.R. She was 90.

In the attack in the Capitol, Ms. Lebrón and the other assailants fired from a spectator's gallery just above the House floor, raining as many as 30 bullets into a chaotic chamber and wounding five congressmen.

Ms. Lebrón was imprisoned for 25 years and widely condemned as a terrorist, although proponents of Puerto Rican independence hailed her and her associates as revolutionary heroes. She ascended into a leftist pantheon with figures like Che Guevara, becoming the subject of books and artwork.

Ms. Lebrón remained proud of the shooting, which came two years after Puerto Rico, formerly a territory of the United States, became a commonwealth, adopting its own constitution as ratified by Congress and approved by President Harry S. Truman. She dismissed that status as only more colonization and demanded complete independence. On the day of the shooting she fully expected to give up her life.

Her political convictions never disappeared. In her 80s she was arrested twice for protesting an American military base on Puerto Rico's island of Vieques. She served 60 days in jail.

But in her latter decades Ms. Lebrón came to believe that civil disobedience, like that at Vieques, was not only more moral than violence, but it was more effective.

"There is no need now to kill for freedom," she said in 1998.

After her release from prison, Puerto Ricans

of all political leanings would hail her on the street — she typically dressed in black — as a sort of national elder. They called her only Doña Lolita. No last name was necessary.

On the blustery, rainy day of the shooting 56 years ago, Ms. Lebrón was a stylishly dressed 34-year-old woman with the looks of the beauty queen she had been as a youth. She wore bright lipstick.

At 2:32 P.M., with 243 representatives in attendance, firecrackers suddenly seemed to be exploding in the House chamber, interrupting a debate about Mexican farm workers. Congressmen dived and fell, though none were killed.

Piercing the confusion was the voice of Ms. Lebrón: "Viva Puerto Rico!" Pointing it at the ceiling, she emptied the chambers of a big Luger pistol, holding it in two hands and waving it wildly. She then threw down the pistol and whipped out a Puerto Rican flag, which she waved but never managed to unfurl completely. As she shouted, her companions trained their weapons on the House floor.

PRISON-BOUND: Ms. Lebrón in police custody after opening fire in the United States Capitol in 1954.

After she was arrested, the police found a note in her purse. "My life I give for the freedom of my country," it read.

Ms. Lebrón was convicted of five counts of assault with a dangerous weapon and sentenced to serve from 16 years and 8 months to 50 years in prison. Her colleagues, Rafael Cancel Miranda, Andres Figueroa Cordero and Irving Flores Rodríguez, were convicted on more serious counts and each sentenced to 25 to 75 years in prison.

Although Ms. Lebrón fired eight shots, she was cleared of assault with intent to kill because she had not fired at the House floor. All four shooters were later sentenced to an additional six years in another trial for seditious conspiracy.

Dolores Lebrón de Perez was born on Nov. 19, 1919, in Lares, P.R., a small town where her father was a coffee plantation foreman. She finished eighth grade, and she was elected "Queen of the Flowers of May" in a beauty pageant.

She had a daughter and a son, both of whom died years ago. Ms. Lebrón is survived by her husband, Dr. Sergio Irizarry; a sister; and two grandchildren.

In the 1940s Ms. Lebrón moved to New York seeking a better life, and found work as a seamstress. She became a follower of Pedro Albizu Campos, a nationalist leader. Deciding a drastic event was needed to highlight his cause, he assigned Ms. Lebrón to lead it, making her responsible for every detail.

"I had all the secrets, all the plans," she told The Washington Post Magazine in 2004. "Me and me alone."

The planning was not perfect. The conspirators got lost on the way to the Capitol from Union Station and had to ask a pedestrian for directions.

During the trial, Ms. Lebrón repudiated an argument by her own lawyer that the conspirators were mentally unsound, shouting "No! No! No!"

When the prosecution let a Puerto Rican flag drag on the floor, she whispered to her lawyer and he successfully objected.

In prison, she built an altar in her cell and said she had repeated ecstatic religious visions. She refused to apply for parole because that would have meant apologizing.

In 1979, President Jimmy Carter, saying he was acting out of "humane considerations," released Ms. Lebrón and two other assailants, a move that was expected to clear the way for the release of four Americans being held in Cuban prisons. He had released the fourth assailant in 1978 because he had cancer.

Many Puerto Ricans opposed the clemency. Puerto Rico's nonvoting representative in Congress at the time, Baltasar Corrado del Río, said the assailants had been "kept in jail for their criminal conduct, not their political beliefs."

Ms. Lebrón remained defiant, saying her release "was done for political expediency and not because of a concern for human rights."

— *By Douglas Martin*

TONY JUDT

Historian in the Public Square

JAN. 2, 1948 - AUG. 6, 2010

TONY JUDT, the author of "Postwar," a monumental history of Europe after World War II, and a public intellectual known for his sharply polemical essays on American foreign policy, the state of Israel and the future of Europe, died on Aug. 6 at his home in Manhattan. He was 62.

The death was announced in a statement from New York University, where he had taught for many years. The cause was complications of amyotrophic lateral sclerosis, known as Lou Gehrig's disease, which he learned he had in September 2008. In a matter of months the disease left him paralyzed and able to breathe only with mechanical assistance, but he continued to lecture and write.

"In effect," Mr. Judt wrote in an essay published in January in The New York Review of Books, "A.L.S. constitutes progressive imprisonment without parole."

Mr. Judt (pronounced Jutt), who was British by birth and education but who taught at American universities for most of his career, began as a specialist in postwar French intellectual history, and for much of his life he embodied the idea of the French-style engaged intellectual.

An impassioned left-wing Zionist as a teenager, he shed his faith in agrarian socialism and Marxism early on and became, as he put it, a "universalist social democrat" with a deep suspicion of left-wing ideologues, identity politics and the emerging role of the United States as the world's sole superpower.

His developing interest in Europe as a whole, including the states of the former Eastern Bloc, led him to take an active role in the unfolding Velvet Revolution in Czechoslovakia; it culminated in "Postwar: A History of Europe Since 1945" (2005), a richly detailed survey embracing countries from Britain to the Balkans. In the words of one reviewer, the book has "the pace of a thriller and the scope of an encyclopedia."

Mr. Judt was well known for his essays on politics and current affairs in journals like The New York Review of Books, The New Republic, The Times Literary Supplement and The London Review of Books.

"He had the unusual ability to see and convey the big picture while, at the same time, going to the heart of the matter," said Mark Lilla, who teaches intellectual history at Columbia University. "Most academics do neither — they float in between. But Tony was able to talk about the big picture and explain why it matters now."

Tony Robert Judt was born in the East End of London on Jan. 2, 1948, and grew up in Putney. His parents, although secular and apolitical Jews, encouraged him to join the Labor Zionist youth organization Dror as a way to meet friends. He became a fervent convert to the cause, spending summers working on a kibbutz in Israel and serving as Dror's national secretary from 1965 to 1967.

"I was the ideal recruit: articulate, committed and uncompromisingly ideologically conformist," he wrote in an autobiographical sketch for The New York Review of Books in February.

After he passed the entrance examinations to King's College, Cambridge, he volunteered as an auxiliary with the Israeli Defense Forces during the Six-Day War, acting as an interpreter for other volunteers in the newly conquered Golan Heights. There he lost faith in the Zionist mission and began to see Israel as a malign occupying power whose self-definition as a Jewish state, he later argued, made it "an anachronism."

Mr. Judt returned to Britain disabused and highly skeptical of the radical political currents swirling around him at Cambridge, where he earned a bachelor's degree in history from King's College in 1969. After studying for a year at the École Normale Supérieure in Paris, he returned to King's College and earned a doctorate in 1972.

"I'm regarded outside N.Y.U. as a looney-tunes leftie self-hating Jewish communist; inside the university I'm regarded as a typical old-fashioned white male liberal elitist. I like that."

His dissertation, on the French Socialist Party's re-emergence after World War I, was published in France as "La Reconstruction du Parti Socialiste: 1921-1926" (1976). In 1979 he followed up with "Socialism in Provence, 1871-1914: A Study in the Origins of the Modern French Left," and in 1986 he published "Marxism and the French Left: Studies on Labour and Politics in France, 1830-1981."

These relatively specialist works led to two interpretive studies of French postwar intellectual life: "Past Imperfect: French Intellectuals, 1944-1956" (1994) and "The Burden of Responsibility: Blum, Camus, Aron and the French Twentieth Century" (1998).

Casting his lot with the nonideological liberals, like Raymond Aron and Albert Camus, who dared to criticize the Soviet Union and third-world revolutionary movements, Mr. Judt subjected Sartre and others to a withering critique that came as a shock to many French and American intellectuals. His target, he wrote, was "the uneasy conscience and moral cowardice of an intellectual generation."

Fluidly written, with a strong narrative drive and an insistent, polemical edge, both books established Mr. Judt as a historian whose ability to see the present in the past gave his work an unusual air of immediacy. Increasingly he inclined toward free-ranging inquiry across disciplines, as reflected in the essay collection "Reappraisals: Reflections on the Forgotten Twentieth Century" (2008).

"A historian also has to be an anthropologist, also has to be a philosopher, also has to be a moralist, also has to understand the economics of the period he is writing about," Mr. Judt told the online magazine Historically Speaking in 2006. "Though they are often arbitrary, disciplinary boundaries certainly exist. Nevertheless, the historian has to learn to transcend them in order to write intelligently."

In 1987, after teaching at Cambridge, the University of California at Berkeley and Oxford, he began teaching at N.Y.U. There, in 1995, he helped found the Remarque Institute with a bequest from Paulette Goddard, the widow of the writer Erich Maria Remarque. Under his directorship, it became an important international center for the study of Europe, past and present. His skepticism about the future of the European Union found expression in a sharply polemical, pamphlet-length book, "A Grand Illusion?: An Essay on Europe" (1996).

His first two marriages ended in divorce. He is survived by his wife, the dance critic Jennifer Homans, and their two sons.

His views on Israel made Mr. Judt an increasingly polarizing figure. He placed himself in the midst of a bitter debate when, in 2003, he outlined a one-state solution to the Israel-Palestinian problem in The New York Review of Books, proposing that Israel accept a future as a secular, binational state in which Jews and Arabs enjoyed equal status.

In 2006, a scheduled talk at the Polish Consulate in Manhattan was abruptly canceled for reasons later hotly disputed, but apparently under pressure, explicit or implicit, from the Anti-Defamation League and the American Jewish Committee.

Leon Wieseltier, the literary editor of The New Republic, told The New York Observer at the time that Mr. Judt, on Israel, "has become precisely the kind of intellectual whom his intellectual heroes would have despised." Mr. Judt's name had been removed from the masthead of the magazine, where he had been a contributing editor, after his article on the one-state solution.

He expressed surprise that he should be defined by his position on one issue and expressed distaste for public controversy, while showing an unmistakable relish for the cut and thrust of public debate.

"Today I'm regarded outside New York University as a looney-tunes leftie self-hating Jewish communist; inside the university I'm regarded as a typical old-fashioned white male liberal elitist," he told The Guardian of London in January 2010. "I like that. I'm on the edge of both; it makes me feel comfortable."

His discovery in 2008 that he had Lou Gehrig's disease did not deter him from his work.

In October 2010, wrapped in a blanket and sitting in a wheelchair with a breathing device attached to his nose, Mr. Judt spoke about social democracy before an audience of 700 at N.Y.U. He turned that lecture into a small book, "Ill Fares the Land," published in March 2011 by Penguin Press.

During the lecture, his last public appearance, he told the audience that some of his American friends felt that seeing him talk about A.L.S. would be uplifting. But he added, "I'm English, and we don't do 'uplifting.'"

He did write about his illness. In an essay in The New York Review of Books, he wrote, "In contrast to almost every other serious or deadly disease, one is thus left free to contemplate at leisure and in minimal discomfort the catastrophic progress of one's own deterioration."

But history remained uppermost in his mind. In "Ill Fares the Land," he turned his attention to a problem he regarded as acute: the loss of faith in social democracy, which had brought prosperity to so many European countries after World War II, and in the power of the state to do good.

"The historian's task is not to disrupt for the sake of it, but it is to tell what is almost always an uncomfortable story and explain why the discomfort is part of the truth we need to live well and live properly," he told Historically Speaking. "A well-organized society is one in which we know the truth about ourselves collectively, not one in which we tell pleasant lies about ourselves."

— *By William Grimes*

AUG

PATRICIA NEAL

An Acting Life of Accolades and Anguish

JAN. 20, 1926 - AUG. 8, 2010

PATRICIA NEAL, who made her way from Kentucky's coal country to Hollywood and Broadway, winning an Academy Award and a Tony, but whose life alternated almost surreally between triumph and tragedy, died on Aug. 8 at her home in Edgartown, Mass., on Martha's Vineyard. She was 84.

She had lung cancer, a friend told The Associated Press. Ms. Neal had a home in Manhattan as well.

Ms. Neal received her Oscar, as best actress, for her performance in 1963 as the tough, shopworn housekeeper who does not succumb to Paul Newman's amoral charm in "Hud." By then she had already endured the death of her first child and a calamitous injury to her infant son, who was brain-damaged in an accident. Then came three strokes, a year after the Oscar, leaving her in a coma for three weeks.

Afterward she was semiparalyzed and unable to speak.

But she learned to walk and talk again with the help of her husband, the British writer Roald Dahl. And in 1968, despite a severely impaired memory that made it difficult to recall dialogue, she returned to the screen as the bitter mother who used her son as a weapon against her husband in the screen version of Frank Gilroy's play "The Subject Was Roses." Once again she was nominated for an Oscar.

Ms. Neal's career started swiftly and brilliantly. Before she was 21 she won a Tony and a New York Drama Critics' Circle Award for her Broadway debut in "Another Part of the Forest" by Lillian Hellman. Her picture was on the cover of Life magazine.

Signed by Warner Brothers, she went to Hollywood as the sought-after young actress of her day. She had talent, a husky, unforgettable voice and an arresting presence, but no training for the camera. Of her movie debut opposite Ronald Reagan in the comedy "John Loves Mary" (1949), Bosley Crowther, the movie critic for The New York Times, wrote that she showed "little to recommend her to further comedy jobs."

Yet Ms. Neal had already been assigned the role that Barbara Stanwyck coveted — the leonine Dominique in the film adaptation of Ayn Rand's best-selling novel "The Fountainhead" (1949). As Dominique was swept away by the godlike architect Howard Roark, Ms. Neal, at 23, fell in love with the 48-year-old movie star who played Roark, Gary Cooper. Their affair lasted three years but ended when Mr. Cooper chose not to leave his family.

"The Fountainhead" was a failure. Ms. Neal saw it at a Hollywood premiere. "You knew, from the very first reel, it was destined to be a monumental bomb," she said. "My status changed immediately. That was the end of my career as a second Garbo."

Ms. Neal's next movie, "Bright Leaf" (1950), an epic story of a 19th-century tobacco farmer played by Cooper, was also a failure. Ill served by Warner Brothers, Ms. Neal acquired screen technique while being wasted in mediocre movies. The exceptions were the screen version of John Patrick's play "The Hasty Heart" (1950) and "The Breaking Point" (1950), based on Ernest Hemingway's "To Have and Have Not."

"Warners finally let me know they weren't so keen on my staying on," Ms. Neal once said. "They didn't fire me. I took the hint."

She was 27 and apparently washed up after five years and 13 movies when Hellman insisted that Ms. Neal star in the Broadway revival of her play "The Children's Hour" in 1952. It was at Hellman's house that Ms. Neal met Dahl, then a writer of macabre short stories; they would marry and have five children in a troubled, 30-year marriage.

In 1957, Ms. Neal triumphantly returned to the screen in Budd Schulberg's "A Face in the Crowd," directed by Elia Kazan. Showing a range she had lacked before, she was praised for her portrayal of a radio reporter who builds the career of a folksy guitarist (played by Andy Griffith).

As the 1950s ended, she appeared to great acclaim in Tennessee Williams's "Suddenly Last Summer" on the London stage and in "The Miracle Worker" on Broadway, then went on to even greater screen success in "Hud" and "In Harm's Way" with John Wayne. Riding the crest, she signed to star in the John Ford movie "Seven Women." But at 39 and pregnant with her fifth child, she suffered the strokes.

Patsy Lou Neal was born in the coal mining town of Packard, Ky., on Jan. 20, 1926, to a mine manager and the daughter of the town doctor. Ms. Neal grew up in Knoxville, Tenn. At 10, she attended an evening of monologues in the basement of the Methodist church and wrote a note to Santa Claus: "What I want for Christmas is to study dramatics." By high school, Patsy Neal was giving monologues at social clubs and had won the Tennessee State Award for dramatic reading.

In 1942, before her senior year, she was chosen to apprentice at the prestigious Barter Theater in Virginia. After two years as a drama major at Northwestern University, she headed to New York, where she worked as an understudy before replacing Vivian Vance in a road company production of "Voice of the Turtle," which

THAT OSCAR GLOW: Ms. Neal at her home in England, in 1964, two days after winning an Academy Award for her role in "Hud."

During her affair with Cooper she became pregnant and had an abortion, according to the autobiography "As I Am" (1988), written with Richard DeNeut. "If I had only one thing to do over in my life," she wrote, "I would have that baby."

Eager to have children, she married Dahl in 1953, even though she did not love him then, she wrote. A former R.A.F. fighter pilot who became a renowned writer of often darkly humorous children's books ("James and the Giant Peach," "Charlie and the Chocolate Factory"), Dahl took control of Ms. Neal's life. After their 4-month-old son, Theo, was left brain-damaged when his baby carriage was crushed between a taxicab and a bus on a New York street in 1960, Dahl decided that they would move to the village of Great Missenden in England. Two years later, their eldest daughter, Olivia, who was 7, died of measles encephalitis, perhaps for want of sophisticated medical care that would have been available in a big city.

had been produced on Broadway by Alfred de Liagre. He had insisted that this patrician-looking new actress call herself Patricia.

Her big break came as a backwoods girl who allies herself with the devil in a summer stock production of "Devil Takes a Whittler" in Westport, Conn. Eugene O'Neill, who became her mentor, saw the performance, and so did much of the Broadway establishment. In less than 24 hours she had two offers to star on Broadway. Ms. Neal turned down Richard Rodgers's offer of the lead in "John Loves Mary" for Hellman's "Another Part of the Forest."

Hollywood soon called, and she signed a seven-year contract with Warner Brothers that included the starring role in the film version of "John Loves Mary." In other studio roles she played a woman waiting to see if her child survived a plane crash in "Three Secrets" (1950) and John Wayne's love interest in "Operation Pacific" (1951).

A contract at Fox followed, and she played opposite Tyrone Power in the espionage thriller "Diplomatic Courier" (1952) and worried through the science fiction film "The Day the Earth Stood Still" (1951).

Still, Ms. Neal continued to work in film and in guest appearances on television. In "Breakfast at Tiffany's" (1961), she played an older woman who supports a young writer (George Peppard) who falls in love with the gentlemen's escort Holly Golightly (Audrey Hepburn).

Ms. Neal survived the strokes in 1965 in part because of the knowledge Dahl had acquired when Theo had eight brain operations. After the shunt that drained fluid from Theo's brain kept clogging, Dahl worked with a retired engineer and a neurosurgeon to design and manufacture a better one, the Wade-Dahl-Till valve.

When Ms. Neal collapsed in their Beverly Hills house, Dahl knew enough about her symptoms to call a leading neurosurgeon. Fourteen days after a seven-hour operation, the surgeon told Dahl that his wife would live but added, "I'm not sure whether or not I've done her a favor."

Dahl badgered her into getting well, pressing her to walk and arranging for hours of physical and speech therapy. She learned to read again. Six months after her brain operation, Ms. Neal gave birth to a healthy daughter.

Early in 1967 Dahl announced that Ms. Neal was ready to perform and that she would give a speech in New York that spring at a charity dinner for brain-damaged children. Terrified, Ms. Neal worked day after day to memorize the speech, which she delivered to thundering applause. As she wrote in her autobiography, "I knew at that moment that Roald the slave driver, Roald the bastard, with his relentless scourge, Roald the Rotten, as I had called him more than once, had thrown me back into the deep water. Where I belonged."

A few months later Frank Gilroy and the director Ulu Grosbard journeyed to Great Missenden to discuss a role in a film version of Mr. Gilroy's "The Subject Was Roses." "We didn't know whether she could memorize a line," Mr. Grosbard said later. "The memory element was the uncertain one. But when we started to shoot, she hit her top level."

Ms. Neal's illness and recovery became the subject of a television movie in 1981, with Glenda Jackson and Dirk Bogarde playing Patricia and Roald. Two years later, Ms. Neal and Dahl were divorced after Ms. Neal discovered that her husband had been having a long affair with one of her best friends. Dahl died in 1990.

Ms. Neal is survived by her four children, a brother, a sister, 10 grandchildren and step-grandchildren, and a great-grandchild.

In her later years Ms. Neal was often seen in guest roles in television series like "Little House on the Prairie" and "Murder, She Wrote." In 1999 she had a small role as the title character, a Southern dowager who commits suicide, in Robert Altman's comedy "Cookie's Fortune."

Ms. Neal also put much time and energy into raising money for brain-injured children and adults and establishing the Patricia Neal Rehabilitation Center in Knoxville. In dozens of speaking engagements, she showed that a brain injury was not necessarily the end of life or of joy.

"I can't see from one eye," she said in 1988. "I've been paralyzed. I've fallen down and broken a hip. Stubbornness gets you through the bad times. You don't give in."

— *By Aljean Harmetz*

TED STEVENS

Alaska's Champion in the Senate

NOV. 18, 1923 - AUG. 9, 2010

TED STEVENS, the former United States senator who helped shape modern Alaska with federal laws and billions in federal dollars, died on Aug. 9 in a plane crash while on a fishing trip there. He was 86.

Mr. Stevens was one of five people killed when the single-engine craft crashed into a mountainside in remote southwest Alaska after weaving through the mountains in clouds, rain and darkness on its way to a fishing lodge. Many of the nine on board had strong connections to his political career. Mr. Stevens had survived a plane crash in Alaska in 1978, suffering injuries while his first wife, the former Ann Cherrington, and four others were killed.

Serving in the Senate for 40 years, longer than any other Republican, Mr. Stevens was known as a fierce and often hot-tempered advocate for his state.

But that long and productive Senate career ended ignominiously in October 2008, when a federal jury in the District of Columbia found that he had concealed more than $250,000 in gifts. It convicted him on seven felony counts. Eight days later, as he sought a seventh term, voters turned him out of office, giving his seat to Mayor Mark Begich of Anchorage, a Democrat.

The following April, the conviction was thrown out by Judge Emmet G. Sullivan at the request of Attorney General Eric H. Holder Jr. During the trial, the judge had chided prosecutors for withholding information from the defense, and now Mr. Holder said they had concealed interview notes in which the chief witness against Mr. Stevens told a story different from the one he had told on the stand.

Mr. Stevens said the case against him had shaken his faith in the judicial system. But after Mr. Holder's and Judge Sullivan's actions, he said, "My faith has been restored."

Mr. Stevens liked to remind Alaskans of what he had done for them. "From frozen tundra," he said in his 2008 campaign, "we built airports, roads, ports, water and sewer systems, hospitals, clinics, communications networks, research labs and much, much more." He drew large amounts of military spending to the state as well as money for small businesses.

ELECTORAL VERDICT: After Mr. Stevens's 40 years in the Senate, his 2008 corruption trial cost him his re-election. The conviction was later thrown out.

Mr. Stevens's legislative work in the 1970s included passing major bills settling native land claims that had been left in limbo when statehood was established in 1959; creating the Trans-Alaska Pipeline, which made the state rich; and protecting the state's fisheries from exploitation.

In 2000, the State Legislature named Mr. Stevens the Alaskan of the Century, saying he "represents Alaska's finest contribution to our national leadership." In his farewell speech on Nov. 20, 2008, he told the Senate, "Working to help Alaska achieve its potential has been and will continue to be my life's work."

But he was roundly and repeatedly criticized for the billions he funneled to his state. The watchdog group Citizens Against Government Waste said Mr. Stevens got Alaska more dollars per capita than any other state, often through earmarks, the pet projects that lawmakers attach to legislation.

"Ted Stevens was a prolific procurer of pork-barrel projects," said Tom Schatz, the group's president, when Mr. Stevens left the Senate. "While his friend Senator Robert Byrd was called 'the king of pork,' Ted Stevens was the emperor of earmarks. Since we started counting in 1991, Senator Stevens has accumulated 1,452 projects worth $3.4 billion. That is a record amount."

Mr. Stevens fiercely defended earmarks, saying Alaska had special needs because the federal government owned much of its land; because the state's rugged terrain and severe weather required particular help; because, as the 49th state, Alaska needed to catch up with its elders; because its proximity to Russia made it strategically important; and because its oil and gas were national resources.

The most well-known earmark he fought for was a $450 million allocation for two bridges in Alaska, the so-called bridges to nowhere. When

Senator Tom Coburn, Republican of Oklahoma, proposed shifting the money to Louisiana to rebuild a highway wrecked by Hurricane Katrina, Mr. Stevens warned that he would wreak havoc.

"If you want a wounded bull on the floor of the Senate, pass this amendment," he said. The measure was defeated, 82 to 15, but Alaska later dropped the project.

Mr. Stevens's conviction, for seven violations of the Ethics in Government Act, did not allege that he had traded any of this spending for personal favors. The bulk of the gifts, which he failed to report on a Senate form, consisted of renovations to his home in Girdwood, Alaska. They were paid for by Bill Allen, a longtime friend and the owner of an oil services construction company.

Testifying in court, Mr. Stevens said that his wife, Catherine, had been in charge of the renovation and that he did not know what Mr. Allen had provided.

After the government moved to throw out his conviction, within months of his election defeat, Mr. Stevens expressed dismay at the political cost, both to him and to his party, saying, "It is unfortunate that an election was affected by proceedings now recognized as unfair."

Theodore Fulton Stevens was born on Nov. 18, 1923, in Indianapolis, the third of four children of George A. Stevens and the former Gertrude S. Chancellor. The family later moved to Chicago, where his father lost his job as an accountant after the 1929 stock market crash. His parents divorced, and after his father died, young Ted moved to Manhattan Beach, Calif., to live with an aunt.

Joining the Army Air Corps in World War II, Mr. Stevens flew transport planes over the perilous "Hump" route in the eastern Himalayas to take supplies into China from India. He was awarded two Distinguished Flying Crosses and two Air Medals.

After the war, he graduated from the University of California, Los Angeles, and Harvard Law School. He joined a law firm in Fairbanks, Alaska, in 1953 and soon afterward became the federal prosecutor there. In 1956, he went to Washington, D.C., to work in the Department of the Interior on Alaska statehood.

Moving back to Alaska, he opened a law firm in Anchorage, served in the Legislature and made two unsuccessful runs for the Senate before he was appointed to fill a vacancy in December 1968. He was elected to fill the last two years of the term in 1970 and easily won reelection until his defeat in 2008. Republicans made him their Senate whip in 1977, though he was defeated in a bid for majority leader by Bob Dole in 1984.

In December 1978 Mr. Stevens was aboard a twin-engine Lear jet when it crashed at Anchorage International Airport while returning from the capital, Juneau. Five people on the plane, including Mr. Stevens's first wife, Ann, 49, were killed. Mr. Stevens, one of two passengers to survive, was hospitalized with head, neck and arm injuries.

In 1980, he married Catherine Chandler.

Besides his second wife, survivors include five children from his first marriage, a daughter from his second marriage and 11 grandchildren.

Mr. Stevens often expressed contempt for those he called "extreme environmentalists" for their opposition to development in Alaska.

"Most of them are hired people who are just hucksters selling slick-backed magazines and national memberships," he said in 1990. But in 2006, he opposed construction of the Pebble Mine, a vast open pit to extract gold, copper and molybdenum, saying it would threaten the Bristol Bay salmon fishery.

He was critical of environmental objections to drilling for oil in the Arctic National Wildlife Reserve. In 2003, after another effort to open up the area for drilling had failed, he said: "People who vote against this today are voting against me. I will not forget it."

Though generally conservative in his votes, Mr. Stevens questioned President Ronald Reagan's level of military spending, supported the Title IX legislation to give women equal access in institutions receiving federal aid, backed spending for public radio, supported a ban on smoking in federal buildings and endorsed tougher fuel efficiency standards for cars and trucks.

When he faced a tough Senate debate, Mr. Stevens wore a tie featuring the image of the Incredible Hulk, the comic book superhero.

"I'm a mean, miserable S.O.B.," he once proclaimed as appropriations chairman.

Indeed, in the halls of Congress, he was known for his temper; it was voted the "hottest" on Capitol Hill in 2006 in a poll of Congressional staff members by Washingtonian magazine.

Mr. Stevens did not argue with the characterization. "I didn't lose my temper," he once said. "I know right where it is."

— *By Adam Clymer*

DAVID L. WOLPER

The Maestro of the Mini-Series

JAN. 11, 1928 - AUG. 10, 2010

David L. Wolper, an award-winning movie and television producer best known for the groundbreaking mini-series "Roots," died on Aug. 10 at his home in Beverly Hills, Calif. He was 82.

Mr. Wolper produced hundreds of films and television shows, including the hit 1983 mini-series "The Thorn Birds," a romantic drama set in Australia, with Richard Chamberlain and Rachel Ward. But he made his biggest mark with "Roots," shown in eight parts on ABC in 1977.

The saga of an African-American family's journey from Africa to slavery and then to emancipation, "Roots," based on the best-selling book by Alex Haley, was not the first mini-series, but it was the first to have a major influence on American culture, igniting a lively national discussion about race. Starring LeVar Burton, Ben Vereen and many others, "Roots" was one of the highest-rated entertainment programs in television history and won nine Emmy Awards.

Another of Mr. Wolper's productions, "The Hellstrom Chronicle" (1971), a film concerned with mankind's real and imagined difficulties with insects, won an Academy Award.

Mr. Wolper was a tireless showman and a flamboyant organizer of major events. He oversaw the opening and closing ceremonies of the 1984 Summer Olympic Games in Los Angeles, replete with sky divers, break dancers and 84 pianists playing music by George Gershwin. He again dazzled an international television audience when he choreographed a celebration in New York Harbor on July 4, 1986, to observe the 100th anniversary of the dedication of the Statue of Liberty, in which several thousand rockets were set off against a backdrop of hundreds of majestic tall ships.

Mr. Wolper gained notice at first as a producer of documentaries and fictionalized accounts of historical events. He drew his share of criticism: it was sometimes suggested that his documentaries were not sufficiently probing, that his so-called docudramas took too many liberties with the facts, that he was more showman than historian.

Critics were also cool to many of his big-screen productions, among them "If It's Tuesday, This Must Be Belgium" (1969), "I Love My Wife" (1970) and "One Is a Lonely Number" (1972). But he fared better with "Willy Wonka & the Chocolate Factory" (1971) and "L.A. Confidential" (1997), which was nominated for nine Oscars and won two.

"The Bridge at Remagen" (1969), about a World War II battle in Germany, was probably the Wolper movie that attracted the most attention — not for what was on the screen, but because his production company was run out of Czechoslovakia when the Soviet Army invaded.

Mr. Wolper scored an early success in 1963 with the television documentary "The Making of the President 1960," based on Theodore H. White's best-selling book about John F. Kennedy's quest for the White House. It won four Emmys, including program of the year.

A tireless showman and a flamboyant organizer of major events, Mr. Wolper dazzled audiences with fantastical ceremonial displays and compelling docudramas.

He also found success in television in the 1960s with the series "Biography," "Hollywood and the Stars" and "The Undersea World of Jacques Cousteau." In the 1970s he branched out into sitcoms, producing "Chico and the Man" and "Welcome Back, Kotter" with James Komack.

David Wolper (he had no middle name, but used the middle initial L to distinguish himself from an uncle, also named David Wolper) was born on the East Side of Manhattan on Jan. 11, 1928, the only child of Irving S. Wolper, a businessman, and the former Anna Fass. As a teenager he spent a lot of time watching movies, and people noticed that he had a knack for selling things.

After graduating from Columbia Grammar and Preparatory School, he entered Drake University in Des Moines, remained there a year, then transferred to the University of Southern California for two more years. He left the university at the end of his junior year because he thought he could make money by purchasing old movies and selling them to television stations all over the country. He was right.

In 1958, sensing that film footage of the Soviet satellite Sputnik would be worth something, he purchased 6,000 feet of it from Artkino, the official Soviet distributor, and used it as the basis for the documentary "The Race for Space," which he sold to more than 100 stations in the United States after all three networks had turned it down.

Making documentaries for television, he soon learned, was not easy. The networks had large news and public affairs departments staffed by seasoned journalists, and network executives tended to be wary of documentaries produced by outsiders.

Undaunted, Mr. Wolper began Wolper Productions on a shoestring. The company's early projects included "The Rafer Johnson Story" (1961), "Hollywood: The Golden Years" (1961) and "D-Day" (1962). Reviews were mixed, but viewers were receptive. By the mid-1970s Wolper Productions had grown from two people in a one-room office to more than 200 employees using 40 cutting rooms.

In 1971 Mr. Wolper produced "Appointment With Destiny," a series that mixed historical footage with dramatic re-enactments. John J. O'Connor, writing in The New York Times, criticized it as "pure fiction cleverly masquerading as reality." Mr. Wolper responded in a letter to the editor: "How else can we approach the past? Shall we leave it, defeated and ignorant, because we cannot fully reconstruct it any more than we can relive it?"

Married three times, Mr. Wolper is survived by his wife of 36 years, the former Gloria Hill; two sons; a daughter by his second wife, the former Margaret Dawn Richard; and 10 grandchildren.

Mr. Wolper remained active as a producer of mini-series and documentaries well into the 1990s. Besides "The Thorn Birds," his noteworthy later productions included the Civil War drama "North and South" (1985). In 2002 he revisited his most famous production with the television special "Roots: Celebrating 25 Years."

Mr. Wolper was inducted into the Academy of Television Arts and Sciences' Hall of Fame in 1989. In 2003 he published an autobiography, written with David Fisher, titling it simply "Producer."

— *By Richard Severo*

BRUNO S.

The Enigma of Berlin

JUNE 2, 1932 - AUG. 11, 2010

HE WROTE SONGS and sang them on the streets of Berlin. One told of a poor boy who grows up wishing for a little horse. The horse arrives years later pulling his mother's hearse.

The man who sang the songs — in a croaky voice, accompanying himself on the accordion and glockenspiel — was known as Bruno S. He was a street musician, a painter of pictures, a forklift operator and, at one time, a mental patient. But perhaps most remarkably, he was the lead actor in a movie that won the Grand Jury Prize at the Cannes International Film Festival in 1975.

His full name, which he seldom used, was Bruno Schleinstein. He died on Aug. 11 at the age of 78 in Berlin.

Werner Herzog, one of the innovators of postwar German cinema, twice in the 1970s cast Bruno to play pretty much himself, a damaged but somehow transcendent character.

The first of those films, the one that won at Cannes, was "The Enigma of Kaspar Hauser" (1974), based on a true story. In the film the character played by Bruno appears in a square in 19th-century Nuremburg. He cannot speak and can barely stand, having apparently been kept in a kind of dungeon. The only clue to his identity is a paper giving his name as Kaspar and asking that he be taken into service as a soldier.

Kaspar is taught to speak and to read and write, and then, in a fashion as mysterious as his appearance, he is murdered.

Bruno's acting moved Richard Eder of The New York Times to write: "Kaspar's extraordinary face, his eyes strained wide to see better, his whole posture suggesting a man trying to swallow, trying to grasp a world of strangeness, is the film's central image."

As he learns to speak, Kaspar finds much of society repulsive. "Every man is a wolf to me," he says. He has no ego: "Nothing lives less in me than my life."

Bruno Schleinstein was born on June 2, 1932, most likely in Berlin. Some accounts say

IN CHARACTER: Bruno S., right, in a still from Herzog's 1977 film, "Stroszek." A Berlin street musician, he gained wide recognition when Werner Herzog tapped him as a leading man.

his mother, a prostitute, had beaten him so badly when he was 3 that he became temporarily deaf. This led to his placement in a mental hospital, where he was the subject of Nazi experiments on mentally disabled children.

Nobody visited him, not even relatives he knew. He spent 23 years in institutions, including jails and homeless shelters. When on his own, he broke into cars for a warm place to sleep.

As an adult he held various jobs — his forklift work was at a steel plant — and began to sing in courtyards around Berlin in the oral tradition that inspired Brecht's "Threepenny Opera."

He didn't sing songs, Bruno said; he transmitted them. One song, "Thoughts Are Free," concerned the impossibility of finding refuge even in one's thoughts.

Mr. Herzog first glimpsed Bruno in a 1970 documentary about street musicians.

"I instantly knew he could be the leading character in 'Kaspar Hauser,'" Mr. Herzog said in an interview with NPR in 2006. Bruno did not want his name known, and so Mr. Herzog began calling him "the unknown soldier of cinema." Mr. Herzog said Bruno would have moments of "utter despair" and start talking, sometimes screaming, in the middle of a shot and continue in that way for two hours.

Bruno's second film, "Stroszek" (1977), was based on his life; Mr. Herzog had written the script expressly for him. Some scenes were shot in Bruno's own apartment. In the film, Bruno befriends a prostitute and moves with her and his aging landlord to the mythical Railroad Flats, Wis., where they live in a trailer. Bruno, who refers to himself in the third person in the film, has sharp comments about America. "Bruno is still being pushed around," he says, "not physically but spiritually; here they hurt you with a smile."

Bruno said in interviews that he had never wanted to be a movie star, and in time the benefits of fame faded, other than the occasional free haircut by a friendly barber.

"Everybody threw him away," Bruno said of himself.

He continued to carve out a life with his music and artwork, some of which was compelling enough to be exhibited at shows of so-called outsider art, including one in New York. When playing for street audiences, he never asked for money. Sometimes a friend would pass a hat for him. He drew a small pension. He apparently had no survivors.

In 2002, the German filmmaker Miron Zownir made a documentary called "Bruno S.— Estrangement Is Death." In it, Bruno seems to answer the many who worried that he had been exploited by Mr. Herzog.

"I have my pride, and I can think," he said, "and my thinking is clever."

— *By Douglas Martin*

DAN ROSTENKOWSKI

Power Broker on Capitol Hill

JAN. 2, 1928 - AUG. 11, 2010

Dan Rostenkowski, who mastered the craft of brokering and compromise to become one of the nation's most influential congressmen but whose imprisonment on fraud charges came to symbolize the excesses of power, died on Aug. 11 at his vacation home on Benedict Lake in Wisconsin. He was 82 and also lived in Chicago, in the house where he was raised.

His longtime spokesman, Jim Jaffe, confirmed the death, saying Mr. Rostenkowski had been treated for lung cancer for some time. In the 1990s he was treated for prostate cancer.

Mr. Rostenkowski, the son of a ward heeler and alderman from Chicago, was reared by the Cook County Democratic political machine under its longtime leader, Mayor Richard J. Daley, and won a seat in the Illinois legislature almost right out of college. First elected to the House of Representatives in 1958 at 30, he was its youngest member for many years.

From the beginning, the plainspoken Mr. Rostenkowski showed a knack for deal-making, often with his Republican colleagues, and in 1961 it helped him land a coveted seat on the House Ways and Means Committee, the powerful tax-writing panel. He served on the committee for most of his 36 years in Congress, 13 of them as its chairman, from 1981 to 1994, and was a central figure in shaping Congressional tax policy.

HOUSE LEADER: Mr. Rostenkowski, center, conferring with House Speaker Tip O'Neill, left, and Representative Charles Rangel in 1986.

As a young lawmaker, Mr. Rostenkowski helped write the legislation that created Medicare in 1966. As the committee's chairman, he helped fashion laws on taxes, trade and welfare. In 1983, he brokered the deal that led to the passage of a bill that kept the Social Security system solvent.

"During that period, my daughters said there's not going to be a Social Security system for them — that it's going to go belly up," he said in an interview in 1990. "Congress was concerned, and legislators made the difficult decisions and enacted a balanced compromise of tax increases and benefit reductions that saved the system from going bankrupt."

Mr. Rostenkowski also forged compromises that led to the 1986 tax reform act, a major rewriting of the federal tax code that sharply reduced nominal tax rates and eliminated vast numbers of loopholes, special preferences and tax-avoidance schemes.

The Social Security and tax laws were both passed when power in Washington was divided between a Democratic House and the Republican administration of President Ronald Reagan. Yet legislative achievements were almost a sidelight to Mr. Rostenkowski's true passion: the cajoling, arm-twisting and posturing that are the stuff of Washington lawmaking. He was so good at the game that for a time in the 1970s he was under consideration to succeed the House speaker, Carl Albert of Oklahoma.

But his candidacy for the post was hurt by the violence in the streets of Chicago during the 1968 Democratic National Convention, and the post went to Thomas P. O'Neill Jr. of Massachusetts. Still, Mr. Rostenkowski had become a significant force in the House, gaining entry to a small circle of the most powerful figures on Capitol Hill.

Republicans came to rely on him as a bridge to the Democratic leadership, and presidents of both parties sought his support in advancing their legislative agendas. He was especially close with Presidents Reagan and Bill Clinton and the elder George Bush.

"Rostenkowski over the years has built a reputation on the Hill as likable, earnest, cautious and absolutely trustworthy," Time magazine wrote in 1981. "Among the show horses of Congress, he is a workhorse."

But Mr. Rostenkowski's esteem and power on Capitol Hill eroded and then collapsed, starting in 1992, when a federal grand jury began investigating reports of wrongdoing in the House post office. Mr. Rostenkowski was pushed to the center of the scandal after investigators asserted that he had bought $22,000 in stamps from the House post office with public money and may have converted them to cash.

The federal inquiry lasted two years, during which Republicans, led by the Georgia congressman Newt Gingrich, accused Democrats of corruption and held up the accusations against Mr. Rostenkowski as symptomatic.

Mr. Rostenkowski showed a knack for deal-making.

In 1994, Mr. Rostenkowski was formally charged with 17 counts of abusing his Congressional payroll by paying at least 14 people who did little or no official work; trading stamp vouchers for at least $50,000 in cash; misusing his office's expense accounts to charge Congress for $40,000 in furniture and fine china and crystal; misusing personal vehicles and paying for them with $70,000 in House funds; and obstruction of justice.

Mr. Rostenkowski fought back. "I did not commit any crimes," he told reporters. "My conscience is clear, and my 42-year record as an elected official is one I am proud to once again run on."

Continuing his re-election campaign, he was beaten by a Republican, Michael P. Flanagan, in the watershed 1994 midterm elections in which Republicans won control of both the House and the Senate. The House post office scandal was widely viewed by political historians as a factor in that electoral triumph.

Two years later, as his federal trial approached, with a long prison sentence looming, Mr. Rostenkowski, the veteran power broker, negotiated his last important deal, pleading guilty to two counts of mail fraud. He served 15 months in federal prisons in Minnesota and Wisconsin and finished his sentence by spending two months in a halfway house and paying a $100,000 fine.

On his release Mr. Rostenkowski issued an unapologetic statement that expressed some bitterness at how he was treated. "Bureaucracies all have a certain mindless logic," he wrote. "I'll reserve my critique of America's criminal justice system for another day. I do believe that a strong case can be made for doing things better."

Mr. Clinton, as he prepared to leave the White House, pardoned Mr. Rostenkowski in December 2000.

Daniel David Rostenkowski was born in Chicago on Jan. 2, 1928, the only son and youngest of three children, in a house built by his grandfather in the city's 32nd Ward. His father, Joseph P. Rostenkowski, was the ward's alderman from 1933 to 1955. His mother, Priscilla R. Rostenkowski, died in 1949 when her son was 21.

Tall and strong, the young Rostenkowski attended St. John's Military Academy in Delafield, Wis., where he played three sports and was skilled enough in baseball to attract an invitation from Connie Mack to try out for the Philadelphia Athletics. Reluctantly, he turned down the offer, abiding by his father's wishes that he pursue a career in politics. It was during this period that Mr. Rostenkowski changed his last name to Rosten, which he kept through much of his 20s.

After serving in the Army in Korea with the Seventh Infantry Division, he attended Loyola University in Chicago, graduating in 1951. The next year he ran for the Illinois House of Representatives and won. After a term as a state senator, he was elected to Congress in 1958 for the first of 18 terms.

His survivors include his wife, LaVerne, whom he married on May 12, 1951, and three daughters. His youngest daughter died in 2007.

Mr. Rostenkowski's later career included stints as a political commentator on the Chicago television station WFLD, and as a college teacher and the head of Danross Associates, a consulting firm in Chicago.

And just as he did during his political career, Mr. Rostenkowski continued to keep his family home in the 32nd Ward, transformed from a neighborhood of immigrants into an enclave of young professionals. When asked about his loyalty to the neighborhood, he replied, "I felt like I should live where the people I represented lived."

— *By Keith Schneider*

EDWIN NEWMAN

Newsman and Language Maven

JAN. 25, 1919 - AUG. 13, 2010

EDWIN NEWMAN, the genteelly rumpled, genially grumpy NBC newsman who was equally famous as a stalwart defender of the honor of English, has died in Oxford, England. He was 91.

He died of pneumonia on Aug. 13, his lawyer, Rupert Mead, said, adding that Mr. Newman and his wife had moved to England in 2007 to live closer to their daughter.

Mr. Newman, recognizable for his balding head and fierce dark eyebrows, was known to three decades of postwar television viewers for his erudition, droll wit and seemingly limitless penchant for puns. (There was, for example, the one about the man who blotted his wet shoes with newspapers, explaining, "These are The Times that dry men's soles.") He began his association with NBC in the early 1950s and was variously a correspondent, anchor and critic there before his retirement in 1984.

An anchor on the "Today" show in the early 1960s and a familiar presence on the program for many years afterward, Mr. Newman also appeared regularly on "Meet the Press." He won seven New York Emmy Awards for his work in the 1960s and '70s with NBC's local affiliate, WNBC-TV, on which he was a drama critic and the host of the interview program "Speaking Freely."

He also moderated two presidential debates — the first Ford-Carter debate in 1976 and the second Reagan-Mondale debate in 1984 — and covered some of the signal events of the 20th century, from the coronation of Queen Elizabeth II to the assassination of President John F. Kennedy.

'FOR NBC NEWS ...': With his genteelly rumpled appearance, Mr. Newman was a staple of television news for decades.

Mr. Newman's best-known books, both published by Bobbs-Merrill, are "Strictly Speaking: Will America Be the Death of English?" (1974) and "A Civil Tongue" (1976). In them he declared what he called "a protective interest in the English language," which, he warned, was falling prey to windiness, witlessness, ungrammaticality, obfuscation and other depredations.

But Mr. Newman "was never preachy or pedantic," Brian Williams, the anchor and managing editor of the NBC "Nightly News," said in a statement after Mr. Newman's death.

"To those of us watching at home," Mr. Williams added, "he made us feel like we had a very smart, classy friend in the broadcast news business."

Edwin Harold Newman was born in New York City on Jan. 25, 1919, the second of three children of Myron Newman and the former Rose Parker. He graduated from George Washington High School in Washington Heights in Manhattan and in 1940 earned a bachelor's degree in political science from the University of Wisconsin, where he worked on the campus newspaper. He was briefly a graduate student in government at Louisiana State University before finding work in print journalism. (Mr. Newman's older brother, Morton, known professionally as M. W. Newman, was a reporter at The Chicago Daily News.)

Edwin Newman's first journalism job was as a "dictation boy" in the Washington bureau of the International News Service. He next joined United Press, to which he returned after serving in the Navy from 1942 to 1945. He later worked in the Washington bureau of the progressive New York newspaper PM before joining the Tufty News Service, founded in 1935 by Esther Van Wagoner Tufty, a Washington journalist.

In 1947 Mr. Newman joined the Washington bureau of CBS News, where he helped the commentator Eric Sevareid prepare his nightly radio broadcasts. Two years later he moved to London to work as a freelance journalist, joining NBC as a correspondent there in 1952. He went on to become the network's bureau chief in London, Rome and Paris before settling in New York in 1961.

Mr. Newman was fond of saying that he had "a spotless record of being in the wrong place at the wrong time," as he told Newsweek in 1961. There was the time in 1952, for instance, that he left London for Morocco, only to learn on arriving that King George VI of England had just died.

But in fact Mr. Newman helped cover numerous historic events, among them the shootings of Robert F. Kennedy, the Rev. Dr. Martin Luther King Jr., George Wallace and Ronald Reagan. He announced the death of President John F. Kennedy on NBC radio. He also narrated many NBC television documentaries.

His role as a moderator for presidential debates seemed only fitting, for it was the dense thicket of political discourse, Mr. Newman often said, that helped spur him to become a public guardian of grammar and usage.

Among the sins that set his teeth on edge were idiosyncratic spellings like "Amtrak"; jargon of any kind; "hopefully" as a sentence adverb (he was said to have had a sign in his office reading, "Abandon 'Hopefully' All Ye Who Enter Here"); "y'know" as a conversational stopgap; a passel of prefixes and suffixes ("de-," "non-," "un-," "-ize," "-wise" and "-ee"); and using a preposition to end a sentence with.

This prescriptive approach to English did not win favor with everyone. In an article in The Atlantic in 1983, the linguist Geoffrey Nunberg took Mr. Newman and the author Richard Mitchell to task for writing "books about the language that rarely, if ever, cite a dictionary or a standard grammar; evidently one just knows these things."

Mr. Newman's other books include a comic novel, "Sunday Punch" (1979). Other honors were an Overseas Press Club Award in 1961 and a Peabody Award in 1966.

His survivors include his wife, the former Rigel Grell, and a daughter.

Mr. Newman helped cover numerous historic events.

Despite his acclaim, Mr. Newman's constitutional waggishness kept him from taking himself too seriously. In 1984, the year he retired from NBC, he appeared on the network as a host of "Saturday Night Live." (One sketch portrayed a distraught woman phoning a suicide hotline. Mr. Newman answers — and corrects her grammar.) A few years before that he delivered the news on David Letterman's NBC morning show. He was also a frequent guest on the game show "Hollywood Squares."

In 1996 Mr. Newman shocked the journalistic establishment by serving as the anchor of the USA cable channel program "Weekly World News," a short-lived television version of the supermarket tabloid. Among the "news" items Mr. Newman introduced was a report on a South Seas island tribe that worshipped the boxing promoter Don King.

"Apparently it is thought that my presence lends some authority," Mr. Newman told The Washington Post that year. He added, "If I'm leading into a story about a couple with a poltergeist in their lavatory, I have to do it soberly."

— By Margalit Fox

ABBEY LINCOLN

Inhabiting Every Song

AUG. 6, 1930 - AUG. 14, 2010

ABBEY LINCOLN, a singer whose dramatic vocal command and tersely poetic songs made her a singular figure in jazz, died on Aug. 14 in Manhattan. She was 80 and lived on the Upper West Side.

Ms. Lincoln's career encompassed outspoken civil rights advocacy in the 1960s and fearless introspection in more recent years, and for a time in the 1960s she acted in films, including one with Sidney Poitier.

Long recognized as one of jazz's most arresting and uncompromising singers, Ms. Lincoln gained similar stature as a songwriter only over the last two decades. Her songs, rich in metaphor and philosophical reflection, provide the substance of her final album, "Abbey Sings Abbey," released on Verve in 2007. As a body of work, the songs formed the basis of a three-concert retrospective presented by Jazz at Lincoln Center in 2002.

Her singing style was unique, a result of bold projection and expressive restraint. She was often likened to Billie Holiday, her chief influence, for the way she could inhabit the emotional dimensions of a song. But Ms. Lincoln had a deeper register and a darker tone, and her phrasing was more declarative.

"Her utter individuality and intensely passionate delivery can leave an audience breathless with the tension of real drama," the jazz writer Peter Watrous wrote in The New York Times in 1989. "A slight, curling phrase is laden with significance, and the tone of her voice can signify hidden welts of emotion."

She had a profound influence on other jazz vocalists, not only as a singer and composer but also as a role model. "I learned a lot about taking a different path from Abbey," the singer Cassandra Wilson said. "Investing your lyrics with what your life is about in the moment."

Ms. Lincoln was born Anna Marie Wooldridge in Chicago on Aug. 6, 1930, the 10th of 12 children, and raised in rural Michigan. In the early 1950s, she headed west in search of a singing career, spending two years as a nightclub attraction in Honolulu, where she met Ms. Holiday and Louis Armstrong. She then moved to Los Angeles, where she encountered the accomplished lyricist Bob Russell.

It was at the suggestion of Mr. Russell, who had become her manager, that she took the name Abbey Lincoln, a symbolic conjoining of Westminster Abbey and Abraham Lincoln. In 1956, she made her first album, "Affair ... a Story of a Girl in Love" (Liberty), and appeared in her first film, the Jayne Mansfield vehicle "The Girl Can't Help It." Her image in both cases was decidedly glamorous: On the album cover she was depicted in a décolleté gown, and in the movie she sported a dress once worn by Marilyn Monroe.

For her second album, "That's Him," released on the Riverside label in 1957, Ms. Lincoln kept the seductive pose but worked convincingly with a modern jazz ensemble that included the tenor saxophonist Sonny Rollins and the drummer Max Roach. In short order she came under the influence of Mr. Roach, a bebop pioneer with an ardent interest in progressive causes. As she later recalled, she put the Monroe dress in an incinerator and followed his lead.

The most visible manifestation of their partnership was "We Insist! Max Roach's Freedom Now Suite," issued on the Candid label in 1960, with Ms. Lincoln belting Oscar Brown Jr.'s lyrics. Now hailed as an early masterwork of the civil rights movement, the album radicalized Ms. Lincoln's reputation. One movement had her moaning in sorrow, then hollering and shrieking in anguish — a stark evocation of struggle. A year later, after Ms. Lincoln sang her own lyrics to a song called "Retribution," her stance prompted one prominent reviewer to deride her in print as a "professional Negro."

Ms. Lincoln, who married Mr. Roach in 1962, was for a while more active as an actress than a singer. In 1964 she starred with Ivan Dixon in the film "Nothing but a Man," a tale of the Deep South in the 1960s, and in 1968 she was the title character opposite Mr. Poitier in the romantic comedy "For Love of Ivy," playing a white family's maid. She also acted on television in guest-starring roles in the 1960s and '70s.

A VOICE TO BE HEARD: Over her 40-year career, Ms. Lincoln went from glamorous songstress to jazz innovator and civil rights advocate.

But with the exception of "Straight Ahead" (Candid), on which "Retribution" appeared, she released no albums in the 1960s. And after her divorce from Mr. Roach in 1970, she took an apartment above a garage in Los Angeles and withdrew from the spotlight for a time. She never remarried.

Ms. Lincoln is survived by two brothers and a sister.

During a visit to Africa in 1972, Ms. Lincoln received two honorary appellations from political officials: Moseka, in Zaire, and Aminata, in Guinea. (Moseka would occasionally serve as her surname.) She began to consider her calling as a storyteller and focused on writing songs.

Moving back to New York in the 1980s, Ms. Lincoln resumed performing, eventually attracting the attention of Jean-Philippe Allard, a producer and executive with PolyGram France. Ms. Lincoln's first effort for what is now the Verve Music Group, "The World Is Falling Down" (1990), was both a commercial and a critical success.

Eight more albums followed in a similar vein, each produced by Mr. Allard and enlisting top-shelf jazz musicians like the tenor saxophonist Stan Getz and the vibraphonist Bobby Hutcherson. In addition to elegant originals like "Throw It Away" and "When I'm Called Home," the albums featured Ms. Lincoln's striking interpretations of material ranging from songbook standards to Bob Dylan's classic "Mr. Tambourine Man."

For "Abbey Sings Abbey" Ms. Lincoln revisited her own songbook exclusively, performing in an acoustic roots-music setting that emphasized her affinities with singer-songwriters like Mr. Dylan. Overseen by Mr. Allard and the American producer-engineer Jay Newland, the album boiled each song to its essence and found Ms. Lincoln in weathered voice but superlative form.

When the album was released in May 2007, Ms. Lincoln was recovering from open-heart surgery. In her Upper West Side apartment, surrounded by her own paintings and drawings, she reflected on her life, often quoting from her own song lyrics.

After she recited a long passage from "The World Is Falling Down," one of her more prominent later songs, her eyes flashed with pride. "I don't know why anybody would give that up," she said. "I wouldn't. Makes my life worthwhile."

— By Nate Chinen

JAMES J. KILPATRICK

A Forceful Conservative Voice

NOV. 1, 1920 - AUG. 15, 2010

JAMES J. KILPATRICK, a forceful and sometimes combative conservative voice for half a century as a newspaper columnist, author and television personality, died on Aug. 15 in Washington. He was 89.

A prolific writer and a sharp debater, Mr. Kilpatrick was widely remembered for his heated intellectual combat with the liberal journalist Shana Alexander on "60 Minutes." When he was not tackling national issues, he took aim at flabby prose and bureaucratic absurdities.

In the mid-1950s, Mr. Kilpatrick became something of a national figure, articulating constitutional arguments justifying the policy of "massive resistance" to the Supreme Court's decision outlawing school segregation. But as the South changed, so did Mr. Kilpatrick, who dropped his fervent defense of segregation a decade later.

Writing in Nation's Business magazine in 1978, Mr. Kilpatrick defined his ideological stance.

"Conservatives believe that a civilized society demands orders and classes, that men are not inherently equal, that change and reform are not identical, that in a free society men are children of God and not wards of the state," he wrote.

"Self-reliance is a conservative principle," he continued. "The work ethic is a conservative ethic. The free marketplace is vital to the conservative's economic philosophy."

James Jackson Kilpatrick was born on Nov. 1, 1920, in Oklahoma City, and grew up there as the son of a lumber dealer. He received a degree in journalism from the University of Missouri and was hired as a reporter by The Richmond News Leader of Virginia in 1941.

An energetic newsman, he became a favorite of Douglas Southall Freeman, the paper's longtime editor, and was named its chief editorial writer in 1949, when Mr. Freeman retired. Two years later, Mr. Kilpatrick was appointed the paper's editor.

In 1953, he persuaded the governor of Virginia to grant a pardon to a black handyman serving a life sentence for killing a police officer. A News Leader investigation he led had concluded that the man was falsely charged.

Mr. Kilpatrick's views on the larger issue of race came to the fore after the Supreme Court's 1954 Brown decision outlawing school segregation. In a series of editorials, he provided a framework for Southern politicians who were resisting the court's decision.

Mr. Kilpatrick popularized the doctrine called interposition, according to which individual states had the constitutional duty to interpose their separate sovereignties against federal court rulings that went beyond their rightful powers and, if necessary, to nullify them, an argument traced to the writings of Thomas Jefferson, James Madison and John C. Calhoun.

He debated on television with the Rev. Dr. Martin Luther King Jr. and wrote on race and states' rights in "The Sovereign States: Notes of a Citizen of Virginia" in 1957 and "The Southern Case for School Segregation" in 1962.

At times, Mr. Kilpatrick went beyond constitutional arguments. In 1963, he drafted an article for The Saturday Evening Post with the proposed title "The Hell He Is Equal," in which he wrote that "the Negro race, as a race, is in fact an inferior race."

But the magazine's senior editor, Thomas B. Congdon Jr., decided not to publish the article after four black girls were killed in the

Birmingham, Ala., church bombing. As recounted in the 2006 book "The Race Beat" by Gene Roberts and Hank Klibanoff, Mr. Congdon viewed Mr. Kilpatrick's article as in "bad taste" and "inflammatory."

Mr. Kilpatrick ultimately acknowledged that segregation was a lost cause and re-examined his earlier defense of it.

"I was brought up a white boy in Oklahoma City in the 1920s and 1930," he told Time magazine in 1970. "I accepted segregation as a way of life. Very few of us, I suspect, would like to have our passions and profundities at age 28 thrust in our faces at 50."

DEBATING RACE: Mr. Kilpatrick in 1962, the year he wrote "The Southern Case for School Segregation." He later changed his views.

Apart from surveying the national scene, Mr. Kilpatrick exposed overbearing local laws and judicial rulings.

His campaign got under way in 1959, when a pedestrian who climbed across the hood of a car that had blocked a downtown Richmond intersection was hauled into court by the driver, an off-duty policeman, and fined $25 for malicious mischief. That inspired Mr. Kilpatrick to create the Beadle Bumble Fund, named for the Dickens character in "Oliver Twist" who proclaimed "the law is a ass."

The fund, Mr. Kilpatrick said, was devoted to "poking fun and spoofing the hell out of despots on the bench." It paid the fines of victims of legal travesties in the Richmond area with contributions from readers.

Mr. Kilpatrick railed against turgid prose in a 1984 book, "The Writer's Art." In his "On Language" column for The New York Times Magazine, William Safire wrote that Mr. Kilpatrick's essays on "the vagaries of style are classics."

Mr. Kilpatrick left The News Leader in 1966 after embarking on a column for the Washington Star Syndicate, "A Conservative View," which was carried by newspapers throughout the country. Writing later for Universal Press Syndicate, which took over the Washington Star Syndicate, he continued "A Conservative View" until 1993, when he began a weekly column, "Covering the Courts." He ended that column in January 2008 and discontinued his other remaining column, "The Writer's Art," in January 2009.

In the 1970s, he sparred with Nicholas von Hoffman and later with Ms. Alexander on the "Point-Counterpoint" segment of "60 Minutes." The Kilpatrick-Alexander clashes on issues like the Vietnam War and the women's movement were parodied on TV's "Saturday Night Live" by Dan Aykroyd and Jane Curtin. Mr. Aykroyd would proclaim, "Jane, you ignorant slut," and Ms. Curtin would reply, "Dan, you pompous ass."

While based in Washington, Mr. Kilpatrick owned a home in the Blue Ridge Mountains of Virginia. His columns with a Scrabble, Va., dateline extolled the joys of rustic life.

His first wife, the former Marie Louise Pietri, died in 1997.

Mr. Kilpatrick is survived by his wife, Marianne Means, a Washington columnist whom he married in 1998, as well as three sons, four stepdaughters, seven grandchildren, nine stepgrandchildren and seven great-grandchildren.

At his country home, Mr. Kilpatrick flew two flags, the Stars and Stripes and another alongside it that seemed to embody his views on the rights of individuals confronting the powers of the state. That flag, from the era of the American Revolution, bore the image of a snake and the words "Don't Tread on Me."

— *By Richard Goldstein*

BOBBY THOMSON

A Legend With One Swing

OCT. 25, 1923 - AUG. 16, 2010

BOBBY THOMSON, who swatted the most famous home run in baseball history — the so-called shot heard 'round the world — for the New York Giants against the Brooklyn Dodgers on Oct. 3, 1951, to cap baseball's most memorable pennant drive, died on Aug. 16 at his home in Savannah, Ga. He was 86.

Partly because of the fierce rivalry between the Giants and the Dodgers; partly because it was broadcast from coast to coast on television; and partly because it was indelibly described in a play-by-play call by the Giants radio announcer Russ Hodges, Thomson's three-run homer at the Polo Grounds endures as perhaps baseball's most dramatic moment. It was a stirring conclusion to the Giants' late-summer comeback, known as the Miracle of Coogan's Bluff, and a vivid symbol of victory snatched from defeat (and vice versa).

"I can remember feeling as if time was just frozen," Thomson once said. "It was a delirious, delicious moment."

It was the bottom of the ninth inning in the third game of a three-game playoff. The Giants were down by two runs and the count was no balls and one strike. The pitcher Ralph Branca, who had just come into the game, delivered a high fastball to Thomson, perhaps a bit inside. In the radio broadcast booth, Hodges watched the baseball fly off Thomson's bat.

"There's a long drive ... it's gonna be ... I believe — the Giants win the pennant! The Giants win the pennant! The Giants win the pennant! The Giants win the pennant!

"Bobby Thomson hits into the lower deck of the left-field stands! The Giants win the pennant, and they're going crazy, they're going crazy! ...

"I don't believe it, I don't believe it, I do not believe it!"

Thomson's home run propelled the Giants to a 5-4 victory, he and Branca became bonded as baseball's ultimate hero and goat, and the moment became enshrined in American culture. In 1999, the United States Postal Service issued a stamp commemorating Thomson's drive, and Don DeLillo used the baseball he hit as a relic of memory in the acclaimed 1997 novel "Underworld."

Robert Brown Thomson was born on Oct. 25, 1923, in Glasgow and arrived in the United States at age 2. The son of a cabinetmaker, he grew up on Staten Island and signed with the Giants' organization for a $100 bonus in 1942 out of Curtis High School.

A right-handed batter with good power and excellent speed, Thomson was in his fifth full season with the Giants in 1951. He got off to a slow start, playing center field, then went to the bench in May when the Giants called up a 20-year-old rookie named Willie Mays. But Thomson was playing regularly again by late July, this time at third base, and he hit better than .350 over the final two months of the season.

In mid-August, the Giants trailed the first-place Dodgers by 13 1/2 games. "The Giants is dead," the Dodgers' manager, Charlie Dressen, had proclaimed. But they went on a 16-game winning streak, and they tied the Dodgers for the National League lead on the season's final weekend.

The Giants won the playoff opener, 3-1, at Ebbets Field, behind Thomson's two-run homer off Branca, the Dodgers starter. But the Dodgers romped, 10-0, the next day at the Polo Grounds.

On Wednesday afternoon, the teams returned to the Polo Grounds to play for the pennant. It was an overcast day, and the attendance was just 34,320 — some 22,000 below capacity — for a duel of pitching aces, the Giants' Sal Maglie against the Dodgers' Don Newcombe.

Thomson blundered in the second inning, trying to stretch a hit into a double while his teammate Whitey Lockman was standing at second base; Thomson was tagged out in a rundown. His fly ball tied the score at 1-1 in the seventh, but in the eighth he let two ground balls get by him at third base for singles in the Dodgers' three-run rally, giving them a 4-1 lead.

PENNANT CLINCHER: Thomson, left, heading for home after hitting the "shot heard 'round the world."

In the bottom of the ninth, the Giants had runners on second and third with one run in and one out. Dressen removed Newcombe and waved in Branca to face Thomson, who had hit 31 home runs that season, two against Branca.

"I kept telling myself: 'Wait and watch. Give yourself a chance to hit,'" Thomson remembered.

Branca threw a fastball and Thomson moved his bat slightly but took a strike.

Branca delivered a second fastball, and this time Thomson sent the ball on a line toward the 16-foot-high green wall in left field. "Sink, sink, sink," Branca told himself.

The Dodgers' Andy Pafko slumped against the wall as the ball cleared the top and landed in the lower deck.

Thomson galloped around the bases as Branca began a long walk to the center-field clubhouse. Eddie Stanky, the Giants' second baseman, and Leo Durocher, the manager, hugged each other in a madcap dance in the third-base coach's box and grabbed at Thomson as he reached the bag. He broke away and arrived at home plate with a leap, surrounded by teammates who carried him on their shoulders.

"Now it is done," Red Smith wrote in The New York Herald Tribune. "Now the story ends. And there is no way to tell it. The art of fiction is dead. Reality has strangled invention. Only the utterly impossible, the inexpressibly fantastic, can ever be plausible again."

Thomson's home run eventually became entangled in revelations of a sign-stealing operation conducted by the Giants in 1951, related by the sports columnist Dave Anderson of The New York Times in his book "Pennant Races" (1994) and by Joshua Prager in The Wall Street Journal in 2001 and in his book "The Echoing Green" (2006).

Prager reported that several players on the 1951 Giants, including Thomson, had confirmed that they stole opposing catchers' signals for much of the season via a buzzer system using a "spy" with a telescope in the center-field clubhouse at the Polo Grounds. But Thomson told Prager that he was not tipped off to the kind of pitch Branca would be throwing when he hit the pennant-winning homer.

In an interview in July, Branca said he felt that Thomson did receive a signal from the Giants' bullpen that a fastball was coming on that fateful pitch.

"When you took signs all year, and when you had a chance to hit a bloop or hit a home run, would you ignore that sign?" Branca said. "He knew it was coming. Absolutely."

The rest of Thomson's career was anticlimax. He performed no World Series miracles as the Giants were beaten by the Yankees in six games. He was traded to the Milwaukee Braves in February 1954, but soon afterward broke an ankle sliding in an exhibition game. He played for the Giants again in 1957, then with the Chicago Cubs, the Boston Red Sox and the Baltimore Orioles. He retired after the 1960 season with a .270 batting average and 264 home runs over 15 years.

After leaving baseball, Thomson, a quiet, modest man, became a sales executive with the Westvaco paper-products company, now part of MeadWestvaco. "I wanted to get a responsible job, stay home more with my wife and daughter and live a normal life," he said.

He is survived by two daughters and six grandchildren. His wife, Elaine, died in 1993. Thomson lived in Watchung, N.J., until 2006, when he moved to Savannah to be near one of his daughters.

In an interview the day after Thomson's death, Mays, who was on deck when the epic homer was hit, recalled how grateful he was to Thomson for helping him adjust to the major leagues when he arrived with the Giants as a rookie in 1951 and Durocher put him in center field.

"Leo wanted him to move to third base," Mays said of Thomson. "He didn't have a problem with that. That's class."

Thomson appeared with Branca at old-timers' games, baseball dinners and autograph shows. They donated much of the money they made to charity and forged a certain closeness.

At one joint appearance on the 40th anniversary of his home run, Thomson remarked that "Ralph didn't run away and hide."

Branca responded, "I lost a game, but I made a friend."

— By Richard Goldstein

FRANK KERMODE

Self-Made Man of Letters

NOV. 29, 1919 - AUG. 17, 2010

FRANK KERMODE, who rose from humble origins to become one of England's most respected and influential critics, died on Aug. 17 at his home in Cambridge, England. He was 90.

His death was announced by The London Review of Books, which he helped create and to which he frequently contributed.

The author David Lodge called Mr. Kermode "the finest English critic of his generation," and few disagreed with that assessment.

The author or editor of more than 50 books published over five decades, Mr. Kermode was probably best known for his studies of Shakespeare. But his range was wide, reaching from Beowulf to Philip Roth, from Homer to Ian McEwan, from the Bible to Don DeLillo. Along the way he devoted individual volumes to John Donne, Wallace Stevens and D. H. Lawrence. Unrelentingly productive, he published "Concerning E. M. Forster" just last December.

His collections of literary criticism and lectures — among them "The Sense of an Ending: Studies in the Theory of Fiction," "The Genesis of Secrecy" and "The Art of Telling: Essays on Fiction" — became standard university texts. The poet and critic Allen Tate called "The Sense of an Ending" "a landmark in 20th-century critical thought."

Mr. Kermode also wrote for the general book-reading audience, chiefly in The London Review of Books and The New York Review of Books, and his judgments were typically measured but pointed, whether reviewing John Updike or Zadie Smith. His pungent take on Updike's series of "Bech" novels managed at once to express a certain awe at the writer's talents while discounting the books in question, calling them "works of the left hand."

Yet despite the variety of his work, he almost invariably tied what he wrote to a recurring central concern: what the English literary critic Lawrence S. Rainey, writing in the London newspaper The Independent, described as "the conflict between the human need to make sense of the world through storytelling and our propensity to seek meaning in details (linguistic, symbolic, anecdotal) that are indifferent, even hostile, to story."

For instance, in his best-known book, "The Sense of an Ending," Mr. Kermode analyzed the fictions we invent to bring meaning and order to a world that often seems chaotic and hurtling toward catastrophe. Between the tick and the tock of the clock, as he put it, we want a connection as well as the suggestion of an arrow shooting eschatologically toward some final judgment.

Yet as he pointed out in "The Genesis of Secrecy," narratives, just like life, can include details that defy interpretation, like the Man in the Mackintosh who keeps showing up in Joyce's "Ulysses," or the young man who runs away naked when Jesus is arrested at Gethsemane in the Gospel according to Mark.

Mr. Kermode's critics sometimes faulted him for a deliberately difficult style and for what Mr. Lodge called "intellectual dandyism." In "The Art of Telling," Mr. Kermode suggested that innovative French approaches to literary criticism like structuralism and deconstructionism might eventually find a place in the mainstream, but he took to task some of the more radical attempts to subvert traditional texts through gender or racial perspectives. In "An Appetite for Poetry" (1989), he reaffirmed his belief in the value of reading literary classics as a way of gauging both ideals of permanence and the forces of change.

The view of him as uppermost an establishmentarian was only reinforced in 1974, when he attained what is considered the pre-eminent post in English literary criticism: the King Edward VII chair of English literature at King's College, Cambridge University, an appointment made by the crown at the suggestion of the prime minister. He was knighted in 1991.

But even his detractors respected him for his brilliance, his evenhandedness and his humaneness. The critic Richard Poirier, reviewing "Puzzles and Epiphanies" (1962) for The New York Review of Books, praised Mr. Kermode's criticism for its freedom from "polemical or theoretical limitations" and for possessing "the power, which Arnold required of good criticism, 'to ascertain the master-spirit in the literature of an epoch.'"

"There was nothing left for me except to become a critic. ..."

John Frank Kermode was born on Nov. 29, 1919, in Douglas, Isle of Man, the only son of John Pritchard Kermode, a storeroom keeper who earned three pounds a week, and the former Doris Kennedy, a farm girl who had been a waitress. She had given her son his unwanted "habit of deference" and had inspired his love of words, as he wrote in his 1995 memoir, "Not Entitled."

He transcended his unpromising background beyond all expectations, winning scholarships to the local high school and to Liverpool University, from which he graduated in 1940. He learned to read Greek and Latin as well as French, Italian and German, and he went on to become a professor of Renaissance and modern English literature.

Yet as a child he was a disappointment to his father, "being fat, plain, shortsighted, clumsy, idle, dirty," as Mr. Kermode wrote in "Not Entitled," "and very unlikely to add to the family store of sporting cups and medals."

He devoted a full third of that book to the six years he spent in the Royal Navy, much of it in Iceland, after graduating from Liverpool, rising to the rank of lieutenant. But he chose not to write about his two marriages, the first to Maureen Eccles, from 1947 to 1970, the second to Anita Van Vactor; or his son and daughter, both of whom survive him. Nor did he mention his knighthood.

Mr. Kermode wrote modestly, perhaps ruefully, of his career prospects, concluding that his incapacity "at least to be able to surmise how very complicated things are done" — or "even simple ones" — prevented him from becoming a playwright or novelist.

"It was also emerging that my poetry wasn't up to much," he added, "so there was nothing left for me except to become a critic, preferably with a paying job in a university."

That career took him to teaching positions in English and American universities and eventually to his appointment in 1967 as Lord Northcliffe professor of modern English literature at University College London, where he was credited with helping to introduce contemporary French critical theory to Britain.

Before taking that post, he also served as co-editor (with Melvin J. Lasky) of the prestigious magazine Encounter, where he succeeded the poet Stephen Spender in 1964. But he resigned in 1966 on learning that the magazine, sponsored by the Congress of Cultural Freedom, had received money from the Central Intelligence Agency.

From London he went on, seven years later, to his prestigious chair at Cambridge, leaving in 1982, in part because of an unsuccessful tenure battle on behalf of the structuralist-oriented film and literary scholar Colin MacCabe, then a junior lecturer.

Mr. Kermode then moved to the United States and taught at several universities, including Columbia, where for many years he was the Julian Clarence Levi professor emeritus in the humanities.

His writing, though, reached beyond academia. His "Shakespeare's Language" (2000) — which traced the development of the playwright through the evolution of his poetry and concluded that "Hamlet" signified a major turning point — was a best seller in England.

At the time, Mr. Kermode worried about the book's accessibility, telling The Irish Times: "What I do is despised by some younger critics, who want everything to sound extremely technical. I spent a long time developing an intelligible style. But these critics despise people who don't use unintelligible jargon."

Perhaps there was a touch of sarcasm in the comment, a bit of grumbling. But he clearly had little patience for critics who seemed to write only for other critics. As he wrote in "Pieces of My Mind: Essays and Criticism 1958-2002," criticism "can be quite humbly and sometimes even quite magnificently useful." But it must also "give pleasure," he added, "like the other arts."

— *By Christopher Lehmann-Haupt*

MARIO OBLEDO

The Back Seat for Hispanics Would Not Do

APRIL 9, 1932 - AUG. 18, 2010

Mario G. Obledo, who slept on the floor with 12 siblings as the child of illegal immigrants and went on to become a leading champion of Hispanic-American rights and an acid critic of stereotypical treatment of Mexicans, died on Aug. 18 in Sacramento. He was 78.

The cause was a heart attack, his wife, Keda Alcala-Obledo, said.

Mr. Obledo, the founder and leader of major Hispanic-American organizations, was called the "Godfather of the Latino Movement."

His overarching accomplishment was to help usher Hispanics toward the center of the American political discussion, declaring that they would no longer "take a back seat to anyone." Known just as Mario, in the manner of his ally Jesse Jackson, he helped forge alliances with other minorities and build political power by registering hundreds of thousands of Hispanics to vote.

During the administration of Gov. Jerry Brown, he became the first Hispanic chief of a California state agency: health and welfare, the largest in both budget and workers. In 1982, he was the first Hispanic citizen to mount a serious run for governor of California. When President Bill Clinton presented him with the Presidential Medal of Freedom in 1998, the citation said that Mr. Obledo had "created a powerful chorus for justice and equality."

HONORED AS HERO: Mr. Obledo with President Bill Clinton after being awarded the Presidential Medal of Freedom in 1998.

His approach was as unsubtle as it was impassioned. He created a national commotion in the 1990s by protesting the stereotypical Mexican accent of the Chihuahua in Taco Bell commercials. When someone put up a sign at the California border reading, "Illegal Immigration State," he threatened to burn it down personally.

He ignited an explosive response in 1998 when he said in a radio interview that Hispanics were on the way to taking over all of California's political institutions. He suggested that people who did not like it should go back to Europe.

In the face of criticism that Hispanics had lagged behind blacks in creating political and civil rights institutions, he created and led many. These included the Mexican American Legal Defense and Educational Fund, the Hispanic National Bar Association, the Southwest Voter Registration Education Project and the National Coalition of Hispanic Organizations.

He was president of the League of United Latin American Citizens and chairman of the National Rainbow Coalition, the liberal political organization that grew out of Mr. Jackson's 1984 presidential campaign.

Mario Guerra Obledo was born in San Antonio on April 9, 1932, and grew up in a tiny house on an alley off a dirt street. His father died when he was 5, and he and his 12 brothers and sisters had to hustle to find chores to help supplement welfare to pay the $5-a-month rent and other expenses.

His mother hammered into him the importance of education, telling him that "teachers are second to God." The pharmacist he started working for at 12 urged him to go to college. His four brothers were convicted of crimes like burglary, robbery and narcotics, but he himself was never jailed.

"I was involved in everything, I guess, that everyone else was," he said in an interview with The New York Times in 1982. "I just never happened to get caught in a serious situation that would embitter me to the point where I would continue in that pattern."

Mr. Obledo entered the University of Texas at Austin in 1949, then interrupted his studies to enlist in the Navy in 1951. He specialized in radar technology and was on a ship during the Korean War. He returned to the university and graduated with a degree in pharmacy. He worked as a pharmacist while earning a law degree from St. Mary's University in San Antonio.

One day, another young lawyer, Pete Tijerina, spotted Mr. Obledo at a dinner for the League of United Latin American Citizens. Mr. Tijerina was pondering how to start a legal organization to fight for the rights of Hispanics in the United States. "I need a guy like him," Mr. Tijerina recalled thinking.

The two men founded the Mexican American Legal Defense and Educational Fund with $2.2 million from the Ford Foundation and guidance from the NAACP Legal Defense and Educational Fund.

They had no trouble finding injustices. They filed a suit saying a utility had discriminated against Hispanic job candidates by having a height requirement, and they won. They forced schools to desegregate, courts to reform jury selection, swimming pools to integrate and businesses to take down signs barring Mexicans from entering.

"Discrimination was so widespread, I claimed that filing a lawsuit was like picking apples off a tree," Mr. Obledo said in an interview.

He joined the Harvard Law School faculty as a teaching fellow for eight months in 1975. Then Governor Brown of California named him secretary of health and welfare. He held the post for seven years, and sharply increased the number of minorities working in the agency. After losing badly in his bid for California's Democratic nomination for governor, he practiced law and consulted.

Besides his wife, Mr. Obledo is survived by nine brothers and sisters and three children by his first wife, the former Mary Robles: two daughters; a son; and four granddaughters.

Saying he was alarmed at what he saw as rising anti-Hispanic sentiment in immigration and education, he re-emerged in the late 1990s to take on issues as diverse as the exclusion of a Latino float from a Fourth of July parade and cutbacks in bilingual education — not to mention that Taco Bell Chihuahua.

In 1987, he wrote a letter to The Los Angeles Times protesting proposals to raise excise taxes on gasoline, liquor and cigarettes. He said the taxes disproportionately harmed the poor.

He accepted The Times's editorial argument that such taxes would help limit consumption and that this was good. But then he zeroed in: "Is it our government's intention to deny these everyday items only to the poor?"

— *By Douglas Martin*

BILL MILLIN

The Gallant Piper of D-Day

JULY 14, 1922 - AUG. 18, 2010

Bill Millin, a Scottish bagpiper who played highland tunes as his fellow commandos landed on a Normandy beach on D-Day and lived to see his bravado immortalized in the 1962 film "The Longest Day," died on Aug. 18 in a hospital in the western England county of Devon. He was 88.

Mr. Millin was a 21-year-old private in Britain's First Special Service Brigade when his unit landed on the strip of coast the Allies code-named Sword Beach, near the French city of Caen at the eastern end of the invasion front chosen by the Allies for the landings on June 6, 1944.

By one estimate, about 4,400 Allied troops died in the first 24 hours of the landings, about two-thirds of them Americans.

The young piper was approached shortly before the landings by the brigade's commanding officer, Brig. Simon Fraser, who as the 15th Lord Lovat was the hereditary chief of the Clan Fraser and one of Scotland's most celebrated aristocrats. Against orders from World War I that forbade playing bagpipes on the battlefield because of the high risk of attracting enemy fire, Lord Lovat, then 32, asked Private Millin to play on the beachhead to raise morale.

When Private Millin demurred, citing the regulations, he recalled later, Lord Lovat replied: "Ah, but that's the English War Office. You and I are both Scottish, and that doesn't apply."

After wading ashore in waist-high water that he said caused his kilt to float, Private Millin reached the beach, then marched up and down, unarmed, playing the tunes Lord Lovat had requested, including "Highland Laddie" and "Road to the Isles."

With German troops raking the beach with artillery and machine-gun fire, the young piper played on as his fellow soldiers advanced through smoke and flame on the German positions, or fell on the beach. The scene provided an emotional high point in "The Longest Day."

In later years Mr. Millin told the BBC that he did not regard what he had done as heroic. When Lord Lovat insisted that he play, he said, "I just said 'O.K.,' and got on with it." He added: "I didn't notice I was being shot at. When you're young, you do things you wouldn't dream of doing when you're older."

He said he found out later, after meeting Germans who had manned guns above the beach, that they didn't shoot him "because they thought I was crazy."

From the beach, Private Millin moved inland with the commandos to relieve British paratroopers who had seized a bridge near the village of Ouistreham that was vital to German attempts to bring in reinforcements. As the commandos crossed the bridge under German fire, Lord Lovat again asked Private Millin to play his pipes.

Bill Millin was born in Glasgow on July 14, 1922, the son of a policeman, and lived with his family in Canada as a child before returning to Scotland. In 1954 he married Margaret Mary Dowdel. A widower, he is survived by their son.

After the war, he worked on Lord Lovat's estate near Inverness, but found the life too quiet and took a job as a piper with a traveling theater company. In the late 1950s, he trained in Glasgow as a psychiatric nurse and eventually settled in Devon, retiring in 1988. He visited the United States several times, lecturing on his D-Day experiences.

He recalled how British commandos cheered and waved as he played his bagpipes, though he said he felt bad as he marched among ranks of wounded soldiers needing medical help. But those who survived the landings offered no reproach.

"I shall never forget hearing the skirl of Bill Millin's pipes," one commando, Tom Duncan, said years later. "As well as the pride we felt, it reminded us of home, and why we were fighting there for our lives and those of our loved ones."

— *By John F. Burns*

JUNE 6, 1944: Private Millin, right foreground, storms the beach at Normandy, bagpipes in hand.

JACKSON GILLIS

If You Watched It, He Probably Wrote It

AUG. 21, 1916 - AUG. 19, 2010

COPS AND DETECTIVES, doctors and lawyers, spies and cowboys, heroes, superheroes and semi-superheroes. These are staples of television drama, and one of the unsung people who stapled them was Jackson Gillis, a prolific slogger in the trenches of television writing whose career spanned more than four decades and whose scripts put words in the mouths of Superman, Perry Mason, Columbo, Wonder Woman, Zorro, Tarzan, Napoleon Solo, Jessica Fletcher and, in a manner of speaking, Lassie.

Mr. Gillis died on Aug. 19 in Moscow, Idaho. He was 93.

Mr. Gillis was not an award winner — he was nominated for a single Emmy, in 1972, for an episode of "Columbo" — but his résumé traces a remarkable path through the evolution of prime time. His niche was the plot-driven tale of distress, in which danger disturbs the serene status quo, is cranked up to crisis dimensions and is resolved with dispatch by the protagonist, all in a neat half-hour or hour.

The formula stayed remarkably consistent during his career — and it has remained so — but Mr. Gillis showed he could adapt to the tenor of the times.

In the 1950s, his dialogue, in "The Adventures of Superman" and "Lassie," for example, was replete with homespun clichés (if sometimes winkingly so) and not especially subtle repartee. In the 1960s, when he wrote for shows like "I Spy" and "The Man From U.N.C.L.E.," with their wisecracking secret agents, he incorporated the hip lingo that television, however tentatively, was invoking to reflect the decade. Later, in "Columbo," he helped define the low-key nature of the title character (played by Peter Falk), with lines that were understated and wry.

Jackson Clark Gillis was born in Kalama, Wash., on Aug. 21, 1916. His father, Ridgway, a highway engineer, moved the family to California when Jackson was a teenager; his mother, the former Marjorie Lyman, was a piano teacher. He went to Fresno State University and graduated from Stanford. He acted after college, working in Britain and at the Barter Theater in Virginia. (Gregory Peck was also in the company at the time.)

His scripts put words in the mouths of Superman, Perry Mason, Columbo, Wonder Woman, Zorro, Tarzan, Napoleon Solo, Jessica Fletcher and, in a manner of speaking, Lassie.

"One play he did was by George Bernard Shaw, who came to see the play and sent him a postcard afterward criticizing his exit," his daughter, Candida Gillis, wrote in an e-mail. "I have the postcard."

Mr. Gillis served as an Army intelligence officer in the Pacific during World War II. After his discharge, he and his wife moved to Los Angeles, where he began writing for radio, including the mysteries "The Whistler" and "Let George Do It."

He shifted to television in the early 1950s; his first regular assignment was for a cop show, "I'm the Law," which starred George Raft as a New York City police detective. He wrote numerous episodes of "The Adventures of Superman," beginning in 1953, and from 1954 to 1960 he was a frequent contributor of heroic canine feats and communicative barks for "Lassie."

He spent several years writing for "Perry Mason," beginning in 1959. He also wrote popular serials for children that appeared on "The Mickey Mouse Club": "The Adventures of Spin and Marty," about boys living on a ranch; and two adventures featuring the teenage amateur detective brothers the Hardy Boys, "The Mystery of the Applegate Treasure" and "The Mystery of the Ghost Farm."

Mr. Gillis's 62-year marriage to Patricia Cassidy, whom he met when they were fellow actors at the Barter Theater, ended with her death in 2003.

In addition to his daughter, who lives in Moscow, he is survived by a brother and a grandson.

Ms. Gillis said in a telephone interview that as she was growing up, the soundtrack of the house was the constant rat-a-tat of her father's typewriter, and certainly what is most impressive about Mr. Gillis's career is its sheer breadth. He worked on "Racket Squad," "Sugarfoot," "The Fugitive," "Lost in Space," "The Wild, Wild West," "Mission: Impossible," "Mannix," "The Mod Squad," "Bonanza," "Ironside," "Land of the Giants," "Hawaii Five-O," "Medical Center," "Starsky and Hutch," "Police Woman" and "Murder, She Wrote."

His daughter described him as a freelance worker bee who was never a Hollywood insider. When he brought her to the studio, he would warn her not to stare at anyone she recognized.

"He was not impressed by the business," she said, adding that he didn't watch much television himself.

"He watched football," Ms. Gillis said. "He thought most of what was on TV was junk."

— *By Bruce Weber*

CORINNE DAY

A Fashion Photographer Who Refused the Airbrush

FEB. 19, 1962 - AUG. 27, 2010

Corinne Day, whose frank, unadorned photos of a teenage Kate Moss in the early 1990s helped inaugurate a new era of gritty realism in fashion photography that came to be called "grunge," died on Aug. 27 at her home in Denham, a village in Buckinghamshire, England.

The cause was a cancerous brain tumor. Ms. Day was 45, according to her Web site, but public records indicate she was 48.

Ms. Day's passion to record the most profound human experiences with a camera was never more evident than the day in 1996 when the tumor was discovered after she had collapsed in New York. She promptly asked her husband to shoot pictures of her, and they continued the project through her treatment and decline.

"Photography is getting as close as you can to real life," she said, "showing us things we don't normally see. These are people's most intimate moments, and sometimes intimacy is sad."

Ms. Day built her reputation on unrelenting visual honesty. She refused to airbrush the bags from under models' eyes or de-emphasize their knobby knees. She eschewed pretty locations or even studios in favor of shooting people in their own environments.

It added up to a startling detour from the glossy world of supermodels — "subversion," in Ms. Day's own phrase.

There were two career-defining moments along the way, both involving Ms. Moss. The first was in 1990, when some of the first published fashion photographs of Ms. Moss, taken by Ms. Day, appeared in the British magazine The Face. One showed Ms. Moss topless; another suggested she was naked. She wore a mix of designer and secondhand clothes and no makeup over her freckles, and her expression was sincere. The photos seemed to usher in a new age of anti-fashion style. Artlessness became art. Some called it "grunge."

ARTIST AND MUSE: Ms. Day, right, with model Kate Moss. Both were instrumental in each other's career.

The second moment, in 1993, was a shoot for British Vogue that featured a pale and skinny Ms. Moss in mismatched underwear. A public outcry ensued, as some claimed that Ms. Moss's waifish figure seemed to imply she was suffering from an eating disorder or drug addiction.

On her agent's advice, Ms. Moss stopped working with Ms. Day, with whom she had become close friends. Ms. Day said she was tired of taking fashion pictures, anyway.

"I think fashion magazines are horrible," she said in an interview with the British newspaper The Observer in 1995. "They're stale and they say the same thing year in and year out."

The grunge aesthetic took hold for several years in designer imagery of the 1990s, most visibly in Calvin Klein's influential fragrance and jeans campaigns, and also in street fashion, with the throwaway style of flannel shirts and distressed jeans, as popularized by Kurt Cobain and the burgeoning Seattle music scene.

Ms. Day eventually took fashion photos again, including ones of Ms. Moss that are in the permanent collection of the National Portrait Gallery in London. But her aspiration was to document the lives of the people she knew best, and her "Diary," published in 2000, told visual stories, including those of a single mother struggling to survive.

Corinne Day was born in Ealing, a town in west London. She said that her mother had run a brothel and that her father had robbed banks. They divorced when she was 5, and her grandmother raised her. As a girl, she said, she liked to spend hours in the photo booth at Woolworth's with her friends.

Ms. Day left school at 16, worked briefly as a trainee in a bank, then flew around the world as an airline courier. A photographer she met on a plane suggested that she take up modeling, and she did, for Guess Jeans.

In Japan she met a filmmaker, Mark Szaszy, who taught her to use a camera — they would later marry — and she began taking pictures of the drab private lives of her fellow models, who seemed so glamorous in public.

"There was a lot of sadness," she said in an interview with The Guardian in 2000. "We couldn't buy the clothes we were photographed in, couldn't go out and do the things we would have liked to do as teenagers."

She took her work to the art director at The Face, who asked her to shoot some fashion pictures. She prowled the modeling agencies with a Polaroid and found Ms. Moss, whom she likened to "the girl next door." They lived, worked and prospered together for three years.

"Corinne's pictures, you might say, made Kate, and Kate made Corinne's reputation," The Evening Standard said in 2007.

Ms. Day is survived by her husband as well as her parents and two brothers.

Even at the height of her celebrity, in 1993, Ms. Day told The Guardian that her personal sartorial goal was to look "unstyled."

"I don't take fashion too seriously," she said.

— *By Douglas Martin*

JOHN FREEBORN

The One Downed Plane That Haunted Him

DEC. 1, 1919 - AUG. 28, 2010

SEVENTY YEARS AGO, John Freeborn was one of the Royal Air Force's leading fighter pilots, acclaimed for his exploits off Dunkirk and in the air above English villages during the Battle of Britain.

Of the nearly 3,000 Allied fliers who dueled with German aircraft in that battle, thwarting Hitler's ambition to conquer Britain, none logged more combat hours than Wing Commander Freeborn. He was credited with shooting down at least 12 German planes during World War II, and he was twice decorated with Britain's Distinguished Flying Cross.

But Mr. Freeborn, who died on Aug. 28 at the age of 90, was also a central figure in a long-remembered episode of "friendly fire" — one that brought him anguish throughout his long life.

'IT'S ONE OF OURS': Mr. Freeborn never forgot the pilot he shot down.

On Sept. 6, 1939, three days after Britain had gone to war with Germany, Mr. Freeborn, flying a Spitfire fighter, was among a group of pilots sent aloft from their base at Hornchurch to intercept what were reported to be German planes headed toward the Essex coast in southeast England. Mr. Freeborn and a pilot flying alongside him each shot down a plane.

But it was a case of war jitters. There were no German aircraft. What Mr. Freeborn and the other pilot presumed to be German planes were in fact a pair of British Hurricane fighters, which had also been sent up, from the nearby North Weald airbase.

Pilot Officer Montague Hulton-Harrop, the flier shot down by Mr. Freeborn, became the first British fighter pilot killed in the war. The other Hurricane pilot shot down that day survived.

Mr. Freeborn, accused by his commanding officer of disregarding a last-minute order to hold his fire, was court-martialed. But he maintained that his commander had lied — that he had, in fact, been told to attack. He was exonerated together with his fellow Spitfire pilot, the affair attributed to miscommunication.

In May 1940, Mr. Freeborn took part in covering the British Expeditionary Force's escape from Dunkirk when German forces were overrunning France. He shot down two German planes, but his Spitfire was later downed. He was rescued, and he returned to England.

When the Battle of Britain raged in the summer of 1940, Mr. Freeborn returned to combat with his No.74 Squadron, a unit with a tiger's face as its emblem and the motto "I Fear No Man."

On Aug. 11, the "tiger" squadron flew into battle four times in a span of eight hours and reported destroying 23 German planes — 3 of them downed by Mr. Freeborn himself — and damaging 14 others.

Mr. Freeborn came to the United States in 1942 to train American fighter pilots, then returned to England to escort bombers on missions off the French and Dutch coasts. He became one of Britain's youngest wing commanders in 1944, overseeing a fighter unit based in southern Italy.

Mr. Freeborn's death, in Southport, in northwest England, was announced on the 74 Squadron Association's Web site by his biographer, Bob Cossey, author of "A Tiger's Tale" (2002).

(In 2009, Mr. Freeborn collaborated with Christopher Yeoman on a memoir, "Tiger Cub.")

Mr. Cossey said that Mr. Freeborn was his squadron's last surviving Battle of Britain pilot.

John Connell Freeborn was born on Dec. 1, 1919, in Middleton, England, outside Leeds. His father was a bank manager.

He joined the R.A.F. in 1938, and left military service in 1946, working as a regional manager for a soft-drink distributorship.

He is survived by a daughter from his marriage to his first wife, Rita, who died in 1980. His second wife, Peta, died in 2001.

Mr. Freeborn never forgot about the British pilot he shot down in those frenzied first days of World War II. In a 2004 interview with the author Gavin Mortimer, reprinted in the Smithsonian's Air & Space magazine on Mr. Freeborn's death, he recalled how that episode could have become even more tragic if another pilot had not intervened after Pilot Officer Hulton-Harrop was shot down.

"I think I would have shot down more if it weren't for Hawkins," he said of that fellow flier. "He got in the way, and I was shouting at him to get out of the bloody way, either shoot or let me shoot. But then he said, 'It's one of ours.'"

In September 2003, Mr. Freeborn visited Pilot Officer Hulton-Harrop's grave in a churchyard near the old North Weald airfield.

"I think about him nearly every day," Mr. Freeborn told the BBC in 2009. "I always have."

"I've had a good life," Mr. Freeborn said, "and he should have had a good life, too."

— *By Richard Goldstein*

VANCE BOURJAILY

In the Thick of Postwar Literature

SEPT. 17, 1922 - AUG. 31, 2010

Vance Bourjaily, a novelist whose literary career, like those of Norman Mailer and James Jones, emerged out of World War II and whose ambitious novels explored American themes for decades afterward, died on Aug. 31 in Greenbrae, Calif. He was 87.

Mr. Bourjaily (pronounced bor-ZHAY-lee) never achieved the top rank of recognition that was predicted for him in 1947 after publication of his first novel, "The End of My Life." But he had a long and substantial career in letters of the sort that was far more prevalent a half-century ago than it is today.

Not only a serious novelist, Mr. Bourjaily was also a teacher who spent more than 20 years at the Iowa Writers' Workshop and five years at the University of Arizona before becoming the first director of the Master of Fine Arts program in creative writing at Louisiana State University. He worked as a journalist and an editor. He wrote short stories, essays and reviews.

He was also a serious literary socialite.

"Everyone came to Bourjaily's parties in the early 1950s," Esquire magazine said about him in the 1980s, naming Mr. Mailer, Mr. Jones, William Styron and others as attendees. At one party Mr. Bourjaily introduced Mr. Jones to the actor Montgomery Clift, a pairing that would lead to one of Mr. Clift's signature roles, the brooding bugler Prewitt in the film version of Mr. Jones's novel "From Here to Eternity."

Mr. Bourjaily's novels often explored what it meant to be an American at a particular historical moment. His second book, "The Hound of Earth" (1955), grounded in the cold war, is about an Army scientist who has gone

AUG

AWOL in guilt-ridden flight after contributing to the development of the atomic bomb. His third, "The Violated" (1958), a psychologically astute profile of four characters over 25 years — a period with World War II at its center — prompted the critic Irving Howe to write that Mr. Bourjaily was "one of the few serious young novelists who has tried to go directly toward the center of postwar experience."

His other books include "Confessions of a Spent Youth," a picaresque, autobiographical tale largely about the war and sex; "The Man Who Knew Kennedy," which tells of the decline into suicide of a young man who seemingly has everything, and which reflects Mr. Bourjaily's view that the nation's golden postwar years were curtailed by the assassination of the president in 1963; and "Brill Among the Ruins," a Vietnam-era parable focusing on a middle-age Midwestern lawyer.

Novelist, teacher and bon vivant. Though Mr. Bourjaily never achieved the top rank of recognition, he had a long and substantial career.

As generally well reviewed as these and other books of his were, Mr. Bourjaily seemed always to be measured against his first, "The End of My Life," which was commissioned by the editor Maxwell Perkins while Mr. Bourjaily was still in the Army. The novel, about a young man coping with his war experiences, was lavishly praised by the critic John W. Aldridge in his influential book "After the Lost Generation." Mr. Aldridge drew comparisons to Fitzgerald and Hemingway.

"No book since 'This Side of Paradise' has caught so well the flavor of youth in wartime," Mr. Aldridge wrote, "and no book since 'A Farewell to Arms' has contained so complete a record of the loss of that youth in war."

Vance Nye Bourjaily was born in Cleveland on Sept. 17, 1922. His father, Monte Ferris Bourjaily, a Lebanese immigrant, was a journalist who became editor of the United Features Syndicate. His mother, Barbara Webb, wrote feature articles and romance novels.

After his parents divorced when he was 12, Mr. Bourjaily split time with them in New York and Virginia. He went to Bowdoin College in Maine, but interrupted his studies to serve in the war, first as an ambulance driver for the American Field Service in Syria, Egypt and Italy, and later as an Army infantryman in Japan.

He returned to Bowdoin to complete his degree after the war, but as he said in a 1987 radio interview, for a lot of college students of the era "our education was the Second World War."

Mr. Bourjaily lived for a time in San Francisco, where he was a feature writer for The San Francisco Chronicle, and then moved to New York, site of the memorable parties. He was a founder of Discovery, a short-lived literary journal of some cachet, and wrote reviews of Broadway shows for a new publication, The Village Voice. He left the city for Iowa and the writers' workshop in 1957.

Mr. Bourjaily's first marriage, to Bettina Yensen, ended in divorce. Two of their children survive him, a daughter and a son, Philip, of Iowa City, an outdoors writer who wrote a book with his father titled "Fishing by Mail: The Outdoor Life of a Father and Son."

He is also survived by his wife, Yasmin Mogul, a former student he married in 1985, as well as their son, a brother, two half-sisters, a stepdaughter, four grandchildren and a stepgranddaughter.

Besides being an avid outdoorsman, Mr. Bourjaily was a jazz aficionado and an amateur cornet player. (He bought his first instrument when he left the Army with his mustering-out pay.) His novel "The Great Fake Book" (1987) has an amateur jazz cornetist as a protagonist, and at Iowa he was known for organizing jam sessions (and parties and pig roasts) at his farm, Redbird, outside of Iowa City.

"Vance was a key member of the workshop," Marvin Bell, a poet who was Mr. Bourjaily's longtime colleague at the writers' workshop, said in a telephone interview after Mr. Bourjaily's death. "Not only for his teaching. For his socializing. There was a lot of socializing."

— *By Bruce Weber*

LAURENT FIGNON

A Cyclist Admired if Not Loved

AUG. 12, 1960 - AUG. 31, 2010

LAURENT FIGNON, one of France's greatest and most enigmatic cyclists, who alienated fans even as he won the Tour de France in back-to-back years before losing the event in 1989 to the American Greg LeMond in the race's closest finish, died in Paris on Aug. 31. He was 50.

His death was confirmed by the French cycling federation. In April 2009, Fignon, who lived in Paris, learned that he had advanced cancer of the digestive tract and that it had spread to his lungs.

From 1982 to 1993, Fignon won more than 75 races and earned as much as $900,000 a year. His victories included the Giro d'Italia (Tour of Italy) in 1989 and the Milan to San Remo Classic in 1988 and 1989. He won the Tour de France in 1983 and 1984. But as he said years after the 1989 race, "Nobody talks about the two Tours I won, only about the one I lost."

The more than century-old Tour de France, the world's premier bicycle race, lasts three weeks. In 1989, it covered 3,285 miles, including the final day's 15.5-mile (25-kilometer) time trial from Versailles to Paris. At the start of the day, Fignon was the overall leader and LeMond was second, 50 seconds behind.

In a time trial, the riders start one by one. LeMond was the next-to-last starter and Fignon the last, starting two minutes apart. LeMond, helped by an aerodynamic helmet and new triathlon handlebars, kept up an almost superhuman pace in the time trial and averaged 33.8 miles (54.4 kilometers) an hour, still a Tour record.

Fignon, his blond ponytail blowing, could not match that pace, and LeMond won the trial by 33 seconds and the Tour by 8 seconds. The Tour director, Christian Prudhomme, speaking to The Associated Press, said of Fignon, "I remember that lost look in his eyes on the finish line at the Champs-Élysées, which contrasted with Greg LeMond's indescribable joy."

ENIGMATIC CHAMPION: Fignon during the final lap of the Tour de France in 1983.

In 2003, a survey of Tour journalists, authors and former riders voted the time trial the Tour de France's greatest race.

The defeat effectively ended Fignon's career, though he did not retire until 1993.

In a statement after Fignon's death, Lance Armstrong, the American seven-time Tour champion who has been treated for cancer, called Fignon a "dear friend" and "always a friendly face with words of advice."

Yet as much as the French public adores its cycling stars, there was little love for Fignon. He was remote and brusque and could be willful, even arrogant, never reluctant to snatch victory away from deserving teammates in a race. He struck photographers, and ignored reporters and fans. Journalists awarded him their Prix Citron, the lemon prize for the least likable rider in the 1989 Tour.

"At least I won something," he later said.

Fignon also generated ill will among his fellow riders. In his 2009 autobiography, "We Were Young and Carefree," published last year, he said drug use had been common among racers, an accusation many of them angrily denied. He admitted to having used cortisone, amphetamines and other drugs, and twice failed doping tests.

"In those days, everyone did it," he wrote.

Laurent Fignon was born on Aug. 12, 1960, in Paris. He rode his first race at 15 and won more than 50 races as an amateur.

He won his first Tour in 1983, when he was not quite 23 and was known mainly as a lieutenant to his team leader, Bernard Hinault, who could not seek his fifth Tour victory that year because of tendinitis in his right knee. Fignon later taunted Hinault when Hinault became his main rival on another team.

Fignon was the rare rider at the time to wear glasses and to read books. Having spent a term in veterinary school — "college" to most others in the bicycle racing world — he was nicknamed the Professor.

That changed to the Playboy after he won the Tour and began showing up at late-night discos, cocktail parties and celebrity ski weekends.

In later years, he organized semiclassic one-day races and then operated the Paris-Nice race for a few years. Bicycles were marketed under his name. Most recently, he opened a hotel in the foothills of the Pyrenees and was a commentator at bicycle races for France 2 television. During the last Tour de France, he sounded weakened by his illness — his voice gravelly, sometimes a whisper — but characteristically grumpy and perceptive.

He is survived by his wife, Valerie, whom he married in 2008; a son; and a daughter from a previous marriage.

Fignon spoke openly about his illness, saying in interviews that he suspected his drug use as an athlete had led to the cancer. Last January, he told the magazine Paris Match: "I do not want to die at 50 years. I love life, love to laugh, travel, read, eat well like a good Frenchman. I'm not afraid of death. I just do not want it."

— *By Frank Litsky and Samuel Abt*

EILEEN NEARNE

No One Would Have Guessed Her Past

MARCH 15, 1921 - SEPT. 2, 2010

AFTER SHE DIED IN EARLY SEPTEMBER, a frail 89-year-old alone in a flat in the British seaside town of Torquay, Eileen Nearne, her body undiscovered for several days, was listed by local officials as a candidate for what is known in Britain as a council burial, or what in the past was called a pauper's grave.

But after the police looked through her possessions, including a Croix de Guerre medal awarded to her by the French government after World War II, the obscurity Ms. Nearne had cultivated for decades began to slip away.

Known to her neighbors as an insistently private woman who loved cats and who revealed almost nothing about her past, Ms. Nearne has emerged as a heroine in the tortured story of Nazi-occupied France, one of the secret agents who helped prepare the French resistance for the D-Day landings in June 1944. And the anonymity she treasured for so long has now been denied her in death.

On Sept. 21, a funeral service was held in Torquay featuring a military bugler and piper and an array of uniformed mourners. A red cushion atop her coffin bore her wartime medals. Eulogies celebrated her as one of 39 British women who were parachuted into France by the Special Operations Executive, a wartime agency known as "Churchill's secret army," which recruited more than 14,000 agents to conduct espionage and sabotage behind enemy lines.

Funeral costs were paid by the British Legion, the country's main veterans organization, and by donors who came forward after the circumstances of Ms. Nearne's death made front-page news in Britain. In accordance with her wishes, her ashes were to be scattered at sea.

Ms. Nearne, known as Didi, volunteered for work that was as dangerous as any that wartime Britain had to offer: operating a secret radio link from Paris that was used to organize weapons drops to the French resistance movement and to shuttle messages back and forth between controllers in London and the resistance.

After several narrow escapes, she was arrested by the Gestapo in July 1944 and sent to the Ravensbruck concentration camp near Berlin. Ravensbruck was mainly intended for women, and tens of thousands of them died there. But Ms. Nearne, unlike other women working for the Special Operations Executive who were executed in the Nazi camps, survived.

As she related in postwar debriefings, documented in Britain's National Archives, the Gestapo tortured her — beating her, stripping her naked, then submerging her repeatedly in a bath of ice-cold water until she began to black out from lack of oxygen. Yet they failed to force her to yield the secrets they sought: her real identity, the names of others working with her in the resistance and the assignments given to her by London. She was 23 at the time.

AGENT ROSE: Ms. Nearne parachuted into Nazi-occupied France to set up a secret radio link.

The account she gave her captors was that she was an innocent and somewhat gullible Frenchwoman named Jacqueline Duterte, and that she had been recruited by a local businessman to transmit radio coded messages that she did not understand.

She recalled one interrogator's attempts to break her will: "He said, 'Liar! Spy!' and hit me on the face. He said, 'We have ways of making people who don't want to talk, talk. Come with us.'"

From Ravensbruck, Ms. Nearne, her head shaved, was shuttled eastward through an archipelago of Nazi death camps. After first refusing to work in the camps, she changed her mind, seeing the work assignments as the only means of staying alive.

In December 1944 she was moved to the Markleberg camp, near Leipzig, where she worked on a road-repair gang for 12 hours a day. But while being transferred yet again, she and two Frenchwomen escaped and linked up with American troops.

Even then, her travails were not over. American intelligence officers at first identified her as a Nazi collaborator and held her at a detention center with captured SS personnel until her account, that she was a British secret agent, was verified by her superiors in London.

Asked by her postwar debriefers how she kept up hope, she replied: "The will to live. Will power. That's the most important. You should not let yourself go. It seemed that the end would never come, but I always believed in destiny, and I had a hope."

"If you are a person who is drowning, you put all your efforts into trying to swim."

Ms. Nearne was born on March 15, 1921, into an Anglo-Spanish family that later moved to France, where she grew up speaking French.

The family fled to Spain ahead of the German occupation of France and arrived in Britain in 1942. Ms. Nearne, her older sister, Jacqueline, and their brother, Francis, were recruited by the Special Operations Executive. In March 1944, Didi Nearne followed her sister in parachuting into France and remained there, under the code name Agent Rose, after her sister was airlifted back to Britain.

The Gestapo had infiltrated many of the Allied spying networks, and Ms. Nearne lived on a knife's edge. On a train journey to a new safe house south of Paris, her cover came close to being blown when a German soldier offered to carry her suitcase, which contained her secret radio. After telling him that it contained a gramophone, she hurriedly got off the train and walked with the case the rest of the way.

Describing how she lived undercover, she said after the war: "I wasn't nervous. In my mind, I was never going to be arrested. But of course I was careful. There were Gestapo in plain clothes everywhere. I always looked at my reflection in the shop windows to see if I was being followed."

In July 1944, the Gestapo arrived at her Paris hideout moments after she had completed a coded transmission. She burned the messages and hid the radio, but the Germans found the radio and the pad she had used for coding the transmissions.

Parts of her story were later told in books written about wartime secret operations, including the 1966 history "SOE in France, 1940-1944," by Michael Foot, part of a government history series by authors given special access to secret government records.

But wartime friends said after her death, on Sept. 2, that she had found it difficult to adjust to peacetime life, and a medical report in the government archives said she was suffering from psychological symptoms brought on by her wartime service. She never married, and she lived alone after her sister died in 1982.

Friends said that she withdrew into herself and shunned all opportunities to earn celebrity from her wartime experiences. In 1993, she returned to Ravensbruck for a visit, but otherwise she cherished her anonymity. As she told an interviewer several years before she died: "It was a life in the shadows, but I was suited for it. I could be hard and secret. I could be lonely. I could be independent. But I wasn't bored. I liked the work. After the war, I missed it."

— *By John F. Burns*

PAUL CONRAD

Drawing With a Skewer

JUNE 27, 1924 - SEPT. 4, 2010

In the Watergate scandal, he drew Richard M. Nixon nailing himself to a cross. He stood Dick Cheney at a vast graveyard of veterans, saying, "For seven years, we did everything to keep you safe." And on the frieze over the United States Supreme Court, he etched the hallowed words: "Of the insurance co's. By the insurance co's. And for the insurance co's."

Paul Conrad's editorial cartoons in The Los Angeles Times, The Denver Post and other papers slashed presidents, skewered pomposity and exposed what he saw as deception and injustice for six decades. Subjects squirmed. Readers were outraged and delighted. And he won a host of awards, including three Pulitzer Prizes.

"No one's ever accused me of being objective," he liked to say of his take-no-prisoners career, which branched into sculpture, books and helium balloons. At the age of 86, Mr. Conrad, who lived in Rancho Palos Verdes, Calif., died of natural causes at his home on Sept. 4.

In the tradition of Thomas Nast, whose caricatures hounded a corrupt Boss Tweed from power in New York in the 19th century, and of Herbert R. Block, the renowned Herblock of The Washington Post, Mr. Conrad captured complex issues and personalities in simple pen-and-ink drawings that touched the major political fights of his era.

Wars, elections, scandals, the legerdemain of politicians and the shenanigans of charlatans — all were grist for the Conrad Truth Machine, a moveable feast that began at The Denver Post in 1950, went to The Los Angeles Times in 1964 and, after 1993, was syndicated in publications that had printed his work for decades. He won Pulitzers in 1964, 1971 and 1984.

"Conrad's name strikes fear in the hearts of men all over the world," the humorist Art Buchwald wrote, with echoes of the Shadow and Superman. "Where there is corruption, greed or hypocrisy, everyone says, 'This is a job for Conrad.' "

POWER OF THE PEN: Mr. Conrad's incisive political cartoons angered subjects and delighted readers.

He was a Democrat with liberal leanings and relished attacking Republicans. His Nixon was a sly, secretive scoundrel in need of a shave. He made the Nixon "enemies list," and his taxes were audited four times. Ironically, he later secured the Nixon lecture chair at the president's alma mater, Whittier College, in 1977-8.

In 1968, Mr. Conrad drew Gov. Ronald Reagan of California on his knees retrieving papers marked "law and order," "patriotism" and "individual liberty" from under the feet of former Gov. George C. Wallace of Alabama, a presidential candidate. "Excuse me, Mr. Wallace," he says, "you're stepping on my lines." As president, Mr. Reagan became Napoleon, "The War Powers Actor."

But Mr. Conrad also took aim at Democrats. President Lyndon B. Johnson and Vice President Hubert H. Humphrey were cowboys riding a Dr. Strangelove bomb as it plunged toward Vietnam in 1968. Years later, when Robert S. McNamara, the former defense secretary, expressed regrets over the war, Mr. Conrad drew him at the Vietnam Veterans Memorial in Washington, beside the names of 58,000 dead, saying, "Sorry about that."

In the 1976 and 1980 presidential campaigns, Mr. Conrad rendered Jimmy Carter with a toothy grin of vacuity. He portrayed yuppies as rich brats, reporters as backward donkey riders and himself as a scruffy artist — a lanky drudge in shirt sleeves with a jutting chin, horn-rimmed glasses and thinning hair — who drew six cartoons a week, inspired by news.

"I decide who's right and who's wrong, and go from there," he told Writer's Digest.

Paul Francis Conrad and his twin brother, James, were born in Cedar Rapids, Iowa, on June 27, 1924, sons of Robert H. Conrad and Florence Lawler Conrad. Paul drew his first cartoon on the wall of a parochial school boys' lavatory. After graduating from high school, he went to Alaska and worked in construction.

He joined the Army in 1942 and was in the invasions of Guam and Okinawa. In 1946, he enrolled at the University of Iowa. His grades were mediocre, but his cartoons for the college newspaper impressed teachers, who sent samples to The Denver Post. The paper hired him after graduation.

In 1953, he married Barbara Kay King; they had four children. His wife, children and a granddaughter survived him.

With syndication, his popularity grew exponentially. Soon after his first Pulitzer, he joined The Los Angeles Times. He often focused on nonpolitical subjects. When Apollo 11 landed on the moon in 1969, he conceived a mailbox awaiting the astronauts. A 1964 vision showed the moon looming larger in four rocket porthole panels, the last at the landing site, revealing a parking meter with an expiration flag: "Violation."

In 1993, Mr. Conrad accepted a buyout and left The Times. But he continued to produce cartoons that were syndicated for years.

He drew Mr. Nixon and George W. Bush side by side, chubby pals in beanies, called "Tweedledumb and Tweedledumber." After the 2008 election, he depicted Gov. Sarah Palin of Alaska, the losing vice-presidential candidate, holding a smoking AK-47 in one hand and, in the other, the trunk of a dead G.O.P. elephant.

Much of his work was collected in books. A PBS documentary, "Paul Conrad: Drawing Fire," was aired in 2006.

In the 1980s, he became a helium balloon enthusiast. He also sculptured bronze busts of presidents — George W. Bush in a 10-gallon hat atop a pair of cowboy boots with nothing in between — and other prominent Americans. Many have been exhibited at the Los Angeles County Museum of Art.

In 1991 he created "Chain Reaction," a 26-foot mushroom cloud of chain links and concrete. The sculpture stands outside the Santa Monica Civic Center. "This is a statement of peace," the artist's inscription says. "May it never become an epitaph."

— *By Robert D. McFadden*

JOHN W. KLUGE

Builder of a Media Empire

SEPT. 21, 1914 - SEPT. 7, 2010

John W. Kluge, who parlayed a small fortune from a Fritos franchise into a multibillion-dollar communications empire that made him one of the richest men in America, died on Sept. 7 at a family home in Charlottesville, Va. He was 95.

Mr. Kluge created Metromedia, the nation's first major independent broadcasting entity, which grew to include seven television stations, 14 radio stations, outdoor advertising, the Harlem Globetrotters, the Ice Capades, radio paging and mobile telephones.

An immigrant from Germany, Mr. Kluge (pronounced KLOOG-ee) came to the United States in 1922 and took his first job at the age of 10 as a payroll clerk for his stepfather in Detroit. He made his first million by the time he was 37.

He made his first billion in 1984, when he took Metromedia private in a $1.1 billion leveraged buyout and then liquidated the company, more than tripling his take.

He sold the television stations, including WNEW in New York, for more than $2 billion to Rupert Murdoch, who was expanding his communications empire. His sale of 11 radio stations brought close to $290 million. The outdoor advertising business went for $710 million. The Harlem Globetrotters and the Ice Capades, which together had cost the company $6 million, brought $30 million.

In 1986, Forbes magazine listed Mr. Kluge as the second-richest man in America (after Sam Walton, the founder of Wal-Mart Stores). By 2010 he had dropped to 109th on the list with a fortune of $6.5 billion, a reflection in part of the collapse in 2008 of two restaurant chains owned by Metromedia, Bennigan's and Steak and Ale.

Mr. Kluge had no patience for those he called "self-important corporation types cut out of the same cookie cutter" who stuck to what was safe. He often took Wall Street by surprise, but as the financial analyst Allen J. Gottesman said in 1986: "Whatever he does works out real well. You always assume there was a good reason, and you usually find out later that it was a good move."

Not everything he touched turned to gold. In 1965 he bought Diplomat magazine in Washington and tried to change it from a society sheet into a serious publication of world affairs. "I lost a million dollars before I ever knew I lost it," he said.

Three years later he negotiated a proposed $300 million merger of Metromedia with Transamerica only to join in calling off the deal "by mutual consent" in a two-paragraph statement months later, saying a merger would "adversely affect" the growth plans of both companies.

But he never lost his zest for developing new businesses or his taste for complex financial deals.

"I love the work because it taxes your mind," he said in an interview for this obituary in 1986. "Years ago, I could have taken a few million dollars and joined the country club and gotten into this pattern of complaining about the world and about the tax law."

He was critical of corporation executives who are hungry for the limelight. There were no public relations officers on his payroll. He liked to do business behind an unmarked door. His interview with The Times was one of the few he ever gave.

"I think a great deal of publicity becomes an obstacle," he said. "I'd love to be in the woodwork all my life. I enjoy it when I know who the other people are and they don't know who I am."

But it was inevitable that people would come to know who he was, first in the business world as the man with the Midas touch and then as a generous contributor to schools and hospitals.

In his later years his name appeared in the society columns as the host for charity parties that he and his third wife, Patricia, gave on their yacht, the Virginian, or as a guest at dinner dances. (He taught dancing at an Arthur Murray studio when he was in college.) He grew flowers and collected paintings, African sculpture and Indian, Chinese, Greek and Egyptian objets d'art.

But nothing gave him more pleasure than putting a deal together. And the creation of Metromedia, considered a triumph of financial structuring, may have been Mr. Kluge's greatest pleasure of all.

The most satisfying day in his life, he said, was the day Barney Balaban of Paramount told him, "Young man, you bring me $4 million and

MEDIA MOGUL: Mr. Kluge in 2007, at the announcement of his $400 million gift to Columbia University. In the background are New York mayor Michael Bloomberg, far left, and Rep. Charles Rangel.

you'll be able to have the Paramount stock in the Metropolitan Broadcasting Company."

With that $4 million, Mr. Kluge got into the television business as chief executive of Metropolitan, then consisting of two stations — WNEW and, in Washington, WTTG — and two radio stations. He renamed the company Metromedia in 1961 because he intended to expand it beyond broadcasting.

Mr. Kluge held to a simple maxim: make money and minimize taxes. He made it his business to study the tax code. In 1981, for example, he received tax benefits when he bought buses and subway cars from New York's Metropolitan Transportation Authority and then leased them back to the authority for a tax savings of $50 million over five years.

He also found a way to enhance the company's revenue by marrying the profits of broadcasting to the depreciation that came with billboard advertising.

"I sold the banks the idea that the Ford Motor Company that advertises on radio and television would also advertise on billboards," he recalled. "From a financial orientation, if you took the pretax profits of radio and television and the depreciation of outdoor advertising, you increase the cash flow. I impressed the bank so much that I borrowed $14 million and got our money back in 27 months."

John Werner Kluge was born Sept. 21, 1914, in Chemnitz, Germany. His father died in World War I. After his mother remarried, John was brought to America by his German-American stepfather to live in Detroit. The stepfather, Oswald Leitert, put him to work as a boy in the family contracting business.

Mr. Kluge said he left home when he was 14 to live in the house of a schoolteacher. "I was driven to have an education," he said.

He worked hard, and successfully, to lose his foreign accent and to win a scholarship to college. He first attended Detroit City College (later renamed Wayne State University) before transferring to Columbia University when he was offered a full scholarship and living expenses.

At college he distributed Communist literature. "I was never an official member of the Communist Party, but I was quite liberal," he said. What got him in trouble was his card playing. At one point the dean warned him that he was in danger of losing his scholarship.

"I told him, 'Dean, you will never catch me gambling again,'" he recalled, "and it was then that I realized that the dean of Columbia University didn't understand the English language. I had told him he'd never *catch* me gambling again."

Mr. Kluge channeled his fondness for gambling into high-stakes finance. "I don't really get comfortable when I haven't got something at risk," he said. Even as a billionaire twice over, he borrowed money to leverage his next ventures.

Mr. Kluge graduated from Columbia in 1937 and went to work for a small paper company in Detroit. Within three years he went from shipping clerk to vice president and part owner.

After serving in Army intelligence in World War II, he turned to broadcasting and, with a partner, created the radio station WGAY in Silver Spring, Md., in 1946. "It cost us $90,000," he recalled. "I went up and down the street on Georgia Avenue in Silver Spring to get investors."

In the 1950s he acquired radio stations in St. Louis, Dallas, Fort Worth, Buffalo, Tulsa, Nashville, Pittsburgh and Orlando. Meanwhile, he invested in real estate and expanded the New England Fritos corporation, which he had founded in 1947 to distribute Fritos and Cheetos in the Northeast, adding Fleischmann's yeast, Blue Bonnet margarine and Wrigley's chewing gum to his distribution network.

In 1951 he formed a food brokerage company, expanding it in 1956 in a partnership with David Finkelstein, and augmented his fortune selling the products of companies like General Foods and Coca-Cola to supermarket chains.

Mr. Kluge served on the boards of numerous companies, including Occidental Petroleum, Orion Pictures, Conair and the Waldorf-Astoria Corporation, as well as many charitable groups, including United Cerebral Palsy.

His philanthropy through the John W. Kluge Foundation was prodigious. About a half-billion dollars went to Columbia alone, mainly for scholarships for needy and minority students. One gift, of $400 million, was to be given to the university when he died.

Mr. Kluge also contributed to the restoration of Ellis Island and in 2000 gave $73 million to the Library of Congress, which established the Kluge Prize for the Study of Humanities.

Mr. Kluge and his third wife, the former Patricia Rose Gay, lived in a Georgian-style house on a 6,000-acre farm near Charlottesville called Albemarle House. He had another home in New Rochelle, N.Y., on Long Island Sound, and an apartment in Manhattan, where he kept much of his art collection, including works by Alberto Giacometti, Frank Stella and Fernando Botero.

Mr. Kluge became acquainted with the woman who would become his third wife when she was in her mid-20s and he was about 60. "At one party," he said, "she cooked the dinner and then she did a belly dance on the table and I said to myself, 'Where have I been all my life?'"

A small scandal erupted in 1985 when Mrs. Kluge was chairwoman of a charity ball in Palm Beach, Fla., attended by Charles and Diana, the prince and princess of Wales. The British press disclosed that a nude photograph of Mrs. Kluge had been published a decade before in a British magazine called Knave, which was owned by her first husband. To avoid embarrassment, the Kluges were traveling abroad on the night of the ball.

Their marriage ended in divorce in 1991, and Mrs. Kluge received a big settlement as well as the Virginia estate. He married again, to Maria Tussi Kuttner, who survives him. Two earlier marriages, to Yolanda Galardo Zucco and Theodora Thomson Townsend, also ended in divorce.

Mr. Kluge is also survived by his two sons, a daughter, a grandson and three stepchildren.

A convert to Roman Catholicism when he married his third wife, Mr. Kluge said he often went to church. He had planned to be buried in a crypt in a chapel he built on the grounds of Albemarle but changed his mind after the house was awarded to his third wife in the divorce.

Mr. Kluge acknowledged that he had been ruled by his ambitions, and traced them to the struggles of his boyhood. He recalled a conversation he had had with friends in college about their aspirations. "One fellow said he wanted to be a lawyer, another a doctor," he said. "I said one thing — that the only reason I wanted money was that I was always afraid of being a charity case and of being a ward someplace. That's what really drove me all my life."

— *By Marilyn Berger*

BARBARA HOLLAND

Defender of Small Vices

APRIL 5, 1933 - SEPT. 7, 2010

BARBARA HOLLAND, a best-selling writer whose humorous essays sang the simple pleasures of drinking martinis, cursing and eating fatty foods, died on Sept. 7 at her home in Bluemont, Va. She was 77.

The cause was lung cancer, her daughter said.

In her essay collection "Endangered Pleasures: In Defense of Naps, Bacon, Martinis, Profanity, and Other Indulgences" (1995), Ms. Holland put forward a hedonist's credo:

"Joy has been leaking out of our life. We have let the new Puritans take over, spreading a layer of foreboding across the land until even ignorant small children rarely laugh anymore. Pain has become nobler than pleasure; work, however foolish or futile, nobler than play; and denying ourselves even the most harmless delights marks the suitably somber outlook on life."

She even mounted a defense of smoking, which, along with drinking, she identified as her principal hobbies. Appalled readers found comfort in her next collection, a celebration of rural life titled "Bingo Night at the Fire Hall: The Case for Cows, Orchards, Bake Sales & Fairs" (1997), but she returned to contrarian form in "The Joy of Drinking" (2007).

"I was getting sick and tired of being lectured by dear friends with their little bottles of water and their regular visits to the gym," she explained to The Washington Post in 2007. "All of a sudden, we've got this voluntary prohibition that has to do with health and fitness. I'm not really in favor of health and fitness."

EAT, DRINK, BE MERRY: Ms. Holland celebrated the joys of life's wicked pleasures.

Late in her career, she drew on her childhood and youth to write the memoir "When All the World Was Young" (2005), a best-selling bittersweet account of growing up in the 1940s and '50s. Critics responded enthusiastically to her compelling portrait of a sensitive, acutely observant girl desperate to find a place in the world, and the light touch with which she handled dark themes. Molly Jong-Fast, in The Chicago Tribune, wrote, "Imagine Lauren Bacall narrating 'Tristram Shandy.'"

Ms. Holland was born Barbara Murray on April 5, 1933, in Washington and grew up in Chevy Chase, Md. Her mother, the former Marion Hall, was a Swarthmore graduate who studied law for a year at Columbia but gave up a career to marry and rear five children. She divorced when Barbara was quite young and married Thomas Holland, a lawyer for the Department of Labor.

Barbara loathed her stepfather, and his dark, looming presence inspired her vivid picture of patriarchy's heavy hand in postwar America. "My friends and I were all deathly afraid of our fathers, which was right and proper and even biblically ordained," she wrote. "Fathers were angry; it was their job."

Her mother later wrote popular children's books under the name Marion Holland, including "A Big Ball of String" and "The Secret Horse." She also passed along a sharp, pithy verbal style. "Any fool can be a Yankees fan," she once told her daughter. "It takes real talent to be a Senators fan."

After graduating from high school, and undergoing an illegal abortion that she describes unsparingly in her memoir, Ms. Holland struck out on her own, landing on her feet with a low-level job at Hecht's department store in Washington. For the first time she enjoyed independence, a cherished state to which she devoted a book, "One's Company: Reflections on Living Alone" (1992).

While working as an advertising copywriter in Philadelphia, she began contributing short fiction, essays and articles to magazines like McCall's, Seventeen, Redbook and Ladies' Home Journal.

Her three marriages ended in divorce. Besides her daughter, she is survived by two brothers, two sisters, two sons and two grandchildren.

Her other books include "Hail to the Chiefs: How to Tell Your Polks From Your Tylers" (1990), "Wasn't the Grass Greener?: A Curmudgeon's Fond Memories" (1999) and "They Went Whistling: Women Wayfarers, Warriors, Runaways, and Renegades" (2001). She also wrote the children's books "The Pony Problem" (1977) and "Prisoners at the Kitchen Table" (1979).

Her fight for ground to stand on as a young woman remained central to her reading of the world. A steady paycheck and self-respect were the keys to her brand of feminism, not the allowance and room of one's own proposed by Virginia Woolf.

"No, Mrs. Woolf," she wrote in her memoir. "A job, Mrs. Woolf."

— *By William Grimes*

IRWIN SILBER

For an Editor, Song Was a Way to Speak Out

OCT. 17, 1925 - SEPT. 8, 2010

IRWIN SILBER, who as a founder and the longtime editor of the folk-music magazine Sing Out! was a prime mover behind the folk-music revival of the 1950s and '60s and who famously treated Bob Dylan to a public scolding for abandoning his political songs, died on Sept. 8 in Oakland, Calif. He was 84.

The cause was complications of Alzheimer's disease, his son Frederic said.

Mr. Silber, an ardent leftist, found common cause with Woody Guthrie, Pete Seeger, Lee Hays and others who regarded folk music as a form of political protest and a way of affirming the dignity of working people. In 1946, he and other folk-music supporters founded People's Songs Inc., which published a bulletin "to create, promote and distribute songs of labor and the American people." Mr. Silber became the group's executive secretary.

After People's Songs went under in 1949, having exhausted its meager funds on Henry Wallace's failed 1948 presidential campaign, Mr. Silber, Mr. Seeger and others founded Sing Out!

Mr. Silber borrowed the title for the magazine from the third verse of "The Hammer Song" (later known as "If I Had a Hammer"), written in 1949 by Mr. Seeger and Mr. Hays, with its refrain "I'd sing out danger, I'd sing out a warning, I'd sing out love between all my brothers (and my sisters) all over this land."

The song appeared on the cover of the first issue, in May 1950.

Mr. Silber assumed the title of editor within a few issues and continued in that post until 1967, steering the magazine through a heady period in which a growing audience embraced Southern blues singers, guitar and banjo pickers from the Appalachians and a new generation of protest singers like Joan Baez and Mr. Dylan.

Under Mr. Silber, the magazine printed, for the first time, "Sixteen Tons," "This Land Is Your Land," "Michael Row the Boat Ashore," "Bells of Rhymney" and "Cotton Fields."

"He was one of a handful of people who can be called the architects of the folk revival, other than the performers themselves, and he helped move the music forward," said Mark D. Moss, the current editor of Sing Out! "A lot of people thought of folk music as a white guy writing his own songs and playing guitar, but Irwin went deeper, presenting songs from different cultures in different languages. He always saw this as an empowering, people-up movement."

Mr. Silber, who wrote a monthly column called "Fan the Flames," kept the pages lively. In an open letter to Mr. Dylan in November 1964, he accused him of becoming a sellout more interested in his own image and his entourage than in his audiences.

REVIVALIST: For Mr. Silber, folk music was a meaningful form of political protest.

"I saw at Newport how you had somehow lost contact with people," Mr. Silber wrote, referring to that year's Newport Folk Festival. "It seemed to me that some of the paraphernalia of fame were getting in your way."

Even worse, he argued,

Mr. Dylan had turned away from the political protest songs that first brought him fame. "Your new songs seem to be all inner-directed now, inner-probing, self-conscious — maybe even a little maudlin or a little cruel on occasion," Mr. Silber wrote. "And it's happening onstage, too. You seem to be relating to a handful of cronies behind the scenes now — rather than to the rest of us out front."

Mr. Dylan was not amused. Mr. Silber is often proposed as a target of the Dylan song "Positively Fourth Street." One line goes: "You say I let you down. You know it's not like that./ If you're so hurt, why then don't you show it?"

Irwin Silber was born on Oct. 17, 1925, in Manhattan, where he attended Seward Park High School. Politically active from an early age, he joined the Young Communist League, the American Student Union and American Youth for Democracy while still in his teens.

At Brooklyn College he formed the American Folksay Group, a politically minded folk-music and folk-dancing organization. After graduating in 1945 with a bachelor's degree in English, he developed a close relationship with the musicians and folklorists, like Alan Lomax, who were presenting and preserving folk music.

He would later be brought before the House Un-American Activities Committee for questioning, but he managed to deflate the atmosphere of high drama. On being asked what subject he had taught at the Communist-sponsored Jefferson School of Social Science, he answered, truthfully, "Square dancing." He left the Communist Party in the late 1950s.

After leaving Sing Out!, Mr. Silber wrote for Guardian, a radical weekly, and was its executive editor from 1972 to 1978.

Mr. Irwin's first two marriages ended in divorce. In addition to his son, he is survived by his wife, the singer Barbara Dane; another son; a daughter; two grandchildren; two stepsons; a stepdaughter; two stepgrandchildren; and one step-great-grandchild.

Besides editing Sing Out!, Mr. Silber recorded protest songs from liberation movements around the world on the Paredon label, which he and Ms. Dane founded in 1970 and ran until the early 1980s.

He published many important folk-song collections, notably "Songs of the Civil War" (1960), "The Great Atlantic and Pacific Song Book" (1965), "Songs of the Great American West" (1967) and, with Fred Silber, "Folksinger's Wordbook." He also wrote "Press Box Red" (2003), a biography of Lester Rodney, the sports editor of The Daily Worker.

— By William Grimes

GEORGE WILLIAMS

Evolution, He Found, Starts With the Gene

MAY 12, 1926 - SEPT. 8, 2010

George C. Williams, an evolutionary biologist who helped shape modern theories of natural selection, died on Sept. 8 at his home on Long Island, near Stony Brook University, where he taught for 30 years. He was 84.

Dr. Williams played a leading role in establishing the now-prevailing, though not unanimous, view among evolutionary biologists that natural selection works at the level of the gene and the individual and not for the benefit of the group or species.

He is "widely regarded by peers in his field as one of the most influential and incisive evolutionary theorists of the 20th century," said Douglas Futuyma, a colleague and the author of a leading textbook on evolution.

Dr. Williams laid out his ideas in 1966 in his book "Adaptation and Natural Selection." In it, he seized on and clarified an issue at the heart of evolutionary theory: whether natural selection works by favoring the survival of elements as small as a single gene or its components, or by favoring those as large as a whole species.

Asking questions evolution didn't seem to answer: Why is there menopause? Why do we grow old and die?

He did not rule out the possibility that selection could work at many levels. But he concluded that in practice this almost never happens, and that selection should be understood as acting at the level of the individual gene.

In explaining an organism's genetic adaptation to its environment, he wrote, "one should assume the adequacy of the simplest form of natural selection" — that of variation in the genes — "unless the evidence clearly shows that this theory does not suffice."

The importance of Dr. Williams's book was immediately recognized by evolutionary biologists, and his ideas reached a wider audience when they were described by Richard Dawkins in his book "The Selfish Gene" (1976).

Those ideas have continued to draw attention because group selection still has influential advocates. In highly social organisms like ants and people, behaviors like altruism, morality and even religion can be more directly explained if selection is assumed to favor the survival of groups.

Dr. Williams had a remarkably open turn of mind, which allowed him always to consider alternatives to his own ideas. David Sloan Wilson, a leading advocate of group selection, recalled in an interview that as a graduate student he once strode into Dr. Williams's office saying he would change the professor's mind about group selection. "His response was to offer me a postdoctoral position on the spot," Dr. Wilson said.

Dr. Wilson did not take the position but remained close to Dr. Williams, though the two continued to differ. One matter of dispute was whether a human being and the microbes in the gut and the skin could together be considered a superorganism created by group selection. Dr. Williams did not believe in superorganisms. (Nonetheless, when Dr. Wilson came to visit him one day, Dr. Williams had taped to his door a hand-lettered sign reading, "Superorganisms welcome here.")

Dr. Williams's interests extended to questions that evolution seemed not to answer well: Why should a woman forfeit her chance of having more babies by entering menopause? Why do people grow old and die when nature should find it far easier to maintain a body than to build one?

An important article he wrote in 1957 on the nature of senescence led to a collaboration with Dr. Randolph Nesse, a psychiatrist at the University of Michigan. Together they developed the concept of Darwinian medicine, described in the 1995 book "Why We Get Sick." There the authors offered Darwinian explanations for questions like why appetite decreases during a fever or why children loathe eating dark green vegetables.

Dr. Williams pursued his ideas even to results that he found disturbing. "He concluded that anything shaped by natural selection was inevitably evil because selfish organisms outproduced those that weren't selfish," Dr. Nesse said.

Dr. Williams acknowledged that people had moral instincts that overcome evil. But he had no patience with biologists who argue that these instincts could have been brought into being by natural selection.

"I account for morality as an accidental capability produced, in its boundless stupidity, by a biological process that is normally opposed to the expression of such a capability," Dr. Williams wrote starkly in 1988.

In the field of evolutionary theory, "George was probably the most influential author in the

1960s," said William Provine, a historian of evolution at Cornell University. But by choosing important subjects, Dr. Williams remained relevant. His ideas were approachable because he wrote in clear, simple prose and largely without the use of mathematics, an almost obligatory tool for most evolutionary biologists today.

George Christopher Williams was born on May 12, 1926, in Charlotte, N.C. After serving in the Army from 1944 to 1946, he studied at the University of California, Berkeley, where he received a bachelor's degree in zoology in 1949. He earned a Ph.D. in biology at U.C.L.A. in 1955. He joined the State University of New York at Stony Brook (now Stony Brook University) in 1960 and worked there until his retirement in 1990.

He is survived by his wife, Doris Williams, who is also a biologist, as well as a son, three daughters and nine grandchildren. He died of Parkinson's disease, his wife said.

Though a major expositor of evolutionary theory, Dr. Williams was always aware that his explanations were a work in progress and that they might in principle be superseded by better ones. Evolutionary theory, as stated by its great 20th-century masters Ronald Fisher, J. B. S. Haldane and Sewall Wright, "may not, in any absolute sense, represent the truth," Dr. Williams wrote at the conclusion of his book on adaptation, "but I am convinced that it is the light and the way."

— *By Nicholas Wade*

KEVIN MCCARTHY

Immortalized by 'Body Snatchers'

FEB. 15, 1914 - SEPT. 11, 2010

KEVIN McCARTHY, the suave, square-jawed actor who earned accolades in stage and screen productions of "Death of a Salesman" but who will always be best known as the star of the 1956 science fiction movie "Invasion of the Body Snatchers," died on Sept. 11 in Hyannis, Mass. He was 96 and lived in Sherman Oaks, Calif.

His death, at Cape Cod Hospital, was confirmed by his daughter Lillah McCarthy.

Mr. McCarthy, whose sister was the celebrated author Mary McCarthy, was 35 and a veteran of seven Broadway plays when Elia Kazan cast him as Biff, the troubled elder son of Willy Loman, in the London stage production of "Death of a Salesman," Arthur Miller's Pulitzer Prize-winning 1949 drama about delusion and the common man. His portrayal of Biff in the 1951 film version earned him an Oscar nomination for best supporting actor.

Five years and four forgettable films later, Mr. McCarthy was cast in a low-budget B movie about a small California town where the residents are gradually replaced by pods from outer space. The pods, resembling giant cucumbers, bubble and foam as they slowly turn into creepy, emotionless duplicates of the townspeople.

Miles Bennell (Mr. McCarthy), a handsome bachelor doctor, and Becky Driscoll (Dana Wynter), a beautiful local divorcée, spend the movie trying to escape podification — mostly just by staying awake; the transformation takes place while people are sleeping — and warn others. (Ms. Wynter died in 2011.)

The movie, selected for the National Film Registry in 1994 and named one of the Top 10 science fiction films of all time by the American Film Institute in 2008, came to be regarded as a metaphor for the paranoia of the era's Communist witch hunts.

But the film's leading man, like many moviegoers at the time, saw it differently, as a warning about mindless conformity.

"I thought it was really about the onset of a kind of life where the corporate people are trying to tell you how to live, what to do, how to behave," Mr. McCarthy told The Bangor Daily News in Maine in 1997.

Over the decades Mr. McCarthy came to embrace the cult immortality he achieved with "Body Snatchers," but he played hundreds of other roles in feature films and on television for decades, including multiple appearances on series from "Studio One" in the 1950s to "The District" in 2000. On stage he toured the United States as Harry S. Truman in the one-man show "Give 'Em Hell, Harry" for 20 years or more.

THEY'RE COMING! Mr. McCarthy in a scene from the 1956 classic "Invasion of the Body Snatchers."

Kevin McCarthy was born on Feb. 15, 1914, in Seattle, the son of Roy Winfield McCarthy and the former Therese Preston. Both parents died in the influenza epidemic of 1918, and their four children were sent to live with relatives in Minneapolis. After five years of near-Dickensian mistreatment, described in Mary McCarthy's memoirs, the youngsters moved in with their maternal grandfather.

After graduating from high school in Wisconsin, Mr. McCarthy, with an eye toward a diplomatic career, studied at the School of Foreign Service at Georgetown University. He changed his mind, however, and transferred to the University of Minnesota, where he became interested in acting.

After moving to New York he made his Broadway debut in 1938 in "Abe Lincoln in Illinois," landing a small part in a cast led by Raymond Massey. After serving as a military police officer during World War II, he became an early member of the Actors Studio, New York's bastion of Method acting.

Mr. McCarthy never abandoned the stage. The 18 Broadway productions in which he appeared included Moss Hart's "Winged Victory" (in which he was billed as Sgt. Kevin McCarthy), the political drama "Advise and Consent," Chekhov's "Three Sisters" and Kurt Vonnegut's irreverent "Happy Birthday, Wanda June."

Mr. McCarthy matured quickly into roles as judges, generals, politicians and other men of power — sometimes not very nice ones. On "Flamingo Road," the soapy 1980s television series, he was a greedy small-town Florida millionaire. In the film "The Best Man" (1964), he was a presidential candidate's henchman, specializing in dirty tricks; he played a similarly ignoble political type in "The Distinguished Gentleman" (1992). In "Innerspace" (1987) he was a devious industrial spy; in "Buffalo Bill and the Indians" (1976), a grabby publicist.

And though he did relatively little science fiction after "Body Snatchers," he did star in the horror comedy "Piranha" (1978) as a mad scientist breeding killer fish. He also made a cameo appearance in the 1978 remake of "Body Snatchers," playing a man who throws himself at the car driven by Donald Sutherland (the remake's star), shouting, "Help! They're coming! Listen to me!" and sounding much like his character in the original film.

His bad guys weren't always all bad. He was a roguish poker player in "A Big Hand for the Little Lady" (1966) and Marilyn Monroe's attractive but distant ex-husband in "The Misfits" (1961).

He married the actress Augusta Dabney in 1941, and they had three children. They divorced in 1961. (She died in 2008.) In 1979 he married Kate Crane, a lawyer, and they had two children. Ms. Crane survives him, as do three daughters, two sons, a stepdaughter, a brother and three grandchildren. Mary McCarthy died in 1989.

Mr. McCarthy continued acting well into his 90s. His last screen appearances were in 2009 in "Wesley," an 18th-century costume drama, and the short film "I Do."

"I try to get as much work as I possibly can," he told The San Diego Union-Tribune in 1991. "I love to work. I love to be in things."

Interviewers rarely asked him about subjects beyond "Invasion of the Body Snatchers." and he rarely complained, despite his long list of other credits. One story he loved to tell was about leaving Ms. Wynter a nostalgic trans-Atlantic telephone message one day. "Becky," he said, "it's Miles. Wake up!"

— *By Anita Gates*

HAROLD GOULD

You'll Recognize the Face

DEC. 10, 1923 - SEPT. 11, 2010

Harold Gould, a widely recognizable character actor in film and television who specialized, especially late in his career, in playing suave, well-dressed gentlemen in popular sitcoms, died on Sept. 11 in Woodland Hills, Calif. He was 86.

The cause was prostate cancer, said Jaime Larkin, a spokeswoman for the Motion Picture and Television Fund. Mr. Gould lived at its retirement community.

Mr. Gould was probably best known for two television roles in which he played dignified, self-possessed and understanding men trying to look out for the women in their lives. In the 1970s, on "The Mary Tyler Moore Show" and later on its spinoff, "Rhoda," he played Martin Morgenstern, the father of Rhoda Morgenstern (Valerie Harper), the best friend of Mary Richards (Ms. Moore). It was a role for an effortless charmer; Martin was the patient and consoling parent, a foil for his brassy wife, Ida (Nancy Walker).

A decade and a half or so later, he was a regular guest star on "The Golden Girls" as a sweetly dashing widower who courts the sweetly ditzy Rose Nylund (Betty White).

Mr. Gould, who had a Ph.D. in dramatic speech and literature from Cornell, taught acting in college before he became a professional actor. But in spite of his late start, few actors can boast a résumé as long.

Mr. Gould appeared on and Off Broadway in New York and in regional theaters around the country, including "King Lear" at the Utah Shakespeare Festival in 1992. He played dozens of character roles in movies, including the dapper grifter Kid Twist in "The Sting" (1973), the Oscar-winning buddy picture that starred Paul Newman and Robert Redford as con men; a Russian count in Woody Allen's sendup of epic literature, "Love and Death" (1975); and a greedy corporate executive named Engulf in Mel Brooks's 1976 slapstick, "Silent Movie."

But Mr. Gould was most of all a fixture on television with a familiar face, with or without what came to be his signature mustache. His credits are a roster of some of the most popular shows of the past several decades. In the 1960s he appeared on "Dennis the Menace," "The Donna Reed Show," "Hazel," "National Velvet," "Perry Mason," "Mister Ed," "Dr. Kildare," "The Twilight Zone," "The Virginian," "12 O'Clock High," "The Fugitive," "Judd for the Defense" and "Hogan's Heroes," among other shows. In 1965, he played Marlo Thomas's father in the pilot episode of "That Girl." (Lew Parker played the part in the series.)

In the 1970s, in addition to "Mary Tyler Moore" and "Rhoda," he was seen on "Cannon," "Mannix," "Hawaii Five-O," "Medical Story," "Police Story," "Family," "Soap" and "The Love Boat." In a 1972 episode of "Love, American Style" that was the progenitor of the hit series "Happy Days," he played Howard Cunningham, the Middle American father of the Middle American son played by Ron Howard. (In the series the father was played by Tom Bosley, see page 117.)

In the 1980s Mr. Gould appeared on "St. Elsewhere," "Webster," "Trapper John, M.D.,"

APPRECIATION

Oh, Him. I Remember Him.

By scanning earth's television broadcasts long after we are gone, other civilizations will be able to make certain judgments about human society. How among untold billions of lives, a few were deemed worthy of repeated and copious observation. Milton Berle, Mary Tyler Moore, Ted Danson, Oprah Winfrey, Simon Cowell: Truly these were giants of the species.

But there were others whose status might inspire mystery. Like the man in this photo. Who is that guy? Note to anthropologists: He's Harold Gould.

There are character actors. And then there is Mr. Gould. Mr. Gould and his mustache were one of the hardest-working, most-familiar duos in Hollywood. He had the face you could place, if not attach a name to.

Mr. Gould didn't start acting until his late 30s, but then he didn't stop. His talent runs like DNA through nearly 50 years of movies and TV. Some actors make mountainous careers out of a handful of parts. Not Mr. Gould, who had no blockbuster roles. Using bit parts like mosaic tiles, he built an awesome résumé.

He was Martin Morgenstern, Rhoda's father in "The Mary Tyler Moore Show" and "Rhoda." He was the crime lord Honore Vachon on "Hawaii Five-O." He was on "The Rockford Files," "The Love Boat," "Gunsmoke," "I Dream of Jeannie," "Get Smart," "The Golden Girls" and dozens of other shows better and worse. He was a grifter in "The Sting," a Russian nobleman in "Love and Death." He was Marlo Thomas's father in the pilot of "That Girl."

He was, in other words, that guy. And they are not making many more like him.

"They don't write parts for character people anymore," said Saratoga Ballantine, a producer of a new, unreleased documentary, "Troupers," about character actors who kept working past 80.

They include Mr. Gould and her father, Carl Ballantine, who died last year. (You know him, too: Lester Gruber, "McHale's Navy.") "Everybody's beautiful and Botoxed these days," Ms. Ballantine said. "Everyone's starting to look alike."

Looking alike is not what Mr. Gould did. He had other dimensions: a doctorate in dramatic speech and literature, a long career teaching drama in college, a family and grandchildren. He had all the parts of a satisfying life, plus a thousand others.

— *By Lawrence Downes*

"L.A. Law" and "Night Court"; in the 1990s, on "Dallas," "Lois and Clark," "Touched by an Angel" and "Felicity"; and in this century on "The King of Queens," "Judging Amy" and "Cold Case."

Harold Vernon Goldstein was born on Dec. 10, 1923, in Schenectady, N.Y. His father worked for the Post Office. Harold served in the Army during World War II, seeing action in France as a mortar gunner. On his return he graduated from New York State College for Teachers (now University at Albany, the State University of New York) and enrolled in the graduate drama program at Cornell. He taught drama at Randolph-Macon Woman's College in Lynchburg, Va., and the University of California, Riverside.

Mr. Gould is survived by his wife, the former Lea Shampanier, whom he married in 1950; a daughter; two sons; and five grandchildren.

— By Bruce Weber

CLAUDE CHABROL

The Hitchcock of the New Wave

JUNE 24, 1930 - SEPT. 12, 2010

Claude Chabrol, the director who helped give rise to the French New Wave and who went on to make stylish, suspense-filled films that were often compared to those of Alfred Hitchcock, died on Sept. 12 in Paris. He was 80.

The death was announced by Christophe Girard, the chief cultural affairs official in Paris. Mr. Chabrol had been hospitalized for "severe anemia," his press agent, Eva Simonet, said.

Mr. Chabrol was a young film critic working for the magazine Cahiers du Cinéma alongside François Truffaut, Eric Rohmer and Jean-Luc Godard when a family inheritance allowed him to form his own production company. In 1956 he produced and wrote the screenplay for the short film "Coup de Berger," which was directed by Jacques Rivette, then used his own money to finance "Le Beau Serge" (1957).

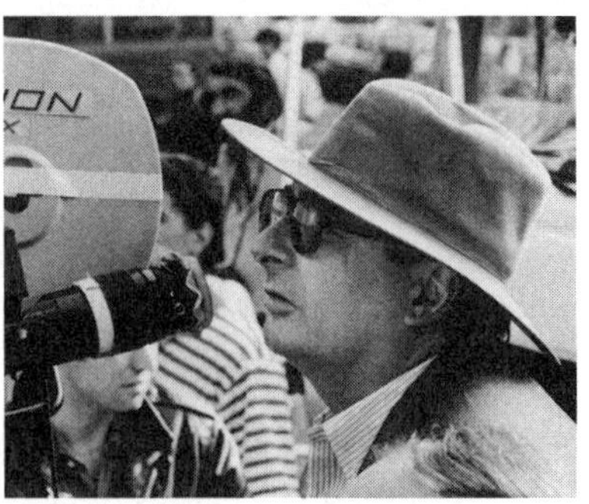

SOCIAL CRITIC: Mr. Chabrol's films explored issues of class and sexuality.

"Le Beau Serge" and a subsequent Chabrol film, "Les Cousins" (1958), are often cited as the opening volley of the French New Wave. "Le Beau Serge" ("Handsome Serge") is an acerbic study of a smug Parisian, François (played by Jean-Claude Brialy), who returns to the provincial village of his youth and tries to rescue his former best friend, Serge (Gérard Blain), from a seemingly pointless, working-class existence. The film established the piercing antibourgeois themes that would shape much of the rest of Mr. Chabrol's career. It also demonstrated, to a professionally closed and aesthetically conservative French film industry, that an outsider could break into the system and make a commercially successful, critically acclaimed film.

This lesson was not lost on his colleagues.

Mr. Truffaut followed Mr. Chabrol's example with "The 400 Blows" (1959) and Mr. Godard with "Breathless" (1960); both men became internationally successful and established La Nouvelle Vague (The New Wave) as a phenomenon.

While never quite equaling the fame of Mr. Truffaut and Mr. Godard, Mr. Chabrol continued to explore questions of class and sexuality in films like "Les Bonnes Femmes" (1959) and "L'Oeil du Malin" (1961). An unabashed admirer of the American cinema, Mr. Chabrol also happily accepted more commercial assignments, including the thriller "Landru" (1962).

Like the Hollywood professionals he admired, Mr. Chabrol refused few projects that came his way. As a result he averaged two or three films a year through the 1960s and '70s, alternating personal films like the suspenseful "La Femme Infidèle" ("The Unfaithful Wife") in 1968 with international co-productions like the dual-language "La Decade Prodigieuse"/"Ten Days' Wonder" (1971), starring Anthony Perkins, Michel Piccoli and Orson Welles.

Frequently working with the cameraman Jean Rabier and the screenwriter Paul Gégauff, Mr. Chabrol, in more than 50 films, developed an elegant, formally distant style, built around controlled camera movements that often seemed to be describing the imprisonment of his characters in a stifling social order. His style was studiously cool, his detachment from his characters disguising a deeper compassion for their plight as victims of a hypocritical middle-class moralism. He employed close-ups with discretion, as if he were declining to violate the privacy of his characters out of a concern for bourgeois propriety. But behind the well-bred manners could be found a sly, mocking sense of humor, a quality Mr. Chabrol carried over to his frequent appearances on French talk shows.

"Stupidity is infinitely more fascinating than intelligence," Mr. Chabrol once observed. "Intelligence has its limits while stupidity has none. To observe a profoundly stupid individual can be very enriching, and that's why we should never feel contempt for them."

"Le Boucher" ("The Butcher," a 1969 Hitchcockian thriller starring Stéphane Audran as a schoolteacher attracted to an Algerian war veteran (Jean Yanne) who may be a serial killer, became a commercial and critical hit in the United States. Other films, like the broadly comic "Docteur Popaul" (1972), starring Jean-Paul Belmondo, were barely seen outside France. Referring to the uneven critical reception of his work, Mr. Chabrol is said to have remarked, "You have to accept the fact that sometimes you are the pigeon, and sometimes you are the statue."

Mr. Chabrol made some 25 films with Ms. Audran, who was his wife from 1964 to 1980. Many of those belong to what has come to be known as the "Hélène" cycle, after the name Mr. Chabrol frequently gave to the elegant, reserved but erotically vulnerable characters he created for her. In "Violette" (1977), Ms. Audran appeared as the mother of the main character, Violette Nozière, a young woman secretly addicted to depravity, memorably played by Isabelle Huppert.

It was Ms. Huppert who took up the role of Mr. Chabrol's muse when she was reunited with him for "Story of Women" (1988), and they worked together in a long series of films that included "Madame Bovary" (1990), "La Cérémonie" (1995) and "Comedy of Power" (2006).

In 2008 he celebrated his 50th year as a filmmaker by working for the first time with another giant of the French cinema, the actor Gérard Depardieu, on the police thriller "Bellamy," Mr. Chabrol's final film. "Bellamy" is a low-key thriller about a Parisian police commissioner (Mr. Depardieu) who interrupts his vacation to investigate a murder. It was released in France in 2009 and opened in the United States in October through IFC Films.

Mr. Chabrol was born in Paris on June 24, 1930, the son of a pharmacist who dwelt in the same sort of bourgeois social environment that the son went on to satirize. He spent much of his childhood in Sardent, a village in central France, where he passed the war years running a film club. He returned to Paris to study law, but he dropped out to study pharmacology (his father's profession) and eventually ended up with a degree in literature.

His passion for the cinema led him first to a job as a publicist for Twentieth Century-Fox, then to writing reviews and interviews for various publications, including Art and Les Cahiers du Cinéma. He immersed himself in the city's film culture and met other aspiring directors. In 1955, he and Mr. Truffaut interviewed Mr. Hitchcock on the set of "To Catch a Thief," and two years later he and Mr. Rohmer wrote an influential study of Mr. Hitchcock's films.

Mr. Chabrol married Agnès Marie-Madeleine Goute in 1952. It was her inheritance that allowed him to establish his production company in the early '50s. They had two sons, Jean-Yves and Mathieu Chabrol, the latter a composer who has scored most of his father's films since the 1980s. His marriage to Stéphane Audran produced one son, Thomas, an actor who has appeared in many films for his father and other directors. Mr. Chabrol's survivors also include his third wife, Aurore Pajot, who acted as his script supervisor from 1968 on and whom he married in 1981; and Ms. Pajot's daughter, Cécile Maistre, who was an assistant director on his films and wrote the script with him for "The Girl Cut in Two" (2007).

In 2004 Mr. Chabrol was awarded the European Film Prize for his body of work. In an interview the year before, Mr. Chabrol shrugged off those who labeled him the Gallic Hitchcock but reassured his admirers that he would continue to make thrillers.

"I like using the thriller genre because when people go see a thriller — unless it's really worthless — they never say, 'We've wasted our time,'" he said. "It's a good way to make people feel like going and not complain too much. Because you don't make a film to express your ideas. You make a film to distract people, to interest them, perhaps to make them think, perhaps to help them be a little less naïve, a little better than they were."

— *By Dave Kehr*

MANFRED GANS

A Wartime Mission: To Find His Parents

APRIL 27, 1922 - SEPT. 12, 2010

He was 16 when his parents sent him to England, fearing for his life as a Jew in Nazi Germany, and when war broke out he clamored to join the British armed forces. His fluency in German earned him a spot with a secret commando unit. And with that, Manfred Gans would set off on a mission: to find his parents.

Mr. Gans — or Capt. Freddy Gray, as he was identified by the British Army — and his fellow commandos were assigned to interrogate enemy prisoners as the Allies made their way across France and the Netherlands and into Germany. In March 1945, he helped free his hometown, the ancient walled city of Borken, where he had been born on April 27, 1922. His house, on the outskirts of town, had been used as a Nazi headquarters; the wine cellar was a torture chamber. His parents, Moritz and Else Fraenkel Gans, had been taken away.

Mr. Gans was determined to find them, though he had no idea if they had survived the war. He asked his superior officers to grant him a leave. They gave him a Jeep and a driver, and the two embarked on a journey that would take them across hundreds of miles of German-held territory.

Because his father, a prosperous merchant, had been the first Jew to serve on the Borken

DETERMINED SON: Mr. Gans, far left, with his mother, grandmother and father in 1945. A British captain, Mr. Gans traveled hundreds of miles to find his parents in German concentration camps.

City Council, it was likely that his parents had been taken to Theresienstadt, the "show" concentration camp that the Nazis had used in propaganda films. Though it was not a death camp, thousands of prisoners were taken from there to the gas chambers. By the end of the war, thousands would starve at Theresienstadt.

Early in May 1945, Mr. Gans and his driver crossed over the Sudeten Mountains into Czechoslovakia and approached the barbed-wire fences at Theresienstadt, outside Prague.

"There were German divisions manning their guns that could have easily killed them" along the way, said Steven Karras, author of "The Enemy I Knew: German Jews in the Allied Military in World War II" (2009).

Russian troops had seized the camp, and they let Mr. Gans and his driver through.

"There were a massive number of people in there, all terribly crowded; most were too weak to get out of the way," Mr. Gans recounted to Mr. Karras. "People were practically crawling through our legs."

At the camp office, a young girl scrolled through the "endless list" of prisoners. Then, Mr. Gans recalled, "she looked up and said: 'You're lucky, they're still here. They are alive.'"

The girl escorted Mr. Gans to where his parents were housed. She went in first to prepare them.

His parents stepped outside. "My father was so decimated, if I had met him on the street I would not have recognized him," Mr. Gans said. "When they saw me, my parents were totally swept up — crying, shocked."

A crowd gathered and started singing.

"A group of Zionist girls came and gave my mother flowers," Mr. Gans said.

Mr. Gans died on Sept. 12 at his home in Fort Lee, N.J., his son, Daniel, said. He was 88.

After the war, Mr. Gans and his parents separated again. He returned to England; they settled in Israel, joining their eldest son, Carl, who had moved to Palestine in 1936 and changed his name to Gershon Kaddar.

In England, Mr. Gans earned a degree in

chemical engineering from the University of Manchester and later immigrated to the United States. He found work with an engineering company in Manhattan. In 1982, he opened his own consulting firm in Hoboken, N.J.

Besides his son, Mr. Gans is survived by a daughter; his brother, Mr. Kaddar; his companion, Esther Okin; and three grandchildren. His wife of 43 years, the former Anita Lamm, died in 1991.

Moritz Gans died in 1980; his wife died two years later. Their third son, Theo, who had fled to England in 1939, died in 1996.

In his book, Mr. Karras told of more than two dozen German Jews who had fought with the Allied forces during the war. Of their stories, Mr. Gans's was clearly among the most unusual. But "not only unusual," Mr. Karras said. "It was epic."

— *By Dennis Hevesi*

ANTONINA PIROZHKOVA

Keeper of a Flame Stalin Couldn't Extinguish

JULY 1, 1909 - SEPT. 12, 2010

Antonina Pirozhkova, who as the widow of the renowned short-story writer Isaac Babel campaigned for more than half a century to keep his literary legacy alive after his execution by Stalin's N.K.V.D., and who wrote a memoir about the last seven years of his life, died on Sept. 12 at her home in Sarasota, Fla. She was 101.

Ms. Pirozhkova, a rising young engineer, met her future husband shortly after she began working at the State Institute for Metallurgical Design in Moscow in 1932. She was 23. He was 38 and separated from his first wife, Yevgenia Gronfein.

The two began living together in 1934, and in 1937 she gave birth to a daughter, Lidiya.

After her husband's arrest in 1939, Ms. Pirozhkova (pronounced peer-ush-KOVE-uh) was advised by an interrogator for the N.K.V.D., the secret police, to forget the matter. "Regulate your life," she was told. Instead she spent the next 15 years trying to discover her husband's fate.

In 1954 she received his death certificate. It bore the false date of March 17, 1941, implying that he had died during World War II. Ms. Pirozhkova then successfully lobbied for Mr. Babel's official rehabilitation, which was granted later in 1954.

Not until the mid-1990s did accurate information emerge about Mr. Babel's date of execution, Jan. 27, 1940, and about the 20-minute trial that took place the day before he was shot. He had been charged with belonging to an anti-Soviet Trotskyite organization and with spying for France and Austria.

During and after her life with Mr. Babel, Ms. Pirozhkova continued her engineering career. At the Metroproekt Institute, which she joined in 1934 and where she rose to chief designer, she helped plan the crown jewels of the Moscow subway system: the Mayakovsky, Pavelets, Kiev, Arbat and Revolutionary Square stations.

For many years Ms. Pirozhkova was the only woman employed as a subway engineer in the Soviet Union.

After retiring in 1965, she devoted her life to reclaiming her husband's legacy, fighting with the authorities for permission to publish his works, organizing public memorials and commemorations of his birth and helping scholars do research in her personal archives, stored in her apartment in Moscow.

She was particularly concerned with securing the return of unpublished manuscripts seized by the N.K.V.D. Their fate remains unknown. In 1972 she compiled and published, in Russian, "I. Babel Recalled by His Contemporaries," a collection of firsthand biographical material. Mr. Babel's "1920 Diary," which she transcribed, presented the raw material that the author drew on for "Red Cavalry," his most celebrated work. The diary was published in the United States by Yale University Press in 1995.

The two-volume collection of Mr. Babel's works that Ms. Pirozhkova compiled and edited remains the most complete edition in Russian. It was published in 1990.

Her memoir, "At His Side: The Last Years of Isaac Babel," was published in the United States by Steerforth Press in 1996 and in 2001 appeared in a Russian edition.

Sharply written and full of insights about Mr. Babel's character and life under Stalin, the book was well received. "Babel would have enjoyed Ms. Pirozhkova's book, concise and full of bright incident," Richard Lourie wrote in The New York Times Book Review.

Ms. Pirozhkova recalled Mr. Babel's dismay at her haphazard reading habits, which he tried to correct by drawing up a list of the "hundred books that every educated person needs to read." It included a volume titled "The Instincts and Morals of Insects." She recounted evenings spent with Soviet cultural giants like the film director Sergei M. Eisenstein and visits by foreign luminaries like André Gide and André Malraux.

But her most telling lines concerned Mr. Babel, portrayed as generous, shrewdly observant, subversively witty and, despite the shadow of the executioner's ax, coolly fascinated by the secret police.

She recalled riding to the Lubyanka, the N.K.V.D. headquarters, on the night of Mr. Babel's arrest in a car with two N.K.V.D. thugs. "I could not say a single word," she wrote. "Babel asked the secret policeman sitting next to him, 'So, I guess you don't get much sleep, do you?' And he even laughed."

Antonina Nikolaevna Pirozhkova was born on July 1, 1909, in Krasny Yar, a village in Siberia. Her father died when she was 14, and she supported the family by tutoring fellow students in math.

Her high school diploma noted her "outstanding abilities" in mathematics, physics and literature, and in 1926 she entered Tomsk Technological Institute, where she studied construction and engineering.

After graduating with an advanced degree in engineering in 1930, she was assigned to one of the Soviet Union's prize industrial projects: Kuznetskstroi, a large metallurgical plant being built near Novokuznetsk.

After working on the Moscow subway, she was assigned to the Moscow Institute of Transportation Engineers, where, as a teacher in the Bridges and Tunnels Department, she trained subway designers and wrote two sections for the standard textbook "Tunnels and Subways." In 1996 she moved with her daughter to the Washington suburbs to be near her grandson and his wife. In addition to her daughter, she is survived by a grandson and a great-grandson.

When Ms. Pirozhkova arrived with Mr. Babel at the Lubyanka, she and her husband kissed. He told her, "Someday we'll see each other," and walked into the building without looking back.

"I turned to stone, and I could not even cry," Ms. Pirozhkova wrote. "For some reason I kept thinking, 'Will they at least give him a glass of hot tea? He can't start the day without it.'"

— *By William Grimes*

TRUTH-SEEKER: Ms. Pirozhkova with her husband, Isaac Babel, in 1935.

SEPT

DODGE MORGAN

Around the World in 150 Days

JAN. 15, 1932 - SEPT. 14, 2010

DODGE MORGAN, the first American to sail solo nonstop around the world, a feat in which he cut the previous record time nearly in half, died on Sept. 14 in Boston. He died of cancer. He was 78 and lived on Snow Island in Harpswell, Me., a 30-acre sanctuary that he owned and where he moored six sailboats.

Aboard the 60-foot sloop American Promise, Mr. Morgan slipped into the port of St. George, Bermuda, at 1:31 P.M. on April 11, 1986, completing the 27,000-mile circumnavigation in 150 days 1 hour 6 minutes. He had sailed out of Bermuda on Nov. 12, 1985. The voyage — often through roiling seas and occasionally past icebergs — shattered the previous record of 292 days set by a British sailor, Chay Blyth, in 1971.

A flotilla of small boats, a throng of well-wishers and a bagpiper welcomed Mr. Morgan to shore that day. His wife, Manny, and his two children handed him a cheeseburger and a bag of popcorn.

The voyage had not started well. Mr. Morgan first set sail on Oct. 14, 1985, from Portland, Me. But he had to put in at Bermuda when the sloop's electronic steering system failed. It took several weeks of repairs before he could restart his intended nonstop adventure.

Heading southeast from Bermuda, Mr. Morgan circled the tip of Africa and went east across the Southern Pacific, past Cape Horn, and then north to Bermuda. "I found that the solitude didn't bother me so much," he told The New York Times a day after arriving. "I felt that the worst thing that could happen was death, but I came to terms with that before I left."

On board had been 650 pounds of tools and spare parts, about 300 pounds of clothing and 1,600 pounds of food, most of it freeze-dried. But no cheeseburgers.

Dodge David Morgan was born in Malden, Mass., on Jan. 15, 1932, one of three children of Russell and Ruth Dodge Morgan. His marriage to the former Manny Hoyt ended in divorce. He is survived by his fiancée, Mary Beth Teas, a son and a daughter.

Although Mr. Morgan had worked at his uncle's boatyard on Cape Cod as a teenager, his voyage was made possible by his entrepreneurial skills. In 1983, he sold his electronics firm, Controlonics, in Westford, Mass.—which he had started in 1971 with $25,000 — for $35 million. He used money from the sale to commission the American Promise, for $1.5 million, and, after the voyage, to invest in two weekly newspapers, The Maine Times and The Casco Bay Weekly. He later sold the newspapers and started a company that manufactures headsets.

27,000 MILES: Mr. Morgan celebrating as he completed a solo sail around the globe, April 11, 1986.

The American Promise

was well equipped. There were six cameras aboard, three above deck and three below. The voyage was later featured in an eight-part PBS series, "Adventure."

Footage taken on the 109th day, as the boat rounded Cape Horn, showed Mr. Morgan taking off his foul-weather gear, putting on a tuxedo jacket and toasting himself with three splits of Champagne.

Four days out from Bermuda, he asked, "How do you prepare to see people after five months?" The first thing to do, he said, is "take a shower."

— *By Dennis Hevesi*

JOHN GOEKEN

A Telephone Game Changer

AUG. 22, 1930 - SEPT. 16, 2010

John D. Goeken, a tenacious entrepreneur who founded the long-distance carrier MCI, which changed the shape of the nation's telephone industry by challenging the monopoly of the American Telephone and Telegraph Company, died on Sept. 16 in Joliet, Ill. He was 80.

The cause was esophageal cancer. He lived in Plainfield, Ill., near Chicago.

Mr. Goeken, known as Jack, had a long track record of creating communications companies, often in the face of stubborn opposition and heavy skepticism. His ventures include Airfone and In-Flight Phone, which are credited with establishing air-to-ground telephones, and the digital network used by FTD florists.

Probably his most important achievement was MCI, which he began as a two-way-radio business in the early 1960s. The company later helped transform the telephone industry, bringing lower-cost long-distance service to millions of American households and businesses.

Mr. Goeken helped set in motion the breakup of AT&T when MCI, in league with the Justice Department, filed an antitrust suit against the giant phone company in 1974. It led to a settlement in which AT&T agreed to break itself apart a decade later. That allowed AT&T, nicknamed Ma Bell, to supply long-distance service and seven regional companies, known as the Baby Bells, to provide local phone service.

Mr. Goeken (pronounced GOH-ken) started his company, originally called Microwave Communications Inc., after being discharged from the Army, where he had learned about microwave technology. At the time, truckers who traveled between Chicago and St. Louis could not use two-way radios to speak with their home offices because their radio signals covered only shorter distances. Mr. Goeken's answer was to construct a network of microwave towers along the routes between the two cities; radio signals could then be relayed from one tower to the next.

In 1971, the Federal Communications Commission granted MCI the right to compete with AT&T for long-distance service throughout the United States, and three years later MCI filed its antitrust suit against AT&T, accusing it of unfairly thwarting the expansion of competition in the long-distance market.

Mr. Goeken left MCI the same year, 1974, after a disagreement over the direction of the company with William G. McGowan, whom he had brought in when MCI became a long-distance phone company for consumers.

Mr. Goeken had wanted MCI to cater more to business customers than the general public. Mr. McGowan went on to become the longtime chairman of MCI Communications, as the company was later known. Mr. Goeken kept an ownership stake when he left.

He soon went on to new projects, including establishing the computer network known as FTD Mercury, which florists use to wire flower orders. And though many in the phone industry were skeptical that executives would want to make calls from the air, he founded Airfone. He sold an interest in that business to the GTE Corporation to raise cash, but eventually left after a disagreement with GTE over the running of the operation.

PHONES TO FLOWERS: Mr. Goeken started MCI, Airfone and FTD Mercury.

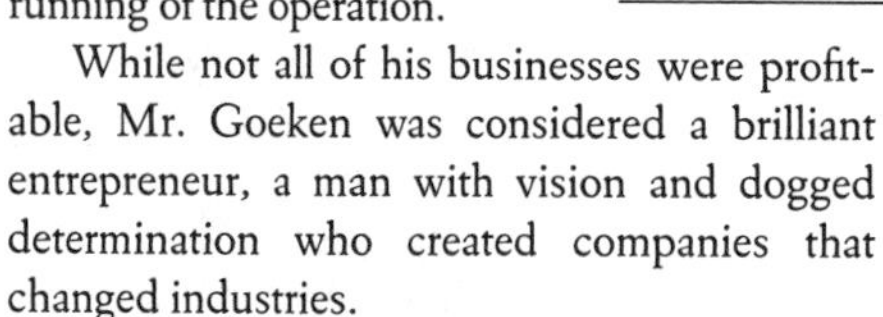

While not all of his businesses were profitable, Mr. Goeken was considered a brilliant entrepreneur, a man with vision and dogged determination who created companies that changed industries.

In 1995, he started the Goeken Group, a holding company to foster new ventures. His most important new business was PolyBrite International, an LED lighting company developing energy-efficient technology to replace traditional bulbs.

John D. Goeken was born on Aug. 22, 1930, in Joliet, where his father was a Lutheran minister. He stayed close to Joliet all his life, Patricia A. Schneider, executive vice president of the Goeken Group, said, and developed a passion for flying, becoming a pilot.

Mr. Goeken is survived by his wife of 59 years, Mona Lisa Goeken, whom he had met in high school; his daughter; a son; and seven grandchildren.

Ms. Schneider said Mr. Goeken was known as "Jack, the Giant Killer" for his business battles. But Ms. Schneider, who knew him for 35 years, said that for all the creative energy and innovation Mr. Goeken had brought to his businesses, he did not change much in his own life. He and his wife lived in the same house in Plainfield for more than 40 years.

— *By Graham Bowley*

JOYCE BEBER

Leona Helmsley's Image Maker

NOV. 20, 1929 - SEPT. 17, 2010

Being fired by a client is hardly an adman's dream, but being fired by Leona Helmsley can make you a legend — especially if it happens four times. So it was with Joyce Beber.

Ms. Beber had a significant hand in promoting the Helmsley hotel empire. It was Ms. Beber who concocted the advertisements portraying Mrs. Helmsley as persnickety hotel royalty with a hawklike eye for the missing towel, the uneven window shade or the erring maid.

And it was Ms. Beber's agency that came up with the idea of calling Mrs. Helmsley "Queen of the Palace," playing on her ownership of the Helmsley Palace Hotel — though

Mrs. Helmsley claimed complete credit for it.

Yet the famously capricious Mrs. Helmsley was hard to satisfy. Even more, Ms. Beber had to sue her three times to be paid.

"You could say I gave her the royal flush," Mrs. Helmsley said of Ms. Beber in an interview with Playboy magazine in 1990.

The fact is that Ms. Beber, who died on Sept. 17, loved to give credit to clients. That was part of how she and her business partner, Elaine Silverstein, built a Miami-based national advertising agency, Beber Silverstein & Partners, starting in 1972, when it was unusual for women to run an ad shop.

The agency is now part of the Beber Silverstein Group, a diversified communications and marketing company led by Ms. Beber's daughter Jennifer Beber. The younger Ms. Beber said her mother, who was 80, died of leukemia in Miami.

While its revenues trailed those of the big Madison Avenue agencies when Ms. Beber and Ms. Silverstein were running the firm, it was noted for the quality of its accounts, among them Humana hospitals and insurance, Steinway pianos, the Knight-Ridder newspaper chain and the National Education Association.

The agency's Helmsley campaign pictured Mrs. Helmsley as an autocrat whose attention to detail knew no limit. The concept, featuring glossy photos of Mrs. Helmsley, was first used in advertisements for the Harley Hotel in Manhattan. Occupancy rates shot up to 87 percent, from 25 percent, in four months.

The campaign expanded to the Helmsley Palace and other hotels, with the slogan "The queen stands guard." Adweek hailed "a new chapter in U.S. hotel advertising."

Before meeting Mrs. Helmsley, Ms. Beber said, she was told to follow Disraeli's advice on talking to Queen Victoria: "When it comes to flattery, lay it on with a trowel."

So she did. In the midst of Ms. Beber's assiduously obsequious interview, Mrs. Helmsley complained about flimsy towels and commiserated with a former guest by phone about a noisy air-conditioner. Inspiration struck: Queen Leona ruled her kingdom with an iron fist to benefit guests.

The causes of the agency's firings are mixed. The first time, Mrs. Helmsley wanted to save money by doing advertising in-house. Another time, Mrs. Helmsley was upset that Ms. Beber had added Donald Trump, a competitor, as a client. Mrs. Helmsley dismissed the agency again after she was convicted of tax evasion in 1992, partly blaming the Beber agency for her legal troubles, for having raised her profile, Jennifer Beber said. (Howard J. Rubenstein, the spokesman for Helmsley Enterprises, declined comment.)

On still another occasion, Ms. Beber angered Mrs. Helmsley for having introduced her to a man whom Mrs. Helmsley fell for romantically and hired for a top job, then fired after learning he was gay.

Jennifer Beber pointed out that her mother was rehired after each firing except the last.

It was Ms. Beber who concocted the advertisements portraying Mrs. Helmsley as persnickety hotel royalty with a hawklike eye for the missing towel, the uneven window shade or the erring maid.

Ms. Beber was born Joyce Sacks on Nov. 20, 1929, in Brooklyn. She attended a yeshiva before going to high school in Manhattan, where she had moved at 12. She graduated from Purdue with a degree in English, then from Columbia Journalism School.

Jennifer Beber said her mother eventually got a job in the social services department of Mount Sinai Hospital in Manhattan because she or her parents had decided that it was time to marry a doctor. She and Dr. Charles Beber were married in 1956, and moved to Miami two years later.

In addition to her daughter, Ms. Beber is survived by her husband; another daughter, a brother and four grandchildren.

A feminist lecture by Gloria Steinem inspired her to pursue a career, and a cousin in advertising urged her to pursue his. She and Ms. Silverstein — both mothers with children at home and with no advertising experience — began with one desk and an investment of $7,000.

An early client was the American Jewish Committee, of which Dr. Beber was an officer. Another was a local florist with a $50,000 ad budget: Ms. Beber's idea was to sell flowers by subscription, and it worked. Hundreds more clients followed over four decades.

One campaign for Florida tourism ruffled feathers, because of its slogan: "Florida. The rules are different here." Ms. Beber had to explain she was promoting exotic experience, not lawlessness.

One different rule: "You must remove your wingtips before going swimming." Another: "You must get suntanned in a place you've never been tanned before."

— *By Douglas Martin*

JILL JOHNSTON

Lesbian Separatist

MAY 17, 1929 - SEPT. 18, 2010

JILL JOHNSTON, a longtime cultural critic for The Village Voice whose daring, experimental prose style mirrored the avant-garde art she covered and whose book "Lesbian Nation: The Feminist Solution" spearheaded the lesbian separatist movement of the early 1970s, died in Hartford on Sept. 18. She was 81 and lived in Sharon, Conn.

The cause was a stroke, her spouse, Ingrid Nyeboe, said.

Ms. Johnston started out as a dance critic, but in the pages of The Voice, which hired her in 1959, she embraced the avant-garde as a whole, including happenings and multimedia events.

"I had a forum obviously set up for covering or perpetrating all manner of outrage," Ms. Johnston wrote in a biographical statement on her Web site, jilljohnston.com.

In the early 1970s she began championing the cause of lesbian feminism, arguing in "Lesbian Nation" (1973) for a complete break with men and with male-dominated capitalist institutions. She defined female relations with the opposite sex as a form of collaboration.

"Once I understood the feminist doctrines, a lesbian separatist position seemed the commonsensical position, especially since, conveniently, I was an L-person," she told The Gay and Lesbian Review in 2006. "Women wanted to remove their support from men, the 'enemy' in a movement for reform, power and self-determination."

At a debate on feminism at Town Hall in Manhattan in 1971, with Germaine Greer, Diana Trilling and Jacqueline Ceballos of the National Organization for Women sharing the platform with Norman Mailer, the moderator, and with a good number of the New York intelligentsia in attendance, Ms. Johnston caused one of the great scandals of the period.

After reciting a feminist-lesbian poetic manifesto and announcing that "all women are lesbians except those that don't know it yet," Ms. Johnston was joined onstage by two women. The three, all friends, began kissing and hugging ardently, upright at first but soon rolling on the floor.

Mailer, appalled, begged the women to stop. "Come on, Jill, be a lady," he sputtered.

The filmmakers Chris Hegedus and D. A. Pennebaker captured the event in the documentary "Town Bloody Hall," released in 1979. Mary V. Dearborn, in her biography of Mailer, called the evening "surely one of the most singular intellectual events of the time, and a landmark in the emergence of feminism as a major force."

Ms. Johnston continued to write on the arts but took a strong political line with a marked psychoanalytic slant evident in "Jasper Johns: Privileged Information" (1996), which explored the artist's works as a series of evasions and subterfuges rooted in conflict about his homosexuality, and in the two volumes of her memoirs: "Mother Bound" (1983) and "Paper Daughter" (1985), both of them subtitled "Autobiography in Search of a Father."

'I WAS AN L-PERSON': Ms. Johnston in Manhattan in 1985.

Jill Johnston was born on May 17, 1929, in London and taken to the United States as an infant by her mother, Olive Crowe, after her father had abandoned them both. She was reared by a grandmother in Little Neck, on Long Island.

Throughout her childhood she believed that her parents had divorced, but in 1950, when The New York Times ran a short obituary about her father, an English bell maker named Cyril F. Johnston, she learned the truth.

Her mother informed her that she and Johnston had never married. A lifelong fascination with this absent figure, whose company, Gillett & Johnston, supplied bells and carillons to churches and cathedrals all over the world, motivated her to write "England's Child: The Carillon and the Casting of Big Bells" (2008), a biography of her father and a history of bell making.

After earning a bachelor's degree from Tufts in 1951 and studying dance at the University of North Carolina, Greensboro, she began writing for The Dance Observer. She was soon hired by the fledgling Voice to write the weekly column Dance Journal, which ran until the mid-1970s.

The revolutionary currents of the time found expression in her increasingly wayward Voice column, which soon took in all aspects of the counterculture and by the late 1960s had become a freewheeling series of dispatches about her adventures in the arts and on the road.

"Now I was a chronicler of my own life, by '60s standards perhaps not too egregiously adventurous and experimental, but in a newspaper in full public view, in the most fractured Dada style of work I had admired as a critic — a rather wild spectacle in those woolly times," she wrote on her Web site.

She developed a singular prose style — what the writer Pattrice Jones called "part Gertrude Stein, part E. E. Cummings, with a dash of Jack Kerouac thrown in for good measure."

One 1964 column began: "Fluxus flapdoodle. Fluxus concert 1964. Donald Duck meets the Flying Tigers. Why should anyone notice the shape of a watch at the moment of looking at the time?"

Ms. Johnston soon shed this style and her amorphous politics, which she described in "Lesbian Nation" as her "east west flower child beat hip psychedelic paradise now love peace do your own thing approach to the revolution."

In 1969, members of the Gay Liberation Front, correctly intuiting that the unidentified companion on her weekly adventures, chronicled in The Voice, was a woman, invited her to a meeting. Her political conversion began, and "Lesbian Nation" was published in 1973.

Her marriage to Richard Lanham in 1958 ended in divorce six years later. Besides her spouse, Ms. Nyeboe, whom she married in Denmark in 1993 and in Connecticut last year, she is survived by two children and four grandchildren.

Since the 1980s Ms. Johnston often wrote for Art in America and The New York Times Book Review. She also wrote other books, including "At Sea on Land: Extreme Politics" (2005).

Although Ms. Johnston later said that she regarded "Lesbian Nation" as "a period piece," she held fast to her version of feminism and reaffirmed it in "Admission Accomplished" (1998): "The centrality of the lesbian position to feminist revolution — wildly unrealistic or downright mad, as it still seems to most women everywhere — continues to ring true and right."

— *By William Grimes*

EDDIE FISHER

A Smooth Voice, a Rocky Love Life

AUG. 10, 1928 - SEPT. 22, 2010

Eddie Fisher, whose matinee-idol looks and smooth, romantic voice made him one of the most popular singers of the 1950s, and whose busy love life stole headlines in 1959 when he divorced Debbie Reynolds to marry Elizabeth Taylor, died on Sept. 22 at his home in Berkeley, Calif. He was 82.

The cause was complications of hip surgery, his daughter Tricia Leigh Fisher said.

With his boyish looks and pulsing delivery, Mr. Fisher was a lethal heartthrob for a generation of teenage girls, who thrilled to chart-topping hits like "Wish You Were Here," "I'm Walking Behind You," "Oh! My Pa-Pa" and "I Need You Now."

Between 1950 and 1956 he had 24 top 10 hits and nearly 50 songs in the Top 40. He reached a wide television audience on his variety show "Coke Time With Eddie Fisher," which NBC broadcast from 1953 to 1957, and "The Eddie Fisher Show," its successor.

Mr. Fisher was irresistible to women, and vice versa. His career suffered badly over his very public and messy divorce from Ms. Reynolds, whom he had married in 1955 and left for Ms. Taylor.

The divorce became a scandal partly because Mr. Fisher and Ms. Reynolds, a hugely popular movie star, had been sold as Hollywood's dream couple, and partly because Ms. Taylor had been married to Mr. Fisher's best friend, the producer Mike Todd, who had died in a plane crash only a year earlier, in 1958.

The gossip columns and magazines feasted on the breakup and the romance for months, and the adverse publicity caused NBC to cancel "The Eddie Fisher Show."

But the marriage ended as sensationally as it had begun when a smoldering romance between Richard Burton and Ms. Taylor, ignited on the set of the 1963 film "Cleopatra," burst into flame before an eagerly watching world. The storied Fisher-Taylor marriage ended in divorce in 1964. Mr. Fisher, an object of worldwide derision as the ousted party, bounced back by marrying the singer Connie Stevens, the third of his five wives.

In his heyday Mr. Fisher was romantically linked with some of Hollywood's most glamorous women, including Kim Novak, Marlene Dietrich and Angie Dickinson. His first autobiography, published in 1981, bore the almost inevitable title "Eddie: My Life, My Loves."

Edwin Jack Fisher was born on Aug. 10, 1928, in Philadelphia. His parents were Jewish immigrants from Russia, and his early singing experience came at the local synagogue.

At 13 he won a singing contest sponsored by the "Horn and Hardart Children's Hour," a radio variety show, and he soon became a regular on the Philadelphia radio station WFIL, where his starting pay of 15 cents — the price of two trolley tokens — rose to $18 a week.

"It takes many qualities to make a good singer, but your boy has the most important quality of all," a local voice teacher told Mr. Fisher's mother. "In his throat there is a thread of gold."

LADIES' MAN: Mr. Fisher flanked by current wife, Debbie Reynolds, right, and future wife, Elizabeth Taylor, in 1958.

While still in high school he sang his way into the Buddy Morrow band, a job that took him to New York and led to an engagement with the Charlie Ventura big band. Too young to appear in nightclubs, he found work as a staff singer at the Grossinger's resort in the Catskills, where his singing caught the attention of Eddie Cantor, who booked him in 1949 on a cross-country show. A contract with RCA soon followed.

"In one year, this boy will be America's most important singer of popular songs," Cantor predicted accurately. In 1950, the year that "Thinking of You" reached No. 5 on the charts and "Bring Back the Thrill" and "Unless" cracked the top 20, Mr. Fisher was voted America's most promising new male vocalist in a poll of disc jockeys conducted by Billboard. He then commanded $1,000 a week as a headliner at the Paramount on Broadway.

In 1951 he was drafted into the Army, which put him to work singing with the Army Band and touring bases overseas. "The Army gave me a lot more than I gave it," Mr. Fisher told The New York Mirror in 1953. "Why, I did shows I never would have done. In the rain, the mud, off the backs of trucks, without a mike and sometimes without even music."

He continued to record while on furloughs and resumed his career, with scarcely a glitch, after completing his two years of service. Stepping back into the headliner role at the Paramount, he began to look like the second coming of Frank Sinatra.

Seeking to capitalize on the golden Fisher-Reynolds marriage, RKO paired the couple in the musical-comedy film "Bundle of Joy" (1956). Mr. Fisher appeared opposite Ms. Taylor in "BUtterfield 8" (1960), in a dramatic role that convinced him and the rest of the world that acting was not his destiny.

The hits became scarcer after the mid-1950s, and RCA dropped him in 1960. He returned to the label and recorded the minor hit "Games That Lovers Play" in 1966. The album of the same title, made with Nelson Riddle, became his top-selling long-playing record.

Mr. Fisher then entered a long slide and filed for bankruptcy in 1970. His career problems were aggravated by addictions to drugs and gambling, which he wrote about frankly in his first memoir and its successor, "Been There, Done That" (1999).

Besides his daughter Tricia Leigh, he is survived by a second daughter from his marriage to Connie Stevens, the actress Joely Fisher; two children from his marriage to Debbie Reynolds, the actress and writer Carrie Fisher and Todd Fisher; and six grandchildren.

— *By William Grimes*

JURE ROBIC

Pedaling 28,000 Miles — Every Year

APRIL 10, 1965 - SEPT. 24, 2010

JURE ROBIC, a long-distance bicyclist who won the grueling Race Across America five times and whose seemingly endless, sleep-eschewing stamina tested the limits of human endurance, died during a training ride on Sept. 24 when he collided with a car on a mountain road in Plavski Rovt, Slovenia, near his home in Jesenice. He was 45.

Primoz Kalisnik, a Slovene journalist and a friend of Robic's, said that the driver of the car, a 55-year-old local man, was not at fault. Robic, he said, was on a mountain bike traveling as fast as 50 miles per hour downhill on a narrow, winding stretch of unpaved road where it was impossible to see around the next bend. He was training for next month's Crocodile Trophy mountain bike race in Australia, Mr. Kalisnik said.

Even in the circumscribed world of ultra-endurance athletes, Robic (his full name is pronounced YUR-eh ROH-bich) was known for his willingness to push his body to extremes of fatigue. Compared by other riders to a machine and known to friends as Animal, he once rode 518.7 miles in 24 hours, a world record.

His training included daily rides or other workouts lasting 6 to 10 hours. Sometimes he put himself through a 48-hour period without sleep: a 24-hour ride followed by a 12-hour break followed by a 12-hour workout. Robic rode an astonishing 28,000 miles — more than the circumference of the Earth — every year.

His five victories in the annual Race Across America, covering about 3,000 miles, are unequaled. (The current course extends from Oceanside, Calif., to Annapolis, Md.)

Unlike the Tour de France, the Race Across America is not a stage race — once it begins, there is no respite until riders give up or cross the finish line — so determining when and how long to sleep is the event's primary strategic element. The winner generally sleeps less than two hours out of 24 and finishes in less than nine days (although Robic's winning time in June was a relatively lethargic 9 days 46 minutes).

Robic won the race in 2005 and two weeks later won Le Tour Direct, a 2,500-mile European version with a course derived from Tour de France routes that included 140,000 feet of climbing, almost the equivalent of starting at sea level and ascending Mt. Everest five times. His time was 7 days 19 hours.

Robic became accustomed to the physical stress. In the later stages of long-distance races, feet swell as much as two sizes and thumb nerves go dull from the pressure of hands on handlebars. After the Race Across America, he had to use two hands to turn a key.

The mental stress may be worse. As each race went on, Robic's temper grew shorter and occasionally exploded. He was prone to hallucinations. More than once he leapt off his bicycle to do battle with threatening attackers who turned out to be mailboxes. Once he imagined he was being pursued by men with black beards on horseback — mujahedeen, he explained to his support team, who encouraged him to ride faster and keep ahead of them.

"In race, everything inside me comes out," Robic said.

GOING TO EXTREMES: A fierce competitor, Robic's friends called him "Animal."

"Good, bad, everything. My mind, it begins to do things on its own. I do not like it, but this is the way I must go to win the race."

Robic was born in Jesenice on April 10, 1965. From 1988 to 1994, he was a member of the Slovene national cycling team, and until recently he was a soldier in the Slovene army, a member of its athletic corps, which allowed him to train full time. (To help motivate him, his crew members, riding in a van behind him, sometimes blared Slovene military music through a loudspeaker.)

Robic's marriage ended in divorce; he is survived by a half brother and a son. A brother, Saso, a former professional skier, committed suicide this year.

"He was two personalities within one body," said Mr. Kalisnik, who called his friend the most popular athlete in Slovenia. "One was very polite and nice when he was not on the bike. During races, he was absolutely the most unpleasant person you could imagine."

— BY BRUCE WEBER

ART GILMORE

A Voice You'd Heard Before

MARCH 18, 1912 - SEPT. 25, 2010

ART GILMORE, whose disembodied voice introduced television shows and narrated hundreds, if not thousands, of movie trailers from the 1940s through the '60s, becoming a trademark of Hollywood self-salesmanship, died on Sept. 25 in Irvine, Calif. He was 98.

Mr. Gilmore actually did some acting, playing full-bodied parts in television shows like "Dragnet," "Emergency!" and "Adam-12." But for most moviegoers and television watchers of his era, Mr. Gilmore was a star without a name or a face; he was even cast as a never-seen radio announcer in several episodes of "The Waltons."

His voice — crisp and articulate, just a tad piercing, cagily pitched to the subject matter and inflected with a precisely calibrated measure of enthusiasm — was as recognizable as a theme song.

Among many other television appearances, Mr. Gilmore was the announcer on "The Red Skelton Show" — "Live! From Television City in Hollywood!" — from 1954 to 1971. He was an announcer of the mid-1950s dramatic anthology series "Climax"; he narrated all 39 episodes of the late 1950s western series "Mackenzie's Raiders." And from 1955 to 1959 he narrated the crime series "Highway Patrol."

"Whenever the laws of any state are broken, each state has a duly authorized organization that swings into action; it may be called the state militia or the state police or the highway patrol," Mr. Gilmore intoned at the start of each weekly episode. "These are the stories of the men whose training, skill and courage have enforced and preserved our state laws."

As the narrator of movie trailers — his wife, Grace, estimated he did 3,000 — Mr. Gilmore was an especially effective pitchman, delivering the language of hype with masterly conviction. Comedies, thrillers, romances, musicals, animation, documentaries — it didn't matter.

Among the films Mr. Gilmore promoted as coming attractions were "Dumbo," "A Place in the Sun," "Roman Holiday," "Shane," "Born Yesterday," "Rear Window," "South Pacific," "War and Peace," "Ocean's 11," "White Christmas" and "Bye Bye Birdie."

"The screen jumps for joy with Glendon

Swarthout's inside story of those uproarious Easter vacations," Mr. Gilmore pronounced in the movie trailer for "Where the Boys Are," a 1960 comedy about college girls on the make. In the one for "It's a Wonderful Life," Frank Capra's life-affirming small-town tale from 1946, Mr. Gilmore asserted, "Never before has any film contained such a full measure of the joy of living." And in a virtuosic bit of melodramatic recitation, he described Alfred Hitchcock's haunting psychodrama "Vertigo" (1958) as "the story of a love so powerful it broke through all the barriers between past and present, between life and death, between the golden girl in the dark tower and the tawdry redhead that he tried to remake in her image."

3,000 TRAILERS: Mr. Gilmore in 1947.

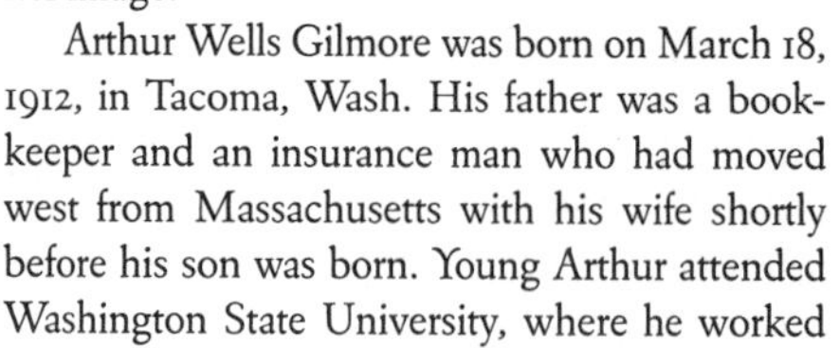

Arthur Wells Gilmore was born on March 18, 1912, in Tacoma, Wash. His father was a bookkeeper and an insurance man who had moved west from Massachusetts with his wife shortly before his son was born. Young Arthur attended Washington State University, where he worked at the campus radio station. He later worked in commercial radio in Seattle and Hollywood, announcing — before the television era — radio shows like "Amos 'n' Andy," "The Sears Radio Theater" and "Red Ryder." In World War II he served in the Navy and for a time in the 1960s was president of the American Federation of Television and Radio Artists, the labor union.

In 1964, on behalf of the Republican presidential candidate Barry Goldwater, Mr. Gilmore introduced a political advertisement titled "A Time for Choosing." Consisting of a speech by Ronald Reagan, the spot helped establish Mr. Reagan's influence in conservative politics.

Besides his wife, Mr. Gilmore is survived by two daughters, two grandchildren and four great-grandchildren.

Mr. and Mrs. Gilmore, 97, met in high school and were married 72 years.

"They dated for eight years before that," their daughter Marilyn Gilmore said.

— *By Bruce Weber*

GLORIA STUART

A Hollywood Comeback at 86

JULY 4, 1910 - SEPT. 26, 2010

Gloria Stuart, a glamorous blonde actress during Hollywood's golden age who was largely forgotten until she made a memorable comeback in her 80s in the 1997 epic "Titanic," died on Sept. 26 at her home in Los Angeles. She was 100.

Ms. Stuart had long since moved on from Hollywood when James Cameron, the director of "Titanic," rediscovered her for the role of Rose Calvert, a 101-year-old survivor of the ship's sinking. She was 86 at the time.

Her performance earned her an Academy Award nomination, for best supporting actress. She was the oldest actress ever to receive one.

Rose's wistful recollections of a love affair aboard the ship as it headed for disaster on its maiden voyage form the frame of "Titanic." Kate Winslet played the character as a young, well-to-do, romantically restless passenger in first class who falls in love with a poor would-be artist in steerage, played by Leonardo DiCaprio. The movie won 11 Oscars and was the top-grossing film of all time until it was overtaken in 2009 by "Avatar," also directed by Mr. Cameron.

Audiences in 1997 had little if any memory of Ms. Stuart's early screen career, but it had been substantial: a total of 46 films from 1932 to 1946. She abandoned movies, she said, after growing tired of being typecast as "girl reporter, girl detective, girl overboard."

"So one day, I burned everything: my scripts, my stills, everything," Ms. Stuart told The Chicago Tribune in 1997. "I made a wonderful fire in the incinerator, and it was very liberating."

In the best of her early movies, Ms. Stuart, a petite and elegant presence, was forced to seek shelter with Boris Karloff in James Whale's classic horror film "The Old Dark House" (1932) and was horrified when Claude Rains, her mad-scientist fiancé, tampered with nature in "The Invisible Man" (1933), also directed by Whale.

She was James Cagney's girlfriend in "Here Comes the Navy" (1934), Warner Baxter's faithful wife in John Ford's "Prisoner of Shark Island" (1936), Shirley Temple's cousin in "Rebecca of Sunnybrook Farm" (1938) and the spoiled rich girl who falls in love with penniless student Dick Powell in "Gold Diggers of 1935."

"Few actresses were so ornamental," John Springer and Jack Hamilton wrote in "They Had Faces Then," a book about the actresses of the 1930s. "But 'undemanding' is the word for most of the roles she played."

After a small role in the limp 1946 comedy "She Wrote the Book," Ms. Stuart had had enough and left the film world, not to be seen again until she appeared in a television movie almost 30 years later.

A STAR REBORN: Ms. Stuart in "The Invisible Man" (1933) and "Titanic" (1997).

Screen Play magazine had called Ms. Stuart one of the 10 most beautiful women in Hollywood, but she was more than a pretty face. She was a founding member of the Screen Actors Guild and helped found the Hollywood Anti-Nazi League, an early antifascist organization.

After she left Hollywood, she taught herself to paint and in 1961 had her first one-woman show, at Hammer Galleries in New York City.

In 1983, the master printer Ward Ritchie taught her to print, and she started a fresh career as a respected designer of hand-printed artists' books and broadsides under her own imprint, Imprenta Glorias. Her print work is in the collections of the Getty Museum in Los Angeles and the Victoria and Albert Museum in London.

Ms. Stuart and Mr. Ritchie also began an autumn romance that lasted until Mr. Ritchie's death in 1996 at the age of 91.

Gloria Frances Stewart was born in Santa Monica, Calif., on July 4, 1910, two years before the Titanic sank. She shortened "Stewart" to "Stuart" when she started in movies "because," she wrote in an autobiography, "I thought — and still do — its six letters balanced perfectly on a theater's marquee with the six letters in 'Gloria.'"

Ms. Stuart attended the University of California, Berkeley, where she met her first husband, the sculptor Gordon Newell. Settling in Carmel, Calif., in 1930, the couple joined a bohemian community whose members included the photographer Edward Weston and the journalist Lincoln Steffens. Ms. Stuart acted at the Golden Bough Theater and wrote for a weekly newspaper.

In 1932, Mr. Ritchie, who was Mr. Newell's best friend, drove her to Pasadena, where she had been offered a role at the prestigious Pasadena Playhouse. "The morning after I opened in Chekhov's 'The Sea Gull,'" Ms. Stuart remembered, "I signed a seven-year contract with Universal."

Soon came movies like "The Girl in 419" (1933), in which she played a mysterious woman who witnesses a murder. Ms. Stuart's social circle included Dorothy Parker, Robert Benchley and other New York intellectuals who had settled at the Garden of Allah hotel while writing and acting in movies. An excellent cook whose oxtail stew with dumplings was praised by M. F. K. Fisher in her book "The Gastronomical Me," Ms. Stuart liked to prepare Sunday dinners for her friends.

Ms. Stuart and Mr. Newell divorced in 1934; later that year she married Arthur Sheekman, a screenwriter who worked on a number of Marx Brothers movies.

After Ms. Stuart gave up on Hollywood, the Sheekmans sailed around the world and settled in New York. They had a daughter, and the family later moved to Italy. It was there she took up painting. Mr. Sheekman died in 1978. Her daughter, Sylvia Vaughn Thompson, collaborated with her mother on the autobiography, "I Just Kept Hoping" (1999). She survives her, as do four grandchildren and 12 great-grandchildren.

Ms. Stuart made brief returns to film and television acting in the 1970s and had a cameo role in the 1982 film "My Favorite Year," in which she danced with Peter O'Toole, who starred as a worn-at-the-edges film idol.

But it was "Titanic," 15 years later, that made Ms. Stuart a celebrity again. She was interviewed on television, invited to Russia for the opening of the movie there and chosen by People magazine as one of the 50 most beautiful people in the world. Her newfound fame resulted in more film and television work into her 90s.

If she had been more famous as an actress, Ms. Stuart might never have won the role of Rose Calvert; Mr. Cameron wanted a lesser-known actress for the part, one who, as Ms. Stuart said in 1997, was "still viable, not alcoholic, rheumatic or falling down."

Ms. Stuart was so viable that it took an hour and a half each day to transform her youthful 86-year-old features into the face of a 101-year-old woman.

When the script of "Titanic" was sent to her, Ms. Stuart told The Chicago Tribune, she thought, "If I had been given plum roles like this back in the old days, I would have stayed in Hollywood."

— *By Aljean Harmetz and Robert Berkvist*

GEORGE BLANDA

Iron Man of the N.F.L.

SEPT. 17, 1927 - SEPT. 27, 2010

George Blanda, a quarterback and placekicker who played professional football longer than anyone else and who retired having scored more points than anyone else, died on Sept. 27. He was 83.

The Oakland Raiders announced his death. Blanda finished his career with the Raiders, playing for them from 1967 until his retirement at 48, just before the 1976 season.

Elected to the Pro Football Hall of Fame in 1981, Blanda played for 26 seasons and was one of only two men to have played in four separate decades. (Jeff Feagles, a punter, is the other.)

He began his career in 1949 with the Chicago Bears, playing for George Halas, the legendary coach and team owner who helped shape pro football in its early years. He finished playing for Al Davis, the Raiders' legendary owner (and onetime coach) who helped shape the contemporary professional game.

Blanda was a reliable kicker with a strong enough leg to have blasted a 55-yard field goal in 1961 and a 52-yarder nine years later. He was also a guileful, gutsy quarterback, a pocket passer who was never known for his arm strength or accuracy, his agility or his foot speed, but who stood up to rushing linemen, saw the whole field and often delivered his best performances when the most was at stake.

GRIZZLED VETERAN: Blanda played football for nearly four decades.

"Blanda had a God-given killer instinct to make it happen when everything was on the line," Davis said to The Sporting News in 1989. "I really believe that George Blanda is the greatest clutch player I have ever seen in the history of pro football."

Davis had a firsthand look at Blanda's most famous stretch of games. On Sunday, Oct. 25, 1970, Blanda stepped in for the Raiders' injured starting quarterback, Daryle Lamonica, and threw for three touchdowns in the fourth quarter to beat Pittsburgh.

The next Sunday, against the Kansas City Chiefs, he kicked a 48-yard field goal, salvaging a tie with eight seconds left in the game. The week after that, against the Cleveland Browns, Blanda entered the game with a little more than four minutes to play and the Raiders down by a touchdown. He threw a touchdown pass, kicked the extra point, drove the team into position for the winning field goal and kicked it — that 52-yarder — with three seconds on the clock.

The next Sunday, he beat Denver with a late touchdown pass; the Sunday after that, he beat San Diego with a last-minute field goal. Five straight weeks he saved the game; he was 43.

"He never got older," The Sporting News once wrote of Blanda. "He just got better. He was the epitome of the grizzled veteran, the symbol of everlasting youth."

George Frederick Blanda was born on Sept. 17, 1927, in Youngwood, in western Pennsylvania, an area that has produced more than its share of Hall of Fame quarterbacks, including John Unitas, Joe Namath and Joe Montana. His father was a coal miner.

Blanda played college football at the University of Kentucky, where his coach was Bear Bryant, who went on to win six national championships at the University of Alabama. In 1949, Blanda was drafted by Halas's Bears, who already had a pair of celebrated quarterbacks in Sid Luckman and Johnny Lujack.

Just before the 1950 season, the Bears traded Blanda to the Baltimore Colts, but the day after the Colts' first-ever game, a 42-0 loss, he was sent back to the Bears.

Halas never warmed up to Blanda as a quarterback, and Blanda spent the first decade of his career mostly as a kicker. He started as a quarterback for one season, 1953, but lost the job because of an injury.

He and Halas never got along. "He was too cheap to even buy me a kicking shoe," Blanda said.

An incident from Blanda's bench-warming days in Chicago, recalled by The Houston Chronicle in 2003, sums up Halas's attitude toward Blanda: "Once, the Bears were getting crushed in the second half and the crowd started to chant, 'We want Blanda. We want Blanda.' Halas looked down the bench and barked, 'Blanda.' George jumped to his feet and ran over to his coach, buckling his helmet. Halas jerked his thumb toward the stands and said, 'Get up there. They're calling for you.'"

Tired of only kicking, Blanda retired before the 1959 season. A year later, however, the American

Football League was born, and Blanda became the starting quarterback for the Houston Oilers, leading them to the league's first two championships.

In one game, he threw seven touchdown passes, a feat only four other professional quarterbacks have equaled. He was voted the A.F.L. player of the year in 1961.

His survivors include his wife, Betty.

Blanda's career record showed 1,911 completions out of 4,007 passes for 26,920 yards, 236 touchdowns and 277 interceptions (including 42 in 1962, a record).

He kicked 335 field goals and more extra points (943) than anyone else in football history. He rushed for nine touchdowns during his career, which gave him a total of 2,002 points, a record at the time.

Blanda was judged to be too old for pro ball after the 1966 season, when the Oilers wanted him to retire. Instead he went to the Raiders. He had only nine more seasons in him.

— By Frank Litsky and Bruce Weber

ARTHUR PENN

With 'Bonnie and Clyde,' a Revolution

SEPT. 27, 1922 - SEPT. 28, 2010

Arthur Penn, the stage, television and motion picture director whose revolutionary treatment of sex and violence in the 1967 film "Bonnie and Clyde" transformed the American film industry, died on Sept. 28 at his home in Manhattan, the day after he turned 88.

The cause was congestive heart failure, his son, Matthew, said.

A pioneering director of live television drama in the 1950s and a Broadway powerhouse in the 1960s, Mr. Penn developed an intimate, spontaneous and physically oriented method of directing actors that allowed their work to register across a range of mediums.

In 1957 he directed William Gibson's television play "The Miracle Worker" for the CBS series "Playhouse 90" and earned Emmy nominations for himself, his writer and his star, Teresa Wright. In 1959 he restaged "The Miracle Worker" for Broadway and won Tony Awards for himself, his writer and his star, Anne Bancroft. And in 1962 he directed the film version of the Gibson text, capturing the best actress Oscar for Ms. Bancroft, the best supporting actress Oscar for her co-star, Patty Duke, and nominations for writing and directing.

Mr. Penn's direction may have also changed American history. He advised Senator John F. Kennedy during his watershed television debates with Richard M. Nixon in 1960 (and directed the broadcast of the third debate). Mr. Penn's instructions to Mr. Kennedy — to look directly into the camera and to keep his responses brief and pithy — helped give Mr. Kennedy an aura of confidence and calm that created a vivid contrast to Nixon, his more experienced but less telegenic Republican rival.

Mr. Penn left his most indelible mark on American culture with "Bonnie and Clyde."

"Arthur Penn brought the sensibility of '60s European art films to American movies," the writer-director Paul Schrader said. "He paved the way for the new generation of American directors who came out of film schools."

Many of the now-classic films of what was branded the New American Cinema of the

1970s — among them Martin Scorsese's "Taxi Driver" and Francis Ford Coppola's "Godfather" — would have been unthinkable without "Bonnie and Clyde" to lead the way.

Loosely based on the story of two minor gangsters of the 1930s, Bonnie Parker and Clyde Barrow, "Bonnie and Clyde" was conceived by its two novice screenwriters, Robert Benton and David Newman, as an homage to the rebellious sensibility and disruptive style of French New Wave films like François Truffaut's "Shoot the Piano Player" and Jean-Luc Godard's "Breathless."

In Mr. Penn's hands, it became something even more dangerous and innovative: a sympathetic portrait of two barely articulate criminals, played by Warren Beatty and a newcomer, Faye Dunaway, that disconcertingly mixed sex, violence and hayseed comedy, set to a bouncy bluegrass score by Lester Flatt and Earl Scruggs.

Not only was the film sexually explicit in ways unseen in Hollywood since the imposition of the Production Code in 1934 — when Bonnie stroked Clyde's gun, the symbolism was unmistakable — it was also violent in ways that had not been seen before. Audiences gasped when a comic bank robbery climaxed with Clyde's shooting a bank teller in the face, and were stunned when this attractive outlaw couple died in a torrent of bullets, their bodies twitching in slow motion as their clothes turned red with blood.

Reporting on the film's premiere on the opening night of the International Film Festival of Montreal in 1967, Bosley Crowther, the chief film critic for The New York Times, was appalled. "Bonnie and Clyde" was "callous and callow" and a "slap-happy color film charade," he wrote. Worse, the public seemed to love it.

"Just to show how delirious these festival audiences can be," Mr. Crowther wrote, "it was wildly received with gales of laughter and given a terminal burst of applause."

Similar reactions by other major critics followed when the film opened in the United States a few weeks later. The film, promoted by Warner Brothers with a memorable tag line — "They're young. They're in love. And they kill people." — floundered at first but soon found an enthusiastic audience among younger filmgoers and won the support of a new generation of critics. "A milestone in the history of American movies," Roger Ebert wrote in The Chicago Sun-Times. In The New Yorker, Pauline Kael described "Bonnie and Clyde" as an "excitingly American movie."

"Bonnie and Clyde" received 10 Oscar nominations but won only two (for Burnett Guffey's cinematography and Estelle Parson's supporting performance). That outcome reflected the Hollywood establishment's ambivalence about a film that seemed to point the way out of the creative paralysis that had set in after the end of the studio system while betraying the values — good taste and moral clarity — that the studios held most dear.

But the breach had been opened: "Bonnie and Clyde" was followed by "Easy Rider," "The Wild Bunch" and a host of other youth-oriented, taboo-breaking films that made mountains of money for Hollywood.

Mr. Penn was now perceived as a major film artist on the European model, a pathbreaker for a group of star directors — including Robert Altman, Terrence Malick, Bob Rafelson and Hal Ashby — who were able to work with comparative artistic freedom through the next decade. The "film generation" had arrived.

Arthur Penn was born on Sept. 27, 1922, in Philadelphia. His father, a watchmaker, and his mother, a nurse, divorced when he was 3, and Arthur and his older brother, Irving (who would achieve renown as one of the 20th century's great photographers), went to live with their mother in New York and New Jersey, changing homes and schools frequently as she struggled to make a living.

Mr. Penn traced his affinity for alienated heroes and heroines to a traumatic childhood. Truffaut's "400 Blows," he once said, "was so much like my own childhood, it really stunned me."

Arthur returned to Philadelphia to live with his father when he was 14 and became interested in theater in high school. He joined the Army in 1943 and, while stationed at Fort Jackson in South Carolina, organized a theater troupe with his fellow soldiers; later, while stationed in Paris, he performed with the Soldiers Show Company.

After the war he took advantage of the G.I. Bill to attend the unconventional Black

Mountain College in North Carolina, where his classmates included John Cage, Merce Cunningham and R. Buckminster Fuller. He went on to study in Italy at the Universities of Perugia and Florence, returning to the United States in 1948. Intrigued by the new, psychologically realistic school of acting that had grown out of the teachings of Konstantin Stanislavski — broadly known as the Method — he studied with the Actors Studio in New York and with Mr. Stanislavski's rebellious disciple, Michael Chekhov, in Los Angeles.

Back in New York, Mr. Penn landed a job as a floor manager at NBC's newly opened television studios. In 1953 an old Army buddy, Fred Coe, gave him a job as a director on "The Gulf Playhouse," also known as "First Person," an experimental dramatic series in which the actors addressed the camera directly. The series, broadcast live, introduced Mr. Penn to writers who would make their names in the television drama of the 1950s, among them Robert Alan Aurthur, Paddy Chayefsky and Horton Foote.

VISIONARY: Mr. Penn's movies paved the way for a new style of filmmaking.

As Mr. Coe moved on to the expanded formats of "The Philco-Goodyear Television Playhouse" and "Playhouse 90," he took Mr. Penn with him. His "Playhouse 90" production of Mr. Gibson's "Miracle Worker," starring Patricia McCormack as Helen Keller and Ms. Wright as the blind girl's determined teacher, Annie Sullivan, was shown on Feb. 7, 1957, and earned glowing reviews for Mr. Gibson and Mr. Penn.

Their television success allowed the two men to return to the original arena of their ambitions, Broadway. With Mr. Coe producing, they mounted Mr. Gibson's play "Two for the Seesaw," about a Midwestern businessman (Henry Fonda) contemplating an adventure with a New York bohemian (Ms. Bancroft). Opening in January 1958, the show was an immediate success.

Sensing themselves on a roll, Mr. Penn and Mr. Coe decided to tackle Hollywood. With Mr. Coe producing, Mr. Penn directed his first film, "The Left Handed Gun" (1958), for Warner Brothers. Based on a Gore Vidal television play, the project was an extension of the "Playhouse 90" aesthetic: a low-budget, black-and-white western about a troubled, inarticulate young man (Paul Newman, in a performance stamped with Actors Studio technique) who happened to be Billy the Kid.

As the critic Robin Wood wrote in a 1969 book about Mr. Penn, "The Left Handed Gun" provides "a remarkably complete thematic exposition of Penn's work." Here already is the theme of the immature, unstable outsider who resorts to violence when rejected by an uncaring establishment — a configuration that Mr. Penn would return to again and again in his mature work.

The film earned mediocre reviews, however, and quickly sank from view. But Mr. Penn had a backup plan. Returning to New York, he mounted "The Miracle Worker" for Broadway with Ms. Bancroft as Annie Sullivan and Ms. Duke as Helen Keller. Mr. Penn's highly physical approach made the show a sensation, and the production ran for 719 performances.

During that run Mr. Penn found time to stage three more hits: Lillian Hellman's "Toys in the Attic"; "An Evening With Mike Nichols and Elaine May," the Broadway debut for that comedy team; and "All the Way Home," an adaptation of James Agee's novel "A Death in the Family."

When Hollywood beckoned again, Mr. Penn returned in strength in 1962 to direct the film version of "The Miracle Worker," which became a popular and critical success.

But he was dismissed from his next project, "The Train," after a few days of filming by its temperamental star, Burt Lancaster. Mr. Penn's subsequent film, "Mickey One" (1965), an absurdist drama about a nightclub comedian (Mr. Beatty) on the run from mobsters, wore its European art-film ambitions on its sleeve and baffled most American critics, though it was admired by the iconoclastic young critics of Cahiers du Cinéma, the French magazine that championed the New Wave.

Mr. Penn had another frustrating experience with "The Chase" (1966), a multi-character, morally complex drama set in a Texas town where the sheriff (Marlon Brando) is on the lookout for a local boy (Robert Redford) who has escaped from prison. Adapted by Ms. Hellman from a Foote play, the drama was taken away from Mr. Penn and re-edited by its producer, Sam Spiegel. But even in its mutilated form, "The Chase" remains one of Mr. Penn's most personal and feverishly creative works.

An embittered Mr. Penn returned to Broadway, where he staged the thriller "Wait Until Dark" with Lee Remick and Robert Duvall. But he eventually returned to Hollywood, summoned by Mr. Beatty to take over the direction of a project originally offered to Mr. Truffaut.

"Frankly, I wasn't all that certain I wanted to make another film," Mr. Penn wrote in an essay for Lester D. Friedman's 2000 anthology, "Arthur Penn's 'Bonnie and Clyde.'" "And if I were to do another film, I felt it should be a story with a broader social theme than a flick about two '30s bank robbers whose pictures I remembered as a couple of self-publicizing hoods holding guns, plastered across the front page of The Daily News."

But Mr. Beatty, who had an option on the property, persuaded Mr. Penn to join the project with promises of autonomy and the rare privilege of having the final cut.

Working with the screenwriters, Mr. Penn eliminated a sexual triangle among Bonnie, Clyde and their disciple C. W. Moss that he felt was too sophisticated for the characters — "farmers or children of farmers, bumpkins most of them," Mr. Penn wrote.

"We talked and moved in the direction of a simpler tale," he added, "one of narcissism, of bravura, and, at least from Clyde's point of view, of sexual timidity."

They had also settled on a tone. "It was to start as a jaunty little spree in crime, then suddenly turn serious, and finally arrive at a point that was irreversible," Mr. Penn wrote.

After the success of "Bonnie and Clyde," Mr. Penn had his choice of Hollywood projects. But he decided to make a small, personal film. "Alice's Restaurant" (1969) revisited many of the social-outsider themes of "Bonnie and Clyde" but in a low-key, gently skeptical, nonviolent manner. Starring Arlo Guthrie and based on his best-selling narrative album about a hippie commune's brush with the law, the film stands as a warm and deeply felt miniature.

By contrast, he seemed to lose his way among the epic ambitions of "Little Big Man" (1970), a sprawling, ironic, anti-western that tried to explain American imperialism through the abstract figure of Jack Crabb (Dustin Hoffman), the sole (though fictional) non-American Indian survivor of the Battle of the Little Bighorn. After that film's disappointing reception, Mr. Penn mostly laid low before returning in 1975 with the modest thriller "Night Moves." Starring Gene Hackman as a Hollywood private detective who loses himself on a case in the Florida Keys, the film made explicit the existential despair that had long permeated American film noir, ending on a daring note of irresolution.

But audiences were losing patience with daring notes, flocking instead to the popcorn pleasures of Steven Spielberg's "Jaws," summer's runaway hit in 1975. Suddenly Mr. Penn's kind of artistically ambitious, personal filmmaking was out of style. He returned to Broadway, where he staged a pair of successes, Larry Gelbart's "Sly Fox" and Mr. Gibson's "Golda."

Mr. Penn's subsequent film career was one of violent ups and downs. A reunion with Mr. Brando for "The Missouri Breaks" (1976) yielded a surreal western with moments of brilliance but a meandering tone. With "Four Friends" (1981), Mr. Penn returned to the subjects of youthful uncertainty and social upheaval.

He seemed less committed to "Target" (1985), a political thriller with Mr. Hackman and Matt Dillon that uneasily matched a father-son conflict with conventional suspense, and "Dead of Winter" (1987), a partial remake of Joseph H. Lewis's 1945 thriller "My Name Is Julia Ross." "I just like to flex my muscles every once in a while and do something relatively mindless," Mr. Penn told Mr. Schickel.

It came as a pleasant surprise, then, when Mr. Penn uncorked the 1989 independent production "Penn & Teller Get Killed," a black comedy in which the two magicians are pursued by a serial killer. Full of wild jokes, bizarre reversals and extravagant gore, the film bristles with a youthful spirit of experimentation.

A dutiful drama of South African apartheid produced by Showtime, "Inside" (1996), would be Mr. Penn's last theatrically released film.

In his last years Mr. Penn returned to television, serving as an executive producer on several episodes of "Law & Order," a series on which his son, Matthew, worked as a director, and directing an episode of "100 Centre Street." One of his final works for the theater was the 2002 Broadway production "Fortune's Fool," an adaptation of Ivan Turgenev's 1848 play. True to Mr. Penn's form, it won Tony Awards for its stars, Alan Bates and Frank Langella.

Mr. Penn met his wife of 54 years, the actress Peggy Maurer, when he auditioned her for a television drama in the 1950s. She survives him. Besides his son, Mr. Penn is also survived by a daughter and four grandsons. Mr. Penn's brother, Irving Penn, died in 2009.

Throughout his career, Mr. Penn never lost his flair for the spontaneous, his remarkable ability to capture an emotional moment in all its pulsing ambiguity and messy vitality.

"I don't storyboard," Mr. Penn explained to an audience at the American Film Institute in 1970s, referring to the practice of sketching out every shot in a film before production begins. "I guess it dates back to my days in live television, where there was no possibility of storyboarding and everything was shot right on the spot — on the air, as we say — at the moment we were transmitting. I prefer to be open to what the actors do, how they interact to the given situation. So many surprising things happen on the set, and I have the feeling that storyboarding might tend to close your mind to the accidental."

— By Dave Kehr

TONY CURTIS

Leading Man With a Comic Touch

JUNE 3, 1925 - SEPT. 29, 2010

Tony Curtis, a classically handsome movie star who came out of the Hollywood studio system in the 1950s to find both wide popularity and critical acclaim in dramatic and comic roles alike, from "The Defiant Ones" to "Some Like It Hot," died on Sept. 29 at his home in Henderson, Nev., near Las Vegas. He was 85.

The cause was cardiac arrest, the Clark County coroner said.

Mr. Curtis, one of the last survivors of Hollywood's golden age, became a respected dramatic actor, earning an Oscar nomination as an escaped convict in "The Defiant Ones," a 1958 Stanley Kramer film. But he was equally adept in comedies; his public even seemed to prefer him in those roles, flocking to see him, to name one, in the 1965 slapstick hit "The Great Race."

As a performer, Mr. Curtis drew on his startlingly good looks. With his dark, curly hair worn in a sculptured style later imitated by Elvis Presley and his plucked eyebrows framing pale blue eyes and full lips, he embodied a new kind of feminized male beauty that came into vogue in the early 1950s.

MADE FOR MOVIES: Mr. Curtis's winning combination of looks and charm made him a box-office star.

A vigorous heterosexual in his widely publicized (not least by himself) private life, he was often cast in roles that suggested sexual ambiguity: his full-drag impersonation of a female jazz musician in "Some Like It Hot" (1959); a slave who attracts the interest of an aristocratic Roman general (Laurence Olivier) in Stanley Kubrick's "Spartacus" (1960); a man attracted to a mysterious blonde (Debbie Reynolds) who turns out to be the reincarnation of his male best friend in Vincente Minnelli's "Goodbye Charlie" (1964).

But behind the pretty-boy looks was a dramatically potent combination of naked ambition and deep vulnerability, both likely products of his Dickensian childhood in the Bronx. Tony Curtis was born Bernard Schwartz on June 3, 1925, to Helen and Emanuel Schwartz, Jewish immigrants from Hungary. Emanuel operated a tailor shop in a poor neighborhood, and the family occupied cramped quarters behind the store, the parents in one room and little Bernard sharing another with his two brothers, Julius and Robert. Helen Schwartz suffered from schizophrenia and frequently beat the boys. (Robert was later found to have the same disease.)

In 1933, at the height of the Depression, the parents found they could no longer provide for their children, and Bernard and Julius were placed in a state institution. (Julius was hit by a truck and killed in 1938.) Returning to his old neighborhood, Bernard became caught up in gang warfare and a target of anti-Semitic hostility. As he recalled, he learned to dodge the stones and fists to protect his face, which he realized even then would be his ticket to greater things.

In search of stability, Bernard made his way to Seward Park High School on the Lower East Side of Manhattan. During World War II he served in the Navy aboard the submarine tender U.S.S. Proteus. His ship was present in Tokyo Bay in 1945 for the formal surrender of Japan aboard the U.S.S. Missouri, which Signalman Schwartz watched through binoculars.

Back in New York, he enrolled in an acting workshop headed by Erwin Piscator at the New School for Social Research, where a classmate was another Seward Park High alumnus, Walter Matthau. He began getting theater work in the Catskills and caught the eye of the casting agent Joyce Selznick, who helped him win a contract with Universal Pictures in 1948. After experimenting with James Curtis as his stage name, he settled on Anthony Curtis and began turning up in bit parts in films like Anthony Mann's "Winchester '73" alongside another Universal bit player, Rock Hudson.

Mr. Curtis's career advanced rapidly at first. He was promoted to supporting player — and billed as Tony Curtis for the first time — in the 1950 western "Kansas Raiders" and became first prize in a Universal promotional contest, "Win a Weekend With Tony Curtis."

In 1951 he received top billing in the Technicolor Arabian Nights adventure "The Prince Who Was a Thief." His co-star was Piper Laurie, and they were paired in three subsequent films at Universal, including Douglas Sirk's "No Room for the Groom," a 1952 comedy that allowed Mr. Curtis to explore his comic gifts.

In 1951 Mr. Curtis married the ravishing MGM contract player Janet Leigh. Highly photogenic, the couple became a favorite of the fan magazines, and their first movie together, George Marshall's "Houdini" (1953), was Mr. Curtis's first substantial hit.

Perhaps the character of Houdini — like Mr. Curtis, a handsome young man of Hungarian Jewish ancestry who reinvented himself through show business — touched something in Mr. Curtis. It was in that film that his most consistent screen personality, the eager young outsider who draws on his charm and wiles to achieve success in the American mainstream, was born.

GIRL TALK: Mr. Curtis with Marilyn Monroe in "Some Like It Hot" (1959).

Mr. Curtis endured several more Universal costume pictures, including the infamous 1954 film "The Black Shield of Falworth," in which he starred with Ms. Leigh but did not utter the line "Yondah lies da castle of my foddah," which legend has attributed to him. His career seemed stalled until Burt Lancaster, another actor who survived a difficult childhood in New York City, took him under his wing.

Mr. Lancaster cast Mr. Curtis as his protégé, a circus performer who becomes his romantic rival, in his company's 1956 production "Trapeze." But it was Mr. Curtis's next appearance with Mr. Lancaster — as the hustling Broadway press agent Sidney Falco, desperately eager to ingratiate himself with Mr. Lancaster's sadistic Broadway columnist J. J. Hunsecker in "Sweet Smell of Success" (1957) — that proved that Mr. Curtis could be an actor of power and subtlety.

The late 1950s and early '60s were Mr. Curtis's heyday. Taking his career into his own hands, he formed a production company, Curtleigh Productions, and in partnership with Kirk Douglas assembled the 1958 independent feature "The Vikings," a rousing adventure film directed by Richard Fleischer. Later that year the producer-director Stanley Kramer cast Mr. Curtis in "The Defiant Ones" as a prisoner who escapes from a Southern chain gang while chained to a fellow convict, who happens to be black (Sidney Poitier).

"The Defiant Ones" may seem schematic and simplistic today, but in 1958 it spoke with hope to a nation in the violent first stages of the civil rights movement. The film was rewarded with nine Oscar nominations, including one for Mr. Curtis as best actor. It was the only acknowledgment he received from the Academy of Motion Picture Arts and Sciences in his career.

Mr. Curtis began a creatively rewarding relationship with the director Blake Edwards with a semi-autobiographical role as a hustler working a Wisconsin resort in "Mister Cory" (1957). That was followed by two hugely successful 1959 military comedies: "The Perfect Furlough" (with Ms. Leigh) and "Operation Petticoat," in which he played a submarine officer serving under a captain played by Cary Grant.

Under Billy Wilder's direction in "Some Like It Hot," another 1959 release, Mr. Curtis employed a spot-on imitation of Mr. Grant's mid-Atlantic accent when his character, posing as an oil heir, tries to seduce a voluptuous singer (Marilyn Monroe). His role in that film — as a Chicago musician who, with his best friend (Jack Lemmon), witnesses the St. Valentine's Day Massacre and flees to Florida in women's clothing as a member of an all-girl dance band — remains Mr. Curtis's best-known performance.

Success in comedy kindled Mr. Curtis's ambitions as a dramatic actor. He appeared in the Kubrick historical epic "Spartacus" and reached unsuccessfully for another Oscar nomination in "The Outsider" (1961), directed by Delbert Mann, as Ira Hayes, a Native American who helped raise the flag at Iwo Jima. In "The Great Impostor," directed by Robert Mulligan, he played a role closer to his established screen personality: an ambitious young man from the wrong side of the tracks who fakes his way through a series of professions, including a monk, a prison warden and a surgeon.

Mr. Curtis's popularity was damaged by his high-profile divorce from Ms. Leigh in 1962, following an affair with the 17-year-old German actress Christine Kaufmann, who was his co-star in the costume epic "Taras Bulba." He retreated into comedies, playing out his long association with Universal in a series of undistinguished efforts including "40 Pounds of Trouble" (1962), "Captain Newman, M.D." (1963) and the disastrous "Wild and Wonderful" (1964), in which he starred with Ms. Kaufmann, whom he married in 1963.

In "The Great Race," Blake Edwards's celebration of slapstick comedy, Mr. Curtis parodied himself as an impossibly handsome daredevil named the Great Leslie. And in 1967 he reunited with Alexander Mackendrick, director of "Sweet Smell of Success," for an enjoyable satire on California mores, "Don't Make Waves."

Mr. Curtis made one final, ambitious attempt to be taken seriously as a dramatic actor with "The Boston Strangler" in 1968, putting on weight to play the suspected serial killer Albert DeSalvo. Again under Richard Fleischer's direction, he gave a rigorously deglamorized performance, but the film was dismissed in many quarters as exploitative and failed to reignite Mr. Curtis's career. That year, he divorced Ms. Kaufmann and married a 23-year-old model, Leslie Allen.

After two unsuccessful efforts to establish himself in series television — "The Persuaders" (1971-72) and "McCoy" (1974-76) — Mr. Curtis fell into a seemingly endless series of unmemorable guest appearances on television (he had a recurring role on "Vegas" from 1978 to 1981) and supporting roles in ever-more-unfortunate movies, including Mae West's excruciating 1978 comeback attempt, "Sextette."

A stay at the Betty Ford Center — he had struggled with drug and alcohol abuse — followed his 1982 divorce from Ms. Allen, but Mr. Curtis never lost his work ethic. He continued to appear in low-budget movies and occasionally in independent films of quality. He took up painting, selling his boldly signed, Matisse-influenced canvases through galleries and stores.

After divorcing Ms. Allen, Mr. Curtis was married to the actress Andrea Savio (1984-92) and, briefly, to the lawyer Lisa Deutsch (1993-94). He married his sixth wife, the horse trainer Jill VandenBerg, in 1998, and with her operated a nonprofit refuge for abused and neglected horses.

In addition to his wife, Mr. Curtis's survivors include his two daughters with Janet Leigh, one who is the actress Jamie Lee Curtis; his two daughters with Christine Kaufmann; and a son with Leslie Allen. A second son with Ms. Allen died of a drug overdose in 1994.

He published "Tony Curtis: The Autobiography," written with Barry Paris, in 1994 and a second autobiography, "American Prince: A Memoir," written with Peter Golenbock, in 2008. In it he described a romance with Marilyn Monroe in 1948, when both were young, relatively unknown performers who had recently arrived in Hollywood. The affair was only a memory when they worked together a decade later, both as major stars, in "Some Like It Hot."

"Somehow working with her on 'Some Like It Hot' had brought a sense of completion to my feelings for her," he wrote. "The more we talked, the more I realized that another love affair had bitten the dust."

In 2002 he toured in a musical adaptation of "Some Like It Hot," in which he played the role of the love-addled millionaire originated by Joe E. Brown in the film. This time, the curtain line was his: "Nobody's perfect."

His final screen appearance was in 2008, when he played a small role in "David & Fatima," an independent budget film about a romance between an Israeli Jew and a Palestinian Muslim. His character's name was Mr. Schwartz.

— *By Dave Kehr*

SHERMAN J. MAISEL

A Force Behind Freddie, Frannie and Ginnie

JULY 8, 1918 - SEPT. 29, 2010

Sherman J. Maisel, an economist and former Federal Reserve governor whose research on housing markets shaped decades of federal policy on mortgages, died on Sept. 29 in San Francisco. He was 92.

His death was announced by the Haas School of Business at the University of California, Berkeley, where Mr. Maisel had taught from 1948 to 1965 and again from 1972 until his retirement in 1986.

Mr. Maisel's research laid the intellectual groundwork for government support of the mortgage market. Well into the 1960s, mortgages were mostly local products, with their availability subject to the flow of deposits into banks and savings and loan institutions. Mr. Maisel found that the structure of the mortgage market tended to suppress home construction during economic downturns, and that the federal government could help buffer the economy from those cyclical swings by supporting a secondary mortgage market.

"His work on housing cycles and mortgage markets was path-breaking," said Kenneth T. Rosen, chairman of the business school's Fisher Center for Real Estate and Urban Economics, which Mr. Maisel helped establish.

President Lyndon B. Johnson named Mr. Maisel to the Fed's board of governors in 1965.

> Mr. Maisel found that the government could help buffer the economy from those cyclical swings in the housing market by supporting a secondary mortgage market.

While Mr. Maisel was on the board, Johnson tapped him to serve on a White House task force on federal mortgage policies. The group proposed allowing the Government National Mortgage Association, or Ginnie Mae, to guarantee securities backed by pools of mortgages. It also proposed freeing Fannie Mae from the constraints of the federal budget so that it could assist the mortgage markets during times of financial stress.

The board's proposals helped create a national mortgage market that relied on bond financing rather than on the strength and liquidity of local banks.

But the proper role of government involvement in housing has come into question since the 2008 takeover of Fannie Mae and its sister company, Freddie Mac, in a bailout that has cost taxpayers billions of dollars. Mr. Rosen said that the sound underwriting that Mr. Maisel advocated had eroded in recent years and that the erosion contributed to the crisis.

Mr. Maisel was at the Fed during a challenging time. As the federal government racked up deficits because of the Vietnam War and the Great Society social programs, the central bank faced pressure from Johnson and his successor, Richard M. Nixon, to keep interest rates low.

The Fed was more deferential to the White House then than it is today, and one outcome was a period of rising inflation that continued through the late 1970s. Mr. Maisel was cautious about what monetary policy could accomplish.

"In my view, changes in monetary policy may be desirable, but they should be used only to a limited degree (and far less than in the past) in attempts to control movements in demand arising from nonmonetary sources," he said in 1972, when he left the Fed after seven years to return to California.

Mr. Maisel's book "Managing the Dollar," an insider's account of the Fed, was published in 1973. "It explained the 'secrets of the temple' in a way that I found relevant to my experience here back in the 1990s," said Janet L. Yellen, who was on the Fed's board from 1994 to 1997 and who became vice chairwoman of the Fed in 2010.

Later, Mr. Maisel helped lead a study of risk and capital adequacy in financial institutions, warning of the danger of letting them make risky loans against deposit insurance funds. Those recommendations were largely ignored; if followed, they might have helped prevent the costly savings and loan crisis of the mid-1980s.

Sherman Joseph Maisel was born on July 8, 1918, in Buffalo. He graduated from Harvard in 1939 and received master's degrees there in 1947 and 1948 and a Ph.D. in 1949. He was a research economist at the Fed in Washington from 1939 to 1941 and served in the Army from 1941 to 1945, rising from private to captain and working at air bases and ordnance depots. He also served a year in the Foreign Service, based in Brussels.

Besides his wife, Lucy Cowdin Maisel, whom he met in 1939, he is survived by a son, a daughter and two grandchildren.

Along with his academic and government work, Mr. Maisel served for a time on the Berkeley school board. As its vice chairman, he survived a 1964 recall vote prompted by voter anger over the board's efforts to reduce racial segregation in junior high schools by redrawing school boundaries.

For both the recall campaign and a vote to pass a bond issue, Mr. Maisel encouraged Berkeley students to register to vote, a phenomenon that contributed to a leftward shift in the city's politics.

Meeting Johnson to discuss the Fed nomination, Mr. Maisel was startled when the president expressed less interest in his economic views than in the politics of the local recall election.

— *By Sewell Chan*

STEPHEN J. CANNELL

The Man Who Owned Prime Time

FEB. 5, 1941 - SEPT. 30, 2010

SEPT

STEPHEN J. CANNELL, one of television's most prolific writers and series creators, whose work encompassed "The Rockford Files," "Wiseguy," "The A-Team" and "The Greatest American Hero," died on Sept. 30 at his home in Pasadena, Calif. He was 69.

The cause was complications of melanoma, his family said.

For 30 years, beginning in the early 1970s, television viewers could hardly go a week without running into a show written by Mr. Cannell. His writing credits include more than 1,000 episodes, primarily of crime dramas, and he is listed as the creator of almost 20 series, some of them long-running hits like "The Rockford Files" and "The Commish" and other flame-outs like "Booker." At one point in 1989, Mr. Cannell's company was producing five series on three networks.

Mr. Cannell's shows opened doors for emerging actors. Johnny Depp was introduced to the wider public in "21 Jump Street." Jeff Goldblum gained wide notice in a short-lived but well-remembered Cannell series, "Tenspeed and Brown Shoe." And "Wiseguy" gave Kevin Spacey a chance to stand out as a villain.

Late in his career Mr. Cannell shifted to crime novels and again proved he had a popular touch. Several of his 16 books, many featuring the detective Shane Scully, were best sellers.

"Most of my things strike to the same theme," Mr. Cannell said in a 2010 interview in Success magazine, "which is not to take yourself so seriously that you can't grow."

His own success mirrored the formula he repeated in his television writing. It was a three-act, feel-good story of overcoming debilitating flaws.

Born on Feb. 5, 1941, in Los Angeles to an affluent family (his father owned an interior design business), Mr. Cannell suffered from extreme dyslexia, which went undiagnosed and all but ruined his school years. Despite inheriting his family's intense work ethic, he failed three grades and was unable to retain a football scholarship to the University of Oregon because of his lackluster academic record.

But a professor there recognized his writing gifts and encouraged him. Once he had broken into television writing, Mr. Cannell was fast and dependable. From early work on shows like "It Takes a Thief" and "Toma," he graduated to more serious efforts, like a script for the notoriously demanding "Columbo."

He was successful and happy, unlike many of his Hollywood writing contemporaries. He married his grade-school sweetheart, Marcia Finch, in 1964. She survives him, along with two daughters, a son and three grandchildren.

It was while banging out a script for "Toma" that Mr. Cannell created a character named Jim Rockford. Like Rockford, Mr. Cannell often pointed out, his lead characters were flawed men who found a way to get the right thing done.

POPULAR TOUCH: Mr. Cannell created hit shows like "The Rockford Files" and "The A-Team."

Rockford was an ex-con turned reluctant detective who would rather crack wise than fight. The series, a hit for seven seasons, reflected a cultural shift away from the perfect physical and moral specimens of the movies and early television and toward more realistic, grittier heroes, in line with the harder reality viewers saw on the evening news.

"That square-jawed good guy began to look like an idiot to us," Mr. Cannell said in an interview in 1999.

Rockford also introduced another staple of Mr. Cannell's best work: humor. The character's wry touch so fit the style of the show's star, James Garner, that he seemed inseparable from the role. By contrast, broad comedy typified "The A-Team," the loud, seemingly mindless action series that ran for five years in the mid-'80s, all but saving the NBC network. The series included set-piece action sequences with explosions and crashing vehicles, and people were hardly ever killed.

Critics and viewers often questioned how a show like that, and other Cannell titles like "Riptide," "Renegade" and the late-night series "Silk Stalkings," could spring from the same mind that created a complex, groundbreaking crime drama like "Wiseguy," a forerunner of "The Sopranos."

Mr. Cannell shrugged off such puzzlement, saying he didn't know why his work ranged so widely. "But I do know it's easier to think of me simply as the guy who wrote 'The A-Team,'" he told The Associated Press in 1993. "So they do."

"I'm generally a very happy guy, because I'm doing what I want," Mr. Cannell said in the Success interview. "I'm willing to tell you that there are people who are much better than I am in writing. I don't have to be the fastest gun in the West."

— *By Bill Carter*

JOSEPH SOBRAN

Hard-Line Columnist

FEB. 23, 1946 - SEPT. 30, 2010

JOSEPH SOBRAN, a hard-hitting conservative writer and moralist whose outspoken antipathy to Israel and what he saw as the undue influence of a Jewish lobby on American foreign policy led to his removal as a senior editor of National Review in 1993, died on Sept. 30 in Fairfax, Va. He was 64 and lived in Burke, Va.

The cause was kidney failure resulting from diabetes, a daughter said.

Mr. Sobran (pronounced SO-brun), one of the conservative whiz kids whom William F. Buckley draft-picked for National Review straight out of college, made his mark with witty, thoughtful essays on moral and social questions. He also wrote a syndicated column for The Los Angeles Times and Universal Press Syndicate. An unapologetic paleoconservative, Mr. Sobran was opposed to military intervention abroad, big government at home and moral permissiveness everywhere.

As a conservative Roman Catholic, he made a particular target of the Supreme Court's decisions legalizing abortion and protecting pornography as free speech. Unlike many of his colleagues, he took little interest in electoral politics or the machinery of government. At the same time, he nourished a libertarian streak that gradually took over, eventually pushing him to declare himself an anarchist.

"I much preferred a literary, contemplative conservatism to the activist sort that was preoccupied with immediate political issues," he wrote in a 2002 essay explaining his conversion to anarchism. "During the Reagan years, which I expected to find exciting, I found myself bored to death with supply-side economics, enterprise zones, 'privatizing' welfare programs and similar principle-dodging gimmickry."

In the mid-1980s he ran into trouble with Mr. Buckley for the first time after writing several columns critical of American policy in the Middle East.

Matters came to a boil in 1993. Mr. Sobran, unhappy with National Review's support for the 1991 Persian Gulf war, and with Mr. Buckley's criticism of his writing on Jews and the Middle East, attacked Mr. Buckley in his "Washington Watch" column in The Wanderer, a traditionalist Roman Catholic weekly.

When informed by National Review's editor in chief, John O'Sullivan, that the column amounted to a letter of resignation, Mr. Sobran was fired.

Mr. Buckley, angry that Mr. Sobran had included conversations from a private dinner that the two had had, and stung by the depiction of him as kowtowing to Manhattan's social elite, wrote in a letter to The Wanderer that the column "gives evidence of an incapacitation moral and perhaps medical, which news is both bad, and sad," adding that Mr. Sobran's criticisms were "a breath-catching libel." The two men later reconciled.

Mr. Sobran's isolationist views on American foreign policy and Israel became increasingly extreme. He took a skeptical line on the Holocaust and said the Sept. 11 terror attacks were a result of American foreign policy in the Middle East, which he believed that a Jewish lobby had directed. Not surprisingly, he spent much of his time defending himself against charges of anti-Semitism.

"Nobody has ever accused me of the slightest personal indecency to a Jew," he said in a speech delivered at a 2002 conference of the Institute for Historical Review. "My chief offense, it appears, has been to insist that the state of Israel has been a costly and treacherous 'ally' to the United States. As of last Sept. 11, I should think that is undeniable. But I have yet to receive a single apology for having been correct."

Michael Joseph Sobran Jr. was born on Feb. 23, 1946, in Ypsilanti, Mich. He studied English and American literature at Eastern Michigan University, where he earned a bachelor's degree in 1969, and went on to do graduate work on Shakespeare, a lifelong preoccupation.

In 1997 the Free Press published "Alias Shakespeare: Solving the Greatest Literary Mystery of All Time," an argument in support of the theory that Shakespeare's plays were written by Edward de Vere, the Earl of Oxford.

While at Eastern Michigan, he sent letters to several professors who objected to an impending visit by Mr. Buckley, rebutting their criticisms point by point. Mr. Buckley later saw the letters and in 1972 offered Mr. Sobran a job writing for National Review.

His two marriages ended in divorce. Mr. Sobran is survived by two daughters, two sons, 10 grandchildren, one great-grandchild and several half-siblings.

In addition to writing his syndicated column, Mr. Sobran regularly appeared on the CBS radio series "Spectrum." He contributed to The Wanderer, The Human Life Review, The American Spectator and other publications. In 1994 he founded Sobran's: The Real News of the Month, a newsletter that ceased publication in the fall of 2007.

He arrived at the conclusion that virtually every act of the federal government since the Civil War was illegal.

Mr. Sobran addressed social issues in his columns, especially questions pertaining to abortion, the family and marriage. Many of his essays were collected in "Single Issues: Essays on the Crucial Social Questions."

He wrote often on the Constitution as well, and as he underwent a slow conversion to anarchism beginning in the late 1980s, he arrived at the conclusion, based on his reading of the 10th Amendment, that virtually every act of the federal government since the Civil War was illegal.

— *By William Grimes*

PHILIPPA FOOT

Philosophy, Ethics and a Life-or-Death Dilemma

OCT. 3, 1920 - OCT. 3, 2010

Philippa Foot, a philosopher who argued that moral judgments have a rational basis, and who introduced the renowned ethical thought experiment known as the Trolley Problem, died at her home in Oxford, England, on Oct. 3, her 90th birthday.

Her death was announced on the Web site of Somerville College, Oxford, where she earned her academic degrees and taught for many years.

In her early work, notably in the essays "Moral Beliefs" and "Moral Arguments," published in the late 1950s, Ms. Foot took issue with philosophers like R. M. Hare and Charles L. Stevenson, who maintained that moral statements were ultimately expressions of attitude or emotion, because they could not be judged true or false in the same way factual statements could be.

Ms. Foot countered this "private enterprise theory," as she called it, by arguing the interconnectedness of facts and moral interpretations. Further, she insisted that virtues like courage, wisdom and temperance are indispensable to human life and the foundation stones of morality. Her writing on the subject helped establish virtue ethics as a leading approach to the study of moral problems.

"She's going to be remembered not for a particular view or position, but for changing the way people think about topics," said Lawrence Solum, who teaches the philosophy of law at the University of Illinois and studied under Ms. Foot. "She made the moves that made people see things in a fundamentally new way. Very few people do that in philosophy."

It was the Trolley Problem, however, that captured the imagination of scholars outside her discipline. In 1967, in the essay "The Problem of Abortion and the Doctrine of the Double Effect," she discussed, using a series of provocative examples, the moral distinctions between intended and unintended consequences, between doing and allowing, and between positive and negative duties — the duty not to inflict harm weighed against the duty to render aid.

The most arresting of her examples, offered in just a few sentences, was the ethical dilemma faced by the driver of a runaway trolley hurtling toward five track workers. By diverting the trolley to a spur where just one worker is on the track, the driver can save five lives.

Clearly, the driver should divert the trolley and kill one worker rather than five.

But what about a surgeon who could also save five lives — by killing a patient and distributing the patient's organs to five other patients who would otherwise die? The math is the same, but here, instead of having to choose between two negative duties — the imperative not to inflict harm — as the driver does, the doctor weighs a negative duty against the positive duty of rendering aid.

By means of such problems, Ms. Foot hoped to clarify thinking about the moral issues surrounding abortion in particular, but she applied a similar approach to matters like euthanasia.

The philosopher Judith Jarvis Thomson added two complications to the Trolley Problem that are now inseparable from it.

Imagine, she wrote, a bystander who sees the trolley racing toward the track workers and can divert it by throwing a switch along the tracks. Unlike the driver, who must choose to kill one person or five, the bystander can refuse to intervene or, by throwing the switch, accept the unintended consequence of killing a human being, a choice endorsed by most people presented with the problem.

Or suppose, she suggested, that the bystander observes the impending trolley disaster from a footbridge over the tracks and realizes that by throwing a heavy weight in front of the trolley he can stop it.

As it happens, the only available weight is a fat man standing next to him. Most respondents presented with the problem saw a moral distinction between throwing the switch and throwing the man on the tracks, even though the end result, in lives saved, was identical.

The paradoxes suggested by the Trolley Problem and its variants have engaged not only moral philosophers but neuroscientists, economists and evolutionary psychologists. It also inspired a subdiscipline jokingly known as trolleyology, whose swelling body of commentary "makes the Talmud look like Cliffs Notes," the philosopher Kwame Anthony Appiah wrote in his book "Experiments in Ethics" (2008).

Philippa Judith Bosanquet was born on Oct. 3, 1920, in Owston Ferry, Lincolnshire, and grew up in Kirkleatham, in North Yorkshire. Her mother, Esther, was a daughter of President Grover Cleveland. Her father, William, was a captain in the Coldstream Guards when he married her mother and later took over the running of a large Yorkshire steel works.

Ms. Foot studied philosophy, politics and economics at Somerville College, where she earned a bachelor's degree in 1942. During World War II, she worked as a researcher at the Royal Institute of International Affairs, sharing a London flat with the future novelist and fellow philosopher Iris Murdoch.

In 1945 Philippa Bosanquet married the historian M. R. D. Foot. The marriage ended in divorce. Ms. Foot is survived by a sister.

Ms. Foot began lecturing on philosophy at Somerville in 1947, a year after receiving her master's degree, and rose to the positions of vice principal and senior research fellow before retiring in 1988. In 1974 she became a professor of philosophy at the University of California, Los Angeles, from which she retired in 1991.

In the 1970s Ms. Foot revisited some of her assertions about the objective nature of morality, allowing a measure of subjectivism to creep into her discussions of topics like abortion and euthanasia. The influence of Wittgenstein, and his linguistic spin on philosophical questions, became increasingly important in her writing, which dealt scrupulously with the various senses, and pitfalls, of terms like "should," "would" and "good."

In "Natural Goodness" (2001), she offered a new theory of practical reason, arguing that morals are rooted in objective human needs that can be compared to the physical needs of

APPRECIATION

Slow Path to a Moral Vision

Ludwig Wittgenstein once said that in philosophy it is hard to work as slowly as you should. When the British philosopher Philippa Foot finally published "Natural Goodness," her first and only book-length statement of her thinking, at age 80 in 2001, an editor at Oxford University Press recalled Wittgenstein's challenge. "Well," he said, "that is a problem that Philippa seems to have solved."

Ms. Foot's philosophical voyage, her "painfully slow journey," as she put it, was long in part because it was uphill. Though born into a family of privilege — her father was a wealthy British industrialist, her mother a daughter of President Grover Cleveland — she was given no formal education ("I was extremely ignorant," she said) and, being a woman, was not expected to go to college.

Spurred on, however, by a governess who recognized her intelligence, Ms. Foot educated herself via correspondence courses and eventually attended Somerville College at Oxford. There, in the clubby, masculine atmosphere of high British learning, she cultivated friendships with a group of young female philosophers, among them Elizabeth Anscombe, who would become a prized student and editor of Wittgenstein's, and Iris Murdoch, the future novelist. (Ms. Foot would marry one of Ms. Murdoch's former boyfriends, the historian M. R. D. Foot.)

The chief obstacle in Ms. Foot's life, however, wasn't educational disadvantage or social prejudice but academic orthodoxy. Returning to Oxford as a graduate student in 1945, after working in London during the war (and living in an intermittently bombed-out apartment with Murdoch), Ms. Foot became troubled by a central assumption of 20th-century moral philosophy: that facts and values are logically independent. According to this view, you can't derive an "ought" conclusion from a series of "is" premises. Nature is composed of objective facts that we can verify through science; values are mere attitudes in our heads that we project onto the world as we like. When we engage in moral disagreement with, say, an unrepentant murderer, reasoned plants and animals and described using the same words.

In a 2001 interview with Philosophy Today, she addressed a colleague's comment that, in her book, she seemed to regard vice as a natural defect.

"That's exactly what I believe, and I want to say that we describe defects in human beings in the same way as we do defects in plants and animals," she said. "I once began a lecture by saying that in moral philosophy, it's very important to begin by talking about plants."

Her most important essays were collected in "Virtues and Vices and Other Essays in Moral Philosophy" (1978) and "Moral Dilemmas: And Other Topics in Moral Philosophy" (2002).

Despite her influence, Ms. Foot remained disarmingly modest. "I'm not clever at all," she told The Philosophers' Magazine in 2003. "I have a certain insight into philosophy, I think. But I'm not clever; I don't find complicated arguments easy to follow."

— *By William Grimes*

---

argument breaks down. We feel it is wrong to kill innocent people; he simply does not. There is no accounting for taste.

In the wake of the news of the concentration camps, Ms. Foot was haunted by the notion that there was no way to overcome a moral standoff with a Nazi rationally. She wanted to argue that moral evaluation ("It is wrong to kill innocent people") is not fundamentally different from factual evaluation ("It is incorrect that the Earth is flat"). A cynic should no more be able to deny the moral implications of a relevant body of evidence than a flat-earther can deny the factual implications of astronomical data. It was Ms. Anscombe, a devoted Roman Catholic, who liberated Ms. Foot, a lifelong atheist, to dare to think in this outmoded fashion. Ms. Foot had been speaking of the conventional contrast of "ought" and "is," and Ms. Anscombe feigned confusion. "She said: 'Of what? What?'" Ms. Foot recalled. "And I thought, My God, so one doesn't have to accept that distinction! One can say, 'What?'!"

Incrementally, over many decades, first at Oxford and then at U.C.L.A., Ms. Foot shaped an alternative moral vision. In the late 1950s she questioned whether you can have a recognizably moral attitude about just any set of facts. (Can you really believe that it is immoral to look at hedgehogs in the light of the moon?) By the 1970s, inspired by Ms. Anscombe's suggestion that she revisit St. Thomas Aquinas's ethical writings, Ms. Foot was arguing that if you focus on traditional virtues and vices like temperance and avarice instead of abstract concepts like goodness and duty, you can see the concrete connections between the conditions of human life and the objective reasons for acting morally. (Why is cowardliness a vice? Because courage is needed to face the world's challenges.) In the '80s, after considering how we evaluate what is "good" for plants and animals, she developed the argument, presented in "Natural Goodness," that vice is a defect in humans in the same way that poor roots are a defect in an oak tree or poor vision a defect in an owl: the latter two assessments have clear normative implications ("oughts"), yet are entirely factual. Even from a secular scientific vantage point, you could locate good and evil in the fabric of the world.

In time, many other thinkers, academic philosophers and popular moralists alike, came to imitate or echo Ms. Foot's efforts to secure moral truth by reflecting on the classical virtues. Looking back, she seemed to appreciate the connection between her distinctive talents and the long arc of her career. "I'm a dreadfully slow thinker, really," she said. "But I do have a good nose for what is important."

— *By James Ryerson*

NORMAN WISDOM

A Slapstick Everyman

FEB. 4, 1915 - OCT. 4, 2010

NORMAN WISDOM, one of Britain's best-loved cinematic clowns, an elfin man of doleful mien who was often described as the rightful heir to Charlie Chaplin, died on Oct. 4 on the Isle of Man. He was 95 and had continued performing until he was 90.

For six decades Mr. Wisdom reigned as one of Britain's most celebrated comics, appearing in films, on television and in live performances. His unabashedly slapstick style — embracing spills, pratfalls and all manner of silly walks — made him one of the last living links to the British music hall tradition. In his trademark cloth cap and too-tight suit, he was a small shambolic Everyman, battered by life but emerging roguishly triumphant in the end.

It was an index of how nobly Mr. Wisdom played the underdog that for decades he enjoyed a cult status in a most unlikely place: Albania. According to many news accounts over the years, his films were among the very few Western pictures shown there during the postwar regime of the Stalinist dictator Enver Hoxha. (Mr. Hoxha apparently chose to interpret Mr. Wisdom's plucky, down-at-the-heels screen persona as anti-capitalist allegory.)

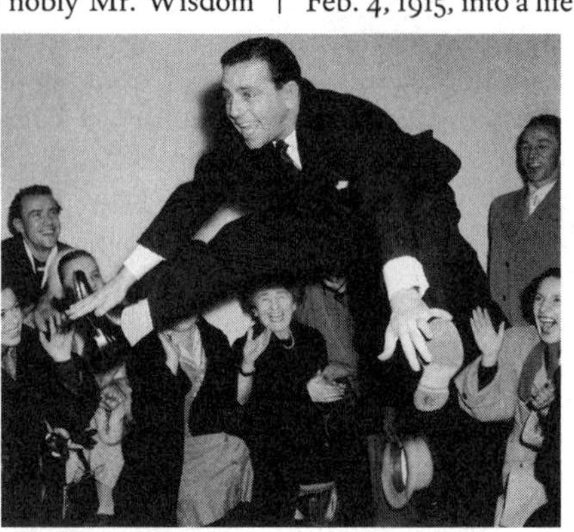

HIGH JINKS: Beloved in Britain, Mr. Wisdom was a cult favorite in an unlikely place: Albania.

The Albanian prime minister, Sali Berisha, declared Oct. 5 an unofficial national day of mourning.

Mr. Wisdom appeared in two Broadway shows, notably the musical "Walking Happy," for which he received a Tony nomination. The show, which ran for 161 performances in 1966 and 1967, had music by Jimmy Van Heusen and lyrics by Sammy Cahn. He later starred in the comedy "Not Now, Darling," which ran briefly in 1970.

His films shown in the United States include "Trouble in Store" (1953) and "Follow a Star" (1959). He was also featured in the Hollywood picture "The Night They Raided Minsky's" (1968).

Norman Wisden was born in London on Feb. 4, 1915, into a life more threadbare than any he portrayed on screen. His mother abandoned the family when he was a boy, leaving Norman and his brother to be reared by their father, a chauffeur of improvident habits and violent temperament. In interviews, Mr. Wisdom recalled having to steal food to survive.

After his father abdicated parental duties altogether, Norman lived in a children's home before striking out on his own when he was about 14. He held a series of knockabout jobs including errand boy, apprentice waiter, ship's cabin boy and army band boy. (The fact that he played no known instrument was apparently no impediment.)

He served with the 10th Royal Hussars in England and India — during that time, he learned to sing and play the trumpet, clarinet, xylophone and much else — and it was in the Army that he developed a flair for entertaining. In 1946, after leaving the service, he began his career in London music halls. Along the way, he changed his name to Wisdom.

Mr. Wisdom was divorced. Survivors include a son, a daughter and grandchildren.

Mr. Wisdom's very English brand of low comedy did not find favor with every American critic. "To put him in a class with Lou Costello would be to flatter him recklessly," the critic Bosley Crowther wrote in The Times in 1956.

But he remained beloved in Britain, where he gave many command performances for the royal family. His most talked-about came in 2000, when he was knighted by Queen Elizabeth II. As widely reported in the British news media, Mr. Wisdom, leaving the ceremony, could not resist stumbling.

The queen, the British press reported, was Most Amused.

— *By Margalit Fox*

SELMA AL-RADI

Saving a Palace in Distress

JULY 23, 1939 - OCT. 7, 2010

On certain dark nights, as a Yemeni legend tells it, Sultan Amir ibn Abd Al-Wahhab would command his servants to set lanterns in the windows of the Amiriya Madrasa, the ornate palace complex he had commissioned at Rada, in southern Yemen. Then, with his daughter by his side, he would ride into the hills above town, to behold his vast edifice ablaze with light.

The sultan was a historical figure, the last ruler of the Tahirid Dynasty, which flourished in Yemen from the mid-15th to early 16th centuries. The Amiriya Madrasa, erected in 1504 and named for him, was then and is now again one of the great treasures of Islamic art and architecture.

Solidly built of limestone and brick, the Amiriya seemed destined to endure as the sultan's monumental legacy. But after he was killed in battle in 1517, the complex was left to decay. The more puritanical rulers who followed him deemed its lavishness a distraction from the sober business of prayer.

That the Amiriya today stands resplendent after five centuries of neglect is due almost entirely to the efforts of one woman, the Iraqi-born archaeologist Selma Al-Radi, who was for many years a research associate at New York University's Institute of Fine Arts.

In an immense undertaking begun in the early 1980s and lasting nearly a quarter-century, Dr. Radi oversaw the return of the complex, brick by brick, to its former glory. What was more, at her direction, the restoration was done using only traditional materials, as well as time-honored construction methods passed down in Yemeni families for generations.

Three stories high and crowned by six large domes, the Amiriya, which reopened in 2005, gleams white as sugar against the sepia landscape. Besides a madrasa, or religious school, it comprises a mosque; residential quarters; and a hammam, or bath, equipped with medieval shower stalls.

Inside, the building is a controlled riot of pattern and color. Walls teem with intricate stucco carving that resemble ivory fretwork. On the soaring vaulted ceilings, geometric and floral designs and Koranic inscriptions are painted in tempera, in brilliant hues of red, orange and green.

In 2007, Dr. Radi and her Yemeni colleague Yahya Al-Nasiri were honored with the Aga Khan Award for Architecture, honoring outstanding architectural achievements throughout the Muslim world.

Dr. Radi died on Oct. 7, at 71. The death, at her home in Manhattan, was of ovarian cancer, her husband, Qais Al-Awqati, said; she also had Alzheimer's disease.

A diplomat's daughter, Selma Al-Radi was born in Baghdad on July 23, 1939. Her father was the Iraqi ambassador first to Iran and later to India, and she was reared in Tehran and New Delhi.

Dr. Radi earned a bachelor's degree from Cambridge in Oriental Studies; a master's degree in art history and Near East archaeology from Columbia; and a Ph.D. in archaeology from the University of Amsterdam.

Where some archaeologists are theoreticians, Dr. Radi was a digger, seldom happier than when she had her hands deep in the grit of history. She excavated at sites in Iraq, Syria, Turkey, Lebanon, Kuwait and Egypt, but it was for her work in Yemen that she would become renowned.

She first saw the Amiriya Madrasa in the late 1970s, when she was helping set up the National Museum of Yemen. One day, she traveled to Rada to visit a Dutch archaeological team that was restoring part of the town.

"I saw this building and said, 'Wow, this we've got to save,'" Dr. Radi told The Guardian of London in 2006. "So I went rushing back to the Dutch embassy and said, 'Help, help, help.'"

By then, the complex was a ruin, with sagging walls, rotting beams and a roof that threatened collapse. Its once-vibrant murals were flaked and faded; its stucco carvings had been obscured by layers of whitewash. The building had long been the de facto town dump, its ground floor filled with the detritus of centuries.

After securing backing from the Dutch and Yemeni governments, Dr. Radi recruited hundreds of local craftsmen. She insisted on traditional materials — baked bricks, mud-and-straw mortar, properly cured local timber — which were both less expensive and more authentic than modern ones like steel and reinforced concrete. (The cost of the entire restoration was about $2 million, a comparatively modest sum for a project of this scale.)

Workers did large tasks like shoring up walls and minute ones like scraping whitewash off the stucco with surgical scalpels, an enterprise that by itself took 15 years. They also revived the lost art of making qudad, a plaster of lime and cinder historically used to waterproof Yemeni buildings. Because there was no local tradition of painting conservation, an Italian team was brought in to restore the Amiriya's lavish tempera murals.

A TREASURE SAVED: Dr. Radi spearheaded the Amiriya Madrasa's 15-year restoration.

Dr. Radi's first marriage, to Muqbil Zahawi, ended in divorce. Besides her husband, Dr. Awqati, she is survived by a son from her first marriage; her mother; and a brother.

Her publications included two books on the Amiriya Madrasa.

In restoring the Amiriya, Dr. Radi did include one nontraditional element: electrical wiring. Now, on many dark nights, the vast edifice is ablaze with light.

— *By Margalit Fox*

ALBERTINA WALKER

Queen of Gospel

AUG. 29, 1929 - OCT. 8, 2010

ALBERTINA WALKER, who started singing in a Baptist choir at 4 years old and went on to become one of America's leading gospel singers, lending her lush contralto voice to a string of hits in the 1950s and '60s with her group the Caravans, died on Oct. 8 in Chicago. She was 81.

Early on, Ms. Walker was a standout even in Chicago's teeming, competitive gospel scene, and she became a protégé of Mahalia Jackson. With her good friend James Cleveland at the piano, she spent many evenings singing and socializing at Ms. Jackson's house, listening to critical advice.

"I had seen Roberta Martin and Mahalia Jackson," she told The Washington Post in 1998. "I wanted to stand up before audiences and deliver the message, win souls for Christ. I wanted to touch dying men and slipping women."

After touring with the Willie Webb Singers, with whom she recorded her first single, "He'll Be There," she joined Robert Anderson and His Gospel Caravan. With the other three singers backing up Mr. Anderson — Elyse Yancey, Nellie Grace Daniels and Ora Lee Hopkins Samson Walker — she formed the Caravans in 1951.

BLESSED WITH TALENT: After forming the Caravans in 1951, Ms. Walker went on to a notable solo career.

"Anderson had an unusual, but pleasing, style of singing behind the beat, which Albertina picked up," said Anthony Heilbut, the author of "The Gospel Sound: Good News and Bad Times" (1971). "You could think of her as his female counterpart."

The Caravans' first big hit, "Mary Don't You Weep," helped make them the most popular gospel group in the United States, with hits like "I Won't Be Back (Sweeping Through the City)," "(I Know) The Lord Will Provide," "Show Me Some Sign," and Ms. Walker's great signature song, "Lord Keep Me Day by Day."

They became known not only for hit songs but also for incubating future stars like Delores Washington, Cassietta George and Dorothy Norwood. Beginning in the 1970s Ms. Walker performed as a soloist with church choirs as her backup. Her first solo venture, "Put a Little Love in Your Heart," released in 1975, was followed by more than 50 albums, including "I Can Go to God in Prayer" and "Joy Will Come."

"Songs of the Church: Live in Memphis" won a Grammy Award in 1995 for the Best Traditional Soul Gospel Album, and in 2001 she was inducted into the Gospel Music Hall of Fame. President George W. Bush honored her in a White House ceremony in 2002.

Albertina Walker, known as Tina, was born on Aug. 29, 1929, on the South Side of Chicago, where she lived her entire life. She was the youngest of nine children. At age 4 she was singing with the youth choir of the West Point Baptist Church, under the direction of Pete

Williams, and before long was performing with the Williams Singers. By 17, she was singing with Mr. Anderson.

Mr. Anderson, although blessed with a top-quality voice himself — he played king to Mahalia Jackson's queen — made a practice of sharing the spotlight with his best singers, Ms. Walker chief among them. She followed his example as leader of the Caravans, stepping aside and letting her top performers shine.

In the early years, singers came and went. All the original members except Ms. Walker left the Caravans within a few years after it was founded. The early recordings, on the States label, featured tight harmonies and a sweet sound. Though popular, the group struggled, touring churches all over the United States but earning little money.

"We would put five to six dollars in the gas tank, drive all the way to New York or Mississippi," Ms. Walker told N'Digo magazine in 2009. "We would pack into one car, nobody had a problem with it either. We would probably make $150 singing, but we would share our rewards and the money would pay a lot of bills back then."

Ms. Walker can be heard in her prime on the album "The Best of the Caravans" (Savoy), and on the CD and DVD compilation "How Sweet It Was: The Sights and Sounds of Gospel's Golden Age" (Shanachie).

With the arrival of a new crop of young singers — Ms. Andrews, Ms. Washington, Ms. Norwood and Ms. Caesar — the Caravans embarked on a hot streak that continued until 1966, when Ms. Caesar and Ms. Anderson left the group. Ms. Walker kept the Caravans going for a time, bringing in the future disco star Loleatta Holloway, but in the 1970s she struck out on her own.

Her later hits included "Please Be Patient With Me," with Reverend Cleveland, and the poignant anthem "I'm Still Here."

"The Lord went all out with this song," Ms. Walker told N'Digo. "I must say, I'm still here, and believe me when I say it, it's been a wonderful life serving the Lord and His people through song."

— *By William Grimes*

ERIC JOISEL

The Astonishing Art of Folding Paper

NOV. 15, 1956 - OCT. 10, 2010

It is no small thing to make a hedgehog. The first time Eric Joisel tried it, it took nearly six years.

But what a hedgehog it turned out to be: folded from a single sheet of paper, each crenellation sharp as the crease in a new pair of trousers, it captures the very essence of hedgehogness.

Mr. Joisel, a solitary Frenchman and one of the most illustrious origami artists in the world, died on Oct. 10 in Argenteuil, outside Paris. He was 53 and lived nearby in Sannois. The cause was lung cancer, said Vanessa Gould, a filmmaker whose 2009 documentary about modern origami masters, "Between the Folds," features him prominently.

Not for Mr. Joisel were the paper boats and wobbly tables that have embodied origami for generations of children. His pieces, which can fetch thousands of dollars, have been exhibited at the Louvre and elsewhere around the world and are in many private collections.

Trained as a sculptor, Mr. Joisel was largely self-taught in origami, and his work resembles

ARTIST, CONJURER: Mr. Joisel, pictured here with a rhinoceros and a concertina, created his sculptures from a single sheet of paper without even a snip of a scissor.

that of no other artist in the genre. Part sculpture, part paper-folding and all rigorous engineering, his art embodies people, animals and fantasy figures in an array of dimensions from palm-size to life-size.

To devise the blueprint for a single figure could take him years. To fold one could take hundreds of hours — a very large work might entail a rectangle of paper measuring more than 15 feet by 25 feet, roughly the size of a New York studio apartment. No two figures were precisely alike.

"Origami is very difficult," Mr. Joisel wrote in English in an introductory passage on his Web site. "When people ask how long it takes me to make a sculpture I say, '35 years,' because that is how long it's taken me to get to this level."

In origami parlance, Mr. Joisel was a wet-folder, dampening his paper so that he could coax it into sinuous curves. His earliest work centered on animals: besides the hedgehog, there was a turtle, a leaping fish, a magnificent sea horse and much else. He later progressed to people, making haunting, atavistic masks and, eventually, entire human forms.

His best-known recent art includes a bevy of musicians, each less than a foot high, with minute sculptured details like furrowed brows and veined, careworn hands. Each holds a tiny instrument — a tuba, a saxophone, a harp, a violin — also made of paper. Other pieces include a set of meticulously costumed characters from the commedia dell'arte.

"Much of his life's work was devoted to studying an expressiveness of human nature that you would never think could be elicited from a piece of paper," Ms. Gould said in an interview.

Mr. Joisel, who had neither life partner nor children, is survived by four siblings.

Eric Joisel was born in Enghien-les-Bains, near Paris, on Nov. 15, 1956. As a young man he studied law and history before becoming a sculptor in clay, wood and stone. Then, in the early 1980s, he encountered the work of Akira

Yoshizawa, the 20th-century Japanese master who was the first person to elevate origami to high-level figurative art.

Mr. Joisel was enthralled by its expressiveness — and by the challenge of conjuring three-dimensional forms from two-dimensional paper without adhesive or a single snip of the scissor. He threw all his earlier sculptures away.

From the early '90s on, Mr. Joisel was a full-time origami maker, his art so labor intensive that despite the prices it commanded he led a markedly threadbare existence. He lived alone by choice, in a modest farmhouse, where he spent hours each day designing, sketching and folding.

"He's so wildly imaginative in a field which often suffers for lack of imagination," Ms. Gould said. "This is a man who lived in a house by himself and made creatures that came from the depths of his imagination."

Mr. Joisel often circulated patterns for his work, and to see one renders his art simultaneously approachable and unattainable. No lay person should even contemplate the hedgehog. It is barely possible, however, to make Mr. Joisel's handsome rat.

All one needs is a square of paper, infinite patience and an entire afternoon.

— *By Margalit Fox*

JOAN SUTHERLAND

Flawless, and Peerless, Soprano

NOV. 7, 1926 - OCT. 10, 2010

Joan Sutherland, one of the most acclaimed sopranos of the 20th century, a singer of such power and range that she was crowned "La Stupenda," died on Oct. 10 at her home in Switzerland, near Montreux. She was 83.

It was Italy's notoriously picky critics who dubbed the Australian-born Ms. Sutherland the Stupendous One after her Italian debut, in Venice in 1960. And for 40 years the name endured with opera lovers around the world. Her 1961 debut at the Metropolitan Opera in New York, in Donizetti's "Lucia di Lammermoor," generated so much excitement that standees began lining up at 7:30 that morning. Her singing of the Mad Scene drew a thunderous 12-minute ovation.

Ms. Sutherland's singing was founded on astonishing technique. Her voice was evenly produced throughout an enormous range, from a low G to effortless flights above high C. She could spin lyrical phrases with elegant legato, subtle colorings and expressive nuances. Her sound was warm, vibrant and resonant, without any forcing. Indeed, her voice was so naturally large that at the start of her career Ms. Sutherland seemed destined to become a Wagnerian dramatic soprano.

Following her first professional performances, in 1948, Ms. Sutherland developed incomparable facility for fast runs, elaborate roulades and impeccable trills. She did not compromise the passagework, as many do, by glossing over scurrying runs, but sang almost every note fully.

Her abilities led Richard Bonynge, the Sydney-born conductor and vocal coach whom she married in 1954, to persuade her to explore the early-19th-century Italian opera of the bel canto school. She became a major force in its revitalization.

Bel canto (which translates as "beautiful song" or "beautiful singing") denotes an approach to singing exemplified by evenness through the range and great agility. The term also refers to the early-19th-century Italian operas steeped in bel canto style. Outside of Italy, the repertory had languished for decades when Maria Callas appeared in the early 1950s and demonstrated that operas like "Lucia di Lammermoor" and Bellini's "Norma" were not just showcases for coloratura virtuosity but musically elegant and dramatically gripping works as well.

Even as a young man, Mr. Bonynge had uncommon knowledge of bel canto repertory and style. Ms. Sutherland and Mr. Bonynge, who is four years younger than she, met in Sydney at a youth concert and became casual friends. They were reacquainted later in London, where Ms. Sutherland settled with her mother in 1951 to attend the Royal College of Music. There Mr. Bonynge became the major influence on her development.

'LA STUPENDA': Ms. Sutherland in her acclaimed 1961 debut at the Metropolitan Opera.

Ms. Sutherland used to say that she thought of herself and her husband as a duo and that she didn't talk of her career "but of ours."

In a 1961 profile in The New York Times Magazine, she said she initially had "a big, rather wild voice" that was not heavy enough for Wagner but didn't realize that it wasn't until she heard "Wagner sung as it should be."

"Richard had decided — long before I agreed with him — that I was a coloratura," she told the magazine.

"We fought like cats and dogs over it," she said, adding, "It took Richard three years to convince me."

In her repertory choices, Ms. Sutherland ranged widely during the 1950s, singing lighter lyric Mozart roles like the Countess in "Le Nozze di Figaro" and heavier Verdi roles like Amelia in "Un Ballo in Maschera." Even then, astute listeners realized that she was en route to becoming something extraordinary.

In a glowing and perceptive review of her performance as Desdemona in Verdi's "Otello" at Covent Garden in London in late 1957, the critic Andrew Porter, writing in The Financial Times, commended her for not "sacrificing purity to power." This is "not her way," Mr. Porter wrote, "and five years on we shall bless her for her not endeavoring now to be 'exciting' but, instead, lyrical and beautiful."

She became an international sensation after her career-defining performance in the title role of "Lucia di Lammermoor" in 1959 at Covent Garden, its first presentation there since 1925. The production, opening on Feb. 17, was directed by Franco Zeffirelli and conducted by the Italian maestro Tullio Serafin, a longtime Callas colleague, who elicited from the 32-year-old soprano a vocally resplendent and dramatically affecting portrayal of the trusting, unstable young bride of Lammermoor.

This triumph was followed in 1960 by landmark portrayals in neglected bel canto operas by Bellini: Elvira in "I Puritani" at the Glyndebourne Festival (the first presentation in England since 1887) and "La Sonnambula" at Covent Garden (the company's first production in half a century).

Ms. Sutherland's American debut came in November 1960 in the title role of Handel's "Alcina" at the Dallas Opera, the first American production of this now-popular work. Her distinguished Decca recording of "Lucia di Lammermoor" was released in 1961, the year of her enormously anticipated Metropolitan Opera debut in that same work, on Nov. 26.

At Ms. Sutherland's first appearance, before she had sung a note, there was an enthusiastic ovation. Following the first half of Lucia's Mad Scene in the final act, which culminated in a glorious high E-flat, the ovation lasted almost 5 minutes. When she finished the scene and her crazed, dying Lucia collapsed to the stage floor, the ovation lasted 12 minutes.

Reviewing the performance in The New

York Times, Harold C. Schonberg wrote that other sopranos might have more power or a sweeter tone, but "there is none around who has the combination of technique, vocal security, clarity and finesse that Miss Sutherland can summon."

Even for some admirers, though, there were limitations to her artistry. Her diction was often criticized as indistinct. But Ms. Sutherland worked to correct the shortcoming and sang with crisper enunciation in the 1970s.

She was also criticized for delivering dramatically bland performances. At 5-foot-9, she was a large woman, with long arms and large hands, and a long, wide face. As her renown increased, she insisted that designers create costumes for her that compensated for her figure, which, as she admitted self-deprecatingly in interviews, was somewhat flat in the bust but wide in the rib cage. Certain dresses could make her look like "a large column walking about the stage," she wrote in "The Autobiography of Joan Sutherland: A Prima Donna's Progress" (1997).

A LAST BRAVA: Ms. Sutherland after her final full-length dramatic performance in 1990.

Paradoxically, Mr. Bonynge contributed to the sometimes dramatically uninvolved quality of her performances. By the mid-1960s he was her conductor of choice, often part of the deal when she signed a contract. Trained as a pianist and vocal coach, he essentially taught himself conducting. Even after extended experience, he was not the maestro opera fans turned to for arresting performances of Verdi's "Traviata." But he understood the bel canto style and was attuned to every component of his wife's voice.

Yet if urging Ms. Sutherland to be sensible added to her longevity, it sometimes resulted in her playing it safe. Other conductors prodded her to sing with greater intensity, among them Georg Solti, in an acclaimed 1967 recording of Verdi's Requiem with the Vienna Philharmonic and the Vienna State Opera Chorus, and Zubin Mehta, who enticed Ms. Sutherland into recording the title role in Puccini's "Turandot," which she never sang onstage, for a 1972 recording. Both projects featured the tenor Luciano Pavarotti, who would become an ideal partner for Ms. Sutherland in the bel canto repertory. Ms. Sutherland's fiery Turandot suggests that she had dramatic abilities that were never tapped.

Joan Alston Sutherland was born on Nov. 7, 1926, in Sydney, where the family lived in a modest house overlooking the harbor. The family garden and the rich array of wildflowers on the hillside near the beach inspired her lifelong love of gardening.

Her mother, Muriel Sutherland, was a fine mezzo-soprano who had studied with Mathilde Marchesi, the teacher of the Australian soprano Nellie Melba. Though too shy for the stage, Ms. Sutherland's mother did vocal exercises every day and was her daughter's principal teacher throughout her adolescence.

Ms. Sutherland's father, William, a Scottish-born tailor, had been married before. His first wife died during the influenza epidemic after World War I, leaving him with three daughters and a son. Ms. Sutherland was the only child of his second marriage. He died on Ms. Sutherland's sixth birthday. He had just given her a new bathing suit and she wanted to try it out. Though feeling unwell, he climbed down to the beach with her and, upon returning, collapsed in his wife's arms. Afterward Joan, along with her youngest half-sister and their mother, moved into the home of an aunt and uncle in the Sydney suburb of Woollahra.

Although Ms. Sutherland's mother soon recognized her daughter's gifts, she pegged her as a mezzo-soprano. At 16, facing the reality of having to support herself, Ms. Sutherland completed a secretarial course and took office jobs while keeping up her vocal studies. She began lessons in Sydney with Aida Dickens, who convinced her that she was a soprano, very likely a dramatic soprano. Ms. Sutherland began singing oratorios and radio broadcasts and made a notable debut in 1947 as Purcell's Dido in Sydney.

In 1951, with prize money from winning a prestigious vocal competition, she and her mother moved to London, where Ms. Sutherland enrolled at the opera school of the Royal College of Music. The next year, after three unsuccessful auditions, she was accepted into the Royal Opera at Covent Garden and made her debut as the First Lady in Mozart's "Zauberflöte."

In the company's landmark 1952 production of Bellini's "Norma," starring Maria Callas, Ms. Sutherland sang the small role of Clotilde, Norma's confidante. "Now look after your voice," Callas advised her at the time, adding, "We're going to hear great things of you."

"I lusted to sing Norma after being in those performances with Callas," Ms. Sutherland told The Times in 1998. "But I knew that I could not sing it the way she did. It was 10 years before I sang the role. During that time I studied it, sang bits of it and worked with Richard. But I had to evolve my own way to sing it, and I would have wrecked my voice to ribbons had I tried to sing it like her."

In 1955 she created the lead role of Jenifer in Michael Tippett's "Midsummer Marriage."

During this period Ms. Sutherland gave birth to her only child, a son, who survives her, along with two grandchildren and Mr. Bonynge, her husband of 56 years.

Immediately after her breakthrough performances as Lucia in 1959, Ms. Sutherland underwent sinus surgery to correct problems with nasal passages that were chronically prone to becoming clogged. Though it was a risky operation for a singer, it was deemed successful.

In the early 1960s, using a home in southern Switzerland as a base, Ms. Sutherland made the rounds, singing in international opera houses and forming a close association with the Met, where she ultimately sang 223 performances. These included an acclaimed new production of "Norma" in 1970 with Ms. Horne in her Met debut, singing Adalgisa; Mr. Bonynge conducted. There was also a hugely popular 1972 production of Donizetti's "Fille du Régiment," with Pavarotti singing the role of Tonio.

Though never a compelling actress, Ms. Sutherland exuded vocal charisma. In the comic role of Marie in "La Fille du Régiment," she conveyed endearingly awkward girlishness as the orphaned tomboy raised by an army regiment, proudly marching in place in her uniform while tossing off the vocal flourishes.

Ms. Sutherland was plain-spoken and down to earth, someone who enjoyed needlepoint and playing with her grandchildren. Though she knew who she was, she was quick to poke fun at her prima donna persona.

"I love all those demented old dames of the old operas," she said in a 1961 Times profile. "All right, so they're loony. The music's wonderful."

Queen Elizabeth II made Ms. Sutherland a Dame Commander of the Order of the British Empire in 1978. Her bluntness sometimes caused her trouble. In 1994, addressing a luncheon organized by a group in favor of retaining the monarchy in Australia, she complained of having to be interviewed by a foreign-born clerk when applying to renew her passport. "A Chinese or an Indian — I'm not particularly racist — but find it ludicrous, when I've had a passport for 40 years," she said. Her remarks were widely reported, and she later apologized.

In retirement she mostly lived quietly at home but was persuaded to sit on juries of vocal competitions and, less often, to present master classes. In 2004 she received a Kennedy Center Honor for outstanding achievement. In 2008, she fell and broke both legs while gardening and was hospitalized for a long period.

Other sopranos may have been more musically probing and dramatically vivid than Ms. Sutherland, but few were such glorious vocalists. After hearing her New York debut in "Beatrice di Tenda" at Town Hall, the renowned Brazilian soprano Bidú Sayão, herself beloved for the sheer beauty of her voice, said, "If there is perfection in singing, this is it."

— *By Anthony Tommasini*

SOLOMON BURKE

From the Pulpit to the Throne (of Soul)

MARCH 21, 1940 - OCT. 10, 2010

SOLOMON BURKE, a singer whose smooth, powerful articulation and mingling of sacred and profane themes helped define soul music in the early 1960s, died on Oct. 10 at Schiphol Airport in Amsterdam on his way to a concert in the midst of a career revival. He was 70 and lived in Los Angeles.

His death was announced by his family, but no cause was given.

Drawing on gospel, country and gritty rhythm and blues in songs like "Cry to Me" (1962), "You Can Make It if You Try" (1963) and "Everybody Needs Somebody to Love" (1964), Mr. Burke developed a vocal style that was nuanced yet forceful. Steeped in church traditions from a young age, he could make a sermon out of any situation, as in "The Price" from 1964, a catalog of the wages of a bad romance. ("You cost me my mother/The love of my father/Sister/My brother too.")

Though he never attained the wide popularity of Otis Redding or James Brown, Mr. Burke had a significant influence on R&B and rock, and he was a favorite of musicians and connoisseurs. Mick Jagger sang several of his songs on early Rolling Stones albums, and Jerry Wexler, the Atlantic Records producer who recorded Mr. Burke at his peak, once affirmed a judgment of him as the best soul singer of all time.

In a genre known for outsize personalities and flamboyant showmanship, Mr. Burke stood out for his sheer boldness and eccentricity. A radio D.J. crowned him the King of Rock and Soul in 1964, and Mr. Burke took the coronation to heart. For the rest of his career he often performed in full royal habit — crown, scepter and robe — and sat on a golden throne onstage. Wide-shaped in his youth, he grew into Henry VIII-like corpulence, and in his later years had to be wheeled to his throne.

An ordained minister, licensed mortician, resourceful entrepreneur and champion raconteur, Mr. Burke inspired almost as much amazement with his offstage persona as he did with his music. A biography on his Web site says that he had 21 children, 90 grandchildren and 19 great-grandchildren. "I got lost on one of the Bible verses that said, 'Be fruitful and multiply,'" he once said. "I didn't read no further."

Born on March 21, 1940, in Philadelphia, Mr. Burke was precocious in the pulpit and at the microphone. His mother and grandmother were preachers (his father plucked chicken at a kosher market) and, according to Peter Guralnick's 1986 book, "Sweet Soul Music: Rhythm and Blues and the Southern Dream of Freedom," Mr. Burke delivered his first sermon at age 7 and by 9 was "widely known as the Wonder Boy Preacher."

Most of his first records, beginning in 1955 for Apollo, an independent label in New York, had clear gospel influences. But before long his songs began to incorporate secular thoughts.

"I love beautiful women, and I'm not going to tell anyone different," Mr. Burke said in an interview in 2002. "Sam Cooke was packing out churches at the same time as me, but when he was singing sacred songs, the young girls were thinking, 'Lord, Jesus, if I could just get with that Sam Cooke. Brother Sam, come over and pray for me one time!' All of that was in the room; it's what life is about."

HIS MAJESTY: In 1964, a radio D.J. proclaimed Mr. Burke the King of Rock and Soul. The title stuck.

Beginning in 1961 with "Just Out of Reach (of My Two Open Arms)," a country song he sang with Elvis Presley-like inflections, Mr. Burke had a string of R&B hits for Atlantic, though he never broke through to mainstream audiences, with Atlantic or any of the labels he recorded for into the 1970s; his highest position on the Billboard pop singles chart was No. 22.

His career revival began in the 1980s, helped by Hollywood. "Everybody Needs Somebody to Love" was featured in the film "The Blues Brothers" in 1980, and in 1987 "Cry to Me" had a prominent role in "Dirty Dancing."

Mr. Burke was inducted into the Rock and Roll Hall of Fame in Cleveland in 2001, and in 2002 he released "Don't Give Up on Me" (Fat Possum/Anti-), with songs by Brian Wilson, Tom Waits, Bob Dylan and others that had been written for Mr. Burke.

He never stopped touring or making records. His most recent album, "Nothing's Impossible" — his first and last collaboration with the celebrated producer Willie Mitchell, who died in January — was released on the E1 label in April. The day he died, he had flown to Amsterdam to perform a sold-out concert there with a Dutch band, De Dijk.

"He was on his way to spread his message of love," his Web site said, "as he loved to do."

— *By Ben Sisario*

BELVA PLAIN

Sagas of Jewish Life

OCT. 9, 1915 - OCT. 12, 2010

Belva Plain, who became a best-selling author at age 59 and whose multigenerational family sagas of Jewish American life won a loyal readership in the millions, died on Oct. 12 at her home in Short Hills, N.J. She was 95.

Ms. Plain's first novel, "Evergreen," published in 1978, spent 41 weeks on The New York Times best-seller list in hardcover and another 20 in paperback. It was made into a mini-series that NBC broadcast in 1985.

"Evergreen" follows Anna, a feisty, red-headed Jewish immigrant girl from Poland in turn-of-the-century New York; her family story continues through several decades and three more books.

Strong-willed women, many of them Jewish and red-haired as well, appear again and again in Ms. Plain's fiction. Some of her novels use historical settings — "Crescent City" was set in the Jewish community of Civil War-era New Orleans. Other books tell stories about contemporary issues, sometimes inspired by the headlines: divorce ("Promises"), adoption ("Blessings"), child sexual abuse ("The Carousel") or babies accidentally switched at birth ("Daybreak"). All of them are full of passion but very little explicit sex.

BEST SELLER: 30 million copies of Ms. Plain's books are in print.

Almost 30 million copies of her books are in print, and they have appeared translated into 22 languages. Twenty of the novels have appeared on The New York Times best-seller list.

The critics were often unimpressed by Ms. Plain's novels. In a review of "Harvest" in The Times in 1990, Webster Schott described Ms. Plain's works as "easy, consoling works of generous spirit, fat with plot and sentiment, thin in nearly every other way and almost invisible in character development."

Such opinions did not stop millions from enjoying her books; readers' comments on Amazon often speak of them as "big, cozy reads." That would have pleased Ms. Plain, who saw nothing wrong with being entertaining. "Even the real geniuses, like Dostoyevsky, entertained," she said.

Belva Plain's own story sounds like something out of a novel. When "Evergreen" became an overnight success, she was a grandmother approaching 60. But she was not a novice; Ms. Plain had been writing for much of her life.

Belva Offenberg was born in New York City on Oct. 9, 1915, a third-generation American of German Jewish descent; her father was a builder. She attended the Fieldston School and graduated from Barnard College in 1939 with a degree in history. She sold her first story to Cosmopolitan ("a very different magazine then," she told an interviewer) when she was 25 and contributed several dozen to women's magazines until she had three children in rapid succession. "I couldn't have done both," she explained.

She married Dr. Irving Plain, an ophthalmologist, in 1941; he died in 1982. Ms. Plain is survived by two daughters, a son, six grandchildren and three great-grandchildren.

Well groomed and conservatively dressed, she looked far younger than her age. "Ladylike" was an adjective often applied both to Ms. Plain and her books. ("Oh," she once responded to an interviewer who had used it, "I certainly hope you don't mean 'prissy.'")

For her own reading, Ms. Plain preferred the classics and spoke of rereading the novels of Anthony Trollope. Many modern novels, she thought, were "sleazy trash."

Ms. Plain's work routine involved making detailed outlines of her books and then writing them in longhand in spiral notebooks, rarely using a typewriter and never a computer. A disciplined worker, she wrote for several hours in the morning five days a week. She produced a 500- or 600-page novel every year or so.

Ms. Plain was fiercely private about her life, but she spoke about her novels, often to Jewish groups.

"I got sick of reading the same old story, told by Jewish writers, of the same old stereotypes — the possessive mothers, the worn-out fathers, all the rest of the neurotic rebellious unhappy self-hating tribe," she said. "I wanted to write a different novel about Jews — and a truer one."

— *By Elsa Dixler*

SOL STEINMETZ

'Lexical Supermaven'

JULY 29, 1930 - OCT. 13, 2010

SOL STEINMETZ, a lexicographer, author and tenured member of Olbom (**n.**, *abbrev.*, ‹ On Language's Board of Octogenarian Mentors), whose opinions on matters semantical, grammatical and etymological were widely sought by the news media, died on Oct. 13 in Manhattan. He was 80 and lived in New Rochelle, N.Y. The cause was pneumonia, his wife, Tzipora, said.

Writing in The New York Times in 2006, William Safire, who knew from language mavens, called Mr. Steinmetz a "lexical supermaven," an accolade that in two scant words draws exuberantly on Greek, Latin, Yiddish and Hebrew. ("Maven," Yiddish for cognoscente, derives from the Hebrew noun *mevin*, "one who knows.")

There are hundreds of thousands of words in English, and Mr. Steinmetz seemed to have his finger on each of them. Over the years, he edited a spate of dictionaries for various publishers; for about five years, until his retirement in the mid-1990s, he was the executive editor of the dictionary division of Random House. There, he edited the Random House Webster's College Dictionary (Random House, 1991), among others.

An ordained rabbi, Mr. Steinmetz was an authority on Yiddish, in all its kvetchy beauty. His books on the subject include "Yiddish and English: A Century of Yiddish in America" (1986) and "Meshuggenary: Celebrating the World of Yiddish" (2002; with Payson R. Stevens and Charles M. Levine).

Mr. Steinmetz was a keen etymologist. In interviews and his own writings, he expounded on the pedigrees of words like "klutz" (from Middle High German *klotz*, "block, log," via Yiddish) and "clone" (from the Greek *klon*, "twig"), which entered English as a noun in 1903.

He was also a master of the first citation, scouring centuries of literature and decades of the airwaves to determine precisely when a particular word or phrase made its debut. "Suit," in the sense of a bureaucrat, for instance, he traced to the television show "Cagney & Lacey" in 1982.

Every book in the Steinmetz home was rife with underlining, Ms. Steinmetz said.

To a broad public, Mr. Steinmetz was perhaps best known as a longtime member of

> A master of the first citation, he traced the word "suit," in the sense of a bureaucrat, to a 1982 episode of the television show "Cagney & Lacey."

Olbom (*first citation:* 1992, W. Safire, *N.Y. Times Mag.*), the band of advisers to Mr. Safire's On Language column in The Times Magazine. Mr. Safire, who wrote the column from 1979 until shortly before his death in 2009, quoted Mr. Steinmetz scores of times.

Sol Steinmetz was born in Budapest on July 29, 1930; his surname is the Yiddish word for stonemason. The family managed to leave Hungary before the outbreak of World War II, traveling first to the Dominican Republic and later to Venezuela.

At 16, the young Mr. Steinmetz settled in New York. He earned a bachelor's degree in English from Yeshiva University, from which he also took rabbinic ordination. Afterward, he studied linguistics at Columbia with the eminent Yiddishist Uriel Weinreich.

During this period Mr. Steinmetz, who had a fine tenor voice, supported himself by working as a cantor.

In 1955 Mr. Steinmetz married Tzipora Mandel — *tzipora* is Hebrew for sparrow, *mandel* Yiddish for almond — and later left graduate school for a job as a pulpit rabbi in Media, Pa.

Mr. Steinmetz began work as a lexicographer in the late 1950s, when he joined the staff of Merriam-Webster. He was later an editor at Clarence L. Barnhart, a dictionary publisher, before joining Random House.

Mr. Steinmetz's survivors include his wife, a brother, two sisters, and three sons. One of Mr. Steinmetz's 12 grandchildren, his grandson Amichai, disappeared in 2009 while trekking in the Himalayas. He has not been found, despite a continuing search. Mr. Steinmetz is also survived by two great-grandchildren.

His other books include "Semantic Antics: How and Why Words Change Meaning" (2008) and "There's a Word for It: The Explosion of the American Language Since 1900" (2010).

In newspaper obituaries, it was long customary to lavish praise on the subjects, noting laudable traits of character. In Mr. Steinmetz's case, one such trait is worthy of mention even today.

"He never had a bad word to say about anyone," said Jesse Sheidlower, the editor at large of the Oxford English Dictionary and a former protégé of Mr. Steinmetz's. "And he knew a lot of bad words."

— *By Margalit Fox*

BENOÎT MANDELBROT

Mother Nature's Mathematician

NOV. 20, 1924 - OCT. 14, 2010

Benoît B. Mandelbrot, a renowned mathematician and intellectual maverick who developed an innovative theory of roughness and applied it to physics, biology, finance and many other fields, died on Oct. 14 in Cambridge, Mass. He was 85. The cause was pancreatic cancer, his wife, Aliette, said.

Dr. Mandelbrot coined the term "fractal" to refer to a new class of mathematical shapes whose uneven contours could mimic the irregularities found in nature.

In a seminal book, "The Fractal Geometry of Nature," published in 1982, he defended mathematical objects that he said others had dismissed as "monstrous" and "pathological." Using fractal geometry, he argued, the complex outlines of clouds and coastlines, once considered unmeasurable, could now "be approached in rigorous and vigorous quantitative fashion."

David Mumford, a professor of mathematics at Brown University, said of Dr. Mandelbrot: "Applied mathematics had been concentrating for a century on phenomena which were smooth, but many things were not like that: the more you blew them up with a microscope the more complexity you found. He was one of the primary people who realized that these were legitimate objects of study."

For most of his career, Dr. Mandelbrot had a reputation as an outsider to the mathematical

APPRECIATION

'Why Is a Cloud the Way It Is?'

Here is a mathematician's nightmare I heard in the 1980s, when that irritating, unconforming, self-regarding provocateur Benoît Mandelbrot was suddenly famous — fractals, fractals everywhere. The mathematician dreamed that Mandelbrot had died, and God spoke: "You know, there really was something to that Mandelbrot."

Sure enough.

Dr. Mandelbrot created nothing less than a new geometry, to stand side by side with Euclid's — a geometry to mirror not the ideal forms of thought but the real complexity of nature. He was a mathematician who was never welcomed into the fraternity ("Fortress Mathematics," he said, where "the highest ambition is to wall off the windows and preserve only one door"), and he pretended that that was fine with him. When Yale first hired him to teach, it was in engineering and applied science; for most of his career he was supported at I.B.M.'s Westchester research lab. He called himself a "nomad by choice." He considered himself an experienced refugee: born to a Jewish family in Warsaw in 1924, he immigrated to Paris ahead of the Nazis, then fled farther and farther into the French countryside.

In various incarnations he taught physiology and economics. He was a nonphysicist who won the Wolf Prize in physics. The labels didn't matter. He turns out to have belonged to the select handful of 20th-century scientists who upended, as if by flipping a switch, the way we see the world we live in.

He was the one who let us appreciate chaos in all its glory, the noisy, the wayward and the freakish, from the very small to the very large. He gave the new field of study he invented a fittingly recondite name: "fractal geometry." But he wanted me to understand it as ordinary.

"The questions the field attacks are questions people ask themselves," he told me. "They are questions children ask: What shape is a mountain? Why is a cloud the way it is?" Only his answers were not ordinary.

Clouds are not spheres — the most famous sentence he ever wrote — mountains are not cones, coastlines are not circles and bark is not smooth, nor does lightning travel in a straight line.

If you closely examine the florets of a cauliflower (or the bronchioles of a lung; or the fractures in oil-bearing shale), zooming in with your magnifying glass or microscope, you see the same fundamental patterns, repeating. It is no accident. They are all fractal. Clouds, mountains, coastlines, bark and lightning are all jagged and discontinuous, but self-similar when viewed at different scales, thus concealing order within their irregularity. They are shapes that branch or fold in upon themselves recursively.

I was following him from place to place, reporting a book on chaos, while he evangelized his newly popular ideas to scientists of all sorts. Wisps of white hair atop his outsize brow, he lectured at Woods Hole to a crowd of oceanographers, who had heard that fractals were relevant to

(continued on page 110)

OCT

(continued from page 109)
cyclone tracks and eddy cascades.
Dr. Mandelbrot told them that he had seen the same channels, flows and back flows in dry statistics of rising and falling cotton prices. At Lamont-Doherty Geological Observatory, as it was then known, the geologists already spoke fractally about earthquakes.
Dr. Mandelbrot laid out a mathematical framework for such phenomena: they exist in fractional dimensions, lying in between the familiar one-dimensional lines, two-dimensional planes and three-dimensional spaces. He revived some old and freakish ideas — "monsters," as he said, "mathematical pathologies" that had been relegated to the fringes of the discipline.

"I started looking in the trash cans of science for such phenomena," he said, and he meant this literally: one scrap he grabbed from a Paris mathematician's wastebasket inspired an important 1965 paper combining two more fields to which he did not belong, "Information Theory and Psycholinguistics." Information theory connected to fractals when he focused on the problem of noise — static, errors — in phone lines. It was always there; on average it seemed manageable, but analysis revealed that normal bell-curve averages didn't apply. There were too many surprises — outliers. Clusters and quirks always defied expectations.

It's the same with brainwaves, fluid turbulence, seismic tremors and — oh, yes — finance.

From his first paper studying fluctuations in the rise and fall of cotton prices in 1962 until the end of his life, he maintained a simple and constant message about extraordinary economic events. The professionals plan for "mild randomness" and misunderstand "wild randomness." They learn from the averages and overlook the outliers. Thus they consistently, predictably, underestimate catastrophic risk. "The financiers and investors of the world are, at the moment, like mariners who heed no weather warnings," he wrote near the peak of the bubble, in 2004, in "The (Mis)behavior of Markets."

Fractals have made their way into the economics mainstream, as into so many fields, though Dr. Mandelbrot was not really an economist; nor a physiologist, physicist, engineer. ...

"Very often when I listen to the list of my previous jobs, I wonder if I exist," he said once. "The intersection of such sets is surely empty."

— BY JAMES GLEICK

establishment. From his perch as a researcher for I.B.M. in New York, where he worked for decades before accepting a position at Yale University, he noticed patterns that other researchers may have overlooked in their own data, then often swooped in to collaborate.

"He knew everybody, with interests going off in every possible direction," Professor Mumford said. "Every time he gave a talk, it was about something different."

Dr. Mandelbrot traced his work on fractals to a question he first encountered as a young researcher: how long is the coast of Britain? The answer, he was surprised to discover, depends on how closely one looks. On a map, an island may appear smooth, but zooming in will reveal jagged edges that add up to a longer coast. Zooming in further will reveal even more coastline.

"Here is a question, a staple of grade-school geometry that, if you think about it, is impossible," Dr. Mandelbrot told The New York Times in an interview this year. "The length of the coastline, in a sense, is infinite."

In the 1950s, Dr. Mandelbrot proposed a simple but radical way to quantify the crookedness of such an object by assigning it a "fractal dimension," an insight that has proved useful well beyond the field of cartography.

Over nearly seven decades, working with dozens of scientists, Dr. Mandelbrot contributed to the fields of geology, medicine, cosmology and engineering. He used the geometry of fractals to explain how galaxies cluster, how wheat prices change over time and how mammalian brains fold as they grow, among other phenomena.

His influence has also been felt within the field of geometry, where he was one of the first to use computer graphics to study mathematical objects like the Mandelbrot set, which was named in his honor.

"I decided to go into fields where mathematicians would never go because the problems were badly stated," Dr. Mandelbrot said. "I have played a strange role that none of my students dare to take."

Benoît B. Mandelbrot (he added the middle initial himself, though it does not stand for a middle name) was born on Nov. 20, 1924, to a Lithuanian Jewish family in Warsaw. In 1936 his family fled the Nazis, first to Paris and then to the south of France, where he tended horses and fixed tools.

After the war he enrolled in the École Polytechnique in Paris, where his sharp eye compensated for a lack of conventional education. His career soon spanned the Atlantic. He earned a master's degree in aeronautics at the California Institute of Technology, returned to Paris for his doctorate in mathematics in 1952, then went on to the Institute for Advanced Study in Princeton, N.J., where he did research.

After several years spent largely at the Centre National de la Recherche Scientifique in Paris, Dr. Mandelbrot was hired by I.B.M. in 1958 to work at the Thomas J. Watson Research Center in Yorktown Heights, N.Y. Although he worked frequently with academic researchers and served as a visiting professor at Harvard and the Massachusetts Institute of Technology, it was not until 1987 that he began to teach at Yale, where he earned tenure in 1999.

Dr. Mandelbrot received more than 15 honorary doctorates and served on the board of many scientific journals, as well as the Mandelbrot Foundation for Fractals. Instead of rigorously proving his insights in each field, he said he preferred to "stimulate the field by making bold and crazy conjectures" — and then move on before his claims had been verified. This habit earned him some skepticism in mathematical circles.

How long is the coast of Britain? "Here is a question, a staple of grade-school geometry that, if you think about it, is impossible. The length of the coastline, in a sense, is infinite."

"He doesn't spend months or years proving what he has observed," said Heinz-Otto Peitgen, a professor of mathematics and biomedical sciences at the University of Bremen. And for that, he said, Dr. Mandelbrot "has received quite a bit of criticism."

"But if we talk about impact inside mathematics, and applications in the sciences," Professor Peitgen said, "he is one of the most important figures of the last 50 years."

Besides his wife, Dr. Mandelbrot, who lived in Cambridge, is survived by two sons and three grandchildren.

When asked to look back on his career, Dr. Mandelbrot compared his own trajectory to the rough outlines of clouds and coastlines that drew him into the study of fractals in the 1950s.

"If you take the beginning and the end, I have had a conventional career," he said, referring to his prestigious appointments in Paris and at Yale. "But it was not a straight line between the beginning and the end. It was a very crooked line."

— *By Jascha Hoffman*

LOUIS HENKIN

Founding Father of Human Rights Law

NOV. 11, 1917 - OCT. 14, 2010

LOUIS HENKIN, a legal scholar credited with creating the field of human rights law and the author of classic works on constitutional law and the legal aspects of foreign policy, died on Oct. 14 at his home in Manhattan. He was 92.

Professor Henkin, who was unusual in combining equal expertise in constitutional law and international law, moved easily between academia and government. His legal scholarship was a fundamental resource for other scholars involved in human rights and international law, and his books addressed to a broader audience — notably "Foreign Affairs and the Constitution," "The Rights of Man Today," "How Nations Behave" and "The Age of Rights" — became required reading for government officials and diplomats.

Through his teaching at Columbia University, where he founded the Center for the Study of Human Rights in 1978 and the Human Rights Institute in 1998, and through seminars run by the Aspen Institute's Justice and Society Program, he trained hundreds of legal specialists and advocates in the field of human rights law.

"It is no exaggeration to say that no American was more instrumental in the development of human rights law than Lou," said Elisa Massimino, the president and chief executive of Human Rights First, an organization Professor Henkin helped found in 1978 under the name Lawyers' Committee for Human Rights. "He literally and figuratively wrote the book on human rights."

Eliezer Henkin was born on Nov. 11, 1917, in present-day Belarus, where his father was a rabbi and Talmudic scholar. In 1923 the family immigrated to the Lower East Side of Manhattan, where Lazar, as his family called him, acquired the nickname Louie. By the time he began studying mathematics at Yeshiva College, where he earned a bachelor's degree in 1937, he had adopted the first name Louis.

On a whim, he applied to Harvard Law School and, after passing the admittance tests, borrowed tuition money from his sister and enrolled. He received his law degree in 1940.

After working as a clerk for Judge Learned Hand at the United States Court of Appeals for the Second Circuit, in Manhattan, he served in the Army during World War II, seeing action in Sicily, Italy, France and Germany.

In 1944, near Toulon, France, he was part of an artillery observation unit that encountered three German officers. Relying on his Yiddish, he convinced the Germans to surrender a force of 78 men to his 13-man unit, a feat for which he was awarded the Silver Star.

On leaving the military, he served as a law clerk for Justice Felix Frankfurter of the United States Supreme Court.

Mr. Henkin, an ardent New Dealer, worked for the State Department's United Nations

"It is no exaggeration to say that no American was more instrumental in the development of human rights law than Lou. He literally and figuratively wrote the book on human rights."

bureau and its Office of European Regional Affairs from 1948 to 1956. He played a main role in negotiating the United Nation's 1951 Refugee Convention, which set forth the standards defining refugees, their rights and the legal obligations of nations toward them.

In 1956 he was invited by Columbia University to spend a year studying the legal issues involved in the control and verification of nuclear weapons, the subject of his first book, "Arms Control and Inspection in American Law" (1958).

Several works on law, foreign policy and diplomacy followed, including "The Berlin Crisis and the United Nations" (1959) and "Disarmament: The Lawyer's Interests" (1964).

After teaching law at the University of Pennsylvania for five years beginning in 1958, he returned to Columbia, where he taught at the law school into his 80s.

His highly influential book "Foreign Affairs and the Constitution" (1972) explored the Constitution's division of power between the president and Congress on matters pertaining to foreign affairs, a quest that took on particular urgency against the backdrop of the Vietnam War.

How did it come about, Professor Henkin asked, that the president gained the initiative in waging war, when, taken as a whole, the Constitution favors Congressional over presidential power?

"Every grant to the president, including those relating to foreign affairs, was in effect a derogation from Congressional power, eked out slowly, reluctantly, and not without limitations and safeguards," Professor Henkin wrote, in a typically lucid and graceful passage.

Over time, however, circumstances trumped principles, he wrote. "The structure of the federal government, the facts of national life, the realities and exigencies of international relations, the practices of diplomacy, have afforded presidents unique temptations and unique opportunities to acquire unique powers," he concluded.

He returned to the subject in 1990 with "Constitutionalism, Democracy and Foreign Affairs," a much more impassioned book, which warned of the dangers of an imperial presidency and insisted on the importance of human rights as a cornerstone of American foreign policy.

Professor Henkin waged a multifront struggle to extend universalist ideas of human rights and the reach of the law. "He pushed back forcefully against the Roman observation that in war — and perhaps in foreign relations generally — the law is silent," Sarah H. Cleveland, a law professor at Columbia, said in an interview with the Columbia Human Rights Law Review in 2007.

In his books, Professor Henkin took on such issues as compliance with international law ("How Nations Behave," 1968) and the underlying principles of human rights ("The Rights of Man Today," 1978).

At the Aspen Institute's Justice and Society Program, which was directed for many years by his wife, Alice Hartman Henkin, a human rights lawyer, he taught international law to more than 300 judges, including four future Supreme Court justices, Ruth Bader Ginsburg, Anthony M. Kennedy, Stephen G. Breyer and Sonia Sotomayor.

Professor Henkin's close ties to the United States government allowed him to serve as a go-between for human rights organizations and Congressional committees drafting rights legislation. He also filed numerous amicus briefs in Supreme Court cases including, most recently, Hamdan v. Rumsfeld, a 2006 case in which the court rejected the Bush administration's plan to try Guantánamo Bay detainees before military commissions.

Professor Henkin is survived by his wife, their three sons and five grandchildren.

Professor Henkin took a lofty view of his own government's international responsibilities. He often felt let down.

"In the cathedral of human rights," he wrote in a well-known passage in a 1979 article, "the United States is more like a flying buttress than a pillar — choosing to stand outside the international structure supporting the international human rights system, but without being willing to subject its own conduct to the scrutiny of that system."

— *By William Grimes*

BARBARA BILLINGSLEY

The Model Mom, Circa 1959

DEC. 22, 1915 - OCT. 16, 2010

BARBARA BILLINGSLEY, who as June Cleaver on the television series "Leave It to Beaver" personified a Hollywood postwar family ideal of the ever-sweet, ever-helpful suburban stay-at-home mom, died on Oct. 16 at her home in Santa Monica, Calif. She was 94.

From 1957 to 1963 and in decades of reruns, the glamorous June, who wore pearls and high heels at home, could be counted on to help her husband, Ward (Hugh Beaumont), get their son Theodore, better known as Beaver (Jerry Mathers), and his older brother, Wally (Tony Dow), out of countless small jams, whether an alligator in the basement or a horse in the garage.

Baking a steady supply of cookies, she would use motherly intuition to sound the alarm about incipient trouble ("Ward, I'm worried about the Beaver") in their immaculate, airy house in the fictional town of Mayfield. (The house appeared to have no master bedroom, just a big door from which Ward and June occasionally emerged, tying their bathrobes.)

Along with the mothers played by Harriet Nelson ("The Adventures of Ozzie and Harriet"), Donna Reed ("The Donna Reed Show") and others, Ms. Billingsley's role became a cultural standard, one that may have been too good to be true but that produced fan mail and nostalgia for decades afterward, from the same generation whose counterculture derided the see-no-evil suburbia June's character represented.

Yes, she acknowledged 40 years later, her role was a picture-perfect reflection of the times. "We were the ideal parents because that's the way he saw it," she said, describing the show as the world seen through the eyes of a child. (The pearls, incidentally, covered up a hollow in her neck. In the beginning of the show, she wore flats; the heels were an attempt to stay taller than the growing boys.)

Ms. Billingsley, a former model and career actress who was married three times and spent part of her career as a working single mother (of two boys, at that), had nothing but respect for June Cleaver. Women who stay at home to care for their children may find in it the best and most important job they'll ever have, she said in an interview for the Archive of American Television in 2000.

"She was a loving, happy, stay-at-home mom," she said of June Cleaver, "which I think is great."

Ms. Billingsley was born Barbara Lillian Combes on Dec. 22, 1915, in Los Angeles, where she attended George Washington High School. She had an early taste of acting when she left Los Angeles Junior College to appear in a short-lived Broadway play, "Straw Hat," taking her stage name from her first husband, Glenn Billingsley, a nephew of Sherman Billingsley, the proprietor of the Stork Club in Manhattan. They had two sons.

After working as a fashion model, Ms. Billingsley returned to Los Angeles, acted in local plays and was signed to a contract by MGM. Her roles were mostly small, in movies like "The Bad and the Beautiful" (1952) with Kirk Douglas, "Shadow on the Wall" (1950) with Ann Sothern and "Three Guys Named Mike" (1951) with Jane Wyman.

Television rescued her from obscurity. Of "Leave It to Beaver," she recalled, "It was a happy experience for me, and very timely." There was never a fight on the set in seven years, she said. After the show ended its run in 1963,

Ms. Billingsley, by then typecast, saw few acting roles.

Her show business career was revived, however, in 1980 by the movie comedy "Airplane!" in which she played a sweet passenger who communicates in "jive" with two streetwise black passengers — an ironic comment on her previous incarnation as America's white-bread mom. After that there were guest appearances on "Mork & Mindy," "The Love Boat," "Murphy Brown" and other shows. From 1984 to 1991 Ms. Billingsley was the voice of the nanny in the animated series "Jim Henson's Muppet Babies."

COOKIES AND PEARLS: Ms. Billingsley played June Cleaver on "Leave It to Beaver" for seven years.

In 1983 she reprised her role as June in a television movie, "Still the Beaver," which reunited her with many members of the original "Leave It to Beaver" cast (but not Hugh Beaumont, who died in 1982). That led to a cable series known first by that name and then as "The New Leave It to Beaver." She also had a small part in an updated 1997 feature-film version of the show.

After her divorce from Glenn Billingsley in 1947, Ms. Billingsley married Roy Kellino. After Mr. Kellino's death in 1956, she married Dr. William Mortenson, a general practitioner. They remained married until Dr. Mortenson died in 1981. She is survived by her two sons.

Many of Ms. Billingsley's later guest appearances were either as June Cleaver or in roles that made wry references to her. But when she was offered scripts that made fun of June, she said, she turned them down.

"She's been too good to me to play anything like that," she said.

— By Michael Pollak

Consuelo Crespi

High-Born and Always Fashionable

MAY 31, 1928 - OCT. 18, 2010

Consuelo Crespi, a New York girl turned Italian countess who helped shape postwar high fashion by modeling, editing Italian Vogue and, perhaps most important, wearing the chic new thing to exactly the right places, died on Oct. 18 in Manhattan. She was 82.

Her death, at Mount Sinai Hospital, following a stroke, came a half-century after she appeared in Life magazine under the headline "High-Born Beauties of Europe as Elegant Sweater Girls," and almost that long since she was a guest at Truman Capote's Black and White Ball in 1966.

"The last of the parties where people weren't

ashamed to be glamorous," she said of the legendary party at the Plaza Hotel.

Countess Crespi moved effortlessly between the artistically effervescent scene in post-Fascist Italy and a New York where fascinated newspapers covered her walks with her dogs, Fu Manchu and Snoopy. A friend of stars like Audrey Hepburn, she was regarded as a social arbiter in both nations at a time when high society had a definite meaning.

The countess's journalism, public relations work and sartorial example helped launch the careers of designers like Valentino, Missoni and Fendi. A regular on best-dressed lists, the countess was inducted into the Fashion Hall of Fame for "faultless taste in dress without ostentation or extravagance."

In the 1970s, Italy presented Countess Crespi with its highest civilian award, for her role in helping the country become a fashion powerhouse.

FASHION INSIDER: Countess Crespi influenced trends as well as designers.

A step toward this recognition had come in 1961, when she arrived in New York from Rome wearing skirts four or five inches longer than what was fashionable. Her look was a bombshell in the circles that cared.

In 1981, when wealthy French women lined up to cancel orders for evening gowns after the election of the Socialist François Mitterrand, Countess Crespi declared that Italian women would never do anything that silly. "They'd rather go down in their taffetas," she told The New York Times.

If Countess Crespi was the ultimate fashion insider, her motives were not entirely altruistic. She did public relations for top designers, even as she edited Vogue's Italian edition. So did her husband, Count Rodolfo Crespi, a top executive at Vogue who was in charge of editions in Mexico and Brazil. Those lengthened hemlines she brought to New York in 1961, for example, were new Fabiani creations that would soon be available in Paris stores.

"I now can't stand the sight of my knees showing," Countess Crespi told The Times.

Her position at the center of the fashion world was underlined by a story told in 2007 by Giancarlo Giammetti, Valentino's longtime business partner. Mr. Giammetti said that in 1973, he and Valentino were thrilled to get an order from Bloomingdale's — until the countess showed up in what Women's Wear Daily described as "a tizzy." She reported that the Valentino coats were being sold in the basement. Mr. Giammetti asked what the basement was. "It's where they sell home detergents," Countess Crespi said in horror.

Consuelo Pauline O'Brien O'Connor was born in Larchmont, N.Y., on May 31, 1928, along with her twin sister, Gloria, who would later marry Frank Schiff, an insurance executive, and take his name.

Mrs. Schiff, whose wearing of a Valentino dress inspired Jacqueline Kennedy to order some for herself, was an editor for Vogue in New York.

After their parents separated, the girls and their mother moved to Nova Scotia. They returned to Manhattan in 1943, and the sisters were spotted as potential models by a French photographer. They appeared on the cover of Look magazine in 1945.

Consuelo was a debutante in 1947, the same year she appeared in a small role in the short-lived Broadway play "Miracle in the

Mountains." She met Count Crespi on a blind date at the Colony restaurant, a beehive of socialites and celebrities. They married three months later, in January 1948.

Count Crespi died in 1985. She is survived by her sister, a daughter, a son, four grandchildren and two great-grandchildren.

Countess Crespi always symbolized a sort of impossible, aristocratic beauty. In 1968, the Broadway producer Hal Prince and his wife had their picture taken for The Times lounging on an elegant sofa. Mr. Prince complained that they resembled Countess and Count Crespi.

"Don't worry, darling," Judy Prince said. "Have you seen them lately? We'll never make it."

Joseph Heller in his novel "Something Happened" (1974), saw larger meaning. Of his character Andy Kagle, he wrote:

"He really thinks that what he does is more important than what he is, but I know he's wrong and that the beautiful Countess Consuelo Crespi (if there is such a thing) will always matter more than Albert Einstein, Madame Curie, Thomas Alva Edison, Andy Kagle and me."

— *By Douglas Martin*

TOM BOSLEY

The Picture of a Father

OCT. 1, 1927 - OCT. 19, 2010

Tom Bosley, a warm-voiced, round-bodied actor who personified paternal authority, especially on Broadway as a big-city mayor in the musical "Fiorello!" and on television as a Middle American dad in the hit comedy "Happy Days," died on Oct. 19 in Rancho Mirage, Calif. He was 83.

The cause was cancer, according to a statement by CBS Films, whose president, Amy Baer, is Mr. Bosley's daughter.

Mr. Bosley is probably best known as Howard Cunningham, the gruff but reliably kind father of teenage children in 1950s Milwaukee in the nostalgic situation comedy "Happy Days," a character he played for a decade beginning in 1974. He was also the title character in the crime series "The Father Dowling Mysteries" and Sheriff Amos Tupper, an ally of the sleuth and mystery writer Jessica Fletcher (Angela Lansbury) in "Murder, She Wrote."

But before he was a television fixture, Mr. Bosley had gained fame on stage, playing Fiorello LaGuardia, the populist mayor of New York, in "Fiorello!" The show, which ran from 1959 to 1961, won the Pulitzer Prize, and Mr. Bosley, a newcomer to Broadway, won a Tony Award for best featured actor in a musical. He never missed one of the show's almost 800 performances.

In his review of the show in The New York Times, Brooks Atkinson summarized the appeal that Mr. Bosley would have for decades to come. Mayor LaGuardia, Atkinson wrote, "is extremely well-played by Tom Bosley, who is short and a trifle portly, has a kindly face, abundant energy and an explosive personality."

Thomas Edward Bosley was born in Chicago on Oct. 1, 1927. His father, Benjamin, worked in real estate; his mother, Dora, was a concert pianist before giving up her musical career to raise two sons. The family suffered through the Depression, and after high school, near the end of World War II, young Tom joined the Navy.

He set his sights on acting after his discharge.

But before leaving Chicago in 1950, he flipped a coin to decide whether to move to New York or Los Angeles. The coin came up in favor of Los Angeles. Still, he demurred.

"I looked in the mirror and said, 'I think I better go to New York and work in the theater,'" he recalled in an interview for the Archive of American Television in 2000. "Because I was short, kind of heavy, and that is not the way to break into the film industry."

MAYOR OF BROADWAY: Mr. Bosley in the title role of the Pulitzer Prize-winning musical "Fiorello!"

In the 1950s, Mr. Bosley studied briefly (and unhappily) with Lee Strasberg and worked in small theaters and in television dramas, notably "Hallmark Hall of Fame" productions like "Born Yesterday" and "Alice in Wonderland." To pay the rent, he was a hat checker at Lindy's and a doorman at Tavern on the Green.

Work came more easily after "Fiorello!" He appeared in several more Broadway shows in the 1960s, though none were especially successful. After a long hiatus, he returned to Broadway in 1994 as Belle's father in the original cast of the Disney musical "Beauty and the Beast."

Mr. Bosley's fatherly appeal was suited to both comedy and drama, and his long résumé as a character actor in the movies stretched across generations of stars, beginning with "Love With the Proper Stranger" (1963) with Natalie Wood and Steve McQueen and "The World of Henry Orient" (1964) with Peter Sellers and continuing into 2010, when he appeared in the romantic comedy "The Back-up Plan" with Jennifer Lopez.

He also made appearances in myriad television series, including "Ben Casey," "Dr. Kildare," "Get Smart," "Mission: Impossible," "The Mod Squad," "Bonanza" and "Bewitched."

In "Happy Days," which was initially set during the mid-1950s but moved into the '60s in its 11-season run, Mr. Bosley played a grumbly sweetheart of a husband to his wife, Marion (Marion Ross), and an unconvincingly stern but wise and understanding father to his children, Richie (Ron Howard) and Joanie (Erin Moran).

Howard Cunningham owned a hardware store, was often seen reading the newspaper in his easy chair and was perpetually befuddled by the behavior of young people. With its mix of cornball humor and family values, the series became a situation comedy landmark, spawning spinoffs and making celebrities of the cast, especially Henry Winkler, who played Richie's charismatic, sweetly renegade friend Arthur Fonzarelli, a k a the Fonz, who referred saucily to Mr. Bosley's character as Mr. C.

In 2004, Mr. Bosley was listed at No. 9 on TV Guide's list of the greatest TV dads of all time.

Mr. Bosley's first marriage, to Jean Eliot, ended with her death in 1978. In addition to his daughter, he is survived by his wife, the former Patricia Carr, whom he married in 1980, a brother, two stepdaughters and seven grandchildren.

In the interview with the television archive, Mr. Bosley said he had suffered stage fright only once. It was very early in his career, before he moved to New York, and he had a small role in a play outside of Chicago that starred Shelley Berman and Geraldine Page. At the first performance, he was obsessively going over his lines backstage and lost track of the progress of the play. He made his entrance several minutes early.

"And Shelley Berman is on one side of the stage, and Geraldine Page is on the other side," he said. "And she turns and looks at me and says, 'Do you mind? We're doing a play here.'"

— *By Bruce Weber*

BOB GUCCIONE

The Sultan of Sex

DEC. 17, 1930 - OCT. 20, 2010

BOB GUCCIONE, who founded Penthouse magazine in the 1960s and built a pornographic media empire that broke taboos, outraged the guardians of taste and made billions before drowning in a slough of bad investments and Internet competition, died on Oct. 20 in Plano, Tex. He was 79.

He had had cancer for some time and at his death was being treated at Plano Specialty Hospital, his family said in a statement.

Mr. Guccione's empire began in London in 1965 with a bank loan, an idea and an accident. The loan was for $1,170. The idea was a new magazine with nude photos to outdo Hugh Hefner's Playboy. And the accident was an old mailing list, so that promotional brochures with pornographic samples went out to clergymen, schoolgirls, old-age pensioners and wives of members of Parliament.

The outcry was huge. And there was a $264 fine for mailing indecent materials. But all 120,000 copies of the first issue of Penthouse sold out in days, and Mr. Guccione, a struggling artist from New Jersey who had been knocking around Europe for more than a decade, was on his way to being a tycoon.

By the early 1980s he was one of America's richest men, king of a $300 million publishing empire, General Media. With a monthly circulation of 4.7 million in 16 countries, the flagship was Penthouse, but there were 15 other magazines — including Omni and Penthouse Forum as well as titles on bodybuilding, photography and computers — in addition to book, video and merchandising divisions.

Forbes listed Mr. Guccione's net worth in 1982 as $400 million. His art collections, worth $150 million, included works by Degas, Renoir, Picasso, Matisse and Chagall. Troves of art and antiques filled his Manhattan home, a 17,000-square-foot double town house on East 67th Street, and his country estate in Staatsburg, N.Y.

Mr. Guccione looked the part of the libidinous pornographer. He was tanned and muscled, and he wore slim pants and silk shirts open to the waist, showing gold chains on a hairy chest. His personality was volatile, but he did not drink, smoke or use drugs.

"He was a mass of contradictions, engendering fierce loyalty and equally fierce contempt," Patricia Bosworth, who had been executive editor of Mr. Guccione's Viva magazine in the 1970s, wrote in Vanity Fair in 2005. "He hired and fired people, then rehired them. He could be warm and funny one minute and cold and detached the next."

Robert Charles Joseph Edward Sabatini Guccione was born in Brooklyn on Dec. 17, 1930, the son of Anthony and Nina Guccione. He was raised Roman Catholic in Bergenfield, N.J., where he considered the priesthood, he said, but decided to be an artist. In 1948 he graduated from Blair Academy, in Blairstown, N.J. At 18 he married the first of his three wives, Lilyann Becker, and had a daughter. The marriage soon failed.

Over the next 12 years he traveled in Europe and North Africa, sketching tourists in cafés and working odd jobs. In Tangier he met Muriel Hudson, an English singer. They traveled together for several years, were married in 1955 and had four children.

In 1960 they settled in London, where he ran a dry-cleaning business, drew cartoons for a syndicate and edited a small newspaper. A mail-order business, selling back issues of men's magazines, put him deep in debt, and his wife left him, taking the children. But Penthouse transformed his life.

With Kathy Keeton, a dancer from South Africa who was his girlfriend, his business partner and later his wife, Mr. Guccione challenged Playboy at the height of the sexual revolution, introducing Penthouse in the United States in 1969 and building it into one of the nation's most successful magazines, a mix of "sex, politics and protest," as it was billed, that took in an estimated $3.5 billion to $4 billion over 30 years.

Its images of women, often shot by Mr. Guccione, left little to the imagination. Compared with Playboy Playmates, as the Hefner centerfold models were known, Penthouse Pets were arrayed in more provocative poses. The magazine infuriated feminists and conservatives; others praised it for breaking taboos.

PLAYBOY RIVAL: Mr. Guccione built his $300 million pornography empire on a $1,170 loan.

Penthouse occasionally ran nude layouts of well-known women, including Madonna. In 1984, sexually explicit photos of Vanessa Williams, taken two years before she became the first black Miss America, appeared in Penthouse. Ms. Williams lost her crown and sued for $500 million, but the suit was dropped and Penthouse reported a $14 million newsstand windfall.

Aside from the battle of the centerfolds, Penthouse offered an aura of class: fiction, celebrity profiles and political articles. It published Alan Dershowitz, Stephen King, Philip Roth, Joyce Carol Oates and J. P. Donleavy as well as interviews with Germaine Greer, Gore Vidal and Isaac Asimov.

Other Guccione magazines made splashes: Viva, featuring male nudes for female browsers, folded in 1978 after five years; Omni, a science and science fiction offering, began in 1978 and ended in 1995. Mr. Guccione employed his children and father in his enterprises.

The dissolution of the Guccione empire took years. A $200 million Penthouse casino in Atlantic City never materialized, and he lost much of his investment. A $17.5 million movie, "Caligula," presenting hard-core sex scenes and graphic violence, was shunned by distributors, and Mr. Guccione lost heavily. He once hired 82 scientists to develop a small nuclear reactor as a low-cost energy source, but it came to nothing and cost $17 million.

The government took chunks of his fortune. In 1985, the Internal Revenue Service demanded $45 million in back taxes. In 1992, he had to borrow $80 million for another tax bill. In 1986, after a scathing federal antipornography report, Penthouse was withdrawn from many newsstands and circulation revenues, a major source of income, fell sharply.

The trend accelerated in the 1990s as Internet pornography grew increasingly available. Mr. Guccione responded with more explicit sexual content that drove advertisers and vendors away, limiting many sales to pornographic bookstores. Ms. Keeton, the president and chief operating officer, died in 1997 at age 58, and friends said her loss had profound effects on Mr. Guccione's business and personal life.

Mr. Guccione, who developed throat cancer in 1998, sold artworks, media properties and his Staatsburg estate as revenues dwindled and debts soared. Penthouse posted a $10 million loss in 2001, General Media filed for bankruptcy in 2003, and he resigned as chairman and chief executive of Penthouse International. Creditors foreclosed on the Guccione mansion, and he moved out in 2006.

Dozens of items from the town house — fireplace mantels, marble columns, even a circular staircase — were auctioned off by a Connecticut gallery in 2009 for a fraction of their presale estimates, with the proceeds going to a charity.

"Kind of gaudy," said Dave Kerr, a prospective buyer looking skeptically over the lot. "It wouldn't work in our house. I guess he lived a different lifestyle."

— *By Robert D. McFadden*

HARVEY PHILLIPS

Mr. Tuba

DEC. 2, 1929 - OCT. 20, 2010

THE TUBA PLAYERS mass by the hundreds every year on the Rockefeller Center ice-skating rink to play carols and other festive fare, a holiday ritual now ingrained in the consciousness of New York.

The tradition began in 1974, the brainchild of Harvey Phillips, a musician called the Heifetz of the tuba. In his time he was the instrument's chief evangelist, the inspirer of a vast solo repertory, a mentor to generations of players and, more simply, Mr. Tuba.

Most tuba players agree that if their unwieldy instrument has shed any of the bad associations that have clung to it — orchestral clown, herald of grim news, poorly respected backbencher best when not noticed, good for little more than the "oom" in the oom-pah-pah — it is largely thanks to Mr. Phillips. He waged a lifelong campaign to improve the tuba's image.

Mr. Phillips died on Oct. 20 at his home, Tubaranch, in Bloomington, Ind. He was 80 and had Parkinson's disease.

Like many towering exponents of a musical instrument, Mr. Phillips left a legacy of new works, students and students of students. But even more, he bequeathed an entire culture of tuba-ism: an industry of TubaChristmases (252 cities in 2009) and tuba minifestivals, mainly at universities, called Octubafests.

"The man was huge in putting the instrument on the map as a solo instrument," said Alan Baer, the New York Philharmonic's tuba player, two of whose teachers were Phillips students. "Our repertory is so limited, and it would be horrible if he had not done the amount of work that he did."

Mr. Phillips's wife, Carol Phillips, said her husband had either commissioned or inspired more than 200 solo and chamber music pieces, many wheedled out of composers, including Vincent Persichetti, by persistence or other methods. "I remember Persichetti was a case of Beefeater gin," she said.

Mr. Phillips once said, "I'm determined that no great composer is ever again going to live out his life without composing a major work for tuba."

Harvey Phillips was born on Dec. 2, 1929, the last of 10 children in a farming family in Aurora, Mo. The family moved often, and he attended high school in Marionville, Mo.

After graduating, Mr. Phillips took a summer job playing tuba with the King Bros. Circus. He left to attend the University of Missouri but was shortly lured away by another circus offer: playing tuba with the Ringling Brothers and Barnum & Bailey Circus. It was the pinnacle of circus bands.

One of the band's duties was to give "alarms": play pieces to alert circus staff in the case of an accident. "Twelfth Street Rag" was the alarm for a high-wire accident, and a signal to send in the clowns to distract the audience, Mr. Phillips said in a New Yorker profile in 1976. He spent three years with the Ringling band.

On a circus trip to New York, where he played duets with the clanging pipes in his hotel room, Mr. Phillips met William Bell, the tuba player of the New York Philharmonic. Mr. Bell soon arranged for him to study at the Juilliard School and become his pupil.

Mr. Phillips spent two years in the United States Army Field Band in Washington but returned to New York, drawn by the many opportunities. He became a successful freelancer, playing regularly with the New York City Opera and New York City Ballet orchestras, recording and making broadcasts.

In 1954 he helped found the New York Brass Quintet. The combination (two trumpets, French horn, trombone and tuba) was less common at the time than it later became. Brass quintets proliferated, a boon for tuba players, because brass players on university faculties needed a tubist colleague to form a group. More tuba professors meant more tuba students.

Mr. Phillips also played jazz, performing in clubs and recital halls. As his reputation grew, composers began writing for him, and Mr. Phillips introduced another rarity, the tuba recital. In 1975 he played five recitals at Carnegie Recital Hall in nine days.

Writing in The New York Times in 1980, the music critic Peter G. Davis said first-time listeners to Mr. Phillips "could scarcely fail to be impressed, and probably not a little astonished, by the instrument's versatility and tonal variety, its ability to spin a soft and sweetly lyrical melodic line, to dance lightly and agilely over its entire bass range, and to bellow forth with dramatic power when the occasion demands."

HEIFETZ OF THE TUBA: Mr. Phillips championed his unwieldy instrument.

Mr. Phillips's entrepreneurial abilities emerged in his New York years, too. He served as the orchestra contractor for Leopold Stokowski, Igor Stravinsky and Gunther Schuller, among others. When Mr. Schuller took charge of the New England Conservatory of Music in Boston, he recruited Mr. Phillips as vice president for financial affairs. Mr. Phillips held the position from 1967 to 1971, commuting to New York for evening performances.

The punishing routine took away from practice and family time. Coming home late one night and missing his family, he took out his tuba while his wife and two of his children slept in the bed nearby and practiced until dawn, playing so softly that they did not wake up, according to the New Yorker profile.

He often practiced in the backseat of his car while his wife drove and their children kept eyes on the road to warn of approaching potholes. "They would yell, 'Daddy, bump!' " Mrs. Phillips said.

In addition to his wife, Mr. Phillips is survived by their three sons.

In 1971 Mr. Phillips joined the faculty of Indiana University. He retired in 1994.

In his tireless efforts to raise the tuba's profile as well as to honor Mr. Bell, his teacher, Mr. Phillips — perhaps touched by the showmanship of his circus past — decided to gather tuba players for a special holiday concert in Rockefeller Center. (Mr. Bell was born on Christmas Day, 1902.)

He called an official there with the suggestion. "The phone went silent," he later recounted. "So I gave the man some unlisted telephone numbers of friends of mine." They included Mr. Stokowski, Leonard Bernstein, André Kostelanetz and Morton Gould. "He called me back in about an hour and said, 'I've spoken with your friends, and you can have anything you want.'"

The Tuba Christmas extravaganzas took off. Volunteers hold them around the country under the auspices of the Harvey Phillips Foundation. Sousaphones and euphoniums are also welcome.

At the tubafests, the musicians play "Silent Night" in honor of their fellows who have died, Mrs. Phillips said. On Dec. 12, 2010, when tuba players gathered again at the skating rink, the carol was played in Mr. Phillips's memory.

— *By Daniel J. Wakin*

ALEX ANDERSON

A Moose, a Squirrel and a Cartoon Classic

SEPT. 5, 1920 - OCT. 22, 2010

ALEX ANDERSON, the cartoonist who first drew Rocky the flying squirrel and his buddy, the bumbling moose Bullwinkle, television characters who captivated young baby boomers in the early 1960s, died on Oct. 22 in Carmel, Calif. He was 90.

Mr. Anderson, whose credit for creating the characters faded from public view until he won a lawsuit in 1996, was not directly involved in the production of the television series, in which Rocky and Bullwinkle typically raced to the aid of those in danger and solved mysteries.

Rocky, in his flight goggles, was the smart one; Bullwinkle, not so bright, would deliver goofy punch lines without always being aware of their meaning. They faced off against no-goodniks like the cold warrish spies Boris Badenov and Natasha Fatale. The shows had a penchant for puns that delighted adults; one episode was titled "The Guns of Abaloney."

OVERDUE CREDIT: Mr. Anderson helped create Rocky and Bullwinkle.

The series, created by Jay Ward (who had been Mr. Anderson's childhood friend) and Bill Scott, made its debut on ABC in 1959 as "Rocky and His Friends." In 1961 it moved to NBC as "The Bullwinkle Show," one of the first prime-time network cartoon series.

"It's one of the most beloved animated cartoon series of all time," Charles Solomon, an animation historian, said. "There's a cadre of baby boomers who didn't know that there was a Boris Godunov until they got older" and discovered Russian history or Russian opera.

Steven Spielberg told The New York Times in 1989, "It was the first time that I can recall my parents watching a cartoon show over my shoulder and laughing in places I couldn't comprehend."

Mr. Anderson, who in 1949 had worked with Mr. Ward in creating "Crusader Rabbit," the first animated series created for television, chose to be a consultant on the Rocky and Bullwinkle shows, said Amid Amidi, co-editor of Cartoon Brew, an online animation news blog. He stayed in San Francisco, where he was an advertising art director, rather than move to Los Angeles.

Alexander Anderson Jr. was born in Berkeley, Calif., on Sept. 5, 1920, the only child of Alexander and Olga Anderson. He graduated from the University of California, Berkeley, and the California School of Fine Arts in San Francisco. In 1938 he began working with his uncle Paul Terry at Terrytoons, the animation studio that created "Mighty Mouse."

After serving in Navy intelligence during World War II, Mr. Anderson teamed with Mr. Ward to create "Crusader Rabbit." The Rocky and Bullwinkle characters were an outgrowth of that collaboration. The television series featured other Anderson creations, including Dudley Do-Right, a Canadian Mountie who pursues the mustachioed Snidely Whiplash.

When Mr. Anderson saw a documentary about the show in 1991 without a mention of his name, he filed suit against Jay Ward Productions, two years after Mr. Ward died.

"I'm thrilled that something I did has become so popular," he told The San Francisco Chronicle. "But I'm sorry that I don't get any credit for it."

An out-of-court settlement was reached in 1996, with a court-mandated acknowledgment of Mr. Anderson as "the creator of the first version of the characters." The settlement included a financial component, which was sealed.

Mr. Anderson, who lived in Pebble Beach, Calif., is survived by his wife, Patricia; four sons; a daughter; 14 grandchildren; and five great-grandchildren.

— *By Dennis Hevesi*

LEO CULLUM

A Gag or Two in Every Issue

JAN. 11, 1942 - OCT. 23, 2010

Leo Cullum, a former TWA pilot who in a parallel career as a cartoonist amused readers of The New Yorker with his blustering businessmen, clueless doctors, venal lawyers and all-too-human dogs and cats, died on Oct. 23 in Los Angeles. He was 68 and lived in Malibu, Calif.

The cause was cancer.

For the last 33 years Mr. Cullum was a classic gag cartoonist whose visual absurdities were typically underlined by a caption reeled in from deep left field:

"I love the convenience, but the roaming charges are killing me," a buffalo says, holding a cellphone up to its ear.

"Your red and white blood cells are normal," a doctor tells his patient. "I'm worried about your rosé cells."

Mr. Cullum had a particular affinity for the animal kingdom, extending well beyond dogs, cats and mice to embrace birds — "When I first met your mother, she was bathed in moonlight," a father owl tells his children — and even the humbler representatives of the fish family. "Some will love you, son, and some will hate you," an anchovy tells his child. "It's always been that way with anchovies."

"There are many ways for a cartoon to be great, not the least of which is to be funny, and Leo was one of the most consistently funny cartoonists we ever had," said Robert Mankoff, the cartoon editor of The New Yorker.

"You're kidding. I thought it was Friday."

Mr. Cullum published 819 cartoons in The New Yorker, the most recent in the issue of Oct. 25. Many were gathered in the collections "Scotch & Toilet Water?," a book of dog cartoons; "Cockatiels for Two" (cats); "Tequila Mockingbird" (various species); and "Suture Self" (doctors).

Leo Aloysius Cullum was born on Jan. 11, 1942, in Newark and grew up in North Bergen, N.J. He attended the College of the Holy Cross in Worcester, Mass., where he earned a degree in English in 1963. On graduating, he entered the Marine Corps as a second lieutenant and underwent flight training in Pensacola, Fla.

In 1966 he was sent to Vietnam, where he flew 200 missions, including secret bombing runs over the Ho Chi Minh Trail in Laos. "Who these were secret from I'm still not sure," Mr. Cullum told Holy Cross magazine in 2006. "The North Vietnamese certainly knew it wasn't the Swiss bombing them."

He went straight from Vietnam to employment with TWA, flying international and domestic flights. He retired in 2002 at age 60 from American Airlines, which had absorbed TWA the year before in a merger.

During layovers he had rekindled a childhood interest in drawing and decided to become a cartoonist. "It looked like something I could do," he told Holy Cross magazine. "I bought some instructional books which explained the format, and I began studying the work of various cartoonists."

Inevitably, he set his sights on The New Yorker. The magazine rejected his early submissions but bought some of his ideas, turning them over to Charles Addams to illustrate. The first one resulted in 1975 in a captionless Addams cartoon of an elderly couple canoeing on a peaceful lake. Their reflection in the water, depicting the husband's actual state of mind, shows him, in a homicidal rage, attacking his wife with his paddle.

After Mr. Addams encouraged him to strike out on his own, Mr. Cullum sold his first magazine cartoon to Air Line Pilot Magazine and soon placed his work with True, Argosy, Saturday Review and Sports Afield.

Before long he cracked The New Yorker. On Jan. 3, 1977, the magazine published his first cartoon, which showed a bathrobed businessman drinking coffee at his desk, surrounded by chickens and speaking into a telephone. The caption read: "No, you're not disturbing me, Herb. I'm up with the chickens this morning."

Mr. Cullum quickly became a regular. By the 1980s he was one of the magazine's most prolific and beloved contributors. He also contributed regularly to The Harvard Business Review and Barron's.

In the aftermath of the 9/11 attacks, Mr. Cullum managed the delicate feat of finding humor when the prevailing national mood was black. The issue of The New Yorker that came out immediately after the attacks carried no cartoons, but Mr. Cullum's was the first cartoon that the magazine's readers saw the following week, on Page 6, under the list of contributors. A woman, turning to the man next to her at a bar, says: "I thought I'd never laugh again. Then I saw your jacket."

His most popular cartoon, from 1998, showed a man addressing the family cat, which is sitting next to the litterbox. "Never, ever, think outside the box," he says.

Mr. Cullum is survived by his wife, Kathy; a brother; and two daughters, the former child actresses Kimberly Berry and Kaitlin Cullum.

In 2006 Mr. Cullum's work appeared in "The Rejection Collection," a book of cartoons rejected by The New Yorker. Asked to complete the sentence "When I'm not cartooning, I ...," he wrote, "am wrestling, then showering, with my demons."

— *By William Grimes*

BURTON ROBERTS

OCT

The Bench Was His Stage

JULY 25, 1922 - OCT. 24, 2010

Burton B. Roberts, a celebrated former justice and chief administrative judge of State Supreme Court in the Bronx and a larger-than-life model for an irascible judge in Tom Wolfe's 1987 best seller, "The Bonfire of the Vanities," died on Oct. 24 in the Bronx. He was 88.

In his courtroom, only Judge Roberts was allowed to be flamboyant. Voluble and blunt, with a fiery temper and a rumbling voice that brooked no nonsense, he drew far more attention — and publicity — than his black-robed colleagues, relentlessly chastising overzealous prosecutors and defense lawyers and even chiding witnesses he deemed out of line.

Out of court, insulated by 14-year terms, multiparty endorsements and wide voter appeal, he denigrated capital punishment, mandatory sentencing laws and public officials who criticized rulings in ways he felt were politically motivated intrusions upon the independence of the judiciary.

And he was not above calling the news media or summoning reporters into his chambers — as he had done when he was an assistant prosecutor in Manhattan and the district attorney in the Bronx earlier in his career — to make sure that the facts, and his point of view, were conveyed accurately to the public.

COLORFUL IN BLACK: Mr. Roberts ruled his courtroom with a fiery temper and flamboyant style.

But to many colleagues, there was more to Judge Roberts than met the ear.

"Despite his image as a tough guy, he's really compassionate," Fernando Ferrer, the former Bronx borough president, said when Judge Roberts retired at the end of 1998 after 25 years as a State Supreme Court justice, the last 11 as the administrative judge in charge of criminal and civil trial courts in the Bronx.

And he was a hero to some he incarcerated.

"I came before Judge Roberts when I was 16," said a man who served two years as a youthful offender in the 1980s, graduated from Pace University with honors, became a New York Mercantile Exchange analyst and never forgot a judge who turned his life around.

"He just seemed to care what happened to me," said the man, who asked not to be identified. "It wasn't the usual assembly-line type of approach to justice."

After Judge Roberts retired from the bench, he joined the law firm of Fischbein Badillo Wagner Harding. He was on the team that defended one of four officers acquitted in the killing of Amadou Diallo, the unarmed West African immigrant who died in a hail of 41 bullets in the Bronx in 1999.

Burton Bennett Roberts was born in New York on July 25, 1922. After earning a bachelor's degree from New York University in 1943, he joined the Army in World War II and saw action as an infantryman in France and Italy, rescued comrades under fire, was wounded and won the Bronze Star for valor. He earned a law degree at N.Y.U. in 1949 and received a master's in law from Cornell University in 1953.

Mr. Roberts was an assistant prosecutor to the Manhattan district attorney, Frank S. Hogan, from 1949 to 1966, and was once knocked out by a defendant. The man, a robbery suspect who said he was being "framed," lunged at Mr. Roberts in court and punched him behind the left ear. Mr. Roberts was unconscious for two minutes, and — although he volunteered — was not allowed to finish the case.

He was a take-no-prisoners prosecutor. Killers, drug dealers, racketeers, even corrupt politicians toppled under his verbal blows. His voice could rise harshly, his face turning beet-red, as he railed before a jury about a defendant's dastardly wrongdoing.

In 1966, he was recruited by the Bronx district attorney, Isidore Dollinger, to be his chief assistant, and when Mr. Dollinger resigned to run for a judgeship two years later, Mr. Roberts became acting district attorney. In 1969, Mr. Roberts, a Democrat, won a full four-year term with the backing of the Democratic, Republican and Liberal Parties. He built his staff from 39 to 100 prosecutors.

He was elected to the court in 1973 and over the next 14 years presided over hundreds of cases, including an arson trial and civil proceedings arising from the Happy Land Social Club fire that killed 87 people in 1990, the worst loss of life in a city fire since the Triangle Waist

Company blaze in 1911. Judge Roberts sentenced the arsonist to 25 years to life and helped negotiate a $15.8 million settlement of civil claims in 1995.

In "The Bonfire of the Vanities," one of the only admirable figures is Myron Kovitsky, a Bronx judge who refuses to be influenced by the press, the public or publicity-seeking prosecutors. Mr. Wolfe modeled the character after Judge Roberts and dedicated the book to him and one of his former assistants, Edward W. Hayes. In the 1990 film version, the judge's name was changed to Leonard White, and he was portrayed by Morgan Freeman.

Judge Roberts was a bachelor until 1982, when, at age 59, he married the former Gerhild Hammer. For the last year he had been living at the Hebrew Home for the Aged in the Riverdale section of the Bronx, where he died of respiratory failure, his niece, Amy Roberts, said. He is also survived by his wife, a brother and three nephews. Another brother died in 2006.

In 1996, when Gov. George E. Pataki and Mayor Rudolph W. Giuliani criticized him for setting bail they considered too low for the accused killer of a police officer, Judge Roberts dismissed their remarks as "the bleatings of public officials who possibly are seeking political advantage."

In his trademark stentorian rumble, he told a reporter for The New York Times: "The judiciary acts as a ballast on our ship of state, and it prevents the ship from being wrecked on the reefs of inappropriate judgment, and should not be steered by the whims of hysterical opinion."

He paused to clear his throat.

"You got that?" he shouted.

— *By Robert D. McFadden*

JOSEPH STEIN

The Old Pro of Broadway

MAY 30, 1912 - OCT. 24, 2010

Joseph Stein, the Tony Award-winning author of "Fiddler on the Roof" and more than a dozen other Broadway musicals, died on Oct. 24 in Manhattan. He was 98.

He died after fracturing his skull in a fall, his son Harry said.

"Fiddler on the Roof," based on Sholem Aleichem's short stories about a Jewish milkman and his family who face terrifying change under the Russian czar in a small village in 1905, opened on Broadway in 1964. Sheldon Harnick's lyrics and Jerry Bock's score captured the high notes of the praise, but Mr. Stein's book hardly went unnoticed.

"It goes beyond local color and lays bare in quick, moving strokes the sorrow of a people," Howard Taubman wrote in his review in The New York Times.

Between memorable songs like "Sunrise, Sunset" and "If I Were a Rich Man," Mr. Stein's dialogue had its own kind of poetry. As Tevye's daughter Hodel prepares to join her future husband in Siberia, she tells her father, "God alone knows when we shall see each other again." He responds, "Then we will leave it in his hands." And just before the show's first big number, Tevye speaks to God: "I realize, of course, that it's no shame to be poor, but it's no great honor, either."

The show won nine Tony Awards, including the one for best musical and Mr. Stein's for best author of a musical. By 1971, when the production became Broadway's longest-running musical (a record since broken several times), it had been produced in 32 countries in 16 languages. The show closed the following year, but it has been revived on Broadway four times, most recently in 2004.

Mr. Stein was already an old Broadway pro when "Fiddler" came along. Just the year before, he had won glowing reviews for "Enter Laughing," a comedy, based on a book by Carl Reiner, about a Jewish boy who wants to become an actor.

He was also a co-writer of two successful shows. "Take Me Along," written with Robert Russell, was a 1959 musical based on Eugene O'Neill's "Ah, Wilderness!" and starred Jackie Gleason and Robert Morse. The 1955 musical "Plain and Fancy," which he wrote with Will Glickman, was a lighthearted story of romance and culture clashes between New Yorkers and the Amish.

A NAME IN LIGHTS: Mr. Stein wrote more than a dozen Broadway musicals, including "Fiddler."

Joseph Stein was born on May 30, 1912, in the Bronx, the son of Charles Stein, a handbag maker, and the former Emma Rosenblum. He received a bachelor's degree from the City College of New York in 1934 and a master's degree in social work from Columbia University in 1937.

Mr. Stein had been a social worker for several years when he happened to meet the comedian Zero Mostel through a mutual friend. Mr. Mostel mentioned that he was looking for comedy material for a radio show, Mr. Stein threw out an idea, and Mr. Mostel paid him $15 for it. His writing career had begun. (Mr. Mostel went on to play Tevye in the original Broadway production of "Fiddler.")

In 1948, Mr. Stein made his Broadway writing debut, creating a single sketch with Mr. Glickman for "Lend an Ear," a musical revue that starred Carol Channing and was choreographed by Gower Champion. And he became part of the writing staff of Sid Caesar's classic 1950s comedy-variety series, "Your Show of Shows."

He also wrote the screenplays for three of his shows — "Fiddler," "Enter Laughing" and the 1949 Broadway flop "Mrs. Gibbons' Boys" — when they were made into films.

While "Fiddler" was still running at the Broadway Theater, Mr. Stein wrote the book for the 1968 Kander and Ebb musical "Zorba," based on the book "Zorba the Greek," which starred Herschel Bernardi as the passionate, moment-seizing, philosophizing title character, a man who "lived as if he was about to die at once," as Clive Barnes wrote in his Times review.

Several of Mr. Stein's shows were revived on Broadway, but he also wrote the books for four more new shows, three of them musicals. His last, "Rags," a 1986 musical about a young immigrant on the sweatshop-era Lower East Side, quickly collapsed under the weight of negative reviews. But it brought Mr. Stein, 74 at the time, his final Tony nomination. The only credited work he did on Broadway after that was some additional text for "Jerome Robbins' Broadway" (1989).

Still, he continued working well into his 90s. In 2007 the Westport Country Playhouse in Connecticut produced "All About Us," a Kander and Ebb musical based on Thornton Wilder's "Skin of Our Teeth," with book by Mr. Stein.

The Times of London called Mr. Stein "the last of the great Broadway book writers." Even his lesser-known works continue to be performed.

Mr. Stein's first marriage, to Sadie Singer, ended with her death in 1974. He married Elisa Loti, an actress, in 1975; she survives him, as do three sons from his first marriage; a stepson; a stepdaughter, Jenny Lyn Bader, a playwright with whom he was working on a new musical, "Heaven Can Wait," at his death; and six grandchildren.

Although he was best known for "Fiddler," he contended that another show had affected him more deeply.

"I do believe in the philosophy of 'Zorba,'" Mr. Stein told The Hartford Courant in 2007, "that life is what you do until the day that you die, so you better make use of all of it so you're proud of what you're doing."

— *By Anita Gates*

GREGORY ISAACS

Reggae's 'Cool Ruler'

JULY 15, 1950 - OCT. 25, 2010

Gregory Isaacs, reggae's "Cool Ruler," whose aching vocals and poignant lyrics about love and loss and ghetto life endeared him to legions of fans of Caribbean music, died on Oct. 25 at his home in London. He was 60.

The cause was lung cancer, said his wife, June Isaacs, who lives in Kingston, Jamaica.

Cat Coore, the guitarist and cellist for the seminal reggae band Third World, has called Mr. Isaacs "the Frank Sinatra of Jamaica" for his elegant vocal phrasing. But as the singer's friend and former manager Don Hewitt observed, "It goes further than that, because Sinatra was not a songwriter."

Mr. Isaacs's nuanced compositions eschewed sentimental cliché and boastful machismo in favor of a sensitive, even vulnerable point of view. But on songs like "Slave Master" and "Hand Cuff," he revealed a more militant side.

Born on July 15, 1950, in the rough Kingston neighborhood Denham Town, Mr. Isaacs picked up the nickname Jah Tooth after a policeman broke one of his teeth. Inspired by the American soul singer Sam Cooke, he got his start on a local radio talent show, "The Vere Johns Opportunity Hour." He was briefly a member of the vocal trio the Concordes before making his name in 1973 with the solo single "All I Have Is Love." Although he established his own Jamaican label and record shop, African Museum, with fellow reggae singer Errol Dunkley, Mr. Isaacs was later signed to the British labels Virgin and Island.

SINGING WITH STYLE: Mr. Isaacs frequently performed in suits, even tuxedos.

While true mainstream success eluded him, few recording artists in any genre could rival his prolific output. He recorded hundreds of albums' worth of original material, starting in the '70s and concluding in 2008 with his final CD, "Brand New Me." His nickname "Cool Ruler" was the title of another album.

Mr. Hewitt said that when Keith Richards of the Rolling Stones was introduced to Mr. Isaacs, Mr. Richards "carried on like he'd met Jesus."

Mr. Isaacs was best known for his 1982 release "Night Nurse," on which he was backed by the renowned band Roots Radics, which he organized in the 1970s. His 1988 album "Red Rose for

OCT

Gregory" proved that he was equally at home singing over the hard-edged digital rhythms of reggae's dancehall era.

He was also renowned for his fashion sense; he performed in the 1978 film "Rockers" wearing a powder-blue tuxedo and black fedora. "He was always dapper," Mrs. Isaacs said. "Very proud, very tidy, very laconic, a man of few words."

But he could be an aggressive businessman, she added. "He always stood up for what he deserved in whichever way he could," she said. "When it came to what was due to him, he had to get that. No ifs, no buts, no maybes."

When he and his wife were arrested for illegal possession of a firearm in 1983, she said, "he took the rap so I could go free" and served time in Kingston's General Penitentiary. He was also arrested repeatedly for possession of cocaine and struggled with addiction for many years.

In addition to his wife, he is survived by his mother, a brother, 12 children and a grandson.

In a 2001 interview, Mr. Isaacs reflected on his legacy. "Look at me as a man who performed works musically," he said. "Who uplift people who need upliftment, mentally, physically, economically — all forms. Who told the people to live with love, 'cause only love can conquer war, and to understand themselves so that they can understand others."

— By Rob Kenner

RICHARD T. GILL

Harvard Economist and, Yes, Opera Singer

NOV. 30, 1927 - OCT. 25, 2010

Richard T. Gill, in all statistical probability the only Harvard economist to sing 86 performances with the Metropolitan Opera, died on Oct. 25 in Providence, R.I. He was 82.

Mr. Gill, a longtime Harvard faculty member who wrote many widely used economics textbooks, did not undertake serious vocal training (which he began as an anti-smoking regimen) until he was nearly 40. At the time, he had seen perhaps 10 operas and rarely listened to classical music.

But after just a few years of study a world-class voice emerged, and Mr. Gill soon forsook chalk and tweed for flowing robes and very large headgear.

A basso profundo, Mr. Gill began performing featured roles with the New York City Opera in the early 1970s. Soon afterward he joined the Met, where between 1973 and 1976 he sang alongside luminaries like Plácido Domingo, Beverly Sills, Kiri Te Kanawa and Shirley Verrett.

At the Met, Mr. Gill's roles included Panthus in "Les Troyens," by Berlioz; Frère Laurent in Gounod's "Roméo et Juliette"; the Commendatore in Mozart's "Don Giovanni"; and the King in Verdi's "Aida."

This was new and dazzling terrain for the author of "Economics and the Private Interest: An Introduction to Microeconomics."

Reviewing a 1975 Met "Boris Godunov" in which Mr. Gill sang the role of Pimen, John Rockwell wrote in The New York Times, "Mr. Gill can be a bit stiff and awkward, dramatically." But, he added, "he has one of the most beautiful, focused lyric basses around."

Reviewing Mr. Gill's "Economic Development: Past and Present" (1963), Industrial and Labor Relations Review found the author "lucid, objective, and eminently readable."

During his 14-year operatic career, Mr. Gill was a guest artist with the companies of Chicago, Houston, Boston, Edinburgh and Amsterdam. At the same time he produced a string of additional books, including "Economics: A Text With Included Readings" and "Great Debates in Economics," a two-volume work he edited. He had earlier published short fiction in The New Yorker and The Atlantic Monthly. In later years he was the host of "Economics USA," a 28-part public television series first broadcast in 1984 and 1985.

> During his 14-year operatic career, Mr. Gill produced a string of books, including "Economics: A Text With Included Readings" and "Great Debates in Economics."

Richard Thomas Gill was born in Long Branch, N.J., on Nov. 30, 1927; his mother, Myrtle, taught piano and voice.

Though he did not study voice formally, Richard was a boy soprano in his church choir and played the clarinet. At 16 he entered Harvard, where he sang in the glee club, interrupting his studies for Army service with the postwar occupation forces in Japan.

Returning to Harvard, Mr. Gill received his bachelor's degree in economics in 1948. After graduate study in philosophy and psychology at Oxford, he was named an assistant dean at Harvard at the age of 21. He earned a Ph.D. in economics from the university in 1956 and was later an assistant professor of economics there.

By his late 30s, shouldering academic and family responsibilities, Mr. Gill was a two-and-a-half-pack-a-day smoker. He made himself quit and, as an incentive to stay on the wagon, began private voice lessons with Herbert Mayer, a respected New York teacher. Mr. Gill enjoyed singing but knew nothing about opera.

For his first lesson, he sang "Drink to Me Only With Thine Eyes."

"My voice gave out halfway through and the teacher yelled, 'Stop, I can't stand it!'" Mr. Gill told Newsweek in 1975.

Mr. Gill persevered, and during the years of rigorous vocal exercise that followed, his neck size grew from 14 to 17 1/2.

As good as he became, he was too scared to sing on campus. "At Harvard, if you even stub your toe in public, it's embarrassing," Mr. Gill told Harvard magazine in 2002.

Finally, after performing small roles in the Boston area, he agreed to sing Count Almaviva in a "Marriage of Figaro" staged at Harvard. The production was directed by John Lithgow (Harvard '67), who went on to no small reputation as an actor, and conducted by John Adams (Harvard '71), who would compose "Nixon in China," among other operas.

Later, during a sabbatical year in England, Mr. Gill was emboldened by well-received auditions at Covent Garden and other European houses. Returning to the United States, he auditioned for the New York City Opera. The company offered him two performances in the 1971 season, at $75 a night.

Mr. Gill quit his tenured job at Harvard and became a fixture at City Opera.

A former resident of Fort Lauderdale, Fla., he also had a home in Chocorua, N.H. Mr. Gill is survived by his wife, the former Elizabeth Bjornson, whom he married in 1950; a sister; three sons; and eight grandchildren.

After retiring from opera in the mid-1980s, Mr. Gill turned his scholarly attention to demographics and the breakdown of the family, writing "Our Changing Population" with Nathan Glazer and Stephan A. Thernstrom and "Posterity Lost: Progress, Ideology, and the Decline of the American Family."

In some respects, Mr. Gill later said, he found the roiling world of opera more appealingly straightforward than the roiling world of academe.

"Performing is a great reality test," he told Newsweek. "There's no tenure in it, and the feedback is much less complicated than you get in academia. When you go out on that stage, you put your life on the line."

— *By Margalit Fox*

MARY EMMA ALLISON

Trick or Treat or, Even Better, a Nickel

MARCH 5, 1917 - OCT. 26, 2010

SIX DECADES AGO, on a fall afternoon, a young woman caught sight of a children's parade. She followed the children, in bright native dress, as they wended their way through the streets of the town. They entered a store, with the woman behind them, and inside the store she encountered a cow.

She followed the cow, and she came to a booth.

On account of the children, the cow and the booth, the woman came up with a world-changing plan. ...

The booth was in Wanamaker's department store in Philadelphia, and it belonged to Unicef. The parade of costumed children (and the cow) was part of a campaign to send powdered milk to needy children overseas.

The woman was a schoolteacher named Mary Emma Allison. Moved by her chance encounter, she and her husband created Trick-or-Treat for Unicef, a Halloween ritual that celebrates its 60th anniversary on Sunday, Oct. 31, and has raised tens of millions of dollars for children worldwide.

COIN COLLECTORS: Mrs. Allison and her children with Unicef milk cartons.

Mrs. Allison died on Oct. 26 at 93. The death, at her home in Lowell, Ind., was announced by Unicef.

Mary Emma Woodruff was born in New Jersey on March 5, 1917. She earned a bachelor's degree from Wheaton College in Illinois and went on to teach elementary school. She later earned a master's degree in library science and worked as a school librarian in Chicago.

At the time of her fateful trip to Wanamaker's, Mrs. Allison was the mother of three young children and the wife of a Presbyterian minister, Clyde Allison. The Allisons, who lived then in the Philadelphia suburbs, had long been concerned with social responsibility. In 1947, they began collecting clothes for children in postwar Europe. As that program drew to a close, they decided to come up with a plan, centered on Halloween, by which American children might help less fortunate ones abroad.

Then, in the autumn of 1949, Mrs. Allison set out with her children to buy winter coats at Wanamaker's. Down the street came the parade.

Mrs. Allison wrote an appeal for a national magazine her husband edited, which was sent to Presbyterian Sunday school teachers. Published before Halloween in 1950, the appeal asked prospective trick-or-treaters to collect coins for Unicef in milk cartons or tins.

There is no accurate record of the takings that first year, but Unicef's orange cardboard box with the coin slot became a ubiquitous presence in the sticky hands of autumn.

Mrs. Allison's husband died last year. Survivors include two daughters and a son, the original trick-or-treaters for Unicef; four grandchildren; and four great-grandchildren.

Since its inception, Trick-or-Treat for Unicef has raised more than $160 million. The money buys food, clean water, milk, medicine and much else for children in more than 150 countries.

All on account of a thoughtful young woman who, driving through town on a long-ago autumn, opted to follow a children's parade.

— *BY MARGALIT FOX*

NÉSTOR KIRCHNER

A Political Impact in Death as in Life

FEB. 25, 1950 - OCT. 27, 2010

NÉSTOR KIRCHNER, the former president of Argentina who led his country out of a crippling economic crisis before being succeeded by his wife, died unexpectedly on Oct. 27, apparently of a heart attack. News of his death created an immediate climate of intense political uncertainty in Argentina.

After complaining of flu symptoms the night before, Mr. Kirchner, 60, lost consciousness early in the morning of the 27th and was taken to a hospital in El Calafate, a town in the southern Argentine province of Santa Cruz. Luis Buonomo, the presidential doctor, said Mr. Kirchner died of sudden cardiac arrest, according to Argentine newspapers. He had undergone two procedures in the last year to clear arterial blockages, the most recent in September 2010.

Mr. Kirchner's death, coming on a national holiday to conduct the census, threw the 2011 elections and the presidency of his wife and political partner, Cristina Fernández de Kirchner, into a state of flux. Mr. Kirchner's popularity had been a significant factor in her election in 2007, and he had wielded substantial influence in her government behind the scenes, particularly in the running of the economy. He had recently served as the head of their Peronist party.

They were one of the world's most powerful political couples, labeled the "penguins" for Mr. Kirchner's close association with his Patagonian home province, Santa Cruz, near the tip of South America. As president, Mrs. Kirchner was more often the public face of their partnership while Mr. Kirchner pulled the levers of the Peronist machinery. He held the governing coalition together by inspiring loyalty in unions and among lower-level politicians using subsidies and patronage and by helping to engineer swift economic growth, even at the cost of inflation.

A STRONG HAND: Mr. Kirchner with voters in 2003. "A ruthless view of politics."

Many Argentines were betting that he, not his wife, would run for president in 2011 in what some called a leap-frog strategy to create a dynasty by passing the presidency between them for multiple terms. Mr. Kirchner was elected in 2003.

Opinion was divided about whether Mr. Kirchner's death would bolster or hurt Mrs. Kirchner's political prospects. Her government, extremely unpopular in her first two years, had been gathering strength in opinion polls as the economy improved.

Argentina has not responded well when presidents or influential spouses have died prematurely. After Eva Perón died in 1952, a military coup three years later ousted her husband, Gen. Juan Perón. Two years after General Perón died in 1974, a military junta overthrew the government of his third wife, Isabel. But the country is far more stable now.

Before running for the presidency, Mr. Kirchner had been a

fairly obscure local politician from Santa Cruz, where he was governor. He was elected in 2003 after garnering only 22.2 percent of the vote in the first round.

He took strong control of the government, standing up to police and military officials and refusing to bend to — and sometimes even to pay — debtors, creditors and the International Monetary Fund. He also pressed Supreme Court justices to resign and overturned amnesty laws for military officers who had been accused of assassinations and torture during the military dictatorship.

"In a very unstable situation he took absolute control," said Mark Jones, a political science professor at Rice University.

Under Mr. Kirchner, the country rode a global commodities boom that increased exports of its agricultural products, stimulated domestic spending and helped get the country out of its economic crisis.

But once the economy stabilized, Mr. Kirchner continued to be contentious, issuing decrees and concentrating power in the executive. Some began to accuse him of authoritarianism.

"He had a ruthless view of politics," said Daniel Kerner, a Buenos Aires-based analyst with Eurasia Group, a risk consultancy. "If you are not the toughest, people will take advantage of you; that's how he saw politics."

— *By Alexei Barrionuevo*

LIANG CONGJIE

A Green Hero in China

AUG. 4, 1932 - OCT. 28, 2010

Liang Congjie, who was a founder of China's first legally recognized environmental group and who came to be honored by international agencies and the Chinese government alike, died in Beijing on Oct. 28. He was 78.

Friends of Nature, the group he established, announced his death on its Web site. It said he died of a lung infection in a Beijing hospital.

Mr. Liang was a historian and teacher at the privately run Academy for Chinese Culture in 1994 when he and three co-workers decided that China's rapid development merited the creation of a citizens' group that would work to solve environmental problems. "We knew from television about Greenpeace, but there wasn't anything like that in China," he told Asiaweek in 2000. "My friends and I began wondering, 'Why not here?' We decided to try."

Unlike Greenpeace, with its aggressive tactics and attention-getting protests, Friends of Nature took a nonconfrontational approach, choosing to urge the national government to use existing laws to address environmental concerns. It established the nation's first bird-watching group and focused on environmental education in primary schools in western China.

Yet the group also won national recognition for sponsoring daring, and sometimes dangerous, efforts to promote environmental protection.

In the 1990s, Friends of Nature helped produce an undercover videotape of officials who were proposing to illegally cut down a stand of virgin forest. The video was broadcast nationally on China's CCTV network and helped persuade the prime minister, Zhu Rongji, to ban logging in virgin forests in 1999.

Friends of Nature also worked to stop the hunting of a rare Tibetan antelope. Hunters killed the leader of antipoaching patrols in the region, but the crusade has drawn worldwide attention; the antelope population tripled to 60,000 animals from 1998 to 2008.

Ma Jun, a friend and fellow environmentalist, described Mr. Liang's relationship with the government as "constructively critical."

FRIEND OF NATURE: Mr. Liang in 1994.

"He was always pushing for a bigger space for civil society in environmental protection," Mr. Ma said in a telephone interview, "but in the meantime he did try to work with the system to promote this course. It isn't easy."

Mr. Liang, he added, "incubated the first generation of environmentalists in China."

Liang Congjie was born into a family known for its reformist bent. His grandfather, the journalist and scholar Liang Qichao, was exiled to Japan for 14 years in 1898 after proposing to Emperor Guangxu of the Qing dynasty that China become a constitutional monarchy.

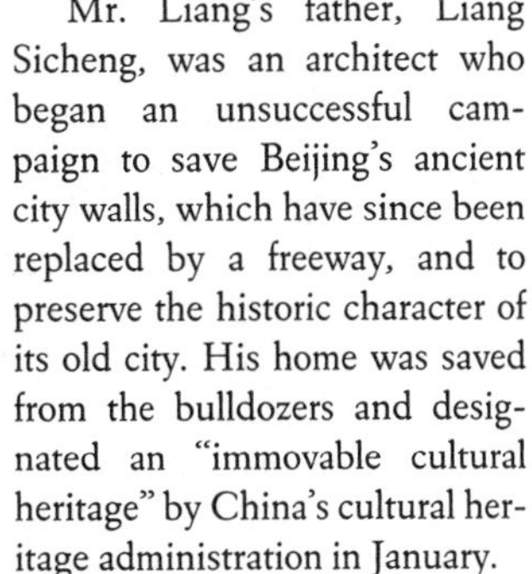

Mr. Liang's father, Liang Sicheng, was an architect who began an unsuccessful campaign to save Beijing's ancient city walls, which have since been replaced by a freeway, and to preserve the historic character of its old city. His home was saved from the bulldozers and designated an "immovable cultural heritage" by China's cultural heritage administration in January.

Mr. Liang is survived by his wife, a son and a daughter.

Friends of Nature said on its Web site that Mr. Liang's family, "hoping to follow his austere nature," planned to hold the simplest possible funeral.

— *By Michael Wines*

JAMES MACARTHUR

'Danno'

DEC. 8, 1937 - OCT. 28, 2010

JAMES MACARTHUR, who played Danno, the boyish-looking but hard-driving sidekick on the long-running television detective show "Hawaii Five-O," died on Oct. 28 in Florida. He was 72.

His agent, Richard Lewis, said Mr. MacArthur died of natural causes but was not more specific.

For 11 of the 12 years that "Hawaii Five-O" first ran on CBS, Mr. MacArthur, as Detective Danny Williams, chased thieves, hit men, swindlers, spies and assorted loonies. His boss was Detective Steve McGarrett, played by Jack Lord, the straitlaced, tight-lipped head of a small, elite police team determined to keep the idyllic islands from turning into a modern Wild West.

When the bad guy was captured, McGarrett would tell his partner, "Book him, Danno!," which became a popular catchphrase.

Most of the original show's main actors are now dead. Mr. Lord died in 1998; Kam Fong, who played Chin Ho Kelly, died in 2002; and Gilbert Lani Kauhi (credited as Zulu), who played Kono Kalakaua, died in 2004.

The original "Hawaii Five-O" ran from 1968 to 1980, making it one of television's longest-running crime shows. It was seen in more than 80 countries. Mr. MacArthur left in 1979. A new version of "Hawaii Five-O" made its debut on CBS in September.

If acting was not in Mr. MacArthur's blood, it was certainly in his upbringing.

James Gordon MacArthur was born in Los Angeles on Dec. 8, 1937. When he was seven months old he was adopted by the actress Helen Hayes and her husband, Charles MacArthur, the playwright best known as the co-author, with Ben Hecht, of "The Front Page."

"They did teach me a lot about the theater just through my life with them," Mr. MacArthur said of his parents in a 1957 interview in Teen Life magazine. Starting as a teenager in summer stock productions, he would go on to a career onstage, in more than a dozen movies and on many television shows.

Mr. MacArthur considered the real start of his acting career the 1955 television production of John Frankenheimer's "Deal a Blow," in which he played a misunderstood teenager on the verge of manhood in trouble with his parents and the law. It was remade in 1957 for the big screen as "The Young Stranger," with Mr. MacArthur reprising the role.

Before "Hawaii Five-O," Mr. MacArthur acted in several Disney adventures, including "Kidnapped" and "Swiss Family Robinson." He had a small but significant role in the taut 1965 cold war thriller "The Bedford Incident." In the rambunctious 1967 film "The Love-Ins," Mr. MacArthur's character hung out in the Haight-Ashbury neighborhood of San Francisco and smoked banana peels.

Besides "Hawaii Five-O," Mr. MacArthur acted in many TV shows, including "Gunsmoke," "Bonanza," "The Love Boat" and "The Untouchables." But it was his appearance in the 1968 movie "Hang 'Em High," a low-budget spaghetti western starring Clint Eastwood, that prompted Leonard Freeman, the creator of "Hawaii Five-O," to cast him.

One of his favorite "Hawaii Five-O" episodes, Mr. MacArthur said, was "Retire in Sunny Hawaii Forever" (1975), because it was one of the rare times that he worked with his mother. Miss Hayes played Danno's Aunt Clara, who visits Hawaii and helps the detectives solve a murder.

SIGNATURE ROLE: Mr. MacArthur as Danno in "Hawaii Five-O."

Mr. MacArthur is survived by his wife of more than 25 years, Helen Beth Duntz; four children; and seven grandchildren. His first two marriages — to the actresses Joyce Bulifant and Melody Patterson — ended in divorce.

— *By Dennis Hevesi*

GEOFFREY CRAWLEY

And the Mysterious Case of the Cottingley Fairies

DEC. 10, 1926 - OCT. 29, 2010

Were there really fairies at the bottom of the garden, or was it merely a childhood prank gone strangely and lastingly awry?

That, for six decades, was the central question behind the Cottingley fairies mystery, the story of two English schoolgirls who claimed to have taken five photographs of fairy folk in the 1910s and afterward.

Set awhirl by the international news media, the girls' account won the support of many powerful people, including one of the most famous literary men in Britain. It inspired books and films, including "Fairy Tale: A True Story" (1997), starring Peter O'Toole, and "Photographing Fairies" (1997), with Ben Kingsley.

From the start, there were doubters. But there was no conclusive proof of deception until the 1980s, when a series of articles by the English photographic scientist Geoffrey Crawley helped reveal the story for what it was: one of the most enduring, if inadvertent, photographic hoaxes of the 20th century.

A polymath who was variously a skilled pianist, linguist, chemist, inventor and editor, Mr. Crawley died on Oct. 29, at 83, at his home in Westcliff-on-Sea, England.

His death followed a long illness, said Chris Cheesman, news editor of the British magazine Amateur Photographer, which first reported the death on its Web site. At his death, Mr. Crawley was the magazine's photo science consultant. Survivors include Mr. Crawley's wife, Carolyn, and a son.

In a telephone interview, Colin Harding, curator of photographic technology at the National Media Museum in Bradford, England, discussed Mr. Crawley's role in the debunking of the Cottingley fairies case. "He took a scientific and analytical approach that was objective to something that had been previously subjective and so full of emotion," he said.

The mystery began innocently enough on a summer day in 1917, in Cottingley, a West Yorkshire village. Two cousins, Elsie Wright, then about 16, and Frances Griffiths, about 10, decided to fool their parents by producing pictures of the fairies they claimed to see in the glen near their house.

They borrowed a glass-plate camera belonging to Elsie's father and returned soon afterward in triumph. Developed, the photograph showed Frances surrounded by whitish forms that resembled stray bits of paper or swans. Their families dismissed the images as childish trickery.

The girls stuck to their story, and later that summer took a second photo, this time of Elsie confronting what appeared to be a gnome. The families remained skeptical but kept the images as private curiosities. They would very likely have remained so had it not been for the intervention of two influential men.

The first was Edward L. Gardner, a leader of the Theosophical Society in Britain, who got wind of the photos in 1920. If they were genuine, he knew, it would advance the cause of theosophy, which believed in the existence of spirit life.

After examining the photos, Gardner concluded that they were real. Wanting to use them to illustrate his public lectures, he had a darkroom technician produce better-quality negatives. New prints made from them showed the fairies clear as day.

The second man was Arthur Conan Doyle. If anyone should have known better, it was he: a trained physician, he had created the single most rational figure in Western literature and was a skilled amateur photographer.

But Conan Doyle was also an ardent spiritualist, an interest amplified by his son's death in World War I. Recruited by Gardner, Conan Doyle soon became an impassioned champion of the photos.

For the girls, there was no turning back. In 1920, using cameras supplied by Gardner and Conan Doyle, they "took" three more fairy photographs.

That December, Conan Doyle used two of their photos to illustrate an article in The Strand magazine, "Fairies Photographed: An Epoch-Making Event Described by A. Conan Doyle." He later wrote a book, "The Coming of the Fairies," defending the images.

For the next 60 years, public interest in the Cottingley fairies waxed and waned. Elsie and Frances gave occasional interviews. Each time they were asked whether they had faked the photos, and each time they gave similar answers: coy, charming and wittily evasive.

In the late 1970s and early '80s, empirical investigation of the case began in earnest. The primary investigators, working independently, included James Randi, the magician and professional skeptic; Joe Cooper, an English journalist; and Mr. Crawley.

Geoffrey Crawley was born in London on Dec. 10, 1926. His father was an avid amateur photographer, and as a boy Geoffrey helped him in his darkroom.

A gifted pianist, the young Mr. Crawley decided to embark on a concert career before switching course and studying French and German at Cambridge. Accomplished at chemistry, he invented Acutol, a chemical developer for black-and-white film, in the 1960s.

From the mid-1960s to the mid-1980s, Mr. Crawley was editor in chief of the magazine British Journal of Photography. His 10-part series exposing the Cottingley fairy photographs as fakes appeared there in 1982 and 1983.

Mr. Crawley had been asked to determine the authenticity of the photos in the late 1970s. "My instant reaction was amusement that it could be thought that the photographs depicted actual beings," he wrote in 2000.

But he came to believe, as he wrote, that "the photographic world had a duty, for its own self-respect," to clarify the record.

Mr. Harding of the National Media Museum said of Mr. Crawley: "What he did was take everything back to empirical principles, ignore everything that had been written previously, go back to the actual cameras, the actual prints, and analyze them in a way that would inform something that was objective."

After acquiring the original cameras, Mr. Crawley painstakingly tested whether they were capable of producing images as crisp and recognizable as those popularized by Gardner and Conan Doyle. He determined that they were not, and that the darkroom alchemy ordered by Gardner had transformed the girls' amateurish blurs into marketable fairies.

In the early 1980s, amid the renewed attention, the cousins came clean, admitting the hoax in The Times of London in 1983.

The girls' plan had been absurdly simple: they used fairy illustrations from a book, which Elsie, a gifted artist, copied onto cardboard, cut out and stuck into the ground with hatpins. They had never set out to deceive anyone beyond their own families.

To the end of her life, Frances, who died in 1986, maintained that the fifth photo in the series was genuine. Elsie, who died in 1988, said that all were fakes.

In the course of his work, Mr. Crawley befriended Elsie, then in her 80s. His writings about the hoax, though rigorously scientific, display great tenderness toward the two country girls whose idle boast of seeing magical creatures captivated a nation convulsed by war and modernity.

"Of course there are fairies — just as there is Father Christmas," Mr. Crawley wrote in the British Journal of Photography in 2000. "The trouble comes when you try to make them corporeal. They are fine poetic concepts taking us out of this at times too ugly real world."

"At least," he went on to say, "Elsie gave us a myth which has never harmed anyone."

"How many professed photographers," he added, "can claim to have equaled her achievement with the first photograph they ever took?"

— *By Margalit Fox*

ELEMENTARY?: When Mr. Crawley was asked to determine the authenticity of Elsie Wright and Frances Griffiths's photographs, he uncovered a decades-old hoax that had fooled Arthur Conan Doyle.

THEODORE SORENSEN

Kennedy's 'Alter Ego'

MAY 8, 1928 - OCT. 31, 2010

THEODORE C. SORENSEN, who as a speechwriter, strategist and counselor did much to shape the narrative, image and legacy of John F. Kennedy, died on Oct. 31 in Manhattan. One of the last surviving links to the Kennedy administration, he was 82.

He had suffered a stroke a week ago and died at New York-Presbyterian Hospital, his wife, Gillian Sorensen, said.

Mr. Sorensen once said he suspected that the headline on his obituary would read "Theodore Sorenson, Kennedy Speechwriter," misspelling his name and misjudging his work, but he was much more. He was a trusted adviser on everything from election tactics to foreign policy.

"You need a mind like Sorensen's around you that's clicking and clicking all the time," Kennedy's archrival, Richard M. Nixon, said in 1962, adding that Mr. Sorensen had "a rare gift" for finding phrases that penetrated the American psyche.

He worked with Kennedy on passages of soaring rhetoric, including the 1961 inaugural address proclaiming that "the torch has been passed to a new generation of Americans" and challenging citizens: "Ask not what your country can do for you, ask what you can do for your country." Mr. Sorensen drew on the Bible, the Gettysburg Address and the words of Thomas Jefferson and Winston Churchill as he helped hone and polish that speech.

First hired as a researcher by Kennedy, a newly elected senator from Massachusetts who took office in 1953, Mr. Sorensen collaborated closely — more closely than most knew — on "Profiles in Courage," the 1956 book that brought Kennedy a Pulitzer Prize and a national audience.

After the president's assassination, Mr. Sorensen practiced law and politics. But in the public mind, his name was forever joined to the man he had served. His first task after leaving the White House was to recount the abridged administration's story in a 783-page best seller simply titled "Kennedy."

Mr. Sorensen held the title of special counsel, but Washington reporters of the era labeled him the president's "intellectual alter ego" and "a lobe of Kennedy's mind." He called these exaggerations, but they were rooted in truth.

Kennedy had plenty of yes-men. He needed a no-man from time to time. The president trusted Mr. Sorensen to play that role in crises foreign and domestic, and he played it well, in the judgment of Robert F. Kennedy, his brother's attorney general. "If it was difficult," Robert Kennedy said, "Ted Sorensen was brought in."

Mr. Sorensen was proudest of a work written in haste, under crushing pressure. In October 1962, when he was 34 years old, he drafted a letter from Kennedy to the Soviet leader, Nikita Khrushchev, which helped end the Cuban missile crisis. After the Kennedy administration's failed coup against Fidel Castro at the Bay of Pigs, the Soviets had sent nuclear weapons to Cuba. They were capable of striking most American cities, including New York and Washington.

"Time was short," Mr. Sorensen remembered in an interview with The New York Times that was videotaped to accompany this obituary. "The hawks were rising. Kennedy could keep control of his own government, but one never knew whether the advocates of bombing and invasion might somehow gain the upper hand."

Mr. Sorensen said, "I knew that any mistakes in my letter — anything that angered or soured Khrushchev — could result in the end of America, maybe the end of the world."

The letter pressed for a peaceful solution. The Soviets withdrew the missiles. The world went on.

Theodore Chaikin Sorensen was born in Lincoln, Neb., on May 8, 1928 — Harry S. Truman's 44th birthday, as he was fond of noting. He described himself as a distinct minority: "a Danish Russian Jewish Unitarian." He was the son of Christian A. Sorensen, a lawyer, and Annis Chaikin, a social worker, pacifist and feminist. His father, a Republican who had named him after Teddy Roosevelt, ran for public office for the first time that year; he served as Nebraska's attorney general from 1929 to 1933.

POLITICAL WORDSMITH: Mr. Sorensen conferring with John F. Kennedy in 1960.

Lincoln, the state capital, was named for the 16th president. Near the Statehouse stood a statue of Abraham Lincoln and a slab with the full text of the Gettysburg Address. As a child, Mr. Sorensen read it over and over. The Capitol itself held engraved quotations; one he remembered was "Eternal vigilance is the price of liberty."

Mr. Sorensen earned undergraduate and law degrees at the University of Nebraska and, on July 1, 1951, at the age of 23, he left Lincoln to seek his fortune in Washington. He knew no one. He had no appointments, phone numbers or contacts. Except for a hitchhiking trip to Texas, he had never left the Midwest. He had never had a cup of coffee or written a check.

Eighteen months later, after short stints as a junior government lawyer, he was hired by John F. Kennedy, the new Democratic senator from Massachusetts. Kennedy was "young, good-looking, glamorous, rich, a war hero, a Harvard graduate," Mr. Sorensen recalled. The new hire was none of those, save young. They quickly found that they shared political ideals and values.

"When he first hired me," Mr. Sorensen recalled, Kennedy said, "'I want you to put together a legislative program for the economic revival of New England.'" Kennedy's first three speeches on the Senate floor — late in the evening, when nobody was around — presented the program Mr. Sorensen proposed.

Kennedy made his mark with "Profiles in Courage," published in January 1956. It was no great secret that Mr. Sorensen's intellect was an integral part of the book. "I've tried to keep it a secret," he said jokingly in his interview with The Times. But Mr. Sorensen drafted most of the chapters, and Kennedy paid him for his work. "I'm proud to say I played an important role," Mr. Sorensen said.

He spent most of the next four years working to make Kennedy the president of the United States. "We traveled together to all 50 states," Mr. Sorensen wrote in his book "Counselor: A Life at the Edge of History," a memoir published in 2008, "most of them more than once, initially just the two of us."

There was no entourage until Kennedy won the Democratic nomination in 1960, and it was not clear at the outset that he could do that, much less capture the White House. "Kennedy was dismissed as being too young, too Catholic, too little known, too inexperienced," Mr. Sorensen said in the interview.

As they crisscrossed the country and built grass-roots support, Mr. Sorensen began to find his voice, as well as Kennedy's. "He became a much better speaker," Mr. Sorensen said. "I became much more equipped to write speeches for him. Day after day after day after day, he's up there on the platform speaking, and I'm sitting in the audience listening, and I find out what works and what doesn't, what fits his style."

The Kennedy White House was never a Camelot, Mr. Sorensen said. "We obviously had our share of mistakes," he said. But he was not ashamed to say he had worshipped Kennedy, and when the president was assassinated in November 1963, he was devastated.

"It was a feeling of hopelessness," he said, "of anger, of bitterness. That there was nothing we could do. There was nothing I could do."

For more than 40 years after he left the White House, Mr. Sorensen practiced law, mostly as a senior partner at the New York firm of Paul, Weiss, Rifkind, Wharton & Garrison. He counseled Nelson Mandela of South Africa, Anwar Sadat of Egypt and other leaders. His life went on, in public and private; he was writing and making speeches well past his 80th birthday. But it was never the same.

In 1970, two years after Senator Robert F. Kennedy was assassinated on the presidential campaign trail, Mr. Sorensen ran for the Senate seat that Robert Kennedy had held in New York. The run was a mistake, he conceded. "I simply thought that if I were to carry on the Kennedy legacy, if I were to perpetuate the ideals of John Kennedy, as Robert Kennedy tried to do, that I would need to be in public office," he said. "Frankly, it was an act of hubris on my part."

In December 1976, out of the blue, President-elect Jimmy Carter offered Mr. Sorensen the post of director of central intelligence.

"I had to make a very quick decision," Mr. Sorensen remembered. "I did not know whether a lawyer and a moralist was suitable for a position that presides over all kinds of lawbreaking and immoral activities. But I wanted to be involved. I wanted to be back in government at a position where I could help things in a sound and progressive way, and so I said, 'Yes, I accept.'"

Opponents of the nomination pointed out a potential problem. More than 30 years before, after the end of World War II, Mr. Sorensen, not yet 18, had registered with his draft board as a conscientious objector to combat. President-elect Carter's top aide, Hamilton Jordan, placed an angry call to Mr. Sorensen, asking why he had not mentioned this suddenly salient fact before accepting the nomination.

"I said, 'I didn't know that the C.I.A. director was supposed to kill anybody,'" Mr. Sorensen recalled. "He wasn't too happy with that answer."

The nomination was withdrawn. That ended Mr. Sorensen's ambition to return to work in Washington.

A stroke in 2001 took away much of his eyesight, but he continued to write and speak and remain active in Democratic politics. He took a particular liking to a freshman senator from Illinois, Barack Obama, when he arrived in Washington in 2005. When Mr. Obama began running for president two years later, Mr. Sorensen endorsed his candidacy and campaigned for him.

"It reminds me of the way the young, previously unknown J.F.K. took off," Mr. Sorensen said in an interview with The Times in 2007.

A year after Mr. Obama took office, Mr. Sorensen acknowledged frustration with his presidency, particularly the decision to send more troops to Afghanistan, a conflict that he called "Obama's Vietnam." But, Mr. Sorensen said, "The foreign policy problems are more difficult than they were in Kennedy's day."

"I still think it was amazing that a man with his skin color — and also he was a liberal Democrat, let's face it — was elected," Mr. Sorensen said in 2009 in an interview in his Manhattan apartment, where a photograph of Mr. Obama joined a tableau of images from the Kennedy administration. "I haven't the slightest doubt that there are a lot of white men who still find it difficult to accept the fact, the reality, that we have a black president in this country."

Mr. Sorensen's 1949 marriage to Camilla Palmer and his 1964 marriage to Sara Elbery ended in divorce. In 1969 he married Gillian Martin. Besides his wife, he is survived by their daughter, three sons from his first marriage, a sister, a brother and seven grandchildren.

Despite his stroke in 2001 and his diminishing eyesight, Mr. Sorensen worked on "Counselor," his memoir, over the next six years. "I still believe that the mildest and most obscure of Americans can be rescued from oblivion by good luck, sudden changes in fortune, sudden encounters with heroes," he concluded. "I believe it because I lived it."

— By Tim Weiner

ANDY IRONS

A Surfing Champion's Early Death

JULY 24, 1978 - NOV. 2, 2010

ANDY IRONS, a three-time world surfing champion from Hawaii whose progressive wave riding and intense rivalry with Kelly Slater invigorated the sport, died on Nov. 2 in a Dallas hotel room while traveling home to Kauai. He was 32.

The cause was a mystery at first. There was no sign of trauma. Irons had struggled with alcohol and drug abuse, so toxicology tests were done. It was not until June 2011, however, that the family announced that he had had a heart attack caused by hardening of coronary arteries.

Irons had been scheduled to compete at the Rip Curl Pro Search, a professional competition in Puerto Rico. But he withdrew because of illness related to dengue fever, a virus transmitted by mosquitoes and associated with tropical areas. Symptoms include severe headache and muscle and bone pain.

While Irons was returning home, his illness worsened during a layover in Dallas. He was discovered in bed by staff members at the Grand Hyatt Hotel at the Dallas/Fort Worth International Airport after failing to respond to a wake-up call.

Irons, an intense and versatile competitor, blended power with innovative aerial maneuvers to signal a new era in the sport. He arrived on surfing's elite world tour in 1998 and rose to dominance. His younger brother, Bruce, followed him on tour. Both had been accomplished Hawaiian amateurs, sharpening their skills on waves along the north shore of Kauai, where they had grown up.

In Hawaii, where the sport was invented, Irons was revered.

"Back in his earliest amateur portion of his career, you knew he was going to be among Hawaii's best when he got to the international level," said Bernie Baker, a contest director in Hawaii who knew Irons for 20 years. The Irons brothers, he added, "were really the mold for all the great kids you see today around the world."

IN HIS ELEMENT: Irons signaled a new era in surfing, blending power and aerial maneuvers.

Irons won 20 events on the professional tour, including a duel with Slater, the nine-time world champion, in the final heat of the final event in 2003 at the celebrated Pipeline Masters. With that signature win, Irons claimed his second of three consecutive world titles, cemented his reputation as one of the sport's greatest surfers and punctured Slater's aura of invincibility.

The rivals engaged in a war of words in the news media before Slater wrested back the title in 2005. The two eventually became friends.

Irons's behavior baffled the surfing world in recent years. He abruptly quit the 2008 tour, citing competitive burnout, then sat out the 2009 season before making a comeback this year, winning the Billabong Pro Teahupoo in Tahiti in September.

Irons alluded to his demons in a documentary produced by his commercial sponsor Billabong, the apparel company. "If I didn't have surfing to get those out of my system," he said, "I would self-destruct."

Irons was expected to compete in the prestigious Vans Triple Crown of Surfing in November on Oahu's north shore, a three-event series he won four times from 2002 to 2006.

After Irons's death, the event in Puerto Rico, at Porta del Sol, was postponed, and surfers and fans held a "paddle out" memorial service. They gathered in the water, forming a circle, then joined hands and raised them to honor Irons.

Philip Andrew Irons was born on July 24, 1978, in Hanalei on Kauai. In addition to his brother, Irons is survived by his mother and father and his wife, Lyndie, who in December gave birth to the couple's first child, a boy.

— *By Matt Higgins*

JERRY BOCK

An Ear for Broadway

NOV. 23, 1928 - NOV. 3, 2010

JERRY BOCK, who wrote his first musical in public school and went on to compose the scores for some of Broadway's most successful shows, including "Fiddler on the Roof," "Fiorello!" and "She Loves Me," died on Nov. 3 in Mount Kisco, N.Y. He was 81 and lived in Manhattan.

His death, of heart failure at a Mount Kisco hospital, came 10 days after the death of Joseph Stein (see page 127), who wrote the book for "Fiddler."

Early on, Mr. Bock wrote music for television and did some work on Broadway, like the score for "Mr. Wonderful" (1956), which starred Sammy Davis Jr. The title song became a standard, along with "Too Close for Comfort."

But Mr. Bock's career shifted into high gear when he met the lyricist Sheldon Harnick. Their first effort, "The Body Beautiful" (1958), about the woes of a prizefight manager, closed in just a few weeks. But it paid a dividend: it caught the attention of George Abbott and Harold Prince, who asked Mr. Bock and Mr. Harnick to work on a new project, a musical about Fiorello H. LaGuardia, the former mayor of New York.

A show's score was not simply an accompaniment for spectacle; it grew naturally out of the story being told, and Mr. Bock proved adept at writing music that reflected both time and circumstance, in this case New York of the 1930s and '40s. "Fiorello!" opened to raves in 1959 and ran for nearly two years. Tom Bosley, who died on Oct. 19 (see page 117), played the feisty mayor.

With songs like "Little Tin Box," "Politics and Poker" and "The Very Next Man," the show was not only a box-office hit but also an award winner, capturing a Pulitzer Prize and six Tonys, including the one for best musical, sharing it with "The Sound of Music" by Rodgers and Hammerstein.

Mr. Bock and Mr. Harnick went on to write the music and lyrics for "Tenderloin" (1960), with Maurice Evans as a crusading clergyman, and "She Loves Me" (1963), with Barbara Cook and Daniel Massey as love-struck workers in a perfume shop in Budapest. Then, in 1964, came their greatest triumph, "Fiddler on the Roof."

With a book written by Mr. Stein and based on stories by Sholem Aleichem, "Fiddler" became an enduring musical portrait of a Jewish community under threat of expulsion by the Russian czar. The show ran until the summer of 1972, and for a while it was Broadway's record holder, with more than 3,200 performances.

Its songs became popular standards: "Sunrise, Sunset," "Matchmaker, Matchmaker," "Tradition" and, of course, the rueful "If I Were a Rich Man," sung by the show's star, Zero Mostel, as Tevye the penniless milkman.

Directed and choreographed by Jerome Robbins, the show received nine Tony Awards — Mr. Bock and Mr. Harnick won as best composer and lyricist — and "Fiddler" went on to become a theatrical staple, frequently revived in the United States and around the world.

In an interview after Mr. Bock's death, Mr. Harnick said he had usually woven in the lyrics after his partner had written the music. In one instance, he said, he became dangerously enraptured by his partner's music.

"I was working a number for 'She Loves Me,'" Mr. Harnick said. "It was called 'Tonight at 8.' I was walking around New York singing the melody to myself, trying to write lyrics, and I stepped in front of a truck. The driver slammed on the brakes, honked his horn. I looked up, startled, and then kept right on walking, working on the song. Jerry told me to be more careful."

WINNING TEAM: Mr. Bock, right, and Mr. Harnick working on "Fiddler" in 1964.

Jerrold Lewis Bock was born on Nov. 23, 1928, in New Haven, the only child of George Bock, a salesman, and the former Peggy Alpert. He grew up in Flushing, Queens, where he wrote his first musical, "My Dream," while still a student at Flushing High School.

When he was a senior at the University of Wisconsin, he and a classmate, Larry Holofcener, wrote another musical, "Big as Life," about Paul Bunyan. After graduation they both went to New York, where they were hired to write songs for "The Admiral Broadway Revue," which evolved into "Your Show of Shows," the popular vehicle for Sid Caesar and Imogene Coca.

In 1955 Mr. Bock and Mr. Holofcener contributed music and lyrics to the musical "Catch a Star," which was a flop, before joining with George Weiss to write the score for "Mr. Wonderful." Mr. Bock married Patricia Faggen in 1950. She survives him, along with their son, their daughter and a granddaughter.

For the Bock-Harnick team, "Fiddler" proved a hard act to follow. "The Apple Tree," a three-act musical drawn from stories by Mark Twain, Frank R. Stockton and Jules Feiffer, was a more modest success, opening in 1966 and closing the next year after 463 performances. Directed by Mike Nichols, it starred Alan Alda and Barbara Harris.

In his review in The Times, Walter Kerr noted that the show "starts high and then scoots downward on a pretty steep slope." The music and lyrics, however, brought Mr. Bock and Mr. Harnick Tony nominations.

They then collaborated on "The Rothschilds" (1970), with a book by Sherman Yellen, based on Frederic Morton's biography about the powerful banking family. The show, starring Hal Linden, Jill Clayburgh (see page 149) and Paul Hecht, overcame a mixed reception and ran for 505 performances. As the show was being prepared, Mr. Bock and Mr. Harnick had a bitter falling out over whether the director, Derek Golby, lacked experience and should be replaced by Michael Kidd.

Mr. Harnick finally went on record about the dispute in 2004. "We had severe artistic differences," he said. "I felt, as many on the staff did, that the director should be fired. Bock was a big defender of him. He was fired, and there was a very big strain between Jerry and I."

The disagreement ended the Bock-Harnick partnership. The bitterness eased over time, and the two men occasionally met to discuss revivals of their shows, but they never wrote another one together.

After "The Rothschilds," and after 14 tumultuous and largely successful years as a creative force on Broadway, Mr. Bock stepped away from the spotlight, more or less for good. A late-career accolade came this year, however, when he shared an Emmy for an original children's song. Its title: "A Fiddler Crab Am I."

— *By Robert Berkvist*

VIKTOR CHERNOMYRDIN

A Bridge Between Russias

APRIL 9, 1938 - NOV. 3, 2010

VIKTOR S. CHERNOMYRDIN, who served as Russia's prime minister during the turbulent transition to a free-market economy in the 1990s and who founded the state-owned gas monopoly Gazprom, died on Nov. 3. He was 72.

The Russian government, in announcing the death, gave no cause.

President Boris N. Yeltsin appointed Mr. Chernomyrdin (pronounced churn-o-MEER-dihn) prime minister in 1992, and he remained in that post through the most painful years of economic turmoil. At first a champion of market reform, he later said he thought that Western economic theory had done "more harm than good."

Mr. Chernomyrdin, a former Soviet oil and gas minister, resisted pressure from reformers to split the gas industry into smaller companies, as the oil and metals industries had done. That decision, to leave the gas industry intact, originated the blend of state control and capitalism that came into vogue under Vladimir V. Putin.

After his death, Mr. Chernomyrdin was recalled throughout Russia as a crucial mediating figure in a country caught between young, inexperienced reformers and the old guard of the Soviet elite.

"Chernomyrdin turned out to be the strongest, most effective and flexible bridge for the extraordinary work of our generation: raising and building a new Russia from the ruins of the totalitarian Soviet system," said Gennadi E. Burbulis, a former Yeltsin adviser and deputy in Russia's lower house of Parliament.

Viktor Stepanovich Chernomyrdin was born in a village in the central Russian Orenburg region on April 9, 1938, at the height of Stalin's purges. The son of a rural truck driver, he worked as a machine operator at an oil refinery and graduated from a technical institute through correspondence courses. He rose through the ranks in the Soviet gas industry, becoming minister the year Mikhail S. Gorbachev came to power.

He remained in charge in 1989, when the ministry was transformed into Gazprom, and made sure its assets stayed intact. When the Soviet Union collapsed in 1991, the supply of heating gas to apartments was never cut off, an accomplishment that the newspaper Nezavisimaya Gazeta credited to the fact that "sly Viktor Chernomyrdin managed to 'rebrand'" the gas ministry and protect it from perestroika-era pressure to sell it off.

Mr. Chernomyrdin enriched himself and his family in the process.

In 2001, Mr. Chernomyrdin was ranked No. 8 on Forbes magazine's list of Russian billionaires, with $1.1 billion. His garage housed a fleet of luxury cars.

Mr. Chernomyrdin was famous for malapropisms. "Government is not the organ in which one uses his tongue only," he told the Russian Parliament. Instructing his detractors, he said, "If your hands are itchy, scratch yourselves in other spots."

But former colleagues remembered a steely politician who helped anchor an often wayward government.

A NEW RUSSIA: Mr. Chernomyrdin helped his country make the transition to a free-market economy.

Vladimir A. Ryzhkov, a former member of Parliament, recalled the day in 1993 when a standoff between Mr. Yeltsin and members of Parliament had brought Russia near civil war. Mr. Chernomyrdin called a meeting with leaders of all of Russia's regions via speakerphone, chatting casually about coal stockpiles and pension payments and the weather.

"Then Chernomyrdin says: 'O.K., guys. You know what's going on in Moscow. I'll tell you what. I am the prime minister, and I have seven ministers sitting here next to me. We have a president, Boris Nikolayevich. He was popularly elected, we are supporting him. Get to work, support the president and don't make any unnecessary movements.'"

Mr. Ryzhkov, who recounted the episode in a radio interview, said the meeting was the "decisive moment" in the crisis.

Two years later, Mr. Chernomyrdin negotiated with the Chechen rebel leader Shamil Basayev, who was holding up to 2,000 hostages in the city of Budyonnovsk. The negotiations were carried live on television, and Russians watched in frozen horror as Mr. Chernomyrdin barked into the phone at Mr. Basayev.

Most of the hostages were released, and Russians credited Mr. Chernomyrdin. "He was very calm," Katya Amachenova, a secretary, said at the time. "He acted like a leader. We haven't seen that in a while."

While serving as prime minister, Mr. Chernomyrdin remained so closely associated with Gazprom that the political party he founded, Our Home Is Russia, was jokingly referred to as "Our Home is Gazprom." His company was allowed to expand lavishly despite falling behind on tax payments.

Mr. Yeltsin fired Mr. Chernomyrdin as prime minister in 1998 but tried to bring him back as the country spiraled into economic crisis. By that point, however, the president's authority was on the wane, and Parliament blocked Mr. Chernomyrdin's appointment.

When Mr. Putin came to power, he replaced Mr. Chernomyrdin as chairman of Gazprom with a little-known adviser, Dmitri A. Medvedev, now the president of Russia. Largely shut out of the halls of power, Mr. Chernomyrdin put his experience in the oil and gas industry to use as ambassador to Ukraine, whose pipelines carry Russian gas to Europe. From 2001 until his retirement in 2009 he played a crucial role in disputes over natural gas prices that caused energy flows to Europe to be shut off on several occasions.

Mr. Chernomyrdin is survived by two sons. His wife of 50 years, Valentina, died in March.

Mr. Chernomyrdin will long be remembered for his fatalistic commentary on a botched monetary overhaul carried out by the Russian Central Bank in 1993. "We wanted to do it better," he declared at a news conference, "but it turned out as usual."

— *By Ellen Barry and Michael Schwirtz*

SPARKY ANDERSON

He 'Let 'Em Win a Lot'

FEB. 22, 1934 - NOV. 4, 2010

SPARKY ANDERSON, who managed Cincinnati's powerful Big Red Machine to baseball dominance in the 1970s and became the first manager to win World Series championships in both the National and American Leagues, died on Nov. 4 at his home in Thousand Oaks, Calif. He was 76.

His death was announced by the Reds, whom he managed to championships in 1975 and '76, and the Detroit Tigers, whom he took to a World Series title in 1984. Anderson had been placed in hospice care at his home because of complications of dementia, his family said in a statement.

Anderson was only 35 when he was named manager of the Reds for the 1970 season, having spent nearly his entire baseball career in the minor leagues.

"Everybody knows the story about how the headline in the paper the day I was hired read, 'Sparky Who?'" he once told The Cincinnati Enquirer. But he began to look the part of a grizzled veteran manager, his hair turning prematurely white and his craggy features suggesting a budding Casey Stengel.

Anderson drew on his keen sense of baseball strategy, his ability to deal with players as individuals and his obsession with winning. He was sometimes called Captain Hook for removing his starting pitchers at the first signs of trouble, but his maneuvering previewed the accepted wisdom of today's game.

The Big Red Machine featured a lineup with the future Hall of Famers Johnny Bench, Joe Morgan and Tony Perez along with Pete Rose, Ken Griffey Sr., George Foster, Dave Concepcion and Cesar Geronimo.

For all his success, Anderson preferred to leave the accolades to his players.

"There's two kind of manager," he said when he was inducted into the Baseball Hall of Fame by the Veterans Committee in 2000. "One, it ain't very smart. He gets bad players, loses games and gets fired. There was somebody like me that I was a genius. I got good players, stayed out of the way, let 'em win a lot, and then just hung around for 26 years."

As his Cooperstown speech suggested, while Anderson was eminently quotable, he was hardly precise with his diction. His wife, Carol, told him to take grammar lessons. His response, as cited by Major League Baseball's Web site: "I told her it ain't gonna help me. Or should I say, 'It ain't gonna help me none?'"

Anderson managed the Cincinnati Reds to four pennants and two World Series titles in the 1970s, a memorable seven-game victory over the Boston Red Sox in 1975 and a sweep of the Yankees in 1976.

After nine years in Cincinnati, he managed Detroit for 16 1/2 seasons, capturing his third World Series championship when the 1984 Tigers defeated the San Diego Padres in five games.

When he retired after the 1995 season, Anderson had won the most games of any manager in both Reds and Tigers history, and his 2,194 victories over all placed him third on the career list, behind Connie Mack and John McGraw. He is now No. 6.

George Lee Anderson was born on Feb. 22, 1934, in Bridgewater, S.D., where his father, LeRoy, painted farmhouses and silos. When he was 8, his family moved to Los Angeles, and he became a batboy for the University of Southern California teams coached by Rod Dedeaux, one of the best-known figures in college baseball.

Anderson played the infield for his high school team, then signed with the Brooklyn Dodgers' minor league system in 1953. While with the Dodgers' Fort Worth farm team, he became known as Sparky for his fiery style.

After being traded to the Phillies' organization, he made it to the major leagues in 1959, a 5-foot-9-inch, 170-pound second baseman who hit .218 with no home runs for a last-place Philadelphia team. Then it was back to the minors, where Anderson played the infield once more and managed.

Anderson was a coach for the expansion San Diego Padres in 1969. Then came the stunning decision by Bob Howsam, the Reds' general manager, to give him the Cincinnati managing job. Anderson was virtually unknown to Reds fans, but Howsam, while previously serving as the St. Louis Cardinals' general manager, had been impressed by his managing skills with their Rock Hill, S.C., farm team.

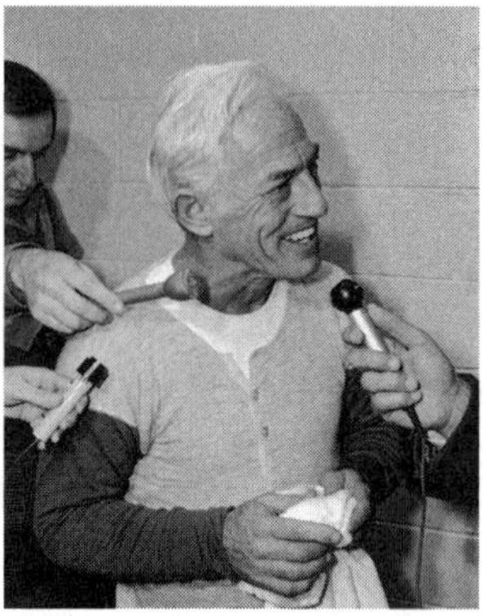

SWEEP: Anderson after his Reds beat the Yankees in the 1976 World Series.

Anderson managed the Reds to pennants in 1970 and 1972, though they were beaten both times in the World Series.

"My rookie year was his first year," Don Gullett, a Reds pitching ace of the 1970s, told The Cincinnati Post in 2000. "Here was a guy coming right out of the minor leagues, and when that happens there's always a question whether he can handle major leaguers.

"But I knew from spring training on that he could do it," Gullett continued, "and he proved it when he won 102 games his first year. He knew his personnel, knew how to motivate, how to discipline, how to push all the right buttons."

The Reds finished second in the National League West to the Los Angeles Dodgers in 1977 and '78. Dick Wagner, concluding his first year as general manager after taking over from Howsam, fired Anderson in November 1978.

Anderson became the Tigers' manager in June 1979 and built on a foundation that included Alan Trammell at shortstop, Lou Whitaker at second base, Kirk Gibson in the outfield and Jack Morris on the pitching staff. His 1984 Tigers got off to a 35-5 start on their way to a World Series championship.

"I wanted to prove the Reds wrong for firing me," Anderson said in his memoir "They Call Me Sparky," written with Dan Ewald (1998). "When the Tigers won in '84, I finally felt vindicated. It wasn't until years after that, though, before I released all the bitterness I should never have allowed to creep into my mind in the first place."

During spring training in 1995, when the club owners brought in replacement players to take the spots of striking major leaguers, Anderson was the only manager who refused to take them on, citing the integrity of the game. He went on unpaid leave, then returned when the regular players came back before the delayed opening of the season. After the Tigers finished fourth in the American League East in 1995, Anderson resigned amid speculation that he would be fired.

Anderson had a record of 2,194-1,834 for his 26 seasons as a manager of both the Reds and the Tigers. Tony La Russa, who won the World Series with the Oakland Athletics in 1989 and the Cardinals in 2006, is the only other manager to have captured World Series championships with teams from both leagues.

In addition to his wife, Carol, Anderson is survived by his sons, his daughter and many grandchildren.

When Anderson was voted into the Hall of Fame in 2001, he chose a Reds cap for his plaque to go with his Hall ring. That was a tribute to Howsam, the Cincinnati general manager who gave a career minor leaguer a chance at the big leagues.

"I never wore a World Series ring," Anderson told The Associated Press. "I will wear this ring until I die."

— *By Richard Goldstein*

JILL CLAYBURGH

Updating the Leading Lady

APRIL 30, 1944 - NOV. 5, 2010

JILL CLAYBURGH, an Oscar-nominated actress known for portraying strong, independent women, most indelibly in "An Unmarried Woman," died on Nov. 5 at her home in Lakeville, Conn. She was 66.

The cause was chronic leukemia, with which she had lived for 21 years, her husband, the playwright David Rabe, said.

Ms. Clayburgh, who began her acting career in the late 1960s, was among the first generation of young actresses — including Ellen Burstyn, Carrie Snodgress and Marsha Mason — to portray characters sprung from the new feminist ethos: smart, capable and gritty, sometimes neurotic, but no less glamorous for all that.

"I guess people look at me and they think I'm a ladylike character," Ms. Clayburgh told The New York Times in 1982. "But it's not what I do best. I do best with characters who are coming apart at the seams."

She was probably best known for her starring role in "An Unmarried Woman," Paul Mazursky's 1978 film about a New Yorker who must right herself after her husband leaves her for another woman. Ms. Clayburgh was nominated for an Academy Award for the performance.

She received another Oscar nomination for "Starting Over" (1979), directed by Alan J. Pakula, in which she played a teacher who embarks on a relationship with a newly divorced man played by Burt Reynolds.

Ms. Clayburgh had earlier starred with Mr. Reynolds in "Semi-Tough" (1977). In 1980 she

APPRECIATION

That Unforgettable 'Unmarried Woman'

In the most famous scene in "An Unmarried Woman," Erica, the title character played by Jill Clayburgh, reacts to the news that her husband wants to leave her with such naturalness, confusion and wounded pride that she captured the imagination of a generation.

"As Miss Clayburgh plays this scene," the critic Vincent Canby wrote in The New York Times in 1978, "one has a vision of all the immutable things that can be destroyed in less than a minute, from landscapes and ships and reputations to perfect marriages."

But she also proved in this, her most influential movie, that a reputation could be made in less than a minute, too.

Has any actor's career ever been more powerfully affected by a prefix? It was the "un" in "Unmarried" that established Ms. Clayburgh's creative power. Women's roles had been changing irrevocably, and a new assertiveness was being established and understood. But the usual story lines of that era followed female characters' quests for independence and authority. Heroines rebelled. They picked themselves up and moved out. They took action.

(continued on page 150)

(continued from page 149)

Their roles were often sharply defined, but Erica's was not. Paul Mazursky, the writer and director, had a divorced friend who described herself as "an unmarried woman" on a mortgage application. Extrapolating from that, he envisioned the story of a Manhattan wife set adrift. But Ms. Clayburgh's shaping of the character was unmistakably her own, just as surely as its impact on female movie audiences was universal. And the unaffected nature of the performance became its most distinctive feature. Ms. Clayburgh didn't have the tics of Diane Keaton, the steel of Jane Fonda, the feistiness of Sally Field, the uncanny adaptability of Meryl Streep. Ms. Clayburgh simply had the gift of resembling a real person undergoing life-altering change. In her signature role, that was enough.

Ms. Clayburgh had been on stage and screen for a decade before giving this definitive performance. But she could be awkwardly miscast and at first often was. She was blond, willowy and beautiful, but she was about as much like Carole Lombard as James Brolin was like Clark Gable ("Gable and Lombard," 1976). Without "An Unmarried Woman" she might never have found her niche.

But once she did, she began a streak. She went on to play an opera star in Bernardo Bertolucci's 1979 "Luna," one of the most conversation-stopping films ever to open the New York Film Festival. She made widely seen comedies about smart, interesting women ("Starting Over," "It's My Turn"). She even turned up on the Supreme Court ("First Monday in October"), a likable presence even in highly unlikely circumstances. "The F.B.I. is wrong in reporting to you that I have no children," her character had to tell senators in the film. "Ideas are my children, and I have hundreds of them."

Then she and her husband, the playwright David Rabe, had real children, Lily and Michael. And though Ms. Clayburgh kept working, her public presence grew more intermittent, the available film roles more motherly or eccentric. (She appeared in the 2006 film version of Augusten Burroughs's "Running With Scissors.") She was so greatly missed that any major appearances were apt to be described as comebacks, but the roles that should have been welcoming hardly existed anymore. Only in life did anyone wonder what had become of all those Ericas 30 years later.

She remained elegant, lovely and so recognizable that she became accustomed to being treated as an avatar. "My God, you've defined my entire life for me," one weeping "Unmarried Woman" fan told her in 2002, and that experience was apparently not unusual for her. When she and Lily, an actress, roomed together in Manhattan in 2005 as both of them prepared for stage appearances, a writer for The Times visited Ms. Clayburgh and still saw her unforgettable movie persona.

"Jill Clayburgh appears to be living in an updated Jill Clayburgh vehicle," Nancy Hass wrote. "Fluttery-yet-determined mom flees comfortable exurban married life to share tiny Manhattan apartment of headstrong, aspiring-actress daughter. Conflict, hilarity and, of course, self-actualization ensue."

For Jill Clayburgh, in both her life and work, that's just what happened.

— *By Janet Maslin*

appeared opposite Michael Douglas in "It's My Turn" and, in 1981, opposite Walter Matthau in "First Monday in October," in which she played the first woman appointed to the United States Supreme Court. In "I'm Dancing as Fast as I Can," a 1982 adaptation of a memoir by Barbara Gordon, Ms. Clayburgh was a driven career woman addicted to Valium.

Jill Clayburgh was born in Manhattan on April 30, 1944, the daughter of Albert, an industrial textile salesman, and Julie Clayburgh. She earned a bachelor's degree in theater from Sarah Lawrence College in 1966.

Ms. Clayburgh made her Broadway debut in 1968 in "The Sudden & Accidental Re-Education of Horse Johnson," a play starring Jack Klugman that ran for five performances. Her other Broadway credits included more successful shows like the Jerry Bock (see page 143) and Sheldon Harnick musical "The Rothschilds" (1970); the Stephen Schwartz musical "Pippin" (1972); and a 1984 revival of Noël Coward's "Design for Living," which also starred Frank Langella and Raul Julia.

Her last Broadway appearance, in 2006, was in a revival of "Barefoot in the Park" at the Cort Theater, with Tony Roberts and Amanda Peet.

Besides Mr. Rabe, whom she married in 1978, Ms. Clayburgh is survived by a daughter, the actress Lily Rabe; a son; a stepson; and a brother.

Her many television credits include guest appearances on "Law & Order," "The Practice" and "Nip/Tuck," and a recurring role on "Ally McBeal" as Ally's mother, Jeannie. Most recently Ms. Clayburgh was a member of the regular cast of "Dirty Sexy Money," broadcast from 2007 to 2009 on ABC.

Despite her acclaim, Ms. Clayburgh, by all appearances, had a healthy sense of herself. "People think about me, 'This wonderful lucky woman, she's got it all,'" she told The New York Times in 1982. "But gee, that's how I feel about Meryl Streep."

— *By Margalit Fox*

SHIRLEY VERRETT

A Soprano Who Soared Over Hurdles

MAY 31, 1931 - NOV. 5, 2010

SHIRLEY VERRETT, the vocally lustrous and dramatically compelling American opera singer who began as a mezzo-soprano and went on to sing soprano roles to international acclaim, died on Nov. 5 at her home in Ann Arbor, Mich. She was 79.

The cause was heart failure after several months of illness, her daughter, Francesca LoMonaco, said.

In her prime years Ms. Verrett was a complete and distinctive operatic artist. She had a plush, powerful voice, thorough musicianship, insightful dramatic skills, charisma and beauty. If she never quite reached mythic status, she came close.

After singing the soprano role of Lady Macbeth in a landmark 1975 production of Verdi's "Macbeth" at La Scala in Milan, demanding Milanese critics and impassioned Italian opera fans called her La Nera Callas (the Black Callas) and flocked to Ms. Verrett's every performance.

Her Lady Macbeth is preserved on a classic 1976 Deutsche Grammophon recording, conducted by Claudio Abbado. And in the early 1980s, she was so popular in Paris that she lived there with her family for three years.

In the early days, like black artists before her, Ms. Verrett experienced racial prejudice, as she recounts in her memoir, "I Never Walked Alone." In 1959 the conductor Leopold Stokowski hired her to sing the Wood Dove in a performance of Schoenberg's "Gurrelieder" with the Houston Symphony, but the orchestra's board would not allow a black soloist to appear. To make amends, a shaken Stokowski took Ms. Verrett to the Philadelphia Orchestra for a performance of Falla's "Amor Brujo," which led to a fine recording.

By her own admission, Ms. Verrett's singing was inconsistent. Even some admiring critics thought that she had made a mistake by singing soprano repertory after establishing herself as one of the premiere mezzo-sopranos of her generation, riveting as Bizet's Carmen and Saint-Saëns's Delila. A contingent of vocal buffs thought that her voice had developed breaks and separated into distinct registers.

To Ms. Verrett the problem was not the nature of her voice but her health. During the peak years she suffered from allergies to mold spores that could clog her bronchial tubes. She could not predict when her allergies would erupt. In 1976, just six weeks after singing Adalgisa in Bellini's "Norma" at the Metropolitan Opera (a role traditionally performed by mezzo-sopranos), she sang the daunting soprano title role on tour with the Met, including a performance in Boston that earned a frenzied ovation. Yet, in 1979, when New Yorkers finally had the chance to hear Ms. Verrett's Norma at the Met, her allergies acted up and undermined her singing, as Ms. Verrett recalled in her memoir. Still, among her 126 performances with the Met, there were many triumphs.

POWERFUL VOICE: Ms. Verrett in the Met's historic 1973 production of "Troyens."

In 1973, when the company opened its historic production of Berlioz's "Troyens," starring Jon Vickers as Aeneas, Ms. Verrett sang not only the role of Cassandra in Part I of this epic opera, but also Dido in Part II, taking the place of the mezzo-soprano Christa Ludwig, who had withdrawn because of an illness. The performance was a tour de force that entered Met annals.

And in the Met's 1978-79 season, Ms. Verrett sang Tosca to Luciano Pavarotti's Cavaradossi in a production of Puccini's "Tosca" that was broadcast live on public television and is available on a Decca DVD.

At her best, Ms. Verrett could sing with both mellow richness and chilling power. Her full-voiced top notes easily cut through the orchestral outbursts in Verdi's "Aida." Yet as Lady Macbeth, during the "Sleepwalking Scene," Ms. Verrett could end the character's haunting music with an ethereal final phrase capped by soft, shimmering high D-flat.

Shirley Verrett was born on May 31, 1931, in New Orleans, one of five children. Her parents, Leon Solomon Verrett and the former Elvira Harris, were strict Seventh-day Adventists. Her father, who ran a construction company and moved the family to Los Angeles when Ms. Verrett was a young girl, was a decent man, Ms. Verrett recalled in her book, though he routinely punished his children by strapping them on the legs.

Her parents encouraged Ms. Verrett's talent but wanted her to pursue a concert career in the mold of Marian Anderson. They disapproved of opera.

When they made their first trip to Europe in 1962 to hear their daughter sing the title role in "Carmen" at the Spoleto Festival, they "got down on their knees and prayed for forgiveness," Ms. Verrett wrote.

In 1951, Ms. Verrett married James Carter, who was 14 years her senior and proved a controlling and abusive husband. Ms. Verrett left that impulsive marriage when she discovered a gun under her husband's pillow. During the first years of her career she was known as Shirley Verrett-Carter.

In 1963 she married Lou LoMonaco, an artist, who survives her, along with her daughter, who was adopted, and a granddaughter.

Her happy marriage came two years after she won the Metropolitan Opera National Council Auditions, having studied at the Juilliard School. Carmen was the role of her 1968 Met debut.

During the late 1970s and 1980s, Ms. Verrett had a close association with Sarah Caldwell, the conductor and stage director who ran the Opera Company of Boston, and won legions of fans in New England.

In 1981, in what was then a bold act of colorblind casting, Ms. Caldwell had Ms. Verrett sing Desdemona in Verdi's "Otello," opposite the tenor James McCracken in the title role. Ms. Verrett's skin color was only somewhat lightened to portray Desdemona. The intensity and vulnerability of her singing cut to the core of the character of the winsome, naïve Desdemona.

Ms. Verrett also sustained a lively rivalry with another black mezzo-soprano-turned-soprano, Grace Bumbry. In later years, she was a professor of voice at the University of Michigan.

In 1994, about to turn 63 and with opera well behind her, Ms. Verrett made her Broadway debut as Nettie Fowler in the Tony Award-winning production of Rodgers and Hammerstein's "Carousel" at Lincoln Center. Nettie's defining moment comes when she sings "You'll Never Walk Alone," which Ms. Verrett adapted for the title of her memoir.

— *By Anthony Tommasini*

ROBBINS BARSTOW

The Auteur of Home Movies

OCT. 24, 1919 - NOV. 7, 2010

Robbins Barstow, a Connecticut man who, movie camera whirring, documented every aspect of his family's life for decades, yielding a vast body of work that formed the cornerstone of the recent home-movie revival and has lately garnered a huge following online, died on Nov. 7 at his home in Hartford. He was 91.

By day, Robbins Barstow was the director of professional development for the Connecticut Education Association, a state teachers' union. By night and in retirement, he was the auteur of tenderly shot documentaries, many of them travelogues, chronicling the ordinary doings of ordinary people in mid-century America.

Mr. Barstow made more than a hundred films in the course of eight decades. In 2008, his best-known, "Disneyland Dream" (1956), a 30-minute account of a family vacation, was named to the National Film Registry of the Library of Congress.

Now comprising 525 films, the registry is heavy with Hollywood masterworks, earmarked for preservation for their cultural or artistic significance. Mr. Barstow's picture is one of the few amateur works on the list; the others include the

SOCIAL DOCUMENT: Mr. Barstow and his family at Disneyland in 1956. "Disneyland Dream," his 30-minute home movie of a family vacation, is part of the National Film Registry.

1963 Zapruder film of the assassination of John F. Kennedy.

In naming "Disneyland Dream" to the registry, the Library of Congress called it "a priceless and authentic record of time and place." The movie is also noteworthy as the uncredited first screen appearance of a young Disneyland employee named Steve Martin, then 11, caught by Mr. Barstow's camera as the boy hawked guidebooks. Mr. Barstow discovered as much only recently, when Mr. Martin — yes, that Steve Martin — wrote to him after seeing the film.

Mr. Barstow, who got his first movie camera at 10, was an ardent champion of home moviemaking. He was also an ardent disseminator of his work, first through neighborhood screenings and later through public-access television. Several years ago, he posted his films on the Internet at archive.org, a digital repository of film, video and much else.

Sixteen of Mr. Barstow's movies can be seen on the site, including "Disneyland Dream," which has been downloaded more than 76,000 times. Another, "Tarzan and the Rocky Gorge" (1936), a stirring jungle drama he made at 16 in the Connecticut woods, has been downloaded more than 150,000 times.

The mere thought of home movies is enough to send most people screaming into the street. But in the 1990s the films began to be rehabilitated, and today are prized by archivists, folklorists and historians as social documents.

Mr. Barstow's films chronicle the stuff of daily life, but they do so artfully, with strong narrative elements. He sometimes "directed" his family, as in a dramatic scene from "Disneyland Dream" in which, on learning they have won a trip to Anaheim, they swoon with theatrical joy on the front lawn.

Though most of his films were silent, Mr. Barstow later added voice-over soundtracks. Before that, he recited live oral narration, carefully scripted and timed, whenever he showed a film.

"It's not raw footage," Dwight Swanson, a board member of the Center for Home Movies, said on Thursday. "He very self-consciously created it and edited it and added special effects." The center sponsors Home Movie Day, an annual celebration of amateur filmmaking in cities around the world. Mr. Barstow was an active participant in the organization.

Robbins Wolcott Barstow Jr. was born on Oct. 24, 1919, in Woodstock, Vt., and was reared in Hartford. His father, a third-generation Congregational minister, was president of what is now the Hartford Seminary.

The younger Mr. Barstow earned a bachelor's degree in English and philosophy from Dartmouth, a master's in education and history from New York University and a Ph.D. in educational administration from the University of Connecticut.

"Disneyland Dream" was born of a nationwide contest. In 1956, the 3M Company offered free trips to Disneyland to the 25 families who best expressed why they loved its signature product, Scotch Tape.

All the Barstows — Mr. Barstow; his wife, Meg; and their three children, Mary, 11; David, 8; and Dan, 4 — entered. So confident were they of victory that Mr. Barstow filmed them composing their submissions round the dining-room table. Then he filmed the postman carrying them away.

Before long, a prize is awarded to little Dan. (His winning entry: "I like 'Scotch' brand cellophane tape because when some things tear then I can just use it.") Swooning ensues. The film goes on to record the family's departure amid confetti-throwing neighbors; Southern California attractions like Knott's Berry Farm; and, finally, Disneyland, then just a year old.

Mr. Barstow was also a conservationist with a special interest in whales; he made several films about endangered species and helped found Cetacean Society International.

His other movies include "Family Camping Through 48 States," Parts 1 and 2 (1957-61).

Mr. Barstow's survivors include the original cast of "Disneyland Dream": his wife, the former Margaret Vanderbeek, whom he married in 1942; his sons and his daughter. He is also survived by both subjects of "Touring Paris With Two Grandchildren" (1992); and a great-grandchild.

Originally, the pleasure in Mr. Barstow's films lay in their wide-eyed enjoyment of the larger world — a world that many mid-century Americans would not otherwise have had the chance to see.

Today, there is pleasure of a bittersweet kind. There is the tree-lined street and the white clapboard house. There is the happy family, dressed alike in Davy Crockett jackets. There are the neighbors, come to wish them godspeed.

As the movie unfolds in faded color on the computer screen, the Barstows' world is as distant and enchanted for modern viewers as Disneyland was for them.

— *By Margalit Fox*

JACK LEVINE

A Very Pointed Paint Brush

JAN. 3, 1915 - NOV. 8, 2010

JACK LEVINE, an unrepentant and much-admired realist artist whose crowded history paintings skewered plutocrats, crooked politicians and human folly, died on Nov. 8 at his home in Manhattan. He was 95. Mr. Levine despised abstract art and bucked the art world's movement toward it, drawing inspiration instead from old masters like Titian and Velázquez. He specialized in satiric tableaus and sharp social commentary directed at big business, political corruption, militarism and racism, with something left over for the comic spectacle of the human race on parade.

"I felt from my early days that good and bad weren't simply aesthetic questions," he told American Artist magazine in 1985. "You have to defend the innocent and flay the guilty."

Mr. Levine burst onto the American art scene in 1937 with a scathing triple portrait remarkable for its bravura brushwork and gleeful vitriol. Titled "The Feast of Pure Reason," it depicted a police officer, a capitalist and a politician seated at a table, their bloated faces oozing malice. Hanging conspicuously in the background was an American flag.

"It is my privilege as an artist to put these gentlemen on trial, to give them every ingratiating characteristic they might normally have, and then present them, smiles, benevolence and all, leaving it up to the spectator to judge the merits of the case," Mr. Levine once said.

The painting was a hot potato. After it was acquired by the Museum of Modern Art in New York, the trustees debated fiercely about whether to exhibit it, lest it offend principal donors.

Similar arguments surrounded Mr. Levine's later work, notably "Welcome Home" (1946). The painting shows an armchair general being honored at an expensive restaurant, a wad of food in one cheek. On his right sits a bored socialite. Two decrepit businessmen in tuxedos make up the rest of the party. The central figure, Mr. Levine said, was "the big slob who is vice president of the Second National Bank and the president of the Chamber of Commerce, only now he's been in the Army."

When "Welcome Home" was included in an exhibition of American culture in Moscow in 1959, the chairman of the House Committee on Un-American Activities mounted a campaign to have it removed. President Dwight D. Eisenhower said, "It looks more like a lampoon than art, as far as I am concerned," but refused to intervene.

The uproar made Mr. Levine a star in the art world. He later told an interviewer, "You get denounced by the president of the United States, you've hit the top."

Jack Levine was born on Jan. 3, 1915, and spent his early childhood in the South End of Boston, the youngest of eight children of immigrant parents from Lithuania. His father was a shoemaker. When he was 8, the family moved to the Roxbury neighborhood, and he began taking children's art classes at the Boston Museum of Art with his friend Hyman Bloom, who also became a well-known painter. The two friends later studied with Harold Zimmerman, a young painter from the museum's art school, at a settlement house in Roxbury.

By a stroke of good fortune, Denman Ross, a patrician professor in Harvard's art department, took Mr. Zimmerman and his two students under his wing. He took Mr. Levine to his home to look at the art treasures on the walls, organized a showing of his drawings at the Fogg Museum while he was still in high school and provided him with a stipend and a studio.

"It is my privilege as an artist to put these gentlemen on trial, to give them every ingratiating characteristic they might normally have, and then present them, smiles, benevolence and all, leaving it up to the spectator to judge the merits of the case," Mr. Levine once said.

With the Depression raging, Mr. Levine signed on with the Works Progress Administration as an artist and, in 1936, two of his paintings were included in "New Horizons in American Art," an exhibition of W.P.A. art at the Museum of Modern Art. After completing "The Feast of Pure Reason," he received his first one-man show at the Downtown Gallery in New York in 1939.

Inspired by old masters like Titian, Velázquez and Goya, and German expressionists like

George Grosz and Oskar Kokoschka, Mr. Levine took a lofty view of art and the artist's mission. "I took my place in the late 1930s as part of the general uprising of social consciousness in art and literature," he said. "We were all making a point. We had a feeling of confidence in our ability to do something about the world."

After the death of his father in 1939, Mr. Levine, a nonobservant Jew, experimented with several formal, Rembrandtesque portraits of Jewish sages and kings. "I think these are the flip side of the satirical work," said Norman Kleeblatt, the chief curator of the Jewish Museum. "They are internal and highly personal."

Mr. Levine later explored his Jewish heritage in a number of paintings on biblical themes, notably "Cain and Abel" (1961) and "David and Saul" (1989).

SATIRICAL REALIST: Mr. Levine in his studio in 1978.

Mr. Levine was drafted into the Army in 1942 and, after doing camouflage painting, spent the war as a clerk on Ascension Island in the South Atlantic. In 1946 he married Ruth Gikow, a painter, who died in 1982. Their daughter survives him, as do two grandchildren.

He returned from the war to an art world in the throes of transformation, as Abstract Expressionism became the dominant painting style, displacing realists like Mr. Levine. He did not go quietly. He referred to abstract painters as "space cadets." Later styles likewise failed to impress him.

Despite retrospective exhibitions at the Institute of Contemporary Art in Boston in 1952 and the Jewish Museum in New York in 1978, the onward march of abstraction and avant-gardism relegated him to the margins.

"I made quite a splash in the art world in the 1930s, and it seems to me that every year since I have become less and less well known," Mr. Levine told David Sutherland, the director and producer of the 1985 documentary "Jack Levine: Feast of Pure Reason."

True to his first artistic impulses, Mr. Levine continued to produce work in a caustic vein. Some works were overtly political, like "Election Night" (1954), a squalid political tableau, and "Birmingham '63," a savage depiction of guard dogs attacking a group of black men. Others were bustling social panoramas in the spirit of Daumier.

"Gangster Funeral," painted in the early 1950s, depicted a crew of thugs in formal attire gathered at the coffin of a slain mob boss. In the grandly conceived diptych "Panethnikon" (1978), Mr. Levine — depicting a semifictionalized gathering of the United Nations Security Council — presented an exuberant portrait of the human race, whose identifiable members included Leonid Brezhnev, Idi Amin and Ibn Saud.

"He never gave up," said Patricia Hills, a professor of art history at Boston University. "He kept the faith. He continued a great tradition of painting, of showing the foibles of people, the human drama and especially the foibles of powerful people."

He spoke of what underlies his art in a speech in 1976. "I am primarily concerned with the condition of man," Mr. Levine said. "The satirical direction I have chosen is an indication of my disappointment in man, which is the opposite way of saying that I have high expectations for the human race."

— *By William Grimes*

ROBIN DAY

His Legacy Is Stacked in Corners

MAY 25, 1915 - NOV. 9, 2010

ROBIN DAY, perhaps Britain's most influential furniture designer since World War II, whose spare, practical and affordable inventions were exemplified by the now ubiquitous "polyprop" chair, died Nov. 9 at his home in Chichester, England. He was 95.

Rare is the human backside that hasn't found solace and support in Mr. Day's most famous creation, a molded polypropylene shell fastened to an enameled bent tubular steel base that has become familiar seating in schools, churches, offices, auditoriums, home patios, kitchens, dens, bedrooms and basements around the world.

Comfortable, durable, inexpensive, lightweight, easy to clean and easy to store, the stackable polyprop chair (or polychair) was developed in 1962 and subsequently mass-produced by Hille, a British manufacturer, whose Web site says the company has sold 14 million of them and produces half a million more each year.

A MODEST BEAUTY: Function was paramount for Mr. Day, shown with his iconic chair.

In 2009, the chair was featured on a first-class British stamp, one of eight examples of memorable British design to be so honored that year. (The others included the miniskirt, the red phone kiosk, the Concorde supersonic jet and the Mini automobile.)

"Robin Day's polypropylene chair is one of those exceptional objects that can genuinely carry the burden of being labeled a humble masterpiece," Deyan Sudjic, director of the Design Museum in London, said after Mr. Day's death.

Mr. Day was among those postwar designers who rejected the ponderous, heavyweight pieces that had characterized home furnishings until then. As he said in 1955, "What one needs in today's small rooms is to see over and under one's furniture."

Taking advantage of new lightweight materials and manufacturing processes, and applying a modern aesthetic in which function and flexibility were crucial, Mr. Day designed storage units, tables, desks, trays, television lounge chairs and other furnishings. He first came to prominence when he and a partner, Clive Latimer, designed a storage system that in 1948 was a winner at the International Competition for Low-Cost Furniture, receiving their $5,000 prize at the Museum of Modern Art in New York.

Both he and his wife, Lucienne Day, a textiles designer, showed their work at the 1951 Festival of Britain, a futuristic display of British ingenuity intended to help propel England from its postwar doldrums.

Mr. Day exhibited his steel and plywood furniture in the Homes and Gardens Pavilion (he also designed the pavilion itself), alongside his wife's vibrantly patterned fabrics and wallpapers. After the festival, the Days were design stars.

"They probably did more than anyone else to lighten and brighten Britain during the postwar period," the design historian Pat Kirkham said in a documentary about the couple that was completed this year.

They were celebrities, interviewed in magazines, photographed at parties, becoming as well known a couple in England as Charles and Ray Eames were in the United States, to whom they were often compared, though the comparison was not entirely just. Though the Days's aesthetics were complementary and they frequently traded ideas, they, unlike the Eameses, worked separately and in distinct fields.

Ronald Henry Day was born into a working-class family — his father was a police constable — on May 25, 1915, in High Wycombe, Buckinghamshire, a town west of London known for furniture production. He attended the Royal College of Art, where he met his wife. They married in 1942. Lucienne Day died this year. Mr. Day is survived by a daughter and a brother.

In contrast with his glamorous image, Mr. Day, an avid mountain climber, considered his work to be just that: work. He never employed a staff, never adopted the computer as a design tool and thought nothing of sitting at the drawing table for 12, 14 or 16 hours a day.

The design philosophy that made him famous was utilitarian; furniture should be functional above all, he believed. It was an outlook that led him to polypropylene, a thermoplastic invented in 1954. Among the first — if not the first — to seize on it as a material suitable for furniture design purposes, Mr. Day went on to create variations on his original polyprop, including an armchair, a school chair and an indoor-outdoor model.

"Things should work well; they should function," Mr. Day said in a 2005 interview with Icon, an architecture and design magazine, adding that "construction techniques, materials and economics are relevant."

"Along with that, hopefully, some poetry and pleasantness in terms of looks," he said. "But these practical things are essential. Without it design is a waste of time."

— By Bruce Weber

BABY MARIE OSBORNE

Seen (by Millions) but Not Heard

NOV. 5, 1911 - NOV. 10, 2010

They called her Baby Marie Osborne, and in silent films nearly a century ago she was America's little sweetheart, a precocious, chauffeured, $1,000-a-week prodigy who could turn on the tears or a sunshine smile and break your heart. She had sparkling eyes and dimpled arms. She also had a lisp, but no matter.

She was a toddler when she made her debut in "Kidnapped in New York," a 1914 potboiler with a tinkling piano to cue the drama. She made 28 more films in five years, including the memorable "Little Mary Sunshine," her 1916 portrayal of a motherless 5-year-old whose love for a drunken father turns him away from the devil brew.

She retired at age 8, and might have lived happily ever after.

But her mother and father turned out to be foster parents who never told her she was adopted and frittered her fortune away before splitting up. She grew up fast, married twice, had a daughter and was divorced and widowed. She worked in a dime store, became a stand-in for Ginger Rogers in the 1930s and wound up draping actors in Hollywood wardrobe departments.

She retired — for real — in 1976.

One of America's earliest child stars, long forgotten except for Internet nostalgia buffs and silent-film aficionados, Baby Marie — Marie Osborne Yeats — died on Nov. 10 at her home in San Clemente, Calif. She was 99. Her daughter, Joan Young, confirmed her death. Five grandchildren also survive her.

SILENT SWEETHART: Ms. Osborne starred in 28 films before retiring at age 8.

With its triumphs, setbacks, poignant struggles and unpredictable turns, her life churned with the stuff of silent films. She was born Helen Alice Myres in Denver on Nov. 5, 1911, the daughter of Roy and Mary Myres. She soon became — under mysterious circumstances — the child of Leon and Edith Osborn, who called her Marie and added the "e" to the surname, apparently to obscure the adoption.

In 1914, the family moved to Long Beach, Calif. Edith Osborn was an actress calling herself Babe St. Clair, and Leon was a theatrical promoter. They rented a room and, unable to afford a baby sitter, took Marie along to the Balboa studios, where they had found work in silent films.

The cute kid was spotted and cast in one of the hundreds of forgettable silents made in 1914. In 1915, the actor-director Henry King put her in "The Maid of the Wild." She showed talent, and Balboa signed her to a contract. Mr. King had "Little Mary Sunshine" written especially for her.

The picture, one of her few that survive, was a huge success and made her an international star. She soon had her own production company and was churning out Baby Marie films. She was cast as an orphan, a child of social climbers, the charmer of a crotchety millionaire, a diplomat, a cupid. She could register fear, shock, delight, pity, sorrow; could cry real tears — and always made things turn out right in the end.

Behind the scenes, her parents squabbled over custody, money and infidelities. In 1919, Baby Marie's career waned. She made a last film, "Miss Gingersnap," and retired. In 1920, The New York American ran a cautionary tale of lost money and bitter divorce under a banner headline: "How Baby Marie's Big Salary Ruined Her Happy Home."

The trauma faded, Baby Marie grew up, silent movies became talkies in the late '20s, and in 1931 Ms. Osborne married Frank Dempsey. They had a daughter, Joan, in 1932, but were divorced four years later. In 1945 she married Murray Yeats, who died in 1975.

In 1933, as her first marriage deteriorated, Ms. Osborne took a job in a dime store. It was a low point. Then came an astonishing call from the superintendent of the Colorado Children's Home, who informed her that she had been adopted as an infant by the Osbornes! And that a man who said he was her real father, H. L. Shriver, had become a tycoon!! And that he had left her a substantial inheritance!!!

Next, with the help of her old mentor, Mr. King, now a major Hollywood director, she got minor parts in a dozen films from 1934 to 1950. She also became a stand-in for Ginger Rogers in "The Gay Divorcee" (1934), "Swing Time" (1936) and "Shall We Dance" (1937), and for Deanna Durbin and Betty Hutton.

In 1954, she joined Twentieth Century-Fox as a costumer. She later became a wardrobe supervisor. Over two decades she draped Jean Simmons, Marlon Brando, John Wayne, Rita Hayworth, Rock Hudson, Robert Redford, Lucille Ball and Elizabeth Taylor. Her work appeared in "Around the World in 80 Days" (1956), "How to Murder Your Wife" (1965), "The Godfather, Part II" (1974) and other films.

She was featured in Michael G. Ankerich's 1993 book, "Broken Silence: Conversations with 23 Silent Film Stars," and in 1999 she was interviewed by Billy Doyle for ClassicImages .com.

"It means little to her that she is regarded by film historians as an icon of film history," Mr. Doyle wrote. "We cannot share her modesty. For historians, her contributions to the film industry give her an almost legendary status as one of the last living witnesses of the crucial early years when Hollywood rose to a position of international importance."

— By Robert D. McFadden

Dino De Laurentiis

Playing to the Critics and *the Crowds*

AUG. 8, 1919 - NOV. 10, 2010

Dino De Laurentiis, the high-flying Italian film producer and entrepreneur whose movies ranged from some of Federico Fellini's earliest works to "Serpico," "Death Wish" and the 1976 remake of "King Kong," died on Nov. 10 at his home in Beverly Hills, Calif. He was 91.

Mr. De Laurentiis's career dated to prewar Italy, and the hundreds of films he produced covered a wide range of styles and genres. His filmography includes major titles of the early Italian New Wave, among them the international success "Bitter Rice" (1949), whose star, Silvana Mangano, became his first wife; two important films by Fellini, "La Strada" (1954) and "Nights of Cabiria" (1957), both of which won Academy Awards; and the film that many critics regard as David Lynch's best work, "Blue Velvet" (1986).

But Mr. De Laurentiis never turned his nose up at unabashed popular entertainments like Sergio Corbucci's "Goliath and the Vampires" (1961), Roger Vadim's "Barbarella" (1968) and Richard Fleischer's "Mandingo" (1975) — several of which hold up better today than some of Mr. De Laurentiis's more respectable productions.

"A producer is not just a bookkeeper, or a banker, or a background. He makes the picture," Mr. De Laurentiis told Cue magazine in 1962. "If the film is a failure, I am responsible. If it is a success, then it is the joint contribution of the actors, director, writers, set designers, musicians and script girl — everybody except the producer. This is a fact of life; I do not complain."

Mr. De Laurentiis was among the first European producers to realize the potential of the international co-production. In the early 1950s, the vertically integrated Hollywood studios were breaking up because of a Justice Department antimonopoly decree, studio-groomed stars were turning into freelance agents, and back lots were beginning to be sold off in favor of using location photography. As a result, the studios started to turn to outside suppliers to keep a steady stream of product coming in for their distribution apparatus.

Mr. De Laurentiis lured Anthony Quinn to Rome for "La Strada," and shortly afterward cast Kirk Douglas in the title role of "Ulysses," a spectacular directed by the Italian film veteran Mario Camerini (with an uncredited assist from the director and cinematographer Mario Bava). Mr. De Laurentiis sold it to Paramount. The formula proved to be a profitable one, allowing Mr. De Laurentiis to pay grandiose salaries to his imported stars while cutting costs by using local technicians.

INTERNATIONAL IMPACT: Mr. De Laurentiis in 1956 with his and Carlo Ponti's Oscars for Fellini's "La Strada."

Actors like Audrey Hepburn and Henry Fonda ("War and Peace," 1956), Anthony Perkins ("This Angry Age," 1958), Vera Miles and Van Heflin ("Five Branded Women," 1960) and Charles Laughton ("Under Ten Flags," 1960) made their way to Italy, where they often performed with other international stars. The results, filmed in a Babel of tongues, were dubbed into different languages for different markets.

At the same time, Mr. De Laurentiis continued to make films for the home market. He had a close relationship with the legendary Italian clown Totò (for whom he produced the 1952 "Totò a Colori," one of the first Italian feature films shot entirely in color) and Alberto Sordi, a rotund comic whose portrayals of middle-class Romans struggling to stay ahead of the game became a projection of the national identity. Mr. De Laurentiis's success, aided by government subsidies that encouraged postwar production in Italy, allowed him to build his own studio, which he named Dinocittà.

Mr. De Laurentiis's empire began to crumble in 1965, when Italy's Socialist government passed regulations that put severe restrictions on what could be called an Italian movie.

With his government subsidies in doubt, his contract with Mr. Sordi coming to an end and a legal battle with Fellini dragging on over unmade projects, Mr. De Laurentiis closed Dinocittà in 1972 and moved to New York, where he opened an office in what was then the Gulf & Western building on Columbus Circle.

In New York, Mr. De Laurentiis began a series of well-known productions, including "Serpico" (1973), "Death Wish" (1974), "Three Days of the Condor" (1975), John Guillermin's big-budget remake of "King Kong" (1976) and "The Shootist (1976), John Wayne's final film.

But the successes alternated with failures, like "King of the Gypsies" (1978) and "Hurricane" (1979), and soon Mr. De Laurentiis was founding and closing production companies with dizzying speed, often selling the rights to his old films to secure the financing for new ones.

Expensive follies, like a hotel opened on Bora Bora (the location of "Hurricane"), an upscale delicatessen on the Upper West Side of Manhattan and a studio complex in North Carolina, strained Mr. De Laurentiis's bottom line, and in later years he was forced to sell many of his properties and rein in his activities.

Still, he persisted through the 1980s and '90s, thanks chiefly to a relationship with Stephen King, many of whose books were filmed by Mr. De Laurentiis, and his ownership of Thomas Harris's first novel in the Hannibal Lecter series, "Red Dragon." Mr. De Laurentiis filmed the Harris novel twice: first in 1986 as "Manhunter," with Brian Cox in the role of the cannibalistic serial killer, and then under the novel's original title in 2002, with Anthony Hopkins back for another turn in the role after becoming a star playing Lecter in the non-De Laurentiis "Silence of the Lambs."

Agostino De Laurentiis was born in Torre

Annunziata, a town in the province of Naples, on Aug. 8, 1919, the third in a family of seven brothers and sisters.

He had four children with Ms. Mangano; their only son died in an airplane crash in 1981. After Ms. Mangano's death in 1989, Mr. De Laurentiis married the American-born producer Martha Schumacher, with whom he had two daughters.

He is survived by his wife and daughters as well as three sisters; five grandchildren, including the chef and Food Network host Giada De Laurentiis; and two great-grandchildren.

In 2001, the Academy of Motion Picture Arts and Sciences honored Mr. De Laurentiis with the Irving G. Thalberg Memorial Award for lifetime achievement.

Mr. De Laurentiis's second wife, as Martha De Laurentiis, continued to work with him as a co-producer. Their most recent projects included "Hannibal Rising" (2007), a prequel to the Lecter saga starring the young French actor Gaspard Ulliel as the apprentice flesh eater.

A master at publicizing his movies and himself, Mr. De Laurentiis made a lot of proclamations that were hard to take seriously. (He referred to his "King Kong" remake as "the greatest love story of all time.") He could also be wryly self-deprecating, as in this explanation of how he became a producer:

"I see my face in the mirror, and I said, 'No, my ambition is not to be an actor.'"

— *By Dave Kehr*

HENRYK GORECKI

A Symphony of Sorrow That Moved So Many

DEC. 6, 1933 - NOV. 12, 2010

HENRYK GORECKI, a renowned Polish composer whose early avant-garde style gave way to more approachable works rooted in his country's folk songs and sacred music and whose Symphony No. 3 — an extended lamentation subtitled "Symphony of Sorrowful Songs" — sold more than a million copies on CD in the 1990s, died on Nov. 12 in Katowice, Poland. He was 76.

Joanna Wnuk-Nazarowa, the general director of the Polish National Radio Symphony Orchestra in Katowice, said Mr. Gorecki, who lived there, had been hospitalized with a lung infection.

With Witold Lutoslawski and Kzysztof Penderecki, Mr. Gorecki (pronounced go-RET-zki) was one of Poland's most revered contemporary composers. His music often played with the extremes of musical expression. In works like "Old Polish Music" (1969), blocks of assertive, high-energy brass writing are juxtaposed with eerie, slow-moving, pianissimo string passages.

His intensely focused "Beatus Vir" (1979) and "Totus Tuus" (1987), both dedicated to Pope John Paul II, draw on the simplicity of traditional chant as well as richly harmonized choral writing and, in the case of "Beatus Vir," monumental orchestral scoring. And in "Already It Is Dusk" (1988), his first string quartet, Mr. Gorecki reconfigures Polish dances and dirges, casting the more outgoing sections in acidic harmonies that give the score a searing, angry edge.

But the work for which Mr. Gorecki is most widely known, the Symphony No. 3 (1976), explores the gradations of a single mood: somber, introspective reflection, conveyed in three long, slow, quiet movements that last nearly an hour. Scored for orchestra and soprano, the work's vocal sections include settings of a 15th-century sacred lamentation, a simple prayer ("Oh Mamma do not cry — Immaculate Queen of Heaven support me always") scrawled by a young girl on the wall of a Gestapo prison in southern Poland, and a plaintive Polish folk song in which a mother grieves for a son lost in war.

Mr. Gorecki surrounds these texts with a compelling amalgam of lush neo-Romanticism; open, entirely consonant tonality; and a gradual unfolding of themes and textures that struck many listeners as a distinctly Eastern European approach to Minimalism.

The work quickly took on a life of its own. In 1985, the French director Maurice Pialat used an excerpt from the symphony on the soundtrack to "Police," a film starring Gérard Depardieu. A recording of the full work, conducted by Ernest Bour, with the soprano Stefania Woytowicz, was released on the Erato label, and though it was packaged as a soundtrack album for "Police" — a film virtually unknown in the United States — it proved a first encounter with Mr. Gorecki's music for many American listeners. Two more recordings were released, both with Ms. Woytowicz as the soloist.

REVERED IN POLAND: Mr. Gorecki's compositions were inspired by his country's folk songs and church music.

But the work did not achieve its explosive success — a surprise, given its unceasingly mournful character — until a recording by the soprano Dawn Upshaw, with David Zinman conducting the London Sinfonietta, was released on the Nonesuch label in 1992. The recording became a radio hit in Britain, where it broke into the Top 10 on the Music Week pop chart, and sold more than a million copies worldwide. For a while, Nonesuch said, it was selling 10,000 copies a day in the United States.

The symphony was subsequently used as soundtrack music in Peter Weir's "Fearless" (1993) and Julian Schnabel's "Basquiat" (1996). Samples of the score were also used in recordings by several pop groups, most notably "Gorecki" by the English band Lamb.

Henryk Mikolaj Gorecki was born in the village of Czernica on Dec. 6, 1933, to parents who were amateur musicians. He began studying the violin when he was 10 and later took up the clarinet and piano. By the early 1950s he was composing songs and piano works while earning a living as a teacher. In 1955, he enrolled at the Music Academy in Katowice, where he was a composition student of Boleslaw Szabelski for five years.

But he was already beginning to make his name in Polish avant-garde circles with works like the Four Preludes (1955) for piano and the contrast-rich Sonata for Two Violins (1957).

In "Epitafium" (1958), for mixed choir and instruments, he began experimenting with the spatial placement of his performing forces. In the Symphony No. 1 (1959) and "Scontri" ("Collisions," 1960), he experimented with Serialism (in which a composer must use all 12 tones of the chromatic scale in equal proportion) and with the textural contrasts — dense clusters versus spare, pointillistic solo lines — that would become a hallmark in his later music.

Mr. Gorecki continued to embrace Serialism through the 1960s, but mixed it with other techniques — including whole-tone harmony and the use of ancient modal scales — that made his music sound bracing and fresh rather than doctrinaire.

He became fascinated with choral and vocal music around 1970, and expanded his stylistic arsenal with folk music and traditional Polish church music. Gradually, he jettisoned Serialism and moved toward the completely tonal, diatonic language that gave the Symphony No. 3 much of its immediate appeal.

Other important works in Mr. Gorecki's catalog include three string quartets — "Already It Is Dusk" (1988), "Quasi Una Fantasia" (1991) and "... Songs Are Sung" (1995), all written for the Kronos Quartet — and the "Kleines Requiem für eine Polka" (1993) for piano and 13 instruments.

Mr. Gorecki joined the faculty of the Music Academy in Katowice in 1968 and became a professor in 1972 and rector from 1975 to 1979. Among his composition students were his son, Mikolaj Gorecki, who survives him, as do his wife, Jadwiga, and his daughter.

Mr. Gorecki left his post at the academy in 1979 to protest the Polish government's refusal to allow Pope John Paul II to visit Katowice. He also composed his Miserere (1981) as a protest, in this case against the government's crackdown on members of Rural Solidarity in Bydgoszcz. But he always insisted on a distinction between his music and his politics.

"My dear, it would be a terrible poverty of life if music were political," he told Bruce Duffie, a radio producer, in a 1994 interview. "I cannot imagine it, because what does this mean — 'political music?' That is why I ignore questions about political music, because music is music. Painting is painting. I can be involved in some political ideals. That would be my personal life."

Last month Bronislaw Komorowski, the president of Poland, visited Mr. Gorecki in the hospital to award him the country's highest honor, the Order of the White Eagle.

"I think about my audience, but I am not writing for them," Mr. Gorecki said in his 1994 interview. "If I were thinking of my audience and one likes this, one likes that, one likes another thing, I would never know what to write. Let every listener choose that which interests him. I have nothing against one person liking Mozart or Shostakovich or Leonard Bernstein, but doesn't like Gorecki. That's fine with me. I, too, like certain things."

— *By Allan Kozinn*

THEODORE KHEEL

In a Labor Standoff, the Crucial Seat at the Table

MAY 9, 1914 - NOV. 12, 2010

THEODORE W. KHEEL, who was New York City's pre-eminent labor peacemaker from the 1950s through the 1980s, a mediator and arbitrator sought after by both City Hall and the White House to help avert or end strikes of crippling consequence, died on Nov. 12. He was 96 and lived in Manhattan.

Mr. Kheel, who played a pivotal role in ending newspaper, teacher and subway strikes in New York, was the go-to guy for mayors, labor leaders and business executives during the post-World War II era, when unions were far more powerful than they are now and a savvy, respected ringmaster was often needed to pressure and cajole all sides to reach a settlement.

Mayor Robert F. Wagner Jr. turned to Mr. Kheel to help end the 114-day newspaper strike of 1962-63, and President Lyndon B. Johnson summoned Mr. Kheel to Washington in 1964 to help mediate 10 days of feverish negotiations that prevented a nationwide rail walkout.

In a flood of articles hailing his successes at resolving myriad conflicts, Mr. Kheel was described as "the most influential peacemaker in New York City in the last half-century" and the "master locksmith of deadlock bargaining." In 1970, The New Yorker called him "the one man best able to keep in working order a substantial portion of the sputtering labor machinery not only in New York City, but over much of the Eastern Seaboard."

Mr. Kheel was not only New York's leading mediator but also its premier arbitrator, deciding more than 30,000 disputes, ranging from whether a new bus service violated the transit union's contract to whether a worker should be suspended because he was seen walking his dog on a day he had called in sick. (An arbitrator's decision is typically binding while a mediator's may not be.)

Even though Mr. Kheel handled disputes for bakers, garbage collectors, plumbers, subway conductors, tugboat captains and undertakers, he was an unabashed bon vivant, fond of fast sports cars and fine food. He once owned a stake in Le Pavillon, a leading French restaurant in Manhattan, and leased wine bin No. 1 at both the Rainbow Room and Windows on the World. He also represented artists, including Robert Rauschenberg and Christo.

Mr. Kheel juggled enough obligations to keep a half-dozen people busy: he was chairman of Republic National Bank, president of the National Urban League from 1956 to 1960 and wrote a 10-volume treatise on labor law.

He also made millions as an entrepreneur. He was the lead investor in the giant Punta Cana resort in the Dominican Republic and chairman of a company that distributed MasterCards to more than 1.4 million union members.

But Mr. Kheel was known above all else for his extraordinary ability to get feuding parties to make concessions to reach a labor agreement, as he did during the 35-day New York City teachers' strike in 1968.

One industrial relations expert said that Mr. Kheel — six feet tall, athletic and dapper in his Saks Fifth Avenue suits — infused the handling of labor disputes with the kind of energy that Fiorello H. LaGuardia had brought to City Hall and George M. Cohan to Broadway. Mr. Kheel had well-honed techniques. Upon entering a negotiation, he first asked each party to tell him what was on its mind, what it hoped to achieve and what it thought of the other side's proposals. He would often have the two sides negotiate across a table until they got so loud and angry that he felt the need to separate them — at which point he often engaged in shuttle diplomacy.

"The essence of mediation is getting information," Mr. Kheel told The New Yorker. "The dirtiest question you can ask in bargaining is, 'What will you settle for?' If you ask that question, you ought to resign, but that's the question you must have an answer to. You get it by asking every question except that. What's left over is the answer."

During the 1962-63 newspaper strike, which involved 10 unions and seven daily newspapers, including The New York Times, The Herald Tribune, The Daily News and The New York Post, Mayor Wagner summoned him 90 days into the walkout. Mr. Kheel arrived at City Hall with two bottles of Champagne to toast what he thought was an imminent settlement. It took another month — 868 hours of bargaining — before an agreement was reached.

Local 6 of the International Typographical Union presented the biggest obstacle, demanding a more generous contract than several other newspaper unions and fearing that the publishers' automation plans would throw its members out of work.

Mr. Kheel shaped the final settlement, which gave the typographical union a larger raise than some unions received and assurances that its members would not lose their jobs.

"I churn the collective bargaining process like butter," Mr. Kheel once said. "It's a butter I hope everyone enjoys, but in any case I'm sure it's a butter everybody can live on."

Theodore Woodrow Kheel was born in Brooklyn on May 9, 1914, named after Theodore Roosevelt and Woodrow Wilson. His father, Samuel, headed a real estate company, and his mother, Kate Herzenstein, ran the company after his father died.

Mr. Kheel was a graduate of DeWitt Clinton High School in the Bronx, Cornell University (1935) and Cornell's law school. The day after passing the New York bar exam, he married Ann Sunstein, whom he had met at Cornell. A journalist and civic leader, she was secretary of the board of the New York Urban League for a quarter-century. She died in 2003. They had five daughters, a son, 11 grandchildren and six great-grandchildren.

RINGMASTER: Mr. Kheel was the top negotiator in labor disputes of the 1960s and '70s.

In 1938, Mr. Kheel joined the legal staff of the National Labor Relations Board. He later worked for the War Labor Board, which was charged with maintaining labor peace to promote the war effort. In 1946, Mayor William O'Dwyer named him deputy director of New York City's new division of labor relations, and a year later he became the division's director.

He returned to private practice in 1948, joining what became Battle, Fowler, Neaman, Stokes & Kheel. In May 1949, he was named impartial arbitrator for the city's private transit industry, settling disputes between the often-militant Transport Workers Union and seven private bus lines. In 1956, Mayor Wagner named him arbitrator for the citywide transit authority, a position he held for 33 years. During that period he handled an average of 1,000 disputes a year.

Michael J. Quill, the transit workers' fiery leader, voiced grudging respect for Mr. Kheel, saying, "Whether we won or lost, we knew we had a fair shake." Over the decades, Mr. Kheel helped mediate more than a dozen transit contracts and helped end the 12-day transit strike of 1966.

In 1974, despite objections from the printers' union, he helped write a landmark contract that enabled the city's newspaper publishers to introduce "cold type," or computerized typesetting. In exchange, the typographical unions' workers were promised lifetime job guarantees.

In 1978, he again helped settle a newspaper strike, this time an 88-day walkout against The Times, The Daily News and The Post.

But Mr. Kheel began losing influence in the early 1980s, after Mayor Edward I. Koch and other critics said he had been partly responsible for the city's financial woes, primarily through overly generous contracts for transit workers and others.

He was active as a philanthropist, heading the Gandhi Society for Human Rights in the 1960s, which helped the Rev. Dr. Martin Luther King Jr. raise money for the civil rights movement, and the Metropolitan Applied Research Center, which helped finance Kenneth B. Clark's research on behalf of civil rights. While in his 80s and 90s he founded Earth Pledge and the Nurture Nature Foundation.

He also joined the law firm of Paul, Hastings, Janofsky & Walker and remained a stalwart supporter of collective bargaining.

In explaining how to reach a settlement, Mr. Kheel once gave this advice: "It is like sculpting an elephant. You chip away everything that doesn't look like an elephant, and what's left is an elephant. When you're trying to get a labor contract, you do the same thing. You chip away everything that doesn't belong in the agreement, and what's left is the agreement."

— *By Steven Greenhouse*

ALLAN SANDAGE

At Home in the Cosmos

JUNE 18, 1926 - NOV. 13, 2010

ALLAN R. SANDAGE, who spent his life measuring the universe, becoming the most influential astronomer of his generation, died on Nov. 13 at his home in San Gabriel, Calif. He was 84.

The cause was pancreatic cancer, according to an announcement by the Carnegie Observatories, where he had spent his whole professional career.

Over more than six decades, writing more than 500 papers, Dr. Sandage ranged across the cosmos, covering the evolution and behavior of stars, the birth of the Milky Way galaxy, the age of the universe and the discovery of the first quasar, not to mention the Hubble constant, a famously contested number that measures the rate of expansion of the universe.

In 1949, he was a young Caltech graduate student, a self-described "hick who fell off the turnip truck," when he became the observing assistant for Edwin Hubble, the Mount Wilson astronomer who discovered the expansion of the universe.

Hubble had planned an observing campaign using a new 200-inch telescope on Palomar Mountain in California to explore the haunting questions raised by that mysterious expansion. If the universe was born in a Big Bang, for example, could it one day die in a Big Crunch? But Hubble died of a heart attack in 1953, just as the telescope was going into operation. So Dr. Sandage, a fresh Ph.D. at 27, inherited the job of limning the fate of the universe.

"It would be as if you were appointed to be copy editor to Dante," Dr. Sandage once said. "If you were the assistant to Dante, and then Dante died, and then you had in your possession the whole of 'The Divine Comedy,' what would you do?"

He was a man of towering passions and many moods, and for years, you weren't anybody in astronomy if he had not stopped speaking to you. Even after retiring from the Carnegie Observatories and becoming ill, he never stopped working; he published a paper on variable stars only last June.

In 1991, Dr. Sandage was awarded the Crafoord Prize in astronomy, the closest thing to a Nobel for a stargazer, worth $2 million.

James Gunn, an astronomer at Princeton, said of Dr. Sandage in an e-mail message, "He was probably (rightly) the greatest and most influential observational astronomer of the last half-century."

Allan Rex Sandage was born in Iowa City, Iowa, on June 18, 1926, the only child of an advertising professor, Charles Harold Sandage, and a homemaker, Dorothy Briggs Sandage. The stars were one of his first loves; his father bought him a commercial telescope.

After two years at Miami University, where his father taught, Allan was drafted into the Navy; he resumed his education at the University of Illinois, earning a degree in physics.

In 1948 he entered graduate school at the California Institute of Technology, where an astronomy program had been started in conjunction with the nearby Mount Wilson Observatory, home of Hubble, among others. As a result, Dr. Sandage learned the nuts and bolts of observing with big telescopes from the founders of modern cosmology, Hubble; Walter Baade, who became his thesis adviser, and Milton Humason, a former mule driver who had become Hubble's right-hand man.

In the years before World War II, there had been a revolution in the understanding of the nature and evolution of stars as thermonuclear furnaces burning hydrogen into helium and elements beyond. Astronomers could now read the ages of star clusters from the colors and brightness of the stars in them.

For his thesis, Dr. Sandage used this trick to date a so-called globular cluster, known as Messier 3, as being 3.2 billion years old, which meant that the universe itself could not be younger than that. In fact, Hubble's own measurements of the cosmic expansion suggested an age of about four billion years — remarkably, even miraculously, consistent.

At the time, astronomers were also still debating whether the universe had had a Big Bang and a beginning at all, not to mention whether it would have an ending as well. An opposing view championed by the British cosmologist Fred Hoyle held that the universe was eternal and in a "steady state," with new matter filling in the void as galaxies rushed away from one another.

Choosing between these models was to be the big task of 20th-century astronomy, and of Dr. Sandage. In 1961 he published a paper in The Astrophysical Journal showing how it could be done using the 200-inch telescope. He described cosmology as the search for two numbers: one was the cosmic expansion rate, known as the Hubble constant; the other, called the deceleration parameter, tells how fast the expansion is being braked by cosmic gravity.

That paper, "The Ability of the 200-inch Telescope to Discriminate Between Selected World Models," may well have been "the most influential paper ever written in any field even close to cosmology," Dr. Gunn said. It was to set the direction of observational cosmology for 40 years, ruling out the Steady State and the Big Crunch and culminating in the surprise discovery in 1998 that the expansion is not slowing down at all but speeding up.

Meanwhile, Dr. Sandage investigated the birth of the galaxy. By analyzing the motions of old stars in the Milky Way, he, Olin Eggen of Caltech and Donald Lynden-Bell of Cambridge showed in a 1962 paper that the Milky Way formed from the collapse of a primordial gas cloud probably some 10 billion years ago. That paper still forms the basis of science's understanding of where the galaxy came from, astronomers say.

In 1959, Dr. Sandage married another astronomer, Mary Connelly, who was teaching at Mount Holyoke and had studied at Indiana University and Radcliffe but did not pursue further research. His longtime collaborator was Gustav Tammann of the University of Basel in Switzerland. Dr. Sandage is survived by his wife and two sons.

We may never know the fate of the universe, he once said, or precisely how fast it is expanding, as the Hubble constant seeks to determine, but the quest and discoveries made along the way were more important and rewarding than the answer anyway.

"It's got to be fun," Dr. Sandage told an interviewer. "I don't think anybody should tell you that he's slogged his way through 25 years on a problem and there's only one reward at the end, and that's the value of the Hubble constant. That's a bunch of hooey. The reward is learning all the wonderful properties of the things that don't work."

— *By Dennis Overbye*

MEASURING THE UNIVERSE: Dr. Sandage readying the 200-inch Hale telescope at the Palomar Observatory in 1974.

FRED GOLDHABER

But to His Gay Students, Just 'Mr. G'

APRIL 23, 1947 - NOV. 15, 2010

Among Mr. G.'s first students back in 1985 were runaways who had been sleeping in a shed down by the docks in Lower Manhattan where the city stored mountains of road salt.

One boy had hitchhiked from Ohio after eight teenagers dragged him into a bathroom at school, bashed his head against a toilet and burned his arm with a cigarette lighter.

Another boy, from New York City, had been abused by his parents after a teacher told them that he was "acting like a faggot." He was kept at home for a year — chained to a radiator, beaten and taken by his father to 42nd Street and forced to have sex with men for money. His father went to prison.

There is no way to know how many of the gay and lesbian youngsters who came under the wing of Mr. G., as he was known, went on to graduate from high school or just found the strength to make their way in the world. But for dozens, at least, he was a hero.

"The kids idolized him."

Mr. G. — Fred Goldhaber — the first and, for a year and a half or so, the only teacher at the Harvey Milk School in Manhattan, the first school in the country with a mission to provide a haven for gay and lesbian students, died of liver cancer on Nov. 15 at his home in Jersey City. He was 63.

He had lived with AIDS for nearly 30 years, his brother, Richard, said.

The Harvey Milk School, named for the gay-rights advocate and San Francisco city supervisor who was killed in 1978, was established in 1985 by what was then called the Institute for the Protection of Lesbian and Gay Youth (now the Hetrick-Martin Institute), with financial support from the New York City Board of Education.

Mr. Goldhaber, who had taught English and remedial reading at Wingate High School in Brooklyn for 17 years, volunteered to teach the incoming class, 22 students who first gathered in April 1985 at a church in Greenwich Village. The school later moved to a building at 2 Astor Place.

Back then it was like an old-time country school, with Mr. G. juggling academic demands: answering questions about physics, correcting spelling tests, going over verb conjugation, keeping an eye out for the girl slumping into sleep.

A longtime member of the New York City Gay Men's Chorus, he laced lessons with song snippets: "Teach me tonight" while assigning homework; "Call me irresponsible" to a girl who had not done her math.

"At his right hand," Time magazine wrote in 1989, "Goldhaber pores over pictures with one student, saying, 'Yes, this is an ion, but is it just an ion or a hydroxide ion? Think about it.' He asks the student on his left, 'Do you really believe 20 times 15 is 30,000?'"

Until 2003, the school was actually what is called a transfer program, meaning students could earn graduate equivalency diplomas or enough credits to graduate from the high school they had left.

Now they can graduate directly from the Milk School. Margie Feinberg, a spokeswoman for the city's Education Department, said about 100 students are enrolled at the Milk School each year, about one-third of whom graduate within four years, a reflection of the difficulties they face.

Stephen Phillips, a professor of education at Brooklyn College who was the city's superintendent of alternative high schools and programs when the Milk School opened, observed Mr. Goldhaber in action.

"The kids idolized him," Mr. Phillips said. "Many of them never would have gotten diplomas had it not been for the way he treated them."

When his brother walked the city's streets, Richard Goldhaber said, "time after time" students "would stop him, hug him and thank him for rescuing them."

Fred Martin Goldhaber was born in Brooklyn on April 23, 1947. His father, Max, was a lawyer; his mother, the former Betty Chatow, was a concert pianist.

He received a bachelor's degree from Brooklyn College in 1968 and a master's degree there a year later, both in education. Besides his brother, Mr. Goldhaber is survived by his companion, Wilfredo Hinds.

When the school celebrated its sixth anniversary in 1991, a student asked, "Will the school survive?"

To which Mr. G. replied, "If you kids do."

Another student said: "I hope there will be a day when there is no gay school. Because, you know, there shouldn't have to be one."

— *By Dennis Hevesi*

ISABELLE CARO

The Cautionary Face of Anorexia

SEPT. 12, 1982 - NOV. 17, 2010

ISABELLE CARO, a French model and actress who became the international face of anorexia when she allowed her ravaged body to be photographed nude for an Italian advertising campaign to raise awareness about the disease, died on Nov. 17. She was 28.

Her friends and family initially kept her death secret. Danièle Gouzard-Dubreuil-Prevot, Ms. Caro's longtime acting instructor, informed The Associated Press on Dec. 29 that she died after returning to France from a job in Tokyo.

Though her anorexia was almost certainly a factor in her death, its exact role was not clear, and her weight at her death was not known. But Ms. Caro weighed only about 60 pounds when she posed, reclining and staring balefully over her right shoulder, for an advertising campaign for the Italian fashion label Nolita in 2007. She was 5 feet 4 inches tall and had battled anorexia since the age of 13.

The image, displayed on billboards and in newspapers as Fashion Week got under way that year in Milan, was shocking. Ms. Caro's face was emaciated, her arms and legs mere sticks, her teeth seemingly too large for her mouth. In large letters, "No — Anorexia" ran across the top of the photograph.

The photo was taken by Oliviero Toscani, celebrated in the fashion industry for his Benetton campaigns in the 1980s and 1990s, which included such provocative images as a close-up of a man dying from AIDS and prisoners on death row.

The Nolita campaign came as the fashion industry was under a spotlight over anorexia, after a 21-year-old Brazilian model, Ana Carolina Reston, died from it in 2006.

"The idea was to shock people into awareness," Ms. Caro said at the time. "I decided to do it to warn girls about the danger of diets and of fashion commandments."

Some groups working with anorexics warned, however, that it did a disservice to those with the disorder. Fabiola De Clercq, the president of Italy's Association for the Study of Anorexia and Bulimia, said that Ms. Caro should be in the hospital and pronounced the image "too crude."

The ads were eventually banned by an Italian advertising watchdog agency, which determined that they exploited the illness.

The campaign gained Ms. Caro widespread attention in Europe and the United States. She subsequently served as a judge on the French version of the reality show "America's Next Top Model" and worked occasionally as a film and television actress.

Ms. Caro often spoke out about her anorexia and her efforts to recover, including an appearance on the VH1 reality series "The Price of Beauty," starring Jessica Simpson.

Ms. Caro's Facebook page said she was born on Sept. 12, 1982. In her 2008 memoir, "The Little Girl Who Didn't Want to Get Fat," she described a tormented childhood dominated by the profound depression that gripped her mother, an artist, when Isabelle was 4. Obsessed with protecting Isabelle, her mother kept her out of school until the age of 11 and forbade her to play with other children, lest she pick up an illness. She often criticized her daughter for being too fat.

"She wanted me to be her little girl forever," Ms. Caro told Italian Vanity Fair in 2007. "So as I started puberty I hated the idea that my body was going to change. I wanted to have the body of a child forever, to make my mother happy."

As a result of her self-imposed diet, she would often lapse into comas and awake delirious, not knowing who she was. At one time, she survived on one square of chocolate a day with a cup of tea, which she consumed a teaspoon at a time, to make it last.

Ms. Caro's long struggle with her disease had alarming ups and downs. In 2006, when her weight dwindled to 55 pounds, she sank into a coma. After months in intensive care, she was advised by a psychologist to break free of her parents, and she moved to Marseille. She also began a blog documenting her struggle with anorexia.

"I still eat almost nothing, but I've stopped vomiting," she said after her photo shoot for Nolita. "I have started to distinguish tastes of things. I have tried ice cream — it's delicious."

This March, she announced with pride that her weight had risen to 93 pounds.

The Swiss singer Vincent Bigler had been working with Ms. Caro on a video for a song he wrote about anorexia called "J'ai Fin." The title is a wordplay in French that means roughly "I am the end" but has the same pronunciation as "I am hungry." He said he wrote the song after being so moved and worried by seeing Ms. Caro on television.

'THE LITTLE GIRL WHO DIDN'T WANT TO GET FAT': Ms. Caro, a model turned anorexia activist, meeting the news media in 2008.

Mr. Toscani said he had visited several hospitals in France, Italy and Germany to find the right model and chose Ms. Caro because she exhibited the classic physical characteristics of advanced anorexia and because her eyes were haunting.

— *By William Grimes*

NORRIS CHURCH MAILER

An 'Eliza Doolittle' Who Made Her Own Name

JAN. 31, 1949 - NOV. 21, 2010

NORRIS CHURCH MAILER, a woman bred in the rural poverty of Arkansas who married Norman Mailer and managed his career and family life while carving out her own niche as a writer, died on Nov. 21 at her home in Brooklyn Heights. She was 61.

The cause was the gastrointestinal cancer that she had had for 11 years, her son John Buffalo Mailer said.

Ms. Mailer, who had grown up as Barbara Jean Davis, was a high school art teacher, former pickle-factory worker and divorced mother when Mr. Mailer came to Russellville, Ark., in 1975 to plug his book-length reflection on Marilyn Monroe. Brooklyn-bred, Harvard-educated, with the first of two Pulitzer Prizes to his credit, he was almost as celebrated for his brawling egocentrism and intellectual provocations as he was for his novels. He was also twice her age and by that point had been married four times.

But as a Book-of-the-Month Club member, she was eager that he sign her copy of "Marilyn." After a few moments of conversation, he was enchanted. She found him "easily the most interesting man I had ever met." She was to give another motive for their magnetic attraction.

"Sex was the cord that bound us together," she wrote.

Within months, she moved to New York where, as she wrote in "A Ticket to the Circus," the memoir she published in 2010, Mr. Mailer became "the Henry Higgins to my Eliza Doolittle." She worked for Wilhelmina Models and changed her name. Norris echoed her first husband's surname, but it was Mr. Mailer, who died in 2007 at 84, who dreamed up Church because he was struck by her having attended Free Will Baptist services three times a week as a child.

She gave birth to John Buffalo in 1978 and spent much of her time taking care of him; her first child, Matthew; and several of Mr. Mailer's seven other children. Mr. Mailer, whom she married in 1980, was by all accounts an attentive father, and at one point seven people were squeezed into the Mailers' apartment on the Brooklyn Heights promenade. All nine children were rounded up for summers in Maine and later Provincetown, Mass.

She was able to enter into her husband's potentially daunting orbit of the famous and the accomplished — people like Woody Allen, Bob Dylan and Jackie Onassis. She also organized her husband's social and family life and defended him against antagonists, like feminists offended by his 1971 volume, "The Prisoner of Sex."

"To me, the humor and irony was inherent," she later wrote. "But you can't transfer the twinkle in the eye to the page, so a lot of people treated everything he said as perfectly serious, like his famous comment that women should be kept in cages. Who would think he was serious about that?"

At one point the two nearly split over Mr. Mailer's infidelities, but he pleaded with her to stay, and she did, wanting to hold the family together. She also confided in a recent interview that she could not think of a single person she would rather have been with.

Making her own cultural mark, Ms. Mailer had nine one-woman art shows and, according to John Buffalo, appeared in several plays. Early in their relationship she showed Mr. Mailer 100 pages of a novel; his response, she recalled, was, "It's not as bad as I thought it would be." She put it away, but it came out in 2000 as "Windchill Summer," a story about coming of age in

Arkansas during the Vietnam War. In 2007 she published a sequel, "Cheap Diamonds," about an aspiring model from Arkansas who arrives in New York in the 1970s.

Whatever her own achievements, friends said she remained down to earth. "I'm not an intellectual," she said in an interview in 2010 with The New York Times. "I pick up People magazine instead of The New York Review of Books and read it first. That's just a fact. I tried very hard to make myself more literate, and I'm not a stupid woman, but some things interest me and some things don't."

FINDING HER NICHE: The Mailers at Radio City Music Hall in 1981.

Although her parents were from Arkansas, she was born on Jan. 31, 1949, in the state of Washington, where her father, James Davis, took a job building a dam while putting his family up in a trailer. By the time she was 2 they had returned to Arkansas, and she grew up in Atkins in a home that had an outhouse.

At the age of 3 she won the title of Little Miss Little Rock. At 20 she married her high school sweetheart, Larry Norris, but they divorced after five years. In addition to John Buffalo and Matthew, survivors include her stepchildren and her mother.

Before she met Mr. Mailer, Ms. Mailer said, she had a fling with the then-unmarried Bill Clinton. She told the story in her memoir. A friend who was in politics told her when Clinton was president, "I guess he slept with every woman in Arkansas except you."

"Sorry," she replied. "I'm afraid he got us all."

— *By Joseph Berger*

INGRID PITT

This Horror Star Knew the Real Thing

NOV. 21, 1937 - NOV. 23, 2010

Lovely and voluptuous, the actress Ingrid Pitt was given a choice early in her film career: pornography or horror. Ms. Pitt, who had spent her childhood in a Nazi concentration camp, later scoured Europe in search of her vanished father and still later was forced to flee East Germany a step ahead of the police, chose horror. It was a genre she knew firsthand.

Ms. Pitt, long celebrated as the first lady of British horror cinema, who starred in sanguinary classics of the 1970s like "The Vampire Lovers," "Countess Dracula" and "The House That Dripped Blood," died, apparently of heart failure, on Nov. 23 in London. She was 73 and had lived in London for many years.

Known for her tousled hair, pneumatic figure and sporadically sharp incisors, Ms. Pitt was closely associated with Hammer Film Productions, the British studio famous for the lurid, the lascivious and the low-budget. The Queen of Scream, the British press called her.

Hammer billed her as "the most beautiful ghoul in the world."

In fact, Ms. Pitt made only a handful of horror films, and not all for Hammer. But her striking, barely clad screen presence and vampirical Middle European accent — it was her real accent — secured her an international cult following that seems likely to remain undead for years to come.

She was also an enthusiastic keeper of her own flame, appearing at horror conventions and maintaining an evocative Web site, pittofhorror.com. So earnestly did Ms. Pitt continue to inhabit her screen persona that she was known on occasion to bite the necks of interviewers — not enough to draw blood but enough for dramatic impact.

QUEEN OF SCREAM: Ms. Pitt in the 1971 film "The House That Dripped Blood."

Ms. Pitt was born in Poland on Nov. 21, 1937. Her precise given name has been lost to time; British news articles have often rendered it as Ingoushka Petrov. Her father was German, her mother a Polish Jew, and in 1942 the Nazis picked the family up. Separated from her father and older sister, she was sent with her mother to the Stutthof concentration camp.

They were held there for three years. In interviews Ms. Pitt spoke of having seen her mother's best friend hanged and her own best friend, a little girl, raped and beaten to death by guards. She recalled lying in the straw, dreaming of being someone else.

After the war she and her mother trudged from one refugee camp to the next, searching for her father and sister. They eventually found them, but by then her father was a broken man. He lived only five years more.

As a young woman Ms. Pitt was determined to be an actress. In the 1950s she joined the Berliner Ensemble, directed by Helene Weigel, the second wife of Bertolt Brecht, and based in East Berlin. A vocal critic of the East German Communist government, Ms. Pitt was pursued by the police on the night of her debut performance, in Brecht's "Mother Courage and Her Children."

Fleeing, she jumped into the River Spree with her costume on, only to be fished out by an American serviceman, Laud Roland Pitt Jr. In fitting dramatic style, she married him soon afterward. That marriage ended in divorce, as did her second, to George Pinches, a British film executive.

Ms. Pitt began her screen career with several minor films in Spain; that she spoke no Spanish was apparently no impediment. Her first significant picture in the United States was "Where Eagles Dare" (1968), starring Richard Burton and Clint Eastwood.

This led to an audition for James Carreras, then the head of Hammer. As Ms. Pitt recounted in a 1997 interview with The Guardian of London, she prepared meticulously:

"I turned up at Jimmy's office in a maxicoat, a mane of hair, lots of makeup and high leather boots," she said. "I walked up to him, threw open my coat like a flasher. I was wearing the tiniest and lowest-cut minidress you can imagine."

She added: "He took me, darling, but not in the way film moguls are said to."

Ms. Pitt is survived by her daughter, Steffanie Pitt-Blake, an actress and graphic designer; her third husband, Tony Rudlin, a former racecar driver; and a grandchild. Her older sister died earlier this year.

Her other films include "The Wicker Man" (1973); "The Asylum" (2000), a horror movie starring her daughter; "Minotaur" (2006); and "Sea of Dust" (2008).

Ms. Pitt wrote several books, including a memoir, "Life's a Scream" (Heinemann, 1999), and "The Ingrid Pitt Bedside Companion for Vampire Lovers" (Batsford, 1998).

Though horror films made her famous, Ms. Pitt rarely watched them. "I don't want to see horror," she told The New Zealand Herald in 2006. "I think it's very amazing that I do horror films when I had this awful childhood. But maybe that's why I'm good at it."

— *By Margalit Fox*

PALLE HULD

The Model for Tintin?

AUG. 2, 1912 - NOV. 26, 2010

Palle Huld, a Danish actor whose fleet, youthful and highly public circumnavigation of the globe as a cowlicked teenager is believed to have inspired the popular comic-book character Tintin, died on Nov. 26 in Copenhagen. He was 98.

Created by the Belgian artist Hergé (the pseudonym of Georges Remi), Tintin was a snub-nosed teenage reporter who traveled the world with his trusty dog, Snowy, doing good deeds and foiling bad men.

The character made his debut in January 1929 in Le Petit Vingtième, the children's supplement of a Belgian newspaper. Over the next half-century (Hergé died in 1983), Tintin's exploits were chronicled in two dozen illustrated books, starting with "Tintin in the Land of the Soviets" in 1930 and ending with "Tintin and Alph-Art," published posthumously in 1986.

Translated into many languages, the books have sold more than 200 million copies worldwide, remain in print and retain an immense following.

A feature film, "The Adventures of Tintin: The Secret of the Unicorn," produced by Steven Spielberg and Peter Jackson, is scheduled to open in 2011.

BOY ADVENTURER: Mr. Huld before the start of his 1928 world trip.

According to many accounts in the European news media over the years, Tintin exists, at least in part, because a young Danish clerk in search of adventure happened to answer a newspaper ad one day.

Mr. Huld's life in the public eye began in 1928, when the Danish newspaper Politiken held a contest to honor the centennial of Jules Verne. The winner would re-enact Phileas Fogg's voyage from "Around the World in Eighty Days," Verne's celebrated 1873 novel.

There were to be some crucial twists: The contest was open only to teenage boys; the winner would circle the globe unaccompanied; and he had to complete the trip within 46 days, using any conveyance but the airplane.

From several hundred applicants, the newspaper chose Palle, a 15-year-old Boy Scout who had left school and was working as a clerk in an automobile dealership.

Palle left Denmark on March 1, 1928, and as he traveled by rail and steamship the world press chronicled his every move, through England, Scotland, Canada, Japan, the Soviet Union, Poland and Germany.

It also chronicled his triumphant homecoming, after just 44 days, to a cheering crowd of 20,000 in Copenhagen. His safe return was "much to the relief of his mother, who had been prescribed sleeping tablets for the duration," as The Copenhagen Post wrote in a profile of Mr. Huld earlier this year.

The young Mr. Huld wrote a book about his adventures, which was published in several languages and appeared in English as "A Boy Scout Around the World" (Coward-McCann, 1929).

Tintin historians (and there are many) have posited various sources for Hergé's hero, including Palle Huld. Mr. Huld seemed to credit the connection, but Hergé was not forthcoming on the subject, and Pierre Assouline, the author of "Hergé: The Man Who Created Tintin," published in English last year, said in an e-mail to The Times that he had never heard of Mr. Huld.

Nevertheless, certain similarities between the intrepid Danish clerk and the intrepid Belgian scribe are indisputable: Like his comic-book incarnation, Palle Huld was fresh-faced and freckled, with a turned-up nose and unruly red hair. On his journey, Palle was often photographed wearing plus-fours, Tintin's breeches of choice.

Palle Huld was born in 1912. He made his stage debut in 1934 at the Royal Danish Theater, with which he remained associated for many years. He also appeared regularly in Danish films and on television before his retirement a decade ago.

Information on survivors could not be confirmed. Mr. Huld is survived, at the very least, by his pen-and-paper incarnation, eternally inquisitive and eternally youthful.

— *By Margalit Fox*

LESLIE NIELSEN

A Comedian Waiting to Emerge

FEB. 11, 1926 - NOV. 28, 2010

Leslie Nielsen, the Canadian-born actor who in middle age tossed aside three decades of credibility in dramatic and romantic roles to make a new, far more successful career as a comic actor in films like "Airplane!" and the "Naked Gun" series, died on Nov. 28 in Fort Lauderdale, Fla. He was 84.

Mr. Nielsen, a tall man with a matinee-idol profile, was often cast as an earnest hero at the beginning of his film career, in the 1950s. His best-known roles included the stalwart spaceship captain in the science fiction classic "Forbidden Planet" (1956), the wealthy, available Southern aristocrat in "Tammy and the Bachelor" (1957) and an ocean liner captain faced with disaster in "The Poseidon Adventure" (1972).

In the 1960s and '70s, as his hair turned white and he became an even more distinguished figure, Mr. Nielsen played serious military men, government leaders and even a mob boss, appearing in crime dramas, westerns and the occasional horror movie.

Then, in the low-budget, big-money-making 1980 disaster-movie parody "Airplane!" he was cast as a clueless doctor on board a possibly doomed jetliner. Some of his lines became catch phrases. ("Surely you can't be serious," one character says. Mr. Nielsen's doctor replies: "I am serious. And don't call me Shirley.")

Critics and audiences alike praised his deadpan comic delivery, and his career was reborn.

"Airplane!" was followed by a television series, "Police Squad!" (1982), from the film's director-writers, David Zucker, Jim Abrahams and Jerry Zucker. It lasted only six episodes, but Mr. Nielsen, his goofy character, Lt. Frank Drebin, and the creators went on to three successful feature-film spinoffs.

(continued on page 180)

APPRECIATION

What Was So Special? Surely You Jest

"Surely you can't be serious."

That line, said not by Leslie Nielsen but to him (by Robert Hays, the ostensible male lead of "Airplane!"), might be taken to sum up Mr. Nielsen's career, or at least the part of it that people are most likely to remember.

Of course Mr. Nielsen could be serious. "I am serious! And don't call me Shirley." And that's what was so funny. He had also, until "Airplane!," been a sober and solid character actor, mostly on television, sometimes playing heavies, sometimes figures of bland authority. And if not for "Airplane!" and the spoofs that followed, he would be recalled now as one of those "hey, it's that guy" guys of an earlier era, lingering in the memory banks of baby boomers and Gen-Xers who watched way too much TV when they were children.

Mr. Nielsen's I.M.D.B. page lists a host of such appearances, on series whose names conjure images of urban decay and embattled masculinity: "Ironside," "Kojak, "Cannon," "Columbo." He also had bigger roles in shorter-lived shows, not all of them about cops (like "Bracken's World" and "The Virginian"). But all the curious researcher may really need to know to understand his peculiar and exemplary cultural trajectory is that he was the captain of the S.S. Poseidon.

Less than a decade separates "The Poseidon Adventure" — the grandest, goofiest and still the most watchable of the disaster flicks of the '70s (thanks mainly to Gene Hackman and Shelley Winters) — from "Airplane!," which appeared in 1980 to finish off that moribund genre and establish an era of spoofery that has not yet ended. By now it is likely that more people are familiar with the parody than with the "Airport" movies that were its targets, along with the older "Zero Hour!" And similarly, younger audiences (which is to say younger than 35 or so) are more likely to recognize Lieut. Frank Drebin, Mr. Nielsen's character in the "Police Squad" franchise, than the battered paladins of law enforcement he was lampooning.

When he died on Nov. 28 at 84, he had transcended both his "Police Squad!" and "Airplane!" roles in part by declining to deviate from them, becoming instead an all-purpose embodiment of the parodic principle itself. What made the old cop shows and disaster movies so susceptible to mockery — to the extent that they could survive in the pop-cultural bloodstream only when dosed with irony — was that their clean-cut, strong-featured heroes represented the last vestiges of a squareness that had been thoroughly routed by the youth culture of the '60s. Pilots, doctors, police detectives, ship captain: these were the kind patriarchal figures whose authority was almost completely undone, but who were still in some way necessary.

"Airplane!," released in the year of Ronald Reagan's election, is full of them. The pranksters who dreamed it up — the brothers David and Jerry Zucker and Jim Abrahams, collectively known as ZAZ

— recruited not only Mr. Nielsen, but also Peter Graves ("Mission: Impossible"), Robert Stack ("The Untouchables") and Lloyd Bridges ("Sea Hunt"), an example of the comic overkill that made the film an instant touchstone among smart alecks weaned on Mad magazine movie satires and the pop irreverence of the first seasons of "Saturday Night Live." So many sonorous voices and furrowed brows in one place! So many dads to make fun of!

But the spirit of ZAZ was more playful and affectionate than rebellious. "Airplane!" and its successors never felt dangerous, subversive or aggressive. And if they thumbed their noses at authority, it was with the implicit assumption that authority could take the joke.

And also, more important, that the joke could be repeated endlessly. Which is pretty much what Leslie Nielsen spent the last 30 years of his life doing. For a while he did sometimes still show up in noncomic roles, on dramatic television series and sometimes in movies like Martin Ritt's "Nuts" (1987), a rather remarkable, fascinatingly bad courtroom drama starring Barbra Streisand as a prostitute on trial for murder. But more often, and almost exclusively by the 1990s, Mr. Nielsen showed up in movies, series and commercials, representing in his own archetypal silver-haired persona an ideal of genial, deadpan nonseriousness. His presence was itself the joke. His afterlife is more likely to be on YouTube, where his best bits can be pulled out of context and assembled into a free-form collage of dour silliness.

This is not to understate his talent. On the contrary. Mr. Nielsen's ability to stay in character, to reel off sublime non sequiturs and koans of cluelessness with a precisely measured balance of dignity and density represents both a rare gift and considerable work. Looking back, it is easy to see that the times required someone like Leslie Nielsen: a handsome silver-haired gentleman of fatherly demeanor willing to commit and submit to any kind of indignity without losing his cool. But only the man himself had exactly the right background.

Not only because he was originally from Canada. That in itself is not special. Lorne Greene — a historical precondition for Leslie Nielsen — was Canadian. So is Lorne Michaels, the godfather of "Saturday Night Live," who helped pave the runway for "Airplane!" So are most people named Lorne and most people who manage to be funny on television or in movies without also being black or Jewish.

No, the uniqueness of Leslie Nielsen is inseparable from the nonspecialness of much of his career, his brilliant lack of distinction. Like many aspiring actors of the postwar era he trained at the Neighborhood Playhouse in New York, absorbing the high-middlebrow culture of the time (studying dance with Martha Graham), taking whatever opportunities came his way and maturing into a reliable and reasonably versatile actor.

The hallmarks of that kind of performer include a willingness to embrace even a half-baked part in a mediocre piece of work and a steadfast refusal to wink, mug or showboat even if circumstances cry out for it. "The Poseidon Adventure" may be a sublimely campy shipwreck, and the cop shows of the '70s may look now like gamy, cynical showcases for wide ties and retrograde social attitudes, but our ability to make jokes about and out of them would be spoiled if they had treated themselves like jokes in the first place.

Self-seriousness was always part of the fun, and no one understood that more completely, or made more of it, than Mr. Nielsen. Surely.

— *By A. O. Scott*

(continued from page 177)

The first, "The Naked Gun: From the Files of Police Squad!" (1988), was followed by "The Naked Gun 2 1/2: The Smell of Fear" (1991) and "The Naked Gun 33 1/3: The Final Insult" (1994). Mr. Nielsen's supporting cast included Priscilla Presley and O. J. Simpson.

Other filmmakers cast Mr. Nielsen in a variety of comedies, including "Repossessed" (1990), an "Exorcist" spoof with Linda Blair; Mel Brooks's "Dracula: Dead and Loving It" (1995); "Spy Hard" (1996); and "2001: A Space Travesty" (2000).

None were received as well as the "Naked Gun" films, but Mr. Nielsen found a new continuing role as the paranoid, out-of-control president of the United States in "Scary Movie 3" (2003) and "Scary Movie 4" (2006).

"Surely you can't be serious," one character says. Mr. Nielsen's doctor replies: "I am serious. And don't call me Shirley."

In keeping with his adopted comic persona, when Mr. Nielsen in 1993 published an autobiography, "Naked Truth," it was one that cheerfully, blatantly fabricated events in his life. They included two Academy Awards, an affair with Elizabeth Taylor and a stay at a rehabilitation center, battling dopey-joke addiction.

In real life he was nominated twice for Emmy Awards, in 1982 as outstanding lead actor in a comedy series for "Police Squad!" and in 1988 as outstanding guest actor in a comedy series for an episode of "Day by Day," an NBC sitcom about yuppies and day care.

Off screen, he was made an Officer of the Order of Canada, the country's highest civilian honor, in 2002.

Leslie William Nielsen was born on Feb. 11, 1926, in Regina, Saskatchewan. The son of a member of the Royal Canadian Mounted Police of Danish heritage and a Welsh mother, he grew up in the Northwest Territories and in Edmonton, Alberta, where he graduated from high school. Jean Hersholt, the Danish-born actor and humanitarian, was an uncle.

Mr. Nielsen enlisted in the Royal Canadian Air Force before his 18th birthday and trained as an aerial gunner during World War II, but he was never sent overseas.

He began his career in radio in Calgary, Alberta, then studied at the Academy of Studio Arts in Toronto and at the Neighborhood Playhouse in New York. This led him to his television debut, in a 1950 episode of "Actors Studio," an anthology series on CBS.

By the time Mr. Nielsen made his film debut, in 1956, he had made scores of appearances in series and performed in one Broadway play, "Seagulls Over Sorrento" in 1952, as a tyrannical Navy petty officer.

He continued to make guest appearances in television series throughout his career, and with great regularity through the 1970s. And he did stage work, touring North America and Britain in a one-man show about the crusading lawyer Clarence Darrow.

His final projects included two 2009 comedies, "Stan Helsing" and "Spanish Movie."

Mr. Nielsen married four times. His first wife (1950-56) was Monica Boyer; his second (1958-73) was Alisande Ullman, with whom he had two daughters; his third (1981 - 83) was Brooks Oliver. Those marriages ended in divorce.

In 2001 he married Barbaree Earl; a resident of Fort Lauderdale, she survives him, as do his daughters.

His elder brother, Erik Nielsen, who was deputy prime minister of Canada from 1984 to 1986, died in 2008.

In a 1988 interview with The New York Times, Leslie Nielsen discussed his career-rejuvenating transition to comedy, a development that he had recently described as "too good to be true."

"It's been dawning on me slowly that for the past 35 years I have been cast against type," he said, "and I'm finally getting to do what I really wanted to do."

— By Anita Gates

SAMUEL T. COHEN

Father of the Neutron Bomb

JAN. 25, 1921 - NOV. 28, 2010

SAMUEL T. COHEN, the physicist who invented the small tactical nuclear weapon known as the neutron bomb, a controversial device designed to kill enemy troops with subatomic particles but leave battlefields and cities relatively intact, died on Nov. 28 at his home in Los Angeles. He was 89.

Unlike J. Robert Oppenheimer and Edward Teller, the respective fathers of the atomic and hydrogen bombs, Mr. Cohen was not well known outside government and scientific circles, although his work for years influenced the international debate over the deployment and potential uses of nuclear arms.

In contrast to strategic warheads, which can kill millions and level cities, and smaller short-range tactical nuclear arms designed to wipe out battlefield forces, the neutron bomb minimized blast and heat. Instead, it maximized a barrage of infinitesimal neutrons that could zip through tanks, buildings and other structures and kill people, usually by destroying the central nervous system, and all other life forms.

While doubters questioned the usefulness, logic and ethics of killing people and sparing property, Mr. Cohen called his bomb a "sane" and "moral" weapon that could limit death, destruction and radioactive contamination, killing combatants while leaving civilians and towns unscathed. He insisted that many critics misunderstood or purposely misrepresented his ideas for political, economic or mercenary reasons.

A specialist in the radiological effects of nuclear weapons, he relentlessly promoted the neutron bomb for much of his life, writing books and articles, conferring with presidents and cabinet officials, taking his case to Congressional committees, scientific bodies and international forums. He won many converts, but ultimately failed to persuade the United States to integrate the device into its tactical nuclear arsenal.

The Reagan administration developed but never deployed the weapons in the 1980s. France, Israel and the Soviet Union were believed to have added versions of the bomb to their arsenals. Western military planners rejected their use in the Vietnam War and regarded them only as a possible deterrent to superior Soviet tank forces in Europe. But the end of the cold war obviated even that purpose.

A graduate of the University of California, Los Angeles, Mr. Cohen was recruited while in the Army in World War II for the Manhattan Project, which developed the first atomic bomb at Los Alamos, N.M. After the war, he joined the RAND Corporation and in 1958 designed the neutron bomb as a way to strike a cluster of enemy forces while sparing infrastructure and distant civilian populations.

Fired via a missile or an artillery shell and detonated a quarter-mile above ground, his bomb limited death to an area less than a mile across, avoiding wider indiscriminate slaughter and destruction. It was not a radioactively "clean" bomb, but its neutrons dissipated quickly, leaving no long-term contamination that could render entire regions uninhabitable.

But many military planners scoffed at the idea of a nuclear bomb that limited killing and destruction, and insisted that deployment would escalate the arms race and make nuclear war more likely. The device was anathema to military contractors and armed services with vested interests in nuclear arsenals. Even peace activists denounced it as "a capitalist weapon" because it killed people but spared the real estate.

Washington rejected the bomb repeatedly. The Kennedy administration said it might jeopardize a test-ban moratorium. The Johnson administration said its use in Vietnam might raise the specter of Hiroshima — Asians again slaughtered by American nuclear bombs — drawing worldwide condemnation. In 1978, President Jimmy Carter said development might impede disarmament prospects.

"It's the most sane and moral weapon ever devised. It's the only nuclear weapon in history that makes sense in waging war. When the war is over, the world is still intact."

In 1981, President Ronald Reagan ordered 700 neutron warheads built to oppose Soviet tank forces in Europe. He called it "the first weapon that's come along in a long time that could easily and economically alter the balance of power." But deployment to the North Atlantic alliance was canceled after a storm of antinuclear protests across Europe. President George H. W. Bush ordered the stockpile scrapped.

By 1982, Mr. Cohen had abandoned his deployment quest. But he continued for the rest of his life to defend the neutron bomb as practical and humane.

"It's the most sane and moral weapon ever devised," he said in September in a telephone interview for this obituary. "It's the only nuclear weapon in history that makes sense in waging war. When the war is over, the world is still intact."

Samuel Theodore Cohen was born in Brooklyn on Jan. 25, 1921, to Lazarus and Jenny Cohen, Austrian Jews who had migrated to the United States by way of Britain. His father was a carpenter and his mother a housewife who rigidly controlled family diets and even breathing habits (believing it unhealthy to breathe through the mouth). The boy had allergies, eye problems and other ailments, and for years was subjected to daily ice-water showers to toughen him up.

The family moved to Los Angeles when he was 4. He was a brilliant student at public schools and U.C.L.A., where he graduated in 1943 with a physics degree. He joined the wartime Army and was posted to the Massachusetts Institute of Technology for advanced training in mathematics and physics.

In 1944 he was tapped for the Manhattan Project to analyze radioactivity in nuclear fission. He worked on Fat Man, the bomb dropped on Nagasaki in 1945, days after Little Boy destroyed Hiroshima.

Mr. Cohen was married twice. His first marriage, to Barbara Bissell in 1948, ended in divorce in 1952. In 1960, he married Margaret Munnemann. She survives him, as do their three children and three grandchildren.

Mr. Cohen joined RAND in Santa Monica in 1947 and 11 years later designed the neutron bomb as a consultant to the Lawrence Livermore National Laboratory. Many technical features of what the Pentagon called an "enhanced radiation weapon" had been known for years, and scientists had theorized about a nuclear device that would release most of its energy as radiation.

All nuclear explosions produce a rain of potentially lethal neutrons, uncharged particles from an atom's nucleus, and Mr. Cohen, by adjusting components and reshaping the bomb shell, limited the blast and released more energy as neutrons — so tiny they passed easily through solid inanimate objects, but killed all living things in their path.

The military successfully tested the bomb, and over the next two decades Mr. Cohen campaigned for its deployment without success. He left RAND in 1969, but continued writing about the bomb. His articles appeared in The Washington Post, The New York Times, The Wall Street Journal and other publications. He was featured in a 1992 segment of the BBC-TV series "Pandora's Box."

Among his books are "Tactical Nuclear Weapons: An Examination of the Issues" (1978);

"The Truth About the Neutron Bomb" (1983); "We Can Prevent World War III" (1985); and a memoir, "Shame: Confessions of the Father of the Neutron Bomb," published on the Internet in 2000.

In recent years, Mr. Cohen warned of a black market substance called red mercury, supposedly capable of compressing fusion materials to detonate a nuclear device as small as a baseball — ideal for terrorists.

Most scientists call the substance mythical, and stories about it, many circulating on the Internet, are widely regarded as spurious.

— *By Robert D. McFadden*

BELLA AKHMADULINA

The Poet Who Flowered in a Thaw

APRIL 10, 1937 - NOV. 29, 2010

Bella Akhmadulina, a poet whose startling images and intensely personal style, couched in classical verse forms, established her as one of the Soviet Union's leading literary talents, died on Nov. 29 at her home in Peredelkino, outside Moscow. She was 73.

Her death was reported by the Russian news agency Itar-Tass, which quoted her husband, Boris Messerer, as saying that she had had a heart attack.

Ms. Akhmadulina came to prominence during the post-Stalin thaw, when a loosening of censorship led to a flowering of the arts. Along with the poets Yevgeny Yevtushenko (her first husband) and Andrei Voznesensky, she became one of the bold new voices in contemporary Russian literature, attracting ecstatic audiences of thousands to readings at concert halls and stadiums.

Her poetry was resolutely apolitical, making her a target of official criticism. Her early poems, usually in rhymed quatrains, offered random observations on everyday life — buying soda from a vending machine, coming down with the flu — in dense, allusive language enriched by coined words and archaisms. A sprightly sense of humor and an audacious way with images marked her from the outset as a distinctive talent.

"More and more severely the shivering/Lashed me, drove sharp, small nails into my skin," she wrote in one of her most famous poems, "A Chill" (sometimes translated as "Fever"). "It was like a hard rain pelting/An aspen and scourging all its leaves."

HONORED BY MOSCOW: Ms. Akhmadulina with Russian president Vladimir I. Putin in 2005.

She later turned to longer forms in works like "My Genealogy" and "Tale About the Rain," both published in the collection "Music Lessons" (1969), or short poems laced into a sequence, notably in the collections "The Secret" (1983) and "The Garden" (1987).

Her themes, as she matured, became more philosophical, even religious, or they dwelled on the nature of poetic language. "O magic theater of a poem,/spoil yourself, wrap up in sleepy velvet./I don't matter," she wrote in one characteristic verse.

Although apolitical as a poet, she openly supported persecuted writers like Boris Pasternak and Aleksandr Solzhenitsyn and political dissidents like Andrei D. Sakharov. In 1979, she fell out of favor by contributing a short story to Vasily Aksyonov's unofficial collection Metropol, a transgression that froze her already chilly relations with the government.

Despite her shaky official reputation, she was always recognized as one of the Soviet Union's literary treasures and a classic poet in the long line extending from Lermontov and Pushkin.

"She was one of the great poets of the 20th century," said Sonia I. Ketchian, the author of "The Poetic Craft of Bella Akhmadulina" (1993). "There's Akhmatova, Tsvetaeva, Mandelstam and Pasternak — and she's the fifth."

Izabella Akhatovna Akhmadulina was born in Moscow on April 10, 1937. Her father was a Tatar, and her mother claimed a mixed Russian-Italian ancestry. During World War II, the family was evacuated to Kazan.

Bella, as she was always known, gravitated to the poetic circle around Yevgeny Vinokurov, and by the mid-1950s she had begun publishing her own work.

She enrolled in the Gorky Literary Institute in Moscow, but her nonpolitical stance as a writer made life difficult for her. Nevertheless, she managed to gain membership in the Writers Union, and her first volume of poetry, "The String," was published in 1962. Thereafter she was published sporadically, although her poetry circulated widely in manuscript form. Her second volume of verse, "A Chill," was published in Germany in 1968.

Early on, the émigré critic Marc Slonim predicted a brilliant future for her. "Her voice has such a purity of tone, such richness of timbre, such individuality of diction, that if her growth continues she will be able some day to succeed Akhmatova," he wrote in "Soviet Russian Literature" (1964), a feat that would make her "the greatest living woman poet in Russia."

Beautiful and charismatic, she married a series of prominent artists, starting with Mr. Yevtushenko, whom she met at a student gathering in 1954. She made an indelible first impression, with her "round, childish face," thick red hair tied in a braid and "slanting Tatar eyes flashing," as he recalled in his 1963 memoir, "A Precocious Autobiography." "This was Bella Akhmadulina, whom I married a few weeks later."

Although Mr. Yevtushenko wrote a series of love poems to her, the marriage did not last, and Ms. Akhmadulina would later claim not to remember the relationship. She went on to marry the short-story writer Yuri M. Nagibin, the children's writer Gennadi Mamlin and the film director Eldar Kuliev before marrying Mr. Messerer, a set designer for the Bolshoi Ballet, in 1974. In addition to her husband, she is survived by two daughters.

With the arrival of glasnost and perestroika, the honors and official acclaim denied her under the Soviet regime came in a torrent. She was awarded the U.S.S.R. State Prize in 1989 and the State Prize of the Russian Federation in 2004. She published several collections of verse in the 1980s and '90s, including "Casket and Key" (1994), "A Guiding Sound" (1995) and "One Day in December" (1996).

Like so many Russian writers, Ms. Akhmadulina stood for more than literary accomplishment. To Russian audiences she embodied the soul of poetry and expressed, in her clashes with the authorities, the moral imperative behind Russian literature.

"There is only one honorable reason for writing poetry — you can't do without it," she said in an interview during her first visit to the United States in 1977. "When a young person comes to ask me, 'Should I, should I not, write poetry?' I say, 'If there's a choice, don't.'"

— *By William Grimes*

STEPHEN SOLARZ

'Representative Pothole,' Who Sought to Fix the World

SEPT. 12, 1940 - NOV. 29, 2010

STEPHEN J. SOLARZ, a nine-term Democratic congressman whose concerns went beyond traffic lights and beach erosion in his Brooklyn district to nuclear weapons, the Middle East and his revelation that Imelda Marcos owned 3,000 pairs of shoes, died on Nov. 29 in Washington. He was 70 and lived in McLean, Va.

His death was caused by esophageal cancer, his wife, Nina, said.

When he was elected to the House in 1974, Mr. Solarz finagled a seat on the Foreign Affairs Committee with the idea that he could appeal to his largely Jewish district by attending to the needs of Israel. He immediately threw himself into foreign policy issues, visiting leaders of Israel, Jordan, Egypt and Syria in his first month on the job. He soon became a leading voice in the House on foreign affairs.

BEYOND BROOKLYN: Mr. Solarz visited more than 100 countries during his nine terms in Congress.

Mr. Solarz was defeated in a Democratic primary in 1992 after being caught up in a scandal involving the bank operated for House members and after his district had been redrawn to facilitate the election of a Hispanic candidate. But his arrival in 1975 was a moment of triumph, both for himself and for his party.

Mr. Solarz was part of a huge class of 75 freshman Democrats who forced changes in the seniority system, giving newer representatives much more influence. The public's interest in global affairs had been heightened by the Vietnam War, and the abuses of presidential power in the Watergate affair had given new steam to Congress.

"I was elected to Congress at precisely the moment in American history when Congress decided it would no longer abdicate its constitutional authority for foreign policy to an executive branch that had lost its claim to presidential infallibility," Mr. Solarz wrote in his preface to "Journeys to War and Peace: A Congressional Memoir," to be published in 2011.

Mr. Solarz would go on to be the first congressman to visit North Korea in 30 years; have a nine-hour conversation with Fidel Castro; introduce a nuclear freeze resolution; help alter Reagan administration policies in Central America and Lebanon; and battle many in his own party when he supported the Persian Gulf war in 1991.

Mr. Solarz visited more than 100 countries, more than earning his nickname, the Marco Polo of Congress. He once got a standing ovation on the floor of the Indian Parliament.

Mr. Solarz was a torrent of activity during his first six months in Congress. According to his office, he made 12 speeches on the House floor, co-sponsored 370 bills, held 11 news conferences, made 24 trips to his district and attended 99 events there, visited 23 subway stations, sent constituents 513,720 pieces of mail and took an 18-day tour of the Middle East.

And he became adept at winning the support of House colleagues. "You don't just win on the merits," Representative Barney Frank of Massachusetts said after Mr. Solarz's death. "He understood legislating."

Mr. Solarz's early battles included an unsuccessful effort to stop the Carter administration's sale of F-15 jets to Saudi Arabia in 1978. The next year, Mr. Solarz was named chairman of the Foreign Affairs Committee's African subcommittee and worked with President Jimmy Carter to thwart the lifting of sanctions against Rhodesia for its racist policies.

In 1981, he gave up his post on the African subcommittee to take over the subcommittee on Asian and Pacific affairs. There he developed a peace plan that helped end the genocide in Cambodia. He returned from his 1980 visit to North Korea with the news that the country's dictator, Kim Il-sung, was interested in improving relations with the United States.

In his 1986 hearings on the Philippines, Mr. Solarz provided irrefutable evidence that President Ferdinand Marcos was misusing foreign aid, leading to the uncovering of the vast United States real estate empire he shared with his wife, Imelda — not to mention Mr. Solarz's blockbuster disclosure about her shoes.

In an interview, Robert Dallek, the presidential historian, praised Mr. Solarz's commitment to building democracy in places like the Philippines, South Korea, Lebanon and Taiwan. "He struck idealistic notes with a lot of his colleagues," Mr. Dallek said.

But he was also pragmatic, said Paul D. Wolfowitz, the former deputy defense secretary and World Bank president, who worked with Mr. Solarz on Asian issues during the Reagan administration. Mr. Solarz, he said, showed that allying with forces fighting repression could be good policy.

"Solarz understood that idealism and realism actually go together," he said.

Stephen Joshua Solarz was born on Sept. 12, 1940, in Manhattan. His parents, Sanford Solarz and the former Ruth Fertig, divorced soon after his birth, and his mother vanished from his life. He was raised first by his father and a stepmother, then by a widowed aunt in Brooklyn after his father divorced again.

His political career began when he was elected president of his sixth-grade class; he was later elected president of the student government at Midwood High School in Brooklyn. After graduating from Brandeis University, where he edited the school newspaper, he entered Columbia Law School. But he quickly became bored by the law and switched his studies, earning a master's degree in public law and government from Columbia.

While at Columbia he joined the ranks of reform Democrats in Brooklyn, and at 25 he helped run the primary campaign of Melvin Dubin, an antiwar candidate for Congress. Mr. Dubin lost, but while working for the campaign Mr. Solarz met Nina Koldin, whom he later married. She survives him, as do his mother, his brothers, his stepson, his stepdaughter and four grandchildren.

Mrs. Solarz had persuaded her husband to run for the State Assembly in 1968 and, using her inheritance, had bankrolled his early campaigns, including his first race for Congress in 1974. She pleaded guilty in 1995 to two criminal charges of writing bad checks against their account at the House bank. Mr. Solarz, despite 743 overdrafts, was not charged.

Before running for Congress, Mr. Solarz served three terms in the Assembly. He lost a race for Brooklyn borough president in 1973 but generally won elections by high margins. He lost his district in 1992, however, when the state's Congressional delegation shrunk to 31 from 34 because of population loss. He chose to run in a district that had been reconfigured to include parts of Queens, Manhattan and Brooklyn to help a Hispanic candidate win. Running against five Hispanic opponents in the Democratic primary, he lost to Nydia M. Velázquez, who went on to win the general election and remains the district's representative.

After his political career Mr. Solarz worked as a consultant and volunteer for nonprofit international organizations. He was a leader of the International Crisis Group, which works with governments and global organizations to quell deadly conflicts.

As a congressman Mr. Solarz was always mindful of local issues, calling himself "Representative Pothole." In 1990, he introduced a bill denying a sports team that leaves a city the right to sue for trademark infringement. The bill grew out of a suit filed by the Los Angeles Dodgers against the Brooklyn Dodgers Sports Bar and Restaurant in Brooklyn. Mr. Solarz wanted to get in one last lick at the team that had fled to the West Coast and broken his borough's heart.

— *By Douglas Martin*

FRANK EMI

A 'No-No Boy' Behind Barbed Wire

SEPT. 23, 1916 - DEC. 1, 2010

For nearly four years, through scorching summer heat, dust storms and frigid winters, 11,000 residents of the United States were forced to live in barracks, surrounded by barbed-wire fences, guard towers and searchlights at the Heart Mountain Relocation Center in the northwest Wyoming desert.

They were among more than 110,000 Japanese-Americans, most from the West Coast, who were herded from their homes to inland detention centers after President Franklin D. Roosevelt, within three months of the attack on Pearl Harbor, issued Executive Order 9066, deeming them threats to national security.

"The military escorted us to the camp with their guns and bayonets, so there really wasn't much thought about standing up for your rights at that time," one internee, Frank Emi, later told the Japanese-American oral history project at California State University, Fullerton.

The phrase he heard among the detainees was "Shikata ga nai" — it can't be helped.

That would change two years later, after the government had begun drafting detainees into the military. Ordered to fight for the country that had imprisoned them, many were defiant, Mr. Emi among them. At Heart Mountain they formed a committee to organize a protest, arguing that they would serve only after their rights had been fully restored. More than 300 detainees in all 10 detention camps joined their cause.

For Mr. Emi, the mantra became "No more shikata ga nai."

Mr. Emi (pronounced EH-me), the last surviving leader of the committee, died on Dec. 1. He was 94 and lived in San Gabriel, Calif.

Not all Japanese-Americans were opposed to serving in the military. After the War Department, at the urging of Japanese-American leaders, decided in 1943 to allow detainees to volunteer for an all-Japanese-American unit, many signed up. Their unit, the 442nd Regimental Combat Team, went to Europe under the rallying cry "Go for Broke!" The 442nd would become one of the most highly decorated regiments in United States history, earning 9,486 Purple Hearts and 21 Medals of Honor.

But when the government decided to start drafting Japanese-Americans in January 1944, scores of internees saw it as the last straw.

"Many of the internees took the reopening of the draft as an unwarranted test of their patriotism," Eric Muller, a professor of constitutional law at the University of North Carolina and the author of "Free to Die for Their Country" (2001), said in an interview. "Some young men decided they had had enough. Why should they and their families, who had lost all of their rights and privileges of citizenship, be asked to shoulder its greatest burden?"

Mr. Emi and six other internees at Heart Mountain formed the Fair Play Committee. They held meetings in mess halls, distributed fliers to all the camps and sought to initiate a court case to re-establish their rights as citizens.

The resisters themselves met resistance in the camps. Some feared they were only doing harm to Japanese-Americans and called them "no-no boys." Some, so proud of the volunteers in the 442nd Regiment, called them cowards and traitors. The Japanese American Citizens League called for them to be charged with sedition.

But as far as Mr. Emi was concerned, as he told The Los Angeles Times in 1993, "We could either tuck our tails between our legs like a beaten dog or stand up like free men and fight for justice."

DRAFT RESISTER: Mr. Emi with a daughter at the Heart Mountain camp in Wyoming.

Charged with draft evasion, all of the more than 300 resisters were sentenced to prison terms of approximately three years.

In separate indictments, Mr. Emi and six other leaders of the Fair Play Committee were charged with conspiracy to counsel draft evasion. Four, including Mr. Emi, were sentenced to four years; two received two-year sentences, and the seventh was acquitted. They were sent to the federal penitentiary in Leavenworth, Kan., where they were surrounded by hardened criminals.

"Frank was a black-belt judo expert," Professor Muller said. "The first thing they did at Leavenworth was stage a judo exhibition in which the little guys threw the big guys. After that nobody bothered them."

Three months after the war, the convictions of the committee leaders were overturned by a federal appeals court; they were released after serving 18 months. The 300 charged as draft resisters lost their appeal, but on Christmas Eve 1947, President Harry S. Truman pardoned them all.

Frank Seishi Emi was born in Los Angeles on Sept. 23, 1916. His parents owned a food market. When his father was injured in a car accident, Mr. Emi dropped out of college to run the business.

He was married and had one child when Executive Order 9066 was issued. The business and the family home were never recovered after the war. He later worked as a postal clerk.

Mr. Emi is survived by his second wife, Itsuko, two daughters, a stepdaughter, a sister, nine grandchildren and four great-grandchildren.

Many Japanese-Americans continued to disapprove of the draft resisters after the war, but as the years went by, attitudes changed, and in 2000, the Japanese American Citizens League, which had once condemned the resisters, formally apologized to them at its national convention in Monterey, Calif.

Two years later, at a league ceremony honoring the resisters, Senator Daniel K. Inouye, Democrat of Hawaii, a veteran of the 442nd Regiment and a Medal of Honor recipient, addressed the crowd in a videotaped message.

"Some young men answered the call to military service," Mr. Inouye said, "and they did so with honor and with great courage. Some young men chose to make their point by resisting the government's order to report for the draft. They too were honorable and courageous."

— By Dennis Hevesi

RON SANTO

A Beloved, and Beleaguered, Cub

FEB. 25, 1940 - DEC. 2, 2010

RON SANTO, a star third baseman of the Chicago Cubs and their longtime broadcaster, who became a revered figure for his exploits on the field and his battle against juvenile diabetes, died on Dec. 2 in a hospital in Arizona, where he lived during the off-season. He was 70.

The cause was complications of bladder cancer, said WGN Radio, where Santo was a Cubs color commentator for the last 21 years.

Playing for the Cubs from 1960 to 1973, then for a final season with the Chicago White Sox, Santo hit 342 career home runs. He won five Gold Glove awards for fielding every season from 1964 to 1968 and was named an All-Star nine times. Although repeatedly passed over for the Baseball Hall of Fame, he was the leading vote-getter in balloting by a veterans committee in 2008.

Santo was an important figure on the 1969 Cubs team that held a wide lead over the Mets in the National League East race before collapsing in yet another notorious chapter for a franchise that has not won a pennant since 1945 or a World Series since 1908. An enduring image from the 1969 season showed a black cat scampering by Santo as he awaited his turn to bat at Shea Stadium in September. But Santo endeared himself to the Bleacher Bums in their hard hats at Wrigley Field that summer by clicking his heels with joy after victories.

That Santo was on a major league field, let alone starring alongside the future Hall of Famers Ernie Banks, Billy Williams and Ferguson Jenkins, seemed remarkable.

When he took a routine physical at 18, Santo was found to have juvenile diabetes.

"I didn't know what it was, so I went to the library and looked it up," he told The Chicago Sun-Times in 1990. "I can still remember the feeling I had when I read the description: life expectancy of a juvenile insulin-dependent diabetic: 25 years. It also stated that it would cause blindness, kidney failure and hardening of the arteries. At that point, I said to myself, 'I'm going to fight this thing and beat it.' That's how badly I wanted to live and be a big league ballplayer."

Santo took insulin but kept his diabetes a secret from the Cubs until he was named to his first All-Star team in 1963, fearing that management's knowledge of his illness might have damaged his career. He did not allow the public to know of his diabetes until his final years with the Cubs.

> "I said to myself, 'I'm going to fight this thing and beat it.' That's how badly I wanted to live and be a big league ballplayer."

After his playing days ended, Santo raised millions of dollars for diabetes research. The disease took a heavy toll on him. He had heart attacks, went through quadruple-bypass surgery, then underwent amputation of his legs, in 2001 and 2002, as a result of circulatory problems.

Using prostheses and walking with a cane, he persevered as a broadcaster, elated when things went right and deflated when the Cubs were, well, the Cubs.

"I think I've personally become more popular as a broadcaster because I'm like they are," Santo told The New York Times in 2008, referring to the fans who regularly pack Wrigley Field. "They love it when I let how I feel out, with the emotions."

Major League Baseball's Web site quoted Banks as calling Santo "one of the greatest competitors I've ever seen."

Banks was known as Mr. Cub. Nonetheless, as Billy Williams once put it: "If you say Chicago Cubs, you say Ron Santo."

Ronald Edward Santo was born on Feb. 25, 1940, in Seattle. He was signed by the Cubs' organization after high school, and when he first entered Wrigley Field, walking alongside Banks, he was transfixed.

"We came out of the clubhouse in left field, and I'm walking down on the grass and I'm looking out to the outfield, and the ivy hadn't quite blossomed yet, but it was close," he told The Denver Post in 2004. "It was like walking on air. There was a feeling of electricity that I've never had."

Santo became a regular in 1961, emerging as a smooth fielder and an outstanding right-handed batter with power. He was durable as well, playing in 390 consecutive games before he was hit in the cheekbone by a pitch from the Mets' Jack Fisher in June 1966.

He had four seasons in which he hit .300, and he hit at least 30 home runs every year from 1964 to 1967. He was a mainstay of a superb Cubs infield of the 1960s, with Banks having switched to first base from shortstop, Glenn Beckert at second base and Don Kessinger at short.

Still, it was not enough to hold off the Mets in 1969, and Santo had never made it to a World Series when he retired after 15 seasons with a career batting average of .277, along with 2,254 hits and 1,331 runs batted in.

For Santo, there was much adversity even beyond his medical travails. His father was an alcoholic who left the family when Santo and his sister were youngsters. His mother remarried, and then in 1973, when his mother and stepfather were driving from California to see him at spring training in Arizona, both were killed in an auto accident.

After various business ventures, Santo began working as a Cubs color commentator on WGN in the early 1990s, occasionally broadcasting alongside the legendary Harry Caray. For the last 15 seasons, he teamed with the play-by-play announcer Pat Hughes.

UNDETERRED BY ILLNESS: Santo, left, covers third base in 1969. Despite being diabetic, Santo was a mainstay of the Cubs' infield for nearly a decade.

Santo is survived by his wife, Vicki, four children; and his grandchildren.

The Cubs retired his No. 10 at Wrigley Field in September 2003, and he stood and waved from the radio booth as the crowd cheered.

When the Cubs had first announced they would fly Santo's number from the left-field foul pole, he told The Associated Press: "There's nothing more important to me in my life than this happening to me. I'm a Cubbie. I'll always be a Cubbie."

— *By Richard Goldstein*

ELAINE KAUFMAN

Feeding and Fussing Over the Famous

FEB. 10, 1929 - DEC. 3, 2010

ELAINE KAUFMAN, who became something of a symbol of New York as the salty den mother of Elaine's, one of the city's best-known restaurants and a second home for almost half a century to writers, actors, athletes and other celebrities, died on Dec. 3 in Manhattan. She was 81.

Her death, at Lenox Hill Hospital, was caused by complications of emphysema, said Diane Becker, the restaurant's manager.

To the patrons she knew at her Upper East Side establishment, Ms. Kaufman was the quirky, opinionated, tender-hearted and imposingly heavyset proprietor who came in almost every night to check on things and schmooze, moving from table to table and occasionally perching herself on a stool at the end of her 25-foot mahogany bar.

With those she did not know, her demeanor varied; some accused her of being rude, though she indignantly denied that she ever was. As she put it, she had little time to explain to dissatisfied customers why they were being directed to tables in the back, known as Siberia, or led to the bar or even turned away, when they could clearly see empty tables along "the line."

"The line" was the row of tables along the right wall of the main room, extending from the front to the back and visible from the entrance. Those tables were almost always saved for the most valued regulars, with or without reservations. One was Woody Allen, who filmed a scene for "Manhattan" at Elaine's.

Elaine's, in fact, was a scene, a lively, celebrated celebrity hangout that all but shouted "New York" to the rest of the country, if not the world. For Billy Joel, in his 1979 hit "Big Shot," the very name connoted an uptown in-crowd. ("They were all impressed with your Halston dress/And the people that you knew at Elaine's.") And in the 2010 movie "Morning Glory," with Harrison Ford, Diane Keaton and Rachel McAdams, the indomitable Ms. Kaufman herself makes a cameo appearance.

Of course, it was an unspoken rule among the patrons never to appear overly impressed or distracted by the famous. This was New York, after all. But there were exceptions. Mick Jagger was one. ("The room grew still," Ms. Kaufman recalled.) Luciano Pavarotti was another. ("Everyone stood up and applauded.") And Willie Nelson proved irresistible. ("He kissed all the women at the bar.")

Once, when a newcomer asked directions to the men's room, Ms. Kaufman replied, "Take a right at Michael Caine."

Ms. Kaufman opened her restaurant in 1963, along an unfashionable block on Second Avenue just north of 88th Street. Soon a loyal clientele began to form, as if by chain reaction.

Almost from the beginning there were writers, many of whom were granted credit privileges when cash was low or nonexistent. And the writers — Gay Talese, George Plimpton, Peter Maas, Dan Jenkins, Joseph Heller, Mario Puzo, Frank Conroy and others — drew editors: Clay Felker, Willie Morris and James Brady, to name a few.

Then came theater, film and television personalities, eager to meet literary lights. And they, having added to the growing cultural cachet, soon attracted the famous from other arenas — sports figures, politicians and gossip-column society — all wanting to be part of the scene.

Elaine's flourished, despite its less-than-stellar reputation for food. For 14 years, it was the site of the New York Oscar-night parties hosted by

Entertainment Weekly. "I live a party life," Ms. Kaufman said in an interview in 1983 in The New York Times. "Elsa Maxwell used to have to send out invitations. I just open the door."

Elaine Edna Kaufman was born in Manhattan on Feb. 10, 1929, one of four children of Joseph and Pauline Kaufman. Brought up in Queens and the Bronx, she graduated from Evander Childs High School in the Bronx and worked at the stamp department at Gimbels, a wholesale fabric house and the long-gone Astor Pharmacy, where she was night cosmetician. She also checked hats and sold cigars at the Progressive Era Political Club in Greenwich Village before being introduced to the restaurant business by Alfredo Viazzi.

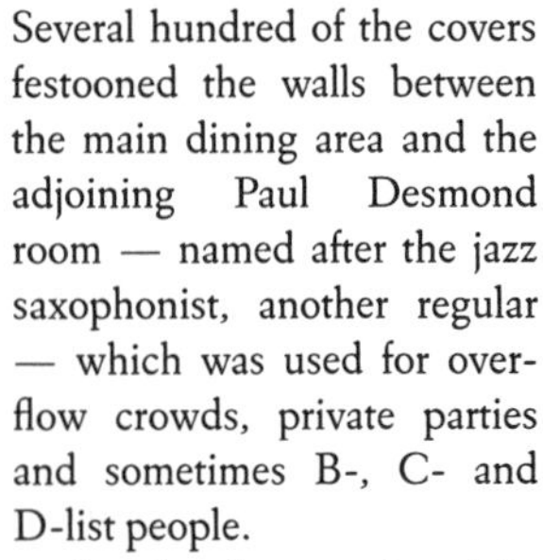

DEN MOTHER: Ms. Kaufman's restaurant was a magnet for writers, actors and sports stars.

Mr. Viazzi, a former seaman and struggling writer, owned Portofino, a Greenwich Village restaurant popular with publishing and downtown theater people, and in 1959 he and Ms. Kaufman, having begun a romantic relationship, joined forces in running it.

When she broke up with Mr. Viazzi four years later, she took her pots and pans, as she put it, and decided to open her own restaurant. "I couldn't afford to open in the Village," she said, "so I found an Austrian-Hungarian restaurant in an area of the Upper East Side which was Siberia then." She bought it with a partner for "$10,000 or $12,000," she said. (Within eight years she was the sole owner.)

Many of her old patrons followed her uptown, and neighborhood celebrities like the painters Helen Frankenthaler and Robert Motherwell, who were married at the time, began dropping in. She was also discovered by the columnists Dorothy Kilgallen and Leonard Lyons.

During the first year, Ms. Kaufman waited on tables herself; one summer Elaine Stritch, unwilling to do summer stock, tended bar.

The restaurant's indifferent décor — the comedian Alan King once said the place was "decorated like a stolen car" — changed little through the years. The rummage from junk shops and $5 light fixtures remained, but one feature continued to grow: the framed covers of books by authors who ate and drank there. Several hundred of the covers festooned the walls between the main dining area and the adjoining Paul Desmond room — named after the jazz saxophonist, another regular — which was used for overflow crowds, private parties and sometimes B-, C- and D-list people.

In the later 1960s Ms. Kaufman bought the low-rise, walk-up building that houses the restaurant as well as the building next to it. The rental apartments above helped finance the restaurant over the years.

Ms. Kaufman treated many of her regular patrons as both friends and extended family, though she had her limits. She had several run-ins with the well known. After an argument with her, Norman Mailer vowed never to return and wrote her an unflattering letter. She scribbled "Boring" across the top and sent it back to him. A day or two later, he was back.

In 1998, Ms. Kaufman was arrested on assault charges after slapping a customer. The case involved a man and a woman who said she had called them "white trash" after they ordered one drink between them. Ms. Kaufman denied using the expression and said she had slapped the man only after "he got in my face." The charges were later dropped, as were civil lawsuits that both Ms. Kaufman and the customer filed.

Ms. Kaufman was married in 1980 to Henry Ball, who was also in the restaurant business. They were divorced in 1984, and he died in later years. Ms. Kaufman, who lived in Manhattan, is survived by three nephews, a niece and several cousins.

Though patronage at Elaine's fell off in the late 1980s, it returned within several years, and the restaurant, which often stays open until the wee hours, once again became a favorite of celebrities. It was a prime destination on summer Sunday evenings, when weekenders returning to the city stopped in for dinner. But on almost any night, the regulars treated it as their club, talking to friends and to Elaine and playing darts, card games and backgammon. The games ended some years ago, but the red-walled ambience remained.

In 2003, Ms. Kaufman was named a Living Landmark by the New York Landmarks Conservancy.

"I've lived just about the most perfect life," Ms. Kaufman said in 1998. "I've had the best time. If I wanted to do something, I did it. Designers designed my clothes and did my apartment. I had house seats for the theater. I was invited to screenings and book parties. I've had fun. What else can you ask in life?"

— By Enid Nemy

PIERRE DE BEAUMONT

A Yankee Count With a Gift for Selling Gadgets

AUG. 1, 1915 - DEC. 4, 2010

Pierre de Beaumont, a nominal nobleman and inveterate tinkerer who founded Brookstone, the gadget-and-gift retailer that is a familiar presence in American shopping malls, died on Dec. 4 at his home in Manchester-by-the-Sea, Mass. He was 95.

With his wife, Mary, Mr. Beaumont began Brookstone in 1965, for $500, in their Berkshires farmhouse. (The company, originally a catalog retailer of hard-to-find tools, was named after their farm.) After learning accounting by correspondence, the couple mailed catalogs to thousands of hobbyists, sowing the seeds of a going concern.

Today Brookstone, based in Merrimack, N.H., has more than 300 brick-and-mortar stores throughout the United States, as well as its catalog and Internet business. Its wares include luggage, massage chairs and remote-control toys. Brookstone's sales in 2009, the most recent year for which figures are available, totaled $430 million, the company said.

If it seems incongruous that so fundamentally Yankee an enterprise was conceived by a French count — for that, technically, was what Mr. de Beaumont was, though he did not noise it about — then it bears noting that he was also a trained engineer who had worked for the Packard Motor Car Company.

Equally incongruous, and even less widely known, was the fact that Mr. de Beaumont happened to own the rights to an emblematic American art form, the "Mutt and Jeff" comic strip, which he had inherited from his mother, a countess and occasional Broadway chorus girl. She had obtained them after a marital dispute that was widely covered in the newspapers and also involved frogs.

Pierre Stuart de Beaumont, familiarly known as Pete, was born in New York on Aug. 1, 1915, while his mother, a French beauty who had married a count, was on a visit there. After Pierre's father, Count de Beaumont, was killed in World War I, his mother, the former Aedita Stuart, settled in New York with her son.

Under the name Gypsy Norman, the countess found work in the chorus of early-1920s Broadway revues, including "Bombo," starring Al Jolson, and "The Whirl of New York."

Pierre de Beaumont attended Harvard, from which he earned a bachelor's degree in engineering in 1938; he later worked for Packard and General Motors.

Meanwhile, the Countess de Beaumont had married — and, in a welter of wooings and suings avidly chronicled in the press, separated from — the cartoonist Harry C. Fisher. Mr. Fisher, known as Bud, had created what became "Mutt and Jeff," the long-popular comic strip about two mismatched tinhorns, in 1907.

In 1925, Mr. Fisher married Countess de Beaumont aboard a trans-Atlantic liner. In 1927, a New York judge granted her a legal separation after she testified, as The New York Times reported, to "her husband's cruelty" in "permitting her to be neglected by his servants while they looked after a number of live frogs he maintained in their former apartment on Riverside Drive."

Mr. Fisher died in 1954. Mrs. Fisher, who apparently never divorced him, retained the rights to "Mutt and Jeff." These later devolved on Mr. de Beaumont.

"Mutt and Jeff" is currently reprinted in syndication in about 40 newspapers worldwide.

Mr. de Beaumont's first marriage, to Barbara Anne Longstreth, ended in divorce. His second wife, the former Mary Deland Robbins Kelley, whom he married in 1960, died in 2001. He is survived by three stepchildren, seven step-grandchildren and seven step-great-grandchildren.

Brookstone was acquired by the Quaker Oats Company in 1980; it is now owned by a consortium led by Osim International, a Singapore retailer.

> With his wife, Mary, Mr. Beaumont began Brookstone in 1965, for $500, in their Berkshires farmhouse. Now it has more than 300 stores.

In founding Brookstone, Mr. de Beaumont identified and closed a small but singular gap in the market. Where else could consumers find, all in one place, sought-after arcana like miniature anvils, wood-rot-cure kits and dental picks (prized by makers of model ships)?

"As far as we could tell, no one else was selling those types of things," he told The Times in 1981. "We didn't know whether it was a hole in the market or a hole to fall into."

— *By Margalit Fox*

DON MEREDITH

The Monday Night Quarterback

APRIL 10, 1938 - DEC. 5, 2010

Don Meredith, a former star quarterback for the Dallas Cowboys who helped changed the perception of professional football with the easy Texas charm and provocative wit he brought to its first prime-time telecasts on Monday nights, died on Dec. 5 in Santa Fe, N.M. He was 72.

The cause was a brain hemorrhage, his lawyer said.

Mr. Meredith always thought of himself as the small-town kid from Mount Vernon, Tex., where his parents, Jeff and Hazel, owned a dry goods store and where his mother swung a tire so he could practice throwing a football at a moving target. He spent much of his life backing away from the nickname Dandy Don, particularly during his secluded later decades in New Mexico.

As a boy, Mr. Meredith dreamed of playing in the Cotton Bowl, 100 miles to the southwest in Dallas, and that was where he played many home games in high school, at Southern Methodist University in Dallas and in the pros. He set passing records for the Cowboys that still stand, including the one for most yards in a game, 460, set on Nov. 10, 1963, against San Francisco.

But it was his sparkling, fun-loving personality that seemed to define him. As a quarterback he sometimes irked the buttoned-down Cowboys coach, Tom Landry, by breaking into a country tune in the huddle; as one of the first color commentators on ABC's "Monday Night Football" he made his down-home ribbing of the loquacious Howard Cosell, one of his two broadcasting partners, a hallmark of the show.

Their spirited banter helped make "Monday Night Football" one of the most popular programs on television, one that soon took its place in the television pantheon, alongside classics like "M*A*S*H," in terms of longevity, ratings and cultural influence. The weekly clash between an opinionated intellectual and a freewheeling spirit drew women to watch football games and caused restaurants and movie theaters to report lower traffic during broadcasts.

"I'd just wait for Howard to make a mistake," Mr. Meredith said in an interview with Sports Illustrated in 2000. "Didn't usually take too long."

In fact, the whole act was planned, by Mr. Cosell. "You wear the white hat, I'll wear the black hat," he said to Mr. Meredith in a rehearsal before the premiere of "Monday Night Football" on Sept. 21, 1970.

Mr. Meredith offered a taste of his breezy, even risky, humor in that first broadcast. In talking about the Cleveland Browns receiver Fair Hooker, Mr. Meredith said, "Fair Hooker — I haven't met one yet."

He later referred to President Richard M. Nixon as Tricky Dick and made what seemed to be a joke about his own marijuana use at a Denver Broncos game. "Welcome to Mile High Stadium — and I really am," he said.

Frank Gifford replaced Keith Jackson as the play-by-play announcer — and straight man of the crew — in the broadcast's second year, and many announcing-team combinations followed over the next decades. ESPN now broadcasts Monday night games.

Joseph Donald Meredith was born on April 10, 1938. In high school, he acted in school plays, scored 52 points in a basketball tournament game, graduated second in his class and won a statewide contest for identifying shrubs. He was an all-American quarterback for two years at Southern Methodist, after turning down Bear Bryant's entreaties to go to Texas A&M, where Mr. Bryant coached before he became an Alabama legend.

The Cowboys coveted the local hero and signed Mr. Meredith to a personal-services contract before the N.F.L. had even granted Dallas a franchise. The Chicago Bears drafted him, and the Cowboys traded future draft picks to get him.

In an interview with The New York Post in 1966, Mr. Meredith said he assumed he would supplant Johnny Unitas as the league's preeminent quarterback in about a year, but Coach Landry thought quarterbacks should ideally have around five years of seasoning before starting. Mr. Meredith mainly sat on the bench the first three years.

As he sat, he grimly regretted not becoming a lawyer or preacher. "It was two years before Landry even spoke to me," he said.

He got his chance to start at quarterback in 1963, and he succeeded by almost any standard. He was named to three Pro Bowls and in 1966 was named the N.F.L.'s most valuable player. But he sustained many injuries and bickered with Mr. Landry about play-calling. Mr. Landry ended up calling plays.

Dallas fans began booing Mr. Meredith after the Cowboys were unsuccessful in the playoffs, losing by inches and seconds to the Green Bay Packers in 1966 and 1967. He retired after nine seasons in 1969 at 31, saying he was eager to try other fields.

But the road to his future was paved after the second loss to Green Bay in an epic battle called the Ice Bowl. Wearing a blood-stained uniform, Mr. Meredith poured out his heart in a postgame interview. CBS was flooded with mail about this soulful, articulate, apparently real-life cowboy.

The interviewer was Mr. Gifford, who recommended Mr. Meredith to Roone Arledge of ABC, who was then planning to bring pro football to prime-time TV. Mr. Arledge wanted a former player with lots of personality.

But Mr. Meredith had already agreed to work for CBS's football coverage. He met Mr. Arledge for lunch and, scribbling contract terms on napkins, agreed to join "Monday Night Football" for $30,000. Mr. Arledge grumbled that the lunch cost him $10,000.

"It's the best $10,000 you'll ever spend," Mr. Meredith said.

IN THE BOOTH: Meredith, center, Howard Cosell and Frank Gifford on ABC's "Monday Night Football" in 1976.

He left the show after the 1973 season for NBC, which promised movies as well as work on N.F.L. coverage. NBC met another condition too: no one would call him Dandy Don. Mr. Meredith returned to the Monday show in 1977 and stayed until ABC's coverage of the 1985 Super Bowl.

After acting in movies and television, he receded into a quiet life in Santa Fe, writing, painting, golfing and acting in a stage production of "The Odd Couple." He played Oscar. Mr. Gifford was Felix.

Mr. Meredith is survived by his wife, Susan, his brother, and his three children.

For many Americans, their most abiding memory of Mr. Meredith was how he suddenly burst into a Willie Nelson song when he decided that a game's fate was sealed. "Turn out the lights," he'd sing, "the party's over."

— *By Douglas Martin and Bill Carter*

ELIZABETH EDWARDS

Triumphs and Troubles on a Political Stage

JULY 3, 1949 - DEC. 7, 2010

Elizabeth Edwards, who as the wife of former Senator John Edwards, gave America an intimate look at a candidate's marriage by sharing his quest for the 2008 presidential nomination as she struggled publicly with incurable cancer and secretly with his infidelity, died on Dec. 7 at her home in Chapel Hill, N.C. She was 61.

Her family confirmed the death, saying Mrs. Edwards was surrounded by her children and other relatives when she died. A family friend said Mr. Edwards was also present. On Dec. 6, two family friends said that Mrs. Edwards's cancer, first diagnosed six years ago, had spread to her liver and that doctors had advised against further medical treatment.

Mrs. Edwards posted a Facebook message to friends on Dec. 6, saying, "I have been sustained throughout my life by three saving graces — my family, my friends, and a faith in the power of resilience and hope." She added: "The days of our lives, for all of us, are numbered. We know that."

In a life of idyllic successes and crushing reverses, Mrs. Edwards was an accomplished lawyer, the mother of four children and the wife of a wealthy, handsome senator with sights on the White House. But their 16-year-old son was killed in a car crash, cancer struck her at age 55, the political dreams died and, within months, her husband admitted to having had an extramarital affair with a campaign videographer.

The scandal over the affair faded after his disclosure in 2008. But in 2009, Mrs. Edwards resurrected it in a new book and interviews and television appearances, telling how her husband had misrepresented the infidelity to her, rocked their marriage and spurned her advice to abandon his run for the presidency, a decision in which she ultimately acquiesced.

Last January, on the eve of new disclosures in a book by a former political aide, Mr. Edwards admitted he had fathered a child with the videographer. Soon afterward, he and Mrs. Edwards separated legally.

Mrs. Edwards, a savvy political adviser who took on major roles in her husband's two campaigns for the White House, learned she had a breast tumor the size of a half-dollar on the day after Election Day 2004, when the Democratic ticket — Senator John Kerry of Massachusetts and Mr. Edwards, his running mate from North Carolina — lost to President George W. Bush and Vice President Dick Cheney.

Radiation and chemotherapy appeared to put the cancer into remission. In a best-selling memoir, "Saving Graces: Finding Solace and Strength From Friends and Strangers" (Broadway Books, 2006), Mrs. Edwards chronicled her fight for survival. But in March 2007, with her husband again chasing a presidential nomination, this time against Senators Barack Obama and Hillary Rodham Clinton, Mr. and Mrs. Edwards disclosed that her cancer had returned.

They said it was malignant and in an advanced stage, having spread beyond the breast and lymph nodes into her ribs, hip bones and lungs. It was treatable but "no longer curable," Mr. Edwards explained. But he said he would continue his bid for the presidency, and Mrs. Edwards said that she, too, would go on with the campaign. "I don't expect my life to be significantly different," she declared.

Mrs. Edwards had always been a dominant figure in her husband's political life. Often called his closest adviser and surrogate, she reviewed his television advertisements and major speeches, helped pick his lieutenants, joined internal debates over tactics and strategy, and sometimes dressed down, or even forced out, campaign aides she thought had failed her husband.

A scathing portrait of Mrs. Edwards's political role, based mainly on unnamed sources, was presented in "Game Change," a book by John Heilemann and Mark Halperin published last January. "The nearly universal assessment" among campaign aides, they wrote, "was that there was no one on the national stage for whom the disparity between public image and private reality was vaster or more disturbing."

Mrs. Edwards's advanced cancer made her a riveting figure, at times overshadowing the candidate himself. In 2007, she was often mobbed by crowds that saw her as courageous. Inevitably, there were questions about putting their marriage on display. People wondered about their values, or whether they were in denial about the cancer. Some accused them of cynically using her illness for political gain.

But Mr. and Mrs. Edwards were undeterred. While she took a yellow chemotherapy pill once a day, her stamina seemed high, she often carried her own bags and put in 16-hour days, and she showed no signs of the disease: her hair was full, her skin color was robust, and she bustled with energy.

Political consultants said American voters yearned for authenticity and character in a candidate, and thought Mr. Edwards had a singular opportunity. But his aides worried, with some justification, that Mrs. Edwards on a podium was too compelling for his good. At a luncheon in Cleveland, some comments from the audience sounded like paeans to her.

"I came to feel the inspiration you exude," said a woman bald from months of chemotherapy and radiation. Another cancer patient called Mrs. Edwards "my angel, my idol, my everything."

Mr. Edwards pitched himself as a populist, up from hardscrabble mill towns to success as lawyer. He stuck to a script of living wages, cuts in greenhouse gases and a timetable for withdrawal from Iraq, with health care as a signature issue.

But many voters were alienated by his 2002 vote for the Iraq war. Falling behind Mr. Obama and Mrs. Clinton in polls, he lost the primary in South Carolina, where he was born, and quit the race in late January 2008. He later endorsed Mr. Obama.

Any lingering hopes for his political future were shattered in August 2008, when he admitted to ABC News that he had had an affair in 2006 with Rielle Hunter, a 42-year-old woman hired to make campaign videos. He denied being the father of her infant daughter, even offering to take a paternity test, and insisted that the affair had occurred when his wife's cancer was in remission and that it was over before he announced his presidential campaign on Dec. 28, 2006. He also said he had not given hush money to Ms. Hunter, although his campaign had paid her $114,000 for videos.

Mrs. Edwards issued a statement supporting her husband. "Although John believes he should stand alone and take the consequences of his action now," she said, "when the door closes behind him, he has his family waiting for him."

WASHINGTON WIFE: Mrs. Edwards at the 2004 Democratic National Convention. She was one of her husband's closest advisers.

But in May 2009, she raised the matter again in interviews and television appearances, including one on "The Oprah Winfrey Show," and in a second memoir, "Resilience: Reflections on the Burdens and Gifts of Facing Life's Adversities."

In the book, she related his admission of infidelity. By his account, she wrote, "on only one night had he violated his vows to me." She grew ill and angry and later tried to make herself believe it had lasted only one night. "It turned out that a single time was not all it was," she said.

She urged him to end his campaign, "to protect our family from this woman, from his act," she wrote. But he refused, she said, and she ended up supporting him, keeping silent about the affair as the campaign continued for a year and a half.

"Being sick meant a number of things to me," she told Ms. Winfrey. "One is that my life is going to be less long, and I didn't want to spend it fighting."

Asked by Ms. Winfrey whether she still loved him, Mrs. Edwards replied, "You know, that's a complicated question."

The couple's separation in 2010, and Mr. Edwards's admission that he had fathered a child with Ms. Hunter, came on the eve of the publication of "The Politician," a tell-all book by Andrew Young, a former campaign aide who had originally said that he was the father of the child, who was born in 2007.

Mrs. Edwards was born Mary Elizabeth Anania on July 3, 1949, in Jacksonville, Fla., the daughter of Vincent J. and Elizabeth Thweatt Anania. Her father was a Navy pilot, and the family moved often in America and abroad.

She attended Mary Washington College in Fredericksburg, Va., then transferred to the

University of North Carolina at Chapel Hill and earned a bachelor's degree in English. She enrolled in the university's law school, where in 1974 she met Mr. Edwards, four years her junior and the son of a textile worker.

After graduating, they were married in July 1977 and began legal careers. In the next two decades, he became a multimillionaire, mostly by winning medical malpractice cases. Her career was low key, in bankruptcy and public service law. Elizabeth preferred her middle name and used her maiden name professionally.

They were not very interested in politics. After the birth of Wade, in 1979, and Catharine, known as Cate, in 1982, they embraced parenthood, he coaching soccer, she joining parent-teacher groups and arranging her work schedule to spend afternoons with the children.

But the storybook family was shattered on April 4, 1996, when Wade, a high school junior, was killed in a car accident driving to the family's beach house. Devastated, the parents stopped working. For months, Mrs. Edwards read her son's textbooks aloud at his grave and spent sleepless nights in online bereavement groups or staring at a weather channel.

Eventually, the couple decided to change their lives. In Wade's name, they established a foundation, created a computer learning lab at his high school and organized scholarships and essay awards. Elizabeth changed her surname to Edwards, began fertility treatments and had two more children — Emma Claire, in 1998, and John, known as Jack, in 2000.

Mr. Edwards went into politics, ran for the Senate in 1998 and handily defeated Lauch Faircloth, the Republican incumbent. Mr. Edwards served one term, deciding to run for president in 2004 rather than for re-election to the Senate. He fell short, but Senator Kerry, who won the nomination, picked him to run for vice president.

Mrs. Edwards soon became her husband's most valued adviser, a role undiminished by her illness. "I trust her more than I trust anybody in the world," Mr. Edwards said a month before abandoning his presidential race. "She's herself, and fearless. I don't think she's intimidated by or afraid of anything."

— *By Robert D. McFadden*

RICHARD C. HOLBROOKE

In Times of Crisis, the Presidents Called

APRIL 24, 1941 - DEC. 13, 2010

RICHARD C. HOLBROOKE, the Obama administration's special representative for Afghanistan and Pakistan since 2009 and a diplomatic troubleshooter who worked for every Democratic president since the late 1960s and oversaw the negotiations that ended the war in Bosnia, died on Dec. 13 in Washington. He was 69 and lived in Manhattan.

Mr. Holbrooke was hospitalized on Dec. 10 after becoming ill while meeting with Secretary of State Hillary Rodham Clinton in her Washington office. Doctors found a tear to his aorta, and he underwent a 21-hour operation. Mr. Holbrooke had additional surgery two days later and remained in critical condition until his death.

In a distinguished career that involved diplomacy in Asia, Europe and the Middle East, Mr. Holbrooke's signal accomplishment was his role as chief architect of the 1995 Dayton peace accords, which ended the war in Bosnia. It was a coup preceded and followed by his peace-keeping missions to the tinderbox of ethnic, religious and regional conflicts that was formerly Yugoslavia.

More recently, Mr. Holbrooke wrestled with the stunning complexity of Afghanistan and Pakistan: how to bring stability to the region while fighting a resurgent Taliban and coping with corrupt governments, rigged elections, fragile economies, a rampant narcotics trade, nuclear weapons in Pakistan and the presence of Al Qaeda — and presumably Osama bin Laden — in the wild tribal borderlands.

One of his main tasks was to press President Hamid Karzai of Afghanistan to take responsibility for security in his country and to confront the corruption that imperils the American mission there. At times, Mr. Karzai refused to see him, but Mr. Holbrooke was undeterred.

"He's an enormously tough customer," Mr. Holbrooke said during one of his periodic breakfasts with reporters who covered his diplomatic exploits. "As you've heard," he added with a smile, "so am I."

He helped his boss, Mrs. Clinton, whom he had supported in her presidential bid, to persuade President Obama to send more troops to Afghanistan. At the same time, he pressed for more aid and development projects to improve the United States' image there. But he died before anyone knew if the experiment would succeed.

A brilliant, sometimes abrasive infighter, he used a formidable arsenal of facts, bluffs, whispers, implied threats and, when necessary, pyrotechnic fits of anger to press his positions. Mr. Obama was sometimes driven to distraction by his lectures.

But Mr. Holbrooke dazzled and often intimidated opponents and colleagues around a negotiating table. Some called him a bully, and he looked the part: the big chin thrust out, the broad shoulders, the tight smile that might mean anything. To admirers, however, including generations of State Department protégés and the presidents he served, his peacemaking efforts were extraordinary.

When President Bill Clinton named Mr. Holbrooke to represent the United States at the United Nations, the president said, "His remarkable diplomacy in Bosnia helped to stop the bloodshed, and at the talks in Dayton the force of his determination was the key to securing peace, restoring hope and saving lives." Others said his work in Bosnia deserved the Nobel Peace Prize. Speaking at the State Department hours after Mr. Holbrooke died, President Obama called him "simply one of the giants of American foreign policy."

Few diplomats could boast of his career accomplishments. Early on, Mr. Holbrooke devoted six years to the Vietnam War: first in the Mekong Delta with the United States Agency for International Development, seeking the allegiance of the civilian population; then at the embassy in Saigon as an aide to Ambassadors Maxwell Taylor and Henry Cabot Lodge Jr.; and finally in the American delegation to the 1968-69 Paris peace talks led by W. Averell Harriman and Cyrus R. Vance.

Mr. Holbrooke was the author of one volume of the Pentagon Papers, the secret Defense Department history of the Vietnam War that cataloged years of American duplicity in Southeast Asia. The papers were first brought to public attention by The New York Times in 1971.

As assistant secretary of state for East Asian and Pacific affairs in the administration of President Jimmy Carter, Mr. Holbrooke played a crucial role in establishing full diplomatic relations with China in 1979, a move that finessed America's continuing commitment to China's thorn in the side, Taiwan, and followed up on the historic breakthrough of President Richard M. Nixon's 1972 visit to China.

During the Clinton presidency, Mr. Holbrooke served as ambassador to Germany in 1993-94, when he helped enlarge the North Atlantic alliance; achieved his diplomatic breakthroughs in Bosnia as assistant secretary of state for European affairs in 1994-95; and was chief representative to the United Nations, a cabinet post, for 17 months from 1999 to 2001.

At the United Nations, he forged close ties to Secretary General Kofi Annan, negotiated a settlement of America's longstanding dues dispute, highlighted conflicts and health crises in Africa and Indonesia, and called for more peacekeeping forces. After fighting erupted in the Democratic Republic of Congo in 1999, he led a Security Council delegation on a mission to Africa. He also backed sanctions against Angolan rebels in 2000.

While he achieved prominence as a cabinet official and envoy to many of the world's most troubled arenas, Mr. Holbrooke was frustrated in his ambition to be secretary of state; he was the runner-up to Madeleine K. Albright, Mr. Clinton's choice in 1997, and a contender when Mr. Obama installed Mrs. Clinton in the post in 2009.

TROUBLESHOOTER: Mr. Holbrooke, shown in 2000, was President Obama's point man in Afghanistan.

Foreign policy was his life. Even during Republican administrations, when he was not in government, he was deeply engaged, undertaking missions as a private citizen traveling through the war-weary Balkans and the backwaters of Africa and Asia to see firsthand the damage and devastating human costs of H.I.V. and AIDS epidemics, genocide and civil wars.

And his voice on the outside remained influential — as an editor of Foreign Policy magazine from 1972 to 1977, as a writer of columns for The Washington Post and analytical articles for many other publications, and as the author of two books. He collaborated with Clark Clifford, a presidential adviser, on a best-selling Clifford memoir, "Counsel to the President" (1991), and wrote his own widely acclaimed memoir, "To End a War" (1998), about his Bosnia service.

Mr. Holbrooke also made millions as an investment banker on Wall Street. In the early 1980s, he was a co-founder of a Washington consulting firm, Public Strategies, which was later sold to Lehman Brothers. At various times he was a managing director of Lehman Brothers, vice chairman of Credit Suisse First Boston and a director of the American International Group.

Richard Charles Albert Holbrooke was born in Manhattan on April 24, 1941, to Dr. Dan Holbrooke, a physician, and the former Trudi Moos. He attended Scarsdale High School in Scarsdale, N.Y., where his best friend was David Rusk, son of Dean Rusk, the future secretary of state. Richard's father died when he was 15, and he drew closer to the Rusk family.

At Brown University, he majored in history and was editor of the student newspaper. He intended to become a journalist, but after graduating in 1962 he was turned down by The Times and joined the State Department as a foreign service officer.

In 1964, Mr. Holbrooke married the first of his three wives, Larrine Sullivan, a lawyer. The couple had two sons and were divorced. His marriage to Blythe Babyak, a television producer, also ended in divorce. In 1995, he married Kati Marton, an author, journalist and human rights advocate who had been married to the ABC anchorman Peter Jennings until their divorce in 1993. He is survived by Ms. Marton, his two sons, a brother and two stepchildren.

After language training, he spent three years working in Vietnam. In 1966, he joined President Lyndon B. Johnson's White House staff, and two years later became a junior member of the delegation at the Paris peace talks. The talks achieved no breakthrough, but the experience taught him much about the arts of negotiation.

In 1970, after a year as a fellow at Princeton, he became director of the Peace Corps in Morocco. He quit government service in 1972 and over the next five years edited the quarterly journal Foreign Policy. He was also a contributing editor of Newsweek International and a consultant on reorganizing the government's foreign policy apparatus.

PEACE BROKER: Mr. Holbrooke, left, with Bosnian president Alija Izetbegovic in 1996, was instrumental in negotiations that led to the end of Bosnia's civil war.

He worked on Jimmy Carter's presidential campaign in 1976, and was rewarded with the post of assistant secretary of state for East Asia and Pacific affairs. When Ronald Reagan and the Republicans took over the White House in 1981, Mr. Holbrooke left the government and for more than a decade focused on writing and investment banking.

When President Clinton took office in 1993, Mr. Holbrooke was named ambassador to Germany. He helped found the American Academy in Berlin as a cultural exchange center.

He returned to Washington in 1994 as assistant secretary of state for European affairs. His top priority soon became the horrendous civil war in the former Yugoslavia, a conflict precipitated by the secession of Croatia, Slovenia, Macedonia and Bosnia. Massacres, mass rapes and displaced populations, among other atrocities, were part of campaigns of "ethnic cleansing" against Muslims.

After months of shuttle diplomacy, Mr. Holbrooke, in 1995, achieved a breakthrough cease-fire and a framework for dividing Bosnia into two entities, one of Bosnian Serbs and the other of Croatians and Muslims. The endgame negotiations, involving the Serbian leader Slobodan Milosevic, President Franjo Tudjman of Croatia and President Alija Izetbegovic of Bosnia, unfolded in Dayton, Ohio, where a peace agreement was reached after months of hard bargaining led by Mr. Holbrooke.

It was the high-water mark of a career punctuated with awards, honorary degrees and prestigious seats on the boards of the Asia Society, the American Museum of Natural History, the National Endowment for Democracy, the Council on Foreign Relations, Refugees International and other organizations. He was 59 when he left the United Nations as the Clinton administration drew to a close.

But there was to be one more task. As Mr. Obama assumed office and attention shifted to Afghanistan, Mr. Holbrooke took on his last assignment. He began by trying to lower expectations, moving away from the grand, transformative goals of President George W. Bush toward something more readily achievable.

But his boss and old friend, Mrs. Clinton, expressed absolute confidence in him. "Richard represents the kind of robust, persistent, determined diplomacy the president intends to pursue," she said. "I admire deeply his ability to shoulder the most vexing and difficult challenges."

—*By Robert D. McFadden*

David E. Sanger contributed reporting from Washington.

BOB FELLER

The Farm Boy Phenom

NOV. 3, 1918 - DEC. 15, 2010

BOB FELLER, who came off an Iowa farm with a dazzling fastball that made him a national celebrity at 17 and propelled him to the Hall of Fame as one of baseball's greatest pitchers, died on Dec. 15 at a hospice near Cleveland. He was 92.

Feller, who had lived in Gates Mills, Ohio, had recently been treated for pneumonia; in August he announced that he had leukemia.

Joining the Cleveland Indians in 1936, Feller became baseball's biggest draw since Babe Ruth, throwing pitches that batters could barely see — fastballs approaching 100 miles an hour and curveballs and sinkers that fooled the sharpest eyes. As Yankees pitcher Lefty Gomez was said to have remarked after three Feller pitches blew by him, "That last one sounded a little low." He became "Rapid Robert" in the sports pages.

A high-kicking right-hander, Feller was a major league phenomenon while still in high school in Van Meter, Iowa. In a spectacular debut as an Indians starter, during his summer vacation, he struck out 15 batters.

Three weeks later he struck out 17, tying Dizzy Dean's major league record. He pitched a no-hitter, the first of three in his 18-year career, when he was 21. (He went on to throw an astonishing 12 one-hitters.) He had more than 100 victories at age 22.

By the end of his brief rookie season, Feller was the best-known young person in America, with the possible exception of Shirley Temple. When he returned for his senior year at Van Meter High School, the governor of Iowa attended a welcome-home ceremony. When the 1937 season opened, Feller's picture was on the cover of Time magazine. And when he graduated from high school in June of that year (he had been tutored while on road trips), NBC Radio carried the ceremony nationwide.

Feller was not particularly big — 6 feet tall and a chunky 185 pounds — but by most estimations he threw harder than anyone who had ever pitched, except perhaps Walter Johnson and Lefty Grove.

Feller's career predated the use of radar guns to measure a pitch's speed, but he was nonetheless able to show exactly how fast he was in a demonstration in August 1946, when he threw 30 pitches through the hole of a photoelectric device before a game in Washington. They averaged 98.6 miles an hour.

"I don't think anyone is ever going to throw a ball faster than he does," Joe DiMaggio was quoted as saying during his epic 1941 season, when he hit in a record 56 consecutive games. "And his curveball isn't human."

Feller capitalized on his fame. During the late 1940s, the average major league salary barely exceeded $10,000, and only DiMaggio, Hank Greenberg and Ted Williams reached $100,000. Feller, in a 1990 memoir, said he earned more than $100,000 in 1946, drawing on a base salary of $50,000 in addition to incentives tied to victories and attendance; the profits from endorsements, most notably for Wheaties and Wilson sporting goods; and the proceeds of a barnstorming tour in which he led major league stars in games against top players from the Negro leagues. His total income climbed to $150,000 the next year, he said.

Feller set a record, since broken, for most strikeouts in a game (18) and struck out 2,581 batters in his career. His three no-hitters included the only one ever thrown on opening day. He led the American League in victories six times and in strikeouts seven times.

Feller entered the Baseball Hall of Fame in 1962 with Jackie Robinson; they were the first to do so in their first year of eligibility since the inaugural inductions 23 years earlier.

Back in 1945, Feller, always outspoken, had created a controversy involving Robinson soon after Robinson had been signed by the Brooklyn Dodgers organization to break baseball's color barrier. After pitching against Robinson in California on a postseason barnstorming tour, Feller told a reporter in Los Angeles that Robinson was too muscle-bound to handle major league pitching and expressed doubt that Robinson would be considered for the big leagues if he were white.

Feller eventually acknowledged that he had been mistaken, but it appears he never expressed regrets directly to Robinson. He did say he had taken pride in giving black players exposure through his barnstorming tours. And in his memoir, "Now Pitching, Bob Feller," written with Bill Gilbert, he said it had been "extra meaningful" for him go into the Hall of Fame "with major league baseball's first black player." Robinson, in turn, said it was a pleasure to be inducted with Feller.

Feller won 266 games in his 18 seasons, all with the Indians, but military service in World War II interrupted his career in his prime and might have deprived him of 100 more victories.

"I know in my heart I would have ended up a lot closer to 400 than 300 if I hadn't spent four seasons in the Navy," Feller once said. "But don't take that as a complaint. I'm happy that I got home in one piece."

Robert William Feller was born on Nov. 3, 1918, in Van Meter, population 300, and grew up nearby on a farm where his father, Bill, devoted himself to hogs, wheat and corn, but most of all to raising a ballplayer.

Bill Feller and his son listened to live broadcasts of Cubs games from Chicago and to re-creations on WHO Radio in Des Moines by a fledgling sportscaster named Ronald Reagan.

The father played catch with his son, bought him a Rogers Hornsby model glove and a flannel baseball uniform, and built a batting cage. When Bob was 12, his father leveled pasture land to create a ballpark, complete with bleachers and scoreboard, and formed a team to showcase Bob against players in their late teens and 20s.

"My father loved baseball and he cultivated my talent," Feller told Donald Honig in Honig's 1975 oral history, "Baseball When the Grass Was Real." "I don't think he ever had any doubt in his mind that I would play professional baseball someday."

RAPID ROBERT: Feller was 17 during his 1936 rookie season and struck out 15 batters in his debut.

Feller was soon blazing the ball past batters in high school and American Legion baseball, and in July 1935 the Indians scout Cy Slapnicka arrived on the Feller farm and signed him at 16. The contract was for a nominal $1 and a baseball autographed by Cleveland players, and the signing was kept a secret; Feller wanted to keep playing high school baseball and basketball. But the secret didn't last. After his junior year, Feller joined the Indians for the summer of 1936, and on July 6, four months before his 18th birthday, he struck out 8 of the 12 batters he faced in an exhibition game against the St. Louis Cardinals' heralded Gashouse Gang. Then came his 15-strikeout game against the St. Louis Browns in his first major league start and, not long afterward, his record-tying 17-strikeout game against the Philadelphia Athletics.

The Indians almost lost Feller in the fall. An independent minor league team in Des Moines still coveted him, and its owner contended that he had been acquired by the Indians in violation of baseball rules that governed the signing of amateurs. The baseball commissioner, Kenesaw Mountain Landis, could have made Feller a free agent, and had he done so Feller would have commanded huge contract offers in a bidding frenzy. But Feller wanted to stay with the Indians, and his father threatened to sue if Landis did not allow that. The commissioner permitted the Indians to keep Feller, and in January 1937 he signed a one-year contract with them for $10,000. He would never spend a day in the minor leagues.

In the 1938 season, Feller threw a one-hitter against the Browns in his first start and struck out 18 Detroit Tigers on the season's final day, breaking the single-game record he shared with Dean. He pitched his opening-day no-hitter on April 16, 1940, stifling the Chicago White Sox, 1-0, at Comiskey Park, then went on to win 26 more games that season. But on the final weekend he was bested by a little-known Tigers rookie named Floyd Giebell as Detroit knocked the Indians out of the race and won the pennant.

Two days after the Japanese attacked Pearl Harbor on Dec. 7, 1941, Feller enlisted in the Navy. He pitched during the spring of 1942 for the Norfolk Naval Training Station team in Virginia, then requested sea duty. After attending gunnery school, he joined the crew of the battleship Alabama in September 1942 and served as chief of a 24-man anti-aircraft battery that saw duty in the North Atlantic and in the Pacific, where it joined eight amphibious invasions.

When he returned from the war, Feller was better than ever, developing a sinker to go with his fastball and curve. He threw his second no-hitter, at Yankee Stadium, in April 1946, and struck out 348 batters that season, listed at the time as a major league record, eclipsing Rube Waddell's 343 for the Athletics in 1904. (Waddell's total was later revised to 349.)

When the Indians won the 1948 American League pennant — their first in 28 years — Feller finally achieved his dream of pitching in a World Series. But he lost the opener to the Boston Braves, 1-0, giving up that one run after he had apparently picked catcher Phil Masi off second base, only to see umpire Bill Stewart rule him safe. The Indians won in six games, but Feller was routed in his only other start in the Series.

Feller pitched his third no-hitter in July 1951, against the Tigers, tying the major league record held by Cy Young and Larry Corcoran. But he had injured his right shoulder during the 1947 season, and after that he was never the strikeout pitcher he had been.

During the 1950s, Feller served as the first president of the Major League Baseball Players Association and helped draw up a new player pension plan.

When the Indians won a league-record 111 games in 1954, Feller was their fourth starter, after Bob Lemon, Early Wynn and Mike Garcia. He did not pitch in the World Series, in which the Indians were swept by the New York Giants, and his dream of winning a Series game went unfulfilled.

He retired after the 1956 season with a career record of 266-162.

For the rest of his life, Feller spoke his mind, denouncing baseball stars enveloped in the steroids scandal, criticizing Pete Rose for lying when he denied betting on baseball, objecting to Muhammad Ali's throwing out the first ball at the 2004 All-Star Game because of Ali's refusal to be drafted during the Vietnam War, and maintaining that the United States had not used enough force to subdue the enemy in Iraq.

Feller remained a familiar face, making promotional appearances on tours of minor league cities and tutoring Indians pitchers during spring training. He was happy to sign autographs, often for a small contribution to the Bob Feller Museum in Van Meter.

In June 2009, at 90, Feller donned an Indians jersey and pitched to three batters in the inaugural Baseball Hall of Fame Classic, a game in Cooperstown, N.Y., between former major leaguers.

Feller's records for single-game strikeouts and career no-hitters would be broken. But his reputation remained undimmed.

When professional baseball celebrated its 100th anniversary at the All-Star Game festivities in 1969, Feller was honored as the game's greatest living right-handed pitcher.

Feller considered Ted Williams the fiercest batter he ever faced. "Trying to sneak a fastball by Ted Williams was like trying to sneak a sunbeam by a rooster in the morning," Feller said in an interview with The Times videotaped to accompany this obituary online.

But Williams had paid Feller a personal tribute every time he was about to face him, preparing himself psychologically by repeating Feller's name over and over.

"That was the test," Williams recalled in David Halberstam's book "Summer of '49." "He was the best, and I wanted to be the best, and three days before he pitched I would start thinking Robert Feller, Bob Feller."

— *By Richard Goldstein*

BLAKE EDWARDS

Brilliant Comedies, Black Farce

JULY 26, 1922 - DEC. 15, 2010

Blake Edwards, a writer and director who was hailed as a Hollywood master of screwball farces and rude comedies like "Victor/Victoria" and the "Pink Panther" movies, died on Dec. 15 in Santa Monica, Calif. He was 88.

His publicist said the cause was complications of pneumonia. Mr. Edwards's wife, the actress Julie Andrews, and other family members were at his side at St. John's Health Center, Mr. Schwam said.

What the critic Pauline Kael once described as Mr. Edwards's "love of free-for-all lunacy" was flaunted in good movies and bad ones: in box-office hits like "Breakfast at Tiffany's" (1961) and "The Pink Panther" (1963) — the first of a series of films with Peter Sellers as the bumbling Inspector Clouseau — and in box-office flops like the musical spy extravaganza "Darling Lili" (1970), starring Ms. Andrews.

"Victor/Victoria" (1982) was Mr. Edwards's last major success, a farce about a starving singer (Ms. Andrews) who pretends to be a homosexual Polish count who performs as a female impersonator. It brought him his only Academy Award nomination, for the screenplay, which was adapted from a 1933 German film written and directed by Reinhold Schünzel.

But he was given an honorary award by the Academy of Motion Picture Arts and Sciences in 2004 for his "extraordinary body of work." That work spanned more than four decades and included a Broadway musical, the detective television series "Peter Gunn" and hit films like the comedy "10" and the drama "Days of Wine and Roses," a portrait of alcoholic despair.

Mr. Edwards had written several zany comic soufflés — among them "Operation Mad Ball" (1957) — when he began directing his own light and buoyant comedies, including "This Happy Feeling" (1958), "The Perfect Furlough" (1958) and "Operation Petticoat" (1959). He later darkened his comedy in films in which middle-aged male protagonists — unlucky womanizers, artists at the end of their creative tethers — are just one banana peel away from disaster.

The critic Andrew Sarris wrote in 1968 that Mr. Edwards had gotten "some of his biggest laughs out of jokes that are too gruesome for most horror films."

In "The Party" (1968), for example, there was a desperate Peter Sellers unable to find a bathroom. In "The Man Who Loved Women" (1983), there was Burt Reynolds staring at the legs of a nurse while dying. And in almost every scene of "S.O.B." (1981), Mr. Edwards wielded a comic ax dipped in cyanide as he took on a movie industry that had alternately embraced and spurned him.

After a series of critical and box-office failures in the late 1960s and early '70s, Mr. Edwards spent several years in self-imposed exile in London and Switzerland. He returned to write and direct three more "Pink Panther" movies between 1975 and 1978, followed by the unexpected critical and commercial success of "10" (1979). One of his most personal films, "10" starred Dudley Moore as a composer whose 42nd birthday causes a whopping midlife crisis and an obsession with a beautiful young woman, played by Bo Derek, whom he considers a perfect 10.

'PRATFALLS AND PAIN': Mr. Edwards's films are a deft mix of wild comedy and dark satire.

A lifelong depressive, Mr. Edwards told The New York Times in 2001 that at one point his depression was so bad that he became "seriously suicidal." After deciding that shooting himself would be too messy and drowning too uncertain, he decided to slit his wrists on the beach at Malibu while looking at the ocean. But while he was holding a two-sided razor, his Great Dane started licking his ear, and his retriever, eager for a game of fetch, dropped a ball in his lap. Trying to get the dog to go away, Mr. Edwards threw the ball, dropped the razor and dislocated his shoulder. "So I think to myself," he said, "this just isn't a day to commit suicide." Trying to retrieve the razor, he stepped on it and ended up in the emergency room.

If that was a shaggy-dog story, it was also the kind of black farce that filled Mr. Edwards's later films. These were often on the far edge of comedy, where sexual pain and sexual pleasure are mixed with politically incorrect stereotypes and a bleak worldview to make audiences laugh and squirm at the same time. In "S.O.B.," a movie director who cannot successfully commit suicide is killed just when his failed movie has been turned into a box-office smash; elsewhere in the film an elderly man who has a heart attack on the beach lies dead on the sand for two days, ignored by everyone except his faithful dog.

Blake Edwards was born William Blake Crump on July 26, 1922, in Tulsa, Okla. He became Blake McEdwards when he was 4, after his mother, Lillian, had married Jack McEdwards, an assistant director and movie production manager. He joined the Coast Guard after high school and was seriously injured at a party one night when he drunkenly dived into a shallow swimming pool. He spent five months in traction at the Long Beach Naval Hospital.

"That particular mix of pain and pratfall is the trademark of all the great Blake Edwards comedies," Vanity Fair wrote of his accident. As he lay in the hospital, Eleanor Roosevelt, on a visit there, solicitously asked how he had been wounded.

Briefly an actor in the studio system, Mr. Edwards played bit parts in more than two dozen movies between 1942 and 1948, usually without screen credit and sometimes loaned to other studios. He was a cadet in "Ten Gentlemen From West Point," an airman in "Thirty Seconds Over Tokyo" and a soldier in "The Best Years of Our Lives." In the late 1940s, having switched to writing, he created the "Richard Diamond" radio series, which starred Dick Powell as a lighthearted detective. Mr. Edwards later directed for Mr. Powell's television anthology series, "Four Star Playhouse."

Mr. Edwards created "Peter Gunn" in 1958. A jazz-soaked detective series, it was his first collaboration with the composer Henry Mancini, who would score almost all of Mr. Edwards's films for the next 30 years. All four of Mr. Mancini's Oscars were for music written for Blake Edwards movies: the score and the original song "Moon River" (lyrics by Johnny Mercer) from "Breakfast at Tiffany's"; the title song from "Days of Wine and Roses" (1962), again with lyrics by Mercer; and the score of "Victor/Victoria," written with Leslie Bricusse.

Although Mr. Edwards was known for his comedies, "Days of Wine and Roses," a harrowing drama about an alcoholic couple, was one of his most successful films. Based on a "Playhouse 90" television play by J. P. Miller, it starred Lee Remick and Jack Lemmon, whom Mr. Edwards often said was his favorite actor. For his part, Mr. Lemmon felt that Mr. Edwards was the right director for the film. As Mr. Edwards recalled in a commentary on a DVD release, Mr. Lemmon had felt that the material was so bleak, it would never have worked without a director who could inject some humor.

Both men were drinking hard in 1962, Mr. Edwards told The Times in 2001, and although he had stopped drinking by the time the shooting began, "the film had as much to do with it as anything did."

Mr. Edwards's string of successful movies ended in the late 1960s. (His attempt at a big-budget slapstick spectacle in 1965, "The Great Race," with Tony Curtis, had been only a modest box-office success.) So, too, did his first marriage, to the actress Patricia Walker. After their divorce, he married Ms. Andrews, the Academy Award-winning musical star, in 1969.

At the time, Ms. Andrews's public image was of the endlessly cheerful governess she had played in "The Sound of Music." In an interview the couple gave Playboy in 1982, Mr. Edwards recalled how, before he had met Ms. Andrews, he got laughs at a party where people were speculating on the reason for her phenomenal success.

"I can tell you exactly what it is," he said he told the partygoers. "She has lilacs for pubic hair."

Ms. Andrews sent Mr. Edwards a lilac bush shortly after they had started dating, she told Playboy, and their marriage lasted 41 years.

The early 1970s were not kind to either of them. "Darling Lili" was a bloated box-office bomb. And what Mr. Edwards called his first "personal" film, the western "Wild Rovers" (1971), was cut to ribbons by the president of MGM, James Aubrey. Mr. Aubrey then took over the editing of Mr. Edwards's next picture, "The Carey Treatment" (1972), before Mr. Edwards had even finished shooting it.

"I felt like an animal who goes off into the weeds and sucks its paw," Mr. Edwards later told a reporter. Instead he went off to England and Switzerland, where he wrote the screenplays for "S.O.B." and "Victor/Victoria."

It was the success of "10" that allowed Mr. Edwards to make those movies. And "10" was his revenge on Mr. Aubrey.

"Right after 'Wild Rovers,' Aubrey called me into his office and told me he hated a screenplay I'd written and refused to pay me the last moneys due on it," Mr. Edwards told Playboy. Mr. Edwards said he responded, "You don't have to pay me, but give me the script back." That script became "10."

Audiences and critics turned away from Mr. Edwards's last films, including "That's Life!" (1986), with Mr. Lemmon as an architect on the eve of his 60th birthday and Ms. Andrews as his wife, who may or may not have cancer, and "Sunset" (1988), a murder mystery hooked together with an elegiac look at the silent film industry. His final film, released in 1993, was "Son of the Pink Panther," a poorly received attempt to revive that franchise starring Roberto Benigni.

But he had one last triumph. He wrote and directed a stage version of "Victor/Victoria," which opened on Broadway in 1995, with Ms. Andrews reprising her movie role. It played for almost two years. In recent years he had been working on two musicals he hoped to bring to Broadway.

He is survived by a daughter and a son from his first marriage; two daughters with Ms. Andrews; a stepdaughter — Ms. Andrews's daughter from her marriage to the Broadway designer Tony Walton — and several grandchildren.

If there were scattered disappointments in a long career that by any measure was a smashing success, Mr. Edwards took them in stride, he said. Besides, he once said, "in what business in the world can you have more fun, be creative while you're having fun, be funny and work at being funny, work really nice hours and get paid a lot of money for doing it?"

But being funny had a larger purpose, he said. "My entire life has been a search for a funny side to that very tough life out there," he told one interviewer. "I developed a kind of eye for scenes that made me laugh to take the pain away."

— *By Aljean Harmetz*

CAPTAIN BEEFHEART

The Surreal Music of Don Van Vliet

JAN. 15, 1941 - DEC. 17, 2010

DON VAN VLIET, an artist of protean creativity who was known as Captain Beefheart during his days as an influential rock musician and who later led a reclusive life as a painter, died on Dec. 17. He was 69 and lived in Trinidad, Calif.

The cause was complications of multiple sclerosis, said Gordon VeneKlasen, a partner at the Michael Werner gallery in New York, where Mr. Van Vliet had shown his art, many of them abstract, colorful oils, since 1985. The gallery said he died in a hospital in Northern California.

Captain Beefheart's music career stretched from 1966 to 1982, and from straight rhythm and blues by way of the early Rolling Stones to music that sounded like a strange uncle of post-punk. He is probably best known for "Trout Mask Replica," a double album from 1969 with his Magic Band.

"Trout Mask Replica" was a bolt-from-the-blue collection of precise, careening, surrealist songs with clashing meters, brightly imagistic poetry and raw blues shouting. It had particular resonance with the punk and new wave generation to come a decade later, influencing bands like Devo, the Residents, Pere Ubu and the Fall.

Mr. Van Vliet's life story is caked with half-believable tales, some of which he himself spread in Dadaist, elliptical interviews. He claimed he had never read a book and had never been to school, and answered questions with riddles. "We see the moon, don't we?" he asked in a 1969 interview. "So it's our eye. Animals see us, don't they? So we're their animals."

The facts, or those most often stated, are that he was born on Jan. 15, 1941, in Glendale, Calif., as Don Vliet. (He added the "Van" in 1965.) His father, Glen, drove a bakery truck.

Don demonstrated artistic talent before the age of 10, especially in sculpture. At 13 he was offered a scholarship to study sculpture in Europe, but his parents forbade him to accept it. They were moving at the time to the Mojave Desert town of Lancaster, where, in high school, Don befriended Frank Zappa.

His adopted vocal style came partly from Howlin' Wolf: a deep, rough-riding moan turned up into swooping falsettos at the end of lines. "When it comes to capturing the feeling of archaic, Delta-style blues," Robert Palmer of The New York Times wrote in 1982, "he is the only white performer who really gets it right."

Mr. Van Vliet enrolled at Antelope Valley Junior College to study art in 1959 but dropped out after one semester. By the early 1960s he had started spending time in Cucamonga, Calif., in Mr. Zappa's studio. The two men worked on what was perhaps the first rock opera, "I Was a Teenage Maltshop" (still unperformed and unpublished), and built sets and wrote some of the script for a film to be titled "Captain Beefheart vs. the Grunt People."

The origins of Mr. Van Vliet's stage name are unclear, but he later told interviewers that he had chosen it because he had "a beef in my heart against this society."

By 1965 a quintet called Captain Beefheart and His Magic Band (the "his" was later changed to "the") was born. By the end of the year the band was playing at teenage fairs and car-club dances around Lancaster and signed by A&M Records to record two singles.

The guitarist Ry Cooder, then a young blues fanatic whose skill was much admired by Mr. Van Vliet, served as pro forma musical director for the next record, "Safe as Milk" (1967), which showed the band working on something different: a rhythmically jerky style, with stuttering melodies. The next album, "Strictly Personal" (1968), went even further in the direction of rhythmic originality.

THE CAPTAIN: Mr. Van Vliet's work influenced punk and new wave music.

But it was "Trout Mask Replica" that drew the widest acclaim. And it was the making of that album that provided some of the most durable myths about Mr. Van Vliet as an imperious, uncompromising artist.

The musicians lived together in a house in Woodland Hills, in the San Fernando Valley; what money there was for food and rent was supplied by Mr. Van Vliet's mother, Sue, and the parents of Bill Harkleroad, the band's guitarist (whom Mr. Van Vliet renamed Zoot Horn Rollo). One persistent myth has it that Mr. Van Vliet, who had no formal ability at any instrument, sat at the piano, turned on tapes and spontaneously composed most of the record in a single marathon eight-and-a-half-hour session.

What really happened, according to later accounts, was that his drummer, John French (whose stage name was Drumbo), transcribed and arranged music as Mr. Van Vliet whistled, sang or played it on the piano, and the band learned the wobbly, intricately arranged songs through Mr. French's transcriptions.

"Trout Mask" offers solo vocal turns that sound like sea shanties; intricately ordered pieces with two guitars playing dissonant lines; and conversations with Mr. Zappa, the record's producer. But its most recognizable feature is its staccato, perpetually disorienting melodic lines.

Band members' accounts have described Mr. Van Vliet as tyrannical; both Mr. French and Mr. Harkleroad have written memoirs with dark details about this period.

Mr. Van Vliet's eccentricity and his skepticism about the music industry had much to do with why his music remained mostly a cult obsession. His band was offered a slot at the Monterey International Pop Music Festival in 1967, but Mr. Cooder had quit a week before, and Mr. Van Vliet was too unnerved to perform. In the following years, when the band was at its creative peak, it played relatively few concerts.

The Magic Band's first records after "Trout Mask Replica," starting with "Lick My Decals Off, Baby," had a more mature sound, but by "Clear Spot," in 1973, the band had turned toward blues-rock. It later made a few ill-conceived concessions to commercialism, and in 1974 the band quit en masse after the critically panned "Unconditionally Guaranteed."

After a long falling-out, Mr. Van Vliet reunited with his old friend Mr. Zappa to tour and make the album "Bongo Fury" in 1975, then assembled a new band to record "Bat Chain Puller," which was never released because of contractual tie-ups. Parts of it were rerecorded in 1978 for an album released by Warner Brothers, "Shiny Beast (Bat Chain Puller)."

When his business affairs cleared in the early 1980s, Mr. Van Vliet made two albums for Virgin, "Doc at the Radar Station" and "Ice Cream for Crow," with a crew of musicians who had idolized him while growing up. The albums were enthusiastically received.

But "Ice Cream for Crow" was his last record; in 1982 he quit music to focus on his painting and moved to Trinidad, near the Oregon border, with his wife, Jan, who is his only survivor.

In the exhibition catalog to a show at the San Francisco Museum of Modern Art, the museum director, John Lane, wrote of Mr. Van Vliet's work, "His paintings — most frequently indeterminate landscapes populated by forms of abstracted animals — are intended to effect psychological, spiritual and magical force."

Some of the images were a continuation of his songwriting concerns, especially those involving animals. A lot of his work dwells on the beauty of animals, on animals acting like humans and even on humans turning into animals. In "Wild Life," he sang, "I'm gonna go up on the mountain and look for bears," and in "Grow Fins," an extraordinary blues from the album "The Spotlight Kid" (1972), he threatened a girlfriend that if she didn't love him better he would turn into a sea creature.

Mr. Van Vliet had rarely been seen since the early 1990s and seldom at his gallery openings.

"I don't like getting out when I could be painting," he told The Associated Press in 1991. "And when I'm painting, I don't want anybody else around."

— *By Ben Ratliff*

EUGENE GOLDWASSER

A 20-Year Quest to Solve Anemia

OCT. 14, 1922 - DEC. 17, 2010

Eugene Goldwasser, a largely unsung biochemist whose 20-year pursuit of an elusive protein led to the development of a widely used anemia drug that became one of the biggest products of the biotechnology industry, died on Dec. 17 at his home in Chicago. He was 88.

The protein Dr. Goldwasser finally isolated and purified while working at the University of Chicago in the late 1970s was erythropoietin, or Epo. Epo tells the body to produce red blood cells, which in turn carry oxygen to the body's tissues. He shared his precious material with a young biotechnology company, which figured out how to produce larger amounts of the protein using genetic engineering.

That company, Amgen, became the world's biggest biotechnology company on the basis of Epo. Sales of the protein, under names like Epogen, Procrit and Aranesp, amount to billions of dollars a year for Amgen, as well as for Johnson & Johnson and Roche.

Most people undergoing kidney dialysis now receive Epo, helping to relieve them of severe anemia, which can sap them of energy. Many cancer patients also get the drug to combat anemia caused by chemotherapy.

"It just continually delighted him that the work he did ended up having an impact on patients," said Dr. Gary Toback, a friend and colleague of Dr. Goldwasser's at the University of Chicago.

Epo has also been used surreptitiously by athletes, most notoriously Tour de France bicycle racers, to increase their endurance. Recent studies have suggested that overuse of the drug can harm patients, leading to declining sales in the last few years.

While Epo has meant huge profits for drug companies, Dr. Goldwasser, whom colleagues described as quiet and self-effacing, won neither fame nor fortune. Although he notified his university about his accomplishment, it never patented Epo, and Dr. Goldwasser did not follow up.

"One percent of one percent of the drug's annual revenues would have funded my lab quite handsomely," he told a university publicist years later.

Eugene Goldwasser was born in Brooklyn on Oct. 14, 1922. When his father's clothing business failed during the Depression, the family moved to Kansas City, Mo., to join a relative in a similar business. After attending high school and a community college there, he transferred as a junior to the University of Chicago on a scholarship, earning a bachelor's degree and, in 1950, a doctorate in biochemistry.

"It ... delighted him that the work he did ended up having an impact on patients."

As far back as 1906, two French researchers had postulated the existence of a substance that prompts the production of red blood cells. But if that substance did exist, it was in such minuscule quantities that no one could find it.

Dr. Goldwasser began to look for it in 1955 at the urging of his mentor, the noted hematologist Leon O. Jacobson. "I estimated several months should see the task completed," Dr. Goldwasser recalled in 1996 in an essay in the journal Perspectives in Biology and Medicine. Instead it took 20 years.

Dr. Goldwasser and colleagues began the work in 1957 by systematically removing different organs from rats to see if the rats became anemic. They concluded that Epo was made in the kidneys, and that helped explain why patients with kidney failure became anemic.

Figuring that animals with anemia would produce more Epo, making the protein easier to find, Dr. Goldwasser spent years visiting a slaughterhouse outside Chicago, injecting sheep with a chemical that would make them anemic. He would collect the blood and try to separate out the various components.

But it turned out that Epo was easier to find in urine than in blood. In 1973, when his search seemed to be at a dead end, Dr. Goldwasser received a letter from Takaji Miyake of Kumamoto University in Japan. Dr. Miyake wrote that he had been collecting urine from people with a disease called aplastic anemia.

As Merrill Goozner wrote in his book "The $800 Million Pill," which recounts the history of Epo, Dr. Miyake met Dr. Goldwasser in 1975 in the lobby of the elegant Palmer House hotel in Chicago. He bowed low and held out a foot-square package wrapped in brightly colored silk. Inside was the dried concentrate of 2,550 liters, or about 674 gallons, of urine.

From that material, Dr. Goldwasser, his assistant Charles Kung and Dr. Miyake purified 8 milligrams of Epo, or about 3 ten-thousandths of an ounce of it, enough to fill a small vial. They published a paper in 1977.

Such a difficult extraction process was not practical for producing enough Epo to use as a drug. But the age of gene splicing was dawning. Knowing some of the protein's composition, Fu-Kuen Lin, a scientist at Amgen, was eventually able to clone the human gene for Epo. The gene was spliced into hamster cells, which churned out enough Epo to sell as a drug.

The drug was tested first in patients undergoing dialysis and suffering debilitating anemia. The only treatment at that time was frequent blood transfusions, which exposed patients to infectious diseases and to a dangerous buildup of iron in their livers.

Epo was "a spectacular success," said Dr. John W. Adamson, who conducted that first trial around 1985 while at the University of Washington. Patients who had so little energy that they had to crawl up stairs became fully functional, he said. Nowadays, owing to Epo, such horribly anemic dialysis patients have "essentially disappeared," said Dr. Adamson, who is now at the University of California, San Diego.

Amgen patented the Epo gene, barely beating out another company, and through litigation has preserved its monopoly for more than 20 years.

Some companies wanting to sell their own versions of Epo have complained that by choosing to work only with Amgen, Dr. Goldwasser, whose research was financed by the National Institutes of Health, had essentially privatized public property. In his 1996 essay, Dr. Goldwasser said he had gotten permission for this from the N.I.H.

Dr. Goldwasser continued research on Epo, retiring from the university in 2002.

He is survived by his second wife, Deone Jackman, three sons from his first marriage, two stepchildren and seven grandchildren. His first wife, Florence Cohen, died in 1981. His own death was caused by kidney failure resulting from a recurrence of prostate cancer, a son said.

Dr. Goldwasser said in his 1996 essay that when he started his quest he had no idea that the results would be so medically useful. "The enormous clinical success of Epo still astonishes me," he wrote.

— *By Andrew Pollack*

SALLY GOODRICH

After 9/11, a Cause in Afghanistan

MAY 12, 1945 - DEC. 18, 2010

JUST THREE MONTHS after losing her son Peter on Sept. 11, 2001, aboard United Airlines Flight 175 — the second plane to crash into the World Trade Center — Sally Goodrich received a diagnosis of ovarian cancer. For three years, through chemotherapy, grief for her son and thoughts of suicide, Ms. Goodrich fought depression while continuing to work as a remedial reading teacher and program coordinator for at-risk children in the North Adams, Mass., school system.

Then, in August 2004, an e-mail from a friend of Peter's arrived from Afghanistan. Maj. Rush Filson, a Marine, asked if Ms. Goodrich and her husband, Donald, could collect school supplies for children in a village southeast of Kabul.

A SON'S LEGACY: Ms. Goodrich in Afghanistan in 2005.

"That was the beginning," Ms. Goodrich later told The Boston Globe. "I call it the moment of grace. I knew Peter would have responded to that e-mail; I knew I had to in his name. For the first time, I felt Peter's spirit back in my life."

That spirit evolved into the Peter M. Goodrich Memorial Foundation, which has since built a school for 500 girls in Logar Province in Afghanistan and supported two smaller schools and an orphanage in Wardak Province.

Ms. Goodrich died of ovarian cancer on Dec. 18 at her home in Bennington, Vt., her husband, Donald Goodrich, said. She was 65.

"The idea that we could go to Afghanistan — where the Afghan people were taken advantage of by Al Qaeda, manipulated, and where the planning for our son's death took place — and provide an alternative way of looking at the world was very appealing to us," Mr. Goodrich told The Associated Press.

With donations from friends, neighbors, schoolchildren, local clubs, Boy Scouts and Girl Scouts, the Goodrich Foundation has so far raised more than $1 million, Mr. Goodrich said.

Besides financing schools, it has also helped exchange students from Afghanistan come to New England, and some have gone on to receive scholarships to colleges like Williams, Mount Holyoke and Bates.

Donations came from all sorts of people.

"We have Jews and Muslims and Christians," Ms. Goodrich told ABC News in 2005. "We have ardent Republicans, and we have Democrats and Red Sox and, I hate to use that word, Yankees. I'm a Red Sox fan."

Peter Goodrich was 33 when he died. "As time went on," Ms. Goodrich said, "I realized that I had, in fact, this opportunity to use my life to continue his."

Sarah Wales Donavan, who was known as Sally, was born in Newton, Mass., on May 12, 1945. She graduated from the University of Vermont in 1967 with a degree in sociology and earned a master's degree in education from Boston University and another master's as a reading specialist from Simmons College.

Besides her husband, Ms. Goodrich is survived by another son, a daughter, three brothers and five grandchildren.

Ms. Goodrich made several trips to Afghanistan, the first in April 2005, to see how construction of the school in Logar Province was coming along. She was greeted as the "kind foreign lady," she said.

"I have regained my sense of trust and hope, and I have seen the best of human nature," she said. "I've been the most unfortunate of women, but I am now the most fortunate of women."

— *By Dennis Hevesi*

FRED FOY

A Famous 'Hi-Yo, Silver'

MARCH 27, 1921 - DEC. 22, 2010

A fiery horse with the speed of light, a cloud of dust and a hearty Hi-Yo, Silver! ... Three times a week on the radio, those words, juxtaposed with the galloping strains of Rossini's "William Tell" overture, captivated generations of midcentury Americans tuned in to "The Lone Ranger." And for a decade, first on the radio and later on television, Fred Foy was the man who intoned those gallant lines, among the most evocative in American broadcasting.

Mr. Foy, who died on Dec. 22, at 89, at his home in Woburn, Mass., was not the first "Lone Ranger" announcer and narrator — the show had begun in 1933, when he was scarcely more than a boy — but he was the last, and almost certainly the best known. From the late 1940s, when he joined the radio show, until the late 1950s, when the TV show went off the air, his was the resonant voice that heralded thrills, adventure and the swift administration of frontier justice by that masked man.

"We had no idea we were creating something that would become an American icon," Mr. Foy told The Daily News of New York in 2003. "We knew it was good, but it was a job. You came in at 3, you checked the script, you did the rehearsal, you made sure the production elements were in place, you went on the air."

On the radio, Mr. Foy was also the announcer for "The Green Hornet" and "Sergeant Preston of the Yukon." On television, he became a staff announcer for ABC in New York, where his duties included "The Dick Cavett Show."

A frequent speaker at old-time radio conventions, Mr. Foy was inducted into the Radio Hall of Fame in 2000.

Frederick William Foy was born in Detroit on March 27, 1921. (He was no relation to the vaudevillian Eddie Foy Sr. or his Seven Little Foys.) Soon after graduating from high school, he took a job with WMBC, a local 250-watt radio station. In 1942 he joined WXYZ in Detroit, the station on which "The Lone Ranger" originated.

Serving in the Army in World War II, Mr. Foy was an announcer for Armed Forces Radio in Cairo. After the war he returned to WXYZ. There, beginning in 1948, he narrated "The Lone Ranger" live in the studio.

Mr. Foy remained with the show until it went off the radio in the mid-1950s; he announced the television version from its inception in 1949 to its demise in 1957. (During the years in which the radio and TV shows overlapped, Mr. Foy was heard on both.)

He played the part of the Lone Ranger exactly once, when Brace Beemer, who acted the role on radio, came down with laryngitis.

VOICE FROM THE PAST: Mr. Foy in 1999.

"I guess I did all right," Mr. Foy told The Daily News, "because we didn't get any complaints."

Mr. Foy's survivors include his wife, the former Frances Bingham, whom he married in 1947; two daughters; a son; and three grandchildren.

Though "The Lone Ranger" enjoyed a prolonged afterlife in television reruns, Mr. Foy received no extra compensation, because his work was done in the era before mandatory residuals.

He did not seem to mind. So proud was Mr. Foy of his association with the show that to the end of his life he recited its introduction for anyone who asked.

— *By Margalit Fox*

ROY R. NEUBERGER

Wall Street's Patron of the Arts

JULY 21, 1903 - DEC. 24, 2010

Roy R. Neuberger, who drew on youthful passions for stock trading and art to build one of Wall Street's most venerable partnerships and one of the country's largest private collections of 20th-century masterpieces, died on Dec. 24 at his home at the Pierre Hotel in Manhattan. He was 107 and had lived in New York City for 101 years.

Mr. Neuberger had set out to study art but ended up as a stockbroker, a life path once likened to Gauguin's in reverse. As a founder of the investment firm Neuberger & Berman, he was one of the few people to experience three of Wall Street's major market crises, in 1929, 1987 and 2008.

Unlike his artistic ability, Mr. Neuberger's wealth had a lasting impact. He accumulated hundreds of paintings and sculptures by Milton Avery, Jackson Pollock, Willem de Kooning and others, becoming one of America's leading art patrons while adhering to the belief that collectors should acquire art being produced in their own time, and then hold on to it, giving the public access but never selling.

The works he gathered are now spread over more than 70 institutions in 24 states, many of them in the permanent collection of the Neuberger Museum of Art, which opened in 1974 on the Purchase College campus of the State University of New York.

The money to buy the works came from his investments at Neuberger & Berman (now

Neuberger Berman), the brokerage and investment firm he founded in 1939 with Robert B. Berman. The firm catered to wealthy individuals but also took on a less-affluent clientele with the establishment, in 1950, of the Neuberger Guardian mutual fund, one of the first funds to be sold without the usual 8.5 percent upfront sales commission.

His art collecting drew on the lessons he learned in the financial world. Each year he would buy more than he had bought the previous year, often purchasing large lots at a time. In 1948, for example, he bought 46 paintings by Avery, whom Mr. Neuberger counted as a close friend. He eventually owned more than 100 Avery works.

"My experience on Wall Street made it possible for me to be comfortable buying a lot of art at once," he later wrote. "In my investment firm, when we like a security after careful analysis, we buy a modest quantity. Sometimes after the purchase, we will find that we like it very much. If a large quantity of the stock then becomes available, and we are still enthusiastic about its value and its future, we will buy in quantity quickly, even though the day before we had no such plan and no knowledge that the stock would be available."

"The same principle," he added, "applied to my purchase of the Avery paintings."

Roy Rothschild Neuberger was born on July 21, 1903, in Bridgeport, Conn. His father, Louis, who was 52 when Roy was born, had come to the United States from Germany as a boy. His mother, the former Bertha Rothschild, was a native of Chicago, a lover of music (she played the piano) and a "nervous, troubled woman from a large, well-to-do Jewish family, not related to the famous Rothschilds," Mr. Neuberger wrote in an autobiography, "So Far, So Good: The First 94 Years" (1997).

His father was half owner of the Connecticut Web and Buckle Company and had an interest in the stock market, owning thousands of shares in a Montana copper company. In 1909, the Neuberger family moved to Manhattan, settling on Claremont Avenue opposite Barnard College on the Upper West Side. Mr. Neuberger attended DeWitt Clinton High School, where in his senior year he was captain of the tennis team that won the Greater New York championship.

"Looking back on my youthful addiction to tennis, I find it not much different from my fascination with the market," Mr. Neuberger wrote in his autobiography. "You have to make fast decisions. You can't wait to think about it overnight."

A similar impatience led him to leave New York University after a single year. He felt, he wrote, "that I could learn much more out in the world of business."

It was while working for two years as a buyer of upholstery fabrics for the department store B. Altman & Company that he said he developed an eye for painting and sculpture, as well as a nose for trading. Books, too, shaped him, notably John Galsworthy's series of novels "The Forsyte Saga," which described the practice among well-to-do English families of educating their children on the European continent, and Floret Fels's biography "Vincent van Gogh."

The Galsworthy tales led Mr. Neuberger to a sojourn in Europe. Using money inherited from his father, he set out in June 1924 for a life of leisure. While living mainly on the Left Bank in Paris, he spent afternoons at a cafe, played in tennis tournaments in Cannes and traveled to Berlin and other European capitals.

In Paris, Mr. Neuberger was inspired by the van Gogh biography to collect and support the work of living artists.

"Of course, to do so, I had to have capital of considerably more than the inheritance that gave me an annual income of about $2,000," he wrote. "In those days you could live very comfortably, almost luxuriously, on $2,000, but you couldn't buy art in quantity. So I decided to go back to work in earnest."

He arrived on Wall Street in the spring of 1929, as the bull market was roaring toward its peak. Hired for $15 a week as a runner for the brokerage firm Halle & Stieglitz, he soon learned all aspects of the business while also managing his own money.

One big trade he executed on his own behalf was designed to hedge his own wealth against the possibility that the stock market might fall from its precarious height. He sold short 100 shares of the Radio Corporation of America, the most popular stock of the era, betting that its price would decline from its lofty level of $500.

In October 1929 came the crash that ushered in the Great Depression, and while Mr. Neuberger's blue-chip stocks fell, his bet against RCA paid off well: the stock's price eventually fell into the single digits. He said he lost only 15 percent of his money in the crash, while many others lost everything.

On June 29, 1932, the Dow Jones industrial average dipped to 42 and Mr. Neuberger married Marie Salant, a graduate in economics from Bryn Mawr who had gone to work in the research department of Halle & Stieglitz two years earlier.

"I can report that by June 29, 1996, the Dow Jones industrial average had climbed to 5,704 and Marie and I had had 64 wonderful years together," Mr. Neuberger wrote. Mrs. Neuberger died in 1997. He is survived by a daughter, two sons, eight grandchildren and 30 great-grandchildren.

Emboldened by his management of his own assets, Mr. Neuberger became a stockbroker at Halle & Stieglitz in 1930. He left to start his own firm, Neuberger & Berman, nine years later. The firm was later acquired by Lehman Brothers, but spun off in 2008 as a stand-alone company with Lehman's bankruptcy. Mr. Neuberger continued to go to his Neuberger Berman office every day until he was 99.

Mr. Neuberger began to build his art collection in the late 1930s, and though he was asked to do so many times, he never sold a painting by a living artist. "I have not collected art as an investor would," he said. "I collect art because I love it."

He preferred to share his love by donating works to museums and colleges. In May 1965, Mr. Neuberger received an anonymous offer to buy his art collection for $5 million, a sum he considered a fortune at the time.

Years later he learned that the offer had come from Nelson A. Rockefeller, then governor of New York. Mr. Rockefeller went on to play a key role in Mr. Neuberger's art collection. In May 1967, while Mr. Neuberger was visiting Mr. Rockefeller at his Pocantico Hills estate in Westchester County, the governor offered to have New York State build a museum to house Mr. Neuberger's collection at the State University campus at Purchase.

Designed by Philip Johnson, the museum opened in May 1974. Mr. Neuberger often said

SHARING THE WEALTH: Mr. Neuberger in the Neuberger Museum of Art at Purchase College in New York. His collection, which includes works by Pollock, de Kooning and O'Keeffe, is housed in more than 70 institutions.

that the true spirit of his collection could be found on the second floor, which held seminal paintings by Pollock, Stuart Davis, Edward Hopper and Georgia O'Keeffe, as well as many Milton Avery works.

Mr. Neuberger made an additional gift of $1.3 million to the State University at Purchase in 1984 and other major gifts to the Museum of Modern Art and the Metropolitan Museum of Art. He served as a president of the New York Society for Ethical Culture and the American Federation of Arts.

Mr. Neuberger's second memoir, "The Passionate Collector," was published in 2003. At a White House ceremony in 2007, President George W. Bush presented Mr. Neuberger with a National Medal of Arts.

Like any collector, Mr. Neuberger rued the ones that got away. He remembered passing up a bargain on a Grant Wood painting and refusing to pay $300 for a Jasper Johns in the late 1950s. One time a dealer offered him a Picasso sculpture for $1,500, but he declined because he was buying works only by American artists. "I was such a square that I stupidly didn't buy it," he told The New York Times in 2003.

Mr. Neuberger bought all his works himself, usually through dealers. And his taste ran toward the bold. "I liked adventuresome work that I often didn't understand," he told The Times as he was celebrating his 100th birthday. "For art to be very good it has to be over your head."

But he said he enjoyed the challenge that the work posed to the viewer. "Those who understand the mysteries of art," he said, "are made happier by doing so."

—*By Edward Wyatt*

ALFRED E. KAHN

Clearing the Runways of Regulators

OCT. 17, 1917 - DEC. 27, 2010

ALFRED E. KAHN, a Cornell University economist best known as the chief architect and promoter of deregulating the nation's airlines, despite opposition from industry executives and unions alike, died on Dec. 27 at his home in Ithaca, N.Y. He was 93.

The cause was cancer, Cornell said in a statement.

Mr. Kahn, a leading regulatory scholar who wielded his influence in both government and academia, helped start a broad movement beginning in the mid-1970s toward freer markets in rail and automotive transportation, telecommunications, utilities and the securities markets.

Before deregulation, the airlines were tightly controlled by the Civil Aeronautics Board, which approved routes and set fares that guaranteed airlines a 12 percent return on flights that were 55 percent full. The changes Mr. Kahn orchestrated resulted in increased competition, lower fares and the rise of low-cost carriers like JetBlue and Southwest. But they also created severe financial problems for the industry, leading to bankruptcies and mergers.

"I have to concede that the competition that deregulation brought certainly was terribly, terribly hard on the airlines and their unions, who had heretofore enjoyed the benefits of protection from competition under regulation," Mr. Kahn said decades later.

He added that he accepted "some responsibility" for the industry's financial problems but noted that the airlines eventually recovered, despite sharply rising oil prices and security costs in response to threats of terrorism.

Before he tackled such national issues, Mr. Kahn served as head of the New York State Public Service Commission, the regulator for electricity, gas, water and telephones. He introduced pricing that varied by season or time of day, producing efficiencies benefiting utilities and consumers.

But Mr. Kahn proved virtually helpless when, as the Consumer Price Index jumped in 1978 to 8 percent, President Jimmy Carter persuaded him to become inflation "czar" as chairman of the ill-fated Council on Wage and Price Stability, a job described by a sympathetic friend as serving as fire chief to a pyromaniac.

FREE-MARKETER: Mr. Kahn conceded that airline deregulation created unforeseen problems for the industry.

Before long, the voluble Mr. Kahn, shunning "recession" as a euphemism, warned of a "very serious depression" if inflation were not tamed. That prompted a private rebuke by the president's chief domestic policy adviser, Stuart E. Eizenstat. In response, Mr. Kahn began referring in public to a possible economic downturn as a "banana," only to be chided by the president of the United Fruit Company. So Mr. Kahn changed his euphemism once again, settling on "kumquat."

Operating without staff of his own and with inflation accelerating to above 10 percent, Mr. Kahn became so frustrated in late 1979 that he asked to be relieved of the job. "I can't figure out why the president doesn't fire me," he joked at the time, adding: "Actually, I do know. Nobody would be foolish enough to take this job."

He made his most significant public policy impact as chairman of the Civil Aeronautics Board, which he joined in 1977 under pressure from Mr. Carter and Vice President Walter F. Mondale. What Mr. Kahn had really wanted was to head the Federal Communications Commission. The civil aeronautics job didn't excite him.

"I don't think it's my highest aspiration to make it possible for people to jet all over the world when the future clearly has to belong to substituting telecommunications for travel," he said in 2008 in an interview for this obituary.

An academic, Mr. Kahn knew almost nothing about the airline business — to him planes were just "marginal costs with wings" — but he quickly mastered the arcana and politics of routes, pricing and costs.

"Fred was clearly the perfect man to lead the airline deregulation effort," John H. Shenefield, a Washington lawyer, said in 2003, describing him as "Carter's field general for deregulation."

Mr. Kahn led the struggle for enactment of the Airline Deregulation Act of 1978, the first total dismantling of a federal regulatory regime since the 1930s.

Washington, he argued, had long fostered airline inefficiency and by thwarting competition was enabling carriers to keep fares artificially high.

The industry was battered by the new law and some smaller cities lost service, but Mr. Kahn stoutly defended his handiwork by saying that many more Americans were flying with greater choice of carriers and at lower fares than ever before.

Alfred Edward Kahn, known as Fred, was born on Oct. 17, 1917, in Paterson, N. J., the son of immigrants from Russia, and came of age during the Depression, which inspired his interest in economics. His father worked in a silk mill and eventually owned one himself.

After taking degrees at New York University and a Ph.D. at Yale, Mr. Kahn went to Washington to work as an economist for the Brookings Institution, the Justice Department's antitrust division and the War Production Board before joining the Army in 1943. His military stint ended with a discharge for poor eyesight after basic training.

After teaching for two years at Ripon College in Wisconsin, he joined the Cornell faculty in 1947 and began an extended academic career there distinguished by a landmark two-volume treatise, "The Economics of Regulation," first published in 1970.

At Cornell, he served as dean of the college of arts and sciences and as a trustee.

He became a favorite of colleagues and students, often holding forth while padding about in stocking feet or sitting with legs slung over the side of his chair.

Mr. Kahn was also an avid Savoyard, appearing in numerous campus productions of the light operas of Gilbert and Sullivan. "I was a ham," he acknowledged, which "made for a special relationship with the students."

Mr. Kahn is survived by his wife, Mary Simmons Kahn, two daughters, a son, a nephew for whom he and his wife were legal guardians, eight grandchildren and two great-grandchildren.

For nearly 30 years Mr. Kahn and his family lived on a large property on Lake Cayuga, the largest of the Finger Lakes, in central New York. To justify what seemed to him an outrageous expense, he forced himself to swim in the lake every day until it was too cold. He continued to swim there into his 90s.

Language was another passion. For more than 25 years he served on the usage panel of the American Heritage Dictionary, and he had a well-known and longstanding revulsion to bureaucratic language, which he let his staff know about four days after arriving at the aeronautics board. Try to write, he told them in a memo, "in straight-forward quasi-conversational, humane prose — as though you were talking to or communicating with real people."

— By Robert D. Hershey Jr.

BILLY TAYLOR

The Professor of Jazz

JULY 24, 1921 - DEC. 28, 2010

Billy Taylor, a pianist and composer and an eloquent advocate for jazz as well as a familiar presence on television and radio for many years, died on Dec. 28 in Manhattan. He was 89 and lived in the Riverdale section of the Bronx.

Dr. Taylor, as he preferred to be called (he earned a doctorate in music education from the University of Massachusetts, Amherst in 1975), was a living refutation of the stereotype of jazz musicians as unschooled, unsophisticated and inarticulate, an image that was prevalent when he began his career in the 1940s and one that he did as much as any other musician to erase.

Dr. Taylor probably had a higher profile on television than any other jazz musician of his generation. He had a long run as a cultural correspondent on the CBS News program "Sunday Morning" and was the musical director of David Frost's syndicated nighttime talk show from 1969 to 1972.

Well educated and well spoken, Dr. Taylor, Ben Ratliff wrote in The New York Times in 1996, came across as "genial professor," which he was: he taught jazz courses at Long Island University, the Manhattan School of Music and elsewhere. But he was also a compelling performer and a master of the difficult art of making jazz accessible without watering it down.

His "greatest asset," Mr. Ratliff wrote, "is a sense of jazz as entertainment, and he's not going to be obscure about it."

A pianist with impeccable technique and an elegant, almost self-effacing style, Dr. Taylor worked with some of the biggest names in jazz early in his career and later led a trio that worked in New York nightclubs and recorded many albums. But he left his mark on jazz less as a musician than as a proselytizer, spreading the gospel of jazz as a serious art form in high school and college lectures, on radio and television, on government panels and foundation boards.

ARTIST AND ADVOCATE: Dr. Taylor was a pianist, composer and champion of jazz as a serious art form.

He also helped bring jazz to predominantly black neighborhoods with Jazzmobile, an organization he founded in 1965 to present free outdoor concerts by nationally known musicians at street corners and housing projects throughout New York City.

"I knew that jazz was not as familiar to young blacks as James Brown and the soul thing," he told The Times in 1971. "If you say to a young guy in Harlem, Duke Ellington is great, he's going to be skeptical until he has seen him on 127th Street."

William Edward Taylor Jr. was born in Greenville, N.C., on July 24, 1921, and grew up in Washington. His father, William, was a dentist; his mother, Antoinette, was a schoolteacher. He had his first piano lesson at 7 and later studied music at what is now Virginia State University. Shortly after moving to New York in 1943 — within two days of his arrival, he recalled — he began working with the tenor saxophonist Ben Webster at the Three Deuces on 52nd Street, and he remained a fixture on that celebrated nightclub row for many years.

Dr. Taylor had the technique, the knowledge and the temperament to straddle the old and the new; his adaptability made him a popular sideman with both swing and bebop musicians and led to his being hired in 1949 as the house pianist at Birdland.

In 1951 he formed his own trio, which was soon working at clubs like the Copacabana in New York and the London House in Chicago. Within a few years he was lecturing about jazz at music schools and writing articles about it for DownBeat, Saturday Review and other publications. He later had a long-running concert-lecture series at the Metropolitan Museum of Art.

He also became one of the few jazz musicians to establish a successful separate career in radio and television. In 1958 he was the musical director of an NBC television show, "The Subject Is Jazz." A year later the Harlem radio station WLIB hired him as a disc jockey; in 1962 he moved to WNEW, but he returned to WLIB in 1964 as both disc jockey and program director, and remained in those positions until 1969. He was later a founding partner of Inner City Broadcasting, which bought WLIB in 1971.

Commercial radio became increasingly inhospitable to jazz in the 1960s, but Dr. Taylor found a home at National Public Radio, where he was a familiar voice for more than two decades, first as host of "Jazz Alive" in the late '70s and most recently on "Billy Taylor's Jazz at the Kennedy Center." That series, on which he introduced live performances and interviewed the performers, made its debut in the fall of 1994 and remained in production until the fall of 2002.

In 1968 Dr. Taylor was appointed to New York City's new Cultural Council, along with Leonard Bernstein, Richard Rodgers and other prominent figures in the arts. He later held similar positions on both the state and federal level and until recently was an adviser to the Kennedy Center for the Performing Arts in Washington.

In 1980 he was a member of an advisory panel that called for greater support for jazz from the National Endowment for the Arts. Many of the panel's proposals were enacted, and Dr. Taylor became a beneficiary of the endowment in 1988, when he received a $20,000 Jazz Masters award. He was also given a National Medal of Arts in 1992.

Dr. Taylor wrote more than 300 compositions. They ranged in scope and style from "I Wish I Knew How It Would Feel to Be Free," a simple 16-bar gospel tune written with Dick Dallas that became one of the unofficial anthems of the civil rights movement in the 1960s, to the ambitious "Suite for Jazz Piano and Orchestra" (1973).

He is survived by his wife, Theodora, and a daughter. A son died in 1988.

For all the energy his other activities required, Dr. Taylor never lost his enthusiasm for performing — or his frustration with audiences that, as he saw it, missed the point. "Most people say, 'Hey, let's go to the nightclub and have a few drinks, and maybe we'll even listen to the music,'" he said. "It's a lack of understanding of the musicians and of the discipline involved.

"This is not to say that playing jazz is all frowning and no fun at all. But because you make it look easy doesn't mean you didn't spend eight hours a day practicing the piano."

— *By Peter Keepnews*

PETE POSTLETHWAITE

To Filmgoers, a Familiar Craggy Face

FEB. 7, 1946 - JAN. 2, 2011

Pete Postlethwaite, a lanky, craggy-faced character actor whose range stretched from sweet sentimentality to acid menace and who was nominated for an Academy Award in 1994 for his role as the father of a man unjustly accused of terrorism in "In the Name of the Father," died on Jan. 2 in Shrewsbury, Shropshire, England. He was 64 and lived on a farm near Bishop's Castle, Shropshire.

The cause was cancer, a friend said.

With a broad nose, prominent ears, high cheekbones and hollow cheeks, Mr. Postlethwaite (pronounced POSS-ul-thwayt) was distinctive looking and rawboned, if not exactly classically handsome. His face was an especially suitable one for the rough-hewn working-class men he often played.

He was widely known in England as a stage and television actor before beginning a busy film career in the 1980s. His first major role was in "A Private Function," with Michael Palin and Maggie Smith, in 1984, and in the 1990s he became familiar to American audiences in "Alien 3," "Waterland," "The Last of the Mohicans" and "The Usual Suspects."

In 1996, he starred as the leader of a local brass band in "Brassed Off," a melancholy and sentimental comedy about the threatened closing of a coal mine in a village in northern England that would also mean the end of the band. His later films included "The Shipping News" and a remake of the 1976 horror film "The Omen."

Last year he was seen in two Hollywood action extravaganzas, as a fisherman and adoptive father of a character loosely based on the mythological figure Perseus in "Clash of the Titans" and as a dying corporate baron in "Inception"; he also played a vicious gangster in Ben Affleck's crime drama "The Town."

"In the Name of the Father" was based on the real-life tribulations of Gerry Conlon, a feckless Irishman wrongly accused in the 1974 Irish Republican Army bombing of two pubs popular with British soldiers in Guildford, England. Mr. Postlethwaite played Giuseppe Conlon, "a father in an unimaginable predicament," as The New York Times described the role, whose complicated relationship with his son (Daniel Day-Lewis) is made even more difficult when he becomes a victim of the prosecution of the crime his son did not commit.

EVERYMAN: Mr. Postlethwaite often played working-class characters.

Peter William Postlethwaite was born on Feb. 7, 1946, into a working-class Roman Catholic family in Warrington, near Liverpool. As a teenager he booked the Beatles to appear at a village hall. His father, William, was a cooper and later a school caretaker. He and his wife, Mary, expected their son to become a priest — as a boy Peter spent two years in a seminary — or a teacher.

As a young man Mr. Postlethwaite did teach for a while — drama and physical education — until he gave it up to pursue acting, a decision that, according to family lore, his mother chided him for until the 1980s, when he had his picture taken with Queen Elizabeth II after appearing in a Royal Shakespeare Company production of "The Taming of the Shrew."

Mr. Postlethwaite studied to be an actor at the Bristol Old Vic and spent his first years as a professional at the Everyman Theater in Liverpool, where he worked with Bill Nighy, Jonathan Pryce and others. He began appearing on television in the 1970s, in both films and series. It was a brazen and brutal performance as a drunken, abusive husband and father in the 1988 film "Distant Voices, Still Lives" that brought him wider attention as a film actor.

He continued to perform onstage throughout much of his career, and two years ago he returned to Liverpool's Everyman as King Lear. Dominic Cavendish wrote in The Telegraph of London, "The journey Postlethwaite takes is beautifully shaded, by turns semi-serious, pensive and pained before arriving, touchingly, at some dazed, carefree state where madness has become his sole means of self-preservation."

Mr. Postlethwaite's survivors include his wife, Jacqui Morrish, a son and a daughter.

— By Bruce Weber

JUDY BONDS

A Crusading Coal-Miner's Daughter

AUG. 27, 1952 - JAN. 3, 2011

Ankle deep in the stream by the house where his coal-mining family had lived for generations, Judy Bonds's 6-year-old grandson, Andrew, scooped up fistfuls of dead fish one day back in 1996.

"What's wrong with these fish?" he asked. "I knew something was very, very wrong," Ms. Bonds told Sierra magazine in 2003. "So I began to open my eyes and pay attention."

Ms. Bonds soon discovered that the fish had been poisoned by debris from the mines in the mountains above the West Virginia hollow where her family had lived since early last century. Within six years, she and her Marfork Hollow neighbors had to abandon their homes.

Ms. Bonds found her mission that day in the stream. For years afterward thousands of people — neighbors, environmental activists, politicians, mining officials, industry regulators and crowds at rallies she organized — heard from the short, round-faced woman known as the godmother of the movement to stop mountaintop-removal coal mining.

Ms. Bonds died of cancer — it had spread from her lungs — on Jan. 3 in Charleston, W.Va., at age 58, said Vernon Haltom, who leads the Coal River Mountain Watch, an advocacy group. He and Ms. Bonds had been its co-directors since 2007.

HOMETOWN HERO: When her community was destroyed by mining, Ms. Bonds took action.

Based in a former post office in Whitesville, W.Va., the organization is dedicated to banning the mining process by which mountaintops are blasted off to expose coal seams, with tons of loose rock cascading into adjacent valleys and carbon dioxide billowing into the atmosphere.

The tumbling rock, called valley fills, clogs streams and rivers and leaches chemicals, previously sealed underground, into water systems.

"There are many things we ought to do to deal with climate change," James E. Hansen, a climatologist at NASA and Columbia University, said after her death, "but stopping mountaintop-removal is the place to start. Coal contributes the most carbon dioxide of any energy source." Carbon dioxide traps heat from the sun and prevents it from escaping the atmosphere.

In 2001, three years after she joined Coal River Mountain Watch as a volunteer, Ms. Bonds became the organization's $12,000-a-year outreach director, a position she accepted after working as a waitress, then manager, at a Pizza Hut while a single mother.

In her new job, she began staging protest rallies, testifying at regulatory hearings, filing lawsuits, picketing mining company stockholders' meetings, organizing letter-writing campaigns. A primary target was the Massey Energy Company, which owned the mines around Marfork Hollow and other Appalachian communities. In 2010 an explosion at the Massey Company's Upper Big Branch mine in Montcoal, W.Va., killed 29 miners in what was the nation's worst mining disaster in 40 years.

"She became the voice for communities around the country fighting mountaintop-removal," Mr. Haltom said of Ms. Bonds. "She spoke to audiences of one person to 6,000."

One of her standard lines was, "Stop poisoning our babies."

In 2003 Ms. Bonds received the Goldman Environmental Prize, an annual $150,000 prize that goes to unrecognized "grassroots environmental heroes."

"Her dedication and success as an activist and organizer have made her one of the nation's leading community activists confronting an industry practice that has been called 'strip mining on steroids,'" the Goldman Foundation said.

For years, Ms. Bonds had envisioned a "thousand-hillbilly march" in Washington. That wish was fulfilled last September, when about 2,000 people joined what was called the Appalachia Rising, leading to the arrest of about 100 protesters outside the White House. But by then she was too ill to join the march.

Julia (she preferred to be called Judy) Belle Thompson was born on Aug. 27, 1952, one of nine children of Oliver and Sarah Thompson. Her father stopped working in the mines at 65 and soon died of black lung disease. Besides her grandson, she is survived by her daughter, two brothers and three sisters.

Danger came with Ms. Bonds's activism: phone threats, insults, physical attacks.

"She was walking right behind me when she got belted by a burly miner's wife," said Dr. Hansen, who in June 2009 joined a march at Marsh Fork Elementary School in Sundial,

W.Va., to protest its proximity to a coal-processing silo and a slurry dam, parts of a 2,000-acre mountaintop-removal site.

"She fought to get a safe new school for the kids," Mr. Haltom said. "In the old one, the kids breathe coal dust in class."

But last April, he continued, "everything came together: a new school at a safe location about 10 miles up the road."

"The kids will start attending class there in the fall of 2012," he said.

—*By Dennis Hevesi*

CYRIL HARRIS

Attuned to the Sound of Music Halls

JUNE 20, 1917 - JAN. 4, 2011

CYRIL M. HARRIS, an acoustical engineer responsible for the sound in many of the most prominent concert halls, theaters and auditoriums in the United States, including the Metropolitan Opera and Avery Fisher Hall in New York, died on Jan. 4 at his home in Manhattan. He was 93.

Mr. Harris was a traditionalist intent on taking the full, resonant sound of the great 19th-century concert halls to their modern descendants, whose cleaner, less ornamented architecture often proved fatal to classical music. In an age of steel, glass and concrete, he favored wood and plaster, an approach that brought a string of triumphs that began in 1966 with the Metropolitan Opera, whose acoustics he designed with the Danish engineer Vilhelm Jordan.

After the Met, he was hired as a consultant on Powell Symphony Hall in St. Louis, the Great Hall at the Krannert Center for the Performing Arts in Urbana, Ill., the three theaters of the John F. Kennedy Center for the Performing Arts in Washington, Orchestra Hall in Minneapolis, Symphony Hall (now Abravanel Hall) in Salt Lake City, the renovation of the New York State Theater at Lincoln Center and, when he was in his 80s, Benaroya Hall in Seattle.

All told, he designed the acoustics for more than 100 halls, most recently the Conrad Prebys Concert Hall at the University of California, San Diego, which opened in 2009.

It was the renovation of Avery Fisher Hall at Lincoln Center in the mid-1970s that put the seal on Mr. Harris as the pre-eminent acoustical engineer in the United States. The hall had been cursed with a long list of acoustical problems from the day it opened in 1962 as Philharmonic Hall and had defeated nearly every effort to overcome its dead spots and lack of reverberation.

Mr. Harris advised the architects Philip Johnson and John Burgee to start from scratch. Concrete floors were replaced with wood, and the ceiling plaster was thickened. Away went the curved side balconies and curved back wall that Mr. Harris had identified as obstacles to the proper diffusion of sound.

Harold C. Schonberg, the classical music critic for The New York Times, wrote that Mr. Harris's acoustical makeover had transformed the hall from "a horror to one of the important acoustic installations of the world."

Reviewing the New York Philharmonic's inaugural concert in the hall, on Oct. 19, 1976, he wrote: "Single instruments stood out in relief. It was almost as if the Philharmonic were one large chamber group. In any part of the dynamic range, too, from the wispiest pianissimo to the most stupendous forte, Fisher Hall came through with extraordinary clarity."

Mr. Harris, judging the result in an interview with Newsweek, said: "I think that my greatest pleasure comes from hearing the musicians say that they don't have to bow or blow so hard — that I've added 10 or 20 years to their careers."

Cyril Manton Harris was born on June 20, 1917, in Detroit. His father, a physician, died in the flu epidemic of 1918, and he was reared as an only child by his mother in Hollywood. He first became interested in acoustics on frequent visits to the Warner Brothers studios, across the street from his junior high school. At the time, the studio's technicians were trying to bring sound to pictures.

He attended the University of California, Los Angeles, where he earned a bachelor's degree in mathematics in 1938 and a master's degree in physics in 1940. At the Massachusetts Institute of Technology he received his doctorate in physics in 1945 and did consulting work on the side, providing solutions to problems like whistling steam pipes and loudly shuddering air-conditioning systems.

While employed as a research engineer for Bell Telephone Laboratories in Murray Hill, N.J., he helped develop a talking typewriter and wrote papers on room acoustics, sound absorption and acoustic impedance. He also wrote, with Vern O. Knudsen, "Acoustical Designing in Architecture," the first of several standard works on acoustics and architecture.

In 1949 he married Ann Schakne, later a book editor at Harper & Row and Bantam, who survives him, as do a daughter, a son and three grandchildren.

In 1952 Mr. Harris accepted a teaching post at Columbia University, where he was professor of electrical engineering in the engineering school and, from 1974 to 1984, the chairman of the division of architectural technology in the graduate school of architecture and planning. One of his first consulting jobs in New York was for Cinema 1 and 2, across the street from Bloomingdale's.

Although he looked to traditional European concert halls or older American performance spaces like Symphony Hall in Boston or Carnegie Hall in New York as models, he often proposed modern equivalents of old solutions. In Minneapolis, for example, he devised a 20th-century counterpart of a 19th-century coffered ceiling by setting plaster cubelike forms into the ceiling.

Dissonant notes occasionally disturbed the chorus of adulation. Although the acoustics at the Kennedy Center's concert hall were pronounced excellent by most critics, musicians griped that they could not hear one another. It was renovated in 1997.

Opinion about Avery Fisher Hall also cooled somewhat over time; the bass remained weak, and brass instruments blared, critics complained. In 1992, the acoustical engineer Russell Johnson was hired to improve the sound onstage.

A GOOD EAR: Mr. Harris in Avery Fisher Hall, one of the hundreds of concert halls for which he designed acoustics.

In 1982, Mr. Harris and the architect I. M. Pei clashed over plans to renovate the Vivian Beaumont Theater in Lincoln Center, and Mr. Pei quit the project, which then stalled.

In the early 1980s, the owners of "21" turned to Mr. Harris for advice on how to tamp down the noise in the Grill Room. He assessed the situation and offered a simple recommendation: do nothing. "Everyone who goes to that room loves the noise," he said.

— *By William Grimes*

GERRY RAFFERTY

Peaking in the '70s, Then a Tumble

APRIL 16, 1947 - JAN. 4, 2011

Gerry Rafferty, a Scottish singer and songwriter who combined a gift for melody, a distinctive voice and a fatalistic worldview to produce 1970s hits like "Stuck in the Middle With You" and "Baker Street," died Jan. 4 in Dorset, England. He was 63.

His death was confirmed by Michael Gray, his former manager, in an obituary he wrote for the London newspaper The Guardian. Various news reports said Mr. Rafferty had been hospitalized for severe liver and kidney problems.

RELUCTANT ROCKER: Mr. Rafferty was successful in an industry he despised.

Mr. Rafferty's 1978 album, "City to City," reached No. 1 in the United States. One track, "Baker Street," made the Top 10 in both Britain and the United States. So did "Stuck in the Middle With You," a song Mr. Rafferty and Joe Egan recorded with their group Stealers Wheel in 1972. That song reached a new generation of listeners when Quentin Tarantino used it in the notorious ear-slicing scene in his 1992 movie "Reservoir Dogs."

In all, Mr. Rafferty sold more than 10 million albums over three decades.

But Mr. Gray, writing in The Guardian, said Mr. Rafferty's success was a shadow of what it might have been. At the peak of his popularity, Mr. Rafferty declined to tour the United States and turned down chances to play with Eric Clapton and Paul McCartney. In his later years his output declined, then stopped altogether as he "spiraled into alcoholism," Mr. Gray said. Mr. Rafferty himself said in a rare interview in 2009 with The Sunday Express that he suffered from depression.

But at his height Mr. Rafferty attracted a following with a synthesis of country, folk and rock music. Reviewing "City to City" in Rolling Stone, Ken Emerson said Mr. Rafferty "writes with the sweet melodiousness of Paul McCartney and sings with John Lennon's weary huskiness."

Mr. Emerson discerned "a prayerful quality" in Mr. Rafferty's voice, reminiscent of "the dim dawn after a dark night of the soul."

Almost from his birth in Paisley, Scotland, on April 16, 1947, Gerald Rafferty knew plenty about life's dark side. He and his mother would hide from his father to avoid being beaten when he stumbled home drunk, Mr. Gray wrote. But music pervaded the family's life, as young Gerry assimilated Roman Catholic hymns, traditional folk music, 1950s pop and even the Irish rebel tunes his deaf father bellowed.

Mr. Rafferty dropped out of school at 15 and went to work in a butcher shop. On weekends he and a friend, Mr. Egan, played in a local group, the Mavericks. After bouncing about a bit, Mr. Rafferty and Mr. Egan reunited in Stealers Wheel, whose 1972 debut album included "Stuck in the Middle."

"Stuck in the Middle," written as a parody of Bob Dylan's songs, ridiculed a music industry cocktail party, complaining, "Clowns to the left of me, jokers to the right, here I am, stuck in the middle with you."

By 1975, Stealers Wheel had broken up after recording three albums, and Mr. Rafferty spent the next three years in legal disputes over contracts. Finally, in 1978, he was free to record again and signed with United Artists. "City to City," a solo effort, was his first album for the label. Its centerpiece song, "Baker Street," featured a saxophone solo by Raphael Ravenscroft that became so popular it was said to spark a global increase in saxophone sales.

Mr. Rafferty went on to record several more albums, including "Night Owl," which made it to the Top Five in England and the Top 20 in the United States in 1979. Other albums followed, some of which garnered good reviews but none of which approached Mr. Rafferty's earlier success.

He contributed a vocal to the soundtrack of the 1983 film "Local Hero" and produced the Proclaimers' 1987 hit "Letter From America."

Mr. Rafferty's marriage to Carla Ventilla ended in divorce. He is survived by a daughter, a brother and a granddaughter.

In the 2009 interview, Mr. Rafferty called the music industry "something I loathe and detest." Nevertheless, he earned nearly $125,000 a year in royalties for "Baker Street" alone.

— By Douglas Martin

MALANGATANA NGWENYA

Political Painter and National Hero

JUNE 6, 1936 - JAN. 5, 2011

Malangatana Ngwenya, one of Africa's best-known contemporary artists, whose phantasmagoric paintings were inspired by political conditions in his home country, Mozambique, died on Jan. 5 in Matosinhos, Portugal. He was 74.

The Pedro Hispano Hospital said he had been admitted on Christmas Day after he became ill while visiting his daughter, but it did not give a cause of death.

Mr. Ngwenya, a beloved national hero in Mozambique, was one of the few African artists to gain substantial worldwide recognition while staying in Africa — an international profile that was enhanced by an expansive personality. He had cosmopolitan tastes; his knowledge of global art was wide; and he was a born performer who composed music, sang songs in five languages and periodically broke into spontaneous dancing.

Even after he took up art full time in 1981 and his fame grew, he remained a highly visible political and civic presence.

Mr. Ngwenya was a founding member of the Mozambique Peace Movement and served as a representative to parliament from 1990 to 1994. He was instrumental in establishing the National Museum of Art of Mozambique in Maputo, the capital, and undertook several large public mural projects. He established cultural programs in his home village, and taught art to children in his home. In 1997 he was named a Unesco Artist for Peace.

Born in Matalana, a village in southern Mozambique, on June 6, 1936, Malangatana Ngwenya (pronounced mah-LANG-gah-tah-nah en-GWEN-yah) attended Swiss Protestant and Roman Catholic missionary schools as a child but did not stay long. He worked on his mother's farm as a herder and studied traditional healing under the tutelage of two uncles.

At 12 he went to Lourenco Marques (now Maputo), Mozambique's capital, and took a job as a servant and ball boy at a colonial tennis club. He went to school at night and developed an interest in painting, which Portuguese members of the tennis club encouraged him to pursue.

In 1959 he exhibited publicly for the first time in a group show; two years later, at 25, he had his first solo exhibition.

BEYOND THE CANVAS: One of Africa's most renowned artists, Mr. Ngwenya used his influence to promote peace.

Simultaneously, he was writing poetry, a lifelong practice. His poems were first published in 1963. At the time, when many African countries were struggling for independence from Europe, he also became politically active. After joining a nationalist guerrilla group called the Front for Liberation of Mozambique, known by the acronym Frelimo, he was arrested by the Portuguese military police and spent 18 months in jail.

In 1971 he traveled to Lisbon on a grant to study printmaking and ceramics. He returned to Mozambique three years later, just before the country separated from Portugal in 1975. He rejoined Frelimo, which as a single-party Communist organization became the new ruling power. Two years later a rival party, supported first by Rhodesia (now Zimbabwe) and then by South Africa, challenged Frelimo and pushed Mozambique into a devastating civil war that dragged on for 16 years.

Most of the paintings and drawings Mr. Ngwenya did during this period were a direct response to the violence he witnessed. Densely packed with figures, they presented lurid, Boschian visions of the Last Judgment and the torments of hell rooted in images related to healing and witchcraft remembered from childhood. It was only after peace was finally declared in 1992 that the content and the look of his work changed: he introduced landscape images and cooled a palette dominated by charred reds and stained whites with greens and blues.

As his international reputation grew, he had solo shows in India, South America and the Caribbean, and two retrospectives in Portugal. He appeared in important surveys in the United States, including "Africa Explores: 20th Century African Art" at the Museum for African Art in 1991 and "The Short Century: Independence and Liberation Movements in Africa, 1945-1994," which traveled the country in 2001 and 2002. In New York, he was represented by the Contemporary African Art Gallery, where he last showed in 2002.

Information on his survivors was not available.

In Mozambique, Mr. Ngwenya was admired for his art and loved for his generosity. William Karg, the director of the Contemporary African Art Gallery, remembered once sharing a Maputo-bound domestic flight with Mr. Ngwenya. The word quickly spread among the African passengers that the artist was on board, and no sooner had the seatbelt sign gone off than people filled the aisles asking him to do sketches for them on any scrap of paper at hand. He accommodated everyone.

— *By Holland Cotter*

DONALD J. TYSON

Going Global With Chicken

APRIL 21, 1930 - JAN. 6, 2011

DONALD J. TYSON, an aggressive and visionary entrepreneur who dropped out of college and built his father's Arkansas chicken business into the behemoth Tyson Foods, one of the world's largest producers of poultry, beef and pork, died on Jan. 6. He was 80 and lived in Fayetteville, Ark.

The cause was complications of cancer, Tyson Foods said.

Shrewd, folksy and often likened to fellow Arkansan Sam Walton, the Wal-Mart tycoon, Mr. Tyson was a risk-taking, bare-knuckle businessman who bought out dozens of competitors, skirted the edge of the law and transformed a Depression-era trucking-and-feed venture into a global enterprise with an army of employees and millions of customers in 57 countries.

SKIPPING THE PINSTRIPES: Mr. Tyson, who oversaw a global company, dressed in the same khaki uniform his employees wore.

Tyson Foods became a household name as he popularized the Rock Cornish game hen as a high-profit specialty item; helped develop McDonald's Chicken McNuggets and KFC's Rotisserie Gold; and stocked America's grocery stores with fresh and frozen chickens — killed, cleaned and packaged in his archipelago of processing plants.

"It was pretty much Don's vision that fueled the company," Mark A. Plummer, an analyst for Stephens Inc., a Little Rock financial services firm, told The New York Times in 1994, the year before Mr. Tyson stepped down after nearly three decades as chairman. "He saw that if you added more convenience by further processing the chicken, consumers would pay for it."

Mr. Tyson grew up on a farm with squawking chickens and became one of the world's richest men, a down-home billionaire who dressed in khaki uniforms like his workers, with "Don" and the Tyson logo stitched over the shirt pockets. He looked like a farmer down at the feed co-op: a short, stocky man with a paunch and a round weather-beaten face, a baldish pate and a gray chin-strap beard.

But he cultivated presidents and members of Congress, threw lavish society parties, took glamorous young women to Wall Street meetings, jetted around the world and spent weeks at a time on his yacht fishing off Brazil or Baja California for the spear-nosed, blue-water trophy marlins that decorated his company headquarters and his homes in Arkansas, England and Mexico.

Critics said his tigerish corporate philosophy

— "grow or die" — led to many acquisitions, notably the bitterly contested purchase of Holly Farms for $1.5 billion in 1989, which made Tyson Foods the nation's No. 1 poultry producer, dwarfing ConAgra and Perdue Farms. But it also led to risky deals, questionable business practices and political ties that produced legal entanglements for him and the company.

Mr. Tyson and his son and future successor, John H. Tyson, were accused of helping to arrange illegal gifts to President Bill Clinton's first-term secretary of agriculture, Mike Espy, including plane trips, lodging and football tickets, when his agency was considering tougher safety and inspection regulations affecting Tyson Foods.

Mr. Espy resigned in 1994, but four years later was acquitted of accepting illegal gifts. In 1997, Tyson Foods pleaded guilty to making $12,000 in such gifts to Mr. Espy and paid $6 million in fines and costs. Don and John Tyson were named unindicted co-conspirators and testified before a grand jury in exchange for immunity from prosecution. (In an unrelated 2004 case, Don Tyson and Tyson Foods agreed to pay $1.7 million to settle a federal complaint that the company did not fully disclose benefits to Mr. Tyson.)

Mr. Tyson's legal problems tainted but hardly overshadowed a career widely regarded as a stunning American success story. But his legacy of aggressive management continued to trouble the company when he served as the semiretired "senior chairman" after 1995 and even after he retired in 2001.

Environmentalists accused Tyson of fouling waterways. Animal rights groups said it raised chickens in cruel conditions. Regulators said it discriminated against women and blacks and cheated workers out of wages. Tyson Foods denied wrongdoing, but paid fines, back wages and penalties to settle some cases.

In 2001 the company and three managers were charged with conspiring for years to smuggle illegal immigrants from Mexico and South America to work in its plants, but all were acquitted.

Marvin Schwartz, who wrote a history of Tyson Foods, "Tyson: From Farm to Market," said its culture reflected its leader. "Don is a gambler, and he's very comfortable taking risks," he said. "And in a state like Arkansas, where there are very few regulatory controls, corporations have more flexibility. The state motto was 'The Land of Opportunity,' and that's why entrepreneurs like Sam Walton and Don Tyson have made it here."

Donald John Tyson was born on April 21, 1930, in Olathe, Kan., to John and Helen Knoll Tyson. They settled in Springdale, Ark., and his father began hauling chickens from farms to markets in the Southeast and Midwest. The boy attended public schools and at 14 started working for his father. After graduating from Kemper Military School in Boonville, Mo., he enrolled at the University of Arkansas, but quit in his senior year in 1952 to join the business, which had added a hatchery and feed mill.

In 1952, he married Twilla Jean Womochil. He is survived by his son, three daughters and two grandchildren.

In 1957, the company built its first poultry-processing plant, and in the 1960s it began buying farms and competitors. It went public in 1963. Two years later, it introduced Rock Cornish game hens, which became enormously popular and profitable. Mr. Tyson became president in 1966 and chairman in 1967 after his parents were killed in a car-train wreck.

Over the next three decades, Tyson grew exponentially. It bought beef, pork and seafood companies, built 60 processing plants and diversified into 6,000 products. It supplied fast-food chains and secured markets abroad. When Mr. Tyson surrendered day-to-day control in 1995, the company ranked 110th on the Fortune 500 list, with sales of $5.2 billion.

Mr. Tyson supported Jimmy Carter, Bill Clinton and George W. Bush for president, along with many charitable, educational and development programs. He called himself a moderate Democrat, but went fishing with Republicans too, and made his Baja California home available for legislative junkets.

"My theory about politics is that if they will just leave me alone, we'll do just fine," he said in 1993. "We pretty much stay home and run chickens."

— *By Robert D. McFadden*

VANG PAO

A Warrior in Laos, a 'King' in Exile

DEC. 1929 - JAN. 6, 2011

VANG PAO, a charismatic Laotian general who commanded a secret army of his mountain people in a long, losing campaign against Communist insurgents, then achieved almost kinglike status as their leader-in-exile in the United States, died on Jan. 6 in Clovis, Calif. He was 81.

He died of pneumonia after celebrating Hmong New Year in Fresno, Calif.

Vang Pao was a general in the official Laotian Army, the chief of a secret Laotian force financed by the Central Intelligence Agency and the undisputed leader of the varied factions of his people, the Hmong. Tens of thousands of them followed him in his flight to Thailand after the Communist victory in 1975. Later, in the United States, he was so revered that some of his people believed he had supernatural powers.

"He is like the earth and the sky," Houa Thao, a Hmong refugee, told The Fresno Bee in 2007.

That year, Gen. Vang Pao was charged with plotting to provide $10 million in arms to antigovernment forces in Laos , but American prosecutors dropped the charges two years later.

Even before President Dwight D. Eisenhower's vow in 1960 that Laos must not fall to the Communists, the country was immersed in conflict. Its importance grew during the Vietnam War, when most of the Ho Chi Minh Trail, the route that North Vietnam used to funnel supplies southward, ran through Laotian territory.

The United States wanted to interdict the supply route, rescue American pilots shot down over Laos and aid anti-Communist forces in a continuing civil war, but it was hampered in doing so publicly because Laos was officially neutral, so the C.I.A. recruited General Vang Pao for the job. At the time, he held the highest rank ever achieved by a Hmong in the Royal Laotian Army, major general.

The Hmong are a tribe in the fog-shrouded mountains separating Laos from southern China, and they were natural allies for the C.I.A. because of their enmity toward Laotian lowlanders to the south, who dominated the Communist leadership.

General Vang Pao quickly organized 7,000 guerrillas, then steadily increased the force to 39,000, leading them in many successful operations, often against daunting odds. William Colby, C.I.A. director in the mid-1970s, called him "the biggest hero of the Vietnam War."

Lionel Rosenblatt, president emeritus of Refugees International, put it more bluntly, telling The New York Times Magazine in 2008 that General Vang Pao's Hmong had been put "into this meat grinder, mostly to save U.S. soldiers from fighting and dying there."

Congressional committees discussed the fighting in Laos in secret at the time, and the press uncovered significant details. But the United States did not officially recognize the Hmong's contribution until 1997, when the Clinton administration authorized a plaque at Arlington National Cemetery saying that the valor of General Vang Pao's troops would never be forgotten.

General Vang Pao was born in December 1929 in a village in northeast Laos, had six years of sporadic schooling and worked as an interpreter for French colonial forces fighting the Japanese in World War II. He became a sergeant in the French colonial army, and, in 1954, an officer in the army of the newly independent Laos.

When the C.I.A. approached him in 1960, he was already fighting Laotian Communists. The next year, he would also fight Communists from Vietnam after they had crossed the Laotian border. The Times in 1971 said that the C.I.A.

did not command the general's army at any level, because his pride and temper would have never permitted it.

The general led troops into combat personally, suffered serious wounds and was known to declare: "If we die, we die together. Nobody will be left behind." About 35,000 Hmong died in battle.

General Vang Pao was also skilled at uniting the 18 clans of Hmong. One technique was to marry women from different tribes, as multiple marriages were permitted in Laos. He had to divorce all but one of his five wives when he went to the United States in 1975, settling on a ranch in Montana.

COMMANDER: Gen. Vang Pao with Hmong troops in 1961. Thousands followed him into exile.

General Vang Pao lived more recently in Southern California and Minnesota, where many of the 200,000 Hmong that followed him to the United States or were born here live. His picture hangs in thousands of homes. His survivors include 25 children and 68 grandchildren.

His funeral, in Fresno, Calif., lasted six days and nights, with 10 cows slaughtered and stir-fried each day. His body was borne on a horse-drawn carriage through the streets of downtown Fresno, where throngs of grieving Hmong lined the way. Scottish bagpipers played "The Green Hills of Tyrol" and two T-28 planes, the aircraft piloted by Hmong guerrilla fighters in the Vietnam War, flew overhead.

The event drew thousands of Hmong, some from as far away as Thailand and France, who strode into Fresno's convention center to say goodbye.

As congressmen and state senators and retired C.I.A. agents filed in to deliver speeches and bow their heads, a scattering of old guerrilla fighters stood outside in the winter sun, puffing on Marlboro cigarettes.

Xa Chao Xiong, 63, was dressed in a camouflage uniform that came not from his years as a jungle warrior but from a local Army surplus store.

"I wear this uniform for my general," he said through a translator. After 20 years in America, he apologized for not knowing English. "Today, I am a soldier again."

Asked by Agence France-Presse to comment on General Vang Pao's death, the Communist government of Laos said, "He was an ordinary person, so we do not have any reaction."

— *By Douglas Martin*

Mark Arax contributed reporting from Fresno, Calif.

FLO GIBSON

The Grande Dame of Audiobooks

FEB. 7, 1924 - JAN. 7, 2011

Flo Gibson, who for decades read soothingly to Americans as they toiled at the gym, behind the wheel or over housework, died on Jan. 7 at her home in Washington. Mrs. Gibson, the universally acknowledged grande dame of audiobooks, was 86.

At her death, Mrs. Gibson was halfway through taping "Les Misérables," which would have been, give or take a title, her 1,134th recorded book.

Mrs. Gibson was the founder of, and chief reader for, Audio Book Contractors, which she ran for nearly three decades from a specially built recording studio in the basement of her home. The company produces audiobooks for sale to libraries and individual consumers.

Audio Book Contractors, which specializes in unabridged recordings of the classics, seeks out an audience for whom a well-told story on tape and the latest bodice-ripper tend to be mutually exclusive. (Mrs. Gibson did record "East Lynne," an 1861 novel by Mrs. Henry Wood that The Chicago Tribune once described as "riveting Victorian smut.")

STORYTELLER: Mrs. Gibson recorded 1,134 books.

Known for her impeccable diction — she was a former radio actress — and scrupulous fealty to the text, Mrs. Gibson narrated everything from "The Wind in the Willows" to capacious adult books like "Pride and Prejudice" (11 hours, 41 minutes) and "Middlemarch," which spans 31 hours, 7 minutes, over 24 cassettes, an effort that took her more than 10 weeks in the studio.

Today, thousands of audiobooks appear annually — read by authors, celebrities and professional voice-over artists — and other companies besides hers do the classics. But Mrs. Gibson's work, colleagues say, was notable on several counts.

For one thing, she was an early entrant in the field, starting out in the mid-1970s recording talking books for the blind for the Library of Congress. She went on to found Audio Book Contractors well before recorded books were commonplace.

For another, she was almost certainly the field's most prolific practitioner. A busy voice-over artist might typically narrate several hundred books in a career; to record more than 1,100, as Mrs. Gibson did, is almost beyond contemplation.

What was more, reviewers agreed that if one were to invest, say, the 36 hours and 7 minutes required to hear "Anna Karenina," then there was no better voice to hear it in than Mrs. Gibson's: deep and throaty, it evoked a firm but favorite schoolteacher and let her juggle men's and women's roles with ease.

Mrs. Gibson was also praised for her meticulous preparation (to tackle the Brontë sisters, she haunted Yorkshire to soak up dialect) and for the intimate compact that appeared to exist between her and the listener. She approached every narration as if she were playing to an audience of one.

Her scrapbooks of fan mail attest to the results. An upholsterer's assistant once wrote Mrs. Gibson to say that her "Pride and Prejudice" had made "the stitches melt down into insignificance" as she labored over an antique chair.

Florence Corona Anderson was born in San Francisco on Feb. 7, 1924. After earning a bachelor's degree in dramatic literature from the University of California, Berkeley, she studied with the noted acting teacher Sanford Meisner at the Neighborhood Playhouse in New York.

She acted in several West Coast radio serials — including "Pat Novak for Hire," which starred a young Jack Webb — before marrying Carlos Gibson, a Peruvian diplomat, and raising four children.

Soon after her youngest child left for college, Mrs. Gibson auditioned for the Library of Congress and was accepted. She later narrated books on tape for several commercial producers before starting Audio Book Contractors in 1983.

As Mrs. Gibson discovered, a narrator's experience of literature differs crucially from a civilian's. Though she adored Henry James, she was often moved to shake her fist and shout at him: "Why don't you punctuate? Why don't you paragraph?" She invariably forgave him, though, and recorded much of his work.

Mrs. Gibson's husband, whom she married in 1947, died in 1989. She is survived by three daughters, a brother and three grandchildren. A son died in 1985.

Audio Book Contractors, which offers hundreds of books on tape and CD, continues to operate. Many of its titles, including dozens narrated by Mrs. Gibson, can also be purchased as digital downloads from audible.com.

What with treadmills and traffic and troublesome chairs, her voice will soothe listeners for decades to come.

— *By Margalit Fox*

PETER YATES

A Briton With a Lens on America

JULY 24, 1929 - JAN. 9, 2011

PETER YATES, a British-born director whose best-known films were well-observed tales of Americana, including the car-chase cop thriller "Bullitt" and the coming-of-age bike-race comedy "Breaking Away," died on Jan. 9 in London. He was 81.

Mr. Yates was nominated for two Academy Awards for directing, for "Breaking Away" (1979), an underdog-triumphs story in which four local teenagers in Bloomington, Ind., take on a privileged team of bicycle racers from Indiana University; and for "The Dresser" (1983), an adaptation of Ronald Harwood's play about an aging theater actor and his long-serving assistant. It starred Albert Finney and Tom Courtenay. (Both films, which Mr. Yates also produced, were nominated for best picture as well.)

Still, Mr. Yates's reputation probably rests most securely on "Bullitt" (1968), his first American film, and particularly on one scene, an extended car chase that instantly became a classic. The film stars Steve McQueen as a conscience-stricken lone-wolf San Francisco detective, and the chase begins with him behind the wheel of a Ford Mustang in a slow, cat-and-mouse pursuit of killers who were in a Dodge Charger. It escalates into high-speed screeches and thuds on city streets and ends in a fiery blast on a highway.

The chase, often paired in discussion with a New York City counterpart from William Friedkin's "French Connection," featured Mr. McQueen doing some of his own driving: a camera placed in the car and peering out the windshield registers the violent shifts in the driver's perspective as the car bounds in chassis-challenging fashion over San Francisco's famous hills.

Mr. Yates's grasp of the American landscape and American characters stretched from coast to coast. He directed Robert Mitchum as a small-time hood desperate to avoid jail time in the low-key crime drama "The Friends of Eddie Coyle" (1973), set in and around Boston; it was especially attentive to the local color and local accents of the George V. Higgins novel on which it was based.

Among Mr. Yates's New York-based films were "For Pete's Sake" (1974), a gag-laced farce set in Brooklyn involving the Mafia, a call-girl operation, cattle rustling and the brassy woman (Barbra Streisand) who gets mixed up in it all; and the 1983 suspense thriller "Eyewitness," set in Manhattan, starring Sigourney Weaver as an ambitious television reporter following a murder story and William Hurt as an informant who may or may not be reliable.

"Breaking Away" and "Eyewitness" were both written by Steve Tesich, a Yugoslavian immigrant with whom Mr. Yates shared a shrewd appreciation of details that perhaps only foreigners might determine were peculiarly American. (Mr. Yates also directed an Off Broadway play by Mr. Tesich, "Passing Game," in 1977.)

"Breaking Away" starred four actors who were unknown at the time (one was Dennis Quaid). They played local Bloomington-ites — or, as they were disparagingly known, "Cutters" — who lived in resentment of the rich college students annually invading their hometown. Mr. Yates and Mr. Tesich used them to illustrate American attitudes about class, education, upward mobility, romance and athletic success.

The film, Vincent Canby wrote in The New York Times, "is so cheerful it almost hurts, but its cheerfulness is grounded in a true appreciation of certain so-called American values (pluck, perseverance, family ties) which, though idealized more often than honored, are a part of the way we see ourselves."

Mr. Yates's career was marked by a willingness to skip from genre to genre, and for a director with so many hits, he had an up-and-down career. Among his other titles, not all well-received, were "John and Mary" (1969), about an anonymous tryst that leads to love, starring Dustin Hoffman and Mia Farrow; "Murphy's War" (1971), a historical drama about a sailor (Peter O'Toole) bent on avenging the sinking of his ship by a German U-boat; "The Deep" (1977), an undersea thriller with Jacqueline Bisset, Robert Shaw and Nick Nolte; "Krull" (1983), a science fiction adventure; and "Eleni" (1985), an adaptation of the memoir by Nicholas Gage about his search for the Communists who executed his mother during the Greek civil war.

OUTSIDER LOOKING IN: Mr. Yates's films captured a particular American worldview.

Peter James Yates was born in England on July 24, 1929. Most sources say his birthplace was Aldershot, Hampshire, about 40 miles southwest of London, though his wife, Virginia, said in an e-mail that it was the village of Ewshot, which is closer to the city. His father was in the military.

He attended the Royal Academy of Dramatic Art in London, and he worked as an assistant director for Jack Cardiff, on "Sons and Lovers" (1960) and Tony Richardson on "A Taste of Honey" (1961). It was a 1967 film, "Robbery," based on the 1963 English heist known as the Great Train Robbery, that impressed Steve McQueen and got Mr. Yates the job directing "Bullitt."

He married Virginia Sue Pope, a New Zealander, in 1960. He is also survived by a son, a daughter and two grandchildren.

— By Bruce Weber

MARGARET WHITING

A Wartime Darling Who Kept on Singing

JULY 22, 1924 - JAN. 10, 2011

Margaret Whiting, a songwriter's daughter who as a bright-eyed teenage singer captivated wartime America and then went on to a long, acclaimed career recording hit songs and performing in nightclubs and on television, died on Jan. 10 in Englewood, N.J. She was 86.

Her daughter and only survivor, Deborah Whiting, said Ms. Whiting died of natural causes at the Lillian Booth Actors' Home, where she had lived since March, having made her home in Manhattan for many years.

Ms. Whiting may not have been a household name like her contemporaries Rosemary Clooney and Ella Fitzgerald, nor was she a singing movie star like Doris Day, but in her heyday she was widely popular in the worlds of big band, jazz, popular music and even country.

Early on, with her schoolgirl smile and wavy blond hair, Ms. Whiting was a favorite interpreter of jazz and popular standards. Her fresh-faced appearance and clear, sturdy voice, tinged with innocence, made her a darling of U.S.O. tours during World War II and the Korean War.

She turned out a string of hit records beginning in the 1940s, became a fixture on radio, appeared on television and later embarked on a nightclub career, touring as late as the 1990s. She was still performing into the 21st century, often at clubs like Arci's Place in Manhattan, where she had been a mainstay of the cabaret scene.

In 2009 she found a wide audience again when her original recording of "Time After Time," a Jule Styne and Sammy Cahn song from 1947, was featured in the film "Julie & Julia," starring Meryl Streep as Julia Child.

A LIFE IN SONG: Ms. Whiting grew up in a musical household.

But it was her association with the lyricist Johnny Mercer that most defined Ms. Whiting's career. Mr. Mercer was writing songs for the movies with Ms. Whiting's father, the popular-song composer Richard A. Whiting, when young Margaret sang for him one night at the family home in Beverly Hills, Calif. She was just 6.

"I came down in my nightgown," she told The New York Times, "sang two songs and went up to bed."

It would become a lasting friendship. After Mr. Whiting died of a heart attack in 1938 at the height of his popularity, Mr. Mercer became a surrogate father of sorts to 13-year-old Margaret, personally overseeing her budding career and signing her immediately after he helped found Capitol Records in 1942. He once told her, "I have two words for you: grow up."

When she was 16, the comedian Phil Silvers asked her to fill in for a missing member of his act at the Grace Hayes Lodge in the San Fernando Valley. It helped start her career. At 18 she recorded the Harold Arlen-Johnny Mercer song "That Old Black Magic" with the bandleader Freddie Slack. The next year it was "Moonlight in Vermont" with the trumpeter Billy Butterfield and his band, followed in 1945 by "It Might as Well Be Spring," with Paul Weston, a Rodgers & Hammerstein tune from the musical "State Fair." That song became a signature for her.

There were more hits, among them "Come Rain or Come Shine," a Mercer-Arlen song from the musical "St. Louis Woman."

In 1948 alone Ms. Whiting had three major hits: "A Tree in the Meadow," "Now Is the Hour" and "Far Away Places." A duet with Mercer, "Baby, It's Cold Outside" (by Frank Loesser), lasted 19 weeks on the Billboard chart in 1949. Her nine duets with the country star Jimmy Wakely, from 1949 to 1951, were sensations. She released albums into the late 1950s with Capitol Records, switched to the Dot and Verve labels but returned to Capitol and recorded her last big hit, "The Wheel of Hurt," in 1966.

Ms. Whiting was a regular performer on television in its first decades, appearing on variety shows hosted by George Jessel, Red Skelton, Jonathan Winters and Nat King Cole. Besides "Julie & Julia," her voice is heard in the films "Bugsy" and "The Cider House Rules." In another, "Valley of the Dolls," she was uncredited as the singing voice of Susan Hayward.

In her long nightclub career, Ms. Whiting was a mentor to younger cabaret singers like K. T. Sullivan and Mary Cleere Haran (see page 284). She played in touring and regional musical theater productions of "Call Me Madam," "Gypsy," "Pal Joey" and "Over Here!" And in 1983 she appeared in the Off Broadway musical "Taking My Turn," in which she delivered the line, "Age doesn't make you boring; boring makes you boring."

"We have been billed as a show about old people, but I don't like that," Ms. Whiting told The Times in an interview at the time. "I call it a musical comedy about living. I mean, in my business, there is no such thing as retiring at 65. You retire when you want to. Right now I'm doing all the things I want to do — this show, television, records, personal appearances. I just gave a pasta demonstration at Bloomingdale's. I don't cook, but they wanted me anyway for pasta Bolognese. I told them, 'Don't ask me to chop or mince.'"

Margaret Eleanor Whiting was born to Richard Whiting and the former Eleanor Youngblood on July 22, 1924, in Detroit, where her father was moonlighting as a piano player in a hotel. As a girl she moved with her parents and sister to New York, where her father worked on Broadway musicals, then to Los Angeles, where he wrote for movies (supplying Shirley Temple with her trademark song "On the Good Ship Lollipop"). He also met Mr. Mercer there and collaborated with him on songs like "Hooray for Hollywood."

Living with her family in Beverly Hills, Ms. Whiting attended a Roman Catholic girls' school and enjoyed a gilded childhood, frolicking at parties with movie stars and music legends, among them Jerome Kern, whom she called Uncle Jerry.

Her younger sister, Barbara, who died in 2004, also became an entertainer, and together they starred in "Those Whiting Girls," a 1950s television series about college coeds.

Ms. Whiting had an early love affair with the actor John Garfield, and her first three marriages ended in divorce: to Hubbell Robinson Jr., a television executive; Lou Busch, a musician with whom she had her daughter; and Richard Moore, a cinematographer who helped found the company Panavision.

In her later years, Ms. Whiting was known to many as the unlikely wife of Jack Wrangler (originally John Stillman), a star of gay pornographic films in the 1970s who went on to become a cabaret and theater producer.

Ms. Whiting and Mr. Wrangler, 22 years her junior, met in the 1970s, lived together for many years and married in 1994. She wrote about their relationship in an autobiography, "It Might as Well Be Spring," saying it was based on similar interests and mutual respect, not sex. When they first became involved, he told her, "I'm gay," to which she replied, "Only around the edges, dear."

Mr. Wrangler helped conceive the 1997 Broadway musical "Dream," a tribute to Mr. Mercer, in which Ms. Whiting starred; it was her only Broadway show.

Mr. Wrangler died in 2009.

Her friend and mentor, Mr. Mercer, died in 1976. But he remained in her thoughts and the subject of stories she told for years afterward. "He was a perfect Southern gentleman until he had three Scotches and two sips," she once said.

One often-repeated story took place in the early 1940s, when she was 19. Mr. Mercer had asked her to sing "Moonlight in Vermont," which he had just heard and felt was ideal for her voice.

"I've never been to Vermont," she said. "How can I sing a song about a place I've never been to? What is the significance of pennies in a stream? What are ski tows?"

"I don't know," Mr. Mercer replied. "I'm from Savannah. We'll use our imagination."

— *By David Belcher*

DAVID NELSON

Ozzie, Harriet, Ricky and Now David

OCT. 24, 1936 - JAN. 11, 2011

DAVID NELSON, the elder son of Ozzie and Harriet Nelson, the brother of Rick Nelson and the last surviving member of the television family that perhaps more than any other stood for the Eisenhower-era middle-class American dream, died on Jan. 11 at his home in Los Angeles. He was 74.

The cause was complications of colon cancer.

At first on radio and, beginning in 1952, on television, "The Adventures of Ozzie and

Harriet" dramatized the gentle conflicts and lapses in communication of the sweet-tempered, well-behaved Nelson clan and brought them into American homes for 22 years.

By today's standards the word "Adventures" can be read as ironic. The plots generally revolved around misunderstandings — a presumed traffic ticket that turns out to be a Christmas card, a pair of mistakenly delivered chairs — and were invariably resolved good-naturedly. Sex, religion, politics and other subjects with argument-starting potential were avoided. Though the show spanned the years from World War II to Vietnam — the radio show began in 1944 and the television show stopped filming, after 14 seasons, in 1966 — the outside world rarely if ever penetrated the comfortable idyll that the Nelson family seemed to inhabit.

"Ozzie and Harriet" laid the groundwork for other mild family sitcoms like "Leave It to Beaver" and "Father Knows Best," but it also had a weirdly postmodern and prescient aspect to it: the four Nelsons were, in some ways, television's first reality stars.

The show was scripted, but the characters were based on the Nelsons themselves, named after the Nelsons themselves and, from 1949, when 12-year-old David and 8-year-old Ricky replaced the actors who had initially voiced their roles on the radio, played by the Nelsons themselves. Their actual Los Angeles home was used in filming, and a reproduction of its interior was built in the studio. When David and Rick married in real life, their wives were incorporated into the show.

David Nelson was probably the least prominent of the four characters, dully mature as a son, quietly sage as an older brother. (In one departure from reality, his character graduated from college and became a lawyer.) Ozzie was the know-it-all dad whose presumptions often got him into trouble and drove the story. Harriet was the wisely, teasingly understanding helpmeet, and young Ricky was the adorable one, the mischievous boy who mispronounced words, made wisecracks, grew up impossibly handsome and became a pop star. His career as a singer took off in 1957 when he performed the Fats Domino song "I'm Walkin'" with a backup band during an episode of "Ozzie and Harriet."

David Oswald Nelson was born on Oct. 24, 1936, in Manhattan. The family lived for a time in Tenafly, N.J., but moved to California when David was about 5. Ozzie Nelson was a popular bandleader, Harriet his lead singer, and they worked together in films and were regulars on Red Skelton's radio show. When Mr. Skelton joined the Army in 1944, Ozzie wrote a script

ART IMITATING LIFE: David Nelson, second from right, who played himself in "The Adventures of Ozzie and Harriet," was the last surviving member of his famous family.

for a show based on his own family, and the Nelsons' future found a new direction. For two years after the show began on television, it continued, with separate scripts, on radio as well.

David graduated from Hollywood High School and attended the University of Southern California. Aside from "Ozzie and Harriet," he had an abbreviated career as an actor, appearing in films like "Peyton Place" (1957), "The Remarkable Mr. Pennypacker" (1959) and "The Big Circus" (1959), in which he played a catcher on a trapeze team, a role that led to his studying circus aerialism and performing as a catcher in an aerial troupe known as the Flying Viennas.

Ozzie Nelson died in 1975, Harriet in 1994. Rick Nelson was killed in a plane crash in 1985. David's first marriage, to June Blair, who appeared on "Ozzie and Harriet," ended in divorce. He is survived by their two sons; his wife of 36 years, Yvonne; her three children, all of whom Mr. Nelson adopted; and seven grandchildren.

During the final years of "Ozzie and Harriet," David directed several episodes. He went on to work as a director of television shows and commercials and to form his own production company.

In 1971, five years after "Ozzie and Harriet" went off the air, Esquire magazine interviewed all the Nelsons about the differences between their real selves and the characters they played on television. It was David who made the most vehement distinctions. One family was real and one wasn't, he said.

"For your sanity you had to keep that clear," he said. "Rick and I had to distinguish between our father and the director telling us what to do. If we got the lines crossed, that's where the arguments started, and I would end up putting my fist through a wall behind the set, because I was that angry."

He added: "We would keep up the front of this totally problemless, happy-go-lucky group. There might have been a tremendous battle in our home, but if someone from outside came in, it would be as if the director yelled, 'Roll 'em.' We'd fall right into our stage roles. You'd get to wondering which was the true thing. It's an awfully big load to carry, to be everyone's fantasy family. How long can you keep protecting that image and never let any of the outside world in?"

— *By Bruce Weber*

ELLEN STEWART

With La MaMa, the Mother of Off Off Broadway

NOV. 7, 1919 - JAN. 13, 2011

ELLEN STEWART, THE FOUNDER, artistic director and de facto producer of La MaMa Experimental Theater Club, a multicultural hive of avant-garde drama and performance art in New York for almost half a century, died on Jan. 13 in Manhattan. She was 91.

Ms. Stewart was a dress designer when she started La MaMa in a basement apartment in 1961, a woman entirely without theater experience and not even much interest in it. But within a few years, and with an indomitable personality, she had become a theater pioneer.

Not only did she introduce unusual new work to the stage; she also helped colonize a new territory for the theater, planting a flag in the name of low-budget experimental productions in the East Village of Manhattan and creating the capital of what became known as Off Off Broadway.

She was a vivid figure, often described as beautiful — an African-American woman whose long hair, frequently worn in cornrows, turned silver in her later years. Her wardrobe was flamboyant, replete with bangles, bracelets and scarves. Her voice was deep, carrying an accent reminiscent of her Louisiana roots.

Few producers could match her energy, perseverance and fortitude. In the decades after World War II her influence on American theater was comparable to that of Joseph Papp, founder of the New York Shakespeare Festival, though the two approached the stage from different wings. Mr. Papp straddled the commercial and noncommercial worlds, while Ms. Stewart's terrain was international and decidedly noncommercial.

Her theater became a remarkable springboard for an impressive roster of promising playwrights, directors and actors who went on to accomplished careers both in mainstream entertainment and in push-the-envelope theater.

Al Pacino, Robert De Niro, Harvey Keitel, F. Murray Abraham, Olympia Dukakis, Richard Dreyfuss, Bette Midler, Diane Lane and Nick Nolte were among the actors who performed at La MaMa in its first two decades. Playwrights like Sam Shepard, Lanford Wilson, Harvey Fierstein, Maria Irene Fornes and Adrienne Kennedy developed early work there. So did the composers Elizabeth Swados, Philip Glass and Stephen Schwartz.

La MaMa directors included the visionary Robert Wilson; Tom O'Horgan (who helped create the rock musical "Hair" at the Public); Richard Foreman, who founded the imaginative Ontological Theater Company; Joseph Chaikin, who founded the Open Theater; and even Mr. Papp, before there was such a thing as the Public Theater. Meredith Monk, the composer, choreographer and director, presented her genre-bending pieces there regularly.

A few La MaMa plays, like the musical "Godspell," moved to Broadway, and others had extended runs in commercial Off Broadway houses.

"Eighty percent of what is now considered the American theater originated at La MaMa," Mr. Fierstein once said in an interview in Vanity Fair, perhaps exaggerating slightly. His play "Torch Song Trilogy" was developed there.

La MaMa became the quintessential theater on a shoestring. Salaries were minimal, ticket prices were low, and profits were nonexistent. For decades Ms. Stewart often swept the sidewalk in front of the theater herself, on East Fourth Street. For many years she lived in an apartment above it.

But an adventurous theatergoer would be rewarded there. More than 3,000 productions of classic and postmodern drama, performance art, dance and chamber opera have been seen on La MaMa's stages. For Ms. Stewart, many were leaps of faith, arising from her belief that what artists need more than anything else is the freedom to create without interference. She would typically appear onstage before a performance, ring a cowbell and announce La MaMa's dedication "to the playwright and all aspects of the theater."

During the earliest days of her theater she supported her family of artists — her children, she called them — with the money she continued to earn designing clothes. She installed a washer and dryer in the basement for the performers, and many a visiting artist slept in her apartment or in the theaters themselves.

She didn't begin directing shows herself until relatively late in her life. She often said she didn't read plays; she read people. Her gifts, as affirmed by a MacArthur Foundation award in 1985, were intuitive and hard to pin down.

"If a script 'beeps' to me, I do it," she said in an interview with The New York Times. "Audiences may hate these plays, but I believe in them. The only way I can explain my 'beeps' is that I'm no intellectual, but my instincts tell me automatically when a playwright has something."

Her programming stretched far wider than the American theater. It was at La MaMa that Andrei Serban, a Romanian director transplanted to the United States, refought the Trojan War with his reinvention of Greek tragedy, "Fragments of a Greek Trilogy," incorporating "Medea," "The Trojan Women" and "Electra." La MaMa became a magnet for the most adventurous European and American companies, including Peter Brook's Paris group. At her death the theater was presenting "Being Harold Pinter," a politically charged production by the Belarus Free Theater, based in Minsk, some of whose members were arrested and others

CULTIVATING TALENT: With La MaMa, Ms. Stewart provided playwrights, actors, directors and composers with the freedom to experiment and create. Many went on to find fame.

forced underground by an authoritarian regime.

La MaMa's range of activity was kaleidoscopic and multicultural, embracing an Eskimo "Antigone," a Korean "Hamlet" and a splashy re-creation of the golden days of the Cotton Club in Harlem, directed by Ms. Stewart herself.

She was a theatrical missionary, scouting new talent abroad and planting La MaMa seeds wherever she went. She produced site-specific performances all over the world — a "Medea" created by Mr. Serban and Ms. Swados, for example, at the ruins in Baalbek, Lebanon, in 1972. Satellite La MaMa organizations sprouted from Tel Aviv to Tokyo. With the $300,000 MacArthur grant, she bought a former monastery in Umbria, Italy, and turned it into an international theater center.

Even when her network of theaters was reduced for economic reasons, she remained the avant-garde's ambassador to the world.

"If the play is good, then it's good," she said when asked about her devotion to experimental work. "If it's bad, that does not change my way of thinking about the person involved. I may be disappointed in production values, but I've never been sorry about anything I put on."

Ms. Stewart was born in Chicago on Nov. 7, 1919, and spent her childhood years there and in Alexandria, La. She was never eager to speak about earlier chapters of her life, and details about them are scarce. She was married at least once and had a son, who died in 1998. Her survivors include an adopted son, who lives in South Korea, and eight grandchildren.

What is known is that she studied to be a teacher at Arkansas State College and worked as a riveter in a defense plant in Chicago during World War II. In 1950 she moved to New York with the intention of going to design school, but ended up having to support herself with a variety of jobs. At one point she was a porter and operated an elevator at Saks Fifth Avenue.

According to a story she often told, on a visit to Delancey Street one Sunday, she met a fabric shop owner who encouraged her dream to become a fashion designer. He gave her fabrics to turn into dresses, and when she wore her own creations to work at Saks, she created such excitement that the store made her a designer.

Her theater career began as a good turn. Her foster brother, Frederick Lights, wanted to be a playwright but had difficulty getting his work staged. Sympathetic to him and to Paul Foster, another aspiring dramatist, she began a theater in 1962 in the basement of a tenement on East Ninth Street.

Everyone already referred to Ms. Stewart as Mama, and one of the actors suggested La MaMa as a name for her space. The theater was called Cafe La MaMa, and later La MaMa E.T.C. (for Experimental Theater Club).

At first people were sometimes literally pulled in off the street to see the shows: Tennessee Williams's "One Arm," Eugene O'Neill's "Before Breakfast," Fernando Arrabal's "Executioner." Ms. Stewart would sometimes present a play — like "The Room," by Harold Pinter — without authorization.

Neighbors initially tried to close the theater down. They thought she was running a brothel, she said in interviews. Otherwise, why would so many white men be visiting a black woman in a basement?

But the shows went on. La MaMa was one of New York's first coffeehouse theaters and became a pillar of Off Off Broadway, which sprang up as alternative theater when Off Broadway began pursuing a more mainstream audience. As word of La MaMa spread, artists flocked to it.

Gradually federal and foundation grants came in, giving added certification to a theater that became an important New York cultural institution.

In 1969, with the help of $25,000 from W. MacNeil Lowry and the Ford Foundation, the company moved to a former meatpacking plant at 74A East Fourth Street, where it created two 99-seat theaters and office space. In 1974 she opened the Annex, a 295-seat theater a few doors down the street in a converted television studio. It was renamed the Ellen Stewart Theater in a gala celebration in November 2009. La MaMa also has an art gallery, a six-story rehearsal and studio building nearby and an extensive archive on the history of Off Off Broadway theater.

Ms. Stewart virtually never stopped working. Despite a variety of ailments, she had been putting on about 70 new productions a year. The shows will go on. The theater said it would continue to present its schedule without interruption, and Mia Yoo, who has been co-artistic director since September 2009, will continue in that capacity.

"When I think about the fact that she is in the last part of her life, even though I've been there a lot of her life, I can't bear the thought of this world without her," Elizabeth Swados said in a 2006 article in the theater journal TDR: The Drama Review. "I can't imagine La MaMa without her. There may be a place called La MaMa that somebody brings good avant-garde international theater to, but it will not be La MaMa. La MaMa is her."

— *By Mel Gussow and Bruce Weber*

DON KIRSHNER

A Leisure-Suited Prime Mover in Pop

APRIL 17, 1934 - JAN. 17, 2011

DON KIRSHNER, a guiding force in pop music as publisher of Brill Building hits like "You've Lost That Lovin' Feelin'" and "Will You Love Me Tomorrow," and as a deadpan Ed Sullivan for Kiss, the Ramones and others with his 1970s television show "Don Kirshner's Rock Concert," died on Jan. 17 in Boca Raton, Fla., where he lived. He was 76.

The cause was heart failure, his family said.

The Brill Building age of pop, named after the Manhattan building where many of its songwriters labored, lasted from the mid-1950s to the mid-1960s and is celebrated for the people behind its innocently aching music: producers like Phil Spector and writing teams like Carole King and Gerry Goffin ("The Loco-Motion").

But behind many of those people was Mr. Kirshner, whose hustle, hit-trained ear and good timing helped shape pop in the days when Tin Pan Alley's song-craft traditions were being mingled with the rhythms of rock.

As a pioneering musical matchmaker, Mr. Kirshner discovered many of the era's best songwriters, prodded them for hits and shopped the results to top artists. Later in the 1960s he married bubblegum to television with two manufactured, semifictitious bands: the Monkees and the cartoon Archies.

MUSIC MAN: In the 1970s Mr. Kirshner was the host of "Rock Concert" on ABC.

"He had a great sense of commerciality and song, the ability to hear a song and know it's a hit," said Charles Koppelman, a music executive who began his career in Mr. Kirshner's company, Aldon.

Yet to music fans who came of age in the 1970s and '80s, Mr. Kirshner is best known as the leisure-suited, monotonous host of the syndicated "Rock Concert," which from 1973 to 1982 presented live performances by acts like Lynyrd Skynyrd, the Sex Pistols, David Bowie and Ted Nugent.

Unlike "American Bandstand" and other early TV rock shows, on which performers lip-synced their music or played a song or two in a sterile studio, "Rock Concert" featured full, loud performances in an arena or club setting. In his spoken introductions, however, Mr. Kirshner often seemed strangely out of place, as if he barely knew the performers he was introducing, which was sometimes the case.

"Someone once told me I had to put on Alice Cooper," he recalled in an interview with The Washington Post in 2004. "I said, 'Well, is she any good?'"

Donald Kirshner was born in the Bronx on April 17, 1934. His father was a tailor. He attended Upsala College in New Jersey. With hopes of being a songwriter, he got his start in the music business when he met a brash young singer named Robert Cassotto at a candy store in Washington Heights in Manhattan. They became partners, working on jingles and pop ditties (their first: "Bubblegum Pop"), but their collaboration ended after Mr. Cassotto — under his new stage name, Bobby Darin — scored a hit in 1958 with "Splish Splash," which he wrote without Mr. Kirshner.

That year Mr. Kirshner founded Aldon with Al Nevins, who had played in a successful instrumental group, the Three Suns. Mr. Kirshner and Mr. Nevins opened an office at 1650 Broadway — a block from 1619 Broadway, the Brill Building — and soon signed two struggling songwriters, Neil Sedaka and Howard Greenfield. By 1962 Aldon had 18 writers on staff.

Aldon's alumni includes Barry Mann, Cynthia Weil, Neil Diamond, Doc Pomus, Mort Shuman, Tommy Boyce and Bobby Hart. To some degree the company operated as an assembly line: teams of writers in piano cubicles churned out songs that would be recorded immediately, as demos or sometimes as finished productions.

In 1963 Mr. Kirshner and Mr. Nevins sold Aldon to Screen Gems, a Columbia Pictures subsidiary, for more than $2 million, and moved to a luxe new office on Fifth Avenue. Meanwhile, with the arrival of the Beatles, the American pop landscape was shifting toward bands that wrote their own material. Mr. Nevins died in 1965.

Yet one of Mr. Kirshner's biggest achievements was an adaptation to the Beatles era. In 1966 he was hired to put together the music for the Monkees, a Beatles-y group assembled by television executives. Mr. Kirshner commissioned songs from many of the best Aldon songwriters, like Mr. Diamond ("I'm a Believer") and the Goffin-King team ("Pleasant Valley Sunday").

When tensions arose with the band, Mr. Kirshner moved on to the Archies, an animated version of the clean-cut comic strip. "I want a band that won't talk back," Mr. Kirshner said.

The Archies' music, performed by uncredited studio musicians, brought bubblegum to its pinnacle: its still-ubiquitous "Sugar, Sugar" was the best-selling song of 1969.

In 1972 Mr. Kirshner began to work with ABC on a live performance show, "In Concert"; he left that show the next year to begin "Don Kirshner's Rock Concert," which had its premiere in September 1973 with the Rolling Stones. He also continued his work as a music executive in the 1970s, signing the band Kansas ("Carry On Wayward Son," "Dust in the Wind") to his CBS-affiliated Kirshner label, but by the early 1980s he had retired.

He is survived by his wife, Sheila, as well as a son, a daughter and five grandchildren.

Though he began his career as a songwriter, Mr. Kirshner said, he realized early that he was better at recognizing talent in others than at creating the work itself.

"My idols were people like Walt Disney, and I feel that what he did with Pinocchio and Mickey Mouse and Minnie Mouse I had the ability to do in my own right — build the stars as a star maker," Mr. Kirshner told The New Yorker in 1993.

"And maybe it's because, you know, I don't read or write music — and I guess I live vicariously through these people, 'cause I don't have the talent myself — but, you know, I'm the man with the golden ear."

— *By Ben Sisario*

MILTON ROGOVIN

Championing the Poor With a Camera

DEC. 30, 1909 - JAN 18, 2011

Milton Rogovin, an optometrist and persecuted leftist who took up photography as a way to champion the underprivileged and who went on to become one of America's most dedicated social documentarians, died on Jan. 18 at his home in Buffalo. He was 101.

Mr. Rogovin chronicled the lives of the urban poor and working classes in Buffalo, Appalachia and elsewhere for more than 50 years. His direct photographic style in stark black and white evokes the socially minded work that Walker Evans, Dorothea Lange and Gordon Parks produced for the Farm Security Administration during the Depression. Today his entire archive resides in the Library of Congress.

Mr. Rogovin (pronounced ruh-GO-vin) came to wide notice in 1962 after documenting storefront church services on Buffalo's poor and predominantly black East Side. The images were published in Aperture magazine with an introduction by W. E. B. Du Bois, who described them as "astonishingly human and appealing."

He went on to photograph Buffalo's impoverished Lower West Side and American Indians on reservations in the Buffalo area. He traveled to West Virginia and Kentucky to photograph miners, returning to Appalachia each summer with his wife, Anne Rogovin, into the early 1970s. In the 1960s he went to Chile at the invitation of the poet Pablo Neruda to photograph the landscape and the people. The two collaborated on a book, "Windows That Open Inward: Images of Chile."

Reviewing a show of the Buffalo photographs at the International Center of Photography in Manhattan in 1976, the New York Times critic Hilton Kramer wrote of Mr. Rogovin: "He sees something else in the life of this neighborhood — ordinary pleasures and pastimes, relaxation, warmth of feeling and the fundamentals of social connection. He takes his pictures from the inside, so to speak, concentrating on family life, neighborhood business, celebrations, romance, recreation and the particulars of individuals' existence."

A DIFFERENT LENS: Mr. Rogovin, an optometrist, took up photography in his 40s.

Milton Rogovin was born on Dec. 30, 1909, in Brooklyn, the third of three sons of Jewish immigrant parents from Lithuania. His parents, Jacob Rogovin and the former Dora Shainhouse, operated a dry goods business, first in Manhattan on Park Avenue near 112th Street and later in the Bay Ridge section of Brooklyn. After attending Stuyvesant High School in Manhattan, the young Mr. Rogovin graduated from Columbia University in 1931 with a degree in optometry; four months later, after the family had lost the store and its home to bankruptcy during the Depression, his father died of a heart attack.

Working as an optometrist in Manhattan, Mr. Rogovin became increasingly distressed at the plight of the poor and unemployed — "the forgotten ones," he called them — and increasingly involved in leftist political causes.

"I was a product of the Great Depression, and what I saw and experienced myself made me politically active," he told The Times in 1994.

He began attending classes sponsored by the Communist Party-run New York Workers School and was introduced to the social-documentary photographs of Jacob Riis and Lewis Hine.

Mr. Rogovin moved to Buffalo in 1938 and opened his own optometric office on Chippewa Street the next year, providing service to union workers. In 1942 he bought his first camera. He also married Anne Snetsky that year before volunteering for the Army and serving for three years in England, where he worked as an optometrist.

Returning to Buffalo after the war (his brother Sam, also an optometrist, managed the practice in his absence), Mr. Rogovin joined the local chapter of the Optical Workers Union and served as librarian for the Buffalo branch of the Communist Party.

In 1957, with cold war anti-Communism rife in the United States, he was called before the House Un-American Activities Committee but refused to testify. Soon afterward, The Buffalo Evening News labeled him "Buffalo's Number One Red," and he and his family were ostracized. With his business all but ruined by the publicity, he began to fill time by taking pictures, focusing on Buffalo's poor and dispossessed in the neighborhood around his practice while living on his wife's salary as a teacher. The photographer Minor White was an early mentor.

His wife, a special education teacher, was a collaborator throughout his career and helped him organize his photographs until her death, in 2003.

Mr. Rogovin's photographs were typically naturalistic portraits of people he met on the street. "The first six months were very difficult," he recalled in a 2003 interview, "because they thought I was from the police department or the F.B.I."

But he gradually built trust, giving away prints of portraits in exchange for sittings. He never told his subjects what to do; they posed in settings and clothing of their own choosing.

Mr. Rogovin began his Storefront Church series in 1961 at the invitation of a friend, William Tallmadge, a professor of music at State University College at Buffalo who was making recordings at a black church on the city's East Side. The success of the series encouraged Mr. Rogovin to devote more and more time to photography and persuaded him that photography could be an instrument for social change.

In 1972 he earned a master's degree in American studies at the University at Buffalo, where he taught documentary photography from 1972 to 1974. The next year he held his first major exhibition, at the Albright-Knox Art Gallery in Buffalo.

Many of his photographs have been published in books, and many are in the collections of museums, including the Bibliothèque Nationale in Paris, the Museum of Modern Art in New York, the J. Paul Getty Museum in Los Angeles and the Victoria and Albert Museum in London. The Library of Congress acquired his archive in 1999.

Mr. Rogovin is survived by a son, two daughters, five grandchildren and four great-grandchildren.

In his later years, as his health declined, Mr. Rogovin used a wheelchair and no longer took photographs. In 2009 he was nominated for a National Medal of Arts but was not selected.

His activism, however, was undimmed — he attended political rallies and antiwar protests into his final years — and his social conscience remained acute.

"All my life I've focused on the poor," he said in 2003. "The rich ones have their own photographers."

— *By Benjamin Genocchio*

APPRECIATION

The Downtrodden Uplifted

In 1994, I was asked to interview Milton Rogovin because I'd written a book about the old Polish East Side of Buffalo. Rogovin had spent years photographing Buffalo's downtrodden Lower West Side. It was like a visitor to Portland, Ore., talking to a resident of Portland, Me., because they both knew something about Portland.

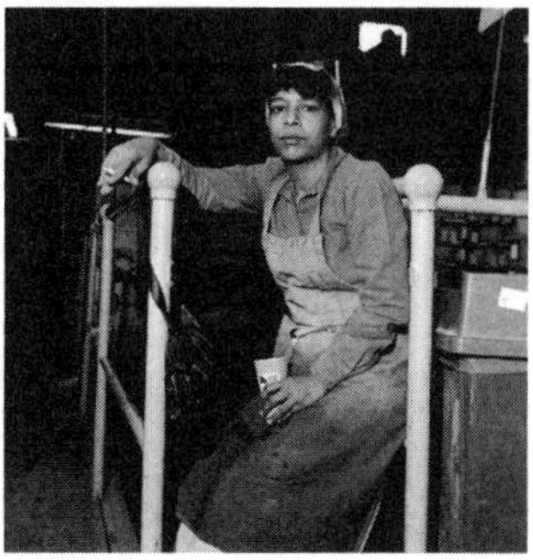

Rogovin's photography was all portraiture, mainly of working people and poor street folk. You learn a lot about him by the way his subjects look at the lens. He found an openness in their faces, a directness, that says a great deal about his candor and empathy.

"I like to photograph people with problems," he told me, and he had an important one in his own life. Rogovin was an optometrist, and committed leftist, who took up photography only in his 40s. In 1957, when he refused to testify before the House Un-American Activities Committee, he was vilified in Buffalo, his business nearly destroyed. Suddenly he had time to explore the storefront churches and streets of Buffalo's Lower West Side.

When I heard that Rogovin had died, I looked again through his two books. "The Forgotten Ones" has a remarkable series called "Working People," from the late 1970s. He shot black-and-white portraits of individuals at work and at home — as the job defined them and as they defined themselves. There is something heroic in the difference, in the ability of these people to step away from their labors and become truer versions of themselves.

In "Triptychs," the subject is time. Rogovin shot three portraits of Lower West Side residents, each taken roughly a decade apart. One by one, his subjects age, their clothes and surroundings alter, but their identities persist. Not everyone he photographed in 1973 was still alive in 1992. It is astonishing how much loss you feel when the third picture in these triptychs is missing. The pathos of that absence says everything about how Rogovin saw the world around him and how clearly he revealed it to us.

— *By Verlyn Klinkenborg*

SARGENT SHRIVER

Answering His Own Call to Public Service

NOV. 9, 1915 - JAN. 18, 2011

R. SARGENT SHRIVER, the Kennedy in-law who became the founding director of the Peace Corps, the architect of President Lyndon B. Johnson's war on poverty, a United States ambassador to France and the Democratic candidate for vice president in 1972, died on Jan. 18 in Bethesda, Md. He was 95.

Mr. Shriver was found to have Alzheimer's disease in 2003 and on Jan. 16 was admitted to Suburban Hospital in Bethesda, where he died. He had been in hospice care in recent months after his estate in Potomac, Md., was sold last year.

White-haired and elegantly attired, he attended the inauguration of his son-in-law, Arnold Schwarzenegger, as the Republican governor of California in the fall of 2003. Mr. Schwarzenegger had joined the family through his marriage to Maria Shriver, a former NBC News correspondent. But in recent years, as his condition deteriorated, Mr. Shriver was seldom seen in public, emerging in one rare instance to attend the funeral of his wife of 56 years, Eunice Kennedy Shriver, a sister of John F. Kennedy; she died in 2009 in Hyannis, Mass., at the age of 88.

As a Kennedy brother-in-law, Mr. Shriver — known as Sarge from childhood — was bound inextricably to one of the nation's most powerful political dynasties. It was an association with enormous advantages, thrusting him to prominence in a series of seemingly altruistic missions. But it came with handicaps, relegating him to the political background and to a subordinate role in the family history.

"Shriver's relationship with the Kennedys was complex," Scott Stossel wrote in "Sarge: The Life and Times of Sargent Shriver," a 2004 biography. "They buoyed him up to heights and achievements he would never otherwise have attained — and they held him back, thwarting his political advancement."

The book, as well as reports in The New York Times, The Washington Post and other publications, suggested that Mr. Shriver's hopes to run for governor of Illinois in 1960 and vice president in 1964 and 1968 were abandoned to help promote Kennedy aspirations, or at least not compete with them. Mr. Shriver's vice-presidential race in 1972, on a ticket with Senator George S. McGovern, and a brief primary run for president in 1976 were crushed by the voters.

Mr. Shriver was never elected to any national office. To political insiders, his calls for public service in the 1960s seemed quixotic at a time when America was caught up in a war in Vietnam, a cold war with the Soviet Union and civil rights struggles and urban riots at home. But when the fogs of war and chaos cleared years later, he was remembered by many as a last vestige of Kennedy-era idealism.

"Sarge came to embody the idea of public service," President Obama said in a statement.

Mr. Shriver's impact on American life was significant. On the stage of social change for decades, he brought President Kennedy's proposal for the Peace Corps to fruition in 1961 and served as the organization's director until 1966. He tapped into a spirit of volunteerism, and within a few years thousands of young Americans were teaching and working on public health and development projects in poorer countries around the world.

After the president's assassination in 1963, Mr. Shriver's decision to remain in the Johnson administration alienated many of the Kennedys, especially Robert, who remained as the United States attorney general for months but whose animus toward his brother's successor was profound. Mr. Shriver's responsibilities deepened, however. In 1964, Johnson persuaded him to take on the administration's war on poverty, a campaign embodied in a vast new bureaucracy, the Office of Economic Opportunity.

From 1965 to 1968, Mr. Shriver, who disdained bureaucracies as wasteful and inefficient, was director of that agency, a post he held simultaneously with his Peace Corps job until 1966. The agency created antipoverty programs like Head Start, the Job Corps, Volunteers in Service to America, the Community Action Program and Legal Services for the Poor. (The Office of Economic Opportunity was dismantled in 1973, but many of its programs survived in other agencies.)

JOINING A DYNASTY: Mr. Shriver married a Kennedy daughter, Eunice.

In 1968, Johnson named Mr. Shriver ambassador to France. It was a time of strained relations. President Charles de Gaulle had recognized Communist China, withdrawn French forces from NATO's integrated military command and denounced American involvement in Indochina. But Mr. Shriver established a working rapport with de Gaulle and was credited with helping to improve relations.

Mr. Shriver returned to the United States in 1970 to work for Democrats in the midterm elections and to reassess his own political prospects. His long-awaited break came two years later when Senator McGovern, the Democratic presidential nominee, picked him as his running mate. Mr. McGovern's first choice, Senator Thomas F. Eagleton of Missouri, was dropped after revelations that he had received electroshock therapy for depression.

The McGovern-Shriver ticket lost in a landslide to the incumbent Republicans, Richard M. Nixon and Spiro T. Agnew. Four years later, Mr. Shriver ran for the Democratic presidential nomination, pledging a renewal of ethics after the Watergate scandal that drove Nixon from the White House. But Mr. Shriver was knocked out early in the primaries and ended his political career.

In later years, he was a rainmaker for an international law firm, Fried, Frank, Harris, Shriver & Jacobson, retiring in 1986. He was also active in the Special Olympics, founded by his wife for mentally disabled athletes, serving as its president and later chairman. And he continued his work with the Sargent Shriver National Center on Poverty Law, an advocacy organization he founded in Chicago in 1967 as the National Clearinghouse for Legal Services.

In 1994, President Bill Clinton awarded Mr. Shriver the Presidential Medal of Freedom. Ten years earlier, President Ronald Reagan conferred the same award on Eunice Shriver. They were the only husband and wife to win the nation's highest civilian honor individually.

In 2008, PBS broadcast a documentary, "American Idealist: The Story of Sargent Shriver." A children's book by Maria Shriver, "What's Happening to Grandpa?," was published in 2004, explaining the effects of Alzheimer's disease. She also took part in a four-part documentary on Alzheimer's presented by HBO in 2009, serving as executive producer of one segment, "Grandpa, Do You Know Who I Am?"

Robert Sargent Shriver Jr. was born in Westminster, Md., on Nov. 9, 1915, the son of his namesake, a banker, and Hilda Shriver. His forebears, called Schreiber, immigrated from Germany in 1721. One ancestor, David Shriver, was a signer of Maryland's Constitution in 1776. The Shrivers, like the Kennedys, were Roman Catholics and socially prominent but not especially affluent.

On scholarships, he attended Canterbury, a Catholic boarding prep school in New Milford, Conn. — John F. Kennedy was briefly a schoolmate — and Yale University, graduating with honors in 1938. He earned a Yale law degree in 1941 and joined the Navy shortly before the attack on Pearl Harbor, becoming an officer on battleships and submarines in the Atlantic and the Pacific and winning a Purple Heart for

APPRECIATION

What I Learned From Sarge

The Irish are still mesmerized by the mythical place that is America, but in the 1960s our fascination got out of hand. I was not old enough to remember the sacrifices of the great generation who saved Europe in the Second World War, or to quite comprehend what was going on in Vietnam. But what I do remember, and cannot forget, is watching a man walk on the moon in 1969 and thinking here is a nation that finds joy in the impossible.

The Irish saw the Kennedys as our own royal family out on loan to America. A million of them turned out on J.F.K.'s homecoming to see these patrician public servants who, despite their station, had no patience for the status quo. (They also loved that the Kennedys looked more WASP than any "Prod," our familiar term for Protestant.)

I remember Bobby's rolled-up sleeves, Jack's jutted jaw and the message — a call to action — that the world didn't have to be the way it was. Science and faith had found a perfect rhyme.

In the background, but hardly in the shadows, was Robert Sargent Shriver. A diamond intelligence, too bright to keep in the darkness. He was not Robert or Bob, he was Sarge, and for all the love in him, he knew that love was a tough word. Easy to say, tough to see it through. Love, yes, and peace, too, in no small measure; this was the '60s, but you wouldn't know it just by looking at him. No long hair in the Shriver house, or rock 'n' roll. He and his beautiful bride, Eunice Kennedy Shriver, would go to Mass every day — as much an act of rebellion against brutal modernity as it was an act of worship. Love, yes,

wounds he sustained at Guadalcanal.

After the war, he joined Newsweek as an editor. He met Eunice Kennedy at a dinner party, and she introduced him to her father, Joseph P. Kennedy. In 1946, Joseph Kennedy hired him to help manage his recently acquired Merchandise Mart in Chicago, then the world's largest commercial building. Mr. Shriver not only turned a profit for the mart but also plunged into Democratic politics.

After a seven-year courtship, Mr. Shriver and Ms. Kennedy were married by Cardinal Francis Spellman at St. Patrick's Cathedral in New York in 1953.

In addition to his daughter, Maria, Mr. Shriver's survivors include four sons and 19 grandchildren.

Mr. Shriver's relationships with the Kennedys were widely analyzed by the news media, not least because of his own political potential. He looked like a movie star, with a flashing smile, dark hair going gray and the kind of muscled, breezy athleticism that went with tennis courts and sailboats. Like the Kennedys, he was charming but not self-revealing, a quick study but not reflective. Associates said he could be imperious, but his knightly public image became indelible.

He took root in Chicago. In 1954, he was appointed to the city's Board of Education, and a year later became its president. In 1955, he also became president of the Catholic Interracial Council, which fought discrimination in housing, education and other aspects of city life.

but love as a brave act, a bold act, requiring toughness and sacrifice.

His faith demanded action, from him, from all of us. For the Word to become flesh, we had to become the eyes, the ears, the hands of a just God. Injustice could, in the words of the old spiritual, "Be Overcome." Robert Sargent sang, "Make me a channel of your peace," and became the song.

The Peace Corps was Jack Kennedy's creation but embodied Sargent Shriver's spirit. Lyndon Johnson declared war on poverty but Sarge led the charge. These, and the Special Olympics, were as dramatic an incarnation of the ideas at the heart of America as the space program.

Robert Sargent Shriver changed the world more than a few times and, I am happy to say, changed my world forever. In the late 1990s, when the Jubilee 2000 campaign — which aimed to cancel the debts that the poorest nations owed to the richest — asked me to help in the United States, I called on the Shriver clan for help and advice. What I got were those things in spades, and a call to arms like a thump in the back.

In the years since, Bobby Shriver — Sarge's oldest son — and I co-founded three fighting units in the war against global poverty: DATA, ONE and (RED). We may not yet know what it will take to finish the fight and silence suffering in our time, but we are flat out trying to live up to Sarge's drill.

I have beautiful memories of Bobby and me sitting with his father and mother at the Shrivers' kitchen table — the same team that gazed over J.F.K.'s shoulder — looking over our paltry attempts at speechifying, prodding and pushing us toward comprehensibility and credibility, a challenge when your son starts hanging round with a bleeding-heart Irish rock star.

Toward the end, when I visited Sarge as a frailer man, I was astonished by his good spirits and good humor. He had the room around him laughing out loud. I thought it a fitting final victory in a life that embodied service and transcended, so often, grave duty, that he had a certain weightlessness about him. Even then, his job nearly done, his light shone undiminished, and brightened us all.

— *By Bono*

By 1959, he had become so prominent in civic affairs that he was being touted as a Democratic candidate for governor of Illinois in 1960.

Mr. Shriver did nothing to discourage reports that he was considering a run. But with the rest of the Kennedy clan, he joined John F. Kennedy's 1960 presidential campaign. As he and other family members acknowledged later, the patriarch, Joseph Kennedy, had told him that a separate Shriver race that year would be a distraction. So he resigned from the Chicago school board and became a campaign coordinator in Wisconsin and West Virginia and a principal contact with minorities.

As the election approached, the campaign learned that the Rev. Dr. Martin Luther King Jr. had been sentenced in Georgia to four months of hard labor for what amounted to a minor traffic violation. Mr. Shriver suggested that Senator Kennedy call a distraught Coretta Scott King, who was terrified that her husband might be killed in prison. His reassuring call, and another by Robert F. Kennedy to a judge in Georgia that led to Dr. King's release, helped produce a windfall of black support for John Kennedy.

Senator Kennedy broached the idea for a volunteer corps in a speech at the University of Michigan and crystallized it as the Peace Corps in an appearance in San Francisco. Mr. Shriver, who as a young man had guided American students on work-and-learn programs in Europe, seemed a natural to initiate it.

After the inauguration, Mr. Shriver, who scouted talent for the incoming administration —

people who came to be known as "the best and the brightest" — was assigned to the task of designing the Peace Corps, which was established by executive order in March 1961.

As director, he laid the foundations for what arguably became the most lasting accomplishment of the Kennedy presidency. As the Peace Corps approaches its 50th anniversary this year, more than 200,000 Americans have served as corps volunteers in 139 countries.

Break mirrors, Mr. Shriver advised graduating students at Yale in 1994. "Yes, indeed," he said. "Shatter the glass. In our society that is so self-absorbed, begin to look less at yourself and more at each other. Learn more about the face of your neighbor and less about your own."

— By Robert D. McFadden

WILFRID SHEED

The Utility Man of Letters

DEC. 27, 1930 - JAN. 19, 2011

Wilfrid Sheed, the wittily satirical man of letters who drew upon his Anglo-American background to write bittersweet essays, criticism, memoirs and fiction about cultural life on both sides of the Atlantic, died on Jan. 19 in Great Barrington, Mass. He was 80.

The cause was a bacterial infection, the family said. Mr. Sheed had recently moved from a nursing home in Southampton on Long Island to one in Great Barrington so he could be closer to his wife, Miriam Ungerer Sheed, who had moved there to live near a daughter. The couple had lived for many years on the East End of Long Island.

Born to the founders of the eminent Roman Catholic publishing house Sheed & Ward, Mr. Sheed was from an early age thrown in with writers, intellectuals and serious thinkers about religion, among them the English writer G. K. Chesterton, who was his godfather. He mined his resources industriously, making for himself a much-admired writing career.

"I guess I sort of backed into writing," Mr. Sheed told Publishers Weekly. "I have taken off from family experiences sometimes as if they were daydreams."

He wrote, in one form or other, for a half-century, without losing much steam. His last book, published in 2007, was a history of American popular music, "The House That George Built: With a Little Help From Irving, Cole and a Crew of About Fifty." Focusing on Mr. Gershwin, it was a critically acclaimed best seller, one that Mr. Sheed had labored over for many years despite debilitating illnesses, dictating parts of it.

As an avid baseball fan whose boyhood fantasies of diamond glory were dashed at 14 by the onset of polio, Mr. Sheed often said that as a writer he could play any position — a utility man of letters. But novelist was clearly a preferred role.

His gently comic fiction focused on self-perceived variations of himself. His early novels concerned American and English schoolboys ("A Middle Class Education" in 1960); a writer of inspirational pieces for minor Catholic publications ("The Hack," 1963); a bore who learns to live with what he is ("Square's Progress," 1965); the beaten-down denizens of a small liberal magazine ("Office Politics," 1966); and a too-brilliant film and theater critic ("Max Jamison," 1970).

His later novels were about a politician stricken with polio as a teenager ("People Will Always Be Kind," 1973); a talk-show host reared by old-line English Catholic parents who couldn't decide whether they hated England or America more ("Transatlantic Blues," 1978); and a writer/publisher engaged in cutthroat literary politics on eastern Long Island while planning the next summer's softball league ("The Boys of Winter," 1987).

Mr. Sheed's characters are almost invariably stricken with an agonized sense of self-awareness, exacerbated by their Roman Catholicism. They all but die of hyperconsciousness, laughing as they go to their fates.

When not writing fiction Mr. Sheed turned out nonfiction like "Clare Boothe Luce" (1982), a gentle portrait — part memoir, part biography — of an emotionally brittle figure in publishing and public affairs whom he knew as a youth, spending a summer in her house. "My Life as a Fan" (1993) was a memoir of rooting for big-league baseball that said fresh things about a dozen clichéd subjects. "In Love With Daylight: A Memory of Recovery" (1995) told of his surviving polio, drug and alcohol addiction, and cancer of the tongue. ("Affliction can land where it likes," he wrote.)

"'Physically challenged' indeed!" he blurted out at one point in that book. "We were challenged and we lost, baby, and that's all she wrote."

Wilfrid John Joseph Sheed was born in London on Dec. 27, 1930, the younger of two children of Francis Joseph Sheed, who emigrated from Australia with a background in law to become a street-corner evangelist, and Maisie Ward, a fellow Catholic Revivalist and author who was eight years her husband's senior and a descendant of a proud English Catholic family.

Together they founded Sheed & Ward (now an imprint of Rowman & Littlefield), which, besides publishing work by Chesterton, published the Catholic social worker Dorothy Day, the historian Hilaire Belloc and the poet Robert Lowell.

In 1933 they moved their principal office to New York, where "for 30-odd years it was the central publishing house of serious Catholicism," William F. Buckley Jr. wrote in a review of Mr. Sheed's "Frank & Maisie: A Memoir With Parents" (1985). That book ranges breezily across several generations, beginning with a great-grandfather, William George Ward, a mathematician, former Anglican priest and militant Catholic follower of Cardinal John Henry Newman.

Of his own youth Mr. Sheed wrote: "All I knew was that no amount of respectability in other sectors could make up for this one eccentricity: we were gypsies, oddities. 'My parents are publishers,' I would emphasize. But their Catholic publishing seemed almost as bizarre as their Catholic tub-thumping in the starchy secularity of England. So I resigned myself to the delicate pleasures of outsiderness at an early age."

Mr. Sheed often said that as a writer he could play any position — a novelist, memoirist, critic.

He immigrated with his family to the United States in 1940 to escape the German blitzkrieg and lived in Torresdale, Pa., a Philadelphia suburb. After a long recuperation from polio, he returned to England with his family in 1946 and attended Downside in Bath before enrolling in Lincoln College, Oxford, where he received a bachelor's degree in 1954 and a master's in 1957.

Returning to the United States, he settled in New York and went to work for Jubilee, a Catholic magazine founded by Edward Rice in 1953 and described by Mr. Sheed as "the Catholic answer to the Beatniks." He started there as a movie and book reviewer and was an associate editor from 1959 to 1966. From 1964 to 1971 he was drama critic and book review editor for Commonweal, the liberal Catholic magazine.

Mr. Sheed regularly wrote book reviews for many publications and was a contributor to The New Yorker, The New York Review of Books and other magazines. He wrote a literary column for The New York Times Book Review, "The Good Word," from 1971 until 1975, and was a Book-of-the-Month Club judge from 1972 to 1988.

His criticism was so lively that it was a continuing argument among his readers as to whether he was a critic who wrote novels or a novelist who wrote criticism. Reviewing "The Good Word: And Other Words," a 1978 collection of Mr. Sheed's essays, John Leonard noted in The Times that Mr. Sheed himself had called his criticism "speculative work like fiction."

"How can we review Mr. Sheed's style?" Mr. Leonard wrote. "It is part Chesterton and part Evelyn Waugh and part Cyril Connolly. He nods at Mr. Cheever, Elizabeth Hardwick and Jean Stafford. He is clean, but sly." But Mr. Leonard concluded: "Behind the warm irony is cold anger. He identifies Tom Wolfe and John Simon as 'moralists,' 'unrelenting,' 'unforgiving' and 'heartless'; he might be looking into a mirror."

Mr. Sheed married Maria Bullitt Darlington in 1957 and they had three children; the marriage ended in divorce in 1967. He is survived by his second wife, Ms. Sheed; a sister; three children from his first marriage; two stepdaughters; and four grandchildren.

He disdained typewriters and computers and preferred to write in longhand, as he did with much of his last book, "The House That George Built."

Garrison Keillor, reviewing that book for The Times, called it "a big rich stew of an homage," adding, "Wilfrid Sheed's jazzy prose is a joy to read."

In the book Mr. Sheed proposes that the jazz era might be defined in terms of women's fashions "and the consequent rise of impulse dancing on improvised dance floors."

"You can't really jitterbug in a hoopskirt or bustle," he wrote. "Swing follows costume, and the big news was that by the 1910s skirts had become just loose enough and short enough to liberate the wearer from the tyranny of twirling through eternal waltzes in ballrooms as big as basketball courts, and freed her to do fox-trots and anything else that could be done in short, quick steps on, if necessary, living room floors with rugs rolled up. So that's what the boys wrote for next. By the 1920s, the whole lower leg could swing out in Charlestons and other abandoned exercises."

— *By Christopher Lehmann-Haupt*

REYNOLDS PRICE

Devoted Voice of the South

FEB. 1, 1933 - JAN. 20, 2011

Reynolds Price, whose novels and stories about ordinary people in rural North Carolina struggling to find their place in the world established him as one of the most important voices in modern Southern fiction, died on Jan. 20 in Durham, N.C. He was 77.

The cause was complications of a heart attack, his brother, Will, said. For many years Mr. Price had lived as a paraplegic after receiving radiation treatment for a spinal tumor, about which he wrote in "A Whole New Life" (1994).

Few writers have made as dramatic an entrance on the American literary stage as Mr. Price, who published his first novel, "A Long and Happy Life," in 1962 to near-universal acclaim for its pungent Southern dialogue, highly wrought prose style and vivid evocation of rural Southern life.

The novel — the tale of Rosacoke Mustian, a young woman desperate to clarify her relationship with an untamable boyfriend, Wesley Beavers — inspired critics to welcome Mr. Price as the brightest literary talent to emerge since the Southern Renaissance in the 1920s and 1930s. In an extraordinary vote of confidence, Harper's Magazine published the novel in its entirety as a supplement.

"He is the best young writer this country has ever produced," the novelist Allan Gurganus said in an interview for this obituary. "He started out with a voice, a lyric gift and a sense of humor, and an insight about how people lived and what they'll do to get along."

Mr. Price staked his claim as a writer to watch with the novel's bravura opening sentence, a paragraph-long curlicue that began, "Just with his body and from inside like a snake, leaning that black motorcycle side to side, cutting in and out of the slow line of cars to get there first, staring due-north through goggles towards Mount Moriah and switching coon tails in everybody's face was Wesley Beavers."

"Some beginning — of a book, of a career," the critic Theodore Solotaroff wrote in Saturday Review in 1970. "Its sheer virtuosity is like that of a quarterback who on the first play of his first professional game throws a 60-yard pass on the run, hitting the receiver exactly at the instant he breaks into the clear; a tremendous assertion of agility, power, timing and accuracy."

His story collection "The Names and Faces of Heroes," published a year later, made it clear that "A Long and Happy Life" was no fluke.

Except for three years he spent in Britain as a graduate student at Merton College, Oxford, Mr. Price lived all his life in northeastern North Carolina, and he would work his home ground in 13 novels and dozens of short stories. Inevitably he drew comparisons to William Faulkner, much to his annoyance, since he regarded himself as a literary heir to Eudora Welty.

He also published poetry, plays, essays, translations from the Bible and three volumes of memoirs. With "A Whole New Life," he attracted a new audience of admirers.

'Like a Banner in Defeat'

With this first sentence of his novel "A Long and Happy Life," published in 1962, Reynolds Price made one of the most arresting debuts in contemporary American fiction:

Just with his body and from inside like a snake, leaning that black motorcycle side to side, cutting in and out of the slow line of cars to get there first, staring due-north through goggles towards Mount Moriah and switching coon tails in everybody's face was Wesley Beavers, and laid against his back like sleep, spraddle-legged on the sheepskin seat behind him was Rosacoke Mustian who was maybe his girl and who had given up looking into the wind and trying to nod at every sad car in the line, and when he even speeded up and passed the truck (lent for the afternoon by Mr. Isaac Alston and driven by Sammy his man, hauling one pine box and one black boy dressed in all he could borrow, set up in a ladder-back chair with flowers banked round him and a foot on the box to steady it) — when he even passed that, Rosacoke said once into his back "Don't" and rested in humiliation, not thinking but with her hands on his hips for dear life and her white blouse blown out behind her like a banner in defeat.

At Duke University, where he taught writing and the poetry of Milton for more than half a century, he encouraged students like Anne Tyler and Josephine Humphreys. Simply by staying in the South and writing about it, he inspired a generation of younger Southern novelists.

"He made this small corner of North Carolina the sovereign territory of his own imagination and showed those of us who went away that the water back home was fine," Mr. Gurganus said.

"We could come back; there was plenty of room for all of us."

Edward Reynolds Price was born on Feb. 1, 1933, in Macon, N.C., a town about 65 miles northeast of Raleigh that he once described as "227 cotton and tobacco farmers nailed to the flat red land at the pit of the Great Depression."

The family, struggling financially, moved from one house to another in nearby towns, but Reynolds, their first child, benefited from the doting attention of cousins, aunts and uncles — all of them, it seemed, gifted storytellers. His early life provided the material for the memoir "Clear Pictures: First Loves, First Guides" (1989). Mr. Price later said of his native county: "I'm the world's authority on this place. It's the place about which I have perfect pitch."

His brother is his only immediate survivor.

Mr. Price enrolled at Duke University, where Eudora Welty read one of his stories, "Michael Egerton," and volunteered to show it to her agent, Diarmuid Russell, who took the young writer on as a client.

After graduating summa cum laude from Duke in 1955, he won a Rhodes scholarship to study at Oxford, where he wrote a thesis on Milton, and developed career-enhancing friendships with the poets Stephen Spender and W. H. Auden and the critic and biographer Lord David Cecil. He wrote about his years in Britain in the third installment of his memoirs, "Ardent Spirits" (2009).

Mr. Spender published the story "A Chain of Love" in the journal Encounter, a coup for Mr. Price, who was also offered a teaching position at Duke when he returned. He was turned down for military service after he stated, without hesitation, that he was homosexual.

His first class included a promising 16-year-old named Anne Tyler. "I can still picture him sitting tailor-fashion on top of his desk, reading to the class from his own work or from one of his students' papers," Ms. Tyler wrote in an e-mail. "He seemed genuinely joyous when we did the slightest thing right."

With his second novel, "A Generous Man" (1966), Mr. Price continued the story of the Mustian clan, to which he would return much later in the 1988 novel "Good Hearts." He later confounded critics with "The Surface of Earth" (1975), an ambitious multigenerational chronicle of the Mayfield family, related by a well-educated, complex narrator much like the author himself.

Self-consciously grand, "The Surface of Earth" was the first part of a trilogy called "A Great Circle." A sequel, "The Source of Light," followed in 1981. Mr. Price completed the series with "The Promise of Rest" in 1995.

Critics divided sharply on the more intricate middle novels, whose prose struck many as mannered. "His interest in Milton is not accidental or incidental," Ms. Humphreys said in an interview. "He has the same fascination with the art of language that that great Baroque poet had. His fiction is word-intense, complex and fancy. But he can take that and combine it with Southern plain talk."

In 1984 Mr. Price discovered that a thin eight-inch malignant tumor called an astrocytoma had wrapped itself around his spinal column just below the neck. Several operations and aggressive radiation therapy to neutralize what he called "the gray eel" left him paralyzed from the waist down.

Despite years of physical torment, Mr. Price entered into a remarkably fecund phase as a writer. "Previously I'd averaged a book every two years at least, so I was hardly a great tree sloth, but I'd always said truthfully that writing was hard for me, very hard, and now it's not," he told The Paris Review in 1991.

A MODEL TO MANY: Encouraged by Eudora Welty, Mr. Price in turn inspired a generation of Southern writers.

Hypnosis therapy, intended to relieve his pain, released a flood of childhood memories that Mr. Price funneled into "Clear Pictures" and "The Tongues of Angels" (1990), which was based on his time as a camp counselor in the Blue Ridge Mountains.

Most important, Mr. Price completed "Kate Vaiden" (1986). Narrated by a 57-year-old North Carolina woman whose lifelong search for love and security has been a series of bitter setbacks, the novel won back many of the critics who were beginning to cool on Mr. Price. It won the National Book Critics Circle prize as the year's best work of fiction.

"Blue Calhoun" (1992), cast as a long letter from the title character to his granddaughter, was also warmly received. The morally shifty but likable narrator, like the lively, irrepressible Kate Vaiden, won readers over.

The undercurrent of Christian charity evident in Mr. Price's previous work became even more pronounced in these and later novels, like "Roxanna Slade" (1998) and "The Good Priest's Son" (2005), in which fallible characters face momentous moral choices. The deepening moral tinge, which some critics found too schematic, was rooted in Mr. Price's Christian faith: he was an unorthodox, nonchurchgoing believer.

"The whole point of learning about the human race presumably is to give it mercy," he told The Georgia Review in 1993.

If Mr. Price shook off the burden of Faulkner, his work remained elusive despite its strong regional flavor and commitment to "the weight and worth of the ordinary," as the novelist Janet Burroway once put it. Mr. Price himself ventured a succinct appraisal for The Southern Review in 1978: "It seems to me they are books about human freedom — the limits thereof, the possibilities thereof, the impossibilities thereof."

— *By William Grimes*

THEONI ALDREDGE

Dazzling Audiences With Needle and Thread

AUG. 22, 1922 - JAN. 21, 2011

THEONI V. ALDREDGE, who won acclaim designing costumes for movies and hundreds of Broadway and Off Broadway productions, including "Annie," "A Chorus Line" and "La Cage aux Folles," died on Jan. 21 in Stamford, Conn. She was 88.

The cause was cardiac arrest, her husband, the actor Tom Aldredge, said.

In a career that lasted more than half a century, Ms. Aldredge was a favorite of top producers and directors on and off Broadway, among them David Merrick, Michael Bennett, Joseph Papp, Gower Champion and Arthur Laurents (see page 442). In film, she won an Academy Award for her work on "The Great Gatsby" and created costumes for many other films, among them "Network," "Semi-Tough," "Moonstruck," "Ghostbusters" and "Addams Family Values."

Her beginnings were auspicious. After designing the costumes for Elia Kazan's production of Tennessee Williams's "Sweet Bird of Youth" in 1959, she was hired by Mr. Merrick for "I Can Get It for You Wholesale," in which Barbra Streisand made her Broadway debut. The same year, 1962, she did the costumes for Edward Albee's "Who's Afraid of Virginia Woolf?"

After being introduced to Mr. Papp, the director of the New York Shakespeare Festival, she designed the costumes for his production of "Measure for Measure" in 1960 and soon became the company's head designer, a position she held for more than 20 years.

In 1984 more than 1,000 of her costumes could be seen in five musicals running simultaneously on Broadway: "A Chorus Line," "Dreamgirls," "La Cage aux Folles," "42nd Street" and "The Rink."

CREATING A LOOK: Ms. Aldredge's costumes appeared in Broadway shows, films, operas and ballets.

She won three Tony Awards for costume design, for "Annie," "Barnum" and "La Cage aux Folles"; she was nominated 11 other times.

"She made people look beautiful, which is a lot harder than you might think," the costume designer Martin Pakledinaz said. "She also had the ability to see a production as a whole, the way one number grew out of the previous number and led into the one after that."

Theoni Athanasiou Vachliotis was born on Aug. 22, 1922, in Salonika, Greece, and grew up in Athens. Her father was the surgeon general of the Greek Army and a member of the Greek Parliament. As a child she fixated on dolls and their clothes — throughout her life she maintained a large doll collection — and by the time she graduated from the American School in Athens in 1949, she had decided on theater as a career.

She enrolled at the Goodman School of Drama in Chicago and, stopping in New York on her way to Chicago, attended a showing of the 1946 film "Caesar and Cleopatra." "A strange thing happened," she told The New Yorker in 1973. "I was overwhelmed by the beauty of the flowing garments worn by Vivien Leigh."

She added: "'People can look so beautiful in clothes,' I said to myself. 'There is a mystery to costume.' And that's when it started."

She made her debut as a costume designer in 1950, creating the clothes for "The Distaff Side," a comedy by John van Druten produced at the Goodman Theater. Within a few years she was teaching costume design at the theater's school.

She also married Mr. Aldredge, an actor who was studying to become a director and who went on to make a successful career in New York. (He currently appears as Steve Buscemi's father in the HBO series "Boardwalk Empire.") He is her only immediate survivor.

After the couple moved to New York in 1959, Ms. Aldredge got off to a quick start when Geraldine Page, who had admired her work at the Goodman, persuaded Mr. Kazan to hire her for "Sweet Bird of Youth."

"I made three outfits for Gerry — a negligee, a robe and a beaded navy blue evening dress with a lighter front because a bird's stomach is always lighter than its back," Ms. Aldredge told Architectural Digest in 1993. "So there you had Tennessee Williams writing, Geraldine Page and Paul Newman acting, and I thought, 'Where do I go from here?'"

Onward and upward, it turned out. She won her first Tony nomination for "The Devil's Advocate" in 1961 and was soon in constant demand on Broadway, designing costumes for "Cactus Flower"; the Edward Albee play "A Delicate Balance"; "Woman of the Year," with Lauren Bacall; the revival of "Private Lives," with Richard Burton and Elizabeth Taylor; "The Secret Garden"; "Nick & Nora"; and the 2006 revival of "A Chorus Line."

She worked on more than 80 productions for Mr. Papp, including "The Threepenny Opera," David Rabe's "Sticks and Bones" and "Hair," which all transferred to Broadway.

Mr. Papp once praised Ms. Aldredge for designing costumes that seemed to develop out of the characters onstage, and she herself insisted on the subservience of her craft. "You don't take over a show," she told The New York Times in 1984. "What you do is enhance it, because the costumes are there to serve a producer's vision, a director's viewpoint and, most importantly, an actor's comfort. To me, good design is design you're not aware of."

In that regard "A Chorus Line" was a challenge, since nearly all the cast members wore slouchy rehearsal clothes until the spectacular closing number, which Ms. Aldredge envisioned as a visual feast of champagne-colored tuxedos and top hats. Bennett had wanted blazing red. No, she told him. Champagne was the color of celebration.

To generate ideas, she sat in on rehearsals, taking Polaroid pictures of each dancer. "I just borrowed from what they brought," she said. "I took it as a compliment if people thought, 'Well, they're wearing their own clothes.'"

Ms. Aldredge designed for opera, ballet and television, as well as the theater, and in a curious detour in the 1980s she produced a ready-to-wear line for Jane Fonda called Jane Fonda Workouts.

For "The Great Gatsby" she generated hundreds of costumes in less than two weeks, a Herculean effort that might account for her irritation when the fashion press turned the spotlight on Ralph Lauren, who took credit for designing the clothes worn by Robert Redford and the film's other male leads. Ms. Aldredge insisted that he had merely executed designs to her specifications.

Michael Gross, in his Lauren biography "Genuine Authentic," wrote that Ms. Aldredge asked Paramount to take Mr. Lauren's name off the film's credits if he continued to bask in the limelight. His name stayed, in a secondary position, but Ms. Aldredge pointedly omitted his name when accepting her Oscar for the film.

The friction with Mr. Lauren was out of character for Ms. Aldredge, who had a history of working happily with even the most high-strung actors. She did know when to draw the line, however.

"Once an actress went overboard with notes to me about how she doesn't wear pink," she told The Chicago Sun-Times in 2006. "I told her, 'Well, don't wear it home then, sweetie. This is the theater.' You kind of have to humor them. If you can't love actors, you probably shouldn't be a costume designer."

— *By William Grimes*

BARNEY HAJIRO

The Medal of Honor Came 56 Years Later

SEPT. 16, 1916 - JAN. 21, 2011

After Barney Hajiro, an Army private, single-handedly wiped out two German machine gun nests and killed two snipers in a gallant charge in World War II, his superiors recommended him for the Medal of Honor. As part of a regiment composed entirely of Japanese-Americans below the officers' ranks, Private Hajiro epitomized the unit's brash motto, "Go for Broke!" In October 1944, in eastern France, he ran 100 yards through a stream of bullets, walked through a booby-trapped area and led the charge up "Suicide Hill" screaming "Banzai!" before taking out the machine gun nests.

He was shot four times, his commanding officer's report said, then insisted that 40 other wounded men be evacuated first.

But he, like Senator Daniel K. Inouye of Hawaii, who was also a member of the regiment, did not initially receive the Medal of Honor, the nation's top military honor, for which he was recommended. Only in 2000, after 56 years and a belated Pentagon review, did President Bill Clinton present the medal to Mr. Hajiro, Senator Inouye and 20 other Asian-American soldiers.

"I nearly gave up hope," Mr. Hajiro said at the time.

Racial prejudice, Mr. Clinton said, had prevented such a ceremony after the war.

"Barney was a good man," Senator Inouye said in an interview after Mr. Hajiro's death. "He didn't go around blowing his own horn. He would just say he was doing something he was supposed to do."

'GO FOR BROKE!': Mr. Hajiro led a charge up "Suicide Hill" in France.

Mr. Hajiro, who had battled cancer, died on Jan. 21 in Honolulu at 94, his family said. He had been the nation's oldest Medal of Honor recipient. His background was modest: born in Hawaii, he dropped out of school in the eighth grade to work for 10 hours a day, at 10 cents an hour, on a sugar plantation. He was a dockworker when he was drafted into the Army in 1942 and assigned to dig ditches. He resented not being allowed to carry arms.

"I didn't bomb Pearl Harbor," Mr. Hajiro said in an interview in 1999. "Why did they blame us?"

As angry about Pearl Harbor as anybody, many Japanese-Hawaiians were eager to fight. Mr. Hajiro was one of the first to volunteer, in March 1943.

The 442nd Regimental Combat Team, a newly formed unit, would go on to be called the most decorated regiment for its size and length of service: its 14,000 men earned 9,486 Purple Hearts, 8 Presidential Unit Citations and 52 Distinguished Service Crosses, the second-highest individual honor in the Army. Mr. Hajiro received three of those.

He and many of his comrades were decorated for the regiment's most celebrated operation, known as "the rescue of the Lost Battalion," in which they saved 211 fellow soldiers trapped in southern France while suffering more than 800 casualties.

One regiment member, Pfc. Sadao S. Munemori, actually did receive a Medal of Honor, posthumously, in 1945, after the Japanese American Citizens League persuaded a Utah senator to take up the soldier's cause. A Filipino-American also won the medal in World War II. But they were the rare exceptions for Asian-Americans.

Their battlefield exploits came under review by the Pentagon in 1996, after the Congressional Black Caucus had prompted a similar look into why no blacks had been awarded the Medal of Honor in World War II. Senator Daniel K. Akaka, Democrat of Hawaii, sought the review of Asian-Americans.

(In the review of African-Americans, seven were awarded the medal in 1997, six posthumously. The seventh, Vernon Baker, died last July.)

Some criticized the reviews of both blacks and Asian-Americans as political pandering, but President Clinton said that facing racial slurs and forced internment, Japanese-Americans had not gotten a fair deal.

James C. McNaughton, the Defense Department historian who led the Asian-American review, said in 2000 that the very fact that the 442nd was segregated amounted to "institutional discrimination." But he said he could find no instance of white officers deliberately ignoring the valor of Asian-American troops.

Of the 22 Asian-Americans whose decorations were upgraded to the Medal of Honor, all but two were Japanese-Americans and members of either the 442nd or the 100th Infantry Battalion, which the 442nd absorbed in 1944. (Of the two others, one was of Filipino heritage and one of Chinese heritage.)

Senator Inouye, who lost his right arm in fierce fighting in Italy, said he and his former comrades had been modest about finally receiving the medal. "Why did we get recognized when there are hundreds of others who did the same thing?" he asked.

Barney Fushimi Hajiro, the oldest of nine children, was born on Sept. 16, 1916, in Puunene, on the island of Maui, where his parents had immigrated from Hiroshima during World War I. The family was so poor that the children were given a bottle of soda only once a year, on New Year's Day. Barney left school as a teenager and would later say his biggest regret was not pursuing his dream of running track.

He fought in Italy, then moved with his unit to eastern France, where he was cited for bravery on Oct. 19 and Oct. 22, 1944, in battles in mountainous terrain.

On Oct. 29, in the fighting that brought him the Medal of Honor, the 442nd was pinned down, its soldiers picked off one by one by Germans on higher ground. Private Hajiro suffered wounds in his face, shoulder and wrist in leading the counterattack.

"I couldn't run backward," he said. "I had to run forward. That's the job of a soldier."

After the war he refused to buy a Japanese car.

Mr. Hajiro, who lived in Waipahu, on Oahu, is survived by his wife, Esther, a son, two brothers, a sister and a grandson.

At Mr. Hajiro's death, Nicholas Oresko, 94, of Cresskill, N.J., became the oldest living Medal of Honor recipient.

Though Mr. Hajiro came to be revered — accepting the French Legion of Honor, serving as grand marshal at county fairs — he never forgot how it was for Japanese-Americans. On the day the Medal of Honor was pinned to his chest, he said, "Even after the war, they still called me a Jap, you know."

— *By Douglas Martin*

DENNIS OPPENHEIM

A Landslide at Exit 52, and Other Artworks

SEPT. 6, 1938 - JAN. 21, 2011

Dennis Oppenheim, a pioneer of earthworks, body art and Conceptual art who later made emphatically tangible installations and public sculptures that veered between the demonically chaotic and the cheerfully Pop, died on Jan. 21 in Manhattan. He was 72.

The cause was liver cancer, his wife, Amy Van Winkle Plumb, said. Mr. Oppenheim had homes in Manhattan and East Hampton on Long Island.

Belonging to a generation of artists who saw portable painting and sculpture as obsolete, Mr. Oppenheim started out in the realm of the esoteric, the immaterial and the chronically unsalable. But he was always a showman, not averse to the circuslike, or to courting danger. For "Rocked Circle — Fear," a 1971 body art piece, he stood at the center of a five-foot-wide circle painted on a New York sidewalk while a friend dropped fist-size stones from three stories above, aiming for inside the circle without hitting the artist. There were no mishaps.

Mr. Oppenheim had a penchant for grandiosity. It was implicit in the close-up photograph of a splinter in his finger, portentously titled "Material Interchange." It was explicit in "Charmed Journey Through a Step-Down Transformer," a Rube Goldberg-like outdoor installation from 1980 that sprawled 125 feet down a slope at the Wave Hill garden and cultural center in the Bronx, its disparate parts suggesting engines, tracks, organ pipes and much else.

Sculptures like these, from Mr. Oppenheim's Factories series, combined aspects of machines and industrial architecture with intimations of mysterious human processes, presenting what he called "a parallel to the mental processing of a raw idea" by both the artist and the viewer.

Many works involved moving parts, casts of animals (whole or partial), upturned or tilted building silhouettes and sound, water and fireworks, which on occasion prompted unscheduled visits by the fire department.

ALWAYS A SHOWMAN: Mr. Oppenheim, with "Blood Breathe" in 2007, created earthworks, body art and Conceptual art, sometimes in circuslike fashion.

An athletic, ruggedly handsome man who maintained a shock of blond hair until his death, Mr. Oppenheim had a knack for the oddly poetic title — as in "A Station for Detaining and Blinding Radio-Active Horses" — and a penchant for the occasional sensational remark. "Korea is a nice place to be," he said after executing sculptural commissions for the 1988 summer Olympics in Seoul, "if your work is hysterical."

Dennis Allan Oppenheim was born in Electric City, Wash., on Sept. 6, 1938. His father was an engineer; his mother promoted his early interest in art. In the mid-1960s he earned a bachelor's degree in fine arts from the California College of Arts and Crafts in Oakland and an M.F.A. from Stanford. He moved to New York in 1966.

He first became known for works in which, like an environmentally inclined Marcel Duchamp, he simply designated parts of the urban landscape as artworks, using engineers' stakes and photographs. Then, in step with artists like Robert Smithson, Walter De Maria and Lawrence Weiner, he began making temporary outdoor sculptures, soon to be known as land art or earthworks. "Landslide," from 1968, for example, was an immense bank of loose dirt near Exit 52 of the Long Island Expressway in central Long Island that he punctuated with rows of steplike right angles made of painted wood.

In other earthworks he cut abstract configurations in fields of wheat; traced the rings of a tree's growth, much enlarged, in snow; and created a sprawling white square (one of Modernism's basic motifs) with salt in downtown Manhattan.

He had his first solo exhibition in New York in 1968, at the John Gibson Gallery, then on East 67th Street in Manhattan, and his work was included in groundbreaking surveys of the new dematerialized art in 1969 at the Kunsthalle Bern in Switzerland and in 1970 at the Museum of Modern Art in New York.

In the mid-1970s, after tiring of the physical demands of body art and subsequently using his children in several works, he turned to custom-made automated marionettes, a solution that brought out his dark humor and theatrical proclivities and led to increasingly elaborate sculptural narratives. One of the first, "Lecture" (1976), centered on a marionette bearing an image of Mr. Oppenheim's face who addressed rows of small chairs on the topic of the art world, talking especially about an artist whose preferred medium was assassination. Only one chair was occupied: by a marionette of a black man.

Mr. Oppenheim's art-making could seem simultaneously driven and lackadaisical, fearless and opportunistic. Few of his contemporaries worked in a broader range of mediums or methods, or seemed to borrow so much from so many other artists. His career might almost be defined as a series of sidelong glances at the doings of artists like Vito Acconci, Mr. Smithson, Bruce Nauman, Alice Aycock (to whom he was married in the early 1980s) and Claes Oldenburg.

Yet few artists could give these borrowings such a personal, sculptural immediacy, as exemplified by "Recall," a 1973 piece. In "Recall," a video monitor shows a close-up of Mr. Oppenheim's mouth as he recalls studying painting as an undergraduate, evoking the obsessive performances and gravelly voiced mumblings of Mr. Acconci, his friend. But in a glamorous, characteristically simple visual touch, the image of Mr. Oppenheim's moving lips is reflected in the shimmering surface of a long, shallow pan of turpentine, the madeleine used to stimulate his memories.

Mr. Oppenheim's first marriage, to Karen Marie Cackett, ended in divorce, as did his second, to Ms. Aycock. In addition to his wife, Ms. Plumb, Mr. Oppenheim is survived by a daughter and son from his first marriage, a daughter from a relationship with Phyllis Jalbert, a son from his relationship with Hélène Poquillion, a sister and two grandchildren.

In the past two decades Mr. Oppenheim turned to smaller, less elaborate pieces whose all-purpose, rather coarsely made forms were generic and instantly legible. Among the 25 or so permanent sculptures from this period, several used enlarged objects in the manner of Pop Art: orange safety cones, Hershey's Kisses, diamond rings, an easy chair, paintbrushes. "Device to Root Out Evil" (1997) is an inverted church, its steeple provocatively stuck in the ground. "Monument to Escape" (2001), a memorial in a Buenos Aires park to victims of the Argentine military dictatorship during the so-called dirty war, is simply a pile of three boxy house forms with bars added to their windows and doors.

His work was the subject of many surveys and retrospectives in the United States and in Europe, including a 1991 exhibition at the P.S. 1 Museum, and is represented in museum collections around the world.

Mr. Oppenheim's best work had a transparency, almost an obviousness, that could seem hokey. But it also took the notion of communication seriously. It refused to talk down.

— *By Roberta Smith*

Poppa Neutrino

David Pearlman: 'The Happiest Man in the World'

OCT. 15, 1933 - JAN. 23, 2011

David Pearlman, an itinerant philosopher, adventurer and environmentalist widely known as Poppa Neutrino, who founded his own church, crossed the Atlantic on a raft made from scrap and invented a theoretically unstoppable football strategy, died on Jan. 23 in New Orleans. He was 77.

He had no fixed abode but had spent the last two years in Burlington, Vt., building and testing a new raft on Lake Champlain that he planned to sail around the globe.

Mr. Pearlman, whose improbable life was chronicled by the New Yorker writer Alec Wilkinson in "The Happiest Man in the World" (2007), became Poppa Neutrino when he was 50.

He had just recovered from a near-mortal illness brought on by a dog bite in Mexico and, considering himself reborn, decided to choose a new name. Neutrino, a nearly undetectable particle with a capacity for constant movement, came immediately to mind.

A lifelong wanderer, he developed a philosophy that emphasized freedom, joy, creativity and antimaterialism, a creed expressed in the rafts he built from discarded materials. The rafts, he wrote on his Floating Neutrinos Web site, "were merely foils for our inner work: an ongoing experiment in human psychology, searching for answers to what makes us function and malfunction, and how to increase our own and others' abilities to create meaningful and fulfilling lives."

William David Pearlman was born on Oct. 15, 1933, in Fresno, Calif., and spent his turbulent childhood in San Francisco. His father, Louis Pearlman, shipped out with the Navy before he was born, and David took his stepfather's last name, Maloney. He later discovered who his real father was and changed his last name to Pearlman.

His mother was a heavy gambler, and the family lived from week to week in cheap hotels, while David attended, fitfully, anywhere from 40 to 50 schools, by his reckoning.

LIFELONG WANDERER: For a time, Mr. Pearlman lived on a paddle-wheel houseboat off Pier 25 in New York City.

Two months after lying his way into the Army at 15, he admitted that he was under age and tried to secure a discharge, a plan that was foiled when his mother insisted to his commanding officer that he was really 18. After the Korean War began, she relented.

Freed from the military, he hitchhiked along Route 66, studied briefly at a Baptist seminary in Texas and became a preacher, spent time with the Beats in San Francisco, founded the First Church of Fulfillment while living in New York, sold life insurance in New Mexico, reported from Vietnam for a small San Francisco newspaper and organized a group of itinerant sign painters he called the Salvation Navy.

In the 1980s, he and his fourth wife, Betsy Terrell, who survives him, formed the Flying Neutrinos, a jazz and rhythm-and-blues band drawn from family members and their many fellow travelers. It is now led by his daughter Ingrid Lucia Marshall, who uses the stage name Ingrid Lucia, and Todd Londagin, a musician he raised as his son.

Mr. Pearlman, who died of congestive heart failure, is also survived by another daughter and another son, a stepdaughter, an adopted daughter and five grandchildren.

In 1988 Mr. Pearlman converted an abandoned barge into a paddle-wheel houseboat, Town Hall, that tied up at Pier 25 on the Hudson River off TriBeCa for several years.

It was then that he began scavenging the material for Son of Town Hall, a 40-foot raft made of discarded timber, foam bricks and plastic bottles lashed together, basketlike, with 3,000 feet of rope abandoned by Con Edison.

"Where did I get this notion?" he said to Mr. Wilkinson. "I have no idea. From the cornucopia of my mind. Somebody put it in there a long time ago, and it came out in this way."

In this it resembled the Neutrino Clock Offense, a system of secret hand signals for football players, based on the face of a clock, designed to let passer and receiver communicate while a play is in progress. Despite his best efforts, Mr. Pearlman was unable to persuade any college teams to adopt it.

In June 1998 Mr. Pearlman set sail from Newfoundland, aiming for France, with his wife, two crew members, three dogs and a piano. After 60 days, the raft reached Ireland, having survived a Force 9 gale that gave him pause.

"I've lived through levels of fear I never thought I had," he told The Evening Standard of London. "The waves were so big and so steep, spitting foam across our raft, that I found the coward in myself."

Nevertheless, he formed plans to circumnavigate the globe on a new raft, the Sea Owl. He abandoned the effort in November when a storm on Lake Champlain drove the raft onto a rocky cliff, where rescue workers hoisted him, his two inexperienced crew members and two dogs to safety.

"The vessel was everything I wanted it to be," he told The Burlington Free Press. "I told the Coast Guard people it was unsinkable. They said, 'Never say that.' They were right. Anything will break up if it's been smashing into a wall for two and a half hours."

— *By William Grimes*

JACK LALANNE

He Got America off the Couch

SEPT. 26, 1914 - JAN. 23, 2011

JACK LALANNE, who combined an obsession with grueling workouts and good nutrition and a gift for salesmanship to become, in the view of many, the founder of the modern physical fitness movement, died on Jan. 23 at his home in Morro Bay, Calif. He was 96.

The cause was respiratory failure resulting from pneumonia.

By his own description Mr. LaLanne was an emotional and physical wreck growing up in the San Francisco area when, at 15, he heard a talk on proper diet. It turned his life around. He started working out with weights when they were an oddity, and in 1936, in only his early 20s, he opened the prototype for the fitness spas to come — a gym, juice bar and health food store — in an old office building in Oakland.

"People thought I was a charlatan and a nut," he remembered. "The doctors were against me — they said that working out with weights would give people heart attacks and they would lose their sex drive." But Mr. LaLanne persevered, and he found a national pulpit in the age of television.

"The Jack LaLanne Show" made its debut in 1951 as a local program in the San Francisco area, then went nationwide on daytime television in 1959. His short-sleeved jumpsuit showing off his impressive biceps, his props often limited to a broomstick, a chair and a rubber cord, Mr. LaLanne pranced through his exercise routines, most notably his fingertip push-ups.

He built an audience by first drawing in children who saw his white German shepherd, Happy, perform tricks.

"My show was so personal, I made it feel like you and I were the only ones there," he told Knight-Ridder Newspapers in 1995. "And I'd say: 'Boys and girls, come here. Uncle Jack wants to tell you something. You go get Mother or Daddy, Grandmother, Grandfather, whoever is in the house. You go get them, and you make sure they exercise with me.'"

His show continued into the mid-1980s.

Long before Richard Simmons and Jane Fonda and the Atkins diet, Mr. LaLanne was a national celebrity, preaching regular exercise and proper diet. Expanding on his television popularity, he opened dozens of fitness studios under his name, later licensing them to Bally. He invented the forerunners of modern exercise machines like leg-extension and pulley devices. He marketed a Power Juicer to blend raw vegetables and fruits and a Glamour Stretcher cord, and he sold exercise videos and fitness books. He invited women to join his health clubs and told the elderly and the disabled that they could exercise despite their limitations.

At 60 he swam from Alcatraz Island to Fisherman's Wharf handcuffed, shackled and towing a 1,000-pound boat. At 70, handcuffed and shackled again, he towed 70 boats, carrying a total of 70 people, a mile and a half through Long Beach Harbor.

He ate two meals a day and shunned snacks.

Breakfast, following his morning workout, usually included several hard-boiled egg whites, a cup of broth, oatmeal with soy milk and seasonal fruit. For dinner he took his wife, Elaine, to restaurants that knew what he wanted: a salad with raw vegetables and egg whites along with fish — often salmon — and a mixture of red and white wine. He sometimes allowed himself a roast turkey sandwich, but never a cup of coffee.

Mr. LaLanne said he performed his exercises until he experienced "muscle fatigue," lifting weights until it was impossible for him to continue. It produced results and, as he put it, "the ego in me" made the effort worthwhile.

A WORKOUT A DAY ... : Mr. LaLanne was an early promoter of weight training.

The son of French immigrants, Jack LaLanne was born in San Francisco on Sept. 26, 1914, and spent his early years on his parents' sheep farm in Bakersfield, Calif. By the time he was 15, the family having moved to the Bay Area, he was pimply and nearsighted, craved junk food and had dropped out of high school. That is when his mother took him to a women's club for a talk by Paul C. Bragg, a well-known speaker on health and nutrition.

That talk, Mr. LaLanne often said, turned his life around. He began experimenting with weights at the Berkeley Y.M.C.A., tossed aside cakes and cookies and studied Gray's Anatomy to learn about the body's muscles. He graduated from a chiropractic school, but instead of practicing that profession he became a pitchman for good health.

He opened his first health studio when he was 21, and a decade and a half later he turned to television. He was first sponsored by the creator of a longevity pill, a 90-year-old man, but it sold poorly and he obtained Yami Yogurt as his new sponsor. "It tasted terrible, so I mixed it with prune juice and fruits," he told The New York Times in 2004. "Nobody thought about it until then. We made the guy a millionaire."

Mr. LaLanne, 5-foot-6 and 150 pounds or so with a 30-inch waist, maintained that he disliked working out. He said he kept at it strictly to feel fit and stay healthy. He built two gyms and a pool at his home in Morro Bay, and began each day, into his 90s, with two hours of workouts: weight lifting followed by a swim against an artificial current or in place, tied to a belt.

"The Jack LaLanne Show" may have run its course in the mid-1980s, but it had a second life in reruns on ESPN Classic. "We have over 3,000 shows," Mr. LaLanne said in 2004. "I own everything."

In September 2007, "Jack LaLanne Live!" made its debut on the online VoiceAmerica Health and Wellness Radio Network. He appeared on it with his wife, Elaine, and his nephew Chris LaLanne, a personal trainer. Mr. LaLanne is survived by his wife, two sons and a daughter.

Mr. LaLanne promoted himself and his calling into his final years, often accompanied at events by his wife, a physical fitness convert but hardly a fanatic. He brimmed with optimism and restated a host of aphorisms for an active and fit life.

"I can't die," he most famously liked to say. "It would ruin my image."

— *By Richard Goldstein*

DAVID FRYE

A Nixon That Had Them in Stitches

NOV. 21, 1933 - JAN. 24, 2011

DAVID FRYE, whose wicked send-ups of political figures like Lyndon B. Johnson, Hubert H. Humphrey and, above all, Richard M. Nixon, made him one of the most popular comedians in the United States in the late 1960s and early '70s, died on Jan. 24 in Las Vegas, where he lived. He was 77.

In the early 1960s Mr. Frye was a struggling impressionist working the clubs of Greenwich Village, relying on a fairly standard repertoire of Hollywood actors. Then he slipped Robert F. Kennedy into his act, basing his impression on a girlfriend's comment that Mr. Kennedy sounded like Bugs Bunny.

Audiences loved it, and Mr. Frye began adding other politicians, capturing not just their vocal peculiarities but also their body language and facial expressions. His L.B.J., with a lugubrious hound-dog face and a Texas twang rich in slushy "s" sounds, became a trademark, as did his bouncy Hubert Humphrey.

But it was Nixon who made his career. Shoulders hunched, his deep-set eyes glowering, Mr. Frye captured the insecure, neurotic Nixon to perfection. "I am the president" — his blustery tag line and the title of a 1969 comedy album he recorded for Elektra — seemed to get at the essence of a powerful politician in desperate need of validation.

"I do Nixon not by copying his real actions but by feeling his attitude, which is that he cannot believe that he really is president," Mr. Frye told Esquire magazine in 1971. Nixon also played the starring role in Mr. Frye's later albums "Radio Free Nixon" (1971), "Richard Nixon Superstar" (1971) and the Watergate satire "Richard Nixon: A Fantasy" (1973).

Mr. Frye added a panoply of political and cultural figures to his act. His William F. Buckley Jr., all darting tongue and wildly searching eyes, was stellar, but he also worked up dead-on impressions of George Wallace, Nelson Rockefeller, David Susskind, Billy Graham, Howard Cosell and a long list of film actors.

It was Nixon, however, who kept Mr. Frye a regular on the top television variety shows and at the big Las Vegas casinos, perhaps because he was one of the few politicians with a truly Shakespearean richness of character. In one skit Mr. Frye even had the president smoking marijuana and reporting, in hushed tones, "I see spacious skies and fruited plains and amber waves of grain."

David Shapiro was born in Brooklyn and attended James Madison High School there. His father, who owned a successful office-cleaning business, was dead set against his son's going into show business, but even at the University of Miami, David was already doing mime impressions in campus productions. Soon he discovered he had an ear for distinctive Hollywood voices like Jimmy Stewart and Cary Grant and began doing vocal impressions as well.

After serving with an Army Special Services unit in France, he returned to New York and developed his act at small clubs while working as a salesman for his father's company. At the Village Gate, where he was filling in for a regular in early 1966, talent scouts saw his Bobby Kennedy imitation and booked him on "The Merv Griffin Show." Soon he was appearing on "The Leslie Uggams Show," "The Smothers Brothers Comedy Hour" and "The Tonight Show."

Nixon came as a gift, but mastering the impression was a struggle. "It took me a long time to get Nixon — but it took the country a long time to get Nixon," Mr. Frye told Esquire.

"Nixon has these brooding eyes that look like my eyes. That helped a lot. But the voice is still the main thing. He has a radio announcer's evenness of speech, very well modulated, and you can't pick out any highs and lows. If I hadn't had to do him, I wouldn't have tried."

LASTING IMPRESSION: Mr. Frye is best remembered for his send-up of Nixon.

Nixon's departure from the scene took most of the air out of Mr. Frye's career. He capitalized on Watergate, although some radio stations refused to play material from "Richard Nixon: A Fantasy," which they thought cut a little too close to the bone for some listeners.

"Today I have regretfully been forced to accept the resignations of 1,541 of the finest public servants it has ever been my privilege to know," Mr. Frye's Nixon intones on the album. "As the man in charge, I must accept full responsibility, but not the blame. Let me explain the difference. People who are to blame lose their jobs; people who are responsible do not."

In another skit, Nixon goes to the Godfather for help. "You want justice?" the Godfather asks. "Not necessarily," Nixon replies.

With Nixon's resignation in August 1974, Mr. Frye lost the best friend an impressionist ever had. He continued to perform and to add new impressions to his act: Jimmy Carter, Anwar el-Sadat of Egypt and Menachem Begin of Israel, among others. He recorded the comedy albums "David Frye Presents the Great Debate" (1980) and "Clinton: An Oral History" (1998). But he never enjoyed anything approaching the fame that the Johnson and Nixon years had given him.

He could see the end quite clearly.

"It's a weird feeling, knowing that you can lose the guts of your act at any time," he told Time in 1974. Nixon's presidential successor, Gerald R. Ford, offered scant hope. "He looks like the guy in a science fiction movie who is the first one to see The Creature," Mr. Frye said.

He is survived by a sister.

— *By William Grimes*

BHIMSEN JOSHI

The Musical 'God' of India

FEB. 1922 - JAN. 24, 2011

"Even Gods Must Die."

So read the headline on the Web site of Open, an English-language Indian magazine, above a tribute to the singer Pandit Bhimsen Joshi. Mr. Joshi, who died on Jan. 24 at 88, was for decades one of the world's most revered singers of Indian classical music. After the announcement of his death, thousands of people thronged Mr. Joshi's home in Pune to pay their respects. He was accorded a state funeral, with a 21-gun salute and dignitaries in attendance.

Mr. Joshi (pronounced JOE-shee) was familiar to a vast public in South Asia through his live concerts, many recordings and performances on

Indian film soundtracks. He also toured Europe, Canada, the United States and elsewhere; his New York engagements included an appearance at Town Hall in 1982.

An artist in the Hindustani, or North Indian, musical tradition, Mr. Joshi was renowned as a master of the khayal, a genre of vocal concert music. Khayals, whose texts can range over subjects including deities, the seasons and love, are sometimes likened to Western lieder for their appearance in concert settings.

Khayals are sung in the traditional melodic modes known as ragas. Unlike lieder, they are highly improvisatory, demanding great artistry of the singer, who manipulates a song's melody, rhythm and tempo each time it is sung. The result is a rigorous yet imaginative rendition of the original song that can unspool for as long as 50 minutes.

MASTER OF KHAYAL: A song by Mr. Joshi could last up to 50 minutes.

In performance Mr. Joshi was said to have a galvanizing effect on his audiences. He had a resonant voice and formidable technique, negotiating with ease the virtuosic melodic runs that are a significant component of khayal improvisation.

He embellished his singing with head, hand and bodily gestures that gathered speed along with the music.

"He was known for his musical creativity; it just sort of flowed out of him," Bonnie C. Wade, a professor of music at the University of California, Berkeley, and an authority on the khayal, said in an interview. "He could sing very fast, he had a good sense of time and he was really enjoyable to listen to."

Mr. Joshi was also known for his musical breadth. He was most closely associated with the Kirana tradition of khayal singing, which emphasizes fluidity of melody. But he also drew freely from India's many other vocal styles. As a result, according to news accounts over the years, his concerts had a pluralistic appeal that could transcend ethnic, linguistic, religious and class lines.

One of some 16 children of a Brahmin schoolmaster, Bhimsen Joshi was born in February 1922 in what is now the Karnataka state of South India. ("Pandit," from which the English word pundit derives, is an honorific title denoting great learning or mastery.)

Captivated by music as a child, he left home very early — at 11, in many accounts — to wander the country in search of a guru who would teach him to sing.

His father eventually found him and took him home, but over time the young Mr. Joshi apprenticed himself to a series of masters of Indian classical song. He made his first recording as a young man, and by the early 1940s was heard regularly on the radio in Bombay, now Mumbai.

In 2008 he was awarded the Bharat Ratna, India's highest civilian honor.

Mr. Joshi was by all accounts a man of appetites, enamored of food and fast cars; he was also widely reported to have struggled with alcoholism in the past.

He was married twice; survivors include four children by his first wife and three by his second.

In an interview quoted in the English-language periodical India Abroad in 1997, Mr. Joshi explained his eclectic approach to his art.

"For a few years after learning music, I did not sing, I only listened; I heard a lot of music of different kinds," he said. "This is an education which is as important as practicing music." He added:

"The singer has to be a great thief. From each person take the best to create your own style."

— *By Margalit Fox*

DANIEL BELL

A Lifelong Engagement With the World

MAY 10, 1919 - JAN. 25, 2011

Daniel Bell, the writer, editor, sociologist and teacher who over seven decades came to epitomize the engaged intellectual as he struggled to reveal the past, comprehend the present and anticipate the future, died on Jan. 25 at his home in Cambridge, Mass. He was 91.

Mr. Bell's output was prodigious and his range enormous. His major lines of inquiry included the failures of socialism in America, the exhaustion of modern culture and the transformation of capitalism from an industrial-based system to one built on consumerism.

Two of Mr. Bell's many books, "The End of Ideology" (1960) and the "Cultural Contradictions of Capitalism" (1978), were ranked among the 100 most influential books since World War II by The Times Literary Supplement in London. In titling "The End of Ideology" and another work, "The Coming of Post-Industrial Society" (1973), Mr. Bell coined terms that have entered common usage.

In "The End of Ideology" he contended — nearly three decades before the collapse of Communism — that ideologies that had once driven global politics were losing force and thus providing openings for newer galvanizing beliefs to gain toeholds. In "The Coming of Post-Industrial Society" he foresaw the global spread of service-based economies as generators of capital and employment, supplanting those dominated by manufacturing or agriculture.

In Mr. Bell's view, Western capitalism had come to rely on mass consumerism, acquisitiveness and widespread indebtedness, undermining the old Protestant ethic of thrift and modesty that writers like Max Weber and R. H. Tawney had long credited as the reasons for capitalism's success.

He also predicted the rising importance of science-based industries and of new technical elites. Indeed, in 1967, he predicted something like the Internet, writing: "We will probably see a national information-computer-utility system, with tens of thousands of terminals in homes and offices 'hooked' into giant central computers providing library and information services, retail ordering and billing services, and the like."

Mr. Bell became an influential editor of periodicals, starting out with The New Leader, a small social democratic publication that he referred to as his "intellectual home." He joined Fortune magazine as its labor editor and in 1965 helped found and edit The Public Interest with his old City College classmate Irving Kristol, who died in 2009.

Though The Public Interest never attained a wide readership, it gained great prestige, beginning as a policy journal that questioned Great Society programs and then broadening into one of the most intellectually formidable of neoconservative publications.

"It has had more influence on domestic policy than any other journal in the country — by far," the columnist David Brooks wrote in The New York Times in 2005.

Mr. Bell also maintained a distinguished academic career. He taught at the University of Chicago in the 1940s, at Columbia as a professor of sociology from 1959 to 1969 — the university awarded him a Ph.D. for his work on "The End of Ideology" — and then at Harvard, where in 1980 he was appointed the Henry Ford II professor of social sciences.

As both a public intellectual and an academic, Mr. Bell saw a distinction between those breeds. In one of his typical yeasty digressions in "The End of Ideology," he wrote: "The scholar has a bounded field of knowledge, a tradition, and seeks to find his place in it, adding to the accumulated, tested knowledge of the past as to a mosaic. The scholar, qua scholar, is less involved with his 'self.'

"The intellectual," he went on, "begins with his experience, his individual perceptions of the world, his privileges and deprivations, and judges the world by these sensibilities."

Mr. Bell may have well been referring to himself in that passage — his intellectual persona self-consciously winking at its detached scholarly twin with whom it conspired in a lifetime of work and experience.

Daniel Bolotsky was born on the Lower East Side of Manhattan on May 10, 1919, to Benjamin and Anna Bolotsky, garment workers and immigrants from Eastern Europe. His father died when Daniel was 8 months old, and Daniel, his mother and his older brother, Leo, moved in with relatives. The family changed the name to Bell when Daniel was 13.

PUBLIC INTELLECTUAL: Mr. Bell, among other things, foresaw the global economy.

Mr. Bell liked to tell of his political beginnings with an anecdote about his bar mitzvah, in 1932. "I said to the Rabbi: 'I've found the truth. I don't believe in God. I'm joining the Young People's Socialist League.' So he looked at me and said, 'Kid, you don't believe in God. Tell me, do you think God cares?'"

Mr. Bell did join the League and as an adolescent delivered sidewalk speeches for Norman Thomas, the Socialist candidate for president. By the time he had graduated from Stuyvesant High School in Manhattan and entered City College in the late 1930s, he was well grounded in the Socialist and Marxist canon and well aware of the leftist landscape, with its bitter rivalries and schisms.

At City College, he had no trouble finding his way to Alcove No. 1 in the cafeteria. There, among the anti-Stalinist socialists who dominated the nook, he found a remarkable cohort that challenged and sustained him for much of his life as it helped to define America's political spectrum over the last half of the 20th century.

Its principal members, in addition to Mr. Bell, included Mr. Kristol, whose eventual move to the right as a founding neoconservative led Mr. Bell to leave The Public Interest in 1972 while steadfastly affirming his friendship for his old school chum.

There was Irving Howe, the critic, professor and editor of the leftist journal Dissent, who remained a Social Democrat. And there was Nathan Glazer, who would become Mr. Bell's colleague in the Harvard sociology department, the author, with Daniel Patrick Moynihan, of "Beyond the Melting Pot," and the architect of strategies for school integration. In 1998 the four men, described as the "New York Intellectuals," were the subjects of a documentary film by Joseph Dorman, "Arguing the World."

The atmosphere of City College in the '30s was supercharged with leftist ideology. There were Communists and Socialists, Stalinists and Trotskyites, all giving vent to their views in the years of the Spanish Civil War just before Hitler's pact with Stalin paved the way to world war.

In the film, Mr. Bell described the atmosphere in the cafeteria as "kind of a heder," referring to the Jewish religious schools where arguing a variety of views and redefining positions was the basis of learning. He graduated in 1939.

The associations Mr. Bell made at City College were fundamental. He also met the sociologist Seymour Martin Lipset and the literary critic Alfred Kazin, whose sister, Pearl Kazin, a book editor, married Mr. Bell in 1960. She survives him, along with a daughter, a son, four grandchildren and one great-grandchild.

Mr. Bell never hesitated to expand and revise his thinking through the years. New editions of his older books often include new prefaces and afterwords that look at his old arguments in the light of new developments in politics and society. And he was always quick to point out what he regarded as misconceptions about his work and his life.

In 2003, for example, an article by James Atlas in The Times described Mr. Bell and Mr. Kristol as neoconservatives who had felt that the Vietnam War had a "persuasive rationale." He answered with a letter that declared, "I was not and never have been a 'neoconservative.' Nor did I support the war."

Indeed, for all the ideological wars he had witnessed, Mr. Bell disdained labels, particularly as they were applied to him. Over the years he would offer his own political profile, declaring what he called his "triune" view of himself: "a socialist in economics, a liberal in politics and a conservative in culture."

— *By Michael T. Kaufman*

Charlie Louvin

In Sweet Country Harmony With His Brother

JULY 7, 1927 - JAN. 26, 2011

Charlie Louvin, a member of one of the pre-eminent brother acts in country music and an inspiration to several generations of rock musicians, died on Jan. 26 at his home in Wartrace, Tenn. He was 83.

The cause was complications of pancreatic cancer, said Michael Manning, a friend of Mr. Louvin's and the producer of his single "Back When We Were Young," his final recording, released last year.

Mr. Louvin achieved his greatest fame with the Louvin Brothers, the popular duo that modernized the close-harmony singing of Depression-era acts like the Blue Sky Boys and the Delmore Brothers and that anticipated the keening vocal interplay of the Everly Brothers.

Typically featuring Mr. Louvin on guitar and lead vocals and Ira, his older brother, on mandolin and high tenor harmonies, the Louvins' 1950s hits also left their mark on the country-rock of the Byrds and others.

"I just could not get enough of that sound," the singer Emmylou Harris said of the Louvin Brothers' music in an interview with The Observer, the British newsweekly, in January 2010. "I'd always loved the Everly Brothers, but there was something scary and washed in the blood about the sound of the Louvin Brothers."

Ms. Harris's breakthrough country hit was a 1975 remake of the duo's "If I Could Only Win Your Love." Resolutely traditional in approach, Mr. Louvin and his brother, who died in an automobile accident in 1965, were proponents of the high, lonesome sound of the southern Appalachian Mountains, where they grew up. Some of their best-known recordings were updates of foreboding antediluvian ballads like "In the Pines" and "Knoxville Girl." Other material centered on the wholesome likes of family and religion, including "The Christian Life," an original that later appeared on "Sweetheart of the Rodeo," the landmark Byrds album featuring the singer Gram Parsons.

Also falling under the duo's sway were alternative-rock acts like Elvis Costello and the band Uncle Tupelo, which recorded a version of the Louvin Brothers' cold-war plaint "Great Atomic Power" in 1992.

Despite their conservative cultural and musical leanings — their initial 1950s hits were recorded without drums, which were commonplace in country music then — the Louvins' greatest acclaim came with the advent of rock 'n' roll, when rebellious sentiments and loud backbeats were in ascendance. They were headliners in a touring revue that included Elvis Presley.

HIGH, LONESOME SOUND: Mr. Louvin with a portrait of himself and his brother Ira. The duo inspired The Byrds and Elvis Costello.

Their biggest single, "I Don't Believe You've Met My Baby," was a No. 1 country hit for two weeks in 1956. They also reached the country Top 10 during the period with songs like "When I Stop Dreaming" and "Cash on the Barrelhead."

The Louvins' popularity waned as the '60s unfolded, and in 1963 declining record sales and Ira's drinking led the brothers to dissolve their partnership and pursue solo careers. Charlie Louvin placed 16 singles in the country Top 40 over the next decade, including "I Don't Love You Anymore," a Top 10 hit in 1964. He went on to make a pair of albums with the singer Melba Montgomery in the 1970s and a record with the bluegrass duo Jim and Jesse in 1982.

By then, Mr. Louvin was known primarily as a star of the Grand Ole Opry, a reputation that persisted into this century, when another wave of rock bands, including the Raconteurs and Cake, embraced his music. In 2007 he released the first of several albums for the New York label Tompkins Square and appeared at the Bonnaroo music festival in Manchester, Tenn.

"Livin', Lovin', Losin': Songs of the Louvin Brothers," a tribute record, won the Grammy Award for best country album in 2004. Mr. Louvin's niece Kathy Louvin was an executive producer.

He was born Charlie Elzer Loudermilk on July 7, 1927, in Section, Ala. One of seven children, he grew up working on the family farm in nearby Henagar, in the northeastern part of the state. John D. Loudermilk, the writer of hits like "Abilene" and "Tobacco Road," was his first cousin.

Reared on the harmonies they learned in church, Charlie and Ira Loudermilk first sang together professionally as the Radio Twins in 1942. They changed their name in 1947 to the Louvin Brothers, believing that Louvin was easier to say and spell than Loudermilk. They also began making records that year, releasing singles on several labels before finding success with Capitol in 1952, after Charlie Louvin's return from the Korean War. More than just singles artists, the Louvins also recorded a series of gospel-themed concept albums, including "Satan Is Real," its outré cover photo depicting the two men before an outsize effigy of the Devil.

The Louvin Brothers were inducted into the Country Music Hall of Fame in 2001.

Mr. Louvin is survived by his wife of 61 years, Betty Harrison Louvin, three sons, three sisters and five grandchildren.

His solo career spanned five decades, but, as he told Terry Gross, the host of National Public Radio's "Fresh Air" program, in 1996, he never got used to singing without his brother.

"When it comes time for the harmonies to come in, I will move to my left because my brother and I always used to use one microphone," he said of performing solo. "Even today, I will move over to the left to give the harmony room, knowing in my mind that there's no harmony standing on my right."

— BY BILL FRISKICS-WARREN

MILTON BABBITT

To Listen to His Music Is to Be Challenged

MAY 10, 1916 - JAN. 29, 2011

MILTON BABBITT, an influential composer, theorist and teacher who wrote music that was intensely rational and for many listeners impenetrably abstruse, died on Jan. 29 in Princeton, N.J. He was 94 and an emeritus professor of composition at Princeton University.

Mr. Babbitt, who had a lively sense of humor despite a reputation for severity that his music fostered, sometimes referred to himself as a maximalist, to stress his musical and philosophical distance from younger contemporaries like Philip Glass, Steve Reich and other Minimalist composers. It was an apt description.

Although he dabbled early in his career with theater music, his Composition for Orchestra (1940) ushered in a structurally complex, profoundly organized style that was rooted in Arnold Schoenberg's serial method.

But Mr. Babbitt expanded on Mr. Schoenberg's approach. In Mr. Schoenberg's system, a composer begins by arranging the 12 notes of the Western scale in a particular order called a tone row, or series, and bases the work on it. Mr. Babbitt was the first to use this serial ordering not only with pitches but also with dynamics, timbre, duration, registration and other elements. His methods became the basis of the "total serialism" championed in the 1950s by Pierre Boulez, Luigi Nono and other European composers.

Mr. Babbitt began exploring this path in Three Compositions for Piano (1947) and Composition for Four Instruments (1948), and adhered to it through his career. He composed prolifically for chamber ensembles and instrumental soloists and created a substantial and varied catalog of vocal works. He also composed a compact but vital group of orchestral pieces and an enduring series of works for synthesizer, often in combination with voices or acoustic instruments.

Mr. Babbitt liked to give his pieces colorful titles, often with puns ("The Joy of More Sextets," for example), and said that in selecting titles he tried to avoid both the stale and the obscure. Yet when Mr. Babbitt explained his compositional approach in essays, lectures and program notes, they could be as difficult to understand as his music. In one program note, he spoke of "models of similar, interval-preserving, registrally uninterpreted pitch-class and metrically durationally uninterpreted time-point aggregate arrays."

He often said that every note in a contemporary composition should be so thoroughly justified that the mere alteration of a tone color or a dynamic would ruin the structure. And although colleagues who worked in atonal music objected when their music was described as cerebral or academic, Mr. Babbitt embraced both terms. He came to be regarded as the standard-bearer of the ultrarational extreme in American composition.

That reputation was based in part on an article published by High Fidelity magazine in February 1958 under the title "Who Cares if You Listen?" The headline was often cited as evidence of contemporary composers' disregard for the public's sensibilities, though Mr. Babbitt objected that it had been added by an editor, without his permission. Still, the article did argue that contemporary composition was a business for specialists, on both the composing and listening ends, and that the public's objections were irrelevant.

"Why refuse to recognize the possibility that contemporary music has reached a stage long since attained by other forms of activity?" Mr. Babbitt wrote. "The time has passed when the normally well-educated man without special preparation could understand the most advanced work in, for example, mathematics, philosophy and physics. Advanced music, to the extent that it reflects the knowledge and originality of the informed composer, scarcely can be expected to appear more intelligible than these arts and sciences to the person whose musical education usually has been even less extensive than his background in other fields."

Listeners who overlooked Mr. Babbitt's philosophical abstractions and thorny analyses — who simply sat back and listened, rather than trying to understand his harmonies and structural processes — often discovered works of great expressive variety.

These range from the intense emotionality of "A Solo Requiem" (1976) to the shimmering surfaces and eerie pictorialism of "Philomel" (1964). The poetic flow of some of his solo piano works have the spirit of advanced jazz improvisations. Indeed, in his "All Set" (1957), for winds, brasses and percussion, he achieved a freely improvisatory feeling within an atonal harmonic context.

Milton Byron Babbitt was born in Philadelphia on May 10, 1916, and grew up in Jackson, Miss. He began studying the violin when he was 4 but soon switched to clarinet and saxophone. Early in his life he was attracted to jazz and theater music. He was making his own arrangements of popular songs at 7 and won a local songwriting contest at 13.

Although the music he went on to write rejected the easily assimilated tonal language of popular music, Mr. Babbitt retained a fondness for theater songs all his life and was said to have an encyclopedic knowledge of the style.

"I grew up playing every kind of music in the world, and I know more pop music from the '20s and '30s," he said in an Internet interview with the New Music Box in 2001. "It's because of where I grew up. We had to imitate Jan Garber one night; we had to imitate Jean Goldkette the next night. We heard everything from the radio; we had to do it all by ear. We took down their arrangements; we stole their arrangements; we transcribed them, approximately. We played them for a country club dance one night and for a high school dance the next."

In 1946, Mr. Babbitt tried his hand at a musical, a collaboration with Richard Koch and Richard S. Childs called "Fabulous Voyage." The work was not produced, but in 1982 Mr. Babbitt published three of its songs, which showed a firm command of the idiom and considerable charm.

Mr. Babbitt set his course toward serious avant-garde composition in 1932, when he played through the scores of some Schoenberg piano music that an uncle had brought home from Europe. At the time, Mr. Babbitt was a 16-year-old philosophy student at the University of Pennsylvania. The next year he became a composition student of Marion Bauer and Philip James at New York University, and in 1935 he began studying privately with Roger Sessions.

In 1938, Mr. Sessions invited Mr. Babbitt to join the Princeton composition faculty, and Mr. Babbitt succeeded him as the William Shubael Conant Professor of Music in 1965. Mr. Babbitt was also on the faculty of several music schools, including Juilliard and the New England Conservatory in Boston. A series of lectures he gave at the University of Wisconsin was published as "Words About Music" in 1987. His articles about music were published as "The Collected Essays of Milton Babbitt" in 2003.

His students included Mario Davidovsky and John Eaton, who have followed in Mr. Babbitt's atonal path (although Mr. Eaton broke away), and the theater composer Stephen Sondheim.

During World War II, Mr. Babbitt taught mathematics at Princeton and undertook secret research in Washington. His extended form of serialism evolved during these years. But after the war he pursued a split musical path, exploring his rigorous serial style in his abstract concert works while completing "Fabulous Voyage" and a film score, "Into the Good Ground" (1949).

In the 1950s Mr. Babbitt was hired as a consultant by RCA, which was developing the most sophisticated electronic-music instrument of the time, the Mark II synthesizer. The Mark II became the centerpiece of the new Columbia-Princeton Electronic Music Center in 1959, and Mr. Babbitt was one of its first directors.

His earliest electronic pieces, Composition for Synthesizer (1961) and Ensembles for Synthesizer (1964), were as intensely organized as his instrumental music had been. He saw the synthesizer as a kind of liberation from the physical limitations of living performers.

"The medium provides a kind of full satisfaction for the composer," he said in an interview with The New York Times in 1969. "I love going to the studio with my work in my head, realizing it while I am there and walking out with the tape under my arm. I can then send it anywhere in the world, knowing exactly how it will sound."

The early synthesizer pieces have become classics, but Mr. Babbitt quickly moved forward, writing works in which electronic soundtracks accompanied live performers. Particularly striking are the vocal works "Vision and Prayer," "Philomel" and "Reflections," for piano and tape. He stopped composing music with an electronic component in 1976, after the Columbia-Princeton studio was vandalized and it was decided that restoring it would be too expensive.

Many of Mr. Babbitt's works have been recorded, and he has always had the loyalty of performers — the soprano Bethany Beardslee and the pianist Robert Miller to name two — willing to devote the effort required to render his music sensibly. In the 1970s and '80s, a generation of young instrumentalists also became his eloquent champions, among them the pianists Robert Taub and the guitarist David Starobin.

Mr. Babbitt's orchestral music is so complex that both the New York Philharmonic, in 1969, and the Philadelphia Orchestra, in 1989,

MAXIMALIST: Mr. Babbitt's music, structurally complex and highly expressive, stood apart from that of his Minimalist contemporaries like Philip Glass.

postponed premieres when the available rehearsal time proved insufficient. He did, however, have champions among top-flight conductors, the most notable being James Levine, who in 1967, at 24, led the premiere of Mr. Babbitt's "Correspondences."

Mr. Babbitt, who lived in Princeton, received a special Pulitzer citation for his life's work in 1982, and in 1986 he was awarded a $300,000 MacArthur Fellowship. He was elected to the National Institute of Arts and Letters in 1965.

Mr. Babbitt's wife, Sylvia, died in 2005. He is survived by a daughter and two grandchildren.

— *By Allan Kozinn*

JOHN BARRY

James Bond's Composer

NOV. 3, 1933 - JAN. 31, 2011

JOHN BARRY, whose bold, jazzy scores for "From Russia With Love," "Goldfinger" and nine other James Bond movies put a musical stamp on one of the most successful film franchises of all time, and who won five Academy Awards as a composer for "Born Free" and other films, died on Jan. 31 in New York. He was 77.

Mr. Barry scored dozens of films, big and small, that called for music to express a wide variety of human emotions and dramatic situations. He composed taut, pulsing, jittery music for the espionage thrillers "The Ipcress File" (1965) and "The Quiller Memorandum" (1966), delivered a sultry sound for the noirish "Body Heat" (1981) and established an offbeat intimacy for "Midnight Cowboy" (1969), with its haunting harmonica theme.

"I like to score the inner feelings of a character — get into their shoes in an imaginative way and take the audience there and enlighten them in a poetic rather than realistic way," he told The New York Times in 2000.

His throbbing, expansive score for "Born Free" (1966) earned him two Oscars, one for best score and the other for best song.

Although he won Oscars for his work on "The Lion in Winter" (1968), "Out of Africa" (1985) and "Dances With Wolves" (1990), he was known first and foremost as the resident composer for most of the Bond films.

The musical template he established was as much a part of the films as Bond's double entendres, Q's gadgetry and Miss Moneypenny's flirtatious repartee. The films began with a catchy song performed by a pop star, its themes picked up and reprised throughout the movie, most effectively when Bond moved from one exotic location to the next or prepared to execute a choice bit of spycraft.

His role in composing the most famous Bond music of all, the theme that has been a signature of the films since "Dr. No" (1962), remains unclear. When he took credit for the theme in an interview with The Sunday Times of London in 1997, the original composer hired for the film, Monty Norman, successfully sued the newspaper for libel, asserting that Mr. Barry had done only the orchestration.

After being called in as a kind of musical special agent for "Dr. No" by the film's producers, Mr. Barry went on to score "From Russia With Love" (1963), "Goldfinger" (1964), "Thunderball" (1965), "You Only Live Twice" (1967), "On Her Majesty's Secret Service" (1969), "Diamonds Are Forever" (1971), "The Man With the Golden Gun" (1974), "Moonraker" (1979), "Octopussy" (1983), "A View to a

Kill" (1985) and "The Living Daylights" (1987).

John Barry Prendergast was born on Nov. 3, 1933, in York, England. His father ran a chain of movie theaters in the north of England, and the boy became entranced by film music early on. Mr. Barry credited the film composers Max Steiner, Erich Korngold and Bernard Herrmann as important influences, as well as Stan Kenton's big band.

"I think the genesis of the Bond sound was most certainly that Kentonesque sharp attack," he told Film Score Monthly in 1996, calling it a brassy wall of sound with notes hitting extreme highs and lows.

He studied piano and took instruction in composition with Francis Jackson, the organist and composer at York Minster. He later played the trumpet with dance bands and, during his military service, with an Army band.

BARRY, JOHN BARRY: His bold, jazzy scores put a musical stamp on the James Bond franchise.

In 1957 he formed the John Barry Seven, a rock 'n' roll band styled after the popular guitar-based instrumental group the Ventures. His group recorded several instrumental hits as well as "Hit and Miss," the theme song for the popular television program "Juke Box Jury."

The band reached its widest audience as the backup group for Adam Faith on the BBC pop show "Drumbeat." When the singer was cast in the 1959 film "Beat Girl," released in the United States as "Wild for Kicks," and the Peter Sellers film "Never Let Go," Mr. Barry came along to write the music.

He quickly found himself in demand at a time when British directors looked to jazz and pop music to create a cool image for their films. He was the composer for "Man in the Middle" (1963), "The Wrong Box" (1966), "The L-Shaped Room" (1962) and "Zulu" (1964).

He inched closer to the center of the British New Wave when he married the actress Jane Birkin in 1965, inspiring Newsweek to call him the man "with the E-type Jag and the E-type wife."

It was his second marriage. He is survived by his fourth wife, Laurie, four children and five grandchildren.

The origins of the James Bond theme are disputed. Mr. Norman, who claimed credit for composing it, traced it to a musical passage from "Bad Sign, Good Sign," a song he had written for a musical version of the V. S. Naipaul novel "A House for Mr. Biswas." With a few adjustments, he said, it became the theme to "Dr. No." The John Barry Orchestra, an expanded version of Mr. Barry's group, performed the theme, with Vic Flick supplying the twangy, Duane Eddy-style guitar sound.

Mr. Barry testified in court in 2001 that he had entered into a secret agreement with the film's producers to write the theme for a flat fee, with Mr. Norman, whose authorship claims he called "absolute nonsense," retaining the credit. He adopted a more circumspect tone after the libel judgment in 2001.

When he was not scoring the Bond movies, Mr. Barry composed the music for films like "The Tamarind Seed" (1974), "The Day of the Locust" (1975), "Robin and Marian" (1976), "The Deep" (1977), "The Cotton Club" (1984), "Peggy Sue Got Married" (1986), "Jagged Edge" (1985) and, perhaps least of all, "Howard the Duck" (1986). He also wrote the theme for the 1970s television series "The Persuaders," with Tony Curtis and Roger Moore.

His scores for "Mary, Queen of Scots" (1971) and "Chaplin" (1992) were nominated for Academy Awards.

Mr. Barry decided to quit the Bond game while the going was still good. "I gave up after 'The Living Daylights' in 1987," he told The Sunday Express of London in 2006. "I'd exhausted all my ideas, rung all the changes possible. It was a formula that had run its course. The best had been done as far as I was concerned."

— *By William Grimes*

RENÉ VERDON

The Flavor of France in 'Camelot'

JUNE 29, 1924 - FEB. 2, 2011

René Verdon, whose position as the White House chef during the Kennedy administration helped him project the allure of classic French cuisine to the American public, died on Feb. 2 in San Francisco. He was 86.

Mr. Verdon brought French culinary flair to the White House, long a headquarters for dull institutional cooking often supplied by outside caterers. Thanks in large part to Jacqueline Kennedy, a walking advertisement for French style, it was a time when the American public was highly receptive to all messages emanating from Paris.

French cooking, in particular, would soon become a passion for home cooks. Just a few months after Mr. Verdon took up his White House post, Julia Child, Louisette Bertholle and Simone Beck published the first volume of "Mastering the Art of French Cooking." Mr. Verdon took full advantage of his platform, elevating standards at the White House overnight and contributing in no small part to the shimmering atmosphere of Camelot.

He shocked Americans used to canned vegetables and iceberg lettuce by tending his own vegetables on the White House roof and arranging for the White House garden designer to plant herbs in the flowerbeds of the East Garden.

THE CHEF: Mr. Verdon at Le Trianon in 1972.

His first official meal at the White House, a lunch for Prime Minister Harold Macmillan of Britain and 16 guests on April 5, 1961, set the new tone: trout in Chablis and sauce Vincent, beef filet au jus and artichoke bottoms Beaucaire, and a dessert he dubbed désir d'avril, or "April Desire," a meringue shell filled with raspberries and chocolate.

The message was clear. No longer would a meal at the White House be a painful duty.

The fall of France came abruptly. Under Lyndon B. Johnson, a "food coordinator" from Texas was hired to cut costs in the White House kitchen. Mr. Verdon was instructed to use frozen vegetables and, in a concession to the simpler tastes of the Johnsons, to prepare, among other delights, a cold garbanzo bean puree, a dish he said was terrible even when it was hot.

"The Johnsons liked to have certain foods, but I think people coming to the White House are not expecting hamburgers, chili con queso or spareribs," he told The New York Times in 1985. "Those foods belong to the land, they do not belong in the dining room."

He resigned his post at the end of 1965 and took a job demonstrating kitchen appliances for Hamilton Beach before moving to California and opening Le Trianon, one of San Francisco's most revered French restaurants in the 1970s and 1980s. His wife, Yvette, said he died of leukemia. He is also survived by a brother.

René Verdon was born on June 29, 1924, in Pouzauges, a village in the Vendée region of western France. His family owned a bakery and pastry shop, and to outdo his two older brothers — one a baker, the other a pâtissier — he decided to become a chef.

He began his apprenticeship at 13 in Nantes and went on to train at Le Berkeley and other restaurants in Paris and at the Hotel Normandy in Deauville. After working on the staff of the

Liberté, operated by the French Line, he immigrated to the United States in 1958. In New York, he worked at the Essex House and at the Hotel Carlyle, where the Kennedy family maintained a penthouse suite.

Mr. Verdon was recommended to Mrs. Kennedy by Roger Fessaguet, the chef at La Caravelle in Manhattan, and his partners. The restaurant was a favorite of the Kennedy family, and Mrs. Kennedy hired Mr. Verdon temporarily to handle the onslaught of official luncheons and dinners for foreign visitors after the inauguration in January 1961. He was hired permanently — at a salary of $10,000 a year plus room and board — a few months later.

He published several cookbooks, including "The White House Chef Cookbook" (1968) and "René Verdon's French Cooking for the American Table" (1974).

— *By William Grimes*

MARIA SCHNEIDER

An Early Mark With 'Last Tango'

MARCH 27, 1952 - FEB. 3, 2011

Maria Schneider, the French actress whose sex scenes with Marlon Brando in "Last Tango in Paris" set a new standard for explicitness on screen, died on Feb. 3 in Paris. She was 58.

A spokesman for her agency, Act 1, said she had died after a long illness but provided no other details.

The baby-faced, voluptuous Ms. Schneider was only 19 when the Italian director Bernardo Bertolucci chose her for the role of the free-spirited, mysterious Jeanne in "Last Tango." She seemed, he said in explaining the choice, "like a Lolita, but more perverse." The part was originally intended for Dominique Sanda, who dropped out after becoming pregnant.

In the film, Jeanne enters into a brief but torrid affair with a recently widowed American businessman, played by Mr. Brando. Their erotically charged relationship, played out in an empty apartment near the Bir-Hakeim Bridge in Paris, shocked audiences on the film's release in 1972, especially a scene in which Mr. Brando pins Ms. Schneider to the floor and, taking a stick of butter, seems to perform anal intercourse. The Motion Picture Association of America gave the film an X rating.

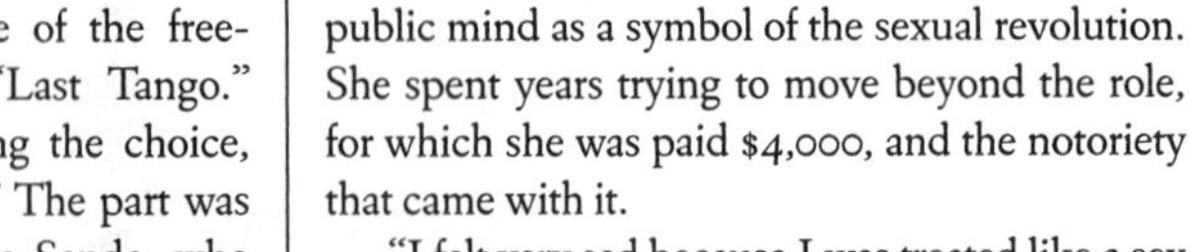

"Last Tango" fixed Ms. Schneider in the public mind as a symbol of the sexual revolution. She spent years trying to move beyond the role, for which she was paid $4,000, and the notoriety that came with it.

"I felt very sad because I was treated like a sex symbol," she told The Daily Mail of London in 2007. "I wanted to be recognized as an actress, and the whole scandal and aftermath of the film turned me a little crazy and I had a breakdown. Now, though, I can look at the film and like my work in it."

X-RATED: Ms. Schneider and Mr. Brando in "Last Tango."

The famous scene, she said, was not in the script and made it into the film only at Mr. Brando's insistence. "I felt humiliated, and to be honest I felt a little raped, both by Marlon and by Bertolucci," she said. "After the scene, Marlon didn't console me or apologize. Thankfully, there was just one take."

Ms. Schneider later appeared opposite Jack Nicholson in "The Passenger" (1975), directed by Michelangelo Antonioni, playing an architecture student known simply as the Girl.

Although she went on to work with important directors like René Clément in "The Baby Sitter" (1975) and Jacques Rivette in "Merry-Go-Round" (1981), her film career declined after the mid-1970s, in part because of a turbulent personal life that included drug abuse, at least one suicide attempt and messy affairs with both men and women.

She walked off the set of "The Baby Sitter" (also known as "Scar Tissue") in Rome and checked herself into a mental hospital to be with her girlfriend at the time. In 1977 she was cast as Conchita in Luis Buñuel's "That Obscure Object of Desire" but left the film after arguing with Mr. Buñuel. Her part was assigned to two actresses, Ángela Molina and Carole Bouquet.

Maria Schneider was born on March 27, 1952, in Paris, the daughter of Marie-Christine Schneider, a Romanian-born model, and the prominent actor Daniel Gélin. She did not meet her father, who refused to acknowledge her, until she was in her teens. She was reared by her mother in a town near the German border and left home at 15 for Paris, where she scratched out a living as a film extra and a model.

Brigitte Bardot, who had worked with Mr. Gélin on several films, was appalled at the girl's situation and intervened, giving her a room in her house and helping find her an agent with William Morris. Ms. Schneider played small parts in "The Christmas Tree," with William Holden and Virna Lisi, and "The Love Mates," with Alain Delon, before being cast in "Last Tango."

Her more recent films included Cyril Collard's "Savage Nights" (1992), Franco Zeffirelli's "Jane Eyre" (1996), Bertrand Blier's "Actors" (2000) and Josiane Balasko's "Cliente" (2008).

"I was too young to know better," she said of "Last Tango" in her Daily Mail interview. "Marlon later said that he felt manipulated, and he was Marlon Brando, so you can imagine how I felt. People thought I was like the girl in the movie, but that wasn't me."

— *By William Grimes*

LENA NYMAN

Shock and Censorship With 'I Am Curious'

MAY 23, 1944 - FEB. 4, 2011

Lena Nyman, the Swedish actress whose performance in the sexually explicit movie "I Am Curious (Yellow)" raised the hackles of censors in the 1960s and helped turn the film into a box office bonanza, died on Feb. 4 in Stockholm. She was 66.

Ms. Nyman went on to a distinguished career after "I Am Curious." In all, she had roles in more than 50 Swedish films and television shows, notably Ingmar Bergman's "Autumn Sonata" in 1978, in which she played the mentally impaired sister to Liv Ullmann's accomplished pianist.

But it was in "I Am Curious" that she made perhaps her most indelible mark. In the film, Ms. Nyman portrayed an intensely serious young woman, also named Lena, who wanders Stockholm as an amateur reporter, raising questions about mores that seem to her to have calcified Swedish life. She asks people if Sweden really is a classless society and badgers union officials about why the labor movement is so conservative.

Searching for her own sexual identity, Lena has a stormy affair with Borje (played by Borje Ahlstedt), after she meets him in a store. They have sex in a tree and on a balustrade in front of the royal palace, among other places.

BOX-OFFICE HIT: A racy film made Ms. Nyman a sensation.

Produced for $160,000 by the Swedish filmmaker Vilgot Sjoman, "I Am Curious (Yellow)" alarmed the United States Customs Service, which in January 1968 banned it from the country as obscene. That November a federal appeals court ruled that the movie was protected by the First Amendment, resulting in its release in March 1969. The movie made $5 million in six months and remained the most financially successful foreign film in the United States for 23 years.

If "the cavemen of the U.S. Customs office" hadn't seized "I Am Curious (Yellow)," Newsweek wrote in March 1969, "there probably wouldn't be thousands upon thousands of people standing on lines today for the privilege of paying $4.50 to see the movie."

Reviews were mixed. "Miss Nyman's performance is monotonous, and her only redeeming vice is her anger, which seems genuine and illimitable," Joseph Morgenstern wrote in Newsweek. In The New York Times, Vincent Canby wrote, "Lena Nyman and Borje Ahlstedt are good, in addition to being perfectly presentable, in the central roles." He added that the sex scenes were "so unaffectedly frank as to be nonpornographic."

In Sweden some critics saw the film as offensive. Because of her full figure, others called Ms. Nyman fat. That did not deter her. In 1968 she again played Lena in "I Am Curious (Blue)," almost a reprise of "Yellow." (The Swedish flag is blue and yellow.)

Ms. Nyman, who was born on May 23, 1944, in Stockholm, had been a student at the National Theater School of Sweden when Mr. Sjoman chose her for "I Am Curious." Information on survivors was not available. The British newspaper The Guardian said she had been married twice, briefly each time. Her manager, Mats Nilemar, said only that she died after a long illness.

Ms. Nyman was stunned by the reaction in her homeland to the "Curious" films, she told The Times in 1974. "You know," she said, "some people get shocked about sex. I was shocked that everyone was so shocked. It was such a quarrel about that movie. Wow!

"You could believe nobody in Sweden had ever seen a naked man or woman."

— *By Dennis Hevesi*

J. PAUL GETTY III

A Kidnapping and a Gruesome Price

NOV. 4, 1956 - FEB. 5, 2011

J. Paul Getty III, who was a grandson of the oil baron once believed to be the richest man in the world and who achieved gruesome notoriety in 1973 when Italian kidnappers severed one of his ears, died on Feb. 5 at his home near London. He was 54.

His son, the actor Balthazar Getty, confirmed the death in a statement by e-mail from one of his agents. Mr. Getty had been wheelchair-bound since 1981, when a drug overdose led to a stroke that left him severely paralyzed, unable to speak and partly blind.

At the time of his abduction, Mr. Getty was just 16 and living on his own in Rome, where his father, J. Paul Getty II, had helped oversee the family's Italian business interests.

Expelled from a private school, the young Mr. Getty was living a bohemian life, frequenting nightclubs, taking part in left-wing demonstrations and reportedly earning a living making jewelry, selling paintings and acting as an extra in movies. He disappeared on July 10, 1973, and two days later his mother, Gail Harris, received a ransom request. No longer married, she said she had little money.

MAIMED, BUT FREE: Mr. Getty after his kidnappers' arrest. His abduction lasted five months.

"Get it from London," she was reportedly told over the phone, a reference either to her former father-in-law, J. Paul Getty, the billionaire founder of the Getty Oil Company, or her former husband, who lived in England.

The ransom demand was for about $17 million, but the police were initially skeptical of the kidnapping claim, even after Ms. Harris received a plaintive letter from her son and a phone call in which a man saying he was a kidnapper offered to send her a severed finger as proof that the boy was still alive. Investigators suspected a hoax or an attempt by the young Mr. Getty to squeeze money out of his notoriously miserly relatives.

"Dear Mummy," his note began, "Since Monday I have fallen into the hands of kidnappers. Don't let me be killed."

The eldest Mr. Getty refused to pay the kidnappers anything, declaring that he had 14 grandchildren and that "If I pay one penny now, I'll have 14 kidnapped grandchildren." His son said he could not afford to pay.

Three months after the abduction, the kidnappers, who turned out to be Calabrian bandits with a possible connection to organized crime, cut off Mr. Getty's right ear and mailed it, along with a lock of his hair, to a Roman newspaper. Photographs of the maimed Mr. Getty, along with a letter in which he pleaded with his family to pay his captors, subsequently appeared in another newspaper.

The kidnappers eventually reduced their demand to about $3 million. According to the 1995 book "Painfully Rich: The Outrageous Fortune and Misfortunes of the Heirs of J. Paul Getty," by John Pearson, the eldest Mr. Getty paid $2.2 million, the maximum that his accountants said would be tax deductible. The boy's father paid the rest, though he had to borrow it from his father at 4 percent interest.

The teenager, malnourished, bruised and missing an ear, was released on Dec. 15. He was found at an abandoned service station, shivering in a driving rainstorm. Nine men were eventually arrested. Two were convicted and sent to prison; the others, including the man prosecutors said was the head of the Calabrian Mafia and the mastermind behind the abduction, were acquitted for lack of evidence.

The year after his release, Mr. Getty married a German photographer — her name has been variously reported as Gisela Zacher and Martine Zacher — and lived with her in New York, where they consorted with the art crowd of Andy Warhol. Mr. Getty became a drug user and a heavy drinker. His grandfather had died in 1976, and after his overdose Mr. Getty sued his father for $28,000 a month to pay for his medical needs.

Mr. Getty's marriage ended in divorce. Besides his son, survivors include his mother, who cared for him after his stroke; a brother; two sisters; a stepdaughter; and six grandchildren and stepgrandchildren.

Some time after Mr. Getty's release, his mother suggested that he call his grandfather to thank him for paying the ransom. Mr. Getty did. His grandfather declined to come to the phone.

— *By Bruce Weber*

MARY CLEERE HARAN

Cabaret Singer With a Big-Band Style

MAY 13, 1952 - FEB. 5, 2011

MARY CLEERE HARAN, a classic popular singer and writer much admired for her cabaret shows celebrating the American songbook, died on Feb. 5 in Deerfield Beach, Fla., two days after a cycling accident. She was 58 and living in Florida, having taken a break from a career that saw her perform in every major New York supper club.

Ms. Haran had just dropped off her résumé at a hotel when she was struck from the side by a car coming out of a driveway, according to a friend. She never regained consciousness at a hospital.

Ms. Haran was a singer and recording artist of remarkable purity whose simple unaffected pop-jazz style echoed big band singers of the 1940s, most notably Ella Fitzgerald. Swinging lightly, she eschewed melodramatic posturing to deliver deep, thoughtful interpretations of standards by Rodgers and Hart, Harry Warren, the Gershwins and others. She had a special love of the wry, wistful lyrics of Hart, to whom she paid tribute in two different shows.

Her stage personality reflected the upbeat, can-do spirit (with zany screwball touches) and subdued glamour of long-ago film stars like Myrna Loy, Irene Dunne and Claudette Colbert. Much as she admired those actresses, her attitude was not that of a besotted fan but of a modern woman with a feminist sensibility who refracted the past through the present.

Comparing Lorenz Hart's lyrics with Richard Rodgers to Oscar Hammerstein's in her 2002 show "Falling in Love With Love: The Rodgers and Hart Story," she remarked that Mr. Hammerstein's lyrics told us what we "*should* feel" versus Mr. Hart's, which told us what "we *did* feel."

A particular singing idol was Doris Day, whom she interviewed in a PBS documentary, "Doris Day: Sentimental Journey," which she also wrote and co-produced. She contributed to the PBS documentaries "Remembering Bing," "Irving Berlin's America," "When We Were Young: The Lives of Child Movie Stars" and "Satchmo."

ECHOING THE PAST: In her shows, Ms. Haran celebrated legends of the American songbook, notably Doris Day.

Doris Day was the subject of Ms. Haran's acclaimed 2007 show at Feinstein's at the Loews Regency, where she made her last major appearance in late 2009 with a Johnny Mercer tribute.

The second of eight children in an Irish Catholic family, Ms. Haran was the daughter of a professor of theater and film at San Francisco City College and grew up enthralled by the music and movies of the 1930s and '40s. As a teenager she was a champion Irish step dancer.

She moved to New York in the 1970s and made her theatrical debut as a band singer in "The 1940s Radio Hour" and appeared Off Broadway in "Manhattan Music," "Swingtime Canteen" and "Heebie Jeebies." On television, she had a recurring role as a nightclub singer in the series "100 Centre Street."

She married twice. A son from her second marriage, to the writer and director Joe Gilford, whom she divorced, survives her, as do six siblings, an uncle, an aunt, a stepmother and several nieces and nephews.

Ms. Haran made her recording debut in 1992 on Columbia with "There's a Small Hotel: Live at the Algonquin." Later albums included "This Funny World: Mary Cleere Haran Sings Lyrics by Hart" (1995), "This Heart of Mine: Classic Movie Songs of the Forties" (1994), "Pennies From Heaven: Movie Songs From the Depression Era" (1998), "The Memory of All That: Gershwin on Broadway and in Hollywood" (1999) and "Crazy Rhythm: Manhattan in the '20s" (2002).

Ms. Haran made her Manhattan cabaret debut in 1985 at Don't Tell Mama. Pianists who accompanied her included Bill Charlap, Fred Hersch and Tedd Firth, but her most frequent partner was Richard Rodney Bennett.

For one of her most popular shows, "An Affair to Remember," in 1994, Ms. Haran visited the 1950s to deconstruct the decade's cultural iconography and affectionately chastise its films for their lack of humor. She joked that she preferred Cole Porter musicals to the heavier fare of Rodgers and Hammerstein. Mr. Porter's, she said, celebrated "fun, sex and money as the most important things in life."

— *By Stephen Holden*

FEB

BRIAN JACQUES

Once Upon a Time There Was a Milkman

JUNE 15, 1939 - FEB. 5, 2011

HE WAS A LONGSHOREMAN AND A LONG-HAUL TRUCKER; a merchant mariner and a railway fireman; a boxer, a bus driver and a British bobby. But it wasn't until he became a milkman that Brian Jacques found his métier.

Nearing midlife, Mr. Jacques (pronounced "Jakes") took a job driving a milk truck in Liverpool, where he was born and lived to the end of his life. On his route was the Royal School for the Blind.

Invited in for a nice cup of tea one day, he volunteered to read to the students. Over time, he grew dissatisfied with the books available — too much adolescent angst, he later said — and vowed to write his own.

He wrote what he called "a proper story," brimming with battle and gallantry. Titled "Redwall" and published in 1986, it became the first installment in what is now a best-selling 21-volume children's fantasy series.

Mr. Jacques died on Feb. 5 in Liverpool, at 71. The death was announced by his North American publisher, Penguin Young Readers Group. The Liverpool newspapers reported that he died after emergency heart surgery.

Set at the pastoral Redwall Abbey in the misty English past, the books are written for children 8 and up. They center on the triumph of good over evil — specifically the hard-won victories of the abbey's resident mice, badgers and squirrels over the marauding rats, weasels and stoats that perennially threaten their peaceable kingdom.

There are quests and riddles; cunning treachery and chivalric derring-do; and, in a feature that became a hallmark of the series, groaning boards spread with sumptuous feasts, lovingly described.

Published in more than 20 countries, the Redwall books have sold more than 20 million copies and inspired an animated series, broadcast on PBS in 2001.

Later titles in the series include "Mossflower" (1988), "Martin the Warrior" (1993), "Doomwyte" (2008) and "The Sable Quean," published in 2010.

A truck driver's son, Brian Jacques was born on June 15, 1939, and reared by the Liverpool docks. At 10, after writing a fine short story about a bird and a crocodile, he was caned by his teacher, who thought it too good to have been the work of a child.

He left school at 15 to work as a merchant seaman, the first in a decades'-long series of blue-collar jobs.

MIDLIFE SUCCESS: Mr. Jacques's "Redwall" children's fantasy series sold millions.

Mr. Jacques's other books include "The Redwall Cookbook" (2005), a collection of recipes for the dishes featured in the series; his unstinting descriptions of food, he often said, sprang from childhood memories of wartime rationing.

He wrote several non-Redwall books, including a series about the Flying Dutchman, the storied ghost ship.

Mr. Jacques's survivors include his wife, Maureen; two sons; and a brother.

His 22nd Redwall book, "The Rogue Crew," was published in May 2011.

As successful as he became, Mr. Jacques could never quite countenance a life in which labor meant sitting in his garden, under an apple tree, with a typewriter.

"I have a working-class ethic," he told The New York Times in 2001. "I get up in the morning, and I still feel guilty about being a famous author."

— *By Margalit Fox*

KEN OLSEN

A Trailblazer in a New World of Computers

FEB. 20, 1926 - FEB. 6, 2011

Ken Olsen, who helped reshape the computer industry as a founder of the Digital Equipment Corporation, at one time the world's second-largest computer company, died on Feb. 6. He was 84.

Mr. Olsen had recently lived with a daughter in Indiana and had been a longtime resident of Lincoln, Mass.

Mr. Olsen, who was proclaimed "America's most successful entrepreneur" by Fortune magazine in 1986, built Digital on $70,000 in seed money, founding it with a partner in 1957 in the small Boston suburb of Maynard, Mass. With Mr. Olsen as its chief executive, it grew to employ more than 120,000 people at operations in more than 95 countries, surpassed in size only by I.B.M.

At its peak, in the late 1980s, Digital had $14 billion in sales and ranked among the most profitable companies in the nation. But its fortunes declined after Digital began missing out on some critical market shifts, particularly toward the personal computer. Mr. Olsen was criticized as autocratic and resistant to new trends. "The personal computer will fall flat on its face in business," he said at one point. And in July 1992, the company's board forced him to resign.

Six years later, Digital, or DEC, as the company was known, was acquired by the Compaq Computer Corporation for $9.6 billion.

But for 35 years the enigmatic Mr. Olsen oversaw an expanding technology giant that produced some of the computer industry's breakthrough ideas.

In a 2006 tribute, Bill Gates, the Microsoft co-founder, called Mr. Olsen "one of the true pioneers of computing," adding, "He was also a major influence on my life."

In a tribute to him in 2006, Bill Gates, the Microsoft co-founder, called Mr. Olsen "one of the true pioneers of computing," adding, "He was also a major influence on my life."

Mr. Gates traced his interest in software to his first use of a DEC computer as a 13-year-old. He and Microsoft's other founder, Paul Allen, created their first personal computer software on a DEC PDP-10 computer.

In the 1960s, Digital built small, powerful and elegantly designed "minicomputers," which formed the basis of a lucrative new segment of the computer marketplace. Though hardly "mini" by today's standards, the computer became a favorite alternative to the giant, multimillion-dollar mainframe computers sold by I.B.M. to large corporate customers. The minicomputer found a market in research laboratories, engineering companies and other professions requiring heavy computer use.

In time, several minicomputer companies sprang up around Digital and thrived, forming the foundation of the Route 128 technology corridor near Boston.

Digital also spawned a generation of computing talent, lured by an open corporate culture that fostered a free flow of ideas. A frequently rumpled outdoorsman who preferred flannel shirts to business suits, Mr. Olsen, a brawny man with piercing blue eyes, shunned publicity and ran the company as a large, sometimes contentious family.

Many within the industry assumed that Digital, with its stellar engineering staff, would be the logical company to usher in the age of personal computers, but Mr. Olsen was openly skeptical of the desktop machines. He thought of them as "toys" used for playing video games.

Still, most people in the industry say Mr. Olsen's legacy is secure. "Ken Olsen is the father of the second generation of computing," said George Colony, who is chief executive of Forrester Research and a longtime industry watcher, "and that makes him one of the major figures in the history of this business."

Kenneth Harry Olsen was born in Bridgeport, Conn., on Feb. 20, 1926, and grew up with his three siblings in nearby Stratford. His parents, Oswald and Elizabeth Svea Olsen, were children of Norwegian immigrants.

Mr. Olsen and his younger brother Stan pursued their passion for electronics in the basement of their Stratford home, inventing gadgets and repairing broken radios. After a stint in the Navy at the end of World War II, Mr. Olsen headed to the Massachusetts Institute of Technology, where he received bachelor's and master's degrees in electrical engineering. He took a job at M.I.T.'s new Lincoln Laboratory in 1950 and worked under Jay Forrester, who was doing pioneering work in interactive computing.

In 1957, itching to leave academia, Mr. Olsen, then 31, recruited a Lincoln Lab colleague, Harlan Anderson, to help him start a company. For financing they turned to Georges F. Doriot, a renowned Harvard Business School professor and venture capitalist. According to Mr. Colony, Digital became the first successful venture-backed company in the computer industry. Mr. Anderson left the company shortly afterward, leaving Mr. Olsen to put his stamp on it for more than 30 years.

In Digital's often confusing management structure, Mr. Olsen was the dominant figure who hired smart people, gave them responsibility and expected them "to perform as adults," said Edgar Schein, who taught organizational behavior at M.I.T. and consulted with Mr. Olsen for 25 years. "Lo and behold," he said, "they performed magnificently."

One crucial employee was Gordon Bell, a DEC vice president and the technical brains behind many of Digital's most successful machines. "All the alumni think of Digital fondly and remember it as a great place to work," said Mr. Bell, who went on to become a principal researcher at Microsoft.

After he left Digital, Mr. Olsen began another start-up, Advanced Modular Solutions, but it eventually failed. In retirement he helped found the Ken Olsen Science Center at Gordon College, a Christian school in Wenham, Mass., where an archive of his papers and Digital's history is housed. His family announced his death through the college.

Mr. Olsen's wife of 59 years, Eeva-Liisa Aulikki Olsen, died in March 2009. A son also died. Mr. Olsen's survivors include another son, a daughter, five grandchildren and his brother Stan.

— *By Glenn Rifkin*

MARIA V. ALTMANN

A Quest to Recover What the Nazis Stole

FEB. 18, 1916 - FEB. 7, 2011

Maria V. Altmann, a Jewish refugee who in her 80s waged a successful legal battle all the way to the United States Supreme Court to force the Austrian government to return paintings by Gustav Klimt that had been seized from her family by the Nazis, died on Feb. 7 at her home in Los Angeles. She was 94.

For more than half a century, five paintings once owned by Ms. Altmann's uncle, Ferdinand Bloch-Bauer — two portraits of his wife, Adele, and three landscapes — had hung in Austrian museums, most recently the Austrian Gallery in Vienna.

All had been seized, along with a large porcelain collection and a sugar refinery, after the Nazi annexation of Austria in 1938. After the war, the Austrian government kept the paintings, on the grounds that Adele, who died in 1925, required in her will that Ferdinand donate the paintings to the state museum after his death, which took place in 1945.

In so doing, the government disregarded the fact that his will had left his estate to his nieces and nephews, including Ms. Altmann, and ignored Adele's less than emphatic language: "I kindly ask my husband."

The most celebrated of the paintings, "Portrait of Adele Bloch-Bauer I," was a commissioned work painted in 1907. It shows a sloe-eyed, elegantly coiffed beauty seated against a gold background in a resplendent gold dress. In a second portrait, painted in pastel tones five years later, Adele stands facing forward, wearing an enormous broad-brimmed hat and a close-fitting white dress.

In 1998, Ms. Altmann became aware of documents in the Austrian government archives uncovered by Hubertus Czernin, a journalist, who had helped reveal the Nazi background of Kurt

Waldheim, the former secretary general of the United Nations. In a series of exposés, Mr. Czernin had also described the nefarious practice under which the Austrian government returned certain looted artworks only if the owners agreed to sign away their rights to other seized art.

FAMILY MATTER: Ms. Altmann with a reproduction of Klimt's "Portrait of Adele Bloch-Bauer I," depicting her uncle's wife. The original, seized in 1938, was recovered and sold for $135 million.

Under pressure to reexamine its Nazi past, the government passed a law in 1998 nullifying such agreements, and the ministry of culture opened its archives to researchers for the first time. Mr. Czernin, examining records at the Austrian Gallery, concluded that Ferdinand Bloch-Bauer had not donated the Klimt paintings to the museum.

"I had never even thought of taking the paintings away," Ms. Altmann told The Daily Telegraph of London in 2007. "I was under the impression that they were theirs."

She hired a lawyer, E. Randol Schoenberg, a friend and the grandson of two Viennese composers, Arnold Schoenberg and Eric Zeisl. Together, the two pursued what most legal experts regarded as a long-shot case.

They filed a claim with a panel commissioned by the Culture Ministry, which in 1999 returned 16 Klimt drawings of Adele Bloch-Bauer and 19 sets of porcelain, but none of the Klimt paintings.

In 2000, balking at the exorbitant expense of pursuing the case in Austria, where costs are calibrated according to the value of the assets at issue, they successfully filed suit in California against the Austrian government, which appealed the ruling.

Ms. Altmann and Mr. Schoenberg won appeals all the way to the Supreme Court, which ruled in 2004 that Ms. Altmann had the right to pursue her claim under the Foreign Sovereign Immunities Act, even though the act had not been passed until 1976.

Mr. Schoenberg, taking a calculated risk, then submitted the case to binding arbitration in Austria and convinced a three-judge panel that the wording of Adele's will was a request, not a command. In January 2006 the panel awarded Ms. Altmann ownership of the five paintings.

With money provided by the businessman and philanthropist Ronald S. Lauder, the Neue Galerie in Manhattan bought the earlier portrait of Adele for $135 million. At the time, it was the largest sum ever paid for a painting. The four other paintings were auctioned by Christie's for $192.7 million and went into private collections.

In 2006, when the Klimts arrived in Los Angeles for an exhibition at the Los Angeles County Museum of Art, Ms. Altmann told The New York Times, "I'm a person of great perseverance."

Maria Viktoria Bloch-Bauer was born on Feb. 18, 1916, in Vienna. The family was wealthy and her father, Gustav, while trained as a lawyer, preferred to live as an aesthete, advising his brother Ferdinand on artistic matters.

As the Nazi threat gathered force, the family scrambled to protect its assets. Ferdinand, whose refinery outside Vienna supplied a fifth of Austria's sugar, set up a trust account with a Swiss bank just days before the Nazi takeover.

It was violated almost immediately, and the business was sold for a fraction of its value to an Austrian businessman with Nazi connections. In 2005, a federal judge in Brooklyn awarded $21 million to Ms. Altmann and descendants of another family with interests in the refinery.

The award was by far the largest to date from a fund of $1.25 billion paid by Swiss banks in 1998 to settle a class-action suit brought by Jewish depositors, who had accused the banks of betraying their trust in order to curry favor with the Nazis.

Ferdinand's palatial summer home near Prague was occupied by Reinhard Heydrich, a principal architect of the Final Solution, and its art treasures, including the Klimts, were dispersed by Ferdinand's court-imposed lawyer, the astoundingly named Erich Führer, a Nazi when the party was still illegal in Austria.

Ms. Altmann's husband, Fritz Altmann, an opera singer whom she married in 1937, was sent to Dachau to pressure his brother, the owner of a cashmere business, to relinquish his overseas assets. After Fritz was released, the couple lived under house arrest. One day, Ms. Altmann gave her guards the slip by claiming that her husband needed to see the dentist. The two boarded a plane to Cologne and made their way to the Dutch border, where, on a moonless night, a peasant guided them across a brook, under barbed wire and into Holland.

They reached the United States in 1940 and eventually settled in Los Angeles, where Mr. Altmann, who died in 1994, worked at a Lockheed plant. Ms. Altmann began selling cashmere sweaters and socks sent by her brother-in-law, who had set up a business in New York.

She did so well that she and her husband went into the clothing business. For years she sold the company's samples from a small shop in Beverly Hills. She later ran a boutique from her home.

Ms. Altmann is survived by three sons, a daughter, six grandchildren and two great-grandchildren.

Ms. Altmann fought the Austrian government with great zest. "They will delay, delay, delay, hoping I will die," she told The Los Angeles Times in 2001, with no end in sight to her case. "But I will do them the pleasure of staying alive."

She did. And victory was sweet. After the paintings arrived in the United States, she told The New York Times: "You know, in Austria they asked, 'Would you loan them to us again?' And I said: 'We loaned them for 68 years. Enough loans.'"

— *By William Grimes*

CHUCK TANNER

With the Pirates, Head of the 'Family'

JULY 4, 1928 - FEB. 11, 2011

Chuck Tanner, whose 19-year career as a big league manager reached its high point in 1979, when he led the Pittsburgh Pirates to a come-from-behind World Series victory over the Baltimore Orioles, died on Feb. 11 at his home in New Castle, Pa. He was in his early 80s.

Infectiously optimistic, Tanner was known for promoting hard-nose play and mollifying disgruntled stars. Though his overall won-lost record with four teams was an undistinguished 1,352-1,381, he was respected for coaxing more victories than expected from rosters with less-than-stellar talent.

His 1979 Pirates, however, had plenty of talent, led by two future Hall of Famers, first baseman Willie Stargell and pitcher Bert Blyleven. They were a rollicking, hard-to-corral bunch that included curmudgeonly stars like third baseman Bill Madlock and outfielder Dave Parker. Tanner's style was to push the action, letting the players swing away when other managers would have them take pitches, encouraging them to steal bases and force opponents to make throws and tags.

"They're aggressive in everything they do: hitting, fielding, pitching, running," a rival manager, Sparky Anderson (see page 147) of the Detroit Tigers, wrote in a scouting report prepared for The New York Times. "They do everything with abandon, because that's the way Chuck Tanner wants it. He's an aggressive manager, a manager who doesn't go by the book. That's why Pittsburgh is such an exciting team."

Under Tanner's guidance the team coalesced, the players happily adopting the Sister Sledge disco hit "We Are Family" as their theme song. They won 98 games to win the National League Eastern Division crown, then swept the three-game championship series from the Cincinnati Reds to capture the pennant.

In the World Series against the Orioles, the Pirates fell behind three games to one. On the day of the fifth game, when Tanner arrived at Three Rivers Stadium in Pittsburgh, he learned that his mother, who had suffered a stroke two weeks earlier, had died that morning. He managed the rest of the series; the Pirates won three in a row to win it.

UNDERDOG: After falling behind three games to one, Tanner led the Pirates to a 1979 World Series victory.

"My mother was a great Pirates fan," he was reported to have told his team before Game 5. "She knows we're in trouble, so she went upstairs to get some help."

In 1972 Tanner was voted American League manager of the year after his Chicago White Sox went 87-67 and finished second in the A.L. West. The team was led by the moody slugger Dick Allen and the knuckleball pitcher Wilbur Wood, whom Tanner had converted from a reliever to a starter. Wood won 24 games.

Tanner managed the White Sox from 1970 through 1975, the Oakland A's in 1976, the Pirates from 1977 through 1985 and the Atlanta Braves in 1986, 1987 and part of 1988.

He lost his job with the White Sox when the team was sold and the new owner, Bill Veeck, replaced him with Paul Richards. In Oakland, Tanner's team finished a strong second and set an A.L. record for stolen bases. But the team's irascible maverick owner, Charles O. Finley, was intent on dismantling a club that had won championships from 1972 to 1974. In an unusual maneuver, he traded Tanner to Pittsburgh for Manny Sanguillen, a catcher. (Sanguillen would return to Pittsburgh the next season, and he played for Tanner on the 1979 team, getting a key hit to win Game 2 of the World Series.)

Most sources say Charles William Tanner was born in New Castle, near the Ohio border, on July 4, 1929, though the Pirates' Web site said he was born in 1928. He went to high school in nearby Shenango. He spent part of eight seasons in the major leagues as an outfielder, playing for the Milwaukee Braves, the Chicago Cubs, the Cleveland Indians and the Los Angeles Angels, batting an overall .261 with 21 home runs and driving in 105 runs in 982 plate appearances.

He is survived by four sons, including Bruce Tanner, who pitched for the White Sox in 1985. His wife, Barbara, died in 2006.

In the spring of 1980, as the Pirates began their attempt to repeat as champions, Tanner spoke about why he was able to get along with players and command their respect, even those who gave other managers trouble.

"I always remember the players are human beings first," he said.

— *By Bruce Weber*

JOANNE SIEGEL

The Original Lois Lane

DEC. 1, 1917 - FEB. 12, 2011

JOANNE SIEGEL, who as a Cleveland teenager during the Depression hired herself out as a model to an aspiring comic book artist, Joe Shuster, and became the first physical incarnation of Lois Lane, Superman's love interest, died on Feb. 12 in Santa Monica, Calif. She was 93.

Ms. Siegel was married to Shuster's partner and Superman co-creator, the writer Jerry Siegel.

An ambitious high school girl with stars in her eyes, young Joanne Kovacs was trying to earn some money when she posed for the first time as Lois Lane. It was probably 1935, her daughter, Laura Siegel Larson, said, and "somebody had told her modeling was easy." Joanne had placed a classified ad in The Plain Dealer, the Cleveland newspaper, declaring herself available for modeling work and confessing that she had no experience.

Most of the responses to the ad were requests for dates, but one at least seemed serious, and she presented herself to Mr. Shuster and Mr. Siegel, who were developing Superman. (The first Superman comic was published in 1938.)

By that point the character was well along in Mr. Siegel's mind; he knew he wanted her to be a newspaper reporter like the clever Torchy Blane, played by Glenda Farrell, in a series of B movies.

(In one, "Torchy Blane in Panama," from 1938, the title character was played by Lola Lane, a singer and actress who some say influenced the name of Superman's leading lady.)

SUPERMODEL?: Ms. Siegel in the 1940s and an original drawing of Lois Lane.

During the modeling session Joanne struck various poses — draping herself over the arms of a chair, for example, to show how she might look being carried by Superman in flight — and she and Mr. Shuster and Mr. Siegel, who were barely in their 20s, became friends. Mr. Shuster's drawings reproduced her hairstyle and her facial features, though in the most famous of the original drawings Lois is considerably more voluptuous than her model was.

"Joe might have taken a few liberties," Ms. Larson said with a laugh.

Ms. Siegel thus became the first in a long line of Lois Lanes, among them Phyllis Coates, Noel Neill, Teri Hatcher and Erica Durance on television and Margot Kidder in the movies.

Ms. Larson said her mother's irrepressibility, ambition and spunk informed her father's development of the character: "My dad always said he wrote Lois with my mom's personality in mind."

The daughter of Hungarian immigrants, Jolan Kovacs was born in Cleveland on Dec. 1, 1917; classmates and teachers who couldn't or wouldn't pronounce her name properly — YO-lan — called her Joan or Joanne, and the second name eventually stuck.

After her Lois Lane debut, she was an artist's model in Boston and elsewhere. (For a time she used the name Joanne Carter.) During World War II she worked for a California ship builder, supporting the war effort. Returning to New York, she re-established a connection with Mr. Siegel at a fund-raising ball for cartoonists at which, according to family lore, the costumes were judged by Marlon Brando, then in the middle of his Broadway run in "A Streetcar Named Desire."

Both she and Mr. Siegel had been married; she was divorced, and he was soon to be. They married in 1948 and lived in Connecticut and on Long Island before moving to California in the 1960s. In addition to her daughter, she is survived by a sister and two grandsons.

Ms. Siegel worked at a number of jobs during her marriage — as one of California's early car saleswomen, she sold new and used Chevys from a lot in Santa Monica — but much of her life was taken up trying to reclaim the original Superman copyright that Mr. Shuster and her husband sold to Detective Comics in 1937 for $130.

The plight of Mr. Shuster and Mr. Siegel, whose lives were marked by privation, is one of the cautionary tales in the annals of intellectual property. In a series of legal and public relations battles that began in 1947, the families eventually won some compensation from DC Comics (the successor to Detective Comics), and in 2008 a federal judge restored Mr. Siegel's co-authorship share of the original Superman copyrights, though how much money the Siegel family is entitled to is still being adjudicated.

"All her life she carried the torch for Jerry and Joe — and other artists," said Marc Toberoff, the lawyer for both the Siegel and Shuster families. "There was a lot of Lois Lane in Joanne Siegel."

— *By Bruce Weber*

DAVID F. FRIEDMAN

From Nudie-Cuties to Splatter

DEC. 24, 1923 - FEB. 14, 2011

David F. Friedman, a film producer who cheerfully and cheesily exploited an audience's hunger for bare-breasted women and blood-dripping corpses in lucrative and popular low-budget films like "Blood Feast" and "Ilsa: She-Wolf of the S.S.," died on Feb. 14 in Anniston, Ala. He was 87.

Part carnival barker, part adman, part good-natured, dirty-minded adolescent, Mr. Friedman plumbed the low-rent depths of the movie business with a sense of boldness and a sense of fun. In the early 1960s he and a partner, the director Herschell Gordon Lewis, made a handful of films in a genre known as "nudie-cuties," in which young women would perform ordinary household tasks or cavort in sun-dappled settings half-dressed or entirely undressed. (Some of the films were shot at Florida nudist colonies.)

The movies were not openly erotic — there was no sex — but in their deadpan presentation of public nudity, they delivered a naughty, subversive wink at censorship standards.

In 1963, Mr. Friedman and Mr. Lewis made the gleefully gore-soaked "Blood Feast," a groundbreaking film in the horror genre, the first so-called splatter film. It tells the story of a murderous Egyptian caterer in Miami who is especially fond of decapitating women. To promote the film, Mr. Friedman warned viewers that it might be sickening and supplied theaters with airline vomit bags to distribute to customers. Made for $24,500, the film reportedly earned millions.

Mr. Friedman and Mr. Lewis followed "Blood Feast" with two other gore fests that are exemplars of their ilk: "Two Thousand Maniacs!," set in a Southern town during a Civil War centennial celebration in which the townspeople take their revenge for losing the war on visiting Yankees; and "Color Me Blood Red," about a painter who gets his distinctive reds from the blood of his murder victims.

A SENSE OF FUN: Mr. Friedman's campy films had titles like "Ilsa: She-Wolf of the S.S." and "Trader Hornee."

Mr. Friedman made soft-porn films — they had titles like "Trader Hornee" and "The Erotic Adventures of Zorro" — and, while chairman of the Adult Film Association, hard-core ones as well. Perhaps his most famous title was "Ilsa: She-Wolf of the S.S.," about a sadistic and insatiable female Nazi prison guard, generally considered a campy classic of sexploitation.

David Frank Friedman was born in Birmingham, Ala., on Dec. 24, 1923. His father worked for The Birmingham News; his mother was a musician. After his parents divorced, his mother moved to Anniston, and young Dave (as he was always called) became interested in carnivals, card games and scams.

Mr. Friedman started college at Cornell — "He sat next to Kurt Vonnegut in a calculus class," said Mica Brook Everett, a relative and his caretaker — and worked as a film booker and projectionist in Buffalo before serving in the Army during World War II. It was in Army signal school that he was taught the technical basics of movie making. Eventually he went to work for Kroger Babb, a producer and a bit of a huckster whose best-known film, "Mom and Dad," was a 1940s sensation, using medical footage of actual births and walking a line between sex education and sexploitation.

Mr. Friedman's wife, Carol Virginia Everett, whom he met when they were both children in Anniston, died in 2001. Besides Mica Everett and other members of his wife's family, he leaves no survivors.

In the last 20 years, since his films started to reappear on video, Mr. Friedman enjoyed a bit of cult celebrity, appearing frequently at conferences and film festivals.

"He partied like an animal," said Mike Vraney, whose company, Something Weird Video, distributed Mr. Friedman's films. "He ate huge meals, drank and smoked enormous cigars. He lived with gusto."

Mr. Friedman was proud of his work, in a manner of speaking.

"'Blood Feast' is probably the most maligned motion picture American critics have ever ripped asunder," he wrote in his 1990 autobiography, "A Youth in Babylon: Confessions of a Trash-Film King." He went on to quote the review in Variety:

"Incredibly crude and unprofessional from start to finish, 'Blood Feast' is an insult even to the most puerile and salacious audiences. The very fact that it is taking itself seriously makes the David F. Friedman production all the more ludicrous. It was a fiasco in all departments."

Mr. Friedman then wrote: "Herschell and I have often wondered who told the Variety scribe we were taking ourselves seriously."

— *By Bruce Weber*

GEORGE SHEARING

Jazz Piano Virtuoso With a Distinctive Sound

AUG. 13, 1919 - FEB. 14, 2011

GEORGE SHEARING, the British piano virtuoso who overcame blindness to become a worldwide jazz star, and whose composition "Lullaby of Birdland" became an enduring jazz standard, died on Feb. 14 in Manhattan. He was 91.

In 1949, just two years after Mr. Shearing immigrated to the United States, his recording of "September in the Rain" became an international hit and established him as a hot property on the jazz nightclub and concert circuit. It also established the signature sound of the George Shearing Quintet, which was not quite like anything listeners had heard before, or have heard since.

"When the quintet came out in 1949, it was a very placid and peaceful sound, coming on the end of a very frantic and frenetic era known as bebop," Mr. Shearing said in a 1995 interview. What he was aiming for, he said, was "a full block sound, which, if it was scored for saxophones, would sound like the Glenn Miller sound. And coming at the end of the frenetic bebop era, the timing seemed to be right."

The Shearing sound, displaying the harmonic complexity of bebop but eschewing bebop's ferocious energy, was built on the unusual instrumentation of vibraphone, guitar, piano, bass and drums. To get the "full block sound" he wanted, he had the vibraphone double what his right hand played and the guitar double the left. That sound came to represent the essence of sophisticated hip for countless listeners worldwide who preferred their jazz on the gentle side.

The personnel of the Shearing quintet changed many times over the years, but except for the addition of a percussionist in 1953 — the band continued to be called a quintet even after it became a sextet — the instrumentation and the sound remained the same for almost 30 years.

When Mr. Shearing disbanded the group in 1978, it was less because listeners had grown tired of that instrumentation and sound (although the group's popularity, like that of mainstream jazz in general, had declined) than because Mr. Shearing himself had.

"I had an identity. I held on to it for 29 years. Eventually I held on like grim death," he told John S. Wilson of The New York Times in 1986. "The last five years I played on automatic pilot. I could do the whole show in my sleep."

Shortly after breaking up the group, Mr. Shearing said, "There won't be another quintet unless Standard Oil or Frank Sinatra want it." Standard Oil never asked, but in 1981 Mr. Shearing reassembled the quintet for a Boston engagement and a series of Carnegie Hall concerts as Mr. Sinatra's opening act. He returned to the quintet format on occasion after that, but it was never again his main focus.

His preferred format became the piano-bass duo, originally with Brian Torff and later with Don Thompson and Neil Swainson. He also performed with bass and drums and sometimes unaccompanied. In the 1980s and '90s he had great success in concert and on record with the singer Mel Tormé.

By his own estimate Mr. Shearing wrote about 300 tunes, of which he liked to joke that roughly 295 were completely unknown.

He nevertheless contributed at least one bona fide standard to the jazz repertory: "Lullaby of Birdland," written in 1952 and adopted as the theme song of the world-famous New York nightclub where he frequently performed. Both as an instrumental and with words by George David Weiss, it has been recorded by everyone from Ella Fitzgerald to Bill Haley and His Comets, who improbably cut a version called "Lullaby of Birdland Twist" in 1962.

George Albert Shearing was born on Aug. 13, 1919, in the Battersea area of London, the youngest of nine children. His father, James Phillip Shearing, was a coal worker; his mother, the former Ellen Amelia Brightner, took care of the family during the day and cleaned trains at night.

In his autobiography, "Lullaby of Birdland" (2004), written with Alyn Shipton, Mr. Shearing recalled that his first attempts at making music involved throwing bottles from an upstairs window: milk bottles for a classical sound, beer for jazz. More conventionally, he began picking out tunes on the family piano at 3, even though it had some broken keys.

Blind from birth, Mr. Shearing attended the Shillington School for the Blind and the Linden Lodge School for the Blind, both in London. It was at Linden Lodge that Mr. Shearing, captivated by the recordings of American jazz pianists like Art Tatum and Fats Waller, began to study piano.

At first he wanted to pursue classical training. But a teacher, recognizing his gifts as an improviser, discouraged him from taking that path, saying it would be a waste of time. Still, he came to see the value of classical training and later returned to the classics, performing Bach and Mozart on several occasions with symphony orchestras.

Mr. Shearing began his career at 16, when another blind pianist gave up his job playing in a London pub and recommended Mr. Shearing as his replacement. He eventually had his own 15-minute show on the BBC and was voted Britain's best jazz pianist for seven consecutive years in the poll conducted by the magazine Melody Maker.

Glenn Miller and Fats Waller, among others, encouraged Mr. Shearing to try his luck in the United States after World War II ended. But the booking agents there were not impressed. At home he had been billed as "England's Art Tatum" or "England's Teddy Wilson." But when he performed for one American agent he received a curt response: "What else can you do?" It was not enough, he realized, to sound like other pianists. He needed to develop a sound of his own.

Mr. Shearing found it with the help of a fellow Englishman, the jazz critic and pianist Leonard Feather, who, like him, had moved to the United States. Mr. Feather suggested what became Mr. Shearing's signature instrumentation. With Margie Hyams on vibraphone, Chuck Wayne on guitar, John Levy on bass and Denzil Best on drums, Mr. Shearing recorded "September in the Rain" in 1949.

The sound of both the quintet and Mr. Shearing himself was distinctive; he used a so-called locked-hands style, in which his hands played melody and harmony in close quarters, the melody line harmonized by the right hand and doubled by the left hand an octave below. It caught listeners' fancy, and stardom soon followed.

After recording for the MGM label in the early years, Mr. Shearing moved to Capitol and became a mainstay of its roster from 1955 to 1969. Besides recording him with his quintet, Capitol teamed him with the singers Peggy Lee, Nancy Wilson and even Nat (King) Cole, an accomplished jazz pianist in his own right.

'I HAD AN IDENTITY': Mr. Shearing overcame blindness to become a star with a style that embodied hip sophistication for listeners who preferred their jazz on the gentle side.

With the market for jazz shrinking in the late 1960s, Capitol chose not to re-sign Mr. Shearing. A small record company he formed, Sheba, was short-lived. In 1979, a year after disbanding his quintet, he signed with Concord, a jazz label, and his career took off again. It was with Concord that he first recorded with Mel Tormé. Their albums, "An Evening With George Shearing and Mel Tormé" and "Top Drawer," won Grammys for Mr. Tormé but not for Mr. Shearing, who never won one.

In his later years he also recorded unaccompanied; in duet with his fellow pianists Marian McPartland and Hank Jones; and in settings as uncharacteristic as a Dixieland band. He continued performing into his 80s and stopped only after a fall in 2004 and a long hospital stay. He had homes in Manhattan and Lee, Mass.

Mr. Shearing's marriage to Beatrice Bayes ended in divorce. He is survived by his second wife, the former Ellie Geffert, and a daughter.

Mr. Shearing was invited to perform at the White House by three presidents: Gerald R. Ford, Jimmy Carter and Ronald Reagan. He performed for the British royal family as well. The British Academy of Composers and Songwriters gave him the Ivor Novello Award for lifetime achievement in 1993. In 1996 he was invested as an officer in the Order of the British Empire, and 11 years later he was knighted.

"I don't know why I'm getting this honor," he said shortly after learning of his knighthood. "I've just been doing what I love to do."

— *By Peter Keepnews*

FEB

DONALD L. COX

Field Marshal for the Black Panthers

APRIL 16, 1936 - FEB. 19, 2011

DONALD L. Cox, who was at the center of black radical politics as a member of the Black Panther Party high command and who earned a moment of celebrity in 1970 when he spoke at the Leonard Bernstein fund-raising party in Manhattan made notorious by the writer Tom Wolfe, died on Feb. 19 at his home in Camps-sur-l'Agly, France. He was 74.

His wife, Barbara Cox Easley, did not specify a cause. He had been living abroad since the early 1970s, when he fled the country after being implicated in a Baltimore murder.

Known as D. C., Mr. Cox held the title of field marshal with the Panthers, the socialist movement founded by Huey P. Newton and Bobby Seale in Oakland, Calif., in 1966. Mr. Cox was living in San Francisco at the time and became part of a group known as the central committee, which included Mr. Newton, Mr. Seale, Eldridge Cleaver and a handful of others.

Mr. Cox's job was to travel the country to establish and supervise branch offices. But he was also the Panthers' arms expert, writing about the proper use of guns in The Black Panther, the party newspaper, teaching party members to shoot, and even procuring guns. The Panthers embraced the use of guns in the name of black liberation from what they saw as a white racist establishment. Mr. Cox liked to say he was in charge of the Panther military.

He also served the Panthers as a spokesman, and in January 1970 he appeared with a handful of Panthers and some 80 other guests at the Bernstein apartment on Park Avenue. The occasion was a fund-raiser for the legal defense of the New York Panther 21 — 19 men and 2 women who had been indicted on charges of plotting to kill police officers and blow up several sites, including Midtown Manhattan stores, police precinct houses and the New York Botanical Garden in the Bronx.

"Some people think that we are racist, because the news media find it useful to create that impression in order to support the power structure," Mr. Cox told Mr. Bernstein's guests. "They like for the Black Panther Party to be made to look like a racist organization, because that camouflages the true class nature of the struggle."

The fund-raiser was notable for its clash of cultures. As Charlotte Curtis of The New York Times reported, "There they were, the Black Panthers from the ghetto and the black and white liberals from the middle, upper-middle and upper classes studying one another cautiously over the expensive furnishings, the elaborate flower arrangements, the cocktails and the silver trays of canapés."

Among the conversations Ms. Curtis noted was an exchange between Mr. Bernstein and Mr. Cox.

Mr. Bernstein: "Now about your goals. I'm not sure I understand how you're going to achieve them. I mean, what are your tactics?"

Mr. Cox: "If business won't give us full employment, then we must take the means of production and put them in the hands of the people."

Mr. Bernstein: "I dig absolutely."

The event raised nearly $10,000, Ms. Curtis reported. In May 1971, all 21 of the accused Panthers were acquitted. In June 1970, Mr. Wolfe's article, "Radical Chic: That Party at Lenny's," was published in New York magazine. A skewering of Mr. Bernstein and his guests, it advanced Mr. Wolfe's career as a leading proponent of the so-called new journalism. But it was reviled by Mr. Cox. The guests that night, he told Roz Payne, who documented the history of the Panthers in a series of films, "were really a concerned bunch of people."

He added that "it was those media freaks and that bloodsucking Tom Wolfe" who exploited the cause of black liberation to make money from it and "to be part of the machinery that tried to ridiculize it."

PANTHER HIGH COMMAND: From left, June Hilliard, Mr. Cox and Elbert Howard, around 1970.

Donald Lee Cox was born on April 16, 1936, in Appleton, in west central Missouri, where he grew up hunting small game and reading everything he could find about nature and the outdoors.

"I read all the books in the library about snakes," he told Ms. Payne for her film series. (That series has been released on DVD under the title taken from the Panther party platform: "What We Want, What We Believe.")

He moved to San Francisco at 17, by his own account an ignorant country boy who was politically naïve until he joined the Panthers.

But as he explained in interviews, anger had been building up in him over attacks on black people, like the bombing that killed four black girls at the 16th Street Baptist Church in Birmingham, Ala., in 1963. Closer to home, there was the shooting of an unarmed black teenager by policemen that set off a riot in the Hunters Point neighborhood of San Francisco in 1966.

"It was a steady accumulation of pressure," he said, "like a volcano."

Shortly after the Bernstein dinner, Mr. Cox was charged as a conspirator in the July 1969 murder of Eugene Anderson, a Panther who had been a police informer in Baltimore. Mr. Cox said he had had nothing to do with the killing. One of several codefendants was convicted of the crime.

After a warrant was issued for his arrest, Mr. Cox left the country, first living in Algeria and then in France. His first marriage, in San Francisco, ended in divorce. He met Ms. Easley, who lives in Philadelphia, in the 1960s, and though they had not lived together since he left the country, she said, they married in 2006 so that she would have legal standing in his affairs.

In addition to Ms. Easley, he is survived by a daughter, two sons, five grandchildren and a great-grandson.

"He created a very comfortable life here," his wife said in a phone interview from Camps-sur-l'Agly, where she was tending to her husband's matters. But she added that the isolation had begun to wear on him.

"Exile will do that to you," she said.

— *By Bruce Weber*

JUDITH P. SULZBERGER

Physician and Member of The Times Family

DEC. 27, 1923 - FEB. 21, 2011

Dr. Judith P. Sulzberger, a physician whose philanthropy led to the creation of a center for genome studies in her name at Columbia University's College of Physicians and Surgeons, and a member of the family that controls The New York Times, died on Feb. 21 at her home in Manhattan. She was 87.

Family ties inextricably linked Dr. Sulzberger to the newspaper that her grandfather, Adolph S. Ochs, bought in 1896. Its affairs dominated dinner conversations when she was growing up. Her father, Arthur Hays Sulzberger, was publisher from 1935 to 1961; her brother, Arthur Ochs Sulzberger, was publisher for nearly 30 years; and her nephew Arthur Ochs Sulzberger Jr. has been publisher since 1992.

Indeed, for 26 years Dr. Sulzberger served on the board of directors, as did her two sisters, Marian Sulzberger Heiskell, a civic leader who was a director for 34 years, and Ruth Sulzberger Holmberg, who published the family-owned Chattanooga Times and was a director of the New York company for 37 years.

But from an early age, Judith Sulzberger resolved to make her career outside the family newspaper enterprises. She became a doctor and for many years conducted clinical and private practices. She later focused on public-health research, investigating AIDS, infectious diseases, microbiology and genetics.

In the early 1990s, she provided financing for what became the Judith P. Sulzberger Genome Center at Columbia's College of Physicians and Surgeons, her alma mater. The center fosters the advanced study of genetics to identify the risks of disease, improve human health and extend life. For many years, Dr. Sulzberger was a staff member at the college and was in charge of special projects for the genome center and chairwoman of its advisory board.

One of her projects was a study, conducted jointly by the genome center and the Pasteur Institute, into the genetic code of the malaria mosquito. She also supported genetic research into autism and Asperger syndrome, and in 2008 established the Isidore S. Edelman professorship in biochemistry and molecular physics at the college. Dr. Edelman, a faculty member since 1978, founded the genome center in 1991, was its director until 2000 and continued his work until his death in 2004.

Dr. Sulzberger, the author of papers on medical issues, wrote a medical column for the Long Island newspaper The East Hampton Star (she had a home in East Hampton) in the early 1980s. She also wrote a novel, "Younger" (2003). It tells the story of two medical researchers who unravel

SULZBERGER SIBLINGS: From left, Dr. Sulzberger, Arthur Ochs Sulzberger, Ruth S. Holmberg and Marian S. Heiskell in 1991.

secrets of the aging process and become famous. When they fall in love, however, they must grapple with social and scientific issues on a personal level because the woman is 10 years older than her colleague.

Dr. Sulzberger was a director of The Times from 1974 to 2000. She remained a principal owner of the company under a trust that had passed to her and her three siblings on the death of their mother, Iphigene Ochs Sulzberger, in 1990.

At that time the trust, set up under a 1986 agreement intended to preserve family control of the company, held 83.7 percent of the Class B stock, which is not publicly traded and elects 70 percent of the directors. Class A stock, traded on the New York Stock Exchange and widely held, elects 30 percent of the directors, whose number fluctuates slightly from time to time.

Dr. Sulzberger was also on the boards of the Wildlife Conservation Society, the Rainforest Alliance, the Health Sciences Council of Columbia University and the Pasteur Foundation, the New York affiliate of the Pasteur Institute in France.

Judith Peixotto Sulzberger was born in New York City on Dec. 27, 1923, the third child and youngest daughter of Arthur Hays and Iphigene Ochs Sulzberger. When she was 4, Judith caught chicken pox and scarlet fever simultaneously and, running a fever of nearly 105, almost died. A pediatrician gave her a serum that caused an allergic reaction, she went into shock, and her heart stopped. She was revived with adrenaline. The frightening episode had one positive effect: it fueled her interest in medicine.

When Judith's brother, Arthur, was born, their father, who enjoyed writing light verse, prepared an illustrated book describing the boy as having "come to play the Punch to Judy's endless show." Punch became his lifelong nickname.

While raised with nannies, maids, butlers, chauffeurs and tutors, Judith and her siblings were inculcated from childhood with lessons of family responsibility toward The Times, which was portrayed to them by their parents and a family lawyer as a kind of revered public institution that required them to follow certain rules.

"At the philosophical center of the list was the exalted importance of The New York Times — 'the holy New York Times,' as Judy ruefully called it — and the relative insignificance of the family," Susan E. Tifft and Alex S. Jones related in their 1999 book, "The Trust," a history of the Ochs and Sulzberger families and The Times.

Fascinated with science, a serious student and a bit of a rebel who sometimes defied her parents and nannies, Judith attended the Froebel League, a laboratory school for teachers, and Brearley, a private school in New York, where she excelled in biology and graduated in 1942. She was accepted at Vassar and Bryn Mawr but went to Smith College in Northampton, Mass., because her sister Ruth was there.

She did well in college, transferring after three years to Columbia's College of Physicians and Surgeons under a transition program that combined her first year at medical school with her fourth year at Smith, which awarded her a bachelor's degree in 1946. She received her medical degree at Columbia in 1949, and over the next two years interned and was a resident in pathology at Grasslands Hospital in Valhalla, N.Y.

She interrupted her medical career in the 1950s to raise a family. In 1946 she had married

Matthew Rosenschein Jr., a fellow medical student in his final year at Columbia, who became a general medical practitioner. The couple had two children, Daniel and James, and were divorced in 1956.

In 1958, Dr. Sulzberger married Richard N. Cohen, a Yale-educated insurance broker. He formally adopted her sons, who took his surname. The couple had no children and were divorced in 1972. Late in 1972, she married Budd Levinson, a divorced businessman. They were divorced in 1984 but later remarried.

In addition to her husband, she is survived by her sons, three stepchildren and four grandchildren, as well as her siblings, Marian Sulzberger Heiskell, Ruth Sulzberger Holmberg and Arthur Ochs Sulzberger.

Dr. Sulzberger resumed her career in 1957 as a physician in the pathology department at Cornell University Medical College (now the Weill Cornell Medical College, part of New York Presbyterian Hospital). Over the next two decades she worked at various hospitals and clinics in New York and, for a time, in Stamford, Conn.

From 1979 to 1983, she was in private medical practice in East Hampton. From 1985 to 1992, she worked on AIDS research at St. Luke's Roosevelt Hospital Center, and she then focused on genetics.

In 1991, the four children of Iphigene Ochs Sulzberger gave $5 million in their mother's name to Barnard College, her alma mater. In 2005, Dr. Sulzberger and her sisters gave $4 million to Columbia University's Graduate School of Journalism for an advanced management training program for news executives, and another $4 million to the Graduate School of Journalism of the City University of New York, which opened in 2006, for internships and scholarships. Both journalism school gifts were made to honor their brother, Arthur Ochs Sulzberger, the chairman emeritus and former publisher of The Times.

— *By Robert D. McFadden*

FEB

BERNARD N. NATHANSON

60,000 Abortions, Then a Change of Heart

JULY 31, 1926 - FEB. 21, 2011

Dr. Bernard N. Nathanson, a campaigner for abortion rights who, after experiencing a change of heart in the 1970s, became a prominent opponent of abortion and the on-screen narrator of the anti-abortion film "The Silent Scream," died on Feb. 21 at his home in Manhattan. He was 84.

Dr. Nathanson, an obstetrician-gynecologist practicing in Manhattan, helped found the National Association for the Repeal of Abortion Laws (now NARAL Pro-Choice America) in 1969 and served as its medical adviser.

After abortion was legalized in New York in 1970, he became the director of the Center for Reproductive and Sexual Health, which, in his talks as an abortion opponent, he often called "the largest abortion clinic in the Western world."

In a widely reported 1974 article in The New England Journal of Medicine, "Deeper Into Abortion," Dr. Nathanson described his growing moral and medical qualms about abortion. "I am deeply troubled by my own increasing certainty that I had in fact presided over 60,000 deaths," he wrote.

His unease was intensified by the images made available by the new technologies of fetoscopy and ultrasound.

"For the first time, we could really see the human fetus, measure it, observe it, watch it, and indeed bond with it and love it," he wrote in the 1996 book "The Hand of God: A Journey from Death to Life by the Abortion Doctor Who Changed His Mind." "I began to do that."

Despite his misgivings, and his conviction that abortion on demand was wrong, he continued to perform abortions for reasons he deemed medically necessary.

"On a gut, emotional level, I still favored abortion," he told New York magazine in 1987. "It represented all the things we had fought for and won. It seemed eminently more civilized than the carnage that had gone on before."

"I know every facet of abortion."

But, he added, "it was making less and less sense to me intellectually."

In addition to the 60,000 abortions performed at the clinic, which he ran from 1970 to 1972, he took responsibility for 5,000 abortions he performed himself, and 10,000 abortions performed by residents under his supervision when he was the chief of obstetrical services at St. Luke's Hospital in Manhattan from 1972 to 1978.

He did his last procedure in late 1978 or early 1979 on a longtime patient suffering from cancer and soon embarked on a new career lecturing and writing against abortion.

"The Silent Scream," a 28-minute film produced by Crusade for Life, was released in early 1985. In it, Dr. Nathanson described the stages of fetal development and offered commentary as a sonogram showed in graphic detail the abortion of a 12-week-old fetus by the suction method.

"We see the child's mouth open in a silent scream," he said, as the ultrasound image, slowed for dramatic impact, showed a fetus seeming to shrink from surgical instruments. "This is the silent scream of a child threatened imminently with extinction."

The film won the enthusiastic praise of President Ronald Reagan, who showed it at the White House, and was widely distributed by anti-abortion groups like the National Right to Life Committee.

Supporters of abortion rights and many physicians, however, criticized it as misleading and manipulative. Some medical experts argued that a 12-week-old fetus cannot feel pain since it does not have a brain or developed neural pathways, and that what the film showed was a purely involuntary reaction to a stimulus.

Dr. Nathanson accused his critics of rationalizing. Responding to a doctor from Cornell's medical school on the ABC News program "Nightline," he said, "If pro-choice advocates think that they're going to see the fetus happily sliding down the suction tube waving and smiling as it goes by, they're in for a truly paralyzing shock."

He later produced another film, "Eclipse of Reason," about a late-term procedure that critics call partial-birth abortion. He also wrote "Aborting America" (1979), a memoir and social history of the abortion rights movement, and, with Adelle Nathanson, "The Abortion Papers: Inside the Abortion Mentality" (1984).

Bernard N. Nathanson, the son of an obstetrician-gynecologist, was born on July 31, 1926, in Manhattan and grew up on the Upper West Side. He earned a bachelor's degree from Cornell and a medical degree from McGill University in 1949.

After serving as the chief of obstetrics and gynecology for the Northeast Air Command of the Air Force, he established a successful practice in Manhattan.

While interning at Woman's Hospital in Manhattan, he observed the effects of illegal abortions on the mostly poor black and Hispanic women who came under his care, and he soon became convinced that the laws prohibiting abortion must be changed. In 1967, he met Lawrence Lader, a crusading journalist and the author of "Abortion," and soon became caught up in Mr. Lader's plans to organize a movement to agitate for the repeal of laws prohibiting abortions.

Dr. Nathanson earned a degree in bioethics from Vanderbilt University in 1996 and that year was baptized as a Roman Catholic — he described himself up to that time as a Jewish atheist — in a private ceremony at St. Patrick's

Cathedral by Cardinal John J. O'Connor, the archbishop of New York.

His first three marriages ended in divorce. In addition to his fourth wife, Christine, he is survived by a son.

In addressing anti-abortion audiences, Dr. Nathanson often drew gasps by painting himself, in his pro-abortion-rights days, in lurid colors.

"I know every facet of abortion," he wrote in his memoir, adding, "I helped nurture the creature in its infancy by feeding it great draughts of blood and money; I guided it through its adolescence as it grew fecklessly out of control."

— *By William Grimes*

JEAN DINNING

Finding Pop Immortality With 'Teen Angel'

MARCH 29, 1924 - FEB. 22, 2011

That fateful night the car was stalled
upon the railroad track
I pulled you out and we were safe
but you went running back.

Love, death, adolescent angst. It all added up to a song that became almost mythical the minute it was released in October 1959: "Teen Angel."

Mark Dinning, a pop singer of modest renown, sang it. Many American radio stations and the British Broadcasting Corporation refused to play it, saying it was too gruesome. Nonetheless, teenagers soon learned enough about it to make it the No. 1 song for two weeks in February 1960.

FOR YOUNG HEARTS: Ms. Dinning wrote a teenage anthem.

Jean Dinning, Mark's sister, wrote "Teen Angel." She got the title from reading a magazine article about juvenile delinquency that said good kids deserved a flattering name, like "teen angel." She wrote half of the song, then jolted awake one night, as if someone had shaken her and handed her more of the words.

What was it you were looking for
that took your life that night?
They said they found my high school ring
clutched in your fingers tight.

Ms. Dinning died on Feb. 22 in Garden Grove, Calif. She was 86.

Early, tragic death was in the air in 1959. Buddy Holly, Ritchie Valens and the Big Bopper died in a plane crash earlier that year, and memories of James Dean's death in a head-on collision four years earlier were still fresh.

Teenagers in 1960 scooped up Ray Peterson's "Tell Laura I Love Her," the tragic tale of a teenage boy who enters a racing car championship to win prize money to buy Laura a wedding ring. After the inevitable crash, his last words are the title of the song.

"Teenage coffin songs" became a genre, at least to sarcastic disc jockeys.

But if "Teen Angel" captured a moment in time, it also had legs as a piece of popular culture. It was sung at Woodstock by Sha Na Na and was heard in the 1973 movie "American Graffiti."

When a panel chosen by the Recording Industry of America Association, the National

Endowment for the Arts and Scholastic Inc. rated the songs of the 20th century in 2001, "Teen Angel" took 219th place. In Britain, The Observer placed "Teen Angel" on a list of the top 50 teenage anthems since 1940.

Eugenia Dinning, who later changed her name to Jean, was born on March 29, 1924, in Grant County, Okla., where her father lost the farm in the Depression and became a Maytag salesman who moved often. His nine pitch-perfect children improved a succession of church choirs.

Jean and her sisters Lou and Ginger won several amateur contests when Jean was 10. As the Dinning Sisters, they had a 15-minute radio show in Enid, Okla., as teenagers and went on to national fame on NBC radio, in movies and on records.

Their million-seller was "Buttons and Bows" from the 1948 movie "The Paleface" with Bob Hope and Jane Russell (see page 323). Other hits included "A Pretty Girl Milking Her Cow" and "We Fell in Love on the Greyhound Bus."

"The Billboard Book of No. 1 Hits" said Jean first played "Teen Angel" to her brother Mark (whose birth name was Max) at a family dinner. Before the dishes were cleared away, Mark recorded it on a tape recorder. Jean later had several 45s made and mailed him one. When he took it to a record store to play it (he didn't own a record player), an appreciative crowd gathered around the listening booth.

Mark didn't love it at first, but MGM soon persuaded him to record it. It sold more than 2.5 million copies.

The song was copyrighted twice, both times with Ms. Dinning's name and the name of her former husband, Red Surrey. The two had agreed to share credit for any song either one wrote during their marriage, and after they divorced she received full credit for "Teen Angel" as part of the settlement.

Her ex-husband did not figure in her accounts of how the song was composed, though he may have helped shape the music.

Ms. Dinning is survived by her sisters Ginger and Dolores (who succeeded Lou in the group), five children, eight grandchildren and eight great-grandchildren. Mark Dinning died in 1986.

To some, "Teen Angel" raises more questions than it answers. Why was the ring loose in the car? Had he just given it to her? Had it fallen off her finger? Did she not hear the train coming?

The uncertainty is part of the song's appeal, and the narrator desperately wants these answers himself. "Teen angel, teen angel," the song ends, "answer me, please."

— By Douglas Martin

JOSEPH H. FLOM

Mergers, Acquisitions and a Fertile New Field of Law

DEC. 21, 1923 - FEB. 23, 2011

Joseph H. Flom, a pioneering corporate lawyer who helped build Skadden, Arps, Slate, Meagher & Flom into one of the nation's leading law firms, died on Feb. 23 in Manhattan. He was 87.

Mr. Flom was one of the pre-eminent lawyers involved in the costly and risky business of corporate mergers and acquisitions, having risen to prominence in the 1960s as an adviser in proxy battles over control of public companies. Other companies often hired his firm simply to ensure that he and his team could not oppose them.

"Mr. Flom participated, on one side or the other, in virtually every major takeover battle of the last 20 years," the author John Taylor wrote in The New York Times in 1994.

In 1985 alone, Mr. Flom orchestrated Ronald Perelman's $2.7 billion takeover of Revlon and ABC's $3.5 billion sale to Capital Cities. Twenty-three years later he represented Anheuser-Busch in a $52 billion takeover by InBev. He counseled aggressive suitors, among them the corporate raiders James Goldsmith in his run at Crown Zellerbach and T. Boone Pickens in his bid for Unocal. And he erected defenses against hostile takeovers for Federated Department Stores and Chemical Bank.

As Skadden's power grew, Mr. Flom helped shape the giant law firm model that now dominates corporate law: a high-powered collection of specialists, spread out in offices across the country and around the globe.

Joseph Harold Flom was born in Baltimore on Dec. 21, 1923, and grew up in Brooklyn, the son of Itzak Flom, a labor organizer in the Manhattan garment district, and the former Fannie Hirsch. Mr. Flom wrote that he had wanted to go to law school from the age of 6.

After graduating from Townsend Harris High School in Manhattan, he attended night school for two years at City College before enlisting in the Army in World War II.

He never graduated from college, but Harvard Law School admitted him after he completed military service, and he earned a law degree in 1948. At Harvard he was an editor of The Harvard Law Review.

After law school, by his account, many firms turned him down for a job because he was Jewish, but a small new firm in Manhattan run by Marshall Skadden, Leslie Arps and John Slate took him on. He became a partner in 1954 and within a few years effectively took over leadership.

In a 1994 book, "Skadden: Power, Money, and the Rise of a Legal Empire," the journalist Lincoln Caplan portrayed Mr. Flom as a scrappy, sometimes rough-edged iconoclast who retained an outsider's sense of himself in the white-shoe world of corporate law.

"We've got to show the bastards that you don't have to be born into it," Mr. Caplan quoted him telling his colleagues.

Skadden is now one of the largest law firms in the world, with annual revenue exceeding $2 billion and about 2,000 lawyers in 24 offices in the United States and abroad. Mr. Flom was the firm's last surviving original principal.

Malcolm Gladwell devoted a chapter to Mr. Flom in his book "Outliers: The Story of Success" (2008), crediting him with building out and diversifying the firm and anticipating the rise of mergers and acquisitions as a specialty. "For 20 years, he perfected his craft at Skadden," Mr. Gladwell wrote. "Then the world changed and he was ready."

It was in the 1960s that Mr. Flom began making his mark in corporate mergers and acquisitions — hostile takeovers in particular. Lawyers for major corporations tended to look down on that area of law, but as more companies began to consider growth by acquisition, they bypassed their own legal advisers and turned to young Turks like Mr. Flom at Skadden and Martin Lipton of Wachtell, Lipton, Rosen & Katz.

The watershed moment may have come in 1973, when the International Nickel Company of Canada made a hostile bid for ESB Incorporated. Morgan Stanley & Company, the investment bank advising International Nickel, proposed that the company hire Skadden to do the deal. Chosen because of his experience in the specialty, a rarity then, Mr. Flom commanded a team that helped Inco fend off a rival bid by United Aircraft. Inco eventually won ESB for $224 million.

In 1982 Mr. Flom represented the Allied Corporation in its acquisition of Bendix, a fiercely fought $1.96 billion transaction that prompted calls for new federal regulations governing mergers and acquisitions to protect shareholders' interests and guard against concentrations of corporate power.

Some argued that the mergers were hurting the nation's economy by transferring wealth from employees to bondholders and bankers and diverting corporate funds from research and development. Mr. Flom, however, was skeptical about the need for changes.

"Shareholders already have a referendum," he told The New York Times in 1982. "If they don't like the results, they can fire the management, or sell their stock. The system, with all of its problems, is working. There's no justification for questions about economic concentration."

Mr. Flom was known to drive his staff. Lawyers would work around the clock for days to get deals done. (Skadden continues to be regarded as an aggressive, high-pressure firm that commands high fees.)

Concerned that Skadden could become a boutique law firm focused mainly on mergers and acquisitions, Mr. Flom headed an effort to expand into other areas, like real estate, product liability and energy.

To accomplish that, Skadden solicited retainer fees from client corporations that wanted to have the firm on call for mergers and acquisitions work. The clients were then offered the chance to use the retainer fees as credit toward other legal services. (Some said they were pressured into accepting the credits.) The strategy helped convert Skadden into the firm that Mr. Flom had envisioned: not a single expert boutique but a collection of them, offering a range of high-value specialized services to corporate clients.

As a philanthropist, Mr. Flom gave millions of dollars to Harvard Law School, where an endowed professorship bears his name. In 2005, he and the Milton Petrie Foundation donated $10 million to

APPRECIATION

Favoring Bootstraps Over White Shoes

Skadden, Arps, Slate, Meagher & Flom may be the world's most influential corporate law firm. Now usually called Skadden, it is known by the family name of a long-gone partner and not by that of Joseph Flom, who built the firm into a global powerhouse by democratizing the elite practice of corporate law.

Mr. Flom believed fiercely that merit, not your family name or your pedigree, mattered most. That was not the world he entered when he finished Harvard Law School in 1948. He was rejected by Manhattan firms where he hoped to work because he was Jewish or, as he put it, "not an obvious fit." He was finally hired as the first associate at a tiny firm founded that year by three men passed over for partnership at white-shoe firms.

Mr. Flom and Skadden became specialists at counseling about bet-your-company deals because the old-style white-shoe firms had initially spurned the work. The deals soon turned corporate lawyering into a competitive business as companies cast aside long relationships with law firms. As deals became central to corporate life, the competition transformed the world of corporate law firms, with Skadden out front.

Skadden was also a pioneer in hiring from law schools that rarely cracked top firms and in hiring women, Jews, Catholics and minorities as well as ex-surfers, ex-construction workers and others making fresh starts. Merit was their ticket in, and the measure of their success. Mr. Flom was their ideal.

The transformation of corporate lawyering exposed it for what it had pretended not to be: a business. Money became how lawyers kept score, and Skadden became a big winner. The verb "Skaddenize" was coined to describe its aggressive style. Today it is a global firm. "We've got to show the bastards that you don't have to be born into it," Mr. Flom exhorted colleagues. That's what he did.

— By Lincoln Caplan

the school for a center that would study legal issues related to biotechnology and health policy.

He also supported programs at City College of New York; pledged to make sure that college tuition would be covered for a class of 80 Harlem sixth-grade students whom he "adopted" in 1983; and supported Urban America, a development fund that invests in depressed areas. He served as a trustee of the New York University Medical Center and Barnard College and as the mayor's representative on the board of the Metropolitan Museum of Art.

At his firm he helped establish the Skadden Fellowship program, which gives money to recent law school graduates involved in public interest projects. Mr. Flom had homes in Manhattan and Palm Beach, Fla. His first wife, the former Claire Cohen, died in 2007. His survivors include his wife, Judi Sorensen Flom; two sons by his first marriage; his first wife's daughter by an earlier marriage; six grandchildren; and two great-grandchildren.

His colleagues said in interviews that what set Mr. Flom apart was his willingness to step back and let others work on important corporate transactions. When Skadden advised a special committee of RJR Nabisco in 1988 in the $25 billion leveraged buyout of the company by Kohlberg Kravis Roberts & Company, for example, he was only indirectly involved, he said; younger partners took the lead. The transaction was the subject of the 1990 book "Barbarians at the Gate: The Fall of RJR Nabisco," by Bryan Burrough and John Helyar.

In his 1994 book on Skadden, Mr. Caplan described Skadden lawyers in thrall to Mr. Flom, always trying to decode his doodles and cryptic remarks, like "They've taken their best shot, and it was a balloon with no air in it," and "Their phone is off the hook, and no conversation is going to put it back on."

At the height of the mergers and acquisitions wave in the 1980s, Mr. Flom was aware of the value of maintaining good public relations during a takeover, whether to reassure employees or stockholders. But he also sensed the limits of public relations at a time when most of a company's shares were in the hands of institutions and arbitrageurs.

"There's no case in American corporate history that I'm aware of where any major corporation was or was not taken over because the stockholders were told it was a good or bad idea," he said in 1989. "P.R. can't change the dynamics of the marketplace."

— *By Jonathan D. Glater*

SUZE ROTOLO

Alongside Dylan, a Face of '60s Music

NOV. 20, 1943 - FEB. 25, 2011

Suze Rotolo, who became widely known for her romance with Bob Dylan in the early 1960s, strongly influenced his early songwriting and, in one of the decade's signature images, walked with him arm-in-arm for the cover photo of his breakthrough album, "The Freewheelin' Bob Dylan," died on Feb. 25 at her home in Manhattan. She was 67.

The cause was lung cancer, her husband, Enzo Bartoccioli, said.

Ms. Rotolo (she pronounced her name SU-zee ROTE-olo) met Mr. Dylan in Manhattan in July 1961 at a Riverside Church folk concert, where he was a performer. She was 17; he was 20.

"Right from the start I couldn't take my eyes off her," Mr. Dylan wrote in his memoir, "Chronicles: Volume One," published in 2004.

“She was the most erotic thing I’d ever seen. She was fair skinned and golden haired, full-blood Italian. The air was suddenly filled with banana leaves. We started talking and my head started to spin. Cupid’s arrow had whistled past my ears before, but this time it hit me in the heart and the weight of it dragged me overboard.”

In “A Freewheelin’ Time: A Memoir of Greenwich Village in the Sixties” (2008), Ms. Rotolo described Mr. Dylan as “oddly old-time looking, charming in a scraggly way.”

They began seeing each other almost immediately and soon moved in together in a walk-up apartment on West Fourth Street in Greenwich Village.

The relationship was intense but beset with difficulties. He was a self-invented troubadour from Minnesota on the brink of stardom. She was the Queens-bred daughter of Italian Communists with her own ideas about life, art and politics that made it increasingly difficult for her to fulfill the role of helpmate, or, as she put it in her memoir, a “boyfriend’s ‘chick,’ a string on his guitar.”

Her social views, especially her commitment to the civil rights movement and her work for the Congress for Racial Equality, were an important influence on Mr. Dylan’s writing, evident in songs like “The Death of Emmett Till,” “Masters of War” and “Blowin’ in the Wind.” Her interest in theater and art exposed him to ideas and artists beyond the world of music.

“She’ll tell you how many nights I stayed up and wrote songs and showed them to her and asked her: ‘Is this ‘right?’” Mr. Dylan told the music critic and Dylan biographer Robert Shelton. “Because her father and her mother were associated with unions, and she was into this equality-freedom thing long before I was.”

When, to his distress, she went to Italy for several months in 1962, her absence inspired the plaintive love songs “Don’t Think Twice, It’s All Right,” “Boots of Spanish Leather,” “One Too Many Mornings” and “Tomorrow Is a Long Time.”

Mr. Dylan later alluded to their breakup and criticized her mother and sister, who disapproved of him, in the bitter “Ballad in Plain D.”

Ms. Rotolo spent most of her adult life pursuing a career as an artist and avoiding questions about her three-year relationship with Mr. Dylan. (He was, she wrote, “an elephant in the room of my life.”) She relented after Mr. Dylan published his autobiography, appearing as an interview subject in “No Direction Home,” the 2005 Martin Scorsese documentary about Mr. Dylan, before writing “A Freewheelin’ Time.”

Susan Elizabeth Rotolo was born on Nov. 20, 1943, in Brooklyn and grew up in Sunnyside and Jackson Heights, Queens. Her mother, from Boston, was an editor and columnist for L’Unità del Popolo, an Italian-language Communist newspaper. Her father, from Sicily, was an artist and union organizer who died when she was 14.

Artistically inclined, she began haunting Washington Square Park and Greenwich Village as the folk revival gathered steam, while taking part in demonstrations against American nuclear policy and racial injustice. She adopted the unusual spelling of her nickname, Susie, after seeing the Picasso collage “Glass and Bottle of Suze.”

FREEWHEELIN’ ROMANCE: Ms. Rotolo, who inspired many of Bob Dylan’s early songs, on the cover of his 1963 album.

The famous photograph of her and Mr. Dylan, taken by Don Hunstein on a slushy Jones Street in February 1963, seemed less than momentous to her at the time, and she later played down her instant elevation to a strange kind of celebrity status as the girl in the picture.

“It was freezing out,” she told The New York Times in 2008. “He wore a very thin jacket, because image was all.

Our apartment was always cold, so I had a sweater on, plus I borrowed one of his big, bulky sweaters. On top of that I put on a coat. So I felt like an Italian sausage. Every time I look at that picture, I think I look fat."

The album, Mr. Dylan's second, included anthems like "Blowin' in the Wind," "A Hard Rain's A-Gonna Fall" and "Don't Think Twice, It's All Right."

After Ms. Rotolo returned from Italy — a trip engineered by her mother in a move to separate her from Mr. Dylan — the relationship became more difficult. Mr. Dylan was becoming increasingly famous and spending more time performing on the road, and he entered into a very public affair with Joan Baez, with whom he had begun performing.

Ms. Rotolo moved out of their West Fourth Street apartment in August 1963 and, after discovering she was pregnant, had an illegal abortion.

By mid-1964 she and Mr. Dylan had drifted apart. "I knew I was an artist, but I loved poetry, I loved theater, I loved too many things," Ms. Rotolo told The Times. "Whereas he knew what he wanted and he went for it."

In "Chronicles," Mr. Dylan wrote: "The alliance between Suze and me didn't turn out exactly to be a holiday in the woods. Eventually fate flagged it down and it came to a full stop. It had to end. She took one turn in the road and I took another."

In 1967 she married Mr. Bartoccioli, a film editor she had met while studying in Perugia. The couple lived in Italy before moving to the United States in the 1970s. In addition to her husband, she is survived by their son and a sister.

Ms. Rotolo worked as a jewelry maker, illustrator and painter before turning to book art, fabricating booklike objects that incorporate found objects.

She remained politically active. In 2004, using the pseudonym Alla DaPie, she joined the street-theater group Billionaires for Bush and protested at the Republican convention in Manhattan.

— *By William Grimes*

FEB

JAMES MCCLURE

A 'Sagebrush Rebel' in the Senate

DEC. 27, 1924 - FEB. 26, 2011

James A. McClure, a three-term Republican senator from Idaho who epitomized the rugged, independent thinking of Western politicians who used new leadership positions in the 1980s to transform their "sagebrush rebellion" into conservative legislation, died on Feb. 26 in Garden City, Idaho. He was 86.

By 1983 — 10 years after Mr. McClure had left the House of Representatives to join the Senate — Westerners, including six from Rocky Mountain states, held 11 of 20 chairmanships of Senate committees. They used their power to promote land developers' interests and to press for tax cuts, relaxed gun laws, restrictions on abortions and other strongly conservative positions.

Mr. McClure, as chairman of the Senate Energy and Natural Resources Committee, sought to weaken federal restrictions on leasing land to foresters and ranchers; fought to allow some development in protected recreation areas; and defended water projects favored by development interests.

"The political pendulum in the Republican Party has swung to the West," Mr. McClure said in an interview with The New York Times in 1983.

He spoke poetically of the West as "the last frontier," where people could still be adventurous and idealistic, and of Westerners as "the kind of people who say, 'I may do it, but you're not going to make me do it,'" as he told The Washington Post in 1980.

Mr. McClure fought to allow off-road vehicles more freedom on public lands and to stop the designation of some scenic areas as national parks, the strictest category of protection.

RANCHERS' FRIEND: As a senator from Idaho, Mr. McClure fought to privatize federal land in Western states.

"As a general proposition, the environmental community disagreed with him about 100 percent of the time," Gaylord Nelson, the Wisconsin Democratic senator who became counselor for the Wilderness Society, once said of him.

Conservatives took the opposite view. In 1990, Senator Malcolm Wallop, Republican of Wyoming, said of Mr. McClure, "There is no major piece of energy, public lands or natural resources legislation passed in recent years on which he has not left an imprint."

As a member of the sagebrush rebellion, Mr. McClure supported privatizing federal land that in some Western states accounted for more than half the land area. But in many cases he worked with the Reagan administration to take moderate steps in relaxing rules governing federal land.

He was also credited with helping to preserve important Idaho wilderness areas like Sawtooth and Hells Canyon National Recreation Areas. But he fought for the rights of ranchers to continue to graze cattle there.

On energy policy, his specialty, Mr. McClure often pushed for bipartisan agreement on issues like the strategic petroleum reserve, which he helped steer through Congress as insurance against an oil cutoff by foreign suppliers. He met regularly with leaders of oil-producing nations and drove an electric car.

He also became famous on Capitol Hill for reading every word of every bill before voting on it. For many years he signed all his own mail.

As a party leader, he was chairman of the Senate Republican Conference from 1981 to 1985. He lost to Bob Dole in a bid to become Senate majority leader in 1984. But he achieved as much prominence in the 1980s as the chairman of an informal group of Republican conservatives that called itself the Steering Committee. Composed of 16 of the Senate's 41 Republicans, the group sought to press the party to promote the conservative agenda with more gusto.

To further the agenda of the "New Right," as it was called, Mr. McClure proposed that English be made the nation's official language, pushed legislation to limit food stamps and opposed the treaty that transferred control of the Panama Canal to Panama.

He received perfect or near-perfect ratings for his voting record from conservative political groups.

Senator Robert C. Byrd of West Virginia, the Democratic leader, denounced the Steering Committee as "shadowy" and "mysterious." In reply, Mr. McClure thanked him, saying Mr. Byrd had helped the group come out from under its "cloak of anonymity."

James Albertus McClure was born in Payette, Idaho, on Dec. 27, 1924, and served in the Navy during World War II. After graduating from the University of Idaho College of Law in 1950, he went into private practice with his father in Payette.

He went on to become city attorney, then county prosecuting attorney, served three terms in the Idaho State Senate and won election to Congress in 1966. After three terms in Washington as a representative, he was elected to the Senate in 1972.

In 1974, as a first-term senator, he endeared himself to conservatives when he sponsored a law to allow private citizens to own gold coins, bars and certificates. President Franklin D. Roosevelt had barred gold ownership by executive order in 1933. When courts rejected his action, Congress banned gold ownership the next year.

After leaving the Senate in 1990, Mr. McClure worked as a lobbyist on energy and resource issues.

He is survived by his wife, the former Louise Miller, two sons, a daughter, six grandchildren and one great-grandchild. The family said he died of strokes.

Mr. McClure said he decided not to seek a fourth term in the Senate because he felt that Congress could no longer make a "balanced judgment on good information." He said a new breed of legislators voted by sampling the political winds. "Wet-finger politicians," he called them.

— *By Douglas Martin*

EUGENE FODOR

So Promising, so Marketable and so Troubled

MARCH 5, 1950 - FEB. 26, 2011

Eugene Fodor, an American violinist who made international headlines in the 1970s after earning a top prize in the Tchaikovsky Competition and in the 1980s after being arrested on drug charges, died on Feb. 26 at his home in Arlington, Va. He was 60.

The cause was cirrhosis, his wife, Susan Davis, said, adding that Mr. Fodor had struggled with drug and alcohol addiction in recent years.

Known for his dark good looks, ready Western charm and prodigious technique, Mr. Fodor was awarded second prize at the 1974 International Tchaikovsky Violin Competition in Moscow. (No first prize was given that year; Mr. Fodor shared the second-place award with two Soviet violinists.)

At the time his showing was the highest placement in the contest by an American violinist. That, amid the cold war, was enough to ensure him a hero's welcome when he returned home to Colorado (in a well-choreographed publicity stunt, his horse, along with his parents, met him at the airport) and the prospect of a stellar career. The Van Cliburn of the violin, he was called. Mr. Cliburn, a fellow American, had won the Tchaikovsky piano competition in 1958.

A string of international engagements followed, as did a recording contract with RCA. Mr. Fodor performed at the White House and appeared often on "The Tonight Show" with Johnny Carson, where the talk centered as much on his outdoorsmanship as it did on his musicianship.

As a result Mr. Fodor spent much of the 1970s as one of the few classical musicians known to the general public.

If Mr. Fodor was unable to sustain his early golden promise, his story is a cautionary tale of what can happen when a gifted young artist, still personally and musically immature, is turned into a global commodity for a spate of wrong reasons.

Eugene Nicholas Fodor Jr. was born in Denver on March 5, 1950, and grew up on his family's ranch in Morrison, Colo. (He is not related to the Eugene Fodor who published travel guides.)

He began violin lessons at 5; by the time he was 10, he had made his orchestral debut, playing Bruch's Violin Concerto No. 1 with the Denver Symphony.

He later studied at the Juilliard School with Dorothy DeLay and Ivan Galamian, at Indiana University with Josef Gingold, and briefly with Jascha Heifetz.

In 1972 Mr. Fodor came to prominence after winning first prize in the Paganini Competition, an international violin contest in Italy. After his success in the Tchaikovsky two years later — at a time when the classical music industry was keen to broaden its appeal — his handlers leapt at the chance to inject his public image with a liberal dose of beefcake.

Mr. Fodor obliged them by going along with it (a memorable publicity photo of the period showed him astride a horse, shirtless), as did the news media, by eating it up. The Mick Jagger of the violin, he was called, an image he later said he longed to shed.

EARLY FAME: Handsome and charming, Mr. Fodor was packaged as a classical music heartthrob.

In July 1989, Mr. Fodor was arrested on Martha's Vineyard after breaking into a motel room there. Charges against him included breaking and entering and possession of heroin and cocaine with intent to distribute.

He was released on his own recognizance — the judge had refused to accept his Guarnerius violin as surety — and later pleaded guilty to the charge of breaking and entering and not guilty to the drug charges. Under a plea agreement that mandated drug treatment, Mr. Fodor received three years' probation. In interviews afterward he expressed joy in his newfound sobriety and excitement at resuming his career.

But even before Mr. Fodor was arrested his career appeared to fall short of the Olympian heights he had been led to expect. He performed worldwide, but not always with the finest orchestras or in the most prestigious halls, a situation that the arrest only intensified.

Mr. Fodor had made his early reputation with dazzling showpieces by Paganini, Fritz Kreisler and Henryk Wieniawski, and critics took him increasingly to task for what they saw as the triumph of flash over substance.

He relapsed periodically into drugs and alcohol. "He would be clean for years and then start using again," Ms. Davis said in an interview.

Mr. Fodor's personal life was sometimes unsettled. Married in 1978, he and Ms. Davis divorced in 1986. His second marriage, to Sally Swedlund, also ended in divorce. He and Ms. Davis remarried in November.

Besides Ms. Davis, Mr. Fodor is survived by their two daughters and their son, a sister, a brother and two grandchildren.

Last year, in despair over his career, Mr. Fodor stopped playing the violin entirely, Ms. Davis said. He canceled his scheduled concerts.

"It was too painful for him," she said. "He felt like his career had been ripped from him, and he didn't have the great venues to play in anymore, and it just crushed him."

— *By Margalit Fox*

JUDITH COPLON

Love and Espionage in Cold War America

MAY 17, 1921 - FEB. 26, 2011

Judith Socolov, who as a diminutive Barnard graduate named Judith Coplon was convicted of espionage more than 60 years ago after embracing a utopian vision of communism and falling in love with a Soviet agent, died on Feb. 26 in Manhattan. She was 89.

A longtime Brooklyn resident, Ms. Socolov had been living at an assisted-living facility in the Bronx.

Judith Coplon was a 5-foot-tall, 27-year-old political analyst for the Justice Department when F.B.I. agents arrested her and the Soviet agent Valentin A. Gubitchev in 1949 on a Manhattan street. The agents had followed her from Washington, where she had been identified from intercepted Soviet cables.

But her convictions for espionage in 1949 and for conspiracy (with Mr. Gubitchev) in 1950 were overturned — in one case because federal agents overheard conversations with her lawyer, and in the other because she was arrested on probable cause but without a warrant.

Still, the United States Court of Appeals concluded that "her guilt is plain," and Soviet documents released years later supported that conclusion.

"She was a very high priority to the F.B.I.," John Earl Haynes, a cold war historian at the Library of Congress, said in an interview, "because she was clearly in a Justice Department office, the Foreign Agents Registration Section, that was receiving the F.B.I.'s own counterespionage reports."

CODE NAME SIMA: Ms. Coplon in 1949, the year of her arrest.

While her appeals were pending, Ms. Coplon (pronounced COPE-lon) married one of her lawyers, Albert Socolov, a decorated D-Day veteran. The court restricted their honeymoon to within 100 miles of New York City.

After the verdicts were reversed, Ms. Coplon — now Ms. Socolov — lived out of the public eye, raising four children, earning a master's degree in education, publishing bilingual books, supporting progressive causes, tutoring women in prison in creative writing, and, with her husband, running two Mexican restaurants in Manhattan (the Beach House in TriBeCa and Alameda on the Upper West Side).

Ms. Socolov refused to discuss her relationship with Mr. Gubitchev, a Russian working at the United Nations, or her legal ordeal. "The subject of her innocence or guilt was something that she would strictly not address," her daughter, Emily Socolov, said.

"It's very hair-raising to read about your mother being given a code name and moved around like a chess piece," Ms. Socolov added. "Was she a spy? I think it's another question that I ask: Was she part of a community that felt that they were going to bring, by their actions, an age of peace and justice and an equal share for all and the abolishing of color lines and class lines?"

"If these were things that she actually did, she was not defining them as espionage," the daughter continued. "If you feel that what you're doing answers to a higher ideal, it's not treason."

Judith Coplon was born in Brooklyn on May 17, 1921, the daughter of Samuel and Rebecca Moroh Coplon, a toy manufacturer and milliner, respectively. Her great-grandfather, a peddler who had emigrated from Prussia, was a prisoner during the Civil War at Andersonville, the infamous Confederate prison camp.

Ms. Coplon won a good-citizenship award in high school and a full scholarship to Barnard, where she majored in history and was a member of the Young Communist League. She graduated cum laude in 1943, joined the Justice Department in 1944 and, according to the government, was recruited by Soviet intelligence later that year.

In 1948, after intercepting a secret three-year-old Soviet cable, the Venona project, a joint effort by the United States and the United Kingdom to decode Soviet diplomatic communications, identified Ms. Coplon as an agent code-named Sima. The Soviet cable said she would be able "to carry out important work for us in throwing light" on United States counterintelligence.

To snare her, the F.B.I. fed her a false memorandum about atomic power, then followed her in Manhattan on March 30, 1949, using 30 agents and a fleet of radio cars. She and Mr. Gubitchev met up at 193rd Street and Broadway, avoided contact for two hours, then were seen dashing onto a bus at 42nd Street and Broadway. Agents finally caught up with them below the elevated subway line on Third Avenue between 14th and 15th streets. Several secret documents, including the faked memo, were confiscated.

"I was never and am not a Communist," Ms. Coplon later declared. "The only crime I can be said to be guilty of is that I knew a Russian."

She said she had met Mr. Gubitchev at the Museum of Modern Art and fallen in love with him, only to learn he was married. "I will always say that I'm innocent and that I'm being framed," she testified. Ms. Coplon's long-ailing father died at 69 while she was under indictment, and one of her lawyers said the shock of her arrest had hastened his death.

In 1952, after winning the right to a new trial, she remained free on $40,000 bail. The bail money was not returned until 1967, when the Justice Department formally dropped the case.

For years, though, the charges haunted her. "If she felt somebody was looking at her askance or treating her disparagingly," Emily Socolov said, "she thought about that case."

Ms. Socolov emerged in 1981 to defend her husband against accusations that money he had invested for a client was drug-related. He was acquitted.

Mr. Socolov survives her. Besides her daughter, Ms. Coplon is also survived by three sons and four grandchildren.

In their book about the case, "The Spy Who Seduced America," Marcia and Thomas Mitchell wrote that in 1994 Albert Socolov continued to insist that his wife was innocent. But for 60 years the couple shunned publicity.

"We've had all kinds of requests for interviews, for books, but it has been our steady policy to refuse," Mr. Socolov told The New York Times a decade ago. "Other people are interested in posterity. We're not."

— *By Sam Roberts*

DUKE SNIDER

A Prince of New York Baseball

SEPT. 19, 1926 - FEB. 27, 2011

Duke Snider, the Hall of Fame center fielder renowned for his home run drives and superb defensive play in the Brooklyn Dodgers' glory years, died on Feb. 27 in Escondido, Calif. He was 84.

From 1949, his first full season, until 1957, Snider was a colossus in New York, one of three roaming its center fields during the city's golden age of baseball, when at least one New York team played in the World Series each October. Snider and Willie Mays of the Giants and Mickey Mantle of the Yankees were symbols of their teams, as the city's fans — divided into three camps for the last time — argued over who was best: Willie, Mickey or the Duke?

History has since settled Snider in third place, but at the time he had a good case to make. The Dodgers, known fondly as Dem Bums and immortalized by the writer Roger Kahn as "The Boys of Summer," won six National League pennants during Snider's 11 seasons in Brooklyn.

They had a roster full of stellar players — Jackie Robinson, Roy Campanella, Pee Wee

Reese and Gil Hodges among them — but Snider was perhaps the star among stars.

A swift outfielder, a slick fielder and a No. 3 hitter with reliable power in the clutch, he hit 40 or more home runs in five consecutive seasons, something neither Mays nor Mantle ever achieved. He was the only player to hit four home runs twice in a World Series. When he accomplished the feat in 1955, it helped the Dodgers end decades of frustration as they defeated the Yankees to bring Brooklyn its only World Series championship.

As if for good measure, in 1957, before the Dodgers left for Los Angeles, Snider hit the last home run at their famous Brooklyn ballpark, Ebbets Field.

"They used to run a box in the New York papers comparing me to Mickey Mantle and Willie Mays," Snider recalled on the eve of his induction into the Hall of Fame in 1980. "It was a great time for baseball."

The comparisons with Mantle and Mays may have been apt, but they were also hard on Snider, who was known as a perfectionist, a harsh self-critic and a man whose moods could be dark.

As pitcher Carl Erskine, his Dodger roommate, recalled in "Bums," a 1984 book by Peter Golenbock: "Every place he went, no matter how good he was, they'd say, 'His potential is so great, he can do even better.' And this was a real frustration for Duke. He saw himself as not measuring up."

Snider said: "I had to learn that every day wasn't a bed of roses, and that took some time. I would sulk. I'd have a pity party for myself."

Playing for 18 seasons, Snider hit 407 home runs and had 2,116 hits. He batted at least .300 seven times, had a lifetime batting average of .295 and was usually among the league leaders in runs batted in and runs.

Snider excelled in center field, though Ebbets Field denied him the outfield expanse enjoyed by Mays at the Polo Grounds and Mantle at Yankee Stadium. He moved back on the ball brilliantly and unleashed powerful throws.

Edwin Donald Snider was born on Sept. 19, 1926, in Los Angeles and was brought up in nearby Compton. His father, Ward, seeing him return proudly from his first day at school, at age 5, called him the Duke.

Snider signed with the Dodgers' minor league system out of Compton Junior College for a $750 bonus and made his debut in Brooklyn on opening day 1947 with a pinch-hit single against the Boston Braves. But his arrival was hardly noticed. That was the day Robinson broke the major league color barrier.

POWER AND GRACE: Snider, shown rounding a base in 1956, hit 40 home runs in five straight seasons.

Snider was overanxious at the plate and frustrated by the curveball. Branch Rickey, the Dodgers' general manager, and his aide George Sisler, once a great hitter with the St. Louis Browns, worked with Snider in spring training in 1948 to teach him the strike zone. Snider credited Rickey's guidance for making him a Hall of Famer.

Snider flourished in 1949, his first full season with the Dodgers, when he batted .292 with 23 home runs and 92 R.B.I. The next year, a Duke Snider Fan Club was born.

But Snider's moodiness affected his relationship with the fans. When he was booed by Dodgers fans in midsummer 1955 after a prolonged slump, he fumed. As he recalled in "The Duke of Flatbush" (1988), written with Bill Gilbert, he told sportswriters: "The Brooklyn fans are the worst in the league.

They don't deserve a pennant." The complaint made headlines.

Reese, the Dodgers' captain and shortstop who later joined Snider in the Hall of Fame, teased him about his outbursts, and Snider later reflected how "Pee Wee taught me to control my emotions more."

But a year after the tirade against the fans, Snider was chided by some sportswriters as being ungrateful for his good fortune when he collaborated with Kahn for a May 1956 article in Collier's titled "I Play Baseball for Money — Not Fun."

On Sunday afternoon, Sept. 22, 1957, Snider hit two home runs off the Philadelphia Phillies' Robin Roberts. The second drive was the last homer at Ebbets Field. The Dodgers moved to Los Angeles and the Giants went to San Francisco the next season.

Snider was 31 by then, hampered by a sore knee and frustrated by the bizarre dimensions at the Los Angeles Coliseum, where the fence in right-center field was 440 feet away. His production declined in the Dodgers' four seasons there.

After 11 years in Brooklyn and 5 in Los Angeles, Snider was sold before the 1963 season to the Mets for $40,000, joining a dreadful ball club in its second season that was collecting former Dodgers, Giants and Yankees to boost attendance.

Snider was reunited with his Brooklyn teammates Hodges, Roger Craig and Charlie Neal

APPRECIATION

And for a Time, the Duke Was King

"Willie, Mickey and the Duke," the Terry Cashman song about three center fielders, defined New York baseball in the 1950s.

But of the three only Willie Mays and Mickey Mantle earned adulation as arguably the best baseball player ever. Duke Snider never did. For a time, though, in the '50s, the Duke of Flatbush was better than either of them. He hit 407 home runs, almost all for the Dodgers in Brooklyn and Los Angeles, and a few for the Mets and the Giants at the end. But in the '50s he hit more home runs than Mays or Mantle or anybody else in the big leagues.

Duke had it all: a sweet swing, a bazooka arm, springs in his legs. He also had the luck of being virtually the only left-handed slugger in a lineup dominated by right-handed hitters like Jackie Robinson, Roy Campanella, Gil Hodges and Carl Furillo. Snider was usually swinging against right-handed pitching, giving him an edge.

Then again, he didn't really have it all. As he often acknowledged, he had a "big mouth" that tarnished his image and his popularity. After being booed at a game at Ebbets Field one night, he snapped that Brooklyn fans "don't deserve a pennant." That prompted even more boos the next night. He later put his name on a Collier's article confessing that he played baseball only for the money, that he would rather be in California on his avocado farm not far from Los Angeles.

He did return to California, when the Dodgers moved there after the 1957 season, but after bombarding Bedford Avenue beyond the 40-foot-high right-field screen at Ebbets Field, he had to cope with the faraway right-field fence at Memorial Coliseum, a stadium built for the track-and-field events of the 1932 Olympics.

and played for Casey Stengel, who had managed the Yankees in all those World Series games against the Dodgers teams of the 1950s.

Snider hit his 400th homer and got his 2,000th hit as a Met but batted only .243 on a team that lost 111 games.

Just before the 1964 season, the Mets accommodated Snider's desire to play for a contender and return to the West Coast by selling him to the San Francisco Giants. Now Snider was a member of the Dodgers' archrivals. He batted .210 in 91 games, then retired at age 38.

Snider later managed in the Dodgers' and San Diego Padres' farm systems and served as a broadcaster for the Padres and the Montreal Expos.

He is survived by his wife, Beverly, two sons and two daughters.

Snider returned to Brooklyn on a sad note on July 20, 1995, when he appeared in federal court, a couple of miles from where Ebbets Field once stood, as a criminal defendant.

Snider and another Hall of Famer, the former Giants first baseman Willie McCovey, pleaded guilty to tax fraud for failing to report thousands of dollars earned by signing autographs and participating in sports memorabilia shows. "We have choices to make in our lives," Snider said. "I made the wrong choice."

The following Dec. 1, he was sentenced to two years' probation and fined $5,000.

Although he made his home in California,

When Mays arrived at the Coliseum with the San Francisco Giants in 1958, he chirped how the Dodgers had taken "the bat out of Duke's hands," the bat that had hit 40 or more homers a year for five consecutive seasons when 40 home runs was an achievement. By the time the Dodgers moved into their Chavez Ravine palace in 1962, and later with the Mets and the hated Giants, Snider was never the same hitter who had stroked four home runs against the Yankees in the 1952 and 1955 World Series.

As a youngster in Compton, Calif., he got his nickname from his father. The nickname fit a center fielder who was Dodger royalty and arguably a better fielder than Mays or Mantle.

In a 1954 game at Connie Mack Stadium in Philadelphia, he made a catch that his teammate and roommate Carl Erskine described as "the greatest I ever saw." With two on, two out and the Dodgers protecting a one-run lead, Willie Jones hit a soaring drive toward the left-center-field stands. Running to his right, Snider climbed the wall like Spider-Man, stretched his left arm and snagged the ball.

"I figured I had about four steps to the wall," he said that day. "After four steps, I jumped. My right foot dug into the wall. It's wood. Then my left knee scraped the wall and I turned my body. All I know is that the ball was in the webbing when I came down."

He would be a $20-million-a-year player now, but he and Robinson were the highest-paid Dodgers at about $40,000 a year. That magazine article about playing for the money would haunt him in 1995 when he pleaded guilty to tax-fraud charges for not reporting thousands of dollars to the Internal Revenue Service for income from baseball memorabilia shows from 1984 to 1993. He reportedly received a total of more than $100,000 from the shows. He did not receive jail time.

"I made the wrong choice," he said. But for all his wrong choices, he'll always be the Duke of Flatbush to anyone who rooted for the Dodgers in Brooklyn, the Duke who was so proud of having hit the last home run at Ebbets Field, the Duke who didn't need his real name (Edwin) to be part of a song title.

— By Dave Anderson

Snider retained emotional ties to Brooklyn. He made that clear on Sept. 12, 1963, when the Mets gave him a "night" at their home in the Polo Grounds, where the Brooklyn Dodgers had long been the hated foe. Snider's former Brooklyn teammates were introduced — Robinson, Campanella, Erskine, Furillo, Don Newcombe and Ralph Branca. And then Snider moved to the microphone.

"I look up into the stands, and it looks like Ebbets Field," he said. "The Mets are wonderful, but you can't take the Dodger out of Brooklyn."

— *By Richard Goldstein and Bruce Weber*

FRANK BUCKLES

Last of the Doughboys

FEB. 1, 1901 - FEB. 27, 2011

FRANK BUCKLES, who drove an Army ambulance in France in 1918 and came to symbolize a generation of embattled young Americans as the last of the World War I doughboys, died on Feb. 27 at his home in Charles Town, W.Va. He was 110.

He was only a corporal and he never got closer than 30 or so miles to the Western Front trenches, but Mr. Buckles became something of a national treasure as the last living link to the two million men who served in the American Expeditionary Forces in France in "the war to end all wars."

President Obama said in a statement that Mr. Buckles "reminds us of the true meaning of patriotism."

Frail, stooped and hard of hearing but sharp of mind, Mr. Buckles was named grand marshal of the National Memorial Day Parade in Washington in 2007. He was a guest at Arlington National Cemetery on Veterans Day 2007 for a wreath-laying ceremony at the Tomb of the Unknowns. He was honored by Defense Secretary Robert M. Gates at the Pentagon and met with President George W. Bush at the White House in March 2008.

United States senators played host to him at the Capitol in June 2008 for the impending 90th anniversary of the World War I armistice. And he appeared before a Senate subcommittee in December 2009 to support legislation named in his honor to bestow federal status on a World War I memorial on the Washington Mall built in the 1930s.

Sought out for interviews in his final years, Mr. Buckles told of witnessing a ceremony involving British veterans of the Crimean War, fought in the 1850s, when he was stationed in England before heading to France. He remembered chatting with Gen. John J. Pershing, the commander of American troops in World War I, at an event in Oklahoma City soon after the war's end.

And he proudly held a sepia-toned photograph of himself in his doughboy uniform when he was interviewed by USA Today in 2007. "I was a snappy soldier," he said. "All gung-ho."

Frank Woodruff Buckles was born Feb. 1, 1901, on a farm near Bethany, Mo. He was living in Oakwood, Okla., when the United States entered World War I, and he tried to enlist in the Marine Corps at age 16, having been inspired by recruiting posters.

The Marines turned him down as under-age and under the required weight. The Navy did not want him either, saying he had flat feet. But the Army took him in August 1917 after he lied about his age, and he volunteered to be an ambulance driver, hearing that was the quickest path to service in France.

He sailed for England in December 1917 on the Carpathia, the ship that had helped save survivors of the Titanic's sinking in 1912. He later served in various locations in France, including Bordeaux, and drove military autos and ambulances. He was moved by the war's impact on the French people.

"The little French children were hungry," Mr. Buckles recalled in a 2001 interview for the Veterans History Project of the Library of Congress. "We'd feed the children. To me, that was a pretty sad sight."

Mr. Buckles escorted German prisoners of war back to their homeland after the Armistice, then returned to the United States and later worked in the Toronto office of the White Star shipping line.

A LONG LIFE: Mr. Buckles, shown in 2008, outlived every other American who served in World War I.

He traveled widely over the years, working for steamship companies, and he was on business in Manila when the Japanese occupied it after the attack on Pearl Harbor in December 1941. He was imprisoned by the Japanese and lost more than 50 pounds before being liberated by an American airborne unit in February 1945.

After retiring from steamship work in the mid-1950s, Mr. Buckles ran a cattle ranch in Charles Town, and he was still riding a tractor there at age 106.

In April 2007, Mr. Buckles was identified by the Department of Veterans Affairs as one of the four known survivors among the more than 4.7 million Americans who had served in the armed forces of the Allied nations from April 6, 1917, when the United States entered World War I, to Nov. 11, 1918, the date of the armistice.

Two of the four — J. Russell Coffey and Harry Landis — had served stateside in the American Army. Mr. Coffey died in December 2007 at 109; Mr. Landis, in February 2008 at 108. John Babcock, who was born in Canada, served in the Canadian Army in Britain in World War I and held dual American and Canadian citizenship, died in Spokane, Wash., in February 2010 at 109.

The last known veterans of the French and German armies in World War I, Lazare Ponticelli and Erich Kästner, respectively, died a few months apart in 2008; Harry Patch, the last British soldier, died in 2009. (With the death in May of Claude Choules, who served in Britain's Royal Navy, Florence Green, who was a member of Britain's Women's Royal Air Force and who lives in England, is thought to be the only person still living who served in any capacity in the war.)

Mr. Buckles is survived by a daughter. His wife, Audrey, died in 1999.

More than eight decades after World War I ended, Mr. Buckles retained images of his French comrades. And he thought back to the fate that awaited them.

"What I have a vivid memory of is the French soldiers — being in a small village and going in to a local wine shop in the evening," he told a Library of Congress interviewer. "They had very, very little money. But they were having wine and singing the 'Marseillaise' with enthusiasm. And I inquired, 'What is the occasion?' They were going back to the front. Can you imagine that?"

— *By Richard Goldstein*

NECMETTIN ERBAKAN

A Turk Who Faced East

OCT. 29, 1926 - FEB. 27, 2011

Necmettin Erbakan, the first Islamist prime minister of Turkey, whose attempt to turn his country away from the West led the military to depose him in 1997, died on Feb. 27 in Ankara. He was 84.

During his turbulent year as prime minister, Mr. Erbakan boldly challenged Turkey's secular dogma, vowing to create a pan-Islamic currency and rescue Turkey from "the unbelievers of Europe." He embraced the religious government in Iran, allowed female civil servants to wear head scarves to work, and held Islamic feasts in the prime minister's residence.

Mr. Erbakan boldly challenged Turkey's secular dogma, vowing to create a pan-Islamic currency and rescue Turkey from "the unbelievers of Europe."

Yet Mr. Erbakan was also a consummate insider, always dapper in trademark Versace ties. He was among the last survivors of the political generation that ruled Turkey as it struggled toward democracy during the second half of the 20th century, a period punctuated by three military coups. He was often called Hodja, a term of affection accorded to religious teachers or wise men.

Like other political patriarchs of his era, Mr. Erbakan was a nationalist who bowed before the reality of military power. He had no sympathy for the demands of Kurdish nationalists who sought broadened cultural and political rights. Yet he repeatedly pushed for a greater role for religion in public life. His party was banned multiple times. After each shutdown, he reinvented and renamed it.

"He introduced political Islam to Turkey," Sedat Bozkurt, a Turkish journalist, said in a televised interview. "However, the political Islam applied in Turkey differed from the others. One of its elements was Turkish nationalism."

Among Mr. Erbakan's most successful followers was the ambitious candy salesman Recep Tayyip Erdogan, who under his tutelage was elected mayor of Istanbul and is now prime minister. The men split politically, and Prime Minister Erdogan displaced Mr. Erbakan as the hero of Turkey's devout.

"We will always remember him with gratitude as a teacher and a leader," Mr. Erdogan said of Mr. Erbakan, who is survived by two daughters and a son.

Necmettin Erbakan was born on Oct. 29, 1926, in the Black Sea town of Sinop, home in antiquity to Diogenes the Cynic. Mr. Erbakan's father, a judge, sent him to high school in Istanbul. He later compiled an outstanding record as an engineering student. He completed his doctoral work in Aachen, Germany, and worked in that country for several years, specializing in diesel engine design. His German remained fluent and lyrical.

In 1970, stung by the refusal of a center-right party to nominate him for a seat in Parliament, he formed his own political party, which advocated a return to religious values — not an obvious choice for the son of a civil servant. The party survived repeated closings and Mr. Erbakan's several years of exile in Switzerland. Though the party never won nearly enough votes to put him in power, he emerged as a kingmaker. Twice in the 1970s he became deputy prime minister.

In the 1995 election, with the political scene atomized, Mr. Erbakan's party, then called Welfare, finished first with 21 percent of the vote. After striking a coalition deal with another party leader who was eager to control corruption investigations, Mr. Erbakan became prime minister. He immediately began challenging the secular, pro-Western foundations of modern Turkey.

The last straw for his opponents may have been Jerusalem Night, when the Iranian ambassador, evidently with Mr. Erbakan's permission, addressed an audience in the town of Sincan and roused it to a frenzy with lurid calls for fundamentalism and anti-Zionist struggle. Alarmed Turks began taking to the streets, marching behind protest banners reading "Turkey Is Secular and Will Remain So!"

After Mr. Erbakan had been in office for 12 months, military commanders, who consider themselves the ultimate guardians of Turkish secularism, decided to strike against him. They forced him out with a series of threatening memoranda listing his sins. He resigned on Feb. 28, 1997, ousted by what is widely described as Turkey's only postmodern coup.

These events split the religious political movement in Turkey. A group of insurgents, accusing Mr. Erbakan of losing touch with a rapidly changing country, tried to wrest control of the party from him. When they failed, they quit the party; founded their own, calling it Justice and Development; and rocketed to national power.

Mr. Erbakan later became the target of corruption charges. In 2002 he was sentenced to two years and four months in prison on charges of "forgery of personal documents." President Abdullah Gul, who was his foreign policy adviser during his ill-fated year in power, pardoned him.

Mr. Erbakan's party withered into insignificance by clinging to old-style Islamism. His onetime follower, Prime Minister Erdogan, devised a more inclusive political formula that combined respect for religious belief with commitments to democracy, capitalism and Western alliances. That formula — a refined version of the one Mr. Erbakan developed nearly half a century ago — propelled Mr. Erdogan to power and has kept him there for nearly a decade.

— *By Stephen Kinzer*

EDDIE KIRKLAND

He Could Sing the Blues, All Right

AUG. 16, 1923 - FEB. 27, 2011

For more than half a century Eddie Kirkland played the blues, and for much of that time he seemed to have known the blues firsthand.

As a child, he was poor in the Jim Crow South. As an adult, he lived through the deaths of several children, including the murder of the niece he had reared as a daughter. By his own account, he also survived two shootings and spent time on a chain gang.

A guitarist, singer, songwriter and harmonica player, Mr. Kirkland performed with some of the greatest names in blues and soul, including John Lee Hooker and Otis Redding. But he remained somewhat in the shadow of the stars, not as widely known as they and not remotely as well off. (Both conditions, by all accounts, were fine with him.)

He kept a rigorous touring schedule. Until several years ago, he spent more than 40 weeks a year on the road; more recently, he toured two weeks out of every four. His itinerant life long ago earned him the nickname the Gypsy of the Blues.

Mr. Kirkland died on Feb. 27, at 87, in a Tampa, Fla., hospital, from injuries sustained in an automobile accident as he drove between gigs that morning.

According to a spokeswoman for the Florida Highway Patrol, Mr. Kirkland turned into the path of a Greyhound bus on a highway in Homosassa, Fla., near the Gulf Coast. No one aboard the bus was injured.

A longtime resident of Macon, Ga., he had known a life of struggle but also, in his vibrant telling, picaresque adventure. Some adventures can be confirmed. Others may have been part of the mythology that seemed to swirl around Mr. Kirkland — he was known as a charismatic teller of tall tales — and that long infused accounts of his life in the news media.

LIVING THE BLUES: A hard, often tragic, life fueled Mr. Kirkland's music.

What is certain is that in the course of a career that began in the 1930s, Mr. Kirkland became known for his impassioned singing; wailing guitar lines (he was among the first to bring blues guitar into the electric age); vibrant stage presence (he favored bravura headgear like turbans and huge bandannas); and boundless energy, expressed not only musically but also acrobatically. (During at least one performance with the British rock band Foghat, Mr. Kirkland did a back somersault while continuing to play the guitar.)

His many albums include "It's the Blues Man!," "Have Mercy" and "Democrat Blues."

Edward Kirkland was born, he said, to a 12-year-old mother on Aug. 16, 1923; his birth took place in either Dothan, Ala. (according to his family), or in Kingston, Jamaica (according to him). In either case, he was known to have been living in Dothan by the time he was a small child.

He took up his instruments as a boy. When he was 12, as he told it, he joined a traveling medicine show, dancing and playing the harmonica.

Mr. Kirkland is known to have made his way to Detroit in the 1940s, and it was there that he honed his skills as a blues guitarist. By day, he worked on the assembly line at the Ford Motor Company. By night, he performed at Detroit's lively round of house parties, where he met Mr. Hooker, with whom he would collaborate for a number of years. Mr. Kirkland later toured for several years as Mr. Redding's bandleader.

As a songwriter, Mr. Kirkland was best known for his twin singles "The Hawg," Parts 1 and 2, written under the name Eddie Kirk. Issued by Volt Records in the 1960s, they are explosively danceable and feature his moaning harmonica and guitar, plus vigorous grunting.

Mr. Kirkland moved to Georgia in the early 1950s. Sometime afterward, he later said, he killed a man in self-defense. He was sentenced to three years in prison, which, in his telling, included work on a chain gang.

In other incidents, Mr. Kirkland said, he was shot in the head — which he described as having cost him sight in one eye and hearing in one ear — and in the knee.

In 1998, as confirmed by local news accounts, Mr. Kirkland's 15-year-old niece, Monica McNeal, whom he and his wife had raised, was abducted and murdered in Macon.

Mr. Kirkland's first wife, the former Ida Mae Shoulders, died before him, as did two daughters. Survivors include his second wife, Mary, five daughters and two sons from his first marriage, three daughters from his second marriage, and many grandchildren and great-grandchildren.

Through everything, Mr. Kirkland kept on playing. His own hard times, he often observed, were the wellspring of his art. Those of others kept him in business.

"Sometime in your life you're gonna need the blues," Mr. Kirkland told The St. Petersburg Times in 1999. "You been left by a girl? You had bad luck? Listening to the blues'll help you overcome your troubles. As long as people got trouble, I'll still be playing the blues."

— *By Margalit Fox*

JANE RUSSELL

Too Sultry for the Censors

JUNE 21, 1921 - FEB. 28, 2011

JANE RUSSELL, the voluptuous actress at the center of one of the most highly publicized censorship episodes in movie history, the long-delayed release of the 1940s western "The Outlaw," died on Feb. 28 at her home in Santa Maria, Calif. She was 89.

Ms. Russell was 19 and working in a doctor's office when Howard Hughes, returning to movie production after his aviation successes, cast her as the tempestuous Rio McDonald, the object of a romantic rivalry between Doc Holliday and Billy the Kid, in "The Outlaw," which he directed.

A movie poster showing a sultry Ms. Russell in a cleavage-revealing blouse falling off one shoulder as she reclined in a haystack and held a gun quickly became notorious. It seemed only to fuel the determination of film censors to prevent the movie's release because of scenes that by 1940s standards revealed too much of the star's breasts. The Roman Catholic Church was one of the movie's vocal opponents.

Although the film had its premiere and ran for nine weeks in San Francisco in 1943, it did not open in New York until 1947 and was not given a complete national release until 1950. Critics were generally unimpressed by it, but it made Ms. Russell a star. The specially engineered bra that Hughes was said to have designed for his 38D leading lady took its place in cinematic history, although Ms. Russell always contended that she never actually wore it.

She went on to make some two dozen feature films, all but a handful of them between 1948 and 1957 and many of them westerns.

In the western comedy "The Paleface" (1948), she played Calamity Jane opposite Bob Hope, with whom she also starred in "Son of Paleface," the 1952 sequel. In the musical comedy that she called her favorite film, "Gentlemen Prefer Blondes" (1953), she starred with Marilyn Monroe as one of two ambitious showgirls. Her numbers included "Two Little Girls From Little Rock," one of several duets with Ms. Monroe, and the comic lament "Ain't There Anyone Here for Love?" Two years later she starred with Jeanne Crain in "Gentlemen Marry Brunettes," a sequel of sorts, set in Paris.

A number of her movies were musicals, and singing became a large part of her career. She first appeared in Las Vegas in 1957 and was performing in musical shows at small venues as recently as 2008. Although she did considerable stage acting over the years, her sole Broadway appearance was in 1971 in the Stephen Sondheim musical "Company," in which she replaced Elaine Stritch as the tough-talking character who sings "The Ladies Who Lunch."

Ms. Russell was best known in the 1970s and '80s as the television spokeswoman in commercials for Playtex bras, which she promoted as ideal for "full-figured gals" like her.

Ernestine Jane Geraldine Russell was born on June 21, 1921, in Bemidji, Minn., the daughter of Roy and Geraldine Russell. Her mother had been an aspiring actress and a model. "The Girl in the Blue Hat," a portrait of her by the watercolorist Mary B. Titcomb, once hung in the White House, bought by President Woodrow Wilson.

When Jane was 9 months old, before her four brothers were born, her father moved the family to Southern California to take a job as an office manager. He died when Jane was in her teens.

After high school, Jane took acting classes at Max Reinhardt's theater workshop and with Maria Ouspenskaya. She did some modeling for a photographer friend but was working in a chiropodist's office when a photo of her found its way to Hughes's casting people.

In 1943 she married her high school sweetheart, Bob Waterfield, a U.C.L.A. football player who became the star quarterback of the Los Angeles Rams. They adopted a daughter and two sons. (After a botched abortion before her marriage, Ms. Russell was unable to have children. She later became an outspoken opponent of abortion and an advocate of adoption, founding the World Adoption International Fund in the 1950s.)

She and Mr. Waterfield divorced in 1967. The following year she married Roger Barrett, an actor, who died of a heart attack three months after the wedding.

NO PLAIN JANE: Ms. Russell's looks helped make her a star, but by the late '50s her film career was all but over.

In 1974, John Calvin Peoples, a real estate broker and retired Air Force lieutenant, became her third husband, and they were together until his death, in 1999. Ms. Russell had had problems with alcohol, but they became worse after she was widowed again; her grown children insisted that she undergo rehabilitation at the age of 79.

She also turned to conservative politics in her later years.

"These days I'm a teetotal, mean-spirited, right-wing, narrow-minded, conservative Christian bigot, but not a racist," she told The Daily Mail of London in 2003. Bigotry, she added, "just means you don't have an open mind."

By the time she married Mr. Peoples, her acting career was all but over. After appearing in three movies in the mid-1960s, she had a small role in her last film, "Darker Than Amber," a 1970 action drama starring Rod Taylor. She did relatively little television, but her final TV role was in a 1986 episode of the NBC police drama "Hunter."

Her children survive her, as do 8 grandchildren and 10 great-grandchildren.

Ms. Russell was very public about her religious convictions. She organized Bible study groups in Hollywood and wrote about experiencing speaking in tongues. In her memoir, "My Path and My Detours" (1985), she described the strength she drew from Christianity.

A higher power was always there, she wrote, "telling me that if I could just hold tough a little longer, I'd find myself around one more dark corner, see one more spot of light and have one more drop of pure joy in this journey called life."

— *By Anita Gates*

PETER J. GOMES

A Coming Out, and a Life's Mission

MAY 22, 1942 - FEB. 28, 2011

THE REV. PETER J. GOMES, a Harvard minister, theologian and author who announced that he was gay a generation ago and became one of America's most prominent spiritual voices against intolerance, died on Feb. 28 in Boston. He was 68.

The cause was complications of a stroke. Mr. Gomes, who died at Massachusetts General Hospital, lived in Cambridge and Plymouth, Mass.

One can read into the Bible almost any interpretation of morality, Mr. Gomes liked to say after coming out, for its passages had been used to defend slavery and the liberation of slaves, to support racism, anti-Semitism and patriotism, to enshrine a dominance of men over women, and to condemn homosexuality as immoral.

He was a thundering black Baptist preacher and for much of his life a conservative Republican celebrity who wrote books about the Pilgrims, published volumes of sermons and presided at weddings and funerals of the rich and famous. He gave the benediction at President Ronald Reagan's second inauguration and delivered the National Cathedral sermon at the inauguration of Reagan's successor, George H. W. Bush.

At Harvard, Mr. Gomes was the Plummer professor of Christian morals at the School of Divinity and the Pusey minister of Memorial Church, a nondenominational center of Christian life on campus. For decades he was among the first and the last to address undergraduates, greeting arriving freshmen with a sermon on hallowed traditions and advising graduating seniors about the world beyond the sheltering Harvard Yard.

Then, in 1991, he appeared before an angry crowd of students, faculty members and administrators protesting homophobic articles in a conservative campus magazine whose distribution had led to a spate of harassment and slurs against gay men and lesbians at Harvard. Mr. Gomes, putting his reputation and career on the line, announced that he was "a Christian who happens as well to be gay."

When the cheers faded, there were expressions of surprise from the Establishment, and a few calls for his resignation, which were ignored. The announcement changed little in Mr. Gomes's private life; he had never married and said he was celibate by choice. But it was a turning point for him professionally.

"I now have an unambiguous vocation — a mission — to address the religious causes and roots of homophobia," he told The Washington Post months later. "I will devote the rest of my life to addressing the 'religious case' against gays."

He was true to his word. His sermons and lectures, always well attended, were packed in Cambridge and around the country as he embarked on a campaign to rebut literal and fundamentalist interpretations of the Bible. He also wrote extensively on intolerance.

"Religious fundamentalism is dangerous because it cannot accept ambiguity and diversity and is therefore inherently intolerant," he declared in an Op-Ed article in The New York Times in 1992. "Such intolerance, in the name of virtue, is ruthless and uses political power to destroy what it cannot convert."

In his 1996 best seller, "The Good Book: Reading the Bible with Mind and Heart," Mr. Gomes urged believers to grasp the spirit, not the letter, of scriptural passages that he said had been misused to defend racism, anti-Semitism and sexism, and to attack homosexuality and abortion. He offered interpretations that he said transcended the narrow context of modern prejudices.

"The Bible alone is the most dangerous thing I can think of," he told The Los Angeles Times. "You need an ongoing context and a community of interpretation to keep the Bible current and to keep yourself honest. Forget the thought that the Bible is an absolute pronouncement."

But Mr. Gomes also defended the Bible from critics on the left who called it corrupt because passages had been used to oppress people. "The Bible isn't a single book, it isn't a single historical or philosophical or theological treatise," he told The Seattle Gay News in 1996. "It has 66 books in it. It is a library."

Peter John Gomes (rhymes with homes) was born in Boston on May 22, 1942, the only child of Peter Lobo and Orissa White Gomes. His father, born in the Cape Verde Islands off Africa's west coast, was a cranberry bog worker. His mother was a graduate of the New England Conservatory of Music. Peter grew up in Plymouth with literature, piano lessons and expectations that he would become a minister. He was active in the Baptist Church and preached his first sermon at 12.

He worked as a houseman to help pay for his education. After graduation from Plymouth High School in 1961, he attended Bates College in Lewiston, Me., a coeducational liberal arts institution founded by abolitionists in 1855. He majored in history and received a bachelor's degree in 1965; he then earned a bachelor of divinity degree at Harvard in 1968 and was ordained a Baptist minister.

After two years teaching Western civilization at Tuskegee Institute in Alabama, he returned to Harvard in 1970 as assistant minister of Memorial Church. His first book, "History of the Pilgrim Society, 1820-1970," was published in 1971. "The Books of the Pilgrims," written with Lawrence D. Geller, appeared four years later. In 1974 he was named Plummer professor and Pusey minister.

In clerical collar and vestments, Mr. Gomes was a figure of homiletic power in the pulpit, hammering out the cadences in a rich baritone that The New Yorker called a blend of James Earl

'AN UNAMBIGUOUS VOCATION': In 1991, Mr. Gomes, a prominent conservative minister, announced he was gay and pledged "to address the religious causes and roots of homophobia."

Jones and John Houseman. In class, he was a New England patrician: the broad shoulders, the high forehead and spectacles that tilted up when he held his head high, the watch chain at the vest and a handkerchief fluffed at the breast pocket.

Mr. Gomes spoke extensively in the United States and Britain. In 1979, Time magazine called him one of the nation's best preachers. While much of his later life was occupied by scholarly questions of the Bible and homosexuality, he came to abhor the label "gay minister," and pursued a much wider range of studies, on early American religions, Elizabethan Puritanism, church music and the African-American experience.

He also continued to write. Besides volumes of sermons, his books included "The Good Life: Truths That Last in Times of Need" (2002), "Strength for the Journey: Biblical Wisdom for Daily Living" (2003) and "The Scandalous Gospel of Jesus: What's So Good About the Good News?" (2007).

In 2006, he became a Democrat and supported Deval Patrick, who was elected the first black governor of Massachusetts.

— *By Robert D. McFadden*

WALLY YONAMINE

Baseball in Japan Was Never the Same

JUNE 24, 1925 - FEB. 28, 2011

WALLY YONAMINE, who was the first American to play professional baseball in Japan after World War II, has often been compared to Jackie Robinson for "integrating" the Japanese game.

When he made his debut for the Yomiuri Giants in 1951, Yonamine was resented by fans and players alike for his otherness, just as Robinson had been vilified four years earlier when he joined the Brooklyn Dodgers. At a time when anti-American sentiment was rife in Japan — memories of Hiroshima and Nagasaki were still fresh — Yonamine endured catcalls and worse. Rocks and bottles were hurled at him from the stands. The Hawaiian-born son of Japanese parents, he was not only the enemy in the fans' eyes; he was a traitor.

And like Robinson, Yonamine overcame the prejudice and became a beloved star player in Japan, a three-time batting champion. His biographer, Robert K. Fitts, saw him as even more, titling his 2008 book about him "Wally Yonamine: The Man Who Changed Japanese Baseball."

Yonamine died on Feb. 28 in Honolulu at 85. Fitts said the cause was prostate cancer.

Yonamine, he said, was a modest man who never really accepted the comparison to Robinson. "Although I had it rough, Jackie Robinson had it much rougher," Fitts's biography quoted him as saying. "You see, my skin is yellow just like the Japanese."

Remarkably, Yonamine was a pioneering athlete in two sports and in two countries. A speedy running back — 5 feet 9 inches and 180 pounds — he starred for a football team in the Army and, after his discharge, an amateur team in Hawaii, impressing professional scouts enough that he signed with the San Francisco 49ers of the All-America Football Conference, a post-World War II rival to the National Football League. (He never went to college, though he turned down at least one football scholarship, to Ohio State.)

The 49ers, who joined the N.F.L. in 1950, say that Yonamine was the first Asian-American to play pro football.

In his one season with the team, in 1947, he had 19 carries for 74 yards and caught 3 passes for 40 yards, playing just a year after the last of the World War II internment camps for Japanese-Americans was closed down. (In Hawaii, a United States territory then, he and his family had been spared the internment.)

His football career ended during the off-season, when he broke his wrist playing in an amateur baseball league in Hawaii, but his gifts as a hitter and an outfielder had been recognized by Lefty O'Doul, a former major leaguer who managed a minor league team, the San Francisco Seals, and was an adviser to the Yomiuri Giants.

CATCALLS BECAME CHEERS: Yonamine, originally seen as a traitor, won over Japanese baseball fans.

After playing for a year for a Seals affiliate in Salt Lake City, Yonamine took O'Doul's advice and moved to Japan in 1951. A leadoff hitter who sprayed the ball, he hit .311 over 12 seasons in Japan, and when his playing days ended, he was a coach and manager for several Japanese teams until his retirement in 1988. He was elected to the Japan Baseball Hall of Fame in 1994.

Yonamine won over the suspicious and hostile fans as well. In fact, he may have inspired less controversy by being American than he did by his fiercely competitive play. In his debut for the Giants, he bunted for a hit in his first at-bat, a show of daredevilry that became his trademark.

To the orderly and respectful game as the Japanese played it, Yonamine brought what was considered bad behavior: hustling to beat out a sacrifice bunt, sliding hard to take out the pivot man on a double play, expressing outrage at the umpire. In 1956, Yonamine's nose-to-nose encounter with a first base umpire was international news. "The argument got thousands of words in Japanese sports pages," The Associated Press said, "but as in the United States, Yonamine didn't win his point." He had just transferred his football ferociousness to baseball, Yonamine explained.

"On the field he was like Pete Rose, hustling all the time, running people over," Fitts said. "He introduced the hook slide and drag bunt. The Japanese were appalled by it, but then they slowly started adapting it themselves, because they saw it won games."

Kaname Yonamine (his full name was pronounced KA-na-may YO-na-MEE-nay) was born on June 24, 1925, in Olowalu, a village on the island of Maui, where his father, an Okinawan, had moved to find work in the sugar cane fields and met his mother, whose family was from Hiroshima. (He adopted the nickname Wally in high school, and it eventually became his legal name.)

His survivors include his wife, the former Jane Iwashita, two daughters, a son and seven grandchildren. The Honolulu Star-Advertiser said he was also survived by four brothers, two sisters and a great-grandchild.

For all his aggressiveness on the field, Yonamine was known for his humility off it.

"When I came to Japan, I wanted to do three things: to manage a championship team, get into the Hall of Fame and to shake hands with the emperor," Yonamine told Fitts in an interview for a 2005 book, "Remembering Japanese Baseball: An Oral History of the Game."

Having achieved the first two, "I thought that meeting the emperor would be impossible," he went on, "but when I was a scout with the Giants, my wife and I met the emperor and the empress in Los Angeles.

"The audience was in a small room with eight others," he added. "When we were introduced, I automatically stuck my hand out because I was in Los Angeles. And he shook my hand! The empress talked with my wife for over five minutes! As they were walking out of the room, the empress looked at me and took a practice swing! There she was, the empress in the nice kimono and all that, giving me this batting stance!"

— *By Bruce Weber*

FRANK CHIRKINIAN

The Father of Televised Golf

JUNE 3, 1926 - MARCH 4, 2011

FRANK CHIRKINIAN, who defined televised golf as the innovative executive producer and director for CBS's coverage of the Masters tournament for 38 years, died on March 4 at his home in North Palm Beach, Fla. He was 84.

When Mr. Chirkinian first oversaw CBS's coverage of the Masters at Augusta National in Georgia in 1959, televised golf was a black-and-white affair with bulky stationary cameras. He transformed it into a riot of color, using more than two dozen mobile cameras as well as a camera in a blimp along with split screens showing two golfers putting at the same time.

He cut briskly from hole to hole. He showed his audience where the leaders stood in relation to par as play progressed, not simply their total score, and he placed microphones on the greens to pick up chatter between the golfers and their caddies.

"Frank is universally regarded as the father of golf television," Jim Nantz, CBS's longtime lead golf announcer, told the PGA Tour Web site in 2011. "He invented it. He took a sport that no one knew how to televise and made it interesting. He brought the Masters tournament to life."

Mr. Chirkinian, at 5 feet 6, was a commanding presence, known as the Ayatollah for his often brusque orders to his production crew and to the CBS announcers on the course.

"Pat Summerall gave me the name in the late 1970s, when the Shah of Iran was deposed and replaced by Khomeini," Mr. Chirkinian told Golf Digest in 2003. "I admit, reluctantly, that I enjoyed the nickname. If nothing else, it beat being called Adolf."

He added: "In rehearsals I was profane as could be. I ripped everybody. We had seven announcers all wanting air time, and it was important they remember I was the boss. I treated my crew almost like children, and let's face it, sometimes children need to be spanked. It was a form of tough love."

When Brent Musburger broadcast the Masters for the first time, Mr. Chirkinian feared that Mr. Musburger's enthusiasm might overwhelm the stateliness of the course. As he related it to The New York Times, he told Mr. Musburger, "I'll kill you if you raise your voice one-half a decibel."

Mr. Chirkinian also directed coverage of the Winter Olympics, the United States Open tennis tournament, college and pro football, auto racing and thoroughbred racing's Triple Crown for CBS Sports. He was a four-time Emmy recipient.

In 1960, while producing the Georgia-Missouri game in the Orange Bowl, he decided the nose of the Goodyear blimp would be a perfect place for a camera to give viewers

'THE AYATOLLAH': Mr. Chirkinian ruled his control room.

a panoramic view. He placed cameras in the curves at auto races, at the clubhouse turn at Triple Crown thoroughbred races; he focused them on coaches on the sidelines of N.F.L. games, and once caught Philadelphia Eagles linebacker Chuck Bednarik punching an opponent who had dared to offer a handshake.

In February, he was elected to the World Golf Hall of Fame in St. Augustine, Fla. But it became clear to close friends of his that Mr. Chirkinian, who was dying of cancer, would not live long enough to attend the induction ceremony, scheduled for May. So they gathered on Feb. 22 at Emerald Hills Golf Club in West Palm Beach, Fla., called together by John Haas, who jointly owned the club with Mr. Chirkinian, a fine golfer in his own right, until its sale.

They agreed that if he felt up to it, he would tape an acceptance speech for the ceremony.

"Tuesday a week ago, he felt up to it," Mr. Haas said in a telephone interview on the day Mr. Chirkinian died. "He wasn't ambulatory, but we managed to get him to the club. He was brilliant. He's an old trouper, and he really rose to the occasion. We weren't sure he was going to be able to, but he was. He delivered the whole thing, for three or four minutes, and it was tremendous."

Frank Chirkinian, a son of Armenian immigrants, was born on June 3, 1926, in Philadelphia and grew up there. He left the University of Pennsylvania in 1950 to take an assistant director's post at WCAU-TV, the CBS station in Philadelphia, handling a variety of programs, including musicals and cooking shows.

When he impressed CBS management as the director of the 1958 P.G.A. Championship coverage in Havertown, Pa., he was hired to work full time for the network.

For many years while overseeing the Masters, Mr. Chirkinian lived in Augusta. His three marriages ended in divorce. He is survived by a son.

Notwithstanding his aura of dominance, Mr. Chirkinian was determined to let the game of golf show itself off without being overwhelmed by clever TV techniques.

"I showed lots and lots of golfers and lots and lots of golf shots," he told Sports Illustrated in 1995, "and I try never to subordinate the event to my ego. When I die, I want my epitaph to read, 'He stayed out of the way.'"

— *By Richard Goldstein*

Larry Dorman contributed reporting.

DAVID BRODER

Ink on His Fingers and Politics in His Veins

SEPT. 11, 1929 - MARCH 9, 2011

David S. Broder, who skillfully straddled the line between commentary and reportage for more than four decades as a political correspondent and columnist for The Washington Post and who spread his influence on television as a Sunday morning pundit, died on March 9 in Arlington, Va. He was 81.

The cause was complications of diabetes, The Post reported.

Mr. Broder, whose last column was published on Feb. 6, 2011, was often called the dean of the Washington press corps and just as often described as a reporter's reporter, a shoe-leather guy who always got on one more airplane, knocked on one more door, made one more phone call. He would travel more than 100,000 miles a year to write more than a quarter-million words. In short, he composed first drafts of history for an awful lot of history.

Mr. Broder's profile was national: his column was syndicated, and he made more guest appearances on "Meet the Press" than any other journalist. His writing life spanned 11 White House administrations, beginning with Dwight D. Eisenhower's second term, and his career as an observer of Congress was longer than Senator Edward M. Kennedy's tenure as a member of it. Indeed, he covered Mr. Kennedy from before his first election in 1962 through his struggle with cancer and his death.

In a statement, President Obama said Mr. Broder had "built a well-deserved reputation as the most respected and incisive political commentator of his generation."

Mr. Broder reported and opined on a host of candidates' campaigns, not just for national offices but also for state and even local ones. His coverage of state governments was, for a Washington-based reporter, nonpareil. It reflected his belief, as his longtime Post colleague Daniel J. Balz put it, "that not all wisdom resides in Washington."

SUNDAY PUNDIT: Mr. Broder appeared on "Meet the Press" more than any other journalist.

"He had great faith in voters — not just their collective judgment, but their individual ideas," Mr. Balz said in an interview. "His view was always that campaigns should not just be about the candidates, but about voters and what they want to happen. He drew sustenance from door-knocking around the country. It's tedious work, physically difficult, but he did it longer and better and more extensively than anybody ever has, and he demonstrated over the years a great sensitivity to what was stirring in the country that people in Washington were slower to pick up on."

Mr. Broder reported on and analyzed a dozen presidential campaigns for The Post. During the New Hampshire Democratic primary race in 1972, he broke the story that Senator Edmund S. Muskie of Maine, infuriated by attacks on him and on his wife by William Loeb, publisher of The Manchester Union Leader, had wept as he held a news conference on the steps of the newspaper during a February snowstorm.

Mr. Muskie said later that he had been wiping snow from his face, not crying, and he went on to win the primary. But the perception of him as overemotional damaged his campaign and contributed to his failure to gain the nomination, which was won by Senator George McGovern of South Dakota, who was defeated in a general election landslide by President Richard M. Nixon.

For his columns that year, Mr. Broder won the Pulitzer Prize for commentary, his analysis of party politics favoring neither one side nor the other but bringing equal measures of frank admiration and, just as often — perhaps more often — spitting disdain to both. His writing style could be pedestrian, but his strengths were in reading the electorate and in parsing the ambiguities and contradictions of the policies and characters of the candidates and their parties.

"Richard M. Nixon has achieved something rather remarkable in the last four years," he wrote during the 1972 Republican National Convention in Miami. "He has managed to shift the program and politics of the Republican Party vast distances in both the foreign and domestic fields, while reducing the G.O.P.'s liberal and conservative wings to a series of feeble and futile squawks. He has managed this feat by being progressive in his policies and conservative in his politics — which is rather a neat trick even for one as nimble as Mr. Nixon."

Later that year, while traveling with Senator Kennedy as he campaigned for Mr. McGovern and Democratic Congressional candidates,

Mr. Broder assessed the senator's talent for "storing up political due bills."

"He is a superb campaigner," Mr. Broder wrote from Butte, Mont., "whether whipping up an auditorium rally with cheerleader tactics and roundhouse swings at the opposition; charming a dinner crowd, as he table-hops with the local candidates; or patiently posing for photographs with every guest at a fund-raising luncheon. He works hard at this trade, accepts tough schedules without complaint and leaves the money and good will behind. He knows as well as anyone that many of his efforts are in a losing cause."

Mr. Broder's doggedness was legend. In August 1968, after Nixon had unexpectedly named Gov. Spiro T. Agnew of Maryland as his running mate, Nixon said publicly that the only one who was not surprised was Mr. Broder, who had wheedled the information out of Nixon himself — and had written it — some months earlier.

"He has earned his reputation not with flamboyance but with meticulousness," Time magazine wrote about him in a flattering profile. "Refusing to be confined to Washington, he thrives on the grueling cross-country chicken-and-peas circuit. Day in, day out, he lives with politics."

Few, if any, other journalists walked the tightrope between news and opinion as effectively as Mr. Broder. But he had his moments of false prophecy and crossing the line. In 1976, he reported that Morris K. Udall of Arizona had won the Wisconsin Democratic primary, only to learn a few hours later that the winner was Jimmy Carter, the former governor of Georgia. Mr. Broder submitted his resignation, only to be talked out of it by The Post's editor, Benjamin C. Bradlee.

During the impeachment of President Bill Clinton, he wrote critically of the president and later expressed his personal disdain for him in an interview. The Post curtailed his news reporting on the story.

And in recent years he wrote admiringly of Karl Rove, President George W. Bush's former adviser, leading some critics, especially bloggers, to rail against him as a hopeless Washington insider and a Republican mouthpiece.

"Broder, of course, is a gasbag," Paul Begala, the liberal political consultant and commentator, wrote on The Huffington Post in 2007. "The Hindenburg of pundits."

For the most part, however, his political leanings and personal biases remained obscure. "It was a very difficult high-wire act, but he was able to do it," William Safire, the late New York Times columnist, once said. "I don't know how. Maybe he had a way of splitting his professionalism and saying, 'Today I'll be an opinion columnist' and 'Tomorrow I'll be a disinterested reporter.' But you couldn't characterize his politics."

David Salzer Broder was born in Chicago Heights, Ill., on Sept. 11, 1929. He attended public schools there and graduated in 1947 from the University of Chicago, where he was editor of the newspaper and earned a master's degree in political science in 1951.

After two years in the Army, he worked for a newspaper in Bloomington, Ill., The Pantagraph, then moved to The Congressional Quarterly in 1955. Five years later he left the Quarterly for The Washington Star, and in 1965 The New York Times hired him as a political reporter.

His tenure at The Times was brief and unhappy. When he switched to The Post the following year, he left behind a stinging memo criticizing what he called the "endless bureaucratic frustrations" and "parochialism of outlook" at The Times.

By then he had begun almost a second career as a panelist and commentator on television news programs. Slender and bookish-looking, articulate with a considered way of talking though not especially expressive, Mr. Broder was an unlikely television personality. But he came across as sober and reliable, and he became a star of the punditry culture.

He first appeared on "Meet the Press" in 1964, and, when he made his 400th appearance on the program in 2008, he was by far the most frequent guest journalist it had ever had. (Robert Novak, with fewer than 300, was second.) He was also a regular on "Washington Week in Review" on PBS and on CNN's "Inside Politics."

Mr. Broder was the author or co-author of seven books, including "Behind the Front Page" (1987), an examination of how the press covers politics. He expressed disapproval of the seemingly open door between journalism and politics that allowed people who have served in government or on campaigns to become commentators, taking to task, by implication if not by name, figures like Mr. Safire and Mr. Begala.

He also objected to the culture of celebrity journalists, though his television punditry and the many speaking invitations it brought made the complaint more difficult to defend. In 2008, Ken Silverstein, the Washington editor of Harper's magazine, disclosed on his Washington Babylon blog that Mr. Broder had accepted paid speaking engagements that violated Washington Post ethics guidelines. Mr. Broder was rebuked in the pages of The Post by its ombudsman, Deborah Howell. He apologized.

Mr. Broder is survived by his wife of 59 years, Ann, four sons, and seven grandchildren.

His colleagues at The Post spoke of him with familial fondness, remarking that he was slow to adapt to technology. He found it difficult at first to compose at a computer, and for one election cycle he traveled with both a typewriter and a computer in tow, writing his stories on the former before copying it secretarially on the latter.

Mostly, though, they marveled at his skills.

Maralee Schwartz, who edited Mr. Broder at The Post for more than a decade, recalled in a telephone interview that in 2003, when the House of Representatives passed a measure to add a prescription drug benefit to Medicare after a contentious debate that resulted in an all-night session, Mr. Broder, then 74, was virtually the only reporter who stayed to the bitter end.

"Then he wrote a tick-tock the next day," Ms. Schwartz said, using newspaper lingo for the kind of story that describes, minute by minute, the progress of a significant event. "That was David. He believed you had to be there."

— *By Bruce Weber*

MAR

BILL BLACKBEARD

Single-Minded Savior of the Comic Strip

APRIL 28, 1926 - MARCH 10, 2011

In the 1890s, when newspapers were made of sweat and trees and ink, some, amid circulation wars, began to carry a new kind of narrative art form: the comic strip. The strips were devoured daily by readers; on Sundays a new technology, color printing, further enhanced their appeal.

Those early comics were the essence of ephemera, preserved only by libraries and fervent collectors. Then, in the mid-20th century, microfilm let libraries unload decades of newspapers in their unwieldy bound volumes. Mutt and Jeff, Little Nemo, Polly Sleepyhead and the denizens of Gasoline Alley seemed destined to spend eternity as tiny black-and-white ghosts of their once-vibrant selves.

This did not please Bill Blackbeard. An author, editor, anthologist and ardent accumulator who died on March 10 in Watsonville, Calif., at 84, Mr. Blackbeard is widely credited with helping save the American newspaper comic strip from the scrap heap, amassing a collection considered the most comprehensive ever assembled.

His death was confirmed by Social Security records. The death was not made public at the time — Mr. Blackbeard, an enigmatic, somewhat elusive figure, appears to have left no immediate survivors who might have done so — and word of it began percolating in the online world of comics aficionados only in late April 2011. The delay befits a man who spent his life steeped in the news-has-reached-us-by-packet-ship age.

Mr. Blackbeard first brought attention to the comic strip as pop-cultural treasure with "The Smithsonian Collection of Newspaper Comics" (1977), which he edited with Martin Williams. The book teems with images from Mr. Blackbeard's personal archive, which eventually comprised more than 2.5 million strips published between 1893 and 1996, culled from libraries and newspaper morgues across the country.

There were newspapers in the garage, where stacks stretched to the ceiling. There were newspapers in the bedroom. There were newspapers in the living room, where foot traffic was dictated by the paths carved among tottering piles.

In 1997 the archive was acquired by Ohio State University, where it forms part of the Billy Ireland Cartoon Library & Museum. It took six semitrucks to move the collection, more than 75 tons in all.

Those tons previously resided in the San Francisco Academy of Comic Art, the nonprofit institution that Mr. Blackbeard founded in 1967 and ran for decades from his house there. (More precisely, the academy *was* his house there, which he shared with his wife at the time, Barbara.)

To judge from published accounts of the place, Mr. Blackbeard used the same interior decorator as the Collyer brothers. Every horizontal surface — he collected more than comics — was piled with books, magazines, dime novels, penny dreadfuls, pulp paperbacks, Holmesiana and, of course, newspapers: whole papers, loose sheets, Sunday supplements, bound volumes and the torrent of comic strips he had shorn from them all.

There were newspapers in the garage, where stacks stretched to the ceiling. There were newspapers in the bedroom. There were newspapers in the living room, where foot traffic was dictated by the paths carved among tottering piles. There were newspapers in the kitchen. There were newspapers everywhere but the bathroom, and that, Mr. Blackbeard told inquisitors, was only because the humidity would have been bad for them.

It was perhaps just as well that he cared little for comic books, which he called "meretricious dreck."

Meeting Mr. Blackbeard inspired Nicholson Baker, who caught newsprint fever from him, to write "Double Fold: Libraries and the Assault on Paper" (2001), in which Mr. Blackbeard appears.

"The thing about Blackbeard — he is like so many collectors in that he saved something terribly important, but he was single-minded: he saved things with a razor," Mr. Baker, sounding pained, said in a telephone interview. "He had no interest in the women's sections, in the magazine sections, in the beautiful photographs that had nothing to do with comics."

In later years, said Jenny E. Robb, curator of the Billy Ireland Cartoon Library and Museum, Mr. Blackbeard reformed and left bound volumes intact.

William Elsworth Blackbeard was born on April 28, 1926, in Lawrence, Ind., and reared in Newport Beach, Calif. Though "Blackbeard" sounds lifted straight from a comic-strip character, it appears to have been his actual surname.

Entranced by comic strips, young Bill discovered that neighbors were delighted to have him cart away their piles of old newspapers, which he promptly took home. This did not please his mother.

After Army service in Europe in World War II, Mr. Blackbeard studied literature and history at Fullerton College in California. He was later a freelance writer for pulp magazines including Weird Tales.

In the 1960s, wanting to write a history of the American comic strip, Mr. Blackbeard began scouring libraries for old newspapers. But no archive had all the strips he hoped to study, and he hoped to study the entire run of every strip ever published.

He soon learned that the San Francisco Public Library, having microfilmed its newspapers, was about to jettison them. As he had done with his childhood neighbors, he offered to relieve the library of its burden. Word got around, and before long, Mr. Blackbeard had unburdened the Library of Congress, the Chicago Public Library, the Los Angeles Public Library and many others.

Mr. Blackbeard, whose marriage appears to have dissolved in later years, had lived recently in Santa Cruz, Calif.

His other books include several volumes he compiled and edited, among them "The Comic Strip Art of Lyonel Feininger," about the German-American painter who drew strips for The Chicago Tribune; "R. F. Outcault's the Yellow Kid"; and "Sherlock Holmes in America."

Mr. Blackbeard's messianic lifework gave rise to the work of many other scholars, artists and publishers.

"A filmmaker like Martin Scorsese couldn't make what he makes if he had never heard of D.W. Griffith and Orson Welles," Art Spiegelman, who created the Pulitzer Prize-winning graphic narrative "Maus," said in a telephone interview. "Similarly, as my art form develops, it's clear that the future of comics is in the past. And Blackbeard was the granddaddy that gave us all access to it."

— *By Margalit Fox*

MAR

FRANK NEUHAUSER

Winner of the First National Spelling Bee

SEPT. 29, 1913 - MARCH 11, 2011

THE WORD WAS "GLADIOLUS," and though he was only 11, the boy knew it cold. As luck would have it, he grew the flower in his garden back home in Louisville, Ky. He had already outspelled two million schoolchildren for a chance to compete in Washington, and now, on a June night in 1925, he was the last speller standing among nine finalists. Eight had already fallen, felled by the likes of "propeller," "blackguard" and "statistician."

"G-L-A-D-I-O-L-U-S," he said firmly, and with those nine letters, Frank Neuhauser won the first National Spelling Bee.

For his victory, Frank earned $500 in gold pieces and a meeting with President Calvin Coolidge at which, it is safe to assume, few words of any length were exchanged.

In Louisville, there was a parade in his honor. His classmates presented him with a new bicycle.

Mr. Neuhauser, a retired lawyer, died on March 11, at 97, at his home in Silver Spring, Md.

His winning word, a cakewalk by modern standards, harks back to simpler times. The bee was begun as a promotional event by The Louisville Courier-Journal, amid a circulation war with a rival paper. (The Courier-Journal sponsored young Mr. Neuhauser and the next year's winner, Pauline Bell, who trounced the field with "cerise.") From start to finish, the 1925 finals lasted 90 minutes.

Today, the bee, formally known as the Scripps National Spelling Bee, involves 11 million children in local contests throughout the United States and abroad. More than 270 finalists convene in Washington for two days of competition, televised on ESPN. The winner earns cash and prizes worth more than $40,000.

An honored guest at several recent bees, Mr. Neuhauser found himself spelling "gladiolus" for strangers to the end of his life. Later champions have faced a welter of more difficult words, which together read like found poetry: "vignette" (1952) and "soubrette" (1953); "ratoon" (1966) and "shalloon" (1971); "psychiatry" (1948), "narcolepsy" (1976) and "sanitarium" (1938).

The bee has become an object of fascination in popular culture, inspiring, among other things, the 2000 novel "Bee Season," by Myla Goldberg, and its 2005 film adaptation; the 2006 movie "Akeelah and the Bee"; the musical comedy "The 25th Annual Putnam County Spelling Bee," which played on Broadway from 2005 to 2008; and the 2002 documentary film "Spellbound," in which Mr. Neuhauser appears.

For many entrants, the bee now entails near-constant study. Mr. Neuhauser, by contrast, practiced just an hour a night for a few months.

Frank Louis Neuhauser was born in Louisville on Sept. 29, 1913. The family name, whose spelling reflects its German origin, is pronounced NEW-how-zer.

His father, a stonemason, "had a stack of spelling books a half-foot high," as Frank Neuhauser told The Washington Post in 1977, and on rainy weekends gave his son extra drilling at home. The father hoped for rain, the son for sun, so he could play baseball.

Mr. Neuhauser earned an engineering degree from the University of Louisville and a law degree from George Washington University. He was a patent lawyer with General Electric and later with Bernard Rothwell & Brown, a Washington firm.

Mr. Neuhauser is survived by his wife, the former Mary Virginia Clark, three sons, a daughter and five grandchildren.

Though much has changed in the 86 years since "gladiolus," for the time being, at least, one constant remains: The bee's young combatants are still sponsored by newspapers, those tactile, sweet-smelling repositories of words large and small, written on real paper, in real ink.

— *By Margalit Fox*

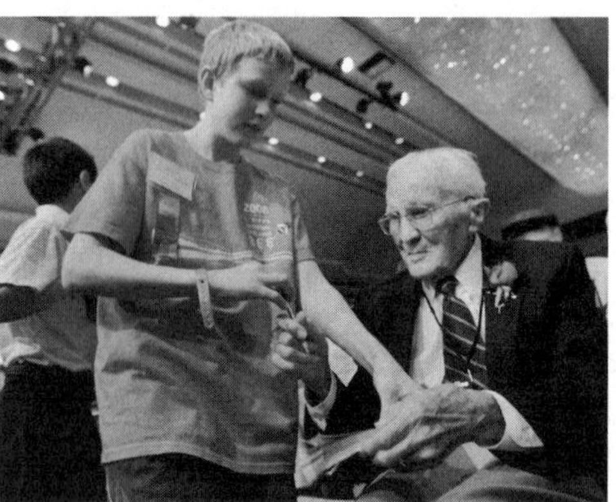

N-O-N-A-G-E-N-A-R-I-A-N: Mr. Neuhauser at the finals of the 2008 Scripps National Spelling Bee.

LEO STEINBERG

A Vivid Writer and Bold Thinker in Art History

JULY 9, 1920 - MARCH 13, 2011

Leo Steinberg, one of the most brilliant, influential and controversial art historians of the last half of the 20th century, died on March 13 at his home in Manhattan. He was 90.

Mr. Steinberg was an admired lecturer, an eloquent writer and an adventurous scholar and critic who loved to challenge the art world's reigning orthodoxies. Though trained in the study of the Renaissance and Baroque eras, he wrote as insightfully about modern art as he did about the old masters.

The titles of his two best-known books, "Other Criteria: Confrontations With Twentieth-Century Art" (1972) and "The Sexuality of Christ in Renaissance Art and in Modern Oblivion" (1983), suggest the range of his interests. The earlier volume, a collection of essays written between 1953 and 1971, includes extended meditations on Picasso and Jasper Johns as well as shorter reviews of artists like Willem de Kooning, Philip Guston and Raoul Hague that he wrote during a brief stint in the mid-1950s as a regular critic for Arts Magazine.

In "Other Criteria" he laid out his philosophical terms. In the essay "The Eye Is a Part of the Mind," first published in 1953, and in the title essay, from 1971, Mr. Steinberg spoke out against formalism, then the dominant approach to art analysis, with its view that a work's artistic value lies not in its content but in its shape, line, color and other visual elements.

"Even nonobjective art continues to pursue art's social role of fixating thought in aesthetic form, pinning down the most ethereal conceptions of the age in vital designs," he wrote in "The Eye Is a Part of the Mind."

In "Other Criteria" he declared, "Considerations of 'human interest' belong in the criticism of modernist art not because we are incurably sentimental about humanity, but because it is art we are talking about."

Such arguments helped liberate a whole generation from the restrictive laws of formalist aesthetics, opening the field to more wide-ranging ways of studying meaning and representation in art.

Mr. Steinberg did not simply substitute interpretation of content for analysis of form. Rather, it was his ability to show how form and content are intertwined that made his writing so revelatory. His ability to discover ever deeper and more interconnected levels of meaning in the form and imagery of an artwork gave his writing a narrative excitement, like that of a detective story.

But it also exposed him to accusations of overinterpretation by his more circumspect colleagues. In his review of Mr. Steinberg's book "Michelangelo's Last Paintings" (1975), the eminent art historian E. H. Gombrich warned against Mr. Steinberg's tendency to speculate on supposedly unprovable meanings. "He has produced a book to be reckoned with," Mr. Gombrich concluded, "but a dangerous model to follow."

For the maverick Mr. Steinberg, however, risk taking was not to be avoided. In his 1967 essay "Objectivity and the Shrinking Self" he lamented the intellectual timidity of the art history of his day. Why, he asked, was the work of younger scholars so tame and conventional? Had the discipline traded humanist imagination for cautious, quasi-scientific professionalism?

Sixteen years later Mr. Steinberg followed up this challenge with one of the most provocative art-historical studies of the 20th century, "The Sexuality of Christ in Renaissance Art and in Modern Oblivion." The book grew out of a question that had apparently occurred to no other modern scholar: Why is it that in so many Renaissance paintings of the Madonna and Child, the infant Jesus' genitals are actively displayed to viewers both within and without the picture?

The explanation, Mr. Steinberg argued, was to be found in Renaissance theology, wherein a major question concerned the humanity of the son of God. Here the possession of reproductive organs proved that Jesus, whatever his metaphysical status, was indeed fully human and subject to human suffering.

"The Sexuality of Christ" drew a divided critical response. Supporters viewed it as a groundbreaking achievement; doubters questioned Mr. Steinberg's interpretation of the visual evidence. Writing in The New York Times Book Review in 1984, the philosopher Richard Wollheim called Mr. Steinberg "one of the sharpest intellects working in the field of art history" but questioned his objectivity.

"The most disturbing aspect of this strange, haunting book, with its great boldness of conception," Mr. Wollheim wrote, "is the resolute silence it maintains on all alternative views." (Mr. Steinberg rebutted Mr. Wollheim's criticism in subsequent editions.)

Mr. Steinberg cut a tall, elegant figure, almost invariably with a cigarette in hand. A heavy smoker, he said in an oral history interview in 1998 that his only fallow period came in the 1960s, when he tried, unsuccessfully, to quit.

The art historian Richard Shiff recalled Mr. Steinberg as all but consumed by art. "He didn't own a car, had no second home," Mr. Shiff said. "He wasn't particularly interested in food, nor in fine clothes. He was not a consumer. I doubt that he ever took vacations. When he traveled it was to see art, or visit an archive."

His analytical mind even showed in his sense of humor, Mr. Shiff added. "He would enjoy the laugh and then want to figure out why the joke was funny."

Why is it that in so many Renaissance paintings of the Madonna and Child, the infant Jesus' genitals are actively displayed to viewers both within and without the picture?

In a field not noted for lively prose, Mr. Steinberg gave academic writing a personal voice: didactic, often urgently polemical, yet generously ruminative, enriched by vivid metaphors, strewn with unfamiliar vocabulary and sometimes idiosyncratic coinages but blessedly free of jargon.

"What he avoids above all is the finishing touch," Mr. Steinberg wrote of Rodin, "his secret dream being to keep every work going like a stoked fire — forever, if possible."

In 1983 Mr. Steinberg became the first art historian to receive an award for literature from the American Academy and Institute of Arts and Letters. His writing skill drew on his own deep reading of literature. "He knew Dickens and Joyce inside out, and he had a better knowledge of Shakespeare and the English novel than many professionals in the field," Helen Vendler, the critic and English professor at Harvard, said in an interview. She befriended him after he gave the Norton Lectures there in 1995-96.

Mr. Steinberg's literary achievement was all the more remarkable for the fact that English was his third language. He was born Zalman Lev Steinberg in Moscow on July 9, 1920, the son of Isaac Nachman Steinberg, a fiercely intellectual lawyer and government figure in revolutionary Russia; his mother, Anyuta Esselson Steinberg, came from a wealthy family, was well educated and had artistic leanings. Lenin appointed Isaac Steinberg commissar of justice, but his outspoken idealism — he wanted to abolish the prison system — led him afoul of the Bolsheviks and into exile. As a boy Mr. Steinberg learned German after his family had moved to Berlin.

Shortly after Hitler took power, the family moved again, this time to Britain, where Mr. Steinberg learned English. At 16 he entered the Slade School of Fine Art at the University of London, receiving his diploma in 1940 for work in sculpture and drawing that he later self-effacingly dismissed as skillful but overly conservative.

After the war the family moved to New York, settling on the Upper West Side of Manhattan. Mr. Steinberg, something of a late bloomer, did freelance writing, editing and translating, taught life drawing and studied philosophy before finally focusing on art history in his mid-30s. Soon publications like Partisan Review and Arts Magazine were publishing his essays, and he drew wide attention for a lecture series he gave at the 92nd Street Y in 1951 titled "An Introduction to Art and Practical Esthetics."

He received his doctorate from the New York University Institute of Fine Art in 1960 for a thesis on the Baroque architect Francesco Borromini. The next year, at the age of 42, he took his first full-time job, as a professor of art history at Hunter College, where he stayed until 1975. He then moved to the University of Pennsylvania, from which he retired in 1991.

He also held professorships and lecturing posts at Stanford, Berkeley, Princeton, Columbia and Harvard, and lectured at museums and galleries around the country. Professor Vendler called his lectures spellbinding.

In 1962 Mr. Steinberg married Dorothy Seiberling, an art editor for Life magazine. The marriage ended in divorce. Mr. Steinberg had no children.

In 2002, after a teaching stint at the University of Texas at Austin, he donated his private collection of 3,200 prints to the College of Fine Arts there. The collection, valued at $3.5 million, includes prints by Michelangelo, Rembrandt, Goya, Matisse, Picasso and Jasper Johns.

Late in life he published "Encounters With Rauschenberg" (2000), based on a lecture about Robert Rauschenberg, and a book about the popularity of Leonardo's "Last Supper" called "Leonardo's Incessant Last Supper" (2001).

In all of Mr. Steinberg's writing is a clear conviction that to study and write about art is far more than an academic pursuit; he believed that in art our deepest human values are at stake.

"It is in the nature of contemporary art to present itself as a bad risk," he wrote in one of his best-known essays, "Contemporary Art and the Plight of Its Public" (1962). "And we the public, artists included, should be proud of being in this predicament, because nothing else would seem to us quite true to life; and art, after all, is supposed to be a mirror of life."

— *By Ken Johnson*

OWSLEY STANLEY

A K A 'Kid Charlemagne': Druggist to the Stars

JAN. 19, 1935 - MARCH 13, 2011

Owsley Stanley, the prodigiously gifted applied chemist to the stars, who made LSD in quantity for the Grateful Dead, the Beatles, Jimi Hendrix, Ken Kesey and other avatars of the psychedelic '60s, died on March 13 in a car accident in Australia. He was 76 and lived in the bush near Cairns, in the Australian state of Queensland.

His car swerved off a highway and down an embankment before hitting trees near Mareeba, a town in Queensland. Mr. Stanley's wife, Sheilah, was injured in the accident.

Mr. Stanley, the Dead's former financial backer, pharmaceutical supplier and sound engineer, was in recent decades a reclusive, almost mythically enigmatic figure. He moved to Australia in the 1980s, as he explained in his rare interviews, so he might survive what he believed to be a coming Ice Age that would annihilate the Northern Hemisphere.

Once renowned as an artisan of acid, Mr. Stanley turned out LSD said to be purer and finer than any other. He was also among the first individuals (in many accounts, the very first) to mass-produce the drug. Its resulting wide availability provided the chemical underpinnings of an era of love, music, grooviness and much else. Conservatively tallied, Mr. Stanley's career output was more than a million doses, in some estimates more than five million.

His was the acid behind the Acid Tests conducted by the novelist Ken Kesey and his Merry Pranksters, the group of psychedelic adherents whose exploits were chronicled by Tom Wolfe in his 1968 book "The Electric Kool-Aid Acid Test." The music world immortalized Mr. Stanley in a host of songs, including the Dead's "Alice D. Millionaire" (a play on a newspaper headline, describing one of his several arrests, that called him an "LSD Millionaire") and Steely Dan's "Kid Charlemagne."

So widely known was Mr. Stanley that he appears in the Encyclopedia Britannica article

GRATEFUL CLIENTS: Mr. Stanley, left, made LSD for celebrities of the 1960s like Jerry Garcia, right.

on LSD under the apparently unironic index term "Augustus Owsley Stanley III (American chemist)." The Oxford English Dictionary contains an entry for the noun "Owsley": "an extremely potent, high-quality type of LSD." In 2007, Mr. Stanley was the subject of a long profile in an issue of Rolling Stone magazine commemorating the 40th anniversary of the Summer of Love.

In short, Mr. Stanley lent the '60s a great deal of its color — color like White Lightning, Monterey Purple and Blue Cheer, the varieties of his LSD that were among the most popular. (He did not, contrary to popular lore, release a product called Purple Haze. In interviews he sounded quite miffed that anything emerging from his laboratory could be thought to cause haziness rather than the crystalline clarity for which he personally vouched.)

He also lent the era much of its sound, developing early, widely admired high-fidelity sound systems for live rock concerts, including the Dead's towering "wall of sound."

Augustus Owsley Stanley III was born on Jan. 19, 1935, to a patrician Kentucky family. His paternal grandfather, for whom he was named, was a congressman, governor of Kentucky and United States senator. (Somewhat prophetically, given his grandson's future pursuits, the elder Mr. Stanley was a vigorous public foe of Prohibition.)

Young Owsley, whose adolescent hirsuteness caused him to be known ever after as Bear, was sent to a military preparatory school in Maryland. He was expelled in the ninth grade for furnishing the alcohol that, as he told Rolling Stone in 2007, had nearly all his classmates "blasted out of their minds" on homecoming weekend.

He briefly attended the University of Virginia before enlisting in the Air Force, where he learned electronics. He later worked in Los Angeles as a broadcast engineer for radio and television stations. He also studied ballet and for a time was a professional dancer.

In 1963, Mr. Stanley enrolled at the University of California, Berkeley. The next year, he encountered LSD, a transformative experience. "I remember the first time I took acid and walked outside," he said in the Rolling Stone interview. "The cars were kissing the parking meters."

Mr. Stanley had found his calling, and at the time it was at least quasi-legitimate: LSD was not outlawed in California until 1966. What he needed to do was learn his craft, which he accomplished, as Rolling Stone reported, in three weeks in the university library, poring over chemistry journals. Soon afterward, he left college and a going concern, the Bear Research Group, was born.

In 1965, he met Mr. Kesey, and through him the Dead. Enraptured, he became their sound man, early underwriter, principal acolyte, sometime-housemate and frequent touring companion. With Bob Thomas, he designed the band's highly recognizable skull-and-lightning-bolt logo. Mr. Stanley also made many recordings of the Dead in performance. Now valuable documentary records of the band's early years, many have been released commercially.

Mr. Stanley remained with the band off and on through the early '70s, when, according to Rolling Stone, his habits became too much even for the Grateful Dead and they parted company. (He had insisted, among other things, that the band eat meat — nothing but meat — a dietary regimen he followed until the end of his life.)

His other clients included John Lennon, who, according to "The Beatles," a 2005 biography by Bob Spitz, contracted to pay Mr. Stanley for a lifetime supply of his wares.

In 1970, after a judge revoked Mr. Stanley's bail from a 1967 drug arrest, he served two years in federal prison. There he learned metalwork and jewelry making, trades he plied in recent years.

Mr. Stanley, who became an Australian citizen in the 1990s, was treated for throat cancer in 2004. He attributed his survival to his carnivorous diet. (A heart attack he had suffered some years earlier he ascribed to childhood broccoli, forced on him by his mother.) He and his wife, Sheilah, had two sons and two daughters, who survive him, as do eight grandchildren and two great-grandchildren.

Though he helped transform the culture, Mr. Stanley asserted that he had never meant to do so. As he told The San Francisco Chronicle in 2007, he had set out only to make a product he knew he could take, because its ingredients were known.

"And my friends all wanted to know what they were taking, too," Mr. Stanley said. "Of course," he added "my 'friends' expanded very rapidly."

— *By Margalit Fox*

MAR

RICHARD WIRTHLIN

With Reagan Every Step of the Climb

MARCH 15, 1931 - MARCH 16, 2011

RICHARD B. WIRTHLIN, the political consultant and pollster who for 20 years helped Ronald Reagan shape his political message and strategies, both in presidential campaigns and in the White House, died on March 16 at his home in Salt Lake City. He was 80.

A Brigham Young University economist turned pollster, Mr. Wirthlin worked with Reagan from 1968 through the end of his presidency, becoming a senior adviser and member of his inner circle while running a public-opinion research company.

He described his role in a 2004 memoir, "The Greatest Communicator: What Ronald Reagan Taught Me About Politics, Leadership, and Life." Reagan, he wrote, "wasn't interested in being told what to say — he intrinsically knew that. He was interested in the most effective way to convey his message."

Mr. Wirthlin supplied that help at a crucial moment in the 1976 Republican primaries, when Reagan's conservative challenge to President Gerald R. Ford for the nomination was flagging. Ford planned to transfer control of the Panama Canal to Panama, and Mr. Wirthlin seized on the issue and pressed Reagan to emphasize his opposition to it.

"Control of the Panama Canal symbolized American autonomy and might," Mr. Wirthlin said in the memoir, written with Wynton C. Hall.

The canal issue helped revive the campaign. Reagan began winning primaries by thundering, "We built it, we paid for it, it's ours, and we are going to keep it."

Reagan ultimately lost the nomination (and the winner of the election, Jimmy Carter, ultimately transferred control of the canal to Panama), but he had laid the groundwork for a successful run four years later, when Mr. Wirthlin would again play a critical role.

In 1980, Mr. Wirthlin, as chief campaign strategist, used polling to help Reagan build a winning coalition that included blue-collar Democrats and evangelical Christians. His advice in frequent memorandums — one was titled "Seven Conditions of Victory" — were closely followed. In March, when Reagan, a former governor of California, had emerged as the almost-certain nominee, Mr. Wirthlin wrote:

"We must position the Governor, in these early stages, so that he is viewed as less dangerous in the foreign affairs area, more competent in the economic area, more compassionate on the domestic issues and less of a conservative zealot than his opponents and the press now paint him to be."

POLLSTER: For 20 years, Mr. Wirthlin helped shape Reagan's political strategy.

One important Wirthlin strategy early in the general election campaign was to use television ads to establish Reagan's qualifications, citing his record in California, before turning to attack President Carter directly, a tactic many in the campaign wanted to adopt quickly.

Mr. Wirthlin also encouraged Reagan to push "pocketbook issues" and to define the election as a referendum on Mr. Carter's leadership in economically troubled times. The strategy produced a pivotal moment when Reagan asked during a debate with Mr. Carter, "Are you better off today than you were four years ago?"

Reagan captured the presidency with ease, and Mr. Wirthlin went on to supervise what was known internally as "The First 90 Days Project," a blueprint of policy goals and the political strategies to achieve them. Some called the White House operations behind the effort "the permanent campaign."

Mr. Wirthlin (Dick Wirthlin to those who knew him) was a regular presence in the Reagan White House, frequently polling and testing the president's speeches with groups holding dial meters to indicate what phrases and emphases they liked or disliked.

Peter Hannaford, a Reagan speechwriter, said in an interview last year that Mr. Wirthlin's importance to Reagan grew in the White House. "It was much more than campaigns," he added. "It was ongoing advice on the things to emphasize."

Mr. Wirthlin advised Reagan for his entire eight years in office, bringing him good news (the public overwhelmingly supported him when he fired striking air traffic controllers in 1981, for example) and bad (the public largely did not believe him when he said he did not know about the sale of arms to Iran to finance the Nicaraguan contras in 1987).

Reagan was said to be reluctant to make decisions based solely on opinion polls. But Mr. Wirthlin proved essential in taking what Reagan had decided to do — or what he was leaning toward doing — and seeing how it might play with the public. He used focus groups, for example, to test American reactions to the themes of speeches Reagan was to give during a visit to Moscow in 1988.

In an interview for this obituary in 2010, Mr. Wirthlin said he was most proud of having helped Reagan, "in a very modest way," set the stage for arms talks with the Soviet Union by first gaining Americans' trust that he would negotiate from a position of strength, having taken "a very strong position early vis-à-vis the Soviets" when he called the Soviet Union an "evil empire."

Mr. Wirthlin, who developed a background in statistics in college, began polling in 1964 when a political scientist he knew asked for help with his own business. "I helped him and found that this was something that I enjoyed," he said in the interview, adding, "Pretty soon I had more business than I could handle, and I decided to set up a firm."

Barry Goldwater, the former Republican senator from Arizona, was an early customer when he ran to regain his Senate seat in 1968 after his crushing defeat in the 1964 presidential campaign against Lyndon B. Johnson. He recommended Mr. Wirthlin to Reagan, who had been elected governor of California in 1966 and had made a weak bid for the 1968 Republican presidential nomination.

Mr. Wirthlin had a low opinion of Reagan at the time, thinking of him as "a heavy-handed, right-wing Hollywood actor," as he wrote in his memoir. But in meeting Reagan he changed his mind. "I found Reagan's belief in his innate optimism paralleled my own," he wrote.

Mr. Wirthlin was measured in his analyses of his polling work. After the 1980 election, he cautioned conservatives against declaring the results a definitive swing to the right. He told a conference at Harvard that the election was more a referendum on President Carter than it was a right-left split. "Ideology did not cut in the vote decision," he said. "The electorate still viewed Reagan as considerably more conservative than themselves, and they did so right through the election."

Richard Bitner Wirthlin was born in Salt Lake City on March 15, 1931, the son of Joseph L. and Madeline Bitner Wirthlin, who had a farm. His father was presiding bishop of the Church of Jesus Christ of Latter-day Saints, responsible for its business side and temporal affairs like the Mormons' welfare program. Richard won letters in football and track in high school.

He earned his bachelor's and master's degrees at the University of Utah and his Ph.D. at the University of California, Berkeley. He said he became interested in economics and politics while doing Mormon missionary work in Switzerland and Austria in 1951.

Mr. Wirthlin's company, originally based in Los Angeles and successively named Decision Making Information, the Wirthlin Group and Wirthlin Worldwide, also did polling for Margaret Thatcher, the British prime minister, among other political clients. The company was sold to Harris Interactive in 2004, and Mr. Wirthlin served on its board until retiring in 2007.

He was active in the Mormon Church throughout his adult life, serving as a bishop and helping to oversee the church's day-to-day affairs. He conducted a survey for the church measuring Americans' attitudes toward Mormons.

Mr. Wirthlin is survived by his wife, the former Jeralie Chandler, whom he married in 1956; four sons, three daughters, a sister and a brother; 27 grandchildren and six great-grandchildren. Another daughter died in 1991.

Mr. Wirthlin's reputation transcended party lines. Peter D. Hart, a Democratic pollster who collaborated on projects with him, said Mr. Wirthlin was important in the field for showing how to integrate different kinds of data — polling, census, political — to measure the electorate's opinions and moods.

"He was a pioneer in terms of data analysis and statistical analysis," Mr. Hart said. "His ability to take a huge volume of information and to make it important, both thematically and strategically, was agenda-setting for those who were to follow him in the polling field."

— *By Adam Clymer*

MAR

FERLIN HUSKY

A Nashville Star Who Broke the Pop Barrier

DEC. 3, 1925 - MARCH 17, 2011

FERLIN HUSKY, the smooth-voiced singer whose 1956 hit "Gone" became the first country single of the Nashville Sound era to cross over to the pop Top 10, died on March 17 at his home in Hendersonville, Tenn. He was 85.

A monumental outpouring of regret, "Gone" established Mr. Husky as a leading proponent of the lush orchestral sound that became the hallmark of the music being made in Nashville during the late 1950s and early '60s. Along with hits by Jim Reeves and Patsy Cline, "Gone" helped country music rebound commercially at a time when the teenage-oriented rock 'n' roll of Elvis Presley and others was cutting into mainstream country record sales.

Mr. Husky had previously recorded an unvarnished take of "Gone," featuring the pedal steel guitarist Speedy West, for Capitol Records in Hollywood in 1952. Released under the pseudonym Terry Preston at the urging of the label's representatives, who insisted that Mr. Husky's real name sounded like a fabrication, the single failed to chart. Four years later, performing under his given name and employing a smooth uptown arrangement, he rerecorded "Gone" for Capitol in Nashville. The single went on to spend 10 weeks at No. 1 on the country charts and climbed to No. 4 on the pop chart.

COUNTRIFIED: Mr. Husky's single "Gone" ruled both the pop and the country charts.

"I talked them into putting more production on the song," Mr. Husky recalled in a 1998 interview with the Texas disc jockey Tracy Pitcox. He added that the producer, Capitol's Ken Nelson, "wasn't thrilled with the arrangement, but after it became a hit he was proud of the song."

Mr. Husky had previously topped the country charts in 1953 with "A Dear John Letter," a duet with the singer Jean Shepard for which he was not originally credited. "Gone," though, secured his presence on the country airwaves, where from 1953 to 1975 he had 41 Top 40 country hits, including "Wings of a Dove," which spent 10 weeks at No. 1 in 1960 and reached the pop Top 20. He also had a pair of Top 10 country hits performing as Simon Crum, a comedic alter ego.

An affable and photogenic performer, Mr. Husky frequently appeared on popular television shows like "The Tonight Show" and in the 1957 movie "Mister Rock and Roll," which starred the disc jockey Alan Freed and featured Chuck Berry, Little Richard and other performers.

The next year he starred, along with Zsa Zsa Gabor, Rocky Graziano, Faron Young and June Carter, in "Country Music Holiday." One of the first country singers to have a star on the Hollywood Walk of Fame, Mr. Husky was also a headliner, with Martha Carson and Mr. Young, at Elvis Presley's 1955 show at the Ellis Auditorium in Memphis.

Ferlin Husky was born on Dec. 3, 1925, in Cantwell, Mo., an unincorporated area about 60 miles south of St. Louis. He learned to play the guitar from an uncle and began singing at parties and dances as a teenager.

Mr. Husky served in the Merchant Marine in World War II and did some amateur boxing during that time. Returning to St. Louis in 1946, he began performing in public, using the name Tex Terry in deference to his parents, who didn't want him to be in show business.

He moved to Bakersfield, Calif., to work as a disc jockey in 1947. A year later he signed with Four Star Records, for which he made several singles before moving to Capitol in 1952. Cliffie Stone, a senior Capitol executive, had previously hired him to replace Tennessee Ernie Ford on the television variety show "Hometown Jamboree." Mr. Husky later joined the cast of the Grand Ole Opry. He was elected to the Country Music Hall of Fame in 2010.

The first major country star to come out of the Bakersfield scene that later produced Buck Owens and Merle Haggard, Mr. Husky was also known for his generosity with up-and-coming performers, including Dallas Frazier and Mr. Owens.

"Buck Owens? I dressed him up, putting some decent clothes on him, and got him with Capitol," Mr. Husky said in a 2004 interview published in the British magazine Country Music People.

Mr. Husky is survived by six daughters, two sons, his companion, the country singer Leona Williams, and 11 grandchildren. Another son died in 1970.

— *By Bill Friskics-Warren*

WARREN CHRISTOPHER

Speaking Softly, a Statesman Who Got Results

OCT. 27, 1925 - MARCH 18, 2011

WARREN M. CHRISTOPHER, the courtly and reserved secretary of state in President Bill Clinton's first term and the chief negotiator for the 1981 release of American hostages in Iran, died on March 18 in Los Angeles. He was 85.

O'Melveny & Myers, the law firm where Mr. Christopher was a senior partner, announced his death, saying he had been ill with kidney and bladder cancer. He lived in Los Angeles.

Methodical and self-effacing, Mr. Christopher alternated for nearly five decades between the top echelons of the federal government and the power centers of legal and political life in California. He served as the Carter administration's point man with Congress in winning ratification of the Panama Canal treaties, presided over the normalization of diplomatic relations with China and conducted repeated negotiations involving the Middle East and the Balkans.

At home, Mr. Christopher investigated racial unrest in Detroit and in the Watts district of Los Angeles and later headed a 1991 commission that proposed major reforms of the Los Angeles Police Department after the beating of a black driver, Rodney King, prompted riots.

As a political operative, he headed Mr. Clinton's 1992 search committee for a vice-presidential running mate, settling on Al Gore, and then directed the transition team of the president-elect, acting as an establishment counterweight on a team dominated by Arkansans new to the national scene. Eight years later, when Mr. Gore was running for president, he directed the search resulting in the selection of Senator Joseph I. Lieberman for the second spot on the Democratic ticket.

When the 2000 election reached a stalemate, Mr. Christopher supervised the recount of disputed votes in Florida before George W. Bush emerged the winner by decision of the Supreme Court.

Mr. Christopher was in overall charge of Mr. Gore's Florida recount effort, although much of the legal strategy was devised by a team of lawyers led by David Boies, the prominent corporate lawyer, and Ronald A. Klain, Mr. Gore's former chief of staff and a onetime partner of Mr. Christopher's at O'Melveny & Myers.

Mr. Christopher came under criticism at the time, and later in "Recount," the 2008 HBO dramatization of the Florida vote dispute, over his handling of the Florida episode. His detractors said he had showed a lack of legal and political aggressiveness against Mr. Bush's legal team, led by James A. Baker III, another former secretary of state. The movie, in particular, portrayed Mr. Christopher as overly concerned with the niceties of the law while Mr. Baker was waging a bare-knuckled campaign on all fronts.

Mr. Klain called it an unfair characterization. "Like all dramatic portrayals, they sought dramatic tension by exaggerating people's personalities," he said. "People often confused Chris's reserved style and personal sense of propriety with a lack of fierceness on behalf of his client. That would be a mistake."

He said it was Mr. Christopher's decision to challenge the Florida result, even as most Republicans and some prominent Democrats were urging Mr. Gore to concede. "People don't remember how controversial that effort was. Without Chris's stature and credibility, I'm not sure we would have gotten as far as we did," Mr. Klain said.

Mr. Bush's ascension to the White House was decreed by five Supreme Court justices, Mr. Klain insisted, not by any flaw in Mr. Gore's legal strategy or Mr. Christopher's leadership. "In all the years since then," he said, "no one has come up with any workable strategic advice on how we could have gotten one of those justices to switch."

CRISIS MANAGER: From hostages in Iran to recounts in Florida, Mr. Christopher led the charge.

In a statement, Mr. Gore described Mr. Christopher as "one of the great statesmen of our era. His quiet, consistently thoughtful demeanor belied a fierce commitment to principle and a brilliant mind. Time and again, his wisdom and skillful diplomacy was invaluable in the conduct of America's foreign policy."

Though widely admired for his even-handedness and equanimity — he was once described as every husband's ideal for a wife's divorce lawyer — Mr. Christopher was also criticized as lacking passionate, big-picture diplomatic vision. Even friends and associates, to whom he was known as Chris or sometimes as "the Cardinal," said they could not discern a guiding geopolitical philosophy, regarding him as more a consummate tactician than as a conceptualizer.

"If we were in a meeting on a crisis, no one would turn to Chris and say, 'You put together the strategy memo,'" a onetime State Department official told The New York Times when Mr. Christopher was named secretary of state. "But everyone would want him to read it, because he'd be very good at implementing it."

Mr. Christopher appeared not to disagree. "My task had been to serve as steward, not proprietor, of an extraordinary public trust," he wrote in "Chances of a Lifetime: A Memoir," published in 2001. But he bristled at criticism that Mr. Clinton's penchant for consultation and his own eagerness to listen had made for seminars, not decisions. "The president's desire to consult and my Norwegian taciturnity didn't prevent us from making the right judgments," he said of one occasion.

Warren Minor Christopher was born on Oct. 27, 1925, in the farming hamlet of Scranton, N.D., one of five children. His father, a local banker, suffered a stroke that the family believed was caused by overwork from his unsuccessful efforts to keep the bank solvent during the Depression. The elder Mr. Christopher died four years later at 53, after the family moved to California.

The unabashed New Deal liberalism that young Warren embraced during this period remained with him throughout his career, even though he made his fortune representing I.B.M., the Lockheed Martin Corporation and other major companies for O'Melveny & Myers, the most traditional and prestigious of Los Angeles law firms, which he eventually led.

Always impeccably dressed and unfailingly polite, Mr. Christopher told an interviewer while secretary of state that "I always thought that I would do things in a conservative way to maximize the progressiveness of my policy positions."

While attending Hollywood High School he delivered newspapers several hours a day. He told friends he had felt discriminated against because of his family's difficult financial circumstances. He entered the University of Redlands at 16, but with the outbreak of World War II he entered a Navy officer program at the University of Southern California and soon served as an ensign in the Navy Reserve on an oil tanker in the Pacific.

After earning degrees at U.S.C. and Stanford's law school, Mr. Christopher won a clerkship with the libertarian Supreme Court justice William O. Douglas, during which he helped draft book chapters.

He joined O'Melveny & Myers in 1950, and later became an adviser and speechwriter for California's newly elected governor, Edmund G. Brown. He was credited with coining the term "responsible liberalism."

Mr. Christopher, made a partner at just 33 in 1958, was named by Governor Brown to the commission investigating the 1965 Watts riots. This brought him to the attention of President Lyndon B. Johnson, who in 1967 lured him back to Washington, until January 1969, as deputy to Attorney General Ramsey Clark.

There, as he focused on racial unrest in Detroit and Washington, he formed a relationship with Cyrus R. Vance. On being installed as secretary of state seven years later, Mr. Vance recommended that President Jimmy Carter ask Mr. Christopher again to take leave from O'Melveny & Myers and become No. 2 at the State Department.

As deputy secretary, his first major task was to shepherd through the Senate the Panama Canal treaties that, in exchange for returning sovereignty over the canal territory to Panama, gave the United States the right to reopen it militarily.

But his tenure is most vividly remembered for the agonizing and prolonged negotiations for the release of 52 hostages held in the American Embassy in Tehran for more than a year after the 1979 Iranian revolution.

Late in 1980 Mr. Christopher shuttled between Algeria, which had become a mediator, and Washington and finally brokered a deal under which the hostages would be released in return for an unfreezing of Iranian assets and a lifting of sanctions.

Even after the agreement was signed on the last full day of the Carter presidency, Iran disavowed a vital element in it, and Mr. Christopher wrote in a 2006 article about lessons learned in dealing with what he called the souk-like "bazaar behavior" of Iranian negotiators.

"To bring them back in line, I directed the pilot of my plane, on a telephone line that I knew was tapped, to warm up the engines," he wrote. "The Iranians quickly dropped their claim and a day later the hostages were released." Mr. Christopher, usually reserved and unemotional, wept at the ultimate success.

> Mr. Gore said of Mr. Christopher: "His quiet, consistently thoughtful demeanor belied a fierce commitment to principle and a brilliant mind."

During the captivity, an American military rescue operation failed, and when Mr. Vance, who had opposed the mission, resigned, Mr. Carter passed over Mr. Christopher, the logical successor, in favor of Senator Edmund S. Muskie.

But Mr. Christopher loyally remained, and a few months after the hostages were released he pointed to what he said was the value of patient negotiation.

"I am thankful to have served a nation so quietly strong that it could preserve its honor, not by retaliation or vengeance, but by preserving the lives of the hostages," he said.

After giving way to Madeleine K. Albright after one term as secretary of state, Mr. Christopher once more returned to O'Melveny & Myers and life in California. He served as president of Stanford's board of trustees and was a longtime director of the Southern California Edison Company.

Mr. Christopher is survived by his wife of 54 years, the former Marie Wyllis, a teacher, as well as by their three children and five grandchildren. He had another child from an earlier marriage.

After leaving public service Mr. Christopher continued to speak out on international issues. In 2002, in an Op-Ed article in The Times, he urged that President George W. Bush rethink "his fixation on attacking Iraq" and focus on what he considered graver threats, like North Korea.

"Even if the optimistic predictions of quick victory prove to be accurate," he wrote more than two months before the invasion, "we would then find ourselves absorbed with the occupation of Iraq and efforts to impose democracy on the fractious elements of that country."

— *By Robert D. Hershey Jr.*

PINETOP PERKINS

A Boogie-Woogie Master of Delta Blues

JULY 7, 1913 - MARCH 21, 2011

Pinetop Perkins, the boogie-woogie piano player who worked in Muddy Waters's last great band and was among the last surviving members of the first generation of Delta bluesmen, died on March 21 at his home in Austin, Tex. He was 97.

From his days in the groups of Mr. Waters and the slide guitarist Robert Nighthawk to the vigorous solo career he fashioned over the last 20 years, Mr. Perkins's accomplishments were numerous and considerable. His longevity as a performer was remarkable — all the more so considering his fondness for cigarettes and alcohol; by his own account he began smoking at age 9 and didn't quit drinking until he was 82. Few people working in any popular art form have been as prolific in the ninth and tenth decades of their lives.

A sideman for most of his career, Mr. Perkins did not release an album under his own name until his 75th year. From then until his death he made more than a dozen records on which he was the leader. His 2008 album, "Pinetop Perkins & Friends" (Telarc), included contributions from admirers like B. B. King and Eric Clapton. His last album, released in 2010, was "Joined at the Hip" (Telarc), a collaboration with the harmonica player Willie Big Eyes Smith. It won a Grammy in 2011 as best traditional blues album.

Mr. Perkins's durability was born of the resilience and self-reliance he developed as a child growing up on a plantation in Honey Island, Miss., in the years leading up to the Great Depression.

"I grew up hard," he said in 2008 in an interview with No Depression, the American roots music magazine. "I picked cotton and plowed with the mule and fixed the cars and played with the guitar and the piano."

"What I learned I learned on my own," he continued. "I didn't have much school. Three years."

The author Robert Gordon, in his book "Can't Be Satisfied: The Life and Times of Muddy Waters," wrote that Mr. Perkins "learned to play in the same school as Muddy — a cotton field, where the conjugation was done with a hoe and the school lunch was a fish sandwich and homemade whiskey."

Originally a guitarist, Mr. Perkins concentrated exclusively on the piano after an incident, in 1943, in which a dancer at a juke joint attacked him with a knife, severing the tendons in his left arm. The injury left him unable to hold a guitar or manage its fretboard.

In 1943 Mr. Perkins moved to Helena, Ark., to work with Mr. Nighthawk. He later joined Sonny Boy Williamson's King Biscuit Boys, before moving on to the band of the slide guitarist Earl Hooker. He also appeared on the recordings that Mr. Nighthawk made for the Chess label and that Mr. Hooker made for Sun in the 1950s. It was for Sun, in 1953, that he cut his first version of "Pinetop's Boogie Woogie," the song that furnished him with his nickname and became his signature number. He appropriated the tune from the repertory of the barrelhouse piano player Clarence Smith, who was also known as Pinetop.

PIANO MAN: Mr. Perkins's playing influenced a generation of rockers.

Mr. Perkins has also been credited with teaching Ike Turner how to play the piano. Rock and pop pianists like Elton John, Billy Joel and Gregg Allman have said they were influenced by his exuberant, down-home style of playing.

Joe Willie Perkins was born on July 7, 1913, in Belzoni, Miss. His parents separated when he was 6. Mr. Perkins, who dropped out of school after the third grade, taught himself the rudiments of blues guitar on a homemade instrument called a diddley bow: a length of wire stretched between nails driven into a wall. He began entertaining at dances and house parties at age 10 and soon learned to play the piano as well. While still in his teens he left Mississippi and traveled to Chicago.

Returning to the Delta, he drove a tractor in the cotton fields, but in the late 1950s he again made Chicago his home. He wasn't very active as musician there, though, until Mr. Hooker enlisted him to appear on an album he was making for Arhoolie Records in 1968. When the pianist Otis Spann left Mr. Waters's band the next year, Mr. Perkins, whose lean gutbucket style contrasted with Mr. Spann's more florid playing, was recruited to replace him.

"I played more of a bluesy type than Spann did," he told Mr. Gordon. "I taught myself off records, Memphis Slim, them old piano players, then added to it. Yeah, hard and loud, beat it to pieces."

Mr. Perkins worked for Mr. Waters for more than a decade, appearing on his acclaimed comeback albums of the late '70s and performing with him in shows; one was the Band's celebrated final concert, billed as "The Last Waltz," in 1976.

Mr. Perkins and other members of the Waters group left and formed the Legendary Blues Band in 1980. Mr. Perkins sang and played piano on that ensemble's records before leaving in the late '80s to concentrate on his solo career.

In addition to his Grammy for "Joined at the Hip," he won one in 2008 for the album "Last of the Great Mississippi Delta Bluesmen: Live in Dallas" (Blue Shoe Project), a collaboration with his contemporaries Henry Townsend, Robert Lockwood Jr. and Honeyboy Edwards. In 2005 he was given a Grammy for lifetime achievement. "Born in the Honey," a documentary about Mr. Perkins's life, was released in 2007.

Hugh Southard, his agent for the last 15 years, said Mr. Perkins had no known survivors.

"What little family I got is in Mississippi," Mr. Perkins said in an interview posted on his Web site, pinetopperkins.com. "A whole lot of them died before I left, and my sister died a long time ago, before my mama did. I had a bunch of friends and people in Chicago, but no family."

— *By Bill Friskics-Warren*

ELIZABETH TAYLOR

At the Pinnacle of Hollywood Glamour

FEB. 27, 1932 - MARCH 23, 2011

Elizabeth Taylor, the Oscar-winning actress who dazzled generations of moviegoers with her stunning beauty and whose name was synonymous with Hollywood glamour, died on March 23 in Los Angeles. She was 79.

Her death, at Cedars-Sinai Medical Center, was caused by complications of congestive heart failure. She had a series of medical setbacks over the years and was hospitalized six weeks earlier with heart problems.

In a world of flickering images, Elizabeth Taylor was a constant star. First appearing on screen at age 10, she grew up there, never passing through an awkward age. It was one quick leap from "National Velvet" to "A Place in the Sun" and from there to "Cleopatra," as she was indelibly transformed from a vulnerable child actress into a voluptuous film queen.

In a career of some 70 years and more than 50 films, she won two Academy Awards as best actress, for her performances as a call girl in "BUtterfield 8" (1960) and as the acid-tongued Martha in "Who's Afraid of Virginia Woolf?" (1966). Mike Nichols, who directed her in "Virginia Woolf," said he considered her "one of the greatest cinema actresses."

When Ms. Taylor was honored in 1986 by the Film Society of Lincoln Center, Vincent Canby wrote in The New York Times, "More than anyone else I can think of, Elizabeth Taylor represents the complete movie phenomenon — what movies are as an art and an industry, and what they have meant to those of us who have grown up watching them in the dark."

Ms. Taylor's popularity endured throughout her life, but critics were sometimes reserved in their praise of her acting. In that sense she may have been upstaged by her own striking beauty. Could anyone as lovely as Elizabeth Taylor also be talented? The answer, of course, was yes.

Given her lack of professional training, the range of her acting was surprisingly wide. She played predatory vixens and wounded victims. She was Cleopatra of the burnished barge; Tennessee Williams's Maggie the cat; Catherine Holly, who confronted terror suddenly last summer; and Shakespeare's Kate. Her melodramatic heroines would have been at home on soap operas.

Joseph L. Mankiewicz, who directed her in "Suddenly, Last Summer" and "Cleopatra," saw her for the first time, in Cannes, when she was 18. "She was the most incredible vision of loveliness I have ever seen in my life," he said. "And she was sheer innocence."

Mr. Mankiewicz admired her professionalism. "Whatever the script called for, she played it," he said. "The thread that goes through the whole is that of a woman who is an honest performer. Therein lies her identity."

It was also Mr. Mankiewicz who said that for Ms. Taylor, "living life was a kind of acting," that she lived her life "in screen time."

The Magnet of Her Personality

Marilyn Monroe was the sex goddess, Grace Kelly the ice queen, Audrey Hepburn the eternal gamine. Ms. Taylor was beauty incarnate. As the director George Stevens said when he chose her for "A Place in the Sun," the role called for the "beautiful girl in the yellow Cadillac convertible that every American boy, some time or other, thinks he can marry."

There was more than a touch of Ms. Taylor herself in the roles she played. She acted with the magnet of her personality. Although she could alter her look for a part — putting on weight for Martha in "Virginia Woolf" or wearing elaborate period costumes — she was not a chameleon, assuming the coloration of a character. Instead she would bring the character closer to herself. For her, acting was "purely intuitive." As she said, "What I try to do is to give the maximum emotional effect with the minimum of visual movement."

Sometimes her film roles seemed to be a mirror image of her life. More than most movie stars, she seemed to exist in the public domain. She was pursued by paparazzi and denounced by the Vatican. But behind the seemingly scandalous behavior was a woman with a clear sense of morality: she habitually married her lovers. People watched and counted, with vicarious pleasure, as she became Elizabeth Taylor Hilton Wilding Todd Fisher Burton Burton Warner Fortensky — enough marriages to certify her career as a serial wife. Asked why she married so often, she said, in an assumed drawl: "I don't know, honey. It sure beats the hell out of me."

FILM ROYALTY: Ms. Taylor, circa 1955, appeared in more than 50 films, starting at age 10.

In a lifetime of emotional and physical setbacks, serious illnesses and accidents, and several near-death experiences, Ms. Taylor was a survivor. "I've been lucky all my life," she said just before turning 60. "Everything was handed to me. Looks, fame, wealth, honors, love. I rarely had to fight for anything. But I've paid for that luck with disasters." At 65, she said on the ABC program "20/20": "I'm like a living example of what people can go through and survive. I'm not like anyone. I'm me."

Her life was played out in print: miles of newspaper and magazine articles, a galaxy of photographs and a shelf of biographies, each painting a different portrait. "Planes, trains, everything stops for Elizabeth Taylor, but the public has no conception of who she is," said Roddy McDowall, who was one of her earliest co-stars and a friend until he died in 1998. "People who damn her wish to hell they could do what they think she does."

There was one point of general agreement: her beauty. As cameramen noted, her face was flawlessly symmetrical; she had no bad angle, and her eyes were of the deepest violet.

One prominent and perhaps surprising dissenter about her looks was Richard Burton, who was twice her husband. The notion of his wife as "the most beautiful woman in the world is absolute nonsense," he said. "She has wonderful eyes," he added, "but she has a double chin and an overdeveloped chest, and she's rather short in the leg."

On screen and off, Ms. Taylor was a provocative combination of the angel and the seductress. In all her incarnations she had a vibrant sensuality. But beneath it was more than a tinge of vulgarity, as in her love of showy jewelry. "I know I'm vulgar," she said, addressing her fans with typical candor, "but would you have me any other way?"

For many years she was high on the list of box-office stars. Even when her movies were unsuccessful, or, late in her career, when she acted infrequently, she retained her fame: there was only one Liz (a nickname she hated), and her celebrity increased the more she lived in the public eye. There was nothing she could do about it. "The public me," she said, "the one named Elizabeth Taylor, has become a lot of hokum and fabrication — a bunch of drivel — and I find her slightly revolting."

Late in life she became a social activist. After her friend Rock Hudson died, she helped establish the American Foundation for AIDS Research and helped raise money for it. In 1997, she said, "I use my fame now when I want to help a cause or other people."

Twice she had leading roles on Broadway, in a 1981 revival of Lillian Hellman's "Little Foxes" and two years later in Noël Coward's "Private

Lives," with Mr. Burton, then her former husband. In the first instance she won critical respect; in the second she and Mr. Burton descended into self-parody. But theater was not her ideal arena; it was as a movie star that she made her impact.

In a life of many surprises, one of the oddest facts is that as an infant she was considered to be an ugly duckling. Elizabeth Rosemond Taylor was born in London on Feb. 27, 1932, the second child of American parents with roots in Kansas. Her father, Francis Lenn Taylor, was an art dealer who had been transferred to London from New York; her mother, the former Sara Viola Warmbrodt, had acted in the theater in New York, under the name Sara Sothern, before she was married. (Ms. Taylor's brother, Howard, was born in 1929.) At birth, her mother said, her daughter's "tiny face was so tightly closed it looked as if it would never unfold."

Elizabeth spent her early childhood in England. It was there, at 3, that she learned to ride horseback, a skill that helped her win her first major role. Just before World War II, the family moved to the United States, eventually settling in Beverly Hills.

An Inauspicious Start

Ms. Taylor's mother shared with her daughter a love of movies and encouraged her to act. Elizabeth made her movie debut in 1942 as Gloria Twine in a forgettable film called "There's One Born Every Minute," with Carl Switzer, best known as Alfalfa, the boy with the cowlick in the "Our Gang" series. The casting director at Universal said of her: "The kid has nothing." Despite that inauspicious debut, Sam Marx, an MGM producer who had known the Taylors in England, arranged for their daughter to have a screen test for "Lassie Come Home." She passed the audition. During the filming, in which Ms. Taylor acted with Roddy McDowall, a cameraman mistakenly thought her long eyelashes were fake and asked her to take them off.

The power of her attraction was evident as early as 1944, in "National Velvet." MGM had for many years owned the film rights to the Enid Bagnold novel on which that film was based, but had had difficulty finding a child actress who could speak with an English accent and ride horses. At 12, Elizabeth Taylor met those requirements, though she was initially rejected for being too short. Stories circulated that she stretched herself in order to fill the physical dimensions of the role: Velvet Brown, a girl who was obsessed with horses and rode one to victory in the Grand National Steeplechase. "I knew if it were right for me to be Velvet," she said, "God would make me grow."

In one scene, her horse, which she called the Pie, seemed to be dying, and Ms. Taylor was supposed to cry — the first time she was called on to show such emotion on screen. Her co-star was Mickey Rooney, a more experienced actor, and he gave her some advice on how to summon tears: pretend that her father was dying, that her mother had to wash clothes for a living and that her little dog had been run over. Hearing that sad scenario, Ms. Taylor burst out laughing at the absurdity. When it came time to shoot the scene, she later said: "All I thought about was the horse being very sick and that I was the little girl who owned him. And the tears came."

Ms. Taylor gave a performance that quite literally made grown men and women weep, to say nothing of girls who identified with Velvet. In his review of the film in The Nation, James Agee, otherwise a tough-minded critic, confessed that the first time he had seen Ms. Taylor on screen he had been "choked with the peculiar sort of adoration I might have felt if we were both in the same grade of primary school."

She was, he said, "rapturously beautiful."

"I think that she and the picture are wonderful, and I hardly know or care whether she can act or not."

The movie made her a star. Decades later she said "National Velvet" was still "the most exciting film" she had ever made. But there was a drawback. To do the movie she had to sign a long-term contract with MGM. As she said, she "became their chattel until I did 'Cleopatra.'"

At first she played typical teenagers (in "Life With Father," "A Date With Judy" and "Little Women"). At 16 she was "an emotional child inside a woman's body," she later said. But in contrast to other child actresses, she made an easy transition to adult roles. In 1950 she played

Robert Taylor's wife in "Conspirator." The same year, she was in Vincente Minnelli's "Father of the Bride," with Spencer Tracy. And, life imitating art, she became a bride herself in 1950, marrying the hotel heir Conrad N. Hilton Jr., who was known as Nicky. After an unhappy nine months, she divorced him and then married the British actor Michael Wilding, who was 20 years older than she.

Could anyone as lovely as Elizabeth Taylor also be talented? The answer, of course, was yes.

By her own estimation, she "whistled and hummed" her way through her early films. But that changed in 1951, when she made "A Place in the Sun," playing her prototypical role as a seemingly unattainable romantic vision. The film, she said, was "the first time I ever considered acting when I was young."

In the film she plays a wealthy young woman of social position who is the catalyst for Montgomery Clift's American tragedy. To the astonishment of skeptics, she held her own with Mr. Clift and Shelley Winters.

"A Place in the Sun" was followed by "Ivanhoe," "Beau Brummel" and "The Last Time I Saw Paris." Then she made two widescreen epics back to back: "Giant," with Rock Hudson and James Dean (who was killed in a car wreck after finishing his scenes), and "Raintree County" with Mr. Clift, who became a close friend. Her role in "Raintree County" (1957), as Susanna Drake, a Civil-War era Southern belle who marries an Indiana abolitionist, earned her an Oscar nomination for best actress. It was the first of four consecutive nominations; the last resulted in a win for "BUtterfield 8."

Ms. Taylor was filming "Cat on a Hot Tin Roof" with Paul Newman in 1958 when her third husband, the impresario Mike Todd, was killed with three others in New Mexico in the crash of a small plane called the Lucky Liz. They had been married little more than a year and had a newly born daughter.

A bereaved Ms. Taylor was consoled by her husband's best friend, the singer Eddie Fisher, who in a storybook romance was married to the actress Debbie Reynolds, one of America's sweethearts. Soon a shocked nation learned that Debbie and Eddie were over and that Mr. Fisher was marrying Ms. Taylor. (In 1993, at an AIDS benefit, Ms. Reynolds appeared on stage 20 minutes before Ms. Taylor and said, to waves of laughter, "Well, here I am, sharing something else with Elizabeth.") Mr. Fisher died in 2010 (see page 70).

After Ms. Taylor finished "Cat on a Hot Tin Roof," MGM demanded that she fulfill her contract and act in a film version of John O'Hara's "BUtterfield 8." Her performance as the call girl Gloria Wandrous brought her an Oscar in 1961 as best actress.

The award was bestowed less than six weeks after she had an emergency tracheotomy in London, where she had been overcome by pneumonia and lost consciousness, prompting one of several times that headlines proclaimed her close to death. She and others felt that the Oscar was given to her more out of sympathy for her illness than in appreciation of her acting.

Next was "Cleopatra," in which she was the first actress to be paid a million-dollar salary. Working overtime, she earned more than twice that amount. The movie was made in Rome and cost so much ($40 million, a record then) and took so long that it almost bankrupted 20th Century-Fox and caused an irrevocable rift between the producer Darryl F. Zanuck and the director, Mr. Mankiewicz.

When "Cleopatra" was finally released in 1963 it was a disappointment. But the film became legendary for the off-screen affair of its stars, Ms. Taylor, then married to Mr. Fisher, and Richard Burton, then married to Sybil Williams.

Opposites Attract

Taylor and Burton: it seemed like a meeting, or a collision, of opposites, the most famous movie star in the world and the man many believed to be the finest classical actor of

APPRECIATION

A Survivor Who Lived Large

The last movie star has died.

Elizabeth Taylor cheated death despite infirmities that repeatedly put her in the hospital and that in 1961 left her with a tracheotomy scar on a neck more accustomed to diamonds. The operation resulted from a bout with pneumonia that left her gasping for air, and it returned her to the big, bountiful, hungry life that was one of her greatest roles. It was a minor incision (she later had the scar removed), but it's easy to think of it as some kind of war wound for a life lived so magnificently.

Unlike Marilyn, Liz survived. And it was that survival as much as the movies and fights with the studios, the melodramas and men (so many melodramas, so many men!) that helped separate Ms. Taylor from many other old-Hollywood stars. She rocketed into the stratosphere in the 1950s, the era of the bombshell and the Bomb, when most of the top female box-office draws were blond, pneumatic and classifiable by type: good-time gals (Betty Grable), professional virgins (Doris Day), ice queens (Grace Kelly). Marilyn Monroe was the sacrificial sex goddess with the invitational mouth. Born six years before Ms. Taylor, she entered the movies a poor little girl ready to give it her all, and did.

Ms. Taylor, by contrast, was sui generis, a child star turned ingénue and jet-setting supernova, famous for her loves (Eddie & Liz, Liz & Dick) and finally for just being Liz. "I don't remember ever not being famous," she said. For her, fame was part of the job, neither a blessing (though the jewels were nice) nor a curse. Perhaps that's why she never looked defeated, unlike those who wilt under the spotlight. In film after film she appears extraordinarily at ease: to the camera born. She's as natural in "National Velvet," the 1944 hit that made her a star at 12, as she is two decades later roaring through "Who's Afraid of Virginia Woolf?," proving once again that beauty and talent are not mutually exclusive, even in Hollywood.

In many respects she was a classic product of the old studio system. Pushed by a quintessential stage mother, she was signed to a contract in 1943 by MGM, which was banking on child talent, much of which was used up by adolescence, either disappearing for good or absorbed into the ranks of character actors. Unlike so many fledgling stars then and now, Ms. Taylor bloomed as a teenager and seemed remarkably relaxed in that newly plush body that soon became a big-screen fetish. She made it all seem so effortless, as did the studio machinery grinding away in the background. "She's the kind of a girl," a reporter for The New York Times wrote in

his generation. What they had in common was an extraordinary passion for each other and for living life to the fullest. Their romantic roller coaster was chronicled by the international press, which referred them as an entity called Dickenliz.

After finishing the film, Ms. Taylor went with Mr. Burton to Toronto, where he was on a pre-Broadway tour with "Hamlet." In Toronto, and later in New York, the two were at the height of their megastardom, accompanied by a retinue as large as that of the Sultan of Brunei and besieged a charmingly naïve 1949 profile, "to whom nice things just happen."

Yet Hollywood and nice don't often keep company, as one after another crash-and-burn studio tell-all attests, and the perils faced by the young, beautiful and exploitable are legion. "Remind me to be around when she grows up," Orson Welles joked after watching the 10-year-old Ms. Taylor shoot a scene in "Jane Eyre." It's a half-funny, queasy comment, and however made in jest (or so you hope), it's also a reminder of the predators that were always lurking and could have swallowed Ms. Taylor whole. That seems particularly the case given how, as she developed (at 16, she was "obviously mature," as the Times reporter put it), she often seemed far too knowing, too womanly for the juvenile and young-lady roles she played.

It was George Stevens, who directed "A Place in the Sun," who gave the young actress her first Elizabeth Taylor role, the one in which everything — her looks, presence and power — came together. Based on Theodore Dreiser's novel "An American Tragedy," it starred Ms. Taylor as an heiress whose allure is so potent it drives a young striver (Ms. Taylor's close friend, Montgomery Clift) to murder his pregnant working-class lover (Shelley Winters). Everything wondrous and mysterious about cinema itself is captured in a dazzling, sensuously lengthy kiss between Ms. Taylor and Mr. Clift that Mr. Stevens shot in tight, almost claustrophobic close-up, filling the frame with beauty made immortal by film. It's an intoxicating vision of bliss if one that — and this is critical to the film's force — has been paid for by the murder of another woman.

Here, the movies seemed to say, was a woman worth killing for. It's hard to think of many actresses, even those die-hard professionals raised inside the old studio bubbles, who could have weathered such an impossible burden. Ms. Taylor managed the role of sex object effortlessly as if it, too, were just part of the job. In contrast to so many other actresses, she seemed as desiring as desirous, with the gift of a thrillingly unladylike appetite. She was a great lover of food, of course, as her cruelly documented weight gains make evident. Yet the appetite that appeared to drive, at times even define her, exceeded mere food to include everything, and her consumption of men, booze, jewels and celebrity itself was an astonishment.

Living large proved a brilliant survival strategy as well as something of a rebuke to the limits of the studio system, both its formulas and false morality, which was all but gone by the time she appeared in "Virginia Woolf" in 1966. Her weight went up and down and the accolades kept coming. She cheated on one husband and then another at a time when adultery was still shocking, and her career kept going. She was a lovely actress and a better star. She embodied the excesses of Hollywood and she transcended them. In the end, the genius of her career was that she gave the world everything it wanted from a glamorous star, the excitement and drama, the diamonds and gossip, and she did it by refusing to become fame's martyr.

— *By Manohla Dargis*

by fans, who turned every public appearance into a mob scene. In New York as many as 5,000 people gathered outside the Lunt-Fontanne Theater on West 46th Street after every performance of "Hamlet," hoping Ms. Taylor was backstage and eager to see the couple emerge.

They were married in 1964, and Ms. Taylor tried without success to keep herself in the background. "I don't think of myself as Taylor," she said, ingenuously. "I much prefer being Burton." She told her husband, "If I get fat enough, they won't ask me to do any more films." Although

GEORGE AND MARTHA: Ms. Taylor and Mr. Burton in the film adaptation of Edward Albee's play "Who's Afraid of Virginia Woolf?"

she put on weight, she continued to act.

The life of Dickenliz was one of excess. They owned mansions in various countries, rented entire floors of hotels and spent lavishly on cars, art and jewelry, including the 69.42-carat Cartier diamond and the 33.19-carat Krupp diamond. (In 2002 Ms. Taylor published "My Love Affair With Jewelry," a coffee-table memoir as told through the prism of her world-class gems.)

Since childhood Ms. Taylor had been surrounded by pets. When she was not allowed to take her dogs to London because of a quarantine rule, she leased a yacht for them at a reported cost of $20,000 and moored it on the Thames.

After "Cleopatra," the couple united in a film partnership that gave the public glossy romances like "The V.I.P.'s" and "The Sandpiper" and one powerful drama about marital destructiveness, the film version of Edward Albee's play "Who's Afraid of Virginia Woolf?" As Martha, the faculty wife, a character 20 years older than she was, Ms. Taylor gained 20 pounds and made herself look dowdy. After she received her second Academy Award for the performance, Mr. Burton, who played Martha's husband, George, offered a wry response: "She won an Oscar for it, he said bitterly, and I didn't, he said equally bitterly."

The Burtons also acted together in "Doctor Faustus" (1968), in which she was a conjured-up Helen of Troy; "The Comedians" (1967), with Ms. Taylor as an adulterous ambassador's wife in Haiti; Franco Zeffirelli's film version of "The Taming of the Shrew" (1967), with Ms. Taylor as the volatile Katharina to Mr. Burton's wife-hunting Petruchio; "Boom!" (1968), based on the Tennessee Williams play "The Milk Train Doesn't Stop Here Anymore," with Ms. Taylor as a rich, ailing woman living on an island; "Under Milk Wood" (1972), an adaptation of the Dylan Thomas play; and "Hammersmith Is Out" (1972), a retelling of the Faust legend in which she played a diner waitress.

On her own, Ms. Taylor was an adulterous Army major's wife in "Reflections in a Golden Eye" (1967), with Marlon Brando; a fading prostitute in "Secret Ceremony" (1968); an aging Las Vegas chorus girl in "The Only Game in Town" (1970), with Warren Beatty; a rich widow who witnesses a murder in "Night Watch" (1973); and a wife who tries to save her marriage through plastic surgery in "Ash Wednesday" (1973).

After 10 high-living and often torrid years (along the way they adopted a daughter), the Burtons were divorced in 1974, remarried 16 months later in a mud-hut village in Botswana, separated again the next February and were granted a divorce in Haiti in July 1976.

Mr. Burton died of a cerebral hemorrhage at 58 in 1984 in Switzerland. Thirteen years later Ms. Taylor said that Mr. Todd and Mr. Burton were the loves of her life, and that if Mr. Burton had lived, they might have married a third time. For years after his death, she told The Times in

2000, she couldn't watch when the films they had made were on television.

After her second divorce from Mr. Burton, she wed John W. Warner, a Virginia politician, and was active in his winning campaign for the United States Senate. For five years she was a Washington political wife and, she said, "the loneliest person in the world." Overcome by depression, she checked into the Betty Ford Center in Rancho Mirage, Calif. She later admitted that she had been treated as "a drunk and a junkie."

Battling Drugs and Food

In addition to alcohol and drugs, she had a problem with overeating, and it became the butt of jokes by the comedian Joan Rivers. ("She has more chins than a Chinese phone book.") Ms. Rivers later apologized to Ms. Taylor through a friend, though Ms. Taylor shrugged off the insults, saying they did not "get me where I live." Ms. Rivers said, "From then on, I was crazy about her." Ms. Taylor wrote a book about her weight problems, "Elizabeth Takes Off: On Weight Gain, Weight Loss, Self-Image & Self-Esteem" (1988).

When she returned to the Ford Center for further treatment, she met Larry Fortensky, a construction worker, who was also a patient. In a wedding spectacular in 1991, she and Mr. Fortensky were married at Michael Jackson's Neverland Valley Ranch in Santa Ynez, Calif., with celebrated guests sharing the grounds with Mr. Jackson's giraffes, zebras and llamas. Although the press was not invited, a photographer parachuted in and narrowly missed landing on Gregory Peck. Five years later, the Fortenskys were divorced. Ms. Taylor, a longtime friend of Mr. Jackson's, was a visible presence at his funeral in 2009.

Through the 1980s and '90s, Ms. Taylor acted in movies sporadically, did "The Little Foxes" and "Private Lives" on Broadway, and appeared on television as Louella Parsons in "Malice in Wonderland" in 1985 and as the aging actress Alexandra Del Lago in Tennessee Williams's "Sweet Bird of Youth" in 1989.

In 1994 she played Fred Flintstone's mother-in-law in "The Flintstones," and in 1996 she made appearances on four CBS sitcoms. In 2001 she and Shirley MacLaine, Joan Collins and Debbie Reynolds made fun of their own images in "These Old Broads," a tepidly received television movie — written by Carrie Fisher, the daughter of Ms. Reynolds and Eddie Fisher — about aging movie stars who despise one another but reunite for a TV special. Ms. Taylor, getting little screen time, played their caftan-wearing agent.

Ms. Taylor was often seen as a caricature of herself, "full of no-nonsense shamelessness," as Margo Jefferson wrote in The Times in 1999, adding, "Whether it's about how she ages or what she wears, she has, bless her heart, made the principles of good and bad taste equally meaningless."

Increasingly, Ms. Taylor divided her time between her charitable works, including various Israeli causes (she had converted to Judaism in 1959), and commercial enterprises, like a line of perfumes. She helped raise more than $100 million to fight AIDS. In February 1997, she celebrated her 65th birthday at a party that was a benefit for AIDS research. After the party Ms. Taylor entered Cedars-Sinai Medical Center for a brain tumor operation.

There were other setbacks. In recent years she had to use a wheelchair because of osteoporosis/scoliosis. In 2009 she had surgery for heart problems. In early 2011 she refused to undergo a back operation, saying she had already had a half-dozen. In February 2011 she entered Cedars-Sinai for the final time with congestive heart failure.

She is survived by two sons, two daughters, 10 grandchildren and four great-grandchildren.

In 2002 Ms. Taylor was among five people to receive Kennedy Center Honors in the performing arts.

Married or single, sick or healthy, on screen or off, Ms. Taylor never lost her appetite for experience. Late in life, when she had one of many offers to write her memoirs, she refused, saying with characteristic panache, "Hell no, I'm still living my memoirs."

— *By Mel Gussow*

William McDonald, William Grimes and Daniel E. Slotnik contributed reporting.

JEAN BARTIK

An Early Programmer Belatedly Recognized

DEC. 27, 1924 - MARCH 23, 2011

JEAN BARTIK, one of the first computer programmers who only later in life won recognition as a pioneer in the technology that came to be known as software, died on March 23 at a nursing home in Poughkeepsie, N.Y. She was 86.

Ms. Bartik was the last surviving member of the group of women who programmed the Eniac, or Electronic Numerical Integrator and Computer, which is credited as the first all-electronic digital computer.

The Eniac, designed to calculate the firing trajectories for artillery shells, turned out to be a historic demonstration project. It was completed in 1946, too late for use in World War II, but it was a milestone in the evolution of modern computing. Ms. Bartik and Frances Elizabeth Holberton, who died in 2001, were the lead programmers among the small team of women who worked on the Eniac.

When the Eniac was shown off at the University of Pennsylvania in February 1946, it generated headlines in newspapers across the country. But the attention was all on the men and the machine. The women were not even introduced at the event.

"For years, we celebrated the people who built it, not the people who programmed it," said David Alan Grier, a technology historian at George Washington University and a senior vice president of the IEEE Computer Society.

The oversight has been somewhat redressed. In 2009, Ms. Bartik received a Pioneer Award from the IEEE Computer Society, and in 2008 she was named a fellow by the Computer History Museum in Mountain View, Calif.

SOFTWARE PIONEERS: Ms. Bartik, right, holding a piece of Eniac in 2002. She and Kay McNulty Mauchly Antonelli, left, helped program it in the 1940s, along with four other women.

The Eniac women were wartime recruits with math skills; their job was initially described as plugging in wires to "set up the machine." But converting the math analysis into a process that made sense to the machine, so that a calculation could flow through the electronic circuitry to completion, proved to be a daunting challenge.

"These women, being the first to enter this new territory, were the first to encounter the whole question of programming," said Paul E. Ceruzzi, a computer historian at the Smithsonian Institution. "And they met the challenge."

Betty Jean Jennings was born on Dec. 27, 1924, in rural Missouri, the sixth of seven children in a farm family whose parents valued education. She attended Northwest Missouri State Teachers College, now Northwest Missouri State University, majoring in math, and it was there that her career path began, in 1945.

Her faculty adviser saw an advertisement one day in a math journal saying the Army was recruiting math graduates for a wartime project in Philadelphia. She applied, was accepted and told to come quickly. She got on the next train, according to her son, Timothy Bartik. "She wanted adventure, and she got it," he said.

In Philadelphia, while working on the Eniac, she dropped the use of the first name Betty, which she never liked. And down the hall at the University of Pennsylvania, she met William Bartik, an engineer working on another Pentagon project. They were married in 1946. (They divorced in 1968.)

After the war, Ms. Bartik joined the Eniac designers, John Presper Eckert and John W. Mauchly, in their effort to develop the Univac, an early commercial computer, which was introduced in 1951. While at the Eckert-Mauchly Computer Corporation — acquired by Remington Rand in 1950 — Ms. Bartik worked on hardware and software for both the Binac, a small computer made for Northrop Aircraft, and the general purpose Univac.

Ms. Bartik called working with the Eckert-Mauchly team on the Eniac and later the Univac a "technical Camelot," a tight-knit group advancing the frontiers of computing.

"This was the most exciting time in her life," said Kathy Kleiman, a technology policy lawyer who has been making a documentary film about the women who programmed Eniac.

Ms. Bartik left the computer industry in 1951 to raise her three children — her son and two daughters, who survive her. She went back to work in 1967. But after holding a series of jobs in programming, training and technical publishing, she was laid off in 1985 as she was nearing 61. Afterward, she could not find another job in the industry.

"There's a lot of age discrimination, then and now, and I see it in my research," said Mr. Bartik, a labor economist.

Ms. Bartik went into real estate instead, and was an agent for the next 25 years.

— By Steve Lohr

MAR

RICHARD LEACOCK

The Camera Was His Unblinking Eye

JULY 18, 1921 - MARCH 23, 2011

Richard Leacock, a filmmaker who helped create the documentary style known as direct camera or cinéma vérité, and who played a pivotal role in making some of the most innovative documentaries of the 1960s, died on March 23 at his home in Paris. He was 89.

Although overshadowed by colleagues like Albert and David Maysles and D. A. Pennebaker, Mr. Leacock was a seminal figure in developing the artistic theories and the small, lightweight camera and sound equipment that led to a new style of reportorial filmmaking, one that had a profound influence not just on nonfiction filmmakers but also on directors, like John Cassavetes, who were seeking a more immediate, spontaneous style.

CINÉMA VÉRITÉ: Mr. Leacock on the set of "Louisiana Story," flanked by director Robert Flaherty and Flaherty's wife, Frances. The film was one of his first jobs.

From the time he made his first documentary film, at the age of 14, Mr. Leacock looked for ways and means that would allow the camera to function as an unblinking observer and allow stories to, as it were, tell themselves — to convey, as he was fond of saying, "the feeling of being there."

A striking example was the 1960 film "Primary," a fly-on-the-wall record of the Democratic primary in Wisconsin that pitted John F. Kennedy against Hubert H. Humphrey. The film, produced by the Time-Life photographic editor Robert Drew and shot by Mr. Leacock with Albert Maysles, Mr. Pennebaker and Terence Macartney-Filgate, offered deadpan, highly revealing scenes of two candidates in the throes of American-style campaigning, in all its tedium and exhaustive repetition.

This was something new in journalistic filmmaking. For the first time, audiences were given a sustained cinematic look behind the curtain of politics and an unvarnished portrait of two candidates going all-out for the brass ring.

Mr. Leacock went on to make many films with Mr. Drew and, after teaming up with Mr. Pennebaker, collaborated on several slice-of-American-life documentaries and "Monterey Pop," an enormously successful concert film that captured artists like Jefferson Airplane, Janis Joplin, the Who, Jimi Hendrix and Otis Redding in their heyday, in 1967.

At the Massachusetts Institute of Technology, where he co-founded the film school and taught for many years, Mr. Leacock influenced aspiring filmmakers like Mira Nair, Ross McElway and Richard Peña, the program director of the Film Society of Lincoln Center.

"He had an eye for character and story," Mr. Drew said in a telephone interview. "While doing unimaginably difficult things with the camera, he could think of character and story and the human factor; that was his great gift."

Richard Leacock, known as Ricky, was born on July 18, 1921, in London and spent his early childhood in the Canary Islands, where his father owned a banana plantation. While still at boarding school in England he filmed "Canary Bananas," about life on the plantation, and made a documentary about the Galapagos Islands while on a school expedition with the ornithologist Richard Lack.

He enrolled at Harvard to study physics and master the technology of filmmaking. At the same time, he worked as a cameraman and assistant editor on several documentaries, notably "To Hear Your Banjo Play" (1941). That film, about a folk festival in Virginia, was one of the earliest documentaries to capture live sound.

In 1942 he dropped out of school to enlist in the United States Army, serving as a combat photographer in the Signal Corps in Burma and China. On returning to the United States, he learned that the pioneering documentarian Robert Flaherty, the director of "Nanook of the North," had just received financing from Standard Oil to make a film about Louisiana.

Mr. Flaherty, who had seen "Canary Bananas" — his daughters had attended Mr. Leacock's school — hired Mr. Leacock as a cameraman and associate producer on "Louisiana Story," which in documentary style told the fictional story of a 12-year-old Cajun boy whose world is transformed when his father allows an oil rig to drill in an inlet behind the family home.

"Louisiana Story" helped push Mr. Leacock toward a new concept of filmmaking.

"I saw that when we were using small cameras, we had tremendous flexibility, we could do anything we wanted and get a wonderful sense of cinema," he told the journal Film Culture in 1961. "The moment we had to shoot dialogue — lip-synch — everything had to be locked down, the whole nature of the film changed."

In 1954 Mr. Leacock made his first solo documentary for the cultural television program "Omnibus." That film, "Toby and the Tall Corn," followed a tent show through the Midwest. By shifting his heavy 35-millimeter cameras around to film the show on different nights from new angles, he was able to achieve some of the variety and immediacy that a later generation of lightweight 16-millimeter cameras would allow.

In Mr. Drew at Time-Life he found a soul mate, a photographic editor who wanted to achieve in film what Life's great photojournalists captured on the page. To that end, Mr. Leacock developed hand-held cameras and recorders that could capture images and sound simultaneously.

With Mr. Leacock as a cameraman and editor, this new technology was put to immediate use on "Primary" and its groundbreaking successors, including "On the Pole," a portrait of the race-car driver Eddie Sachs and the 1960 Indianapolis 500, and "The Children Were Watching," about school integration in New Orleans.

With Mr. Drew, he made two of the most gripping documentaries to come out of the cinéma vérité movement: "Chair," the story of a lawyer's fight to save his client from the electric chair, and "Crisis: Behind a Presidential Commitment," a taut behind-the-scenes diary of the face-off between the Kennedy administration and Gov. George C. Wallace of Alabama over the integration of the University of Alabama.

In 1963 Mr. Leacock formed a production partnership with Mr. Pennebaker. It yielded "Happy Mother's Day," a film, made with Joyce Chopra, about the hoopla surrounding a woman who gives birth to quintuplets.

The partners' other films included "A Stravinsky Portrait," about the composer Igor Stravinsky, and "Chiefs," about a convention of police chiefs.

The partnership dissolved not long after the filmmaker Jean-Luc Godard pulled out of "One A.M." ("One American Movie"), which was intended to be his first American feature, with Mr. Leacock and Mr. Pennebaker filming under his direction. A mélange of footage from the film and documentary footage of the production, called "One P.M." ("One Parallel Movie"), was released in 1972.

In the meantime Mr. Leacock accepted an invitation, with the documentary filmmaker Ed Pincus, to found a film school at M.I.T., where he taught for the next 20 years.

In 1988 he moved to Paris, where he collaborated with his companion, Valérie Lalonde, on several works shot on video, including "Les Oeufs à la Coque" and "A Musical Adventure in Siberia."

Mr. Leacock's two marriages ended in divorce. He is survived by Ms. Lalonde, three daughters, two sons, a half-sister and nine grandchildren.

His memoir, "Richard Leacock: The Feeling of Being There," was to be published in the summer of 2011.

— *By William Grimes*

LEONARD WEINGLASS

Defender of Radicals and Renegades

AUG. 27, 1933 - MARCH 23, 2011

LEONARD I. WEINGLASS, perhaps the nation's pre-eminent progressive defense lawyer, who represented political renegades, government opponents and notorious criminal defendants in a half century of controversial cases, including the Chicago Seven, the Pentagon Papers and the Hearst kidnapping, died on March 23. He was 77 and lived in Manhattan.

Mr. Weinglass was working as a lawyer in racially torn Newark in the late 1960s when he met Tom Hayden, a founder of the activist group Students for a Democratic Society, who was working there as well.

In 1968, when Mr. Hayden was indicted, along with seven others — the case was initially known as the Chicago Eight — for conspiring to incite a riot during the Democratic National Convention in Chicago, he reached out to Mr. Weinglass, who joined William M. Kunstler on the defense team in what turned out to be one of the most raucous trials in American history.

The defendants included Jerry Rubin and Abbie Hoffman, the leaders of the radically counter-cultural Youth International Party (a k a the Yippies), and the mutual disdain between them and Judge Julius J. Hoffman, who presided over the case, became a key element in their lawyers' ability to paint the charges as politically motivated. At one point, Abbie Hoffman referred to the judge as his "illegitimate father" and renounced his last name. After he took the witness stand, Mr. Weinglass began the questioning by asking his name.

"My name is Abbie," Mr. Hoffman said. "I'm an orphan of America."

Five of the defendants were found guilty in the case, but the verdicts were reversed on appeal, and Judge Hoffman, who had ordered one defendant, Bobby Seale of the Black Panthers, shackled and gagged in court, was upbraided in the appeals court ruling for his "deprecatory and often antagonistic attitude toward the defense."

Mr. Seale's case was later severed from that of the other seven.

Mr. Hayden, who roomed with Mr. Weinglass during the trial, said in an interview that the legal spectacle was "a morality play for all of the issues of the '60s." Of Mr. Weinglass, he added, "I would say he was the best courtroom lawyer I've known in my lifetime, and I've known a lot of them."

'OUR ERA'S CLARENCE DARROW': Mr. Weinglass, left, and William Kunstler during a press conference after the verdict in the Chicago Seven trial was announced, Feb. 18, 1970.

Mr. Weinglass said after the trial that the court, obviously biased in his view, had shaken his faith in the law and, along with other events — the Kent State shootings, the invasion of Cambodia — had helped to radicalize him. By 1972 he had moved to Los Angeles and was defending Daniel Ellsberg, a military analyst with the RAND Corporation. Disaffected with the Vietnam War, Mr. Ellsberg and a colleague, Anthony Russo, had copied the secret documents about the government's conduct of the war that became known as the Pentagon Papers and eventually shared them with a reporter for The New York Times, which published them. The case against Mr. Ellsberg and Mr. Russo was eventually dismissed because of misconduct by the government in trying to gather evidence against them.

Mr. Weinglass defended Bill and Emily Harris, the founders of the radical group known as the Symbionese Liberation Army, for the 1974 kidnapping of the newspaper heiress Patricia Hearst, who joined her kidnappers and helped them rob a bank, a crime for which she served two years in prison before her sentence was commuted by President Jimmy Carter. The Harrises were convicted of the kidnapping and served eight years in prison.

In another notorious case, Mr. Weinglass, who had worked with the lawyer Leonard Boudin on the Pentagon Papers defense, defended Mr. Boudin's daughter Kathy Boudin, who, as a member of the radical Weather Underground, had taken part in the robbery of a Brink's security truck in 1981 in which two police officers and a Brink's guard were killed. Ms. Boudin, who did not fire a gun during the robbery but was a passenger in a getaway van, eventually pleaded guilty to murder and robbery charges and served 22 years in prison. She was released on parole in 2003.

"Lenny was the best lawyer I've ever seen picking a jury and cross-examining witnesses," said Martin Garbus, who was Mr. Weinglass's co-counsel on the Kathy Boudin trial. "He was soft, he was gentle, he was not bombastic. You believed he was a man of dignity and honesty."

Leonard Irving Weinglass was born in Belleville, N.J., on Aug. 27, 1933, and grew up in Kearny; he was a high school debater and an end on the football team. His father, Sol, was a pharmacist. He graduated from George Washington University and Yale Law school and was a lawyer for the Air Force before beginning his practice in Newark.

Mr. Weinglass was married once, late in life, and divorced. He is survived by two sisters and a brother. He died of pancreatic cancer at a Bronx hospital.

Over 40 years he represented many other prominent clients, including Angela Davis, the activist and educator who was acquitted of murder, conspiracy and kidnapping charges in the 1970 killing of a California judge; and Amy Carter, the daughter of President Carter, who was arrested along with others, including Abbie Hoffman, during a 1986 protest against the activities of the Central Intelligence Agency at the University of Massachusetts. She was acquitted of trespassing and disorderly conduct charges.

More recently, Mr. Weinglass was involved in the death-row appeals of Mumia Abu-Jamal, whose conviction in the 1981 killing of a Philadelphia police officer has been shrouded in allegations of racism, police corruption and judicial bias; and the Cuban 5, who were convicted in 2001 of conspiracy to commit espionage against the United States but who say they were monitoring Miami-based terrorist groups that target Cuba.

"He filed a brief on March 5 in that case, a post-conviction motion to vacate the conviction of his client," said Michael Krinsky of the New York law firm Rabinowitz, Boudin, Standard, Krinsky & Lieberman, for whom Mr. Weinglass had worked since 1985. Mr. Krinsky, who called Mr. Weinglass "our era's Clarence Darrow," met him in 1969, in Newark.

"That was a rough place to be," he said. "A police department and a city administration that was racist and as terrifying as any in America, and there was Lenny representing civil rights people, political people, ordinary people who got charged with stuff and got beat up by the cops. He did it without fame or fortune, and that's what he kept doing, in one way or another."

— *By Bruce Weber*

LANFORD WILSON

His Marginal Characters Took Center Stage

APRIL 13, 1937 - MARCH 24, 2011

LANFORD WILSON, the Pulitzer Prize-winning playwright whose work — earthy, realist, greatly admired, widely performed — centered on the sheer ordinariness of marginality, died on March 24 in Wayne, N.J. He was 73 and lived in Sag Harbor, on Long Island.

The cause was complications of pneumonia, said Marshall W. Mason, a director and longtime collaborator who is widely considered the foremost interpreter of Mr. Wilson's work.

One of the most distinguished American playwrights of the late 20th century, Mr. Wilson was instrumental in drawing attention to Off Off Broadway, where his first works were staged in the mid-1960s. He was also among the first playwrights to move from that milieu to renown on wider stages, ascending to Off Broadway, and then to Broadway itself, within a decade of his arrival in New York.

His work has also long been a staple of regional theaters throughout the United States.

Mr. Wilson won the 1980 Pulitzer Prize for drama for "Talley's Folly," which played 286 performances on Broadway that year. A one-act, two-character comedy set in his hometown, Lebanon, Mo., the play chronicled the romantic fortunes of a Jewish man (played by Judd Hirsch) and a Protestant woman (Trish Hawkins) in 1944.

"Talley's Folly" was an installment in Mr. Wilson's Talley Cycle, an eventual trilogy. The cycle also comprised "Talley & Son," which played Off Broadway in 1985 and also looked in on the Talley family in 1944, and "Fifth of July," which takes up the family's story in 1977.

"Fifth of July," a comedy that explores the disillusionment of the Vietnam era, came to Broadway in November 1980. The production, which starred Christopher Reeve as Kenneth Talley Jr., a gay, paraplegic Vietnam veteran, ran for 511 performances at the New Apollo Theater; it also starred Jeff Daniels and Swoosie Kurtz.

"Mr. Wilson has poured the full bounty of his gifts into this work," Frank Rich wrote in his review in The New York Times, "and they are the gifts of a major playwright. 'Fifth of July' is a densely packed yet buoyant outpouring of empathy, poetry and humor, all shaped into a remarkable vision."

Mr. Wilson's other Broadway plays include "Burn This" (1987), "Angels Fall" (1983) and "Redwood Curtain" (1993).

His Off Broadway work included "The Hot L Baltimore," about the denizens of a down-at-the-heels residential hotel. The play was the basis of a short-lived television sitcom of the same name, broadcast on ABC in 1975.

Stylistically, the distinguishing hallmark of Mr. Wilson's work was his dialogue — authentic, gritty, often overlapping — be it the speech of his native Missouri or adopted New York. To audiences, his approach gave the experience of eavesdropping on real, bustling people in real, bustling time. (As a young playwright honing his craft, he later explained, he would set himself exercises like writing down the overheard speech of five people talking at once.)

Thematically, his work concerned dissolutions large and small: the rupture of societies, families and individual marriages; the loss of life, love, companionship and sanity.

His characters, drawn true to life if sometimes larger, tended toward the socially marginalized, perhaps no surprise for a man whose identity — Ozark, somewhat rootless, a child of a broken home, gay at a time when it was taboo to be gay —

no doubt made him feel pushed to the margins of mainstream culture himself. (Mr. Wilson was noted for being one of the first mainstream playwrights to create central, meaningful gay and lesbian characters.)

Ragtag collections of prostitutes and pimps, drug addicts and sundry urban nighthawks, the people who populate his plays were unusual theatrical subjects in their day, but were no less sympathetic for that. In many respects, as he made clear in interviews, Mr. Wilson saw his work as the counterpart to the New Realism of post-1960 visual art, in which artists created works that were amalgams of images, often fragmentary, observed in the world around them and ripe for the taking.

THE WAY PEOPLE TALK: Mr. Wilson's plays were acclaimed for their use of authentic overlapping dialogue.

As he also made clear, the subject matter of many of his plays was drawn from his own life.

Lanford Eugene Wilson was born in Lebanon, Mo., on April 13, 1937; his parents divorced when he was a young child. He moved with his mother to Springfield, Mo., and, after she remarried a farmer, to Ozark, Mo.

After studying briefly at Southwest Missouri State College, Mr. Wilson moved to San Diego, where his father was living. Their reunion — not a happy one, though their relationship fared better in later years — became the basis of "Lemon Sky."

That play, first performed in 1970 at the Studio Arena Theater in Buffalo, opened Off Broadway that year at the Playhouse Theater on West 48th Street, and was revived in 1985 at the Second Stage Theater. It was later adapted as a television movie, first broadcast in 1988 and starring Kevin Bacon as the youth who attempts to bond with his estranged father.

In San Diego, the young Mr. Wilson worked at a desultory job in an aircraft plant and took classes at what was then San Diego State College. It was there, in a writing class, that he discovered dialogue and determined to become a writer of short stories.

In the late 1950s, Mr. Wilson moved to Chicago, where he worked as a commercial artist in an advertising agency and took extension classes at the University of Chicago. He wrote a sheaf of short stories that were rejected by all the magazines to which he sent them, and made his first tentative stabs at writing plays.

Mr. Wilson settled in New York in 1962. There, as the reference work Current Biography wrote in 1979, he "saw and disliked every play on Broadway."

He found the ersatz environment of Off Off Broadway, with its theater spaces shoehorned into coffeehouses and church basements, far more congenial. His first produced play, a one-act called "So Long at the Fair," was staged at Caffe Cino, in the Village, in 1963. It concerned a young man, newly arrived in New York, and the young woman who hopes to seduce him.

Reviewing the play, The Village Voice praised the "exactness and inner logic" of the dialogue. Over the years to come, Mr. Wilson's facility for dialogue proved both a great strength and an occasional weakness: critics sometimes took him to task for neglecting other aspects of dramatic construction, like tight plotting, in favor of the rush of pure spoken language.

In 1965, Mr. Wilson attracted attention with "The Madness of Lady Bright," also at Caffe Cino. Its protagonist, Leslie Bright, is a middle-aged gay man confronting a wistful past, a lonely present and an uncertain future.

He garnered still wider attention for his first full-length play, "Balm in Gilead," also staged in 1965, at La MaMa. The play, about low-life characters converging in the New York nightscape, was so successful that Ellen Stewart (see page 240), La MaMa's founder, had to stand on the sidewalk each night and beseech an eager fire marshal not to close the theater, packed to capacity.

His first play to come to Broadway was "The Gingham Dog," about the dissolution of an interracial marriage. It ran for just 19 performances in 1969.

With Mr. Mason, Tanya Berezin and Rob Thirkield, Mr. Wilson founded the Circle Repertory Company, a highly regarded collective of actors, directors, playwrights and others known for its collaborative approach.

Established in 1969 on the Upper West Side as the Circle Theater Company, it later moved to the Sheridan Square Playhouse in Greenwich Village. The company ceased operations in 1996.

Besides producing work by Mr. Wilson, Circle Rep produced plays by Jules Feiffer, Sam Shepard, Larry Kramer and others. Actors associated with the company include William Hurt, Kathy Bates, Barnard Hughes, Cherry Jones and Cynthia Nixon. Mr. Wilson was single at the time of his death. Survivors include two half-brothers and a stepsister.

In an interview quoted in The Times in 2002, Mr. Wilson expounded on his realist, quasidocumentary approach: "I want people to see — and to read — my plays and to say: 'This is what it was like living in that place at that time. People haven't changed a damn bit. We can recognize everyone.'"

— By Margalit Fox

GERALDINE FERRARO

She Ended the Men's Club of National Politics

AUG. 26, 1935 - MARCH 26, 2011

Geraldine A. Ferraro, the former Queens congresswoman who strode onto a podium in 1984 to accept the Democratic nomination for vice president and to take her place in American history as the first woman nominated for national office by a major party, died on March 26 in Boston. She was 75 and lived in Manhattan.

The cause was complications of multiple myeloma, a blood cancer that she had battled for 12 years, her family said in a statement. She died at Massachusetts General Hospital, where she had been undergoing treatment for almost a week.

"If we can do this, we can do anything," Ms. Ferraro declared on a July evening to a cheering Democratic National Convention in San Francisco. And for a moment, for the Democratic Party and for an untold number of American women, anything seemed possible: a woman occupying the second-highest office in the land, a derailing of the Republican juggernaut led by President Ronald Reagan, a President Walter F. Mondale.

It did not turn out that way — not by a long shot. After the roars in the Moscone Center had subsided and a fitful general election campaign had run its course, hopes for Mr. Mondale and his plain-speaking, barrier-breaking running mate were buried in a Reagan landslide.

But Ms. Ferraro's supporters proclaimed a victory of sorts nonetheless: 64 years after women won the right to vote, a woman had removed the "men only" sign from the White House door.

It would be another 24 years before another woman from a major party was nominated for vice president — Gov. Sarah Palin of Alaska, the Republican running mate of Senator John McCain, in 2008. And though Hillary Rodham

Clinton came close to being nominated that year as the Democratic presidential candidate, a woman has yet to occupy the Oval Office. But Ms. Ferraro's ascendance gave many women heart.

Ann Richards, who was the Texas state treasurer at the time and who went on to become governor, once recalled that after the Ferraro nomination, "the first thing I thought of was not winning in the political sense, but of my two daughters." She added, "To think of the numbers of young women who can now aspire to anything."

President Obama said in a statement, "Geraldine will forever be remembered as a trailblazer who broke down barriers for women and Americans of all backgrounds and walks of life."

As Mr. Mondale's surprise choice, Ms. Ferraro rocketed to national prominence, propelled by fervid feminist support, a spirited and sometimes saucy personality, canny political skills and the calculation by Democratic strategists that Reagan might be vulnerable on issues thought to be more important to women.

But it proved to be a difficult campaign. The incumbent Reagan-Bush ticket presented a formidable enough challenge in and of itself, but Ms. Ferraro found herself on the defensive almost from the start, answering critics who questioned her qualifications for high office. Then there were damaging revelations about the finances of her husband, John Zaccaro, forcing Ms. Ferraro to release his tax returns and hold a marathon news conference in the middle of the general election race. Some said she had become a liability to Mr. Mondale and only hurt his chances more.

A former Queens criminal prosecutor, Ms. Ferraro was a vigorous but relatively inexperienced candidate with a better feel for urban ward politics than for international diplomacy. But she proved to be a quick study and came across as a new breed of feminist politician: comfortable with the boys, particularly powerful Democrats like the House speaker, Thomas P. O'Neill Jr., and less combative than predecessors like Representative Bella Abzug of New York.

She was also ideal for television: a down-to-earth, streaked-blond, peanut-butter-sandwich-making mother whose personal story resonated powerfully. Brought up by a single mother who had crocheted beads on wedding dresses to make ends meet, Ms. Ferraro had waited until her own children were school age before going to work in a Queens district attorney's office headed by a cousin.

For the first time, a major candidate talked about abortion with the phrase "If I were pregnant," or about foreign policy with the observation "As the mother of a draft-age son. ..."

In the 1984 race, many Americans found her breezy style refreshing. "What are you — crazy?" was a familiar expression. She might break into a little dance behind the speaker's platform when she liked the introductory music. Feeling patronized by her Republican opponent, Vice President George H. W. Bush, she publicly scolded him.

With Ms. Ferraro on the ticket, Democrats hoped to exploit a so-called gender gap between the parties. A Newsweek poll taken after she was nominated showed men favoring Reagan-Bush 58 percent to 36 percent but women supporting Mondale-Ferraro 49 percent to 41 percent.

For the first time, a major candidate for national office talked about abortion with the phrase "If I were pregnant," or about foreign policy with the personal observation "As the mother of a draft-age son. ..." She wore pearls and silk dresses and publicly worried that her slip was showing.

She also traveled a 55,000-mile campaign trail, spoke in 85 cities and raised $6 million. But in November the Democratic ticket won only one state — Mr. Mondale's Minnesota — and the District of Columbia. And to the Democrats' chagrin, Reagan captured even the women's vote, drawing some 55 percent. Women, it appeared, had opposed, almost as much as men, the tax increase that Mr. Mondale had said would be inevitable. Mr. Mondale, a former senator and vice president under Jimmy Carter, had made that assertion in his acceptance speech as an attempt at straight talking, and it cost him dearly at the polls.

Most election analysts believed that from the start the Democratic ticket had little chance against a popular incumbent who was basking in an economic recovery and proclaiming that it was "morning again in America." Some said the choice of the little-known Ms. Ferraro had been a desperate move to attract the female vote in a daunting election year. Compounding the campaign's woes was a barrage of questions about the Ferraro family finances — often carrying insinuations about ties to organized crime — that not only blemished Ms. Ferraro's stature as the first Italian-American national candidate but also diverted attention from other issues.

A PLACE IN HISTORY: Ms. Ferraro in 1997. Her vice-presidential bid inspired generations of women.

Ms. Ferraro's politics teetered from liberal positions, like her support for the Equal Rights Amendment for women and a nuclear freeze, to conservative ones, like her opposition to school busing and her support for tax credits for private and parochial school parents. In her first race for the House of Representatives, in 1978, from New York's Ninth Congressional District in Queens, a Republican stronghold, her slogan was "Finally, a tough Democrat."

The abortion issue, magnified because she was Roman Catholic and a woman, plagued her campaign. Though she opposed the procedure personally, she said, others had the right to choose for themselves. Abortion opponents hounded her at almost every stop with an intensity seldom experienced by male politicians.

Writing in The Washington Post in September 1984, the columnist Mary McGrory quoted an unnamed Roman Catholic priest as saying, "When the nuns in the fifth grade told Geraldine she would have to die for her faith, she didn't know it would be this way."

Geraldine Anne Ferraro was born on Aug. 26, 1935, in the Hudson River city of Newburgh, N.Y., where she was the fourth child and only daughter of Dominick Ferraro, an Italian immigrant who owned a restaurant and a five-and-dime store, and the former Antonetta L. Corrieri. One brother died shortly after birth, and another, Gerard, died in an automobile accident when he was 3, two years before Geraldine was born.

Geraldine was born at home; her mother, who had been holding Gerard at the time of the crash and who had washed and pressed his clothes for months after his death, would not go to the hospital for the delivery and leave the third brother, Carl, at home.

Geraldine was named for Gerard, but in her book "Framing a Life: A Family Memoir," written with Catherine Whitney, Ms. Ferraro said her mother had emphasized that her daughter was not taking his place.

"Gerry is special," she quoted her mother as saying, "because she is a girl."

Unknown to Ms. Ferraro at the time, her father had repeated trouble with the state liquor authorities and ultimately lost his restaurant license. During the vice-presidential campaign, she learned by reading The New York Post that her father had been arrested on charges of running a numbers racket but had died of a heart attack the morning he was to appear in court. Her mother was arrested as an accomplice, but the charges were dropped after Dominick Ferraro's death, Ms. Ferraro wrote.

She called her father's death, which happened when she was 8, "a dividing line that runs through my life." In her grief, she said, she developed anemia.

Her mother soon sold the store and the family's house and moved to the South Bronx. With the proceeds from the sale of property in Italy that her husband had left her, she sent Geraldine to the Marymount School, a Catholic boarding school in Tarrytown, N.Y. She sent Carl to military school.

Ms. Ferraro's outstanding grades earned her a scholarship to Marymount College in Tarrytown, from which she transferred to the school's Manhattan branch. She commuted there from Queens, where her mother had moved by then. An English major, Ms. Ferraro was editor of the school newspaper and an athlete and won numerous honors before graduating in 1956. "Delights in the unexpected," the yearbook said.

After graduating, Ms. Ferraro got a job teaching in a public grade school in Queens. She later applied to Fordham Law School, where an admissions officer warned her that she might be taking a man's place. Admitted to its night school, she was one of two women in a class of 179 and received her law degree in 1960.

Ms. Ferraro and John Zaccaro, whose family was in the real estate business, were married on July 16, 1960, two days after she passed her bar exam. She was admitted to the New York State bar in 1961, and decided to keep her maiden name professionally to honor her mother. (She was admitted to the United States Supreme Court bar in 1978.)

For the first 13 years of her marriage, Ms. Ferraro devoted herself mainly to her growing family. Donna was born in 1962, John in 1964 and Laura in 1966. Ms. Ferraro did some legal work for her husband's business, worked pro bono for women in Family Court and dabbled in local politics. In 1970 she was elected president of the Queens County Women's Bar Association.

In 1973, after her cousin Nicholas Ferraro was elected Queens district attorney, she applied for and got a job as an assistant district attorney in charge of a special victims bureau, investigating rape, crimes against the elderly, and child and wife abuse.

The cases were so harrowing, she later wrote, that they caused her to develop an ulcer. And the crime-breeding societal conditions she saw, she said, planted the seeds of her liberalism.

One night, before he became governor of New York, Mario M. Cuomo gave Ms. Ferraro and her husband a ride home from a bar mitzvah. She told him she was thinking of running for public office. "What about Congress?" Mr. Cuomo asked.

Ms. Ferraro found her opportunity in 1978, when James J. Delaney, a Democratic congressman from a predominantly working-class district in Queens, announced his retirement. In a three-way Democratic primary for the seat, Ms. Ferraro won with 53 percent of the vote. In the general election campaign, a slugfest against a Republican assemblyman, Alfred A. DelliBovi, she won by 10 percentage points, helped by her law-and-order background.

In the House, Ms. Ferraro was assigned to unglamorous committees but used them to her advantage. On the Public Works and Transportation Committee, she successfully pushed for improved mass transit around La Guardia Airport.

Mr. O'Neill, the speaker, took an immediate liking to her, and in her three terms she voted mostly with her party's leadership. Liberal and labor groups gave her high ratings, though she was less adamant than many liberal Democrats about cutting military spending.

Ms. Ferraro was a co-sponsor of the Economic Equity Act, which was intended to accomplish many of the aims of the never-ratified Equal Rights Amendment. She also supported federal financing for abortions.

"She manages to be threatening on issues without being threatening personally," Representative Barney Frank, Democrat of Massachusetts, told The Chicago Tribune in 1984.

Others were less laudatory. "Some see her as too compromising, too ambitious, too close to the leadership," The Washington Post wrote that same year.

Her friendship with Mr. O'Neill helped her career. Thanks in part to him, she was elected secretary of the Democratic caucus, giving her influence on committee assignments, and in 1983 she was awarded a seat on the powerful budget committee, where she received a crash course in economics. To enhance her foreign policy credentials, she took trips to Central America and the Middle East.

It was Ms. Ferraro's appointment as chairwoman of the 1984 Democratic Platform Committee that gave her the most prominence. In her book "Ferraro: My Story," written with Linda Bird Francke, she said that in becoming the first woman to hold that post she owed much to a group of Democratic women — Congressional staffers, abortion rights activists, labor leaders and others — who called themselves Team A and who lobbied for her appointment.

Even before then, however, Ms. Ferraro's name had been mentioned on lists of potential candidates for vice president, along with Representative Patricia Schroeder of Colorado, the former congresswoman Barbara Jordan and Dianne Feinstein, the mayor of San Francisco. By May 1984, Mr. O'Neill had endorsed her for the No. 2 spot on the ticket. It was, as Ms. Ferraro later put it, "the Good Housekeeping seal of approval."

On July 1, the National Organization for Women threatened a convention floor fight if the Democrats did not choose a woman, and three days later a delegation of Democratic women went to Minnesota to urge Mr. Mondale to do so.

Mr. Mondale made his historic call, asking Ms. Ferraro to be his running mate, on July 11. His campaign believed that she would do well not only among women but also among blue-collar workers. Eight days later, wearing a white dress she had bought on Orchard Street on the Lower East Side of Manhattan, she accepted the Democratic nomination for vice president.

Her campaign was soon stalled by accusations about her personal finances. The storm reached its height in a two-hour press conference on Aug. 21, after Ms. Ferraro had released the tax returns of her husband, Mr. Zaccaro. She responded to question after question in a confident, relaxed manner. Mr. Cuomo called it "one of the best performances I've ever seen by a politician under pressure."

Ms. Ferraro later faced down hecklers in Texas and pro-Reagan auto workers in Illinois. After Vice President Bush was overheard bragging that "we tried to kick a little ass last night," referring to a debate with Ms. Ferraro, she declined to comment directly, though her aides called the remark insulting and demeaning. There were signs at campaign rallies saying, "Give 'em hell, Gerry!"

Everywhere people were adjusting — or manifestly not adjusting — to a woman on a national ticket. Mississippi's agriculture secretary called Ms. Ferraro "young lady" and asked if she could bake blueberry muffins. When a Roman Catholic bishop gave a news conference in Pennsylvania, he repeatedly referred to the Republican vice-presidential nominee as "Mr. Bush" and to the Democratic one as "Geraldine."

Ms. Ferraro's words raised hackles as well. She was criticized for suggesting that Reagan was not a "good Christian" because, she said, his policies hurt the disadvantaged.

Her inability to escape questions about her finances was partly brought on by her husband's initial refusal to release his tax returns. She riled Italian-Americans when she explained, "If you're married to an Italian man, you know what it's like."

When her financial situation was finally disclosed, it turned out that the candidate with the rags-to-riches story had a net worth approaching $4 million, a boat, a full-time uniformed maid and vacation homes on Fire Island in New York and in the Virgin Islands.

Mr. Bush's wife, Barbara, complained that Ms. Ferraro was masquerading as a working-class wife and mother, calling her a "four-million-dollar — I can't say it, but it rhymes with rich."

Her associations and finances revealed one questionable thing after another. The Federal Election Commission fined her 1978 campaign committee for accepting $134,000 in contributions from her husband and children when they were legally allowed to contribute only $4,000.

Evidence also emerged that organized-crime figures had contributed to her campaigns. When a House ethics panel investigated her financial disclosures, it came out that one of Mr. Zaccaro's companies had rented two floors of a building to a pornography distributor.

The disclosures damaged a campaign that was already fighting an uphill battle; Mr. Mondale later said he thought they cost the campaign 15 percentage points in the polls. He also suggested that a male running mate might not have been dissected so severely. After the election, the House ethics committee determined that Ms. Ferraro's financial disclosures had been inadequate. In 1986, the elections commission said one of her campaign committees had improperly allocated funds.

Ms. Ferraro's family experienced legal problems of its own. In 1985, Mr. Zaccaro pleaded guilty to a misdemeanor charge that he had schemed to defraud a mortgage broker. Two years later he was acquitted of attempted extortion in a cable television company's bid to get a Queens franchise. And in 1988 the couple's son, John Jr., was convicted of a felony for selling cocaine in Vermont while a student at Middlebury College.

RUNNING MATES: Ms. Ferraro and Walter Mondale on the campaign trail, July 20, 1984.

After her defeat in 1984, Ms. Ferraro was criticized for appearing in a Diet Pepsi commercial. Feminists in particular called it undignified.

She is survived by her husband, three children and eight grandchildren.

Weary of the spotlight on her family, Ms. Ferraro passed up a chance to challenge Senator Alfonse M. D'Amato, Republican of New York, in his bid for a second term in 1986. But she decided to seek the seat in 1992 and entered the Democratic primary. She finished 10,000 votes (1 percent of the total) behind Robert Abrams, the state attorney general, who lost to Mr. D'Amato in the general election. She again ran for the Senate in 1998 but lost to Charles E. Schumer in the Democratic primary by a lopsided margin.

Ms. Ferraro was later ambassador to the United Nations Human Rights Commission during the Clinton administration and co-host of the CNN program "Crossfire" from 1996 to 1998. She also wrote books and articles and did business consulting.

Near the end of 1998, she learned she had multiple myeloma, a bone-marrow cancer that suppresses the immune system. She was one of the first cancer patients to be treated with thalidomide, a drug used in the 1960s to treat morning sickness that caused severe defects in unborn children.

"Such a strange thing," Ms. Ferraro said in an interview with The New York Times in 2001. "What was terrible for a healthy fetus has been wonderful at defeating the cancer cells."

She addressed her place in history in a long letter to The Times in 1988, noting that women wrote to her about how she had inspired them to take on challenges, "always adding a version of 'I decided if you could do it, I can too.'" Schoolgirls, she said, told her they hoped to be president someday and needed advice.

"I am the first to admit that were I not a woman," she wrote, "I would not have been the vice-presidential nominee." But she insisted that her presence on the ticket had translated into votes that the ticket might have otherwise not received.

In any event, she said, the political realities of 1984 had made it all but impossible for the Democrats to win, no matter the candidates or their gender. "Throwing Ronald Reagan out of office at the height of his popularity, with inflation and interest rates down, the economy moving and the country at peace, would have required God on the ticket," Ms. Ferraro wrote, "and She was not available!"

— *By Douglas Martin*

HARRY COOVER

The Inventor of Super Glue

MARCH 6, 1917 - MARCH 26, 2011

HARRY WESLEY COOVER JR., the man who invented Super Glue, died on March 26 at his home in Kingsport, Tenn. He was 94.

Dr. Coover first happened upon the super-sticky adhesive — formally known as cyanoacrylates — by accident when he was experimenting with acrylates for use in clear plastic gun-sights during World War II. He gave up because they stuck to everything they touched.

In 1951, a researcher named Fred Joyner, who was working with Dr. Coover at Eastman Kodak's laboratory in Tennessee, was testing hundreds of compounds looking for a temperature-resistant coating for jet cockpits. When Mr. Joyner spread the 910th compound on the list between two lenses on a refractometer to take a reading on the velocity of light through it, he discovered he could not separate the lenses. His initial reaction was panic at the loss of the expensive lab equipment.

"He ruined the machine," his daughter, Dr. Melinda Coover Paul, said of the refractometer. "Back in the '50s, they cost, like, $3,000, which was huge."

But Dr. Coover saw an opportunity. Seven years later, the first incarnation of Super Glue, called Eastman 910, hit the market. And not long after, Dr. Coover made an appearance on the television show "I've Got a Secret."

Dr. Coover's secret was that he had invented Super Glue, and the host, Garry Moore, asked him to demonstrate what it could do. A metal bar was lowered onto the stage, and Dr. Coover used a dab of the glue to connect two metal parts together. Then, his daughter said, he grabbed hold of one and was raised in the air on the strength of his invention.

"Then Garry Moore jumped on, too!" she said. "And this is live television. But it worked. It absolutely worked."

Nonetheless, Kodak was never able to capitalize commercially on Dr. Coover's discovery. It sold the business to National Starch in 1980.

Dr. Coover was born in Newark, Del., on March 6, 1917. He studied chemistry at Hobart College in Geneva, N.Y., and then received a master's degree and a Ph.D. in chemistry from Cornell University. He worked at the Eastman Kodak Company until he retired and then worked as a consultant.

In 2004, he was inducted into the National Inventors Hall of Fame.

In 2010, President Obama awarded him the National Medal of Technology and Innovation. Dr. Coover was in the hospital at the time, his daughter said, but his family made sure he was able to get to Washington for the award ceremony.

Dr. Coover held 460 patents by the end of his life. Dr. Paul said her father was particularly proud that Super Glue was used to treat injured soldiers during the Vietnam War. Medics, she said, carried bottles of Super Glue in spray form to stop bleeding.

Besides his daughter, he is survived by two sons and four grandchildren. His wife of more than 60 years, Muriel Zumbach Coover, died in 2005.

Super Glue did not make Dr. Coover rich. It did not become a commercial success until the patents had expired, his son-in-law, Dr. Vincent E. Paul, said. "He did very, very well in his career," Dr. Paul said, "but he did not glean the royalties from Super Glue that you might think."

— *BY ELIZABETH A. HARRIS*

PAUL BARAN

They Said His Ideas for an 'Internet' Wouldn't Work

APRIL 29, 1926 - MARCH 26, 2011

PAUL BARAN, an engineer who defied the skeptics to help create the technical underpinnings for the Arpanet, the government-sponsored precursor to today's Internet, died on March 26 at his home in Palo Alto, Calif. He was 84.

In the early 1960s, while working at the RAND Corporation in Santa Monica, Calif., Mr. Baran outlined the fundamentals for packaging data into discrete bundles, which he called "message blocks." The bundles are then sent on various paths around a network and reassembled at their destination. Such a plan is known as "packet switching."

Mr. Baran's idea was to build a distributed communications network, less vulnerable to attack or disruption than conventional networks. In a series of technical papers published in the 1960s he suggested that networks be designed with redundant routes so that if a particular path failed or was destroyed, messages could still be delivered through another.

Mr. Baran's invention was so far ahead of its time that in the mid-1960s, when he approached AT&T with the idea to build his proposed network, the company insisted it would not work and refused.

"Paul wasn't afraid to go in directions counter to what everyone else thought was the right or only thing to do," said Vinton Cerf, a vice president at Google who was a colleague and longtime friend of Mr. Baran's. "AT&T repeatedly said his idea wouldn't work, and wouldn't participate in the Arpanet project."

In 1969, the Defense Department's Advanced Research Projects Agency built the Arpanet, a network that used Mr. Baran's ideas, and those of others. The Arpanet was eventually replaced by the Internet, and packet switching still lies at the heart of the network's internal workings.

Paul Baran was born on April 29, 1926, in Grodno, Poland. His parents moved to the United States in 1928, and Mr. Baran grew up in Philadelphia. His father was a grocer, and as a boy, Paul delivered orders to customers in a small red wagon.

He attended the Drexel Institute of Technology, which later became Drexel University, where he earned a bachelor's degree in electrical engineering in 1949. He took his first job at the Eckert-Mauchly Computer Corporation in Philadelphia, testing parts of radio tubes for an early commercial computer, the Univac. In 1955, he married Evelyn Murphy, and they moved to Los Angeles, where Mr. Baran took a job at Hughes Aircraft working on radar data processing systems. He enrolled in night classes at the University of California, Los Angeles.

Mr. Baran received a master's degree in engineering from U.C.L.A. in 1959. Gerald Estrin, who was Mr. Baran's adviser, said Mr. Baran was the first student he ever had who actually went to the Patent Office in Washington to investigate whether his master's work, on character recognition, was patentable.

"From that day on, my expectations of him changed," Dr. Estrin said. "He wasn't just a serious student, but a young man who was looking to have an effect on the world."

In 1959, Mr. Baran left Hughes to join RAND's computer science department. He quickly developed an interest in the survivability of communications systems in the event of a nuclear attack, and spent the next several years at RAND working on a series of 13 papers — two of them classified — under contract to the Air Force, titled "On Distributed Communications."

About the same time that Mr. Baran had his idea, similar plans for creating such networks were percolating in the computing community. Donald Davies of the British National Physical Laboratory, working a continent away, had a similar idea for dividing digital messages into chunks he called packets.

When Mr. Baran approached AT&T with the idea to build his proposed network, the company insisted it would not work and refused.

"In the golden era of the early 1960s, these ideas were in the air," said Leonard Kleinrock, a computer scientist at U.C.L.A. who was working on similar networking systems in the 1960s.

Mr. Baran left RAND in 1968 to co-found the Institute for the Future, a nonprofit research group specializing in long-range forecasting.

Mr. Baran was also an entrepreneur. He started seven companies, five of which eventually went public. Mr. Baran's wife, Evelyn, died in 2007. He is survived by a son, three grandchildren and a companion.

In recent years, the origins of the Internet have been subject to claims and counterclaims of precedence. Mr. Baran was an outspoken proponent of distributing credit widely.

"The Internet is really the work of a thousand people," he said in 2001. And in 1990 he said in an interview: "The process of technological developments is like building a cathedral. Over the course of several hundred years, new people come along and each lays down a block on top of the old foundations, each saying, 'I built a cathedral.'

"Next month another block is placed atop the previous one. Then comes along an historian who asks, 'Well, who built the cathedral?' Peter added some stones here, and Paul added a few more. If you are not careful you can con yourself into believing that you did the most important part. But the reality is that each contribution has to follow onto previous work. Everything is tied to everything else."

— By Katie Hafner

DIANA WYNNE JONES

A Weaver of Fantastical Worlds

AUG. 16, 1934 - MARCH 26, 2011

Diana Wynne Jones, whose critically admired stories and novels for children and teenage readers imagined fantastical worlds inhabited by wizards, witches, magicians and ordinary boys and girls, died on March 26 in Bristol, England. She was 76.

Though Ms. Jones never became the household name in the United States that J. K. Rowling did with the Harry Potter franchise, her work was relished by connoisseurs of the young-adult fantasy and science fiction genres. She wrote more than 35 books, including the Chrestomanci series, which focuses on a powerful enchanter who presides over a world in which magic is, in her words, "as common as music." Another popular book, "Howl's Moving Castle"

(1986), about a young girl transformed into an old crone by a spiteful witch, was adapted into a 2004 animated film.

Her books, which draw partly on Norse mythology, created generally recognizable worlds except for the ubiquity of spells, trances and hocus-pocus. Her protagonists were generally clever and curious children whose cleverness and curiosity became useful as they wended their way through convoluted adventures, mostly unaided by the adults in their lives, who routinely disappointed them. Her prose was literate and sonorous, and she wrote with what sounded like an arched eyebrow — perfect for the skeptically wise young person who was her ideal reader.

BEWITCHING: Ms. Jones's stories enchanted readers.

"Jones's fiction is relevant, subversive, witty and highly enjoyable, while also having a distinctly dark streak and a constant awareness of how unreliable the real world can seem," the British critic Christopher Priest wrote in The Guardian of London. "Disguises and deceptions abound. Though avoiding criminally dysfunctional families or unwanted pregnancies, her cleverly plotted and amusing adventures deal frankly with emotional clumsiness, parental neglect, jealousy between siblings and a general sense of being an outcast. Rather than a deliberately cruel stepmother, a Jones protagonist might have a real mother far more wrapped up in her own career than in the discoveries and feelings of her child. The child protagonist would realize this, but get on with the adventure anyway."

Ms. Jones was born in London on Aug. 16, 1934. Her family moved a great deal when she was a child, especially after the onset of World War II. She spent time in Wales, where her father was from, and the family eventually settled in Thaxted, a village in Essex, where her parents ran a cultural center for local teenagers.

As Ms. Jones described them, her parents were distant, chilly people, miserly and neglectful, and perhaps that is where her characters' self-reliance and sense that life must proceed in spite of obstacles was born. In any case, her powers of observation emerged as acute, somewhat critical and wryly mischievous. In an autobiographical essay, she described childhood encounters with two giants of children's literature, Arthur Ransome and Beatrix Potter, and concluded that they both hated children. Of the community in Thaxted, she wrote, "This idyllic place had the highest illegitimate birth rate in the county."

"In numerous families, the younger apparent brothers or sisters turned out to be the offspring of the unmarried elder daughters," she continued, adding that there was one young woman who pretended her daughter was her sister, "and there was a fair deal of incest, too. Improbable characters abounded there, including two acknowledged witches and a man who went mad in the church porch at full moon."

Ms. Jones graduated from St. Anne's College, Oxford. She married a university professor, John A. Burrow, and began writing children's books because the ones she was reading to her own children displeased her. Her skeptical outlook extended to the genre of fiction in which she wrote, and in 1996 she published "The Tough Guide to Fantasyland," a spoof, in the form of a guidebook, of the entire universe of fantasy novels and their too-often-shared conventions.

In addition to the Chrestomanci books — including "Charmed Life" (1977), "The Magicians of Caprona" (1980) and "Witch Week" (1982) — Ms. Jones wrote another series, known as the Dalemark quartet, set in a medieval-like seacoast civilization. Her recent titles include "The Merlin Conspiracy" (2003), about three young people who manage to foil a plot to seize control of the magic of the universe, and "The Game" (2007), about children venturing into an alternate world known as the mythosphere. A new book, "Earwig and the Witch," was published in June 2011.

Ms. Jones, who died of cancer, is survived by her husband, whom she married in 1956, three sons and five grandchildren.

— *By Bruce Weber*

FARLEY GRANGER

Almost a Matinee Idol

JULY 1, 1925 - MARCH 27, 2011

FARLEY GRANGER, who found quick stardom in films like Alfred Hitchcock's "Strangers on a Train" in the 1940s and '50s but who then turned aside from Hollywood to pursue stage and television roles, died on March 27 at his home in Manhattan. He was 85.

Mr. Granger's youthful good looks gave him matinee-idol potential, and he was linked romantically to some of the biggest names of the day, of both sexes. But his passion for stage acting and his discontent with the studio system kept him from reaching Hollywood superstardom. Though he had scores of television and film credits and made a half-dozen Broadway appearances, his best-known performances were two of his earliest: as a preppie thrill-killer in Hitchcock's "Rope" in 1948, and as a tennis player wrongly suspected of murder in "Strangers on a Train" in 1951.

Mr. Granger was born on July 1, 1925, in San Jose, Calif. His father, also named Farley, owned a car dealership, but the stock market crash killed that business, and, hoping to find work, the senior Mr. Granger took the family to Los Angeles. It was an auspicious move for young Farley, an only child: in 1943 a casting director for Samuel Goldwyn saw him in a play called "The Wookie" at a showcase theater and had him come in for a reading. The onlookers included Mr. Goldwyn and Lillian Hellman.

"The war was on, and men were in short supply," Mr. Granger recalled in an interview for this obituary in 2007. Not yet 18, he was cast in the film version of Hellman's "North Star," playing a resident of a Ukrainian village that is invaded by the Nazis. Then, in 1944, came "The Purple Heart," about a downed bomber crew, followed by real-life military service in the Navy.

Mr. Granger had made enough of an impression in his first films that when he finished his Navy stint Mr. Hitchcock borrowed him from Goldwyn for "Rope," and then "Strangers." Mr. Hitchcock, in turn, made an impression on the young actor. "He could make the phone book sound intriguing," Mr. Granger said in his 2007 autobiography, "Include Me Out: My Life From Goldwyn to Broadway," written with his longtime romantic partner Robert Calhoun.

Working with Mr. Hitchcock and spending time with theater pros like Betty Comden and Adolph Green, whom he met on trips to New York, left Mr. Granger feeling trapped by his Goldwyn contract. Goldwyn's choices of movies for him weren't helping. There was, for instance, "Edge of Doom" (1950), in which Mr. Granger's character beats a clergyman to death. "The critics gave it the same kind of beating I had given the priest," he wrote in "Include Me Out."

In 1953 Mr. Granger took the unusual step of buying his way out of the remaining two years of his contract with Goldwyn, freeing him to chase his increasingly insistent dream of working on the stage.

"When I was in Hollywood I used to visit New York, go to the theater, and then go visit in the dressing room," he recalled in a 1977 interview with The New York Times. "I'd cross the stage to get there, and when I did I'd tremble. Hollywood was never a place for me. The stage was the magic."

Mr. Granger moved to New York, but he found that success did not come as quickly for him in the theater as it had in film. "I said, 'Here I am,' and everyone said, 'Terrific' and looked the other way," he remembered in that 1977 interview.

He reacted to this cold shoulder with a humility other Hollywood stars might not have mustered: he decided to learn how to act, studying at schools like the Neighborhood Playhouse in New York. He was also willing to work in Off Broadway, regional and summer stock theaters, touring with the National Repertory Company. In 1959 he made it to Broadway as Fitzwilliam Darcy in "First Impressions," a musical version of "Pride and Prejudice," but the show lasted only 92 performances. Later that year he had another two-and-a-half-month Broadway run in "The Warm Peninsula," part of a cast that included Julie Harris, June Havoc, Larry Hagman and Ruth White.

NEXT STOP, NEW YORK: Mr. Granger, left, in Hitchcock's "Strangers on a Train." He left Hollywood for Broadway.

With his film experience, Mr. Granger found he could supplement his slow-starting stage career with work in the emerging medium of live television. He worked steadily in the 1950s and early '60s in the "Kraft Television Theater" series, "Playhouse 90" and other television-from-theater programs that dotted the broadcast landscape. A favorite among his early television roles, he said, was Morris Townsend in "The Heiress" in 1961, also opposite Ms. Harris.

In the midst of switching his focus from movies to theater and television, Mr. Granger also made the film he would later say he was most proud of: "Senso" (1954), by the Italian director Luchino Visconti, in which Mr. Granger played an Austrian military officer. "Working with Visconti was a unique thing," he recalled, "and that was a difficult role." Later, in the 1970s, Mr. Granger would return to Italy to make films of a much lesser caliber, marketed under names like "Leather and Whips" and "The Red-Headed Corpse."

Mr. Granger's love life was as adventurous as his career choices. He had a longstanding hot-and-cold relationship with Shelley Winters — "the love of my life and the bane of my existence," he called her in his book — which began in his Goldwyn years and included talk of marriage. Another serious love interest was the actress Janice Rule, with whom he had worked Off Broadway in the 1950s. Women who were in his life more briefly included Ava Gardner.

But Mr. Granger, who described himself as bisexual, also had relationships with Leonard Bernstein and Arthur Laurents (see page 442). He met Mr. Calhoun, who died in 2008, while doing a National Repertory Theater tour of which Mr. Calhoun was production manager. Asked about his preferences in the 2007 Times interview, Mr. Granger said, "I've lived the greater part of my life with a man, so obviously that's the most satisfying to me."

He leaves no immediate survivors.

Mr. Granger won an Obie Award in 1986 for his performance as Eldon in the Circle Repertory Company's production of "Talley & Son," by Lanford Wilson (see page 364). His other notable New York productions included "The Crucible" (as John Proctor) on Broadway in 1964 and "The King and I" (as the king) at City Center in 1960. "Farley Granger comes with a fresh point of view — as well as a full head of hair," Brooks Atkinson wrote of the City Center performance in The Times.

For Mr. Granger, the live audience was what made theater superior to filmmaking. "I love getting laughs," he said in an interview in 1982, in the midst of a substantial run as a replacement Sidney Bruhl in "Deathtrap" on Broadway. "Next to sex, laughs are the best things in the world."

— *By Neil Genzlinger*

MAR

GEORGE TOOKER

Mysterious Pictures of a Soulless World

AUG. 5, 1920 - MARCH 27, 2011

GEORGE TOOKER, a painter whose haunting images of trapped clerical workers and forbidding government offices expressed a peculiarly 20th-century brand of anxiety and alienation, died on March 27 at his home in Hartland, Vt. He was 90.

Mr. Tooker, often called a symbolic, or magic, realist, worked well outside the critical mainstream for much of his career, relegated to the margins by the rise of abstraction. As doctrinaire modernism loosened its hold in the 1980s, however, he was rediscovered by a younger generation of artists, critics and curators, who embraced him as one of the most distinctive and mysterious American painters of the 20th century.

He specialized in eerie situations with powerful mythic overtones. Luminous and poetic, his paintings often conveyed a sense of dread, but could just as easily express a lover's rapture or spiritual ecstasy. Whatever the emotion, his generalized figures, with their smoothly modeled sculptural forms and masklike faces, seemed to dwell outside of time, even when placed in contemporary settings.

The harried figures in "The Subway" (1950), gathered in a low-ceilinged passageway, could be characters in a Greek tragedy, stalked by the Furies. In "Landscape With Figures" (1965-66), the disembodied heads of despairing office workers peep out of a mazelike set of cubicles, like the damned in a modern version of the Inferno. The men and women in "Waiting Room" (1957) simply wait, catatonically and existentially, as if they were extras in a play by Beckett or Sartre.

"These are powerful pictures that will stay in the public consciousness," said Thomas H. Garver, author of the monograph "George Tooker." "Everyone can say, 'Yes, I've been in that faceless situation,' even if it's just standing in line waiting to apply for a driver's license."

Mr. Tooker's lyrical, poetic paintings were no less enigmatic than the angst-filled works he called his "protest paintings." In "Sleepers II" (1959), wide-eyed heads, swaddled in a cloudlike blanket, stare fixedly upward, like souls captured midway between death and transfiguration.

"His narratives are so mysterious that viewers have to look deeply into the paintings," said Marshall N. Price, chief curator at the National Academy Museum in New York, which organized a retrospective of Mr. Tooker's work in 2008. "You cannot look quickly at a Tooker and then turn away. And the work is filled with so many references to Renaissance painting, there is so much mysterious iconography, that for art historians it's just fascinating."

George Clair Tooker Jr. was born on Aug. 5, 1920, in Brooklyn and grew up on Long Island, in Bellport, where he studied painting with a local artist. To please his parents, he entered Harvard after attending Phillips Academy in Andover, Mass. At Harvard he studied English but continued to draw and do watercolors.

After graduating in 1942, he enlisted in the Marine Corps' officer candidate school, but the psychological stress of bayonet drill reactivated an old intestinal complaint, and he was discharged from the service on medical grounds.

Mr. Tooker began studying with Reginald Marsh at the Art Students League of New York. There he met the painter Paul Cadmus, who introduced him to egg-tempera technique, which enforced a slower style of painting much more congenial to Mr. Tooker's contemplative nature. Working on wood panels or Masonite board, Mr. Tooker painstakingly built luminous matte surfaces, inch by square inch; soft, powdery colors complemented the rounded forms and fabrics of the paintings.

Mr. Cadmus's exuberant use of homosexual themes in his work also encouraged Mr. Tooker to address that aspect of his identity in paintings like the terrifying, Bruegel-esque "Children and Spastics" (1946), in which a group of leering sadists torment three frail, effeminate men.

Equally influential was Jared French, part of Mr. Cadmus's intimate circle, whose interest in Jungian archetypes and in the frigid, inscrutable forms of archaic Greek and Etruscan art inspired Mr. Tooker to take a more symbolic, mythic approach to his subject matter.

"Symbolism can be limiting and dangerous, but I don't care for art without it," Mr. Tooker told the writer and cultural critic Selden Rodman in 1957. "The kind that appeals to me the most is a symbolism like a heraldic emblem, but never just that alone: the kind practiced by Paolo Uccello and Piero della Francesca."

At the same time, he fended off attempts to define him as a surrealist or a magic realist. "I am after reality — painting impressed on the mind

APPRECIATION

Bureaucracy in Egg Tempera

"Government Bureau," a 1956 painting by George Tooker, was inspired by his maddening encounter with the New York City Building Department. Most people who waste hours in line just end up with sore feet and headaches. Mr. Tooker emerged with one of the best-known depictions of modern alienation and despair.

The painting, in luminous egg tempera, shows people waiting in a vaulted office that seems to stretch to infinity. Clerks stare emptily through glass partitions. No one talks or moves. It's a waiting room; everybody just waits.

Mr. Tooker, a New Yorker who settled in Vermont, did a lot with angst — his paintings of subways, waiting rooms and office cubicles are similarly haunting — but he also made lovely images of rapture and compassion. He said in 2002 that his pictures had gotten happier as he got older.

I wonder what he thought of institutional limbo today. The government bureau is now in our heads. It's the infinite space we inhabit when we languish on hold. The chill light is computer glow. Our isolation may be deeper now than anyone imagined in the 1950s.

My father, a New Yorker who left newspapering to work in a government bureau, had a copy of "Government Bureau" on his office wall. I saw it as a boy and was scarred. Those pale hands and slumped shoulders. The desolate eyes. The unnerving thought that this was my father's idea of decorating. I learned later that his motivation was of the mordant-droll variety. He said the picture was there to remind him how not to do his job.

— *By Lawrence Downes*

so hard that it recurs as a dream," he said, "but I am not after dreams as such, or fantasy."

At the insistence of Lincoln Kirstein, who was Cadmus's brother-in-law, the curator Dorothy C. Miller included Mr. Tooker's work in the "Fourteen Americans" show at the Museum of Modern Art in 1946, and his work also appeared in exhibitions at the Whitney Museum of American Art and other major museums.

With his partner, the painter William Christopher, Mr. Tooker moved into an illegal loft on West 18th Street in Manhattan, making custom furniture to supplement his art income. By the late 1940s he had developed his mature style and settled on the themes that would engage him for the rest of his life: love, death, sex, grief, aging, alienation and religious faith. Working in isolation in rural Vermont after 1960, he produced from two to four paintings a year.

Mr. Tooker's magical images were drawn from mundane experience. The bureaucratic shuffle he experienced when trying to get city permits to renovate a house in Brooklyn Heights led to "Government Bureau" (1956). One of his best-known works, it depicts disconsolate supplicants being stared at, impassively, by workers behind frosted-glass partitions, only their noses and eyes visible. Across the street from his home, the open windows in a Puerto Rican rooming house provided the raw material for his Windows series of the 1950s and '60s, like the young man strumming a guitar while his female lover sleeps behind him in "Guitar" (1957).

In 1973 Mr. Christopher died in Spain, where the two men had been living for six years, plunging Mr. Tooker into a spiritual crisis that he resolved by embracing Roman Catholicism. (He grew up in an Episcopal home but had become nonreligious.) In Mr. Tooker's later work, marked by a new sense of compassion, he often addressed specifically religious themes, notably in "The Seven Sacraments" (1980), an altarpiece he produced for the church of St. Francis of Assisi in Windsor, Vt.

Mr. Tooker, who is survived by a sister, was notoriously reticent about the meaning of his work. "I don't examine it myself, and I don't want to," he once said.

But he did reflect on the change in his later work. "I suppose I don't paint such unpleasant pictures as I used to," he told American Art magazine in 2002. "I got to be known for unpleasant pictures. I think my pictures are happier now, with fewer complaints."

— *By William Grimes*

DAVID E. DAVIS

A New Model of Automotive Journalism

NOV. 7, 1930 - MARCH 27, 2011

David E. Davis Jr., an editor and writer who transformed automotive journalism by bringing an irreverent tone, a literary sensibility and top-notch writers to the magazines Car and Driver and Automobile, died on March 27 in Ann Arbor, Mich. He was 80.

Mr. Davis, a former race-car driver and advertising copywriter for the Chevrolet Corvette, brought a taste for Southern-style storytelling and a penchant for splashy editorial concepts when he signed on at Car and Driver in the early 1960s, first as a writer and later as editor and publisher.

The magazine, a weak sister to publications like Road & Track and Motor Trend, moved into the passing lane under Mr. Davis, a combative swashbuckler who encouraged criticism of the cars it tested, even at the risk of losing advertising, and signed promising young writers, notably a former taxi driver and Chrysler test driver named Jean Lindamood (now Jennings).

Ms. Lindamood's wild adventures behind the wheel became reader favorites, as did Mr. Davis's monthly column, "American Driver," a wayward exercise in which he might veer off into, say, a character sketch of God: "He likes a little Armagnac, but only after the roast has been consumed and the empty Bordeaux bottles cleared away. He drives one of the old fastback Bentley Continentals, and he drives it both vigorously and well."

In the mid-1980s, Rupert Murdoch, the media magnate, asked Mr. Davis to create a new car magazine. Elaborating on ideas he had developed at Car and Driver, Mr. Davis came up with Automobile. With its heavy paper stock and lush color photography, it aimed at the kind of upscale readers who, he told Adweek, "are interested in driving from New York to Los Angeles in a Porsche 911 Turbo" and whose tastes would be attractive to advertisers like Ralph Lauren.

NO BORING CARS!: Mr. Davis, in 1986, with the first issue of Automobile.

Shedding the mechanical focus of Car and Driver, Mr. Davis did away with orthodox test drives and numerical results. Instead, he handed the keys to writers like P. J. O'Rourke, Jim Harrison and David Halberstam and encouraged them to hit the road, have adventures and write about the lived experience of driving a spiffy car.

David Evan Davis Jr. was born on Nov. 7, 1930, in Burnside, Ky. After graduating from high school in Royal Oak, Mich., he studied briefly at Olivet College but soon took an assortment of jobs — selling Volkswagens and Triumphs for a dealer in Ypsilanti, working in a men's clothing store, assembling Fords — before the sight of a Jaguar XK120 inflamed his incipient car lust.

He turned to auto racing, but in 1955, driving in an amateur race in Sacramento, he flipped his MG and nearly destroyed half his face, requiring 18 months of recuperation and reconstructive surgery.

"I suddenly understood with great clarity that nothing in life — except death itself — was ever going to kill me," he said in a commencement address at the University of Michigan in 2004. "No meeting could ever go that badly. No client would ever be that angry. No business error would ever bring me as close to the brink as I had already been."

After selling advertising on the West Coast for Road & Track, he was hired by Campbell-Ewald, the longtime agency for Chevrolet, to write copy for Corvette ads. A colleague, the future novelist Elmore Leonard, coached him on how to put pizazz into his prose, advising him, he told an audience at the Adcraft Club in Detroit in 2003, to "write like you talk, and read aloud everything you write."

In 1962, he began writing for Car and Driver, which had been founded in 1956 as Sports Cars Illustrated and was struggling to compete under a new name. Soon he was named its editor and publisher, but his monthly column got him in trouble. Reviewing the BMW 2002, he wrote that its Blaupunkt radio "could not pick up a Manhattan station from the other side of the George Washington Bridge."

He resigned after being ordered to apologize and returned to Campbell-Ewald as a creativ director. In 1976, he resumed his post at C and Driver, which he moved to Ann Arb from New York two years later. He grew d enchanted with the job after CBS bought magazine from Ziff-Davis Publishing in 19

Many of his columns for Car and Driver and Automobile were reprinted in "Thus Spake David E.: The Collected Wit and Wisdom of the Most Influential Automotive Journalist of Our Time" (1999).

At Automobile, to which he gave the motto "No Boring Cars!," Mr. Davis installed Ms. Jennings as editor, hired Robert Cumberford to write on car design in a monthly column, unleashed the illustrator Bruce McCall and maintained the atmosphere of creative turbulence that had become his editorial style. Being fired by Mr. Davis was a left-handed compliment.

In 1991, Automobile was sold to K-III Communications (renamed Primedia). Mr. Davis, under pressure, turned over the editorship of the magazine to Ms. Jennings in 2000. He stayed on as a columnist and as an editorial director of Motor Trend after it was acquired by Primedia in 2001.

Mr. Davis designed the start-up Internet magazine Winding Road in 2006 and in 2009 returned to Car and Driver as a columnist.

He is survived by his wife, Jean, three children from his first marriage, a stepdaughter, two stepsons, a sister, two grandchildren, nine stepgrandchildren and a great-grandson.

"I see myself as a guest in the homes of several hundred thousand car enthusiasts each month, talking about what I've driven, where I've been and who I've met," he wrote in Car and Driver. "I strive to be entertaining as well as informative, because I want to be liked, to be remembered, to be invited back. It usually works."

— *By William Grimes*

GIL CLANCY

Guiding Hand in the Boxing Ring

MAY 30, 1922 - MARCH 31, 2011

GIL CLANCY, the Hall of Fame boxing manager and trainer who guided Emile Griffith to the welterweight and middleweight championships and who later worked as a boxing matchmaker and TV analyst, died on March 31 in Lynbrook, on Long Island. He was 88.

Clancy trained a host of big-name boxers, including George Foreman, Oscar De La Hoya, 'erry Quarry and Gerry Cooney. But he was st known for his long association with 'fith.

'ancy was teaching in the New York City and training amateur fighters when he 1 Griffith into a Golden Gloves cham- 'as Griffith's trainer and co-manager turned pro in 1958.

.4, 1962, Clancy sent Griffith into Benny Paret, known as Kid, in mpionship bout at Madison

Griffith, a native of the Virgin Islands, had knocked out Paret, a Cuban, to take his championship, had lost it back to him and was seeking it once more.

At the weigh-in for that third bout, as Griffith remembered it, Paret directed a gay slur at him in Spanish. Griffith wanted to attack Paret, but Clancy held him back.

In the 12th round, Griffith pinned Paret into a corner, then delivered a whirlwind of blows to the head with no response from Paret. When the referee finally stopped the fight, Paret collapsed with blood clots in his brain. He died 10 days later.

CHARLES LAUFER

Founding Tiger Beat: The Inside Story!

SEPT. 13, 1923 - APRIL 5, 2011

CHARLES LAUFER, who as a high school teacher in 1955 despaired that his students had nothing entertaining to read and responded with magazines aimed at teenage girls desperate to know much, much more about the lives of their favorite cute stars, died on April 5 in Northridge, Calif. He was 87.

Mr. Laufer's best-known magazine was Tiger Beat, published monthly. With its spinoff publications and its competitors, of which the most popular was 16 Magazine, Tiger Beat had it all covered — or at least what mattered most to girls from about 8 to 14. The Beach Boys' loves! Jan and Dean's comeback! The private lives of the Beatles!

Exclamation points abounded, as many as 50 a page. Pix, as pictures were known, were glossy, glamorous and frequently poster-size. Fax, as facts were known, often included "101 things you never knew about (fill in star's name)": he uses a blue toothbrush!

Titles were catchy, oddly innocent by later standards: "Shaun: A Junk Food Junkie?," "Leif's Sad Childhood," "Bobby's Favorite Type of Girls" and "Marie: Fighting With Donny?"

"Let's face it," Mr. Laufer told Parade magazine in 1979, "we're in the little girl business."

Charles Harry Laufer was born on Sept. 13, 1923, in Newark, where his father, Isadore, owned a taxi company and was a state assemblyman. Charles was a star basketball player in high school before moving to Los Angeles, where he graduated from the University of Southern California. He taught English, journalism and history at two high schools.

To tempt his students to read more, Mr. Laufer, in 1955, started a magazine called Coaster, which later became Teen, and which he sold in 1957. In 1965 he published a one-shot magazine crammed with Beatles photos. It sold 750,000 copies in two days. Later in 1965 he started Tiger Beat. Its mainstay, copied by so-called teenzines to this day, was "guys in their 20s singing La La songs to 13-year-old girls," as Mr. Laufer once put it.

Covering what mattered to girls from 8 to 14.

His brother, Ira, put up half the capital for Tiger Beat, but Charles ran it as publisher. To compete with 16 Magazine, his strategy was to build promotional relationships with production and record companies. But it was often Mr. Laufer's own perspicacity that yielded the advantage. At a screening of new television shows in 1965, he saw the Monkees for the first time and recognized Davy Jones from his performance in "Oliver!" on Broadway. Immediately seeing the Monkees' potential, he put the band on the cover of Tiger Beat. That put the still-struggling publication in the black, and he signed an exclusive deal for special Monkees magazines, Monkees picture books and Monkees love beads, which added to the bonanza.

Tiger Beat also used glossy paper (16 Magazine used newsprint) and a more advanced process for colored pictures. And it gave away bonus posters and ran contests in which readers could compete for stars' personal belongings.

The Laufer brothers sold Tiger Beat in 1978 for a reported $15 million. Its circulation was then 700,000.

Charles Laufer stayed on as a consultant to the new owners for several years, then retired.

Various combinations of his family members have since owned Bop and other teenage publications, as ownership of Tiger Beat passed through five or six companies. In 2003 Mr. Laufer's son, Scott, bought Tiger Beat, which he now publishes with Bop.

Mr. Laufer's first marriage ended in divorce. In addition to his son, he is survived by his brother; his wife of 55 years, the former Dorothy Lacy; four daughters; and 10 grandchildren.

In 1985, Mr. Laufer said it would be hard to duplicate his success if he were just starting. "Today you have rock stars coming out and saying they're bisexual, or you see four-letter words in print," he said in an interview.

Still, some things never change, like the covers of Tiger Beat. The cluttered collages of yesteryear look very much like those of today. Only the faces have changed, from the likes of David Cassidy and Bobby Sherman to Justin Bieber.

— *By Douglas Martin*

APPRECIATION

46 Years Old, and Still Going on 15

Hair floating, skin dewy, eyes free of guile: the boys of Tiger Beat will never hurt you. In crisp photos and squeaky-clean quotes about love, they've been practically interchangeable for more than four decades. It's an archetype that's survived any number of invasions: the Brits, disco, boy bands, the Brat Pack, more boy bands, the Disney Channel, TMZ and more.

Tiger Beat, even now the glossiest of rags, began as an act of capitalist savvy that was also a good deed: acknowledging the interests and burgeoning desires of young women, a group that had been ignored all too often. Started in 1965 near the height of Beatlemania by Charles Laufer and his brother, Ira, Tiger Beat remains the original teen-girl tabloid, providing a steady diet of boyflesh to gaze at longingly, and helping to launch the careers of oodles of similarly coiffed, similarly moisturized young men, some of whom actually grew up to be famous.

In truth, the names of those who have filled the pages — the boys (Davy! Leif! Corey! Luke! Brian!) and the occasional relatable girl (Debbie! Miley!) — don't much matter. Tiger Beat is a see-no-evil, speak-no-evil place holder for young readers not yet ready for the complex questions posed by, say, Seventeen magazine and Judy Blume books. It allows for playacting at desire, before the real, parent-scaring thing comes into play.

But even at its outset, Tiger Beat, innocent and chipper and with a prim 1950s aesthetic, was a bit of a relic. Teen culture was racing toward Woodstock and to more risqué territory beyond, but polished Tiger Beat was basically staying put. And as actual grown-folks magazines began to take an interest in the Justins of the world (Timberlake! Bieber!), and as young stars became more eager than ever to prove themselves to be anything but young, Tiger Beat has remained a naïf. It's still packed with those huge fold-out posters stapled in the center, big gleaming boy beacons meant to be taped to walls and ceilings, the raw material for sweet dreams and future fantasies.

— *By Jon Caramanica*

BARUCH S. BLUMBERG

A Virus Discovered, and Millions Saved

JULY 28, 1925 - APRIL 5, 2011

DR. BARUCH S. BLUMBERG, the Nobel Prize-winning biochemist and medical anthropologist who discovered the hepatitis B virus, showed that it could cause liver cancer and then helped develop a powerful vaccine to fight it, saving millions of lives, died on April 5 in Moffett Field, Calif. He was 85.

His family said he died, apparently of a heart attack, shortly after giving a keynote speech at a NASA conference at the Ames Research Center in Moffett Field, in the San Francisco Bay area. He had been associated with a NASA project to hunt for microorganisms in space.

Dr. Blumberg's prize-winning virology and epidemiology work began in the 1960s at the Fox Chase Cancer Center in Philadelphia and took him and his colleagues on field trips around the world, from Japan to Africa.

The work led to the discovery of the hepatitis B virus in 1967, the first test for hepatitis B in the blood supply and the development in 1969 of the hepatitis B vaccine — the first "cancer vaccine." Dr. Irving Millman, a colleague at the research center, was its co-creator.

Dr. Blumberg's discoveries have been compared to those of Jonas Salk, the developer of the polio vaccine. He shared the Nobel Prize in Physiology or Medicine in 1976 with D. Carleton Gajdusek for their work on the origins and spread of infectious viral diseases. (Dr. Gajdusek had discovered the cause of the kuru, or "trembling disease," prevalent in New Guinea.)

Almost 20 years later, after decades of hepatitis B-related studies and a global search for medicinal plants to treat hepatic infections, Dr. Blumberg began what he called his second career. In 1999 he became the founding director of the National Aeronautics and Space Administration's Astrobiology Institute.

The institute's mission was to oversee research teams in the development of life-detecting devices for planetary rovers and asteroid flybys, and to scrutinize life forms in "extreme" environments on Earth, like the ocean bottom and the geothermal cauldrons that produce geysers. He joined several expeditions himself.

To these seemingly disparate endeavors — investigating disease-causing organisms and postulating alien or primordial life forms — Dr. Blumberg contributed to the understanding of the evolutionary phenomenon called polymorphism, in which a species can adapt to an environment through changes in appearances and functions.

From his base in Philadelphia, where he lived, Dr. Blumberg began investigating viruses with a study of yellow jaundice, so named because of the characteristic vivid yellowing of the eyes and skin. As early as 1940, medical researchers had determined that there were two different forms of virus-induced jaundice: one transmitted as an intestinal infection, the other spread mainly by blood transfusions.

Scientific field trips to pinpoint the agent responsible for blood-borne jaundice were conducted by Dr. Blumberg and his colleagues in the Philippines, India, Japan, Canada, Scandinavia, Australia and Africa. Ultimately it was blood serum from an infected Australian aborigine that yielded the so-called Australian antigen, a protein found on the surface of the hepatitis B virus.

After he and Dr. Millman developed the hepatitis vaccine, they struggled to interest a pharmaceutical company to help develop and produce it. As Dr. Blumberg wrote in an autobiographical essay for the Nobel committee, "Vaccines are not an attractive product for pharmaceutical companies, in that they are often used once or only a few times and they ordinarily do not generate as much income as a medication for a chronic disease that must be used for many years."

> Dr. Blumberg's Nobel Prize-winning discoveries have been compared to those of Jonas Salk, the developer of the polio vaccine.

Moreover, he said, the medical research community in the early 1970s remained skeptical about the claim that a virus had been identified and a vaccine developed.

Ultimately he and Dr. Millman signed an agreement with Merck & Company, whose vaccine laboratories were near Philadelphia.

Dr. Blumberg's discoveries are credited with saving millions of patients from ever developing liver cancer. But in his scientific autobiography, "Hepatitis B: The Hunt for a Killer Virus" (2002), he observed ruefully that hepatic disease continued to kill 1.5 million people a year worldwide — despite the widespread availability of the vaccines he had helped develop — and that 350 million were chronically infected.

Still, he was hopeful. "Life — and death — are full of surprises," he wrote, "and while it may be tempting fate to be too optimistic, it appears likely that within the next few decades this virus will be effectively controlled." (There is still no vaccine for the blood-borne hepatitis C, one of the five known hepatitis viruses.)

Dr. Blumberg traced his fascination with inherited variations in susceptibility to disease to the volunteer service he did during medical school at an isolated mining town in northern Suriname, where he delivered babies, performed clinical services and undertook the first malaria survey done in that region.

He was particularly interested in the sugar plantation workers who had been imported from several continents, among them Hindus from India, Javanese, Africans, Chinese "and a smattering of Jews descended from 17th century migrants to the country from Brazil," he wrote in his Nobel essay. All "lived side by side," he said, but "their responses to the many infectious agents in the environment were very different."

He wrote his first scientific paper based on these studies and would revisit the tropics repeatedly. "Nature operates in bold and dramatic manner in the tropics," he wrote.

By the late 1990s Dr. Blumberg was immersed in astrobiology, as NASA called the new science. Appointed by the NASA administrator, Dan Goldin, to lead the Astrobiology Institute, Dr. Blumberg and his team were asked to address three profound questions: How does life begin and evolve? Does life exist elsewhere in the universe? And what is life's future on Earth and beyond?

As in his disease studies, Dr. Blumberg collaborated with specialists in other fields, including physics, chemistry, geology, paleontology and oceanography as well as biology and medicine, drawing on their expertise, he said, to "help us to recognize biospheres that might be different from our own."

While promoting the development of astrobiological space probes, he recommended equal efforts in the study of earthly "extremophiles," the organisms that somehow thrive in extreme temperatures, pressures and chemical conditions.

In fissures in the deep ocean floor, Dr. Blumberg said, are extremophiles that might resemble the earliest life forms on Earth or other planets. He described Earth as "a place of extremes" during the first few hundred million years of its 4.5-billion-year existence, given to radical climate fluctuations, from searing heat to immobilizing cold, amid constant meteorite bombardments and catastrophic volcanic eruptions.

He speculated that life might have started on Earth at geothermal sites, either underground or in the sea. The NASA venture — since diminished by administrative changes and financing cutbacks — was welcomed by those who advocate a search for extraterrestrial intelligence, known as SETI. Dr. Blumberg joined the board of the SETI Institute in Mountain View, Calif.

But in an interview with The New York Times in 2002, he said he would be "very surprised if we found something in space, that it would look like E.T."

"If we found something more like a virus or a bacteria," he said, "that would be astounding enough."

Baruch Samuel Blumberg (Barry to his friends) was born in New York City on July 28, 1925, the second of three children of Meyer Blumberg, a lawyer, and Ida Blumberg. After attending the Yeshiva of Flatbush in Brooklyn, he went to Far Rockaway High School in Queens (whose graduates also include the Nobel physicists Richard Feynman and Burton Richter).

His undergraduate studies at Union College in Schenectady, N.Y., were interrupted by World War II, when he served as a Navy deck officer on landing ships. Returning to Union College, he completed a bachelor's degree in physics, enrolled in graduate studies of mathematics at Columbia and transferred to Columbia's College of Physicians and Surgeons, earning his M.D. there in 1951.

Dr. Blumberg served a clinical fellowship at Columbia-Presbyterian Medical Center, went to Oxford University's Balliol College for a doctorate in biochemistry, and returned to the United States in 1957 to join the National Institutes of Health, where he headed the Geographic Medicine and Genetics Section until 1964.

Most of his research afterward was conducted at the Fox Chase Cancer Center. Dr. Blumberg was also on the faculty of the University of Pennsylvania and its School of Medicine as a professor of medicine, medical genetics and medical anthropology.

Dr. Blumberg married Jean Liebesman, an artist, in 1954. She survives him, as do two daughters, two sons and nine grandchildren.

Dr. Blumberg saw his Nobel Prize as more than a recognition of his achievements. He said it helped draw renewed attention to his work on a hepatitis B vaccine with enormously beneficial consequences. After receiving the prize, he said, he was invited to China. "I spoke before several thousand people," he told The Times in 2002. "I provided them with a copy of the patent, and now I'm told that it helped to change the direction of what they were doing and led to the saving of a lot of lives."

Saving lives, he said, was the whole point of his career. "Well, it is something I always wanted to do," he said in the 2002 interview. "This is what drew me to medicine. There is, in Jewish thought, this idea that if you save a single life, you save the whole world, and that affected me."

— *By H. Roger Segelken*

GERALD A. LAWSON

An Idea That Transformed the Home Video Game

DEC. 1, 1940 - APRIL 9, 2011

Gerald A. Lawson, a largely self-taught engineer who became a pioneer in electronic video entertainment, creating the first home video game system with interchangeable game cartridges, died on April 9 in Mountain View, Calif. He was 70.

Before disc-based systems like PlayStation, Xbox and Wii transformed the video game industry, before techno-diversions like Grand Theft Auto and Madden NFL, and even before

Pac-Man and Donkey Kong became the obsession of millions of electronic gamers, it was Mr. Lawson who made it possible to play a variety of video games at home.

In the mid-1970s, he was director of engineering and marketing for the newly formed video game division of Fairchild Semiconductor, and it was under his direction that the division brought to market in 1976 the Fairchild Channel F, a home console that allowed users to play different games contained on removable cartridges. Until then, home video game systems could play only games that were built into the machines themselves. Mr. Lawson's ideas anticipated — if they did not entirely enable — a huge international business.

INNOVATOR: Mr. Lawson in 2006 with a Channel F video game console.

In March, Mr. Lawson was honored for his innovative work by the International Game Developers Association, an overdue acknowledgment of an unfamiliar contributor to the technological transformation that has changed how people live.

"He's absolutely a pioneer," Allan Alcorn, a creator of the granddaddy of video games, Pong, said in an interview with The San Jose Mercury News in March. "When you do something for the first time, there is nothing to copy."

Mr. Alcorn was the first design engineer at Atari, whose own cartridge console eventually dominated the home video game market.

At 6 feet 6 inches and well over 250 pounds, Mr. Lawson cut an imposing figure. A modest man but a straight talker who was known to one and all as Jerry, he was among only a handful of black engineers in the world of electronics in general and electronic gaming in particular.

Gerald Anderson Lawson was born in Brooklyn on Dec. 1, 1940, and grew up mostly in Queens. His parents encouraged his intellectual pursuits. His father, Blanton, was a longshoreman by profession and a voracious reader of science books by inclination; his mother, Mannings, was a city employee who was also president of the PTA at the nearly all-white school Jerry attended. There he had a first-grade teacher who changed his life.

"I had a picture of George Washington Carver on the wall next to my desk," he said in a 2009 interview with the publication Vintage Computing and Gaming. "And she said, 'This could be you.'" He went on: "This kind of influence led me to feel, 'I want to be a scientist. I want to be something.'"

As a boy he pursued a number of scientific interests, ham radio and chemistry among them. As a teenager he earned money repairing television sets. He attended both Queens College and the City College of New York, but never received a degree. In the early 1970s he started at Fairchild in Silicon Valley as a roving design consultant. While he was there he invented an early coin-operated arcade game, Demolition Derby. Along with other Silicon Valley innovators, he belonged to a hobbyists' group known as the Homebrew Computer Club. Two of its members were Steve Jobs and Steve Wozniak, later the founders of Apple.

"I was not impressed with them — either one of them, actually," Mr. Lawson said in the 2009 interview, and, though he didn't say why, he declined to hire Mr. Wozniak for a job at Fairchild.

After inventing Demolition Derby, Mr. Lawson was put in charge of the company's video game division. He and his team came up with cartridges that could be loaded with different game programs and then inserted into the console one at a time. This allowed the company to sell individual games separately from the console itself, a business model that remains the cornerstone of the video game industry.

A crucial element of the invention was the use of a new processor, the Fairchild 8; another was a mechanism that allowed for repeated insertion and removal of cartridges without damaging the machine's semiconductors. Video hockey and tennis were programmed into the Channel F console; additional games available on cartridge included Shooting Gallery, Video Blackjack and Alien Invasion.

Mr. Lawson lived in Santa Clara, Calif., and died of complications of diabetes, his wife, Catherine, said. Besides his wife, whom he married in 1965, he is survived by a brother, a son and a daughter.

After he left Fairchild in 1980, Mr. Lawson founded Videosoft, a company that created games, and worked as a consultant.

"I don't play video games that often; I really don't," he said in the 2009 interview. "First of all, most of the games that are out now — I'm appalled by them." Most are concerned with "shooting somebody and killing somebody," he said.

"To me, a game should be something like a skill you should develop — if you play this game, you walk away with something of value."

— By Bruce Weber

Sidney Lumet

Filming a Moral Universe on the Streets of New York

JUNE 25, 1924 - APRIL 9, 2011

Sidney Lumet, a director who preferred the streets of New York to the back lots of Hollywood and whose stories of conscience — "12 Angry Men," "Serpico," "Dog Day Afternoon," "The Verdict," "Network" — became modern American film classics, died on April 9 at his home in Manhattan. He was 86.

"While the goal of all movies is to entertain," Mr. Lumet once wrote, "the kind of film in which I believe goes one step further. It compels the spectator to examine one facet or another of his own conscience. It stimulates thought and sets the mental juices flowing."

Social issues were what energized Mr. Lumet. His best films probed the consequences of prejudice and corruption. But they also celebrated individual acts of courage.

In his first film, "12 Angry Men" (1957), he took his cameras into a jury room where the pressure mounted as one courageous juror, played by Henry Fonda, tenaciously convinced the others that the defendant on trial for murder was, in fact, innocent. (Justice Sonia M. Sotomayor of the United States Supreme Court said the film had an important influence on her law career.)

Almost two decades later, Mr. Lumet's moral sense remained acute when he ventured into satire with "Network" (1976), perhaps his most acclaimed film. Based on Paddy Chayefsky's biting script, the film portrays a television anchorman who briefly resuscitates his fading career by launching on-air tirades against what he perceives as the hypocrisies of American society.

The film starred William Holden, Faye Dunaway and Peter Finch as the commentator turned attack dog whose proclamation to the world at large — "I'm as mad as hell, and I'm not going to take this anymore!" — became part of the American vernacular.

"Network" was nominated for 10 Academy Awards, including best film and best director, and won four: best actor (Mr. Finch), best actress (Ms. Dunaway), best original screenplay

(Mr. Chayefsky) and best supporting actress (Beatrice Straight).

Yet for all the critical success of his films and despite the more than 40 Academy Award nominations they drew, Mr. Lumet (pronounced loo-MET) never won an Oscar for directing, though he was nominated four times. (The other nominations were for "12 Angry Men," "Dog Day Afternoon" and "The Verdict.")

Only in 2005 did the Academy of Motion Picture Arts and Sciences present him with an honorary Academy Award. Manohla Dargis, writing in The New York Times, called it a "consolation prize for a lifetime of neglect."

In 2007, in an interview that was videotaped to accompany this obituary online, Mr. Lumet was asked how it felt to receive an Academy Award at long last. He replied, "I wanted one, damn it, and I felt I deserved one."

That he was more a creature of New York than of Hollywood may have had something to do with his Oscar night disappointments. For Mr. Lumet, location mattered deeply, and New York mattered most of all. He was the quintessential New York director.

"Locations are characters in my movies," he wrote. "The city is capable of portraying the mood a scene requires."

He explored New York early on in "The Pawnbroker" (1964), the story of a Holocaust survivor, played by Rod Steiger, numbed and hardened against humanity by the horrors he has endured, who deals with racketeers in his Harlem pawnshop until his conscience is reawakened by a vicious crime on his doorstep.

The city loomed large in Mr. Lumet's several examinations of the criminal justice system. Police corruption particularly fascinated him, beginning with "Serpico" (1973). The film, based on a book by Peter Maas, was drawn from a real-life drama involving two New York City police officers, David Durk and Frank Serpico, who told the Times reporter David Burnham that they had ample evidence of police graft and corruption.

Their story, published in The Times, led to the mayoral appointment of a commission to investigate the allegations and ultimately to major reforms. Both the book and the film concentrated on Detective Serpico, played by Al Pacino, and his efforts to change the system. Mr. Pacino's performance brought him an Oscar nomination.

Mr. Lumet returned to the theme in 1981 with "Prince of the City," sharing screenwriting credit with Jay Presson Allen. Based on a book by Robert Daley, the film dealt with an ambitious detective, portrayed by Treat Williams, who goes undercover to gather evidence for an investigative commission and winds up alone after being manipulated into destroying the lives and careers of many of those around him.

Mr. Lumet focused on criminals, rather than the police, in "Dog Day Afternoon" (1975), telling the story — again, based on fact — of a botched attempt to rob a Brooklyn bank. Mr. Pacino again starred, this time as Sonny, the leader of an amateurish gang of bank robbers whose plans go awry and who winds up taking hostages and demanding jet transport to a foreign country. (Sonny, it turns out, although he has a wife at home, had planned the robbery to pay for his boyfriend's sex-change operation.) In 2009, the film was added to the National Film Registry by the Library of Congress.

New York, or at least a fantasy version of it, was even the backdrop for Mr. Lumet's most uncharacteristic film, "The Wiz," his 1978 musical version of the "The Wizard of Oz" starring Michael Jackson and Diana Ross. Roundly panned, it was also a box-office failure.

By the time he finished shooting "Night Falls on Manhattan" in 1996, Mr. Lumet had made 38 films, 29 of them on location in New York City. That film, written by Mr. Lumet and based on another Daley novel, "Tainted Evidence," once again looked at the justice system as it moved from a shootout with drug dealers into a revealing courtroom trial.

The courthouse was one of Mr. Lumet's favorite arenas for drama, beginning with "12 Angry Men." He returned to it again in "The Verdict" (1982), with a screenplay by David Mamet and a cast led by Paul Newman as a down-at-the-heels lawyer who redeems himself and his career when he represents a malpractice victim in a legal battle with a hospital.

(continued on page 398)

APPRECIATION

A Hard-Nosed Realist With a Heart

The half-dozen great or almost-great New York movies Sidney Lumet directed from the late 1950s to the early '80s — for the sake of argument, let's specify "12 Angry Men" (1957), "The Pawnbroker" (1964), "Serpico" (1973), "Dog Day Afternoon" (1975), "Network" (1976) and "Prince of the City" (1981) — are hardly period pieces. But nowadays it is almost impossible not to look at them that way. These movies are such vivid time capsules of urban life and cinematic style that it can seem as if they must have been intended as such.

We have grown so accustomed to seeing certain images through bifocal lenses of nostalgia for New York as it was and for movies the way they were that we can miss the present-tense urgency and the journalistic clarity that were hallmarks of Mr. Lumet's tough, unassuming style.

It is tempting, from the safe distance of our self-satisfied, smoke-free 21st century metropolis — where the crime rate is still down and property values and Wall Street profits are rising again — to impose a perverse, rosy halo on the bad old days. Among cinephiles, the habit of romanticizing the movies of the past is even more deeply ingrained. In both cases, what has taken hold is a hazy myth of authenticity: especially in the '70s, we like to imagine, the movies were more realistic, and New York City was more real.

No doubt Mr. Lumet was a realist. The vigor of his best films and the hectic energy of the city they capture are undeniable. To watch those movies in sequence and with some sense of history — as opposed to an antiquarian, fetishistic attention to clothes and haircuts, cinematographic techniques and vanished neighborhood landmarks — is to encounter an episodic chronicle of societal unraveling. Some characters may cling to an idealized picture of the past, but they tend to do so out of fear and anxiety, as their hopes for the future fray and collapse along with the mores and values of the place they call home.

It is only a small exaggeration to say that the six movies I've named constitute an epic of decline, a sprawling, Zolaesque series of narratives whose common theme — discernible only in retrospect — is the crisis of American civic liberalism, as witnessed in its 20th century capital, New York. In our own day, what survives of that worldview, which was always more of an ethos than a political ideology, is subject to distortion and caricature. It is therefore easy to look at a movie like "12 Angry Men" and mock its earnest dedication to using a dramatic medium to hash out social problems. And the didactic, moralizing streak that runs through much of Mr. Lumet's work has provided some critics with a convenient, ready-made case against him. We are supposed to be too sophisticated to require stories that place their themes in the foreground. And also, perhaps, too jaded to be stirred by a dramatic universe built around increasingly battered beliefs in progress, solidarity and fair play.

(continued on next page)

(continued from previous page)

But even if that is so, we surely can't be immune to the pathos of watching those beliefs buffeted by the storms of history. We start out in a jury room where a confident, articulate paladin of right-thinking, commonsensical decency — it could only be Henry Fonda — holds out against the massed forces of bigotry, suspicion and laziness. The defendant, a young man from a poor background on trial for his life, is exonerated, and the anxious, law-abiding citizens who would have railroaded him achieve a unanimity that remains a stirring vision of consensus.

At the time, that vision may have been a noble illusion, a projection of the progressive, problem-solving hopes of the culture. Not long after, it would seem like a dream. Within 20 years, that consensus would shatter, and the picture of those men in that room would look almost unbearably quaint. Neighborhoods would crumble, and racial and ethnic resentments would fester. The institutions in which ordinary people might place their trust, and to which they might commit their honest labor, were discovered to be dysfunctional and corrupt. You could no longer trust the cop on the beat, or believe what you saw on the evening news. Evidence of this can be found in the history books, in the newspaper morgues or in the archived reports of various commissions (Knapp, Kerner, Moynihan).

And also, needless to say, in "The Pawnbroker," "Serpico" and "Network." There are certainly angry men in those movies — they were Mr. Lumet's specialty — but instead of righteously outraged burghers, they looked like raving lunatics. There was Sonny, the would-be bank robber in "Dog Day Afternoon," trying to stir up a crowd of Brooklynites with cries of "Attica! Attica!" as if the mere mention of that bloody prison uprising could turn his crime into political theater. And, of course, most famously, there was poor Howard Beale, exhorting his viewers to go to their windows and cry, "I'm as mad as hell, and I'm not going to take this anymore!"

Mad at what? Not going to take it how? Beale, the role for which Peter Finch won a posthumous Oscar, may be the most famous character in "Network," but the film's moral center is occupied by William Holden's Max Schumacher, who fights a rear-guard action to save his old friend's sanity and his own dignity in the teeth of rampant greed and cynicism. The film is fascinated by Beale's madness, and by the varieties of corporate venality incarnated by Faye Dunaway, Robert Duvall and Ned Beatty, but its heart is with Max.

Holden is a rumpled, weary, half-defeated version of Fonda's juror in "12 Angry Men" (a description that can also apply to the beleaguered detective played by Charles Durning in "Dog Day Afternoon"). It is no accident that Max's fond memories of the past hark back to the broadcast era of Edward R. Murrow, which was also the era of black-and-white, socially conscious television dramas where the young Mr. Lumet started out.

In the history of American movie realism, you might place Mr. Lumet between Elia Kazan and Martin Scorsese. To some extent, this is a matter of chronological happenstance: Mr. Kazan was born in 1909, Mr. Lumet in 1924 and Mr. Scorsese in 1942. Mr. Lumet's career overlapped with both of theirs. Mr. Lumet and Mr. Scorsese in particular were professional contemporaries. They both seem to belong to, and to have defined, the 1970s, the era of "Serpico," "Dog Day

Afternoon" and "Network" and also of "Mean Streets" and "Taxi Driver." But the differences between those studies in urban dysfunction and modern existential woe are not just temperamental or stylistic. They are generational as well. The city in Mr. Scorsese's early films is one from which hope has largely fled, and in which heroism and nihilism are for the most part indistinguishable. Johnny Boy, the character played by Robert De Niro in "Mean Streets," represents an anarchic, disruptive criminality unconstrained by the codes and customs of organized crime. The vigilantism of Mr. De Niro's Travis Bickle in "Taxi Driver," is, if anything, even more pathological: his idea of justice is paranoid, apocalyptic and bloody, and it may be the only justice the city has to offer.

In Mr. Lumet's universe, however, a shadow of the old hope persists, a residual but still potent faith in the possibility of something better. The tired old warhorses — Holden and Durning in "Network" and "Dog Day," Paul Newman in "The Verdict" — are like creatures from the world of Kazan and Clifford Odets who have somehow survived into the age of Travis Bickle. Frank Serpico and Treat Williams's Daniel Ciello in "Prince of the City," conscience-driven heroes taking a stand against systemic corruption, are sons of Terry Malloy from "On the Waterfront," aiming for clarity in a landscape of endless compromise and ambiguity.

It is instructive to look at "Network" alongside Kazan's "Face in the Crowd," from 1957, and Mr. Scorsese's "King of Comedy," released in 1983. All three films take up the vexing, evergreen problem of the media's power to shape and distort reality, and they offer progressively more dire diagnoses of the state of the collective psyche. In "Face" a populist demagogue named Lonesome Rhodes (Andy Griffith) is unleashed on the viewing public by cynical network executives, who quickly see the error of their ways and stuff their rabble-rousing genie back in the bottle before he can do too much damage. The self-correcting mechanisms of liberal institutions are shown to work in the end, and social responsibility prevails over baser instincts, something that happened a lot in the 1950s.

Not so much in the 1970s of "Network," when scruples are sacrificed for ratings and profits. But the scruples at least still register, even in defeat, and the idea of a morally consequential separation between truth and illusion is central to the film's structure. In "The King of Comedy," it has disappeared entirely, as the machinery of celebrity has swallowed up everything else.

But though it seemed, by the 1980s, to have collapsed entirely — and not only on movie screens — the liberal ethic Mr. Lumet represented has proved to have a long afterlife. And not only in his own subsequent films, a number of which (notably "Daniel" and "Running on Empty") deal with political disillusionment and failure. New York realism was revived in the 1980s and after by Spike Lee, whose debt to Mr. Lumet is most apparent in "Clockers," "Summer of Sam" and "The 25th Hour." And while ethically engaged, sprawling city dramas may be rarer on the big screen, they can still be found on television. "The Wire," with its complicated tableaus of commitment and corruption, and its inexhaustible fascination with men at work and with the flawed, vital institutions they work in, is perhaps the most powerful recent evidence that the wise, stubborn, angry humanism Mr. Lumet celebrated and exemplified is still alive.

— *By A. O. Scott*

(continued from page 394)

But Mr. Lumet's concerns could also range more broadly, to issues of national survival itself. One of the most sobering films of the cold war era was his 1964 adaptation of Eugene Burdick and Harvey Wheeler's novel, "Fail-Safe," a taut examination of the threat of accidental nuclear war, with Henry Fonda as the president of the United States and a young Larry Hagman as his Russian-speaking interpreter. The film concludes with a harrowing suggestion of an atomic blast on American soil, rendered as a series of glimpses of ordinary life — children playing, pigeons taking wing — simply stopping. The scenes are from the streets of New York.

Sidney Lumet was born on June 25, 1924, in Philadelphia to Baruch Lumet and Eugenia Wermus, both actors in Yiddish theater. His father was born in Poland and moved his family to New York when Sidney was a baby. By the time he was 4, Sidney was appearing onstage with his father, and he went on to make his Broadway debut in 1935 as a street kid in Sidney Kingsley's "Dead End." He appeared in several more Broadway shows, including Maxwell Anderson's "Journey to Jerusalem" in 1940, in which he played the young Jesus.

After wartime service as a radar technician in the Far East, Mr. Lumet returned to New York and started directing Off Broadway and in summer stock. His big break came in 1950, when he was hired by CBS and became a director on the television suspense series "Danger." Other programs followed, including the history series "You Are There."

His career soared in 1953, when he began directing original plays for dramatic series on CBS and NBC, including "Studio One," "Playhouse 90" and "Kraft Television Theater." He eventually added some 200 productions to his credits, many of them acclaimed and considered important to the early development of television. One highlight was a full-length production of Eugene O'Neill's play "The Iceman Cometh," with Jason Robards as the salesman Hickey.

He returned to the theater to direct Albert Camus's "Caligula," with Kenneth Haigh as the Roman emperor, and George Bernard Shaw's "Man and Superman," among other plays.

Some of Mr. Lumet's early films had their origin in the theater. He directed Anna Magnani and Marlon Brando in "The Fugitive Kind" (1960), an adaptation of Tennessee Williams's play "Orpheus Descending"; he traveled abroad to film part of Arthur Miller's "View From the Bridge" (1962) in Paris, with Raf Vallone, Maureen Stapleton and Carol Lawrence, completing the film on the Brooklyn waterfront; and he returned to the world of O'Neill to film "Long Day's Journey Into Night" (1962), with Katharine Hepburn and Ralph Richardson as the tormented Tyrones. His 1968 adaptation of Chekhov's "Sea Gull," however, was generally deemed uneven despite a stellar cast that included James Mason, Simone Signoret and Vanessa Redgrave.

A trainload of stars turned out for Mr. Lumet's 1974 adaptation of Agatha Christie's "Murder on the Orient Express," the project that took him abroad again, this time to Britain, France and Turkey, to film the famous whodunit in which the detective Hercule Poirot (Albert Finney)

ON LOCATION: Mr. Lumet, center, with Paul Newman, left, Lindsay Crouse, second from right, and an unidentified crew member on the set of "The Verdict," New York City, 1982.

must single out a murderer from a crowd of suspects that included Lauren Bacall, Ingrid Bergman, Sean Connery and John Gielgud.

There was a run of less-than-successful films, including "Running on Empty" (1988), with Judd Hirsch and Christine Lahti as '60s radicals still in hiding from the F.B.I. 20 years after participating in a bombing; the police drama "Q & A" (1990), with a screenplay by Mr. Lumet, about a racist New York detective (played by Nick Nolte); and "Critical Care" (1997), a satiric jab at the American health care system.

In 1995, Mr. Lumet published a well-received memoir, "Making Movies," in which he summed up his view of directorial style: "Good style, to me, is unseen style. It is style that is felt."

He returned to television in 2001 as executive producer, principal director and one of the writers of a new courtroom drama for cable television, "100 Centre Street" (the address of the Criminal Court Building in Lower Manhattan). The series, which ran for two seasons on A&E, had an ensemble cast, with Alan Arkin as an all-too-forgiving judge known as Let-'Em-Go Joe.

The director seemed immune to advancing age. Before long, he was behind the camera again. "Find Me Guilty" (2006), which starred Vin Diesel, was a freewheeling account of the events surrounding the federal prosecution of a notorious New Jersey crime family.

And he marked his 83rd year with the 2007 release of his last feature film, "Before the Devil Knows You're Dead," the bleakly riveting story of two brothers (Philip Seymour Hoffman and Ethan Hawke) propelled by greed into a relentless cycle of mayhem. The film drew raves.

Mr. Lumet's first three marriages — to the actress Rita Gam, Gloria Vanderbilt and Gail Jones, the daughter of Lena Horne — ended in divorce. He married Mary Gimbel in 1980. She survives him, as do two daughters (one is the screenwriter Jenny Lumet), a stepdaughter, a stepson, nine grandchildren and a great-granddaughter. The cause of death was lymphoma. Mr. Lumet also had a home in East Hampton, on Long Island.

Ms. Dargis called Mr. Lumet "one of the last of the great movie moralists" and "a leading purveyor of the social-issue movie." Yet Mr. Lumet said he was never a crusader for social change. "I don't think art changes anything," he said in The Times online interview.

So why make movies? he was asked.

"I do it because I like it," he replied, "and it's a wonderful way to spend your life."

— *By Robert Berkvist*

VIOLET COWDEN

A Band of Sisters Who Flew for Their Country

OCT. 1, 1916 - APRIL 10, 2011

THE PROBLEM WAS SIMPLE but would have disastrous consequences if left unsolved. The United States had entered World War II, and military aircraft were barreling off the assembly lines. But with many military pilots deployed overseas, or soon to be, there was no way to transport the planes from the factories to the airfields where they were urgently needed.

Then someone remembered an untapped source of aeronautic talent: the thousands of American women who were licensed pilots. And so, in 1942, the Women Airforce Service

Pilots — as the contingent of more than a thousand would be named — was born, freeing the men for service overseas.

Attached to the Army Air Forces, the WASPs, as they were known, were the first women to serve as United States military pilots. They performed duties formerly done by men: some ferried new planes to their destinations, others towed targets for aerial gunnery practice, still others were flight instructors.

By all accounts, the women did their jobs capably and ardently — until the men came home and suddenly the Army had no need of them.

Her plane once caught fire on landing; thinking quickly, Mrs. Cowden saved her important papers and her makeup.

Then, unable to work as peacetime pilots, they faded into the 1950s, receiving recognition as military veterans only decades after the war ended.

Violet Cowden, who died at 94 on April 10, was one of those women. In 1943 and 1944, assigned to the Army's Air Transport Command, she flew some of the country's most sophisticated planes, transporting them from factories to domestic airfields or to coastal debarkation points for shipment to foreign theaters.

She was the subject of a documentary, "Wings of Silver: The Vi Cowden Story," released in 2010.

A past president of the national WASP veterans' group, Mrs. Cowden was among about 200 WASPs (fewer than 300 are now living) presented in 2010 with the Congressional Gold Medal, one of the country's two highest civilian awards.

Mrs. Cowden, who flew a plane as recently as last year, lived in Huntington Beach, Calif. She died in nearby Newport Beach.

Ever since she was a child, watching hawks swoop over the family farm, Mrs. Cowden had yearned to fly. She was not quite sure how one went about it, until she discovered a marvelous thing called the airplane.

Violet Clara Thurn was born on Oct. 1, 1916, in a sod house in Bowdle, S.D. In 1936, she earned a teaching certificate from what was then the Spearfish Normal School, in Spearfish, S.D., and stayed in Spearfish to teach first grade. There, she rode her bicycle six miles each way to a local airfield for her first flying lessons. (She had no driver's license.)

She knew immediately that she had found her calling. "The air is such a comfortable place for me," Mrs. Cowden said in 2007 in an interview with the Betty H. Carter Women Veterans Historical Project at the University of North Carolina, Greensboro. "I feel so in oneness with life and with the world and everything when I'm in the air."

After Pearl Harbor was attacked, Mrs. Cowden, by then a licensed pilot, asked to join the Civil Air Patrol but got no reply. "Everybody was joining something," she said in the interview. "So I joined the Navy, because I liked their hats."

She soon heard about the Women's Flying Training Detachment, an early incarnation of the WASPs. Of the 25,000 women who applied, she was one of 1,830 accepted. She had lived for a week on a diet rich in bananas and malted milk to raise her weight from 92 pounds to 100, the required minimum.

She reported to Avenger Field in Sweetwater, Tex., then a place of dust, desolation and rattlesnakes, for six months of rigorous training.

The women banded together through shared ritual. "They'd have picnics in the sky," Mark C. Bonn, who with his wife, Christine, directed "Wings of Silver," said in an interview. "If there was a group of girls picking up two or three planes from the same factory, they would have their lunch on their long trip at the same time. And so they would talk on the radio. 'O.K., I'm having my apple.' 'I'm having my sandwich.'"

Because they were civil service employees and not military personnel, the WASPs had to pay for their own food, lodging and often capacious attire. There were no flight suits for

UNTIL THE MEN CAME HOME: Mrs. Cowden was one of the first women to serve as a United States military pilot. She called the P-51 Mustang, a single-seat fighter plane, "the love of my life."

women then, and Mrs. Cowden, barely more than 5 feet tall, was installed in a men's size 44 for the duration.

Mrs. Cowden, one of 1,074 women to complete training, was assigned to Love Field in Dallas. She logged hundreds of thousands of miles in a variety of planes, including the P-51 Mustang, the swift single-seat fighter she called "the love of my life."

She once delivered a P-51 to the Tuskegee Airmen, the black military squadron. (There were also black women who had graduated from the Tuskegee Institute's pilot training program; they were denied admission to the WASPs.)

Mrs. Cowden worked seven days a week, sleeping on commercial flights that ferried her to and from assignments. She flew in all weather, came down on runways without lights and sometimes took the controls of planes so fresh from the factory that they had never been tested. To fly such a plane, she often said, was like making footprints in soft virgin snow.

Her plane once caught fire on landing; thinking quickly, Mrs. Cowden saved her important papers and her makeup.

Thirty-eight WASPs died in accidents during training or while on duty; others were injured, some seriously.

By late 1944, male pilots began coming home, and they wanted their jobs back.

"We had defeated the Luftwaffe by then, and so our pilots were not dying at the rate that they had been," said Katherine Landdeck, a historian at Texas Woman's University who is an authority on the WASPs. "The whole purpose of the WASP program was to release male pilots for combat duty. By December of '44, the WASPs were no longer releasing them; they were replacing them. And that was the argument that was used against them."

That December, on a day Mrs. Cowden recalled as one of the worst in her life, the Army dissolved the WASPs.

Few airlines would hire a woman as a commercial pilot then. Mrs. Cowden went to work in New York in the only aviation job she could get — behind the ticket counter at Trans World Airlines. It was painful, she later said, to be so close to planes yet so far from the cockpit. She soon left and became a partner in a California ceramics studio, married and had a child. She let her pilot's license lapse, though friends who took her aloft over the years gladly ceded her the controls.

In 1977, President Jimmy Carter signed a bill granting the WASPs recognition as veterans, which allowed them limited benefits.

Mrs. Cowden is survived by a daughter, two sisters and three grandchildren. Her husband, Warren William Cowden, known as Scott, whom she married in 1955, died in 2009.

Though Mrs. Cowden and her colleagues were consigned to the recesses of history, during the war their work was considered so vital that the airlines were ordered to displace any passenger if a WASP needed to be shuttled to an assignment.

This status was brought home to Mrs. Cowden one day after a place was made for her on a commercial flight to Memphis. Disembarking, she faced a throng of women huddled on the tarmac, looking unaccountably disappointed.

Mrs. Cowden had bumped Frank Sinatra.

— *By Margalit Fox*

SIDNEY HARMAN

A Name in High-Fidelity, and Then Journalism

AUG. 4, 1918 - APRIL 12, 2011

Sidney Harman, an audio pioneer who built the first high-fidelity stereo receiver, dabbled in education and government, and made a late-in-life splash by acquiring an antiquated Newsweek magazine and wedding it with a sassy young Web site, The Daily Beast, died on April 12 in Washington. He was 92.

For most of his life, Mr. Harman was known as the scientist-businessman who co-founded Harman/Kardon in 1953 and made high-quality audio equipment for homes and businesses, and later navigational and other devices for cars. He made a fortune, estimated by Forbes at $500 million in 2010, and gave millions to education, the performing and fine arts and other philanthropies.

But Mr. Harman, who was married to former Representative Jane Harman, a nine-term California Democrat who lost a 1998 California gubernatorial primary race largely financed by him, was also a golfing, tennis-playing health enthusiast who leaped out of bed every morning to do calisthenics, a scholar of boundless energy and utopian ideas, and something of a Renaissance man.

He studied physics, engineering and social psychology; was a classical music fan and jazz aficionado; recited Shakespeare by heart; was a civil rights and antiwar activist; created programs to humanize the workplace; was the president of a Quaker college on Long Island; served as President Jimmy Carter's deputy secretary of commerce; published a memoir at 85; and was still active in business in his 90s.

In August 2010, two days before he turned 92, Mr. Harman, who had virtually no media experience, bought Newsweek from the Washington Post Company for a token $1 and some $47 million in liabilities. The Post had sought a deep-pocketed savior who might preserve Newsweek's staff and standards.

Founded in 1933 and acquired by the Post Company in 1961, Newsweek had long trailed Time magazine in circulation and revenue but was known for serious print journalism. But bled by an exodus of staff members, readers and advertisers and under pressures of recession and

Internet competition, the magazine had gone into a financial freefall, losing $30 million in 2009, and seemed rudderless and moribund.

After a shaky courtship, Mr. Harman and Barry Diller, The Daily Beast's owner, agreed to a merger, with Mr. Harman as executive chairman and Tina Brown of The Beast — and of The New Yorker and Vanity Fair before that — as its editor. The two-year-old Web site was also losing millions. Critics called it a noble but impractical venture. Mr. Harman regarded it as the capstone challenge of his diversified career.

His stamp can be seen in the magazine's pages, where a weekly column called "Connecting the Dots" was added at his suggestion, the name reflecting his view of a weekly news magazine's role.

But its attempt to regain readers and advertisers has been a struggle. Figures released in April 2011 by the Publishers Information Bureau showed that the number of advertising pages in Newsweek fell 31 percent compared with the same three months last year.

Mr. Diller said Mr. Harman's estate would assume control of his stake in the magazine.

"Three weeks ago, when he told me of his illness, he said he and his family wanted to continue as partners in Newsweek/Beast in all events," Mr. Diller said. "We will carry on, though we will greatly miss his passionate enthusiasm and belief in the venture."

Sidney Harman was born in Montreal on Aug. 4, 1918, and grew up in New York City, where his father worked at a hearing-aid company. The boy had a paper route and sold discarded magazines. In 1939 he graduated from a branch of City College that became Baruch College, earning a degree in physics. He found an engineering job with the David Bogen Company, a New York maker of loudspeakers. After Army service in 1944-45, he returned to the company and by the early 1950s was general manager.

At a time when sophisticated hi-fi radio required a tuner to capture signals, a pre-amplifier, a power amp and speakers, Mr. Harman and Bernard Kardon, Bogen's chief engineer, quit their jobs in 1953, put up $5,000 each and founded Harman/Kardon. It produced the first integrated hi-fi receiver, the Festival D1000.

It was hugely successful, and by 1956 the company was worth $600,000. Mr. Kardon retired, and in 1958 Mr. Harman created the first hi-fi stereo receiver, the Festival TA230. In later years, the company made speakers, amplifiers, noise-reduction devices, video and navigation equipment, voice-activated telephones, climate controls and home theater systems.

In the 1960s Mr. Harman was an active opponent of the Vietnam War, and for a year taught black pupils in Prince Edward County, Va., after public schools there were closed in a notorious effort to avoid desegregation. From 1968 to 1971 he was president of Friends World College, a Quaker institution in Suffolk County. In 1973 he earned a doctorate from the Cincinnati-based Union Institute and University.

In August 2010, two days before he turned 92, Mr. Harman, who had virtually no media experience, bought Newsweek from the Washington Post Company for a token $1 and some $47 million in liabilities.

In the early 1970s he created a program to provide employees at his Bolivar, Tenn., automotive parts plant with training, flexible hours and work assignments, stock ownership and other benefits that eased tensions with management and raised productivity. It was hailed as visionary and scorned as impractical. But President Carter was impressed, and made him deputy secretary of commerce. He served in 1977-78.

Mr. Harman sold his company to avoid conflicts of interest during his government service, and bought it back a few years later at a profit. Renamed Harman International Industries, with headquarters in Stamford, Conn., he took it public in 1986, was chief executive until 2007 and retired as chairman in 2008. He joined the University of Southern California in 2008 as a polymath professor, lecturing on architecture, medicine, law, economics and other subjects.

He donated $20 million for the Shakespeare Theater Company's Sidney Harman Hall in Washington, and was a trustee of the Aspen Institute, the California Institute of Technology, Freedom House, the Martin Luther King Center for Social Change, the Los Angeles Philharmonic and the National Symphony Orchestra.

Mr. Harman was the co-author, with the pollster Daniel Yankelovich, of "Starting With the People" (1988), an analysis of national policies through a prism of public values. He also wrote an autobiography, "Mind Your Own Business: A Maverick's Guide to Business Leadership and Life" (2003).

His first marriage, to the former Sylvia Stern, who is deceased, ended in divorce. He married the former Jane Lakes, who is 27 years his junior, in 1980. Besides Ms. Harman, he is survived by their two children, four children from his first marriage, two stepchildren and 10 grandchildren.

Mr. Harman's death was caused by complications of acute myeloid leukemia, according to a statement by the family that appeared on The Daily Beast. Family members said they learned of his illness only about a month ago.

"He's a man who needs a project," his daughter Barbara Harman, executive director of the Harman Family Foundation, said when he bought Newsweek. "He will die working — if he does die — and he'll love every minute of it, because he'll pick things to do that are worth doing."

— *By Robert D. McFadden*

ALBERT BACHMANN

A Cold War Warrior Who Was Ready for the Worst

NOV. 26, 1929 - APRIL 12, 2011

Albert Bachmann, Switzerland's least effective but most colorful spymaster, whose dread of a Soviet invasion led him to create a secret intelligence service and guerrilla force unknown to the Swiss government in the 1970s, died on April 12 in Cork, Ireland. He was 81.

Mr. Bachmann, who held the rank of colonel, brought dash and panache to Swiss spy craft in his relatively brief but highly eventful leadership of Swiss military intelligence. A Communist in his younger days, he became a hard-line cold warrior after the 1968 Soviet takeover of Czechoslovakia, which he regarded as the dress rehearsal for a full-scale invasion of Western Europe.

After being appointed to run Swiss intelligence in 1976, he created Project 26, a secret army of 2,000 resistance fighters trained to wage guerrilla warfare against Soviet troops in the event of an invasion.

To ensure the survival of the Swiss state, he bought Liss Ard, a 200-acre estate near Cork, to serve as a refuge and headquarters for a government in exile. In the basement of one of two Georgian houses on the estate he installed a vault for Switzerland's gold reserves.

Loyalists regarded Colonel Bachmann as a fearless visionary. Others agreed with the intelligence agent who dismissed his former boss as "a glorified Boy Scout who saw evil everywhere and believed that he alone possessed the absolute truth about national defense."

Colonel Bachmann came to grief after sending one of his operatives, a management consultant named Kurt Schilling, to spy on Austrian troops carrying out maneuvers near the town of St. Pölten in November 1979.

The need for cloak-and-dagger secrecy was unclear, since the Austrian government had invited observers from all over the Eastern bloc to watch the operations. Mr. Schilling, equipped with maps, binoculars and a notebook, nevertheless spent several days snooping around military barracks and command posts before the Austrian police pounced.

Called "the spy who came in from the Emmentaler," a reference to Switzerland's most famous cheese, Mr. Schilling was put on trial for espionage. His mission, he told the court, was to gauge the ability of the Austrian Army to resist a Soviet attack.

MR. PEEL: Colonel Bachmann used several code names during his tenure as an eccentric Swiss spymaster.

The affair proved deeply embarrassing to Switzerland, and Colonel Bachmann was suspended. Further investigation into his activities exposed Project 26 and related initiatives.

All were a complete surprise to the Swiss defense minister, Georges-André Chevallaz, who found them so outlandish that their architect was briefly suspected of being a double agent.

Colonel Bachmann was soon forced to resign, bringing down the curtain on one of the more intriguing chapters in the history of the cold war.

Project 26 lingered, under various names, until it was dissolved in 1990 after the Swiss government declared it to be a clandestine organization operating outside parliamentary or governmental control.

Albert Bachmann, known as Bert, was born on Nov. 26, 1929, in Albisrieden, now part of Zurich, where his father was a housepainter. He entered the printing trade and joined the Freie Jugend, the youth organization of the Swiss Labor Party, whose politics were communist.

After taking a sharp right turn politically, he performed his compulsory military service and found the army to his liking. He rose through the ranks of the intelligence service, despite his lack of formal education and polish. He was fond of saying that he was the only general staff officer with a mustache and a forearm tattoo.

In 1969 he created a stir as the principal author of "Civil Defense," a primer on popular resistance in case of invasion; 2.6 million copies were printed and distributed throughout Switzerland. Its red cover, and its identification of leftists and intellectuals as internal enemies, earned it sneering comparisons to Mao's Little Red Book.

Undeterred, he headed off on a secret mission of his own to Biafra, then struggling to secede from Nigeria. There, for obscure reasons, he operated under cover as an upper-class Englishman named Henry Peel, one of several colorful code names he favored in his spy work. To the German intelligence services, with whom the Swiss shared information, he was Black Hand.

After being promoted to colonel and named as chief of military intelligence, Colonel Bachmann assumed oversight of Bureau Ha, an unofficial intelligence service created during World War II, and Special Service D, a so-called stay-behind resistance force, similar to secret units created in many NATO countries, which was trained to harry an occupying army. It provided the inspiration for Project 26.

With energy and imagination — perhaps too much of the latter — Colonel Bachmann trained his special agents in the arts of bomb-making, sharpshooting, encryption, assassination and, in a nod to his onetime profession, the printing of pamphlets. Mountain guides were entrusted with the task of shepherding important officials across the Alps.

After being forced into retirement in 1980, Colonel Bachmann moved to Cork, where he dealt successfully in real estate.

"He was an amazing character with a great sense of humor — but a lot of people thought he was a retired banker and not an intelligence officer," a local resident told The Irish Independent.

— *By William Grimes*

WILLIAM A. RUSHER

Rallying Conservatives, No Matter Their Party

JULY 19, 1923 - APRIL 16, 2011

William A. Rusher, who advanced a rising conservative tide in America for more than 50 years as a political strategist, author, syndicated columnist and publisher of William F. Buckley Jr.'s bible of the right, National Review, died on April 16 in San Francisco. He was 87.

Like Mr. Buckley, the founding editor of National Review, Mr. Rusher championed postwar conservatism as a mainstream political movement, which first tasted national success in the Republican presidential nomination of Barry M. Goldwater in 1964 and fulfilled its dream with the election of Ronald Reagan as president in 1980.

A lawyer who helped lay the foundations for conservative ascendancy in the Republican Party, Mr. Rusher was a relentless spokesman for the cause: the author of five books, scores of articles and "The Conservative Advocate," a syndicated column published in newspapers across the country for 36 years. He lectured widely and debated opponents of the left and right on television and radio.

FROM THE RIGHT: Mr. Rusher sought a conservative alliance to replace the G.O.P.

While he never held public office, he entered the fray of several campaigns. He and two colleagues founded the draft-Goldwater movement in 1961. With other prominent conservatives, he opposed the re-election of Richard M. Nixon in 1972 because of the president's overtures to China. In 1976 he started a third party, which faltered, and four years later he became an adviser in Reagan's presidential campaign.

Mr. Rusher's 31-year tenure as publisher of National Review, from 1957 to 1988, paralleled the growth of mainstream conservatism. Founded in 1955 in small, cluttered, Dickensian offices in Manhattan, with a circulation of 16,000, the magazine rose by the 1980s to a pinnacle of influence, with 100,000 readers and Reagan, its ideological godchild, in the White House. Besides overseeing the magazine's business side, Mr. Rusher introduced his column in its pages in 1973.

His first major book, "The Making of the New Majority Party" (1975), was a manifesto for a conservative alliance to replace the Republican Party. Americans calling themselves conservatives were already a majority, he argued, but unaware of it, being politically independent or scattered in Republican and Democratic ranks: people who valued the work ethic, religion and patriotism and opposed Communism, higher taxes and government spending.

In an Op-Ed article for The New York Times in 1975, Mr. Rusher explained how it might work. "The only practical solution, therefore, is for conservative Republicans (broadly represented by Reagan) and conservative Democrats (most of whom have in the past supported Wallace)" — a reference to Gov. George C. Wallace of Alabama — "to join forces in a new majority party, designed to win both the presidency and Congress and replace the G.O.P. in toto as one of America's two major parties."

In 1976, putting his ideas into practice, Mr. Rusher and several colleagues founded the New Majority Party. But it collapsed that summer at a convention in Chicago after a rival group pushed through the presidential nomination of Lester G. Maddox, the former governor of Georgia and an avowed segregationist. Jimmy Carter, the Democrat and also a former Georgia governor, defeated President Gerald R. Ford, the Republican, in the general election.

A month after Reagan's election in 1980, National Review celebrated its 25th anniversary with a party. "I really think this is the watershed moment," Mr. Rusher said. "Conservatism is at the crossroads. And incidentally, our old enemy liberalism has died."

William Allen Rusher was born in Chicago on July 19, 1923, the son of Evan and Verna Self Rusher. His father, a Republican businessman, moved the family to the New York area when William was a boy. He attended school in Great Neck, on Long Island, and in New York City, graduated from Princeton in 1943, served in the Army Air Forces in India in World War II and earned a law degree at Harvard in 1948.

He worked at the New York law firm of Shearman, Sterling & Wright from 1948 to 1956, and was associate counsel of the internal security subcommittee of the United States Senate in 1956 and 1957. As the cold war developed, Mr. Rusher turned increasingly to conservative politics.

When he joined National Review as publisher, vice president and a director in 1957, the magazine was a small conservative ship in a sea of liberal journals. For years, it had deficits of $100,000 or more and was kept afloat largely by Mr. Buckley's earnings from speeches and television appearances.

David B. Frisk, author of the book "If Not Us, Who?: William Rusher, National Review, and the Conservative Movement," said Mr. Rusher's relationship with Mr. Buckley was close but complex. Beyond the business affairs of the magazine, the two often discussed strategies in the developing conservative movement, including Mr. Rusher's opposition to Nixon and his desire to break away from the Republican Party to form a national conservative party.

Mr. Rusher took active roles in the Young Americans for Freedom, founded in 1960 at Mr. Buckley's Connecticut estate, and the American Conservative Union, founded after Goldwater's landslide loss to President Lyndon B. Johnson in 1964. Both organizations promoted conservative ideas and candidates.

In his history, "The Rise of the Right" (1984), Mr. Rusher detailed efforts by conservatives like himself to recoup old and trusted American values, renew the spirit of free enterprise and capture the Republican Party for Goldwater and later the White House for Reagan.

"I do not think it an exaggeration to say that, without William Rusher, the conservative revival in America would not have taken place," Dr. Edward N. Peters, a Roman Catholic canon lawyer, wrote in a review for Reflections magazine. "Rusher has written an amazingly informative account of the return to right thought."

But writing in The New York Times Book Review, Lewis H. Lapham, the former editor of the liberal magazine Harper's, called the book self-serving. "All but singlehandedly, against some pretty heavy odds (i.e., the entire weight, trend and ethos of the 20th century), he rescued the United States of America from death by liberalism," Mr. Lapham wrote. "True, he had a little help from his friends, notably William F. Buckley, the editor of National Review, but mostly it was Bill Rusher."

Mr. Rusher, who never married, left no immediate survivors. He had been living in a retirement home in San Francisco since 2004.

Mr. Rusher joined the Claremont Institute, a conservative research organization in California, in 1989. He ended his syndicated column in 2009.

"Undoubtedly," he wrote in a farewell, "the most important single factor in the growth of conservatism has been the realization, on the part of individual conservatives, that their views were shared by others, and constituted collectively a formidable national influence."

— *By Robert D. McFadden*

MICHAEL SARRAZIN

The Leading Man as Antihero

MAY 22, 1940 - APRIL 17, 2011

Michael Sarrazin, who had a successful run in films of the late 1960s and '70s as an antiheroic leading man, especially in the Depression drama "They Shoot Horses, Don't They?," died on April 17 in Montreal. He was 70.

With his big, soulful eyes and sensitively handsome face, Mr. Sarrazin brought youthful innocence with a dash of countercultural rebelliousness to films like "The Flim-Flam Man" (1967), in which he played a reluctant apprentice to George C. Scott's grifter, and the 1973 television drama "Frankenstein: The True Story," in which he gave a Byronic performance as the monster.

He was in great demand in the 1970s. He played Paul Newman's misunderstood half-brother in "Sometimes a Great Notion" (1971), a pickpocket trainee in the James Coburn caper film "Harry in Your Pocket" (1973), and Barbra Streisand's cabdriver husband in the screwball farce "For Pete's Sake" (1974). He brought a brooding complexity to the title role of the horror film "The Reincarnation of Peter Proud" (1975).

But it was his performance in the 1969 film "They Shoot Horses, Don't They?," a grueling existentialist drama directed by Sydney Pollack, that established him as one of the era's more intriguing antiheroes. He played Robert Syverten, an aimless, unemployed film extra who enters a marathon dance contest with the equally desperate Gloria (Jane Fonda), hoping to win recognition and prize money. Instead, after days spent circling the dance floor, he ends up fatally shooting his partner in a twisted act of mercy.

"You could have paid me a dollar a week to work on that," Mr. Sarrazin told The Toronto Star in 1994. "It hits you bolt upright; I still get really intense when I watch it."

Jacques Michel André Sarrazin was born on May 22, 1940, in Quebec City and grew up in Montreal. After dropping out of high school he acted in theater and television in Montreal and Toronto — he played Romeo to Geneviève Bujold's Juliet in a live production on Canadian television — before being signed by Universal Studios in 1965.

He was assigned to the television series "The Virginian" and the TV movie "The Doomsday Flight" before making his big-screen debut in "Gunfight in Abilene" (1967), starring Bobby Darin and Leslie Nielsen.

"The Flim-Flam Man" put his career on the fast track. He played a drifting Malibu surfer in "The Sweet Ride" (1968) opposite Jacqueline Bisset, with whom he entered into a long romantic relationship, and a raw Confederate recruit (with James Caan) in "Journey to Shiloh"

(1968), before being offered the role of Joe Buck in "Midnight Cowboy."

Universal refused to let him take the role, which went to Jon Voight, but tried to make amends by steering him to Mr. Pollack and "They Shoot Horses." The experience was every bit as demanding off screen as on.

"We stayed up around the clock for three or four days," Mr. Sarrazin told The Toronto Star, adding that the director demanded that the actors remain in character. "Pollack said we should work until signs of exhaustion," he said. "Fights would break out among the men; women started crying. I'd get into terrible fights with Bruce Dern."

'70S SENSITIVITY: Mr. Sarrazin combined youthful innocence and rebelliousness.

His career waned after the mid-1970s and "The Gumball Rally" (1976), his last prominent role. In 1993 he took a French-speaking role in the Canadian comedy "La Florida," about a Quebec family trying to run a shabby motel in Hollywood, Fla. The film was a huge hit in Quebec, and as Romeo Laflamme, an-over-the-hill Canadian crooner and ladies' man, Mr. Sarrazin became a cult figure in Montreal, where he returned to live in his 60s.

Mr. Sarrazin is survived by a brother, a sister and two daughters. He died of cancer, his agent, Michael Oscars, said.

— *By William Grimes*

APR

WILLIAM DONALD SCHAEFER

The Mayor of Maryland

NOV. 2, 1921 - APRIL 18, 2011

William Donald Schaefer, a political showman who captivated voters and infuriated critics for more than three decades as the mayor who rejuvenated decaying Baltimore and then as Maryland's governor and comptroller, died on April 18 at a retirement home in Catonsville, Md. He was 89.

New York had its Fiorello H. La Guardia. Chicago had its Daleys. And Baltimore had William Donald Schaefer: the name on park benches, garbage trucks, office buildings, construction sites, horse races at Pimlico — and on the psyche of Baltimoreans in the 1970s and '80s. It was a kind of anticlimax when he became governor: they called him the mayor of Maryland.

Mr. Schaefer, a Democrat who steamrolled his opponents with up to 94 percent of the ballots, had one of the longest runs in American politics. After 16 years as a city councilman, he won four terms as mayor, from 1971 to 1987; two terms as governor, from 1987 to 1995; and two terms as state comptroller, from 1999 to 2007. His defeat in a 2006 bid for re-election was his first in more than a half-century.

"Bawlamer," as natives call it, was a seedy, shot-and-a-beer factory town when he became mayor. There had been riots in the late 1960s, and residents and businesses were leaving. Its 18th-century core was a shambles of rotting piers and dilapidated warehouses. Gritty row houses and run-down tenements lined the inner-city streets. Neighborhoods ached with poverty, unemployment, drugs and crime.

His methods were unorthodox. He sold 500 abandoned buildings for $1 apiece to urban homesteaders and hundreds of commercial shells for $100 each to businessmen. He twisted bureaucratic arms to get development projects moving. He badgered government authorities for housing and transportation money, solicited private donations, lured new businesses with concessions and enlisted world-class architects.

POLITICAL SHOWMAN: Mr. Schaefer, pictured during his 1983 re-election campaign, captivated voters.

He demolished and rebuilt whole neighborhoods. He had city crews salvage the lintels, fireplaces and marble from derelict buildings and sold them for restoration money. He pushed summer festivals and community theaters. He jawboned professional sports teams to stay put, or come to town. He drove around at night looking for potholes, trash, troublemakers and drug pushers, and got things done.

By the end of his tenure at City Hall, Mr. Schaefer was being hailed for transforming what was once the United States' eighth-largest city into a model of urban renaissance and national tourism. There were new businesses, parks, auditoriums, expressways and transit lines, a new skyline of hotels and office towers, a new convention center and a 28-story pentagonal World Trade Center designed by I. M. Pei.

The centerpiece was Mr. Schaefer's signature Harborplace, a glass waterfront pavilion of restaurants and shops by James Rouse, the developer of New York's South Street Seaport and Boston's Faneuil Hall Marketplace. It had cobblestone walks, a National Aquarium and, on the water, sailboats, a historic frigate, a vintage submarine and a Chesapeake Bay skipjack. It had 18 million visitors its first year, 1980-81.

The transformation was hardly complete. The city's economy and image improved, but critics said that the lives of many citizens had not, that schools had declined, and that poverty, crime, unemployment and drugs had not been subdued. The mayor was widely denigrated as a bully who favored business and promoted himself with clownish gimmicks. (When the aquarium was not finished on time, he jumped as promised into the seal pool wearing a striped Victorian swimsuit and clutching a rubber ducky.)

But defenders insisted that his improvements were substantive and had brought a much-needed sense of pride. When he became governor in 1987, The Baltimore Sun editorialized that Mr. Schaefer had "changed the way the city felt about itself."

William Donald Schaefer was born in Baltimore on Nov. 2, 1921, the son of William Henry and Tululu Irene Skipper Schaefer. He attended public schools and graduated from Baltimore City College in 1939 and the University of Baltimore Law School in 1942. He joined the Army in World War II, became an officer and supervised hospitals in England and Europe.

He practiced real estate law in Baltimore after the war and joined citizens' groups focused on housing and city planning. He was portly, with a long face and solemn eyes, and painfully shy as a young man. He never married and lived most of his life with his mother, until her death in 1983, in two plain Baltimore row houses. After he became governor at 65, his friend since childhood, Hilda Mae Snoops, served as his official hostess in the governor's mansion in Annapolis. She died in 1999.

After two unsuccessful races in the early 1950s, Mr. Schaefer finally won a seat on the City Council in 1955, and he became known as a tireless civic leader as he worked his way up to the council presidency. In a city of 900,000, where blacks were half the population and Democrats outnumbered Republicans 5 to 1, he easily won the mayoral election in 1971, and was soon embarked on his mission to resurrect Baltimore.

His re-election totals ("Vote for Baltimore") in 1975, 1979 and 1983 all exceeded 85 percent. He won the governorship in 1986 with 82 percent of the vote, the biggest landslide ever in a contested statewide race in Maryland, and was re-elected in 1990 with 60 percent. In politics, he used all three of his names, and they were up everywhere, including Pimlico Race Course, where the annual William Donald Schaefer Handicap was inaugurated in 1994.

As governor, he overhauled the state's legal code and was credited with improving education, social programs, transportation and efforts to clean up pollution in Chesapeake Bay. He saw the completion of the publicly financed Oriole Park at Camden Yards in 1992, a project he had pushed as mayor. But he also ignited controversy by commuting the sentences of eight battered women who had killed or assaulted their mates, and suggesting that contraceptives be given to women on welfare and vasectomies to men leaving prison.

Limited to two terms as governor, he joined a Baltimore law firm and held a chair named for him at the University of Maryland. In 1998, after three years out of politics, he won the comptroller's job. His two terms as chief financial officer were relatively unremarkable. But he was in the news for feuding with Gov. Parris N. Glendening, a fellow Democrat, and for criticizing immigrants who could not speak English, saying AIDS victims "brought it on themselves," and ostentatiously ogling a woman at a public meeting.

When he lost his re-election bid in 2006, Mr. Schaefer was asked how he would like to be remembered. "There are two words," he said. "'He cared.' People mock me and make fun of it. But it's the truth."

— *By Robert D. McFadden*

GRETE WAITZ

The Marathon Runner Who Ruled New York

OCT. 1, 1953 - APRIL 19, 2011

GRETE WAITZ, the Norwegian schoolteacher who won more New York City Marathons than anyone else — nine — and whose grace as a champion made her a role model for young runners, especially women, died on April 19 in Oslo. She was 57.

Waitz died after a struggle with cancer — she never revealed what kind — which was diagnosed in 2005. As she underwent treatment, she started a foundation to support cancer patients and encourage them to embrace physical fitness.

In 1991, Runner's World magazine named Waitz the female runner of the quarter-century; some considered her the pre-eminent female distance runner in history. She twice set the world record at 3,000 meters, and she set records at distances of 8 kilometers, 10 kilometers, 15 kilometers and 10 miles.

But it was in the marathon, a 26.2-mile symbol of human endurance, that Waitz distinguished herself most, setting a world record of 2 hours 32 minutes 30 seconds the first time she ran one, in New York in 1978, and then lowering the world standard three more times. In addition to her New York City victories, Waitz won the London Marathon twice, the Stockholm Marathon and the world championship marathon in 1983.

"She is our sport's towering legend," said Mary Wittenberg, the president of the New York Road Runners. "I believe not only in New York, but around the world, marathoning is what it is today because of Grete. She was the first big time female track runner to step up to the marathon and change the whole sport."

Grete Waitz (pronounced GREH-tuh VITES) was not simply a champion; she was also something of a pioneer. At the time of her first New York victory, women's distance running was a novelty. Fewer than 11 percent of the entrants — 938 out of 8,937 — in the 1978 New York marathon were women. (In 2010, almost 36 percent were — 16,253 of 45,350.) And the women's marathon would not be added to the Olympics until the 1984 Summer Games in Los Angeles, where Waitz finished second to Joan Benoit Samuelson.

"I lost a mentor and a role model," Samuelson, 53, said the day Waitz died, a day after Samuelson ran the Boston Marathon in 2:51:29.

"What will endure forever is that she was able to balance a competitive career with the most gracious lifestyle, and a character that emanated good will," Samuelson said.

Remarkably, Waitz, a champion track runner, ran her first marathon as a lark, with the encouragement of her husband, Jack Waitz, who was also her coach. He had told her that a trip to New York would be like a second honeymoon for them. Even in training she had never run more than 13 miles, and the science of the sport was young enough that her dinner the night before the race included shrimp cocktail and filet mignon, hardly the load of carbohydrates that even today's rankest amateurs know to consume. As she recalled in interviews, the last 10 miles of the race were agony, so much so that when she crossed the finish line, she tore off her shoes and flung them at her husband in anger.

"I'll never do this stupid thing again!" she yelled.

But in fact she was hooked. The next year, she finished the race in 2:27:33, beating her record by almost five minutes and becoming the first woman officially to run a marathon faster than two and a half hours. Her legend was assured, and the image of her on the road — small and slight, a quick, efficient stride, her pigtails slicing back and forth — became familiar to television audiences and the thousands of fans lining the marathon route.

A GRACEFUL CHAMPION: Waitz breaking the world record, one she set herself, in the 1980 New York City Marathon.

In Norway, her New York victories made her a national hero; a statue of her stands outside Bislett Stadium, an international sports arena in Oslo, and her likeness

NORIO OHGA

At Sony, American Culture Met Japanese Know-How

JAN. 29, 1930 - APRIL 23, 2011

NORIO OHGA, a onetime opera singer who plunged into consumer electronics, shaped the development of the compact disc and pushed Sony to branch out and capitalize on American entertainment, died on April 23 in Tokyo. He was 81.

Mr. Ohga, who rose to chairman and chief executive of the Sony Corporation, was the driving force behind Sony's move beyond sleek consumer electronics gear, its stronghold, and into music and movies. The biggest steps came when Sony bought CBS Records for $2 billion in 1988 and Columbia Pictures for $3.4 billion a year later.

At the time, when Japan Inc. seemed unstoppable, those acquisitions, along with a Japanese real estate company's purchase of most of Rockefeller Center, were symbols of Japan's rising economic power. There was worried talk of the Japanese commercial "invasion" and the loss of American "cultural assets."

But to Mr. Ohga, the goal was a kind of industrial synthesis, marrying Sony's wizardry in electronics with the West's talent in entertainment. In a statement, Howard Stringer, the current chief executive of Sony, said it was Mr. Ohga's vision that drove "Sony's evolution beyond audio and video products into music, movies and game, and subsequent transformation into a global entertainment leader."

Still, Mr. Ohga wanted to do more than expand Sony's corporate empire. In his view, linking electronics and entertainment would increase the value of each and insure a lucrative future for Sony. "Hardware and software are two wheels on a car," he said over the years.

There were good years in Sony's media businesses. But the real payoff from the electronics hardware and the entertainment software, each theoretically lifting the sales of the other, proved elusive. When Mr. Ohga spoke of software, industry analysts say, he was thinking of the kind that comes from Hollywood, not Silicon Valley.

The vision Mr. Ohga championed, those analysts say, has come to fruition at Apple, in a different guise. Apple, they note, has combined beautifully designed devices, like iPods and iPhones, with software for making media easy to consume and buy. Apple does not own music companies or movie studios, but it controls an online marketplace where media are purchased.

"Sony was a great product company, and Ohga made it better," said Michael A. Cusumano, a professor at the Sloan School of Management at the Massachusetts Institute of Technology. "But Sony did not really get software or the Internet. That wasn't Ohga's domain."

Born on Jan. 29, 1930, in Numazu, 80 miles west of Tokyo, Norio Ohga was the son of a wealthy lumber trader. As a child he had pleurisy, an inflammation in the chest, which exempted him during the war years from working at military factories, as many Japanese youths did. Instead, he practiced the piano and took singing lessons.

"By the time I was 18, I knew I wanted to be a vocalist," Mr. Ohga told The New York Times in 1990. "So just after the war, I had to come to Tokyo."

Mr. Ohga enrolled in the Tokyo National University of Fine Arts and Music, where he demonstrated a strong voice. He also developed strong opinions about a tape recording device that had just been introduced by the company that would become Sony. Mr. Ohga wrote a letter to Sony's co-founder, Akio Morita, detailing the machine's shortcomings for professional musicians and singers.

Mr. Morita, fascinated by this aspiring opera singer's technical knowledge, met with him and hired him as a part-time consultant. In 1954, Mr. Ohga left for West Germany to study music and to start a professional singing career that led to performances throughout Europe and Japan. Yet Mr. Morita kept Mr. Ohga on the payroll and stayed in touch.

In 1957, when Mr. Ohga married Midori Matsubara, a pianist he had met in Germany, Mr. Morita and Sony's elder co-founder, Masaru Ibuka, attended the wedding.

Mr. Ohga eventually surrendered to Mr. Morita's persistence. He joined Sony as a full-time employee in 1959.

Within a few years, Mr. Ohga was placed in charge of the company's design center. "The sleek, matte black finishes and other touches that would make products 'Sony looking' were largely his doing, his taste," said John Nathan, a professor of Japanese studies at the University of California, Santa Barbara, and the author of "Sony: The Private Life" (1999).

Mr. Ohga was also given sway over advertising, branding and even product development. As a rising young executive, he was imposing: tanned, meticulously dressed, imperious. He was also a skilled jet pilot.

In the late 1970s, Sony and Philips demonstrated early compact discs, but the standards for the emerging technology were still in flux. Mr. Ohga worked with Sony engineers and traveled to the Philips laboratory in the Netherlands, pushing for a larger CD format with longer playing time. He insisted on a recording capacity of 75 minutes, so that listeners could enjoy all of Beethoven's Ninth Symphony without interruption.

Sony introduced the first compact disc as a product in 1982. It would change the way people listen to music.

In Mr. Ohga's design philosophy, the miniaturization of electronics was to make devices not merely smaller but also more intimate, affording one-to-one relationships between people and machines. It was the theory behind the Walkman, introduced in 1979, and other Sony successes.

Electronic games held that kind of interactive potential. Mr. Ohga championed the development of the Sony PlayStation video game player, a new product category, which was introduced in 1994.

He became president of Sony in 1982, chief executive in 1989 and chairman in 1994. A year later, he declared that his successor would be Nobuyuki Idei, plucked from relative obscurity in the management ranks. In 1999, Mr. Idei became chief executive while Mr. Ohga stayed on as chairman until 2000. Mr. Idei expanded on Mr. Ohga's vision of combining electronics and media, but Sony struggled under him. In 2005, he was replaced by Mr. Stringer.

Mr. Ohga is survived by his wife, Midori.

Mr. Ohga would sometimes profess his desire to leave the executive suite and return to music. He never did, but owning a major music company had its privileges, including the

JAPAN INC.: Mr. Ohga in front of a portrait of himself and Sony founders Akio Morita and Masaru Ibuka.

chance to take the baton as the guest conductor of symphony orchestras.

In a review of Mr. Ohga's performance at Avery Fisher Hall in 1993, Bernard Holland wrote in The Times that Mr. Ohga had "a dignified and graceful presence at the podium." The musicians played beautifully, it seemed, even if the conductor could not always keep up.

"The Met players," Mr. Holland wrote, "seemed genuinely to like Mr. Ohga and did their best to take care of him."

— *By Steve Lohr*

MADAME NHU

'The Dragon Lady' of South Vietnam

AUG. 22, 1924 - APRIL 24, 2011

MADAME NHU, who as the glamorous official hostess in South Vietnam's presidential palace became a politically powerful and often harshly outspoken figure in the early years of the Vietnam War, died on April 24 in Rome, where she had been living. She was 86 and had spent the last four decades in Rome and southern France. Her sister, Lechi Oggeri, confirmed her death.

Her parents named her Tran Le Xuan, or "Beautiful Spring." As the official hostess to the unmarried president of South Vietnam, her brother-in-law, she was formally known as Madame Ngo Dinh Nhu. But to the American journalists, diplomats and soldiers caught up in the intrigues of Saigon in the early 1960s, she was "the Dragon Lady," a symbol of everything that was wrong with the American effort to save her country from Communism.

In those years, before the United States deepened its military involvement in the war, Madame Nhu thrived in the eye of her country's gathering storm as the wife of Ngo Dinh Nhu, the younger brother and chief political adviser to Ngo Dinh Diem, the president of South Vietnam from 1955 until 1963.

While her husband controlled the secret police and special forces, Madame Nhu acted as a forceful counterweight to the diffident president, badgering Diem's aides, allies and critics with unwelcome advice, public threats and subtle manipulations. Then, after both men were killed in a military coup mounted with the tacit support of the United States, she slipped into obscurity.

In her years in the spotlight, when she was in her 30s, she was beautiful, well coiffed and petite. She made the form-fitting ao dai her signature outfit, modifying the national dress with a deep neckline. Whether giving a speech, receiving diplomats or reviewing members of her paramilitary force of 25,00[illegible] women, she drew photographers like a m[illegible]gnet. But it was her impolitic penchant for [illegible]ying exactly what she thought that drew wor[illegible] attention.

When, during Diem[illegible] early days in power, she heard that the h[illegible]d of the army, Gen. Nguyen Van Hinh, w[illegible] bragging that he would overthrow the [illegible]ident and make her his mistress, she c[illegible]nted him at a Saigon party. "You are n[illegible]going to overthrow this government be[illegible]ou don't have the guts," Time magazi[illegible]ed her as telling the startled general. "A[illegible]u do overthrow it, you will never hav[illegible]cause I will claw your throat out first[illegible]

[illegible]ity for intrigue was boundless," H[illegible]chnau wrote in "Once Upon a Wi[illegible]: Young War Correspondents and D[illegible] the Early Vietnam Battles" (1995). So was her hatred of the American press.

"Madame Nhu looked and acted like the diabolical femme fatale in the popular comic strip of the day, 'Terry and the Pirates,'" Mr. Prochnau wrote. "Americans gave her the comic-strip character's name: the Dragon Lady."

In the pivotal year of 1963, as the war with the North worsened, discontent among the South's Buddhist majority over official corruption and failed land reform efforts fueled protests that culminated in the public self-immolations of several Buddhist monks. Shocking images of the fiery suicides raised the pressure on Diem, as did Madame Nhu's well-publicized reaction. She referred to the suicides as "barbecues" and told reporters, "Let them burn and we shall clap our hands."

GLAMOUR AND GUNS: As official hostess, Madame Nhu was anything but diplomatic.

Tran Le Xuan was born on Aug. 22, 1924, the younger daughter of Nam Tran Chuong, herself the daughter of an imperial Vietnamese princess, and Tran Van Chuong, a patrician lawyer who later became Diem's ambassador to Washington. As a willful girl, she bullied her younger brother, Khiem Van Tran, and was more devoted to the piano and the ballet than to her studies.

She later resisted any arranged marriage, choosing in 1943 to wed one of her mother's friends, Ngo Dinh Nhu. Fifteen years her senior, he was from a prominent Hue family of Roman Catholics who opposed both French colonial rule and the Communist rebels. Tran Le Xuan, raised a Buddhist, embraced her new family's faith as well [illegible]s politics.

As World War II [illegible]d, Vietnam's battle for independence intensif[illegible] [illegible]n 1946, Communist troops overran Hue, ta[illegible] prisoner Madame Nhu, her infant daughte[illegible] [illegible]r aging mother-in-law. They were held [illegible] months in a remote village with little f[illegible] no comforts before being freed by the [illegible]g French. After she was reunited with [illegible]band, the family lived quietly for the next few years, an interlude that Madame Nhu would later refer to as her "happy time." She and her husband would eventually have four children, two boys and two girls.

In 1955, Diem became president of the newly independent South Vietnam, his authority menaced by private armies, gangsters and disloyal officers like General Hinh. Madame Nhu publicly urged Diem to act. This only embarrassed him, and he exiled her to a convent in Hong Kong. Then he reconsidered, took her advice, smashed his opponents and forced Hinh into exile.

Madame Nhu returned, complaining that life in the convent had been "just like the Middle Ages." But then, so was the lot of most Vietnamese women. After winning a seat in the National Assembly in 1956, Madame Nhu pushed through measures that increased women's rights. She also orchestrated government moves to ban contraceptives and abortion, outlaw adultery, forbid divorce and close opium dens and brothels. "Society," she declared, "cannot sacrifice morality and legality for a few wild couples."

Meanwhile, she kept a tight emotional hold on the president. According to a C.I.A. report, Diem came to think of his sister-in-law like a spouse. She "relieves his tension, argues with him, needles him, and, like a Vietnamese wife, is dominant in the household," the report said. It also said that their relationship was definitely not sexual. When Diem, who was notoriously prudish, once questioned the modesty of Madame Nhu's low-cut dress, she was said to have snapped back: "It's not your neck that sticks out, it's mine. So shut up."

In fact, both their lives were on the line. In 1962, renegade Vietnamese Air Force pilots bombed and strafed the presidential palace. Diem was not hurt. Madame Nhu fell through a bomb hole in her bedroom to the basement two floors below, suffering cuts and bruises.

Vietnamese officers were judged by their loyalty to Diem and Nhu, who kept their best troops close to Saigon, to the exasperation of the Americans. As Communist strength grew, the South's internal stresses mounted. Diem sought compromise with dissidents, but he was undercut by the Nhus. In August 1963, thousands of Buddhists were arrested and interned. In Washington, Madame Nhu's father declared that Diem's government had done more damage than even the Communists and resigned as ambassador; her mother, South Vietnam's observer at the United Nations, also quit.

That fall, Madame Nhu went on an American speaking tour, criticizing Diem's critics as soft on communism. She was in Los Angeles on Nov. 1 when news flashed that Diem and her husband had been shot to death in a coup. "The deaths were murders," she told reporters, "either with the official or unofficial blessing of the American government."

Refused permission to return to Vietnam, she and her children moved to Rome to be near her brother-in-law, Archbishop Ngo Dinh Thuc. In July 1966, in a vehemently anti-American interview with a French journalist, she expressed sympathy for the Vietnamese Communists and declared that America preaches "the liberty of the jungle."

In 1967, her eldest daughter, Le Thuy, was killed in an automobile accident in France. In 1986, her parents were found strangled in their Washington home. Her brother, Khiem, was charged in the killings, motivated, according to the authorities, by the fact that he had been disinherited. In 1993, after seven years in a mental hospital, he was declared incompetent but harmless and released.

As time passed, Madame Nhu declined to be interviewed, but in November 1986 she agreed to answer questions in an exchange of letters with The New York Times. In these statements she continued to blame the United States for the fall of South Vietnam and for her brother's arrest. Asked to describe her daily life, she wrote, "Outer life such as writing and reading has never seemed interesting enough to be talked about, while inner life, more than a secret, is a mystery that cannot be so easily disclosed."

— By Joseph R. Gregory

POLY STYRENE

Marianne Elliot-Said Gave Punk a Day-Glo Jolt

JULY 3, 1957 - APRIL 25, 2011

Marianne Elliot-Said, who, as Poly Styrene, the pioneering, braces-wearing frontwoman of the 1970s British band X-Ray Spex, made a place for feminine brashness in punk, died on April 25 in East Sussex, England. She was 53.

She had been treated for cancer at a hospice near her home in St. Leonards-on-Sea, in the south of England.

Ms. Elliot-Said (pronounced sah-EED), the daughter of a Somali father and a British mother who raised her alone, began performing as a free-spirited teenager, leaving home at 15 and ending up in London, where she studied to be an opera singer. In 1976 she released a pop-reggae single under the name Mari Elliot on the GTO label.

But after stumbling on a performance by the Sex Pistols, she was inspired to place an ad in a British music magazine, searching for "young punx who want to stick it together."

After a handful of rehearsals, X-Ray Spex — whose early lineup included Jak Airport, Paul Dean, Rudi Thomson, B P Hurding and Lora Logic — became fixtures on the 1977 London music scene. They performed in Chelsea and at the Roxy, the Covent Garden club that served as a punk incubator, and they added a new instrument, the saxophone, to the chopping guitars and brazen lyrics of the genre.

BRASH: As Poly Styrene, Ms. Elliot-Said, shown in 1977, inspired future female rockers.

The original group released just one album, "Germ Free Adolescents," in 1978, but it became a punk classic, summing up the era's "sass and adrenaline," as Jon Pareles wrote in The New York Times in 2006, reviewing a boxed set of the group's music.

X-Ray Spex toured abroad, playing in Los Angeles and at CBGB in New York, cross-pollinating with acts like Blondie and Richard Hell of the Voidoids. (For the album and the tour, Rudi Thomson replaced Lora Logic, born Susan Whitby and still a schoolgirl, on saxophone.) Ms. Elliot-Said wrote lyrics questioning social mores, commercialism and conformism and, as a boldly styled, biracial young band leader, lived up to them.

As a performer, Ms. Elliot-Said was a rare combination of taunting and cheerful. Dressed in Day-Glo colors — the album cover of "Germ Free Adolescents" has the band in pink, acid green and bright yellow — and bouncing unself-consciously around the stage, she inspired other female musicians, prefiguring movements like riot grrrl.

"Some people think little girls should be seen and not heard," she shouted at the start of X-Ray Spex's best-known anthem, whose punchy title and chorus begins "Oh, Bondage!" and gets vulgar from there. The song, she said later, was inspired partly by Vivienne Westwood's 1970s bondage fashion. But it was her styling that made it stand out.

Poly Styrene's voice on that song "was the most exhilarating voice I ever heard — it was all body," said Kim Gordon of Sonic Youth.

Kathleen Hanna, the riot grrrl progenitor and leader of the bands Bikini Kill and Le Tigre, is often compared to Ms. Elliot-Said musically, but she said she felt unworthy of the comparison. "Poly lit the way for me as a female singer who wanted to sing about ideas," Ms. Hanna wrote on her blog, adding, "Her lyrics influenced everyone I know who makes music."

After X-Ray Spex broke up in 1979, Ms. Elliot-Said retreated from the spotlight, releasing music only sporadically. She joined the Hare Krishna movement. She later received a diagnosis of bipolar disorder.

Though a second X-Ray Spex record, "Conscious Consumer," released in 2005, was not well received, reunion concerts in 1991 and 2008 were. After the second concert, Ms. Elliot-Said began working on a solo album, "Generation Indigo," her first new work in seven years. It was released in March.

Marianne Elliot-Said was born on July 3, 1957, in a London suburb. She is survived by her daughter, Celeste Bell-Dos Santos, who leads the Spanish band Debutant Disco; her mother; a brother; and a sister.

Though in a recent interview Ms. Elliot-Said said she would like to be remembered for something "more spiritual" than her early punk efforts, she was aware of the impact she had on music.

"It's worked out fine," she said in 2008, speaking to the British newspaper The Independent. "I feel better for having been onstage, having been told I never could. I'm starting to think, maybe what I did then is working. Oh, I didn't waste my time. My youth wasn't misspent!"

— *By Melena Ryzik*

JOE PERRY

A Black Star When Football Was Mostly White

JAN. 22, 1927 - APRIL 25, 2011

JOE PERRY, the San Francisco 49ers Hall of Fame fullback who was one of the first black stars in modern professional football, died on April 25 in Tempe, Ariz. He was 84.

Perry, who lived in Chandler, Ariz., had been receiving financial assistance under a National Football League benefits plan aiding former players with dementia, which he had had for 10 years. His wife, Donna, said his physician believed that the dementia was caused by football concussions. She said his brain would be donated to a Boston University facility researching that issue.

Perry, one of pro football's top runners in the decade after World War II, was the first N.F.L. player to rush for more than 1,000 yards in two consecutive seasons, achieving the milestone in 1953 and '54, and he was voted to the all-N.F.L. team in both seasons. He was a three-time Pro Bowl player.

In the mid-1950s, Perry starred in what became known as the Million Dollar Backfield, teaming with Y. A. Tittle at quarterback and Hugh McElhenny and John Henry Johnson at halfback, all of them future Hall of Famers. Perry was inducted into the Pro Football Hall of Fame in Canton, Ohio, in 1969.

Perry was smallish for a fullback at 6 feet and 200 pounds, but he drew on the speed that brought him the nickname the Jet and a knack for finding holes in the defensive line.

"If you saw a hole, you take it," Perry once said, describing his running style. "If you didn't, you kept moving until you did. You run with instinct."

Fletcher Joe Perry was born on Jan. 22, 1927, in Stephens, Ark., and moved with his family to the Los Angeles area as a youngster. His heroes were U.C.L.A.'s black football stars Kenny Washington, Woody Strode and Jackie Robinson, who would later break baseball's color barrier.

Perry played football at Compton Junior College in the Los Angeles area in 1944, then joined the Navy. He was spotted by the 49ers while playing football for the Alameda Naval Air Station in the Bay Area.

Perry joined the 49ers in 1948, their third season in the All-America Football Conference, becoming the team's first black player. Washington and Strode had been signed by the N.F.L.'s Los Angeles Rams two years earlier, and the Cleveland Browns, who won the All-America Football Conference championship in each of its four seasons, featured the black stars Marion Motley and Bill Willis. But there were few other black players in pro football in the 1940s.

Perry recalled how his teammates, including those from the South, provided strong support from the outset.

"If somebody on the other team ever got any idea he wanted to start something, he had to mess with our whole team," Perry told Andy Piascik in "Gridiron Gauntlet" (2009), an oral history of pioneering black players.

But he had been ready to fight back on his own if necessary. "You had two or three bigots on every team, so you heard stuff just about every game," he recalled. "I could take anything they had to say, but if they had ever put their hands on me like they wanted to fight, that would have been something else."

Perry averaged 7.3 yards a carry and ran for 10 touchdowns as a rookie, when he played with the future Hall of Fame quarterback Frankie Albert.

In one game, as Perry remembered it, he had twice burst past Albert as he tried to hand him the football for a play up the middle. "He said, 'Joe, you're like a jet coming through there.' From then on, for as long as I played, I was known as the Jet."

'LIKE A JET': Perry was the first N.F.L. player to rush for more than 1,000 yards in two consecutive seasons.

The 49ers joined the N.F.L. in 1950, after the All-America Football Conference went out of business, and Perry soon made his mark facing pro football's best-known players. He gained 1,018 yards in 1953 and 1,049 yards in 1954 (averaging 6.1 yards a carry) in 12-game seasons. But the 49ers never made it to the N.F.L. championship game in his years with them, coming closest in 1957, when they were beaten by the Detroit Lions in a playoff for the Western Conference title.

Perry was traded to the Baltimore Colts before the 1961 season, played two seasons for them, then returned to the 49ers for his final season.

He gained 9,723 rushing yards in 16 pro seasons, 1,345 yards in the All-America Football Conference and 8,378 yards in the N.F.L., having become the league's career rushing leader until he was surpassed by Cleveland's Jim Brown in October 1963. Perry had 71 rushing touchdowns and 12 as a receiver.

Perry was later a scout and assistant for the 49ers and a sales executive for Gallo wines, and he owned a bowling-supplies store.

In addition to his wife, he is survived by a son, three daughters, a stepdaughter and several grandchildren and great-grandchildren.

Pro football's popularity soared in the decades after he played and the athletes became bigger and faster, but Perry seemed unimpressed.

"When I played, there were a lot of tough guys," he told Football Digest in 2003. "We would play with broken bones and things like that that you don't see nowadays."

— *By Richard Goldstein*

PHOEBE SNOW

A Singer-Songwriter Who Defied Categories

JULY 17, 1950 - APRIL 26, 2011

Phoebe Snow, whose signature hit, "Poetry Man," established her as a leading light of the singer-songwriter movement and whose swooping vocal acrobatics transcended musical genres, died on April 26 in Edison, N.J. She was 60.

Her death, at a hospital in Edison, was caused by complications of a stroke she suffered in January 2010, her manager, Sue Cameron, said. Some sources give Ms. Snow's age as 58, though New Jersey voter records say she was born on July 17, 1950.

"Poetry Man," a lilting guitar-based original song from her 1974 debut album, "Phoebe Snow" (Shelter), catapulted Ms. Snow to fame. The song, with lyrics addressed to a married man, rose to No. 5 on Billboard's Hot 100, and the album went to No. 4 on the album chart. Released as the singer-songwriter movement was at the peak of its influence, the album led to a Grammy nomination for Ms. Snow as best new artist of 1974.

A soaring contralto, Ms. Snow was variously labeled a jazz, blues, pop, funk and gospel artist, depending on the record she released. Few popular singers of her generation combined the technical resources she commanded. She was a renowned interpreter of soul and rock classics, including the Temptations' "Shakey Ground," Barbara Acklin's "Love Makes a Woman," the Buckinghams' "Mercy, Mercy, Mercy" and Aretha Franklin's "Do Right Woman, Do Right Man," which Ms. Snow sang with a roof-raising power.

Phoebe Ann Laub was born in New York City and grew up in Teaneck, N.J. Her mother, Lili, an alumnus of the Martha Graham company, was a dance teacher. Her father, Merrill Laub, was an exterminator who collected and restored antiques.

Phoebe Laub took her professional name from a fictional advertising character created in the early 1900s by the Delaware, Lackawanna & Western Railroad, which named its flagship train the Phoebe Snow. She saw the name on boxcars as the train passed through town.

After graduating from Teaneck High School, Ms. Snow attended Shimer College in Mount Carroll, Ill., for two years but dropped out to perform in clubs. She was married briefly to Phil Kearns, a musician, and they had a daughter, Valerie, who was born with severe brain damage. Her care occupied much of the rest of Ms. Snow's life.

"I've finally settled into realizing that my daughter is what she is," she told The New York Times in 1983. "Any progress she makes is fantastic, but I no longer foresee any miracles happening. I went through phases of the occult and of trying to find every single doctor in the country who could possibly do something. I realize now that I can't move mountains."

Refusing to institutionalize Valerie, who suffered from hydrocephalus and was not expected to live long, Ms. Snow cared for her daughter until her death on March 18, 2007, at age 31.

Ms. Snow, who is survived by her sister and an uncle, maintained that her devotion to her daughter was her greatest accomplishment.

Ms. Snow was discovered at the Bitter End in Greenwich Village in 1972 by Dino Airali, a promotion executive for Shelter Records, based in Tulsa, Okla. Mr. Airali and Phil Ramone produced her first record, which included guest performances by Zoot Sims, the Persuasions and Teddy Wilson.

Besides "Poetry Man," the most striking original song on her debut album is "I Don't Want the Night to End," about a lover who had died. The introspective, quirky coffeehouse torch-singing of that hit was a style she later largely abandoned to pursue various hybrids of hard rock, soul and gospel. Her only other single to reach the top 25 was her 1975 duet with Paul Simon on his gospel song "Gone at Last."

VERSATILE VOICE: Ms. Snow performing at the Ritz in 1989.

After 1975, motherhood took precedence over Ms. Snow's career. Her album "Second Childhood," a moody follow-up to "Phoebe Snow" released by Columbia in 1976, was certified gold, with sales of over 500,000, but it was still considered a commercial disappointment.

Three more Columbia albums followed: the hard-edged "It Looks Like Snow," the medium-soft "Never Letting Go" and the funky

APR

"Against the Grain." She then left Columbia to record for Mirage ("Rock Away," 1981), and Elektra ("Something Real," 1989). "Something Real" was her last album to reach the Billboard album charts.

Her changing labels while owing money to them led to years of legal battles and financial hardship. "With my quick success, I didn't have time to learn the ropes of the music business," she told The Times in 1983. "Because my first record was such a hit, I was terribly spoiled and I thought I couldn't do anything wrong. I was also desperate to make tons of money because of my responsibility to my daughter. And there was no longer any joy in making music."

At the same time, the singer-songwriter movement waned, and the breadth and individuality of her musical personality made marketing her talent to narrow radio formats problematic. Her focus on her daughter also made touring difficult.

In 1994, Ms. Snow performed at the Woodstock 25th Anniversary festival as part of a soul act that included Thelma Houston, Mavis Staples and CeCe Peniston. She was recruited by Donald Fagen, of Steely Dan fame, to participate in the New York Rock and Soul Revue, a series of concerts in which she performed along with Charles Brown, Michael McDonald, Boz Scaggs and others. The project led to a 1991 album recorded live at the Beacon Theater in Manhattan. She also recorded "Have Mercy," a duet with Jackson Browne.

As her record sales diminished Ms. Snow became a highly sought-after voice on commercial jingles for companies like Michelob, Hallmark and AT&T.

In 2003, she released "Natural Wonder," her first album of new original material in 14 years. In 2007, shortly after her daughter's death, Ms. Snow appeared at Birdland, the Manhattan jazz club, where she delivered a blazing performance that showed that her gifts had not diminished.

— *By Stephen Holden*

JOANNA RUSS

Where Few Women Had Gone Before: Science Fiction

FEB. 22, 1937 - APRIL 29, 2011

Joanna Russ, a writer who four decades ago helped deliver science fiction into the hands of the most alien creatures the genre had yet seen — women — died on April 29 in Tucson. She was 74.

Ms. Russ was best known for her novel "The Female Man," published in 1975 and considered a landmark. With that book, which told the intertwined stories of four women at different moments in history, she helped inaugurate the now-flourishing tradition of feminist science fiction. She also published essays, criticism and short fiction.

Ms. Russ was herself the subject of many critical studies, including those collected in "On Joanna Russ," edited by Farah Mendlesohn and published in 2009 by Wesleyan University Press.

The science fiction writer has the privilege of remaking the world. Because of this, the genre, especially in the hands of disenfranchised writers, has become a powerful vehicle for political commentary. In the America in which she came of age, Ms. Russ was triply disenfranchised: as a woman, a lesbian and an author of genre fiction who earned her living amid the pomp of university English departments.

Some critics found her too polemical, but

many praised her liquid prose style, intellectual ferocity and cheerfully unorthodox approach to constructing her fiction, which could include discursions into history and philosophy and sections of quasitheatrical dialogue. (She was originally trained as a dramatist.)

There was palpable anger in Ms. Russ's work, but it was leavened by wit and humor. In a scene from "The Female Man," Janet Evason, who inhabits an idyllic future on Whileaway, a planet without men, visits Earth, where she is promptly hustled onto a television talk show. A dialogue unfolds between Janet and the master of ceremonies:

MC: I — Miss Evason — we — well, we know you form what you call marriages, Miss Evason, that you reckon the descent of your children through both partners. ... I confess you're way beyond us in the biological sciences. ... But there is more, much, much more — I am talking about sexual love.

JE (enlightened): Oh! You mean copulation.

MC: Yes.

JE: And you say we don't have that?

MC: Yes.

JE: How foolish of you. Of course we do.

MC: Ah? (He wants to say, "Don't tell me.")

JE: With each other. Allow me to explain.

She was cut off instantly by a commercial poetically describing the joys of unsliced bread.

Writing in The New York Times in 1983, Gerald Jonas ranked Ms. Russ "among the small band of accomplished stylists in science fiction."

She won a Hugo Award in 1983 for "Souls," a historical fantasy novella about a 12th-century abbess who must defend against invading, sexually brutalizing Norsemen, and a Nebula Award in 1972 for the story "When It Changed," a precursor of "The Female Man." The Hugo, presented by members of the World Science Fiction Convention, and the Nebula, presented by the Science Fiction & Fantasy Writers of America, are considered the Pulitzer Prizes of the genre.

Joanna Russ was born in the Bronx on Feb. 22, 1937. In 1957 she earned a bachelor's in English from Cornell, where she studied with Vladimir Nabokov. In 1960 she received a master's degree in playwriting and dramatic literature from the Yale Drama School.

Ms. Russ was triply disenfranchised: as a woman, a lesbian and an author of genre fiction who earned her living amid the pomp of university English departments.

But by then she had set her sights on science fiction, having published her first story, "Nor Custom Stale," the year before in The Magazine of Fantasy & Science Fiction.

The field was such a male stronghold that through the mid-20th century its handful of female writers often used masculine pseudonyms. (Ursula K. Le Guin, today the best-known woman in science fiction, did not begin publishing until the 1960s.)

In midcentury science fiction by men and women, female characters resembled their earthly counterparts: comely, compliant and domestic. "Galactic suburbia," Ms. Russ derisively called this fictional universe, and she began to push against its confines.

In a series of stories published in the late 1960s, she introduced the heroine Alyx, a quick-witted, not greatly beautiful mercenary, thief and assassin who roams energetically across the centuries from antiquity onward.

Alyx also stars in Ms. Russ's first novel, "Picnic on Paradise," published in 1968; the novel was later reissued with the stories in a compilation volume, "The Adventures of Alyx."

Ms. Russ's feminism is perhaps nowhere more visible than in "The Female Man." It features a contemporary woman, Joanna, and three alter egos: Jeannine, who dwells in a dismal past; Jael, a warrior who inhabits a world in which the war between men and women is literal ("The best way to silence an enemy is to bite out his larynx," she says); and Janet, the utopian.

Ms. Russ, who lived in Tucson, had a brief early marriage that ended in divorce. No known family members survive. The Web site of the

Science Fiction & Fantasy Writers of America said she died of complications of a stroke.

As a scholar, Ms. Russ was known for a study of Willa Cather that invoked Cather's lesbianism, long a taboo subject. She taught at the State University of New York, Binghamton (now Binghamton University, State University of New York); the University of Colorado; the University of Washington; and elsewhere.

Her other books include the novels "We Who Are About to ..." and "The Two of Them," and the nonfiction books "How to Suppress Women's Writing" and "Magic Mommas, Trembling Sisters, Puritans & Perverts," in which she denounces as censorship the antipornography stance of some feminists.

In her critical work, too, Ms. Russ's wit came barreling through. Writing in The Magazine of Fantasy & Science Fiction in 1969, she had this to say about John Boyd's novel "The Last Starship From Earth," published the year before by Berkley Books:

"I forgive Mr. Boyd the anguish his novel caused me and hope he will eventually forgive me the anguish this review may cause him, but for Berkley there is no forgiveness. Only reform. *Don't do it again.*"

— BY MARGALIT FOX

OSAMA BIN LADEN

The Manhunt Ends

1957 - MAY 2, 2011

OSAMA BIN LADEN, the mastermind of the most devastating attack on American soil in modern times and the most hunted man in the world, was killed by United States forces in Pakistan in the early hours of May 2.

"Justice has been done," President Obama declared in a dramatic late-night appearance in the East Room of the White House as he announced to a global television audience that American commandos had finally cornered Bin Laden. He was shot in the head by Navy Seals during a helicopter raid on the compound where he had been hiding in the city of Abbottabad. His body was whisked away and buried at sea.

The news touched off an extraordinary outpouring of emotion as crowds gathered outside the White House, in Times Square and at the ground zero site, waving flags, cheering and shouting "USA, USA!" The death of Bin Laden, who was thought to be 54 years old, came almost 10 years after his terrorist recruits hijacked jetliners on Sept. 11, 2001, in a coordinated attack, killing almost 3,000 people in fireballs of destruction at the World Trade Center and the Pentagon and in a Pennsylvania field.

Bin Laden's radical, violent campaign to recreate a seventh-century Muslim empire redefined the threat of terrorism for the 21st century. With the Sept. 11 attacks, he was elevated to the realm of evil in the American imagination once reserved for dictators like Hitler and Stalin. He was a new national enemy, gloating on videotapes, taunting the United States and Western civilization.

"Do you want Bin Laden dead?" a reporter asked President George W. Bush six days after the Sept. 11 attacks.

"I want him — I want justice," the president answered. "And there's an old poster out West, as I recall, that said, 'Wanted: Dead or Alive.'"

The manhunt was punctuated in December 2001 by a battle at a mountain redoubt in Afghanistan called Tora Bora, near the border with Pakistan, where Bin Laden and his allies were hiding. Despite days of pounding by American bombers, he escaped, and for more than nine years he remained an elusive, shadowy figure frustratingly beyond the grasp of his pursuers and thought to be holed up somewhere in the region plotting new attacks.

IMAGE-CONSCIOUS: Bin Laden styled himself a Muslim ascetic but was media-savvy and careful about his public profile. He appeared in a taped statement broadcast on television on Oct. 7, 2001.

Long before, he had become a hero in much of the Islamic world, as much a myth as a man — what a longtime C.I.A. officer called "the North Star" of global terrorism. A son of the Saudi elite, he had united disparate militant groups, from Egypt to the Philippines, under the banner of his terrorist group, Al Qaeda, and his ideal of a borderless brotherhood of radical Islam.

Terrorism before Bin Laden was often state-sponsored, but he was a terrorist who had sponsored a state. From 1996 to 2001 he bought the protection of the Taliban, then the rulers of Afghanistan, and used the time and freedom to make Al Qaeda — which means "the base" in Arabic — into a multinational enterprise for the export of terrorism.

After the Sept. 11 attacks, the names Al Qaeda and Bin Laden spread to every corner of the globe. Groups calling themselves Al Qaeda, or acting in the name of its cause, attacked American troops in Iraq, bombed tourist spots in Bali and blew up passenger trains in Spain.

To this day, the precise reach of his power remains unknown: how many members Al Qaeda could truly count on, how many countries its cells had penetrated — and whether, as Bin Laden had boasted, he was seeking chemical, biological and nuclear weapons.

He waged holy war with modern methods. He sent fatwas — religious decrees — by fax and declared war on Americans in an e-mail beamed by satellite around the world. Qaeda members kept bomb-making manuals on CDs and communicated through encrypted memos on laptops, leading one American official to declare that Bin Laden possessed better communications technology than the United States. He railed against globalization, even as his agents in Europe and North America took advantage of a globalized world to carry out their attacks, insinuating themselves into the very Western culture he despised.

He styled himself a Muslim ascetic, a billionaire's son who gave up a life of privilege for the cause. But he was media-savvy and image-conscious. Before a CNN crew was allowed to leave after interviewing him in 1997, his media advisers insisted on editing out unflattering shots. He summoned reporters to a cave in Afghanistan when he needed to get his message out, but like the most controlling of corporate chief executives he insisted on receiving written questions in advance.

His reedy voice seemed to belie the warrior image he cultivated, a man whose constant companion was a Kalashnikov rifle, which he boasted he had taken from a Russian soldier he had killed. The world's most threatening terrorist, he was also known to submit to dressings-down by his mother. While he built his reputation on his combat experience against Soviet troops in Afghanistan in the 1980s, even some of his supporters questioned whether he had actually fought.

And though he claimed to follow the purest form of Islam, many scholars insisted that he was glossing over the faith's edicts against killing innocents and civilians. Islam draws boundaries on where and why holy war can be waged; Bin Laden declared the entire world fair territory.

Yet it was the United States, Bin Laden insisted, that was guilty of a double standard.

"It wants to occupy our countries, steal our resources, impose agents on us to rule us and then wants us to agree to all this," he told CNN in the 1997 interview. "If we refuse to do so, it says we are terrorists. When Palestinian children throw stones against the Israeli occupation, the U.S. says they are terrorists. Whereas when Israel bombed the United Nations building in Lebanon while it was full of children and women, the U.S. stopped any plan to condemn Israel. At the same time that they condemn any Muslim who calls for his rights, they receive the top official of the Irish Republican Army at the White House as a political leader. Wherever we look, we find the U.S. as the leader of terrorism and crime in the world."

Visions of Islamic Glory

For Bin Laden, as for the United States, the turning point came in 1989, with the defeat of the Soviets in Afghanistan.

To the United States, which had supported the Afghan resistance with billions of dollars in arms and ammunition, the Soviet retreat was the beginning of the end of the cold war and the birth of a new world order; to Bin Laden, who had supported the resistance with money, construction equipment and housing, it was not only an affirmation of Muslim strength but also an opportunity to recreate Islamic political power and topple infidel governments through jihad, or holy war.

He declared to an interviewer in 1998, "I am confident that Muslims will be able to end the legend of the so-called superpower that is America."

In its place he built his own legend, modeling himself after the Prophet Muhammad, who in the seventh century led the Muslim people to rout the infidels, or nonbelievers, from the Middle East. Just as Muhammad saw the Koran revealed to him amid intense persecution, Bin Laden regarded his expulsions from Saudi Arabia and then Sudan in the 1990s as signs that he was a chosen one.

In his vision, he would be the "emir," or prince, in a restoration of the khalifa, a political empire extending from Afghanistan across the globe. "These countries belong to Islam," he told the same interviewer, "not the rulers."

Al Qaeda became the infrastructure for his dream. Under it, he created a web of businesses — some legitimate, some less so — to obtain and move the weapons, chemicals and money he needed. He created training camps for his foot soldiers, a media office to spread his word and even "shuras," or councils, to approve his military plans and his fatwas.

Bin Laden's radical, violent campaign to recreate a seventh-century Muslim empire redefined the threat of terrorism for the 21st century.

Through the 1990s, Al Qaeda evolved into a far-flung and loosely connected network of symbiotic relationships: Bin Laden gave affiliated terrorist groups money, training and expertise; they gave him operational cover and furthered his cause. Perhaps the most important alliance was with the Taliban, who rose to power in Afghanistan largely on the strength of Bin Laden's aid, and in turn provided him refuge and a base for holy war.

Long before Sept. 11, though the evidence was often thin, Bin Laden was considered in part responsible for the killing of American soldiers in Somalia and Saudi Arabia; the first attack on the World Trade Center, in 1993; the bombing of the Khobar Towers in Saudi Arabia; and a foiled plot to hijack a dozen jets, crash a plane into the C.I.A. headquarters and kill President Bill Clinton.

In 1996, American officials described Bin Laden as "one of the most significant financial sponsors of Islamic extremism in the world,"

Bin Laden was emboldened, summoning Western reporters to his hideouts in Afghanistan to relay his message: He would wage war against the United States and its allies if Washington did not remove its troops from the Persian Gulf region.

"We calculated in advance the number of casualties," Bin Laden gloated.

"So we tell the Americans as a people," he told ABC News, "and we tell the mothers of soldiers and American mothers in general that if they value their lives and the lives of their children, to find a nationalistic government that will look after their interests and not the interests of the Jews. The continuation of tyranny will bring the fight to America, as Ramzi Yousef and others did. This is my message to the American people: to look for a serious government that looks out for their interests and does not attack others, their lands or their honor."

In February 1998, he issued the edict calling for attacks on Americans anywhere in the world, declaring it an "individual duty" for all Muslims.

That June, the grand jury that had been convened two years earlier handed up its indictment, charging Bin Laden, as the leader of Al Qaeda, with conspiracy to attack the United States abroad and with financing terrorist activities around the world.

On Aug. 7, 1998, the eighth anniversary of the United States order sending troops into the gulf region, two bombs exploded simultaneously at the American embassies in Nairobi, Kenya, and Dar es Salaam, Tanzania. The Nairobi bomb killed 213 people and wounded 4,500; the bomb in Dar es Salaam killed 11 and wounded 85.

The United States retaliated two weeks later with strikes against what were thought to be terrorist training camps in Afghanistan and a pharmaceutical plant in Sudan, which American officials contended — erroneously, it turned out — was producing chemical weapons for Al Qaeda.

Bin Laden had trapped the United States in a spiral of tension, in which any defensive or retaliatory actions would affirm the evils that he said had provoked the Qaeda attacks in the first place. In an interview with Time magazine that December, he brushed aside President Clinton's threats against him, and referred to himself in the third person, as if encouraging the notion that he had become larger than life.

"To call us Enemy No. 1 or Enemy No. 2 does not hurt us," he said. "Osama bin Laden is confident that the Islamic nation will carry out its duty."

In January 1999, the United States government issued a superseding indictment that affirmed the stature that Bin Laden had sought all along, declaring Al Qaeda an international terrorist organization in a conspiracy to kill American citizens.

MAY

Reveling in the Horror

After the attacks of Sept. 11, Bin Laden did what had become routine: He took to Arab television. He appeared, in his statement to the world, to be at the top of his powers. President Bush had declared that the nations of the world were either with the Americans or against them on terrorism; Bin Laden held up a mirror image, declaring the world divided between infidels and believers.

Bin Laden had never before claimed responsibility for terrorist attacks. But in a videotape found in the southern Afghan city of Kandahar weeks after Sept. 11, he did precisely that, reveling in the horror of that day.

"We calculated in advance the number of casualties from the enemy, who would be killed based on the position of the tower," he said, speaking to followers in the videotape. "We calculated that the floors that would be hit would be three or four floors. I was the most optimistic of them all."

He smiled, appearing to hunger to hear more approval and noting proudly that the attacks let loose a surge of interest in Islam around the world.

COMMENT

History and the Impact of One Man

Osama bin Laden's mother was about 15 at the time of his birth. Nicknamed "The Slave" inside the family, she was soon discarded and sent off to be married to a middle manager in the Bin Laden construction firm.

Osama revered the father he rarely got to see and adored his mother. As a teenager, he "would lie at her feet and caress her," a family friend told Steve Coll, for his definitive biography "The Bin Ladens: An Arabian Family in the American Century."

Like many people who go on to alter history, for good and evil, Bin Laden lost his father when he was a boy. The family patriarch was killed in a plane crash caused by an American pilot in the Saudi province of Asir. (Five of the Sept. 11 hijackers would come from that province. His brother was later killed in a plane crash on American soil.)

Osama was an extremely shy child, Mr. Coll writes. He was an outsider in his new family but also the golden goose. His allowance and inheritance was the source of his family's wealth.

He lived a suburban existence and was sent to an elite school, wearing a blue blazer and being taught by European teachers. As a boy he watched "Bonanza" and became infatuated by another American show called "Fury," about a troubled orphaned boy who goes off to a ranch and tames wild horses. He was a mediocre student but religiously devout. He made it to university, but didn't last long. He married his first cousin when she was 14 and went into the family business.

I repeat these personal facts because we have a tendency to see history as driven by deep historical forces. And sometimes it is. But sometimes it is driven by completely inexplicable individuals, who combine qualities you would think could never go together, who lead in ways that violate every rule of leadership, who are able to perpetrate enormous evils even though they themselves seem completely pathetic.

Analysts spend their lives trying to anticipate future threats and understand underlying forces. But nobody could have possibly anticipated Bin Laden's life and the giant effect it would have. The whole episode makes you despair about making predictions.

He explained that the hijackers on the planes — "the brothers who conducted the operation" — did not know what the mission would be until just before they boarded the planes. They knew only that they were going to the United States on a mission of martyrdom.

Bin Laden's voice continued to be heard, off and on, for almost the next 10 years as he issued threats, warnings and pronouncements on video and audiotape from wherever he was hiding. As recently as October 2010 he appealed for aid for flood victims in Pakistan and blamed the West for causing climate change.

He long eluded the allied forces in pursuit of him, moving, it was said, under cover of night with his wives and children, at first between mountain caves. When he was finally cornered

As a family man, Bin Laden was interested in sex, cars and work but was otherwise devout. He did not permit photography in his presence. He banned "Sesame Street," Tabasco sauce and straws from his home. He covered his eyes if an unveiled woman entered the room. He liked to watch the news, but he had his children stand by the set and turn down the volume whenever music came on.

As Mr. Coll emphasized in an interview, this sort of devoutness, while not everybody's cup of tea, was utterly orthodox in his society. He was not a rebel as a young man.

After the Soviets invaded Afghanistan, he organized jihadi tourism, helping young, idealistic Arab fighters who wanted to spend some time fighting the invaders. He was not a fighter himself, more of a courier and organizer, though after he survived one Soviet bombardment, he began to fashion a self-glorifying mythology.

He was still painfully shy but returned with an enormous sense of entitlement. In 1990, he wanted to run the Saudi response to the Iraqi invasion of Kuwait. He also thought he should run the family business. After he was shot down for both roles, the radicalism grew.

We think of terrorism leaders as hard and intimidating. Bin Laden was gentle and soft, with a flaccid handshake. Yet his soldiers have told researchers like Peter Bergen, the author of "The Longest War," that meeting him was a deeply spiritual experience. They would tell stories of his ability to avoid giving offense and forgive transgressors.

We think of terrorists as trying to build cells and organizations, but Bin Laden created an anti-organization — an open-source set of networks with some top-down control but much decentralization and a willingness to embrace all recruits, regardless of race, sect or nationality.

We think of war fighters as using violence to seize property and power, but Bin Laden seemed to regard murder as a subdivision of brand management. It was a way to inspire the fund-raising networks, dominate the news and manipulate meaning.

In short, Osama bin Laden seemed to live in an ethereal, postmodern world of symbols and signifiers and also a cruel murderous world of rage and humiliation. Even the most brilliant intelligence analyst could not anticipate such an odd premodern and postglobalized creature, or could imagine that such a creature would gain such power.

I just wish there were a democratic Bin Laden, that amid all the Arab hunger for dignity and freedom there was another inexplicable person with the ability to frame narratives and propel action — for good, not evil.

So far, there doesn't seem to be, which is tragic, because individuals matter.

— By David Brooks

MAY

and killed in his compound in Abbottabad, three of his wives were at home with him and one, the youngest, was in the same room. She was shot in the leg. A son was also killed in the raid, and a young daughter witnessed her father's death. Bin Laden had as many as 20 children as well as many half-brothers and half-sisters. The wives and children at the compound were taken into custody by the Pakistani authorities.

Bin Laden was determined that if he had to die, he, too, would die a martyr's death. His greatest hope, he told supporters, was that if he died at the hands of the Americans, the Muslim world would rise up and defeat the nation that had killed him.

— By Kate Zernike and Michael T. Kaufman;
Tim Weiner contributed reporting.

JACKIE COOPER

America's Boy, Hollywood Survivor

SEPT. 15, 1922 - MAY 3, 2011

JACKIE COOPER, the pug-nosed kid who became America's Boy in tear-jerker films of the Great Depression, then survived Hollywood's notorious graveyard of child stardom and flourished as an adult in television and modern pictures, died on May 3 in Los Angeles. He was 88.

Before the heydays of Shirley Temple and Mickey Rooney, young Jackie, a ragged urchin with a pout and a mischievous half-winked eye, was dreaming up schemes in "Our Gang" comedies and Wallace Beery pictures, like "Treasure Island," that Hollywood churned out for the rialto.

As Americans flocked to escapist movies, he made $2,000 a week, toured the nation and hobnobbed with Bing Crosby, Tallulah Bankhead and Joan Crawford. At 9 he became the youngest Oscar nominee for best actor (a record he still holds), in "Skippy" (1931). Later he dated Lana Turner and Judy Garland and spent weekends on the yacht of MGM's boss, Louis B. Mayer.

By his late teens, though, he seemed washed up, just another fading child star bound for oblivion and the life of drugs, booze and anonymity that became the fate of many of Hollywood's forgotten children.

But he got into television in the 1950s, starring in the sitcoms "The People's Choice" and "Hennesey," and later became an Emmy-winning director of "M*A*S*H" and other hits. He was introduced to a new generation of moviegoers as Perry White, editor of The Daily Planet, in four "Superman" films. And he earned his star on Hollywood's Walk of Fame.

Along the way he became a Navy musician in World War II and a daredevil race-car driver, was married three times and had four children, made and lost fortunes, and drank heavily and underwent psychiatric treatment. He also ran across the father who had deserted him in infancy — and left without saying a word to him.

"Of all the kid stars, I think I came through with more of my buttons intact," he wrote in his best-selling memoir, "Please Don't Shoot My Dog" (1981, with Dick Kleiner), titled after a director's malicious trick to get him to cry for the cameras when he was 9.

"Rooney is doing well now," he went on, "but only after eight marriages and a lengthy professional dry spell. Judy Garland and her tortured soul are gone. All the kid stars had a tough row to hoe because the public smothered them with so much love, they couldn't grow up, and after that, they never could find enough love to flourish."

It was a strange life on the borders of fantasy and reality. He was born John Cooper Jr. in Los Angeles on Sept. 15, 1922, the only son of his namesake and the former Mabel Leonard. He never knew his father, a musician who one night said he was going out for cigarettes and never came back.

Jackie grew up among grasping relations. From age 3 he was dragged down to the studio gates by his grandmother for the chance of $2 and a box lunch for a day's work as an extra. His mother, a rehearsal pianist for "Fox Movietone Follies of 1929," got him a singing role when he was 6, and he was soon a pro.

Over the next few years his childhood consisted of shenanigans with a gaggle of child actors under a $1,300-a-week contract. He appeared in 15 Hal Roach "Our Gang" comedies, including "Teacher's Pet" and "School's Out" (both 1930) and "Love Business" (1931).

In 1931 he was lent to Paramount to star in "Skippy," a tale of a clever boy and his dog, directed by his uncle, Norman Taurog, who got him to cry on camera by having his dog dragged off the set and "shot," complete with sound effects. Jackie did not win the Academy Award, but he was catapulted to stardom.

"This youthful player gives a truly remarkable portrayal in a film that is endowed with wholesome amusement and affecting tenderness," Mordaunt Hall applauded in The New York Times. "Master Cooper is extraordinarily natural. He awakens sympathy even when he is not strictly obedient, which, it might be said, is more the rule than the exception."

Besides "Treasure Island" (1934), in which he played Jim Hawkins to Wallace Beery's crusty Long John Silver, Jackie teamed with Beery in "The Champ" (1931), about a drunken fighter and his son; "The Bowery" (1933); and "O'Shaughnessy's Boy" (1935). Fans and Hollywood image-makers called the team magical, but the magic was only celluloid deep. "I really disliked him," Mr. Cooper said.

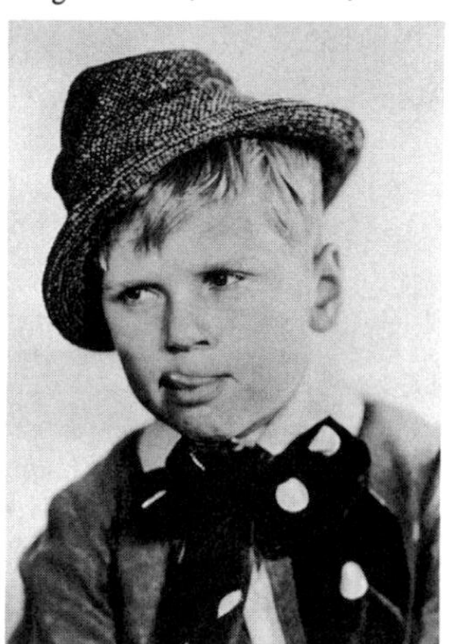

PUG-NOSED NOMINEE: Jackie Cooper, age 9, in "Skippy." The role earned him an Oscar nomination.

There were more Jackie Cooper films, including "That Certain Age" (1938) with Deanna Durbin, and Fritz Lang's "Return of Frank James" (1940), but most were forgettable. Facing teenage retirement, he joined the Navy and spent part of World War II in the Pacific, drumming in Claude Thornhill's band.

Mr. Cooper married June Horne in 1944. They had one son and were divorced in 1949. He married Hildy Parks in 1950 and was divorced in 1951. He and Barbara Kraus were married in 1954 and had a son and two daughters. One daughter died in 1997, the other in 2009, the same year his wife died.

After the war, acting jobs came sporadically. His skills were rusty for live television. He argued with directors. In 1949 he appeared on Broadway in the comedy "Magnolia Alley," which flopped. After that he played Ensign Pulver in a road production of "Mister Roberts," reprising the role the next year in London.

After his second divorce, his confidence ebbed and he drank. He also became fascinated with car racing. He was good at it, but realized after a 90-mile-an-hour spinout in a Ferrari — a narrow escape that left his wife sobbing in the stands — that he was risking too much. He underwent therapy for years.

In the 1950s he appeared on "Lux Video Theater," "The Philco Television Playhouse," "The United States Steel Hour" and "Kraft Television Theater" and starred in and occasionally directed two sitcoms. In one, "The People's Choice," from 1955 to 1958, he played a politician with a basset hound, Cleo, whose droll thoughts were given voice on the soundtrack; in the other, "Hennesey," from 1959 to 1962, he played a Navy doctor.

From 1964 to 1969 Mr. Cooper was a production executive for Screen Gems, the TV subsidiary of Columbia Pictures, where he worked on the sitcoms "Bewitched," "The Donna Reed Show" and "Hazel" and the soap opera "Days of Our Lives."

He won a directing Emmy in 1974 for "M*A*S*H," and another in 1979 for "The White Shadow." He also directed episodes of "McMillan & Wife," "Quincy," "The Rockford Files" and other shows.

In Mr. Cooper's four "Superman" films, from 1978 to 1987, it was not hard to see in the aging editor the scrunched-up face of the towheaded child star.

After retiring, he raised thoroughbred horses and appeared occasionally in Hollywood retrospectives. He had homes in Beverly Hills and Palm Springs, Calif.

In his memoir he recalled his close encounter with the father who had abandoned him. Driving cross-country in 1951, he stopped at a garage. A mechanic recognized him and said his father, John Cooper Sr., lived upstairs, had pictures of him and often spoke of him with pride.

"Let me tell him you're here," the man suggested.

"No, please don't," Mr. Cooper replied. "I don't need to be confused."

He drove away.

— *By Robert D. McFadden*

ARTHUR LAURENTS

Broadway Milestones Are Etched With His Name

JULY 14, 1917 - MAY 5, 2011

Arthur Laurents, the playwright, screenwriter and director who wrote and ultimately transformed two of Broadway's landmark shows, "Gypsy" and "West Side Story," and created one of Hollywood's most well-known romances, "The Way We Were," died on May 5 at his home in Manhattan. He was 93.

Mr. Laurents once described writers as "the chosen people" and said he was happiest when sitting alone and putting his "daydreams and fantasies down on paper."

He did so in various genres. His film credits include Hitchcock's "Rope"; "Anastasia," with Ingrid Bergman; and "The Turning Point," with Anne Bancroft and Shirley MacLaine. His screenplay for "The Way We Were," with Robert Redford and Barbra Streisand, was adapted from his novel by the same name.

But the stage was his first love, and he wrote for it for 65 years, turning out comedies and romances as well as serious dramas that often explored questions of ethics, social pressures and personal integrity. Early on, he once said, he realized that "plays are emotion," not simply words strung together, and it became his guiding principle.

A milestone was "West Side Story," the 1957 musical for which Mr. Laurents's book gave a contemporary spin to the tale of Romeo and Juliet. The Montagues and the Capulets, the families of the doomed young lovers, were now represented by the Jets and the Sharks, warring street gangs in Manhattan.

It was a plot device that had been discussed several years earlier by Mr. Laurents, the director and choreographer Jerome Robbins and the composer Leonard Bernstein. Bernstein was initially going to write both the music and lyrics, but he eventually accepted Mr. Laurents's suggestion that a co-lyricist could ease the burden of composition. Mr. Laurents then brought in a talented newcomer named Stephen Sondheim, who eventually wrote all the lyrics for what became his Broadway debut.

"What we really did stylistically with 'West Side Story' was take every musical theater technique as far as it could be taken," Mr. Laurents wrote in a 2009 memoir. "Scene, song and dance were integrated seamlessly; we did it all better than anyone ever had before." Two years later, with "Gypsy," Mr. Laurents helped create what is regarded as one of Broadway's best musicals.

With music by Jule Styne and lyrics by Mr. Sondheim, "Gypsy" is the story of the striptease artist Gypsy Rose Lee as told through the story of her domineering mother, Rose. The show, directed by Robbins and starring Ethel Merman as Rose, was a hit. (Mr. Laurents did not write the screenplay for the less-successful 1962 film version with Rosalind Russell.)

Mr. Laurents directed a 1974 revival of "Gypsy" in London and on Broadway with Angela Lansbury in the lead, then staged it again on Broadway in 1989 with Tyne Daly as Rose. Bernadette Peters starred in the 2003 Broadway revival, directed by Sam Mendes.

Four years later Mr. Laurents agreed to direct a limited-run revival of "Gypsy" as part of the Encores! summer concert series at City Center in Manhattan. This time, Patti LuPone played Momma Rose. The production, he decided, would be a tribute to his longtime partner, Tom Hatcher, who had urged him to direct it before he died in 2006. Mr. Laurents was determined, as he put it, to make it "an Event."

The stage was his first love, and he wrote for it for 65 years, turning out comedies and romances as well as serious dramas that often explored questions of ethics, social pressures and personal integrity.

In his 2009 memoir, "Mainly on Directing: 'Gypsy,' 'West Side Story,' and Other Musicals," Mr. Laurents recalled making "discovery after discovery about every character" as he planned the revival. The process, he wrote, "became as exciting as directing a new play."

The City Center production of "Gypsy" was a triumph for both Mr. Laurents and Ms. LuPone, and in March 2008 a full-fledged staging of it opened to rave reviews on Broadway. The show received seven Tony Award nominations, including one for Mr. Laurents, who was on the verge of his 91st birthday. The winners included Ms. LuPone, as best leading actress in a musical.

Yet another version of "Gypsy" was being proposed in January 2011, when Mr. Laurents, still working into his 90s, met with Mr. Sondheim and Ms. Streisand about a new film adaptation, with Ms. Streisand as Rose.

Mr. Laurents also credited Mr. Hatcher, his partner, with providing the spark that led to the hit revival of "West Side Story" in 2009. Mr. Hatcher had seen a production of it in Bogotá, Colombia, and suggested that a Broadway revival could benefit from having the Sharks, whose members were of Puerto Rican heritage, speak Spanish.

"And there it was," Mr. Laurents wrote, "the reason for a new production. It excited me and now I wanted to direct it." (A few months after the opening, some of the Spanish lyrics were changed back to English.)

As he saw it, the challenge was "erasing the '50s without violating what made 'West Side Story' the classic it has become." For one thing, he was determined to find the right cast — performers who could act as well as they could dance and sing. The much-anticipated revival opened in March 2009 to largely enthusiastic reviews.

A compact, elegant man, Mr. Laurents could be as convivial as a raconteur and as equally blunt. In a single interview in 2004 he dismissed a Sondheim-Burt Shevelove musical adaptation of Aristophanes' "Frogs" and said Nathan Lane had "made it worse" in a Lincoln Center production, called Jerome Robbins "a monster," described David Hare's play "Stuff Happens" as "a paste job," and branded Robert Anderson's "Tea and Sympathy" as "a fraud."

Mr. Laurents collected his share of brickbats as well. At various times critics deemed his work predictable, preachy or sentimental.

He made his Broadway debut in 1945 with "Home of the Brave," a play about a young Jewish soldier traumatized by witnessing the death of his best friend during a combat mission on an island in the Pacific during World War II. When the play, a look at anti-Semitism in the military, was adapted for the screen by Carl Foreman in 1949, the central character became a black G. I., but the theme of destructive prejudice was unchanged.

The late 1940s found Mr. Laurents in Hollywood, trying his luck as a screenwriter. His first effort, "Rope" (1948), had its origins in a play called "Rope's End," by Patrick Hamilton, which had first been adapted by Hume Cronyn. Mr. Laurents's version became the framework for Alfred Hitchcock's 1948 film about two friends (Farley Granger and John Dall) who decide to commit a murder. (Mr. Granger died on March 27, see page 376.) Mr. Laurents went on to collaborate with Philip Yordan on the screen adaptation of Yordan's play "Anna Lucasta" (1949). The film starred Paulette Goddard as the black-sheep daughter of a conniving family.

After that, Mr. Laurents came back to New York and resumed writing for the theater. In "The Bird Cage" (1950), he portrayed the dark goings-on at an outwardly glamorous night club. The club owner, played by Melvyn Douglas, is cruel and unscrupulous, even in his dealings with his wife (Maureen Stapleton), and ultimately leaves his world in ruins. The play was dismissed as an unconvincing melodrama.

He found his footing again with "The Time of the Cuckoo" (1952), a comedy-drama in which an unmarried American woman (Shirley Booth) who is open to romance journeys to Venice. A hit with theatergoers, the play was adapted for the screen under the title "Summertime" as a vehicle for Katharine Hepburn in 1955. In 1965 Mr. Laurents reworked the play into the book for the modestly successful musical "Do I Hear a Waltz?," which had music by Richard Rodgers and lyrics by Mr. Sondheim.

Mr. Laurents didn't begin writing seriously until he had finished college, but he admitted to becoming stage-struck while still a boy, saying he had loved being taken to the theater, especially to musicals. Born on July 14, 1917, he grew up in the Flatbush section of Brooklyn. His father was a lawyer, his mother a teacher.

TRIUMVIRATE: Mr. Laurents, center, with Richard Rodgers, left, and Stephen Sondheim in 1964 as they worked on the musical "Do I Hear a Waltz?" Mr. Laurents also teamed with Mr. Sondheim on "West Side Story" and "Gypsy."

He attended Erasmus Hall High School in Brooklyn and then went to Cornell University, where, he recalled, he spent most of one school year reading plays. Back in New York, he enrolled in an evening writing class at New York University and sold his first radio play to CBS for $30. The two leading female roles were played by an aspiring actress named Shirley Booth. His career was barely under way when he was drafted into the Army in 1941, but he spent the war years far from combat, first assigned to writing training films, then radio propaganda shows.

By then he had long since cast off whatever remaining doubts he had about his homosexuality. In "Original Story By," a memoir published in 2000, he was frank about his gay encounters, saying he lost count of the sexual experiences he had while in the Army, referring to his partners as "those unremembered hundreds." Tom Hatcher, a former actor and real estate developer, would be his companion for 52 years.

Mr. Laurents managed to keep one foot in theater and the other in films, though his Hollywood career was suspended in the late 1940s when he was accused of Communist sympathies and blacklisted for several years. He had been active in civil rights causes and had joined a Marxist study group but had not been a member of the Communist Party. Still, the anti-Communist publication Red Channels labeled him a subversive.

His first screenplay after his return was for "Anastasia" (1956), in which Ingrid Bergman gave an Academy Award-winning performance as the woman who was thought by some to be the sole survivor of Russia's imperial family. Mr. Laurents also adapted Françoise Sagan's novel "Bonjour Tristesse" for a 1958 film with a cast including Deborah Kerr, David Niven and Jean Seberg.

One of Mr. Laurents's less successful Broadway offerings was "A Clearing in the Woods" (1957), with Kim Stanley as a neurotic woman haunted by her past.

In 1960 he added directing to his theater credits when he staged his comedic fairy tale "Invitation to a March" on Broadway, with a cast that included Celeste Holm, Eileen Heckart and Jane Fonda. He went on to direct the musical "I Can Get It for You Wholesale" (1962), which featured the Broadway debut of Barbra Streisand, as a garment district secretary. He then wrote the book for and directed "Anyone Can Whistle" (1964), which had a score by Mr. Sondheim and starred Angela Lansbury as the mayor of a moribund town.

"Entertainment is dessert. It needs to be balanced by the main course: theater of substance."

Mr. Laurents won the first of his three Tony Awards in 1968 for "Hallelujah, Baby!," named best musical of the year. With a book by Mr. Laurents, music by Jule Styne and lyrics by Betty Comden and Adolph Green, the show followed the rising fortunes of a young black couple (Leslie Uggams and Robert Hooks) in the first half of the 20th century.

With the 1972 publication of his first novel, "The Way We Were," Mr. Laurents laid the foundation for one of his best-remembered screenplays. His 1973 film adaptation starred Ms. Streisand as a Jewish political activist and Mr. Redford as the smoothly ambitious screenwriter she marries. A plot element was the entanglement of Ms. Streisand's character in the Hollywood red scare, for which Mr. Laurents drew on his own experience.

His last Hollywood venture was "The Turning Point" (1977), a drama set in the world of dance. Directed by Herbert Ross, the film portrayed two former ballerinas (Ms. MacLaine and Ms. Bancroft) who have taken different paths in choosing between family and career. It also featured Mikhail Baryshnikov as a young dancer who has an affair with Ms. MacLaine's daughter (Leslie Browne), a budding ballet star. "The Turning Point" was nominated for 11 Oscars, including one for Mr. Laurents's screenplay, though it did not win any.

He returned to Broadway in 1983 as the director of "La Cage aux Folles," which had music and lyrics by Jerry Herman and a book by Harvey Fierstein about a gay couple (George Hearn and Gene Barry) who preside over and entertain at a St. Tropez nightclub where the main attraction is a drag revue. Mr. Laurents won a Tony for his staging.

Mr. Laurents also wrote and directed the musical "Nick and Nora," in 1991. That show, with music by Charles Strouse and lyrics by Richard Maltby Jr., was based on Dashiell Hammett's "Thin Man" characters, the polished investigators Nick and Nora Charles, and starred Barry Bostwick and Joanna Gleason. It lasted for only nine regular performances, and Mr. Laurents later summed it up as the "biggest and most public flop of my career."

His output during the next decade, none of it on Broadway, included "The Radical Mystique" (1995), in which complacent liberals are shaken into reality by revolutionary goings-on; and "Jolson Sings Again," which once again evoked the Hollywood blacklist. "Attacks on the Heart" (2003) was about an American filmmaker whose relationship with a Turkish woman sours after the 9/11 terrorist attacks. "New Year's Eve," which had its premiere in the spring of 2009, was about an aging actress and her family. And "Come Back, Come Back, Wherever You Are," which opened in the fall of 2009, was a portrait of a grieving family.

In these plays as in much of his earlier work, he explored questions of self-deception and honesty, guilt and innocence, love and loyalty. That was in keeping with his belief that a writer's job was not only to entertain but also to illuminate.

"Entertainment is dessert," he wrote in a 1995 essay in The New York Times; "it needs to be balanced by the main course: theater of substance."

— By Robert Berkvist

KATE SWIFT

Finding Sexism in the Words We Read

DEC. 9, 1923 - MAY 7, 2011

Kate Swift, a writer and editor who in two groundbreaking books — "Words and Women" and "The Handbook of Nonsexist Writing" — brought attention to the sexual discrimination embedded in ordinary English usage, died on May 7 in Middletown, Conn. She was 87.

Ms. Swift seized on the issue of sexist language after she and Casey Miller, her companion, formed a professional editing partnership in 1970 and were hired to copy-edit a sex education manual for junior high school students.

The stated goal of the manual was to encourage mutual respect and equality between boys and girls, but Ms. Swift and Ms. Miller, who died in 1997, concluded that the author's intent was being undermined by the English language.

"We suddenly realized what was keeping his message — his good message — from getting across, and it hit us like a bombshell," Ms. Swift said in a 1994 interview for the National Council of Teachers of English as part of a project called The Women in Literacy and Life Assembly.

"It was the pronouns! They were overwhelmingly masculine gendered."

The partners turned in a manuscript with suggestions that sex-identifying singular pronouns be made plural, or that pronouns be avoided altogether, and that word order be changed so girls preceded boys as often as the reverse.

"The publisher accepted some suggestions and not others, as always happens," Ms. Swift said. "But we had been revolutionized."

Now, they wrote in the preface to their first book, "Words and Women," "everything we read, heard on the radio and television, or worked on professionally confirmed our new awareness that the way English is used to make the simplest points can either acknowledge women's full humanity or relegate the female half of the species to secondary status."

Ms. Swift and Ms. Miller also wrote two attention-getting essays on the subject in 1972: "Desexing the English Language," which appeared in the inaugural issue of Ms. magazine, and "One Small Step for Genkind," which was published in The New York Times Magazine. "Words and Women: New Language in New Times" followed in 1976. An updated version was published in 1991.

The book illustrated the implicit biases in spoken and written English, highlighting the time-honored phrases "all men are created equal" and "land where our fathers died," the persistent identification of women by Miss and Mrs., and the journalistic habit of describing women as divorcées or blondes, who might be pert, dimpled or cute.

Some of the authors' proposals gained traction. Many newspapers, textbooks and public speakers avoid "fireman" and "stewardess" nowadays. Other ideas fell by the wayside, notably "genkind" as a replacement for "mankind," or "tey," "ter" and "tem" as sex-neutral substitutes for "he/she," "his/her" and "him/her."

Barbara Peabody Swift, known as Kate, was born on Dec. 9, 1923, in Yonkers, to a journalistic family. Her paternal grandfather, J. Otis Swift, wrote a daily nature column, "News Outside the Door," for The New York World and its successor, The World-Telegram, for 40 years. Her father and mother were both newspaper and magazine journalists.

Ms. Swift grew up in Hastings-on-Hudson, N.Y., and attended Connecticut College before earning a journalism degree from the University of North Carolina in 1944. After working as a copy runner in the NBC newsroom in New York, she enlisted in the Women's Army Corps as a writer and editor for the Army's information and education department.

> "The way English is used to make the simplest points can either acknowledge women's full humanity or relegate the female half of the species to secondary status," Ms. Swift wrote in the book "Words and Women."

She was a writer for the Port of New Orleans, an editorial assistant at Time and a news writer for the public relations department of the Girl Scouts of America before becoming a science writer on the public-affairs staff of the Museum of Natural History in Manhattan in 1954, serving as the press liaison for the Hayden Planetarium. In 1965 she became the director of the news bureau of the school of medicine at Yale.

She lived in East Haddam, Conn., and Georgetown, Me. A marriage ended in divorce. She is survived by a brother and a half-sister.

Although Ms. Swift and Ms. Miller followed up their first book with a style guide, "The Handbook of Nonsexist Writing," in 1980, Ms. Swift insisted that she had no interest in policing the language.

"We just wanted to give people the background, to make them aware of what was happening right underneath their noses," she said of the handbook. "We didn't want to tell people, Do This or Don't Do That!"

— *By William Grimes*

SEVE BALLESTEROS

A Daring Golfer With Winning Ways

APRIL 9, 1957 - MAY 7, 2011

SEVE BALLESTEROS, the charismatic Spaniard who became one of the finest golfers of his era, winning the Masters twice and the British Open three times, died on May 7 at his home in the coastal town of Pedreña in northern Spain, where his struggle with brain cancer drew wide attention in the sports world. He was 54.

Ballesteros was only 19 and virtually unknown when he was thrust into the golf spotlight in July 1976 at the British Open at Royal Birkdale. On the final hole he hit a brilliant chip shot between two bunkers that landed four feet from the cup. He then sank his putt to tie Jack Nicklaus for second place behind Johnny Miller after leading for three rounds.

That daring chip, coming after a string of miraculous shots that rescued him from wild drives into dunes and bushes, caught the golf world's attention and defined his swashbuckling kind of game.

WORLD CLASS: In 1980, Ballesteros became the first European to win the Masters.

With a passion for perfection, uncommon intensity and a stellar short game, Ballesteros helped propel Europe's rise in the Ryder Cup competition with the United States while winning five major championships in a 10-year span. At Augusta National in 1980, he became the first European and, at 23, the youngest player to win the Masters. (Tiger Woods was 21 when he won the Masters in 1997, replacing Ballesteros as the youngest.) Ballesteros won the Masters again in 1983, the British Open in 1979, 1984 and 1988, and the World Match Play Championship five times.

"I think he comes as close to a complete player as anybody I've ever seen," his fellow golfer Ben Crenshaw told Sports Illustrated in 1985. "He can hit every shot in the bag, and do it with the style and look of a champion."

Ballesteros won 45 events on the European Tour and was its earnings leader six times. He was in the vanguard of world-class Spanish golfers, preceding José Maria Olazábal, Miguel Ángel Jiménez and Sergio García. But he had a limited presence in the United States, winning just four PGA Tour events in addition to his Masters triumphs.

Ballesteros was something of a golf magician. In addition to his spectacular recoveries from wild drives, he could balance three golf balls on top of one another, a favorite trick. Handsome and spirited, he was a favorite of the television cameras, as Frank Hannigan, senior executive director of the United States Golf Association, remarked at the 1985 Masters.

"He's made for this medium," Hannigan said. "They come in close for a shot, and they can't miss. You can see his thought processes. For me, he is more fun to watch than any player in the world."

But his dash could be deceiving. He was extraordinarily disciplined, a master of concentration. "I'm so deeply immersed in my game plan and my play that I'm virtually oblivious to outside sights and sounds," he wrote in his 1991 book "Natural Golf," written with John Andrisani.

"I never hear my playing partner's clubs rattling, and I rarely ever hear the gallery applauding. I'm grinding as hard as I can inside my bubble."

His death was mourned throughout professional golf. At the Spanish Open in Terrassa — the tournament where Ballesteros began his professional career in 1976 and had his final European Tour victory in 1995 — players wore black ribbons on their caps and stood in a light rain for a moment of silence. Olazábal wept on the shoulder of his countryman Jiménez.

In Charlotte, N.C., at the Wells Fargo Championship, players reflected on his legacy after receiving bleak news about his failing health the day before he died. Phil Mickelson said that beyond Ballesteros's impact on the game, "the greatest thing about Seve is his flair and his charisma."

"Because of the way he played the game of golf, you were drawn to him," Mickelson added. "You wanted to go watch him play."

In an e-mail message, Nicklaus said Ballesteros "was able to create shots, invent shots and play shots from anywhere."

"I have watched him play 1-irons out of greenside bunkers when just fooling around," Nicklaus wrote. "He could get up and down out of a garbage can."

Severiano Ballesteros (pronounced buy-yuh-STAY-ros) was born on April 9, 1957, in Pedreña, where his father, a former Spanish-champion rower, was a farmer. His three older brothers, Baldomero, Manuel and Vicente, were golf pros, as was his uncle Ramon Sota.

As a boy, Seve batted stones with a homemade golf club on the beaches near his family's stone farmhouse. When he was 8, his brother Manuel gave him a 3-iron, and he began to caddie at a prestigious golf club in Santander, near his home. He won the caddie championship there at age 12 with a 79, sneaked onto the course at night to practice his shots, quit school at 14 and turned pro at 16.

Ballesteros won his first major when he captured the 1979 British Open at Royal Lytham & St. Annes in England, and it was there, on the 16th hole of the final round, that he made one of his most storied shots. With his ball in a parking lot, he hit a sand wedge to the green, then sank a 20-foot putt for birdie and went on to win by three shots, besting Nicklaus. In this case, however, it wasn't a matter of Ballesteros's being out of control on a drive. He had deliberately hit to the parking lot to take advantage of the prevailing winds.

In winning the 1980 Masters, Ballesteros led or was tied for the lead after each round, but he ran into trouble late on the final day, three-putting the 10th hole, hitting twice into Rae's Creek and sending his drive on the 17th hole onto the seventh green. At one point, he was only two shots ahead, but he won by four, a margin he reprised in winning the 1983 Masters.

Apart from his individual achievements, Ballesteros was instrumental in Europe's emergence on the Ryder Cup scene after players from the continent were allowed to join with British and Irish players beginning in 1979. Americans had dominated the competition for a decade.

Ballesteros played on eight Ryder Cup squads, including the 1987 team that achieved the Europeans' first triumph in America, at Muirfield Village in Dublin, Ohio. He was the nonplaying captain of Europe's team in 1997, when the Valderrama Golf Club on Spain's Costa del Sol played host to the event, the first time the Ryder Cup had been held on the Continent.

Ballesteros's last European Tour victory came at the Spanish Open in 1995; a chronic back problem curtailed his play after that. His biggest disappointment, he said, was his failure to win a United States Open championship; his often erratic play proved costly on the Open's customarily narrow fairways and high roughs.

Ballesteros was inducted into the World Golf Hall of Fame in 1999 and retired in an emotional news conference at Carnoustie before the 2007 British Open. In recent years, he ran a golf-course design business.

He learned he had a cancerous brain tumor after fainting at Madrid's international airport while waiting to board a flight to Germany on Oct. 6, 2008. That month he had the first of four surgical operations and was cared for at his home in Pedreña.

The next March, in an interview with Marca, a Spanish sports newspaper, he spoke openly about his cancer and the 300,000 get-well cards he had received from around the world as he underwent chemotherapy.

"I'm not called Seve Ballesteros," the paper quoted him as saying, "I'm called Seve Mulligan, because I've had the luck to be given a mulligan, which in golf is a second chance."

He is survived by two sons, a daughter and three brothers. His marriage to Carmen Botín ended in divorce in 2004.

In 1988, when he won a major for the last time, Ballesteros displayed the elements that had been his trademark: he was erratic but overwhelmingly brilliant. He had two bogeys in one 11-hole stretch of the final round of the British Open, but he also had six birdies and an eagle in that span, finishing with a 65 to beat Nick Price by two shots. On the 16th hole, he hit a 9-iron from 135 yards that stopped three inches from the cup.

"It was the best round of my life so far," Ballesteros said. "That shot at 16 was one of my two best."

The victory came at Royal Lytham & St. Annes, the site of that memorable approach shot in his first British Open nine years earlier. Holding the champion's silver cup aloft, Ballesteros said, "This time I didn't hit from the parking lot."

— *By Richard Goldstein;*
Larry Dorman contributed reporting from Charlotte, N.C.

LEO KAHN

Selling Steno Pads, Filing Cabinets and, of Course, Staples

DEC. 31, 1916 - MAY 11, 2011

Leo Kahn, whose success in pioneering big-box, warehouse-style supermarkets persuaded him to join with another entrepreneur in 1986 to found Staples, the retail empire that calls itself the "office superstore," died on May 11 in Boston. He was 94.

Staples brought to office supplies the strategy that worked so well for Toys "R" Us: stock the store with a huge variety of items — from paper clips to executive chairs — and price them at a deep discount.

Small businesses, which could not benefit from the discounts available to big companies, flocked to Staples' ever-expanding chain of stores. Today the company has sales of $25 billion, employs 91,000 people and operates in 26 countries.

Mr. Kahn went on to start two chains of health food stores, Fresh Fields and Nation's Heartland, which combined sharp attention to the demands of fitness-conscious consumers with price-conscious marketing.

"Leo Kahn is betting that he's seen the future of natural foods retailing, and it's wearing a suit and tie, not sandals," Regardies, a business magazine, said in 1992. The bet paid off: Whole Foods bought both chains in the 1990s at a hefty profit for Mr. Kahn.

Mr. Kahn's partner in starting Staples was Thomas G. Stemberg, who had previously been his biggest competitor in the New England grocery business. Mr. Stemberg, a leader in introducing nonbranded generic merchandise, started his own chain of discount groceries to compete with Mr. Kahn's.

An indication of the rivalry's intensity came when Mr. Kahn ran ads guaranteeing his customers the best price on Thanksgiving turkeys. Mr. Stemberg parried with his own ads promising that his company would match the lowest advertised price on turkeys. Technically, that made Mr. Kahn's claim untrue, a point Mr. Stemberg made to the Massachusetts attorney general's office. Mr. Kahn withdrew his ads.

Mr. Stemberg found himself out of a job in 1985, after he complained to his bosses about the sale of First National Supermarkets' warehouse division, which he headed. It had been sold to the Supermarket General Corporation, of which Mr. Kahn was chairman. Mr. Kahn had taken that job after selling his own food company, Purity Supreme, to Supermarket General for $80 million in 1984.

Part of the reason Mr. Kahn had been attracted to First National was that acquiring it meant getting Mr. Stemberg on his team. So the two men, both Harvard alumni, went to a Harvard basketball game and traded ideas for starting a new venture in specialty retailing.

After several Fridays visiting shopping malls and rigorous analysis of the retail market, they decided that Mr. Stemberg's proposal to concentrate on office supplies was the right one.

Mr. Kahn invested the first $500,000 in Staples. In May 1986, the first Staples store opened in Brighton, Mass. A dozen yellow writing pads that would have cost $11.55 from a traditional office-supply dealer went for $3.99.

Leo Kahn was born in Medford, Mass., on Dec. 31, 1916, to parents who had emigrated from Lithuania. He graduated from Harvard and Columbia Journalism School, worked as a reporter at a small Massachusetts newspaper and served as a navigator for the Army Air Forces in World War II. He joined his father's wholesale grocery company and started a new retail division, which became Purity Supreme.

He first built small stores, then supermarkets. The company came to include the Heartland Food Warehouse, which Inc. magazine called "the first successful deep-discount warehouse supermarket in the country."

After his success with Staples, Mr. Kahn, who had made his fortune discounting prices, took on a new challenge: the upscale market. His inspiration was the Bread & Circus health food stores in the Boston area, which he visited repeatedly. He recognized a new kind of affluent consumer, one concerned about physical fitness, food contamination and the environment.

Instead of buying Bread & Circus, he opened his own Fresh Fields store in Washington in 1991. Money magazine named it the nation's "store of the year" in 1993. In 1996, Whole Foods bought what had become a 22-store Fresh Fields chain. Three years later, it bought another group of Mr. Kahn's stores, Nature's Heartland, in the Boston area.

After his success in discounting prices, Mr. Kahn took on the upscale market. He recognized a new kind of customer, one concerned about physical fitness and the environment.

Mr. Kahn's wife of 11 years, the former Dorothy Davidson, died in 1975. He is survived by his second wife, the former Emily Gantt; two sons, a daughter, two stepdaughters, eight grandchildren and three stepgrandchildren.

When he was in the grocery business, Mr. Kahn aided a black-owned company that was opening supermarkets in areas of Boston that lacked them by using his influence to get good deals on wholesale food. His philanthropy included endowing two professorships at Harvard and encouraging education about the Holocaust.

In 1987, Forbes magazine asked Mr. Kahn if there were any high-margin areas still to be addressed by "category killers" like Staples. He mentioned back support and other orthopedic supplies; panty hose and lingerie; and telephone installation.

— *By Douglas Martin*

BERNARD GREENHOUSE

Elevating the Once-Lowly Cello

JAN. 3, 1916 - MAY 13, 2011

BERNARD GREENHOUSE, an internationally acclaimed cellist and a founding member of the Beaux Arts Trio, long considered the most eminent piano trio in the world, died on May 13 at his home in Wellfleet, Mass., on Cape Cod. He was 95.

The Beaux Arts, founded in 1955 by Mr. Greenhouse, the violinist Daniel Guilet and the pianist Menahem Pressler, was known for its refined musicality and remarkable continuity of personnel. Mr. Greenhouse, for instance, played with the group for 32 years until retiring in 1987.

The trio, which in its last incarnation comprised Mr. Pressler, the violinist Daniel Hope and the cellist Antonio Meneses, disbanded in 2008. But for more than five decades, it toured worldwide and made many celebrated recordings. The most esteemed is almost certainly its complete cycle of Haydn's 43 extant piano trios, made for the Philips label during Mr. Greenhouse's tenure.

Mr. Greenhouse began his career at midcentury as a soloist, but he shouldered a triple onus: he was a cellist; a restrained, contemplative player; and, before long, a member of a piano trio.

Though he played well-received solo recitals in the late 1940s, concert presenters rarely booked cellists then; the instrument was thought capable of little more than ooming and pahing at the bottom of an orchestra. (The situation obtained until the 1960s, when a series of televised master classes by Pablo Casals sent the cello's popularity soaring.)

What was more, though Mr. Greenhouse had an impeccable command of his instrument, he was by temperament and choice not a flashy player. Unlike the bravura style of many marquee cellists, which typically involves a huge sound, intense vibrato and unbridled emotionalism, his work leaned toward subdued, thoughtful interpretations.

A GLOBAL AUDIENCE: Mr. Greenhouse in 2002. He helped found the Beaux Arts Trio and played with it for 32 years.

Piano trios faced their own obstacles. For chamber-music lovers, the string quartet, with its evenly married sonorities and vast repertory, was the ensemble of choice. The sonic challenge entailed in combining a violin and a cello with a piano, akin to pairing gentle breezes with a thunderclap, was something performers were rarely willing to take on.

As a result, there were few high-level piano trios at the time the Beaux Arts began. Those that did exist were generally shotgun affairs, created when three

SAMMY WANJIRU

A Long-Distance Runner With Many Miles to Go

NOV. 10, 1986 - MAY 15, 2011

SAMMY WANJIRU, who set a blistering pace to shatter the 24-year-old Olympic record in the marathon in Beijing in 2008, becoming the youngest winner of the event, died on May 15 in Nyahururu, Kenya. He was 24.

Reports by the Kenyan police about the cause of death were conflicting. One police report said he had jumped from a balcony after his wife came home and found him with another woman. But a national police spokesman said Wanjiru had committed suicide. The Kenyan authorities said they would open an inquest to determine whether Wanjiru deliberately jumped, was pushed or intended to commit suicide.

MARATHON MILESTONE: Wanjiru in 2008 after shattering an Olympic record in Beijing and winning a gold medal.

Wanjiru had been going through a troubled period. In December he was charged with threatening his wife and a maid with an illegally obtained AK-47 assault rifle. He was also charged with hitting a security guard at his estate with the butt of the firearm. His wife withdrew the attempted-murder charge, saying she and Wanjiru had reconciled, but he was scheduled to appear in court on the firearms charge.

Wanjiru had twice been attacked at his home by bandits, probably because of his wealth earned from running, and he might have felt he needed a firearm for protection, his agent, Federico Rosa, said.

For all of Kenya's dominance in long-distance running, no Kenyan had won the Olympic marathon until Wanjiru did in Beijing at age 21, winning it in 2 hours, 6 minutes and 32 seconds on a blistering day that reached 86 degrees. Given the heat, many considered it the greatest marathon ever run, even though it was not a world record. Wanjiru won the race in warm-up shoes because he had left his racing shoes in Kenya.

He became known for starting races fast, darting ahead of runners who were worried about using up their energy too quickly. In Beijing's hot, humid conditions, he said, "I had to push the pace to tire the other runners."

Returning home with his gold medal, he was made an elder of his village.

Within two years Wanjiru, at 23, became the youngest person to win four major marathons: Chicago in 2009 and in 2010 and London in 2009 in addition to the Olympics race in 2008.

Raila Odinga, the prime minister of Kenya, called Wanjiru one of his country's "sure bets for gold" at the 2012 Olympics in London. His death, he said, was "a big blow to our dreams."

Wanjiru broke the world record for the half-marathon three times, and his time of 58:33 at the Hague in March 2007 is still the second best, behind the current world record of 58:23, set by Zersenay Tadese of Eritrea in 2010.

Wanjiru won the Chicago Marathon in 2009

with a record time of 2:05:41. His 2:05:10 in the London Marathon that year, his best marathon time, also set a record, though it has since been surpassed. But he never achieved his goal of running the marathon in less than two hours. The present world record is 2:03:59, set by Haile Gebrselassie of Ethiopia in Berlin in 2008.

David Bedford, the race director for the London Marathon, said, "He was in my opinion the best marathon runner ever and was likely to break the world marathon record."

Samuel Kamau Wanjiru, who is survived by a daughter in addition to his wife, grew up in Nyahururu, the rural village where he died. He started running as a means of transportation and impressed people with his speed.

But his family could not afford to send him to training schools for running, and he dropped out of school in the seventh grade. A Japanese scout spotted him, however, and he ended up going to Japan to complete high school and become a champion runner.

In the weeks before his death, he had been training in Eldoret, Kenya's running capital, and planned to run the San Diego Marathon in June. Rosa said that he spoke to Wanjiru the day before he died and that Wanjiru was planning to travel home to pay some bills and meet with his lawyer regarding the firearm case.

"He had the special gift of the champion," Rosa said. "Besides a big talent, champions have what I could call an arrogance. They know they are stronger than the others. He was so focused on winning, not to be famous or to get a lot of money, but just to show that he was the best."

— *By Douglas Martin and Jeré Longman*

HARMON KILLEBREW

He Swung for the Fences, and Cleared Them

JUNE 29, 1936 - MAY 17, 2011

Harmon Killebrew, the Hall of Famer who developed the strength to hit home runs by lifting 10-gallon milk cans as an Idaho farmhand and grew up to be one of the most feared sluggers of his generation, died on May 17 at his home in Scottsdale, Ariz., four days after announcing he was ending treatment for esophageal cancer. He was 74.

Killebrew said in December that he had begun treatment for the cancer at a Mayo Clinic branch near his home. On May 13, he said his doctors had told him his illness was incurable. "With profound sadness" he was ending treatment, he said in a statement released by the Minnesota Twins, which had made him the centerpiece of the franchise through the 1960s and early '70s. "I have exhausted all options."

Killebrew hit 573 home runs in 22 major league seasons, starting with the Washington Senators and continuing with the organization when it moved to Minnesota and became the Twins. He set an American League home run record for right-handed batters that endured for more than three decades, until Alex Rodriguez of the Yankees hit his 574th in 2009. When Killebrew turned to broadcasting in 1975, only Babe Ruth had hit more home runs in the A.L. At his death, he was No. 11 in career major league home runs.

Signed out of an Idaho high school, he had a slow start, making his debut with the Senators in 1954 only six days away from his 18th birthday and playing little in his first few seasons, though he wore the uniform of one of baseball's lowly franchises. He had little speed, his career batting average was only .256, and he was never known for defensive play; he played first base, third base and the outfield and never won a Gold Glove award.

But he led or tied A.L. hitters in home runs six times and hit 40 or more homers in eight seasons. He drove in 100 or more runs nine times. He won the A.L. Most Valuable Player award in 1969 when he led the league in home runs with 49, tying his single-season high, and in runs batted in with 140, his career best.

He helped take the Twins to the pennant in 1965, when they lost to the Los Angeles Dodgers in the World Series, and to West division titles in 1969 and 1970. He played in 13 All-Star Games and was inducted into the Baseball Hall of Fame in 1984.

And he wowed the crowds when his 5-foot-11, 210-pound frame connected at the plate.

"They'd go out of any ballpark," said Lou Gorman, a former Boston Red Sox general manager who died in April, speaking to The Hartford Courant in 2007. "Some of the ones that he hit would go out of the Grand Canyon."

Harmon Clayton Killebrew was born on June 29, 1936, in the farming community of Payette, Idaho, where his father, a former college football player, tutored him in sports. With the powerful chest and broad shoulders he developed working on dairy farms, he gained a reputation for hitting long balls in high school, where he was also a star quarterback.

That batting prowess caught the attention of Herman Welker, a United States senator from Idaho and a baseball fan. Welker recommended him to Clark Griffith, the Senators' owner, and Griffith sent Ossie Bluege, a former Senators manager, to scout him.

"I was set to go to Oregon to play college baseball and football," Killebrew once said. "It rained the night Mr. Bluege was there. They burned gasoline to dry the infield, and then I hit a ball over the left-field fence — first one to do it, 435 feet into a beet field."

Killebrew dropped his college plans and signed a three-year contract with the Senators' organization that included a $12,000 bonus. As a so-called bonus baby, he was required to remain with the team for at least two years. He played sparingly, but a tip he received from the future Hall of Fame slugger Ralph Kiner served him well. Kiner suggested that he stand closer to the plate and concentrate on pulling the ball.

When Killebrew finally became a regular for the Senators in 1959, he tied for the league lead in home runs with 42 despite the long distances to the left-field stands at Griffith Stadium.

The Senators moved to the Minneapolis-St. Paul area in 1961, and Killebrew emerged as the slugging heart of lineups that included other outstanding hitters like Rod Carew, Tony Oliva and Bob Allison.

Killebrew had a mild temperament, but his ability to crush a baseball, and the easy play on his name, brought him the nickname Killer. In 1962, he became the first of only four batters to hit a ball over the left-field roof at Tiger Stadium. In 1967, he hit the longest home run in the history of Metropolitan Stadium in Bloomington, Minn., a drive off the California Angels' Lew Burdette that traveled some 530 feet.

Killebrew complemented his physical talent with fierce concentration.

"I always tried to watch the pitcher and his complete windup from the moment he had the ball in his glove all the way through his motion, and tried to follow it all the way out of his hand, all the way to home plate," he told Fay Vincent, a former baseball commissioner, in Vincent's oral history, "We Would Have Played for Nothing."

As Killebrew put it, "I could pretty much tell when he released the ball what kind of pitch it was going to be and where it might end up at the plate."

In addition to his 573 home runs, Killebrew had 2,086 hits — not a single one on a bunt, by his account — and 1,584 R.B.I. His late-career at-bats were often as the designated hitter. In his last season, 1975, he played for the Kansas City Royals.

After his playing days ended, he was a broadcaster for the Oakland Athletics and the Angels as well as for the Twins, and he owned an insurance company and an auto dealership.

In the last decade, he promoted hospice care and, as he said in his statement, he was "educating people on its benefits." He chose to receive hospice care after ending cancer treatments.

"I look forward to spending my final days in comfort and peace with Nita by my side," Killebrew said, referring to his second wife. His survivors also include nine children from his two marriages. His marriage to his first wife, Elaine, ended in divorce.

Killebrew was scheduled to throw out the first pitch at the Twins' home opener in April at Target Field, but his illness kept him from the ceremony. His former teammate Oliva substituted for him, tossing a baseball to Killebrew's grandson Casey, a high school baseball player in suburban Minneapolis, who has honored him by wearing his No. 3. In the hours after Killebrew's death, groundskeepers placed a plastic-encased black-and-white photograph of Killebrew beneath home plate. It was to remain there for the rest of the season.

'KILLER': Killebrew had 573 home runs and, he said, not a single bunt.

Killebrew was the face of the Twins' franchise in his time and a huge fan favorite. A bronze statue capturing his swing stands outside the stadium.

"I loved the fans because they were down-to-earth Midwestern people," The Star Tribune of Minneapolis once quoted him as saying. "The people in the Upper Midwest were the same kind of people I grew up around in Idaho."

He made sure that his autographs for young fans were legible.

"I had a doctor's signature," the former Twins outfielder Torii Hunter told The Star Tribune in recalling the time Killebrew looked at his autograph several years ago. "I had a 'T' and an 'I' and a dot-dot. He said, 'What the hell is this?' He said, 'If you play the game this long, make sure people know who you are.' "

Killebrew hit many memorable home runs, but his first one remained a favorite. He got it in 1955, against a Detroit left-hander.

"It came off Billy Hoeft of the Tigers at Griffith Stadium," Killebrew told Rich Westcott in "Splendor on the Diamond," a book of interviews with baseball stars.

"Frank House was the catcher. When I came to the plate, he said, 'Kid, we're going to throw you a fastball.' I didn't know whether to believe him or not. I hit it out. It was one of the longest home runs I ever hit. As I crossed the plate, House said, 'That's the last time I ever tell you what pitch is coming.' "

— *By Richard Goldstein*

GARRET FITZGERALD

Steering Ireland Toward Peace

FEB. 9, 1926 - MAY 19, 2011

Garret FitzGerald, who served twice as Irish prime minister, helped set the stage for peace in Northern Ireland and shifted the tone of Ireland's relations with Britain, died on May 19 in Dublin. He was 85.

Across the country, flags were lowered to half-staff on government buildings, and a

Ms. Carrington, one of the last surviving links to the world of André Breton, Man Ray and Miró, was an art student when she encountered Ernst's work for the first time at the International Surrealism Exhibition in London in 1936. A year later she met him at a party.

The two fell in love and ran off to Paris, where Ernst, more than 25 years her senior, left his wife and introduced Ms. Carrington to the Surrealist circle. "From Max I had my education," she told The Guardian of London in 2007. "I learned about art and literature. He taught me everything."

She became acquainted with the likes of Picasso, Dalí and Tanguy. With her striking looks and adventurous spirit, she seemed like the ideal muse, but the role did not suit. Miró once handed her a few coins and told her to run out and buy him a pack of cigarettes. "I gave it back and said if he wanted cigarettes, he could bloody well get them himself," she told The Guardian. "I wasn't daunted by any of them."

MORE THAN A MUSE: Ms. Carrington, an intimate of Max Ernst, with one of her works in 2005.

Encouraged by Ernst, she painted and wrote. In 1939 she produced her first truly Surrealist work, "The Inn of the Dawn Horse (Self-Portrait)." Now in the collection of the Metropolitan Museum of Art, it shows an androgynous-looking woman seated in a room with a rocking horse on the wall, extending her hand to a hyena.

Her interest in animal imagery, myth and occult symbolism deepened after she moved to Mexico and entered into a creative partnership with the émigré Spanish artist Remedios Varo. Together the two studied alchemy, the kabbalah and the mytho-historical writings Popol Vuh from what is now Guatemala.

"She was a seeker and a searcher," said Whitney Chadwick, a professor of art at San Francisco State University and the author of "Women Artists and the Surrealist Movement"(1991). "In her work, she always sought to define moments when one plane of consciousness blends with another."

In the 1940s and '50s Ms. Carrington made a small number of carved wooden sculptures, and in her 80s and 90s she produced large-scale bronze sculptures of fantastical quasi-human forms, both comic and horrific, like "How Doth the Little Crocodile." Located on one of Mexico City's most prominent avenues, that work depicts a lizardlike oarsman steering a crocodile vessel and its four lizardy passengers on a voyage to places unknown.

Leonora Carrington was born on April 6, 1917, in Clayton Green, Lancashire, England. Her father was a wealthy textile manufacturer, and she grew up in a grand house, Crookhey Hall, where her Irish nanny entranced her with folk tales.

Her parents, both Roman Catholic, sent her to convent schools, from which she was expelled for eccentric behavior. At their wits' end, they sent her to study at Mrs. Penrose's Academy of Art in Florence. On returning to Britain, she enrolled in the art school recently established by the French modernist Amédée Ozenfant.

Her father was dead set against her becoming an artist and had insisted that she be presented as a debutante at the court of George V. Her mother was at least mildly encouraging, and, little suspecting the impact it might have, gave her a copy of Herbert Read's new book on Surrealism, published in 1936. It had a reproduction of an Ernst work on the cover.

After Ernst left his wife in 1938, he and Ms. Carrington left Paris and settled in Provence, near Avignon, but the outbreak of World War II put an end to their idyll. Ernst was imprisoned, first by the French and then by the Germans, and Ms. Carrington suffered a breakdown. She described the abusive treatment she received at a mental hospital in Spain in a memoir, "Down Below." She and Ernst never reunited.

After entering into a marriage of convenience with Renato Leduc, a Mexican writer and friend of Picasso's, Ms. Carrington made her way to New York, where she had solo shows at the Pierre Matisse Gallery and was included in group shows at Peggy Guggenheim's Art of This Century gallery and at the Museum of Modern Art.

After her marriage was dissolved, she moved to Mexico and lived in Mexico City for the rest of her life, with interruptions. There she married Emeric Weisz, a Hungarian photographer who had been Robert Capa's darkroom manager in Paris. Mr. Weisz spirited three cardboard valises filled with negatives of Capa photographs of the Spanish Civil War from Paris to Marseilles, where he was arrested and sent to an internment camp in Algiers. The negatives, believed lost, resurfaced in Mexico City in 2008.

Ms. Carrington is survived by their two sons and five grandchildren.

Ms. Carrington wrote short stories and novels in the same Surrealist vein as her artwork. In 1988, Dutton published "The House of Fear: Notes From Down Below," an anthology of her work, and "The Seventh Horse and Other Tales." And in 2004 she was the subject of Susan Aberth's "Leonora Carrington: Surrealism, Alchemy and Art."

— *By William Grimes*

JEFF CONAWAY

After 'Taxi' and 'Grease,' a Struggle

OCT. 5, 1950 - MAY 27, 2011

JEFF CONAWAY, the personable actor who won television fame on the sitcom "Taxi" and movie success in the musical "Grease" and who later publicly struggled with drug and alcohol abuse, died on May 27 in Los Angeles. He was 60.

He died of complications of pneumonia at Encino Tarzana Medical Center after being taken off life support the day before, a talent representative, Phil Brock, said.

Mr. Conaway was found unconscious at his home in the Encino section of the city on May 11 and was medically kept in a coma without ever regaining consciousness, Mr. Brock said. Mr. Conaway, he said, had had severe back problems and was treating himself with painkillers while in weakened health.

Mr. Conaway's addictions to alcohol and drugs were well known because of his appearances in 2008 on the reality series "Celebrity Rehab With Dr. Drew," starring Drew Pinsky. Mr. Conaway often appeared high and belligerent on the show. He had agreed to participate against the wishes of his agents, Mr. Brock said.

Mr. Conaway said numerous back surgeries were responsible for his addiction to painkillers.

In early 2010 he had a serious fall that left him with a brain hemorrhage, a broken hip and a fractured neck.

He spoke openly of his problems in 2008 when he appeared on Howard Stern's radio show and told the host, "I've tried to commit suicide 21 times." Asked about his methods, he replied, "Mostly it's been with pills."

CANDID ACTOR: Mr. Conaway's dependence on drugs and alcohol became well known.

In late February and early March, Mr. Conaway and his girlfriend of seven years, Victoria Spinoza, a singer who records as Vikki Lizzi, filed temporary restraining orders against each other, trading accusations of theft and physical violence.

Mr. Conaway had continued to work in films and television in recent years, but his acting career had plummeted since his greatest popularity, in the late 1970s and early '80s.

The film version of "Grease," starring John Travolta and Olivia Newton-John as improbable high school sweethearts — the rebellious Danny Zuko and the wholesome Sandy — opened in June 1978, with Mr. Conaway in the supporting role of Kenickie, Mr. Travolta's bad-boy sidekick. The tough-talking but vulnerable Kenickie goes through his own trauma, believing that his girlfriend, Rydell High's bad girl Rizzo (Stockard Channing), may be pregnant.

Three months later, "Taxi," a sitcom about a group of New York cabdrivers, had its premiere on ABC. The show's ensemble cast included Judd Hirsch, Danny DeVito, Andy Kaufman, Tony Danza, Christopher Lloyd and Marilu Henner. Mr. Conaway's character, Bobby Wheeler, was a vain and handsome aspiring actor who never seemed to get a break in his show business career.

In an admiring review of the show in 1979, John J. O'Connor, writing in The New York Times, described a scene in which Bobby had accidentally let his friend Tony's two pet fish die. "I guess it was just their time," Bobby tells Tony desperately, adding that maybe the deaths were "one of those murder-suicide things."

The series lasted five seasons, but Mr. Conaway left after the fourth. "I kept doing the same scene for three years," he told The Toronto Star in 1989. "I was underused."

Jeffrey Charles William Michael Conaway was born on Oct. 5, 1950, in New York City. His parents, a struggling actress and an advertising man, divorced when he was a boy, and he divided his time between his mother's apartment in Flushing, Queens, and his maternal grandparents' home in South Carolina.

He began acting as a child and made his Broadway debut when he was 10 in a small part in "All the Way Home," a well-received adaptation of James Agee's novel "A Death in the Family," starring Colleen Dewhurst, Arthur Hill and Lillian Gish.

Growing up, he modeled, appeared in commercials and played in a rock band. He spent a year at the North Carolina School of the Arts, then transferred to New York University. But because of a job offer, he never graduated.

That job was in the original Broadway production of "Grease," which opened in 1972. He understudied several roles but was never cast as Kenickie, the role that made him famous in the film version. He eventually took over the role of Danny, the romantic lead.

A few years after "Taxi," Mr. Conaway returned to Broadway in a new musical, "The News," in which he played the editor of a big-city tabloid. But the reviews were negative, and the show closed after three nights. He continued to appear in films and did television again, most successfully in the 1990s science fiction series "Babylon 5."

His last film work was as the voice-over narrator in two fantasy dramas, "Dante's

Inferno Documented" and "Dante's Purgatorio Documented." His final screen appearance was in the film "Dark Games," a thriller to be released in the summer of 2011.

Mr. Conaway married and divorced three times. After an early marriage that lasted less than a year, he married Rona Newton-John, the sister of his "Grease" co-star, in 1980. They divorced in 1985. His marriage to Keri Young in 1990 ended in the early 2000s. His survivors include two sisters and a stepson, Emerson Newton-John, a race-car driver.

When Mickey Rourke, after fighting his own battles with addiction, earned an Oscar nomination for his performance in "The Wrestler" in 2009, an interviewer asked Mr. Conaway what he thought about Mr. Rourke's comeback.

"Hollywood can be a very stinging town," Mr. Conaway said. "They say it's a forgiving business. It's not that forgiving."

— *By Anita Gates*

GIL SCOTT-HERON

A Social Critic in Song

APRIL 1, 1949 - MAY 27, 2011

Gil Scott-Heron, the poet and recording artist whose syncopated spoken style and mordant critiques of politics, racism and mass media in pieces like "The Revolution Will Not Be Televised" made him a strong voice of black protest in the 1970s and an important influence on hip-hop, died on May 27 in Manhattan. He was 62.

'BLUESOLOGIST': Mr. Scott-Heron performing onstage, around 1970. His music drew on blues, jazz and poetry.

The cause was not immediately known. He had become ill after returning from a trip to Europe and entered a Manhattan hospital, where he died. He was a longtime resident of Harlem.

Mr. Scott-Heron often bristled at the suggestion that his work had prefigured rap. "I don't know if I can take the blame for it," he said in an interview in 2010 with the music Web site The Daily Swarm. He preferred to call himself a "bluesologist," drawing on the traditions of blues, jazz and Harlem renaissance poetics.

Yet, along with the work of the Last Poets, a group of black nationalist performance poets who emerged alongside him in the late 1960s and early '70s, Mr. Scott-Heron established much of the attitude and the stylistic vocabulary that would characterize the socially conscious work of early rap groups like Public Enemy and Boogie Down Productions. His work continues to be sampled by stars like Kanye West.

"You can go into Ginsberg and the Beat poets and Dylan, but Gil Scott-Heron is the manifestation of the modern word," Chuck D, the leader of Public Enemy, told The New Yorker in a profile of Mr. Scott-Heron in 2010. "He and the Last Poets set the stage for everyone else."

Mr. Scott-Heron's early ambitions were literary rather than musical. He was born in Chicago on April 1, 1949, and reared in Tennessee and New York. His mother was a librarian and an English teacher; his estranged father was a Jamaican soccer player.

In his early teens, Mr. Scott-Heron wrote detective stories, earning him a scholarship to the Fieldston School in the Bronx, where he was one of 5 black students in a class of 100. Following in the footsteps of Langston Hughes, he went to the historically black Lincoln University in Pennsylvania. At 19 he wrote his first novel, a murder mystery called "The Vulture." A book of verse, "Small Talk at 125th and Lenox," and a second novel, "The Nigger Factory," soon followed.

Working with a college friend, Brian Jackson, Mr. Scott-Heron turned to music in search of a wider audience. His first album, "Small Talk at 125th and Lenox," was released in 1970 on Flying Dutchman, a small label, and included a live recitation of "Revolution" accompanied by conga and bongo drums. Another version of that piece, recorded with a full band including the jazz bassist Ron Carter, was released on Mr. Scott-Heron's second album, "Pieces of a Man," in 1971.

"Revolution" established Mr. Scott-Heron as a rising star of the black cultural left, and its cool, biting ridicule of a nation anesthetized by mass media has resonated with the socially disaffected of various stripes — campus activists, media theorists, coffeehouse poets — for four decades. With sardonic wit and a barrage of pop-culture references, he derided society's dominating forces as well as the gullibly dominated:

The revolution will not be brought to you by the Schaefer Award Theater and will not star Natalie Wood and Steve McQueen or Bullwinkle and Julia.

The revolution will not give your mouth sex appeal.

The revolution will not get rid of the nubs.

The revolution will not make you look five pounds thinner, because the revolution will not be televised, brother.

During the 1970s, Mr. Scott-Heron was seen as a prodigy, but he never achieved more than cult popularity. He recorded 13 albums from 1970 to 1982, and was one of the first acts the music executive Clive Davis signed after starting Arista Records in 1974. In 1979, Mr. Scott-Heron performed in "No Nukes" benefit concerts at Madison Square Garden, and in 1985 he appeared on the all-star anti-apartheid album "Sun City."

But by the mid-1980s he had begun to fade, his recording output slowing to a trickle. He struggled publicly with addiction. Since 2001, he had been convicted twice for cocaine possession. He served a sentence at Rikers Island in New York for parole violation.

Mr. Scott-Heron often bristled at the suggestion that his work had prefigured rap. "I don't know if I can take the blame for it," he said.

Commentators sometimes used Mr. Scott-Heron's plight to support their contention that New York's drug laws were unjustly harsh.

His friends were horrified by his decline. In interviews he dodged questions about drugs, but the writer of the New Yorker article reported witnessing Mr. Scott-Heron's crack smoking and finding him so troubled by his ravaged appearance that he avoided mirrors. "Ten to 15 minutes of this, I don't have pain," he was quoted as saying as he lighted a glass crack pipe.

That depiction stood in contrast to the musician who had once mocked the psychology of addiction. "You keep sayin' kick it, quit it, kick it, quit it!" he said in his 1971 song "Home Is Where the Hatred Is." "God, did you ever try to turn your sick soul inside out so that the world could watch you die?"

His survivors include a half-brother, a son and two daughters. Mr. Scott-Heron had been working on his memoirs at his death, according to his British publisher, Jamie Byng, who said he hoped to publish them in part.

Despite his personal struggles, Mr. Scott-Heron remained an admired figure in music. He made concert appearances and was sought after as a collaborator. In 2010, the XL label released "I'm New Here," his first album of new material in 16 years. Richard Russell, a British record producer who met Mr. Scott-Heron at Rikers Island in 2006 after writing him a letter, produced the album.

Reviews of the album inevitably called Mr. Scott-Heron the "godfather of rap," but he made it clear he had different tastes.

"It's something that's aimed at the kids," he once said of rap. "I have kids, so I listen to it. But I would not say it's aimed at me. I listen to the jazz station."

— *By Ben Sisario*

ROSALYN S. YALOW

In a Male Preserve, Persistence Paid Off

JULY 19, 1921 - MAY 30, 2011

Rosalyn S. Yalow, a medical physicist who persisted in entering a field largely reserved for men to become only the second woman to earn a Nobel Prize in Medicine, died on May 30 in the Bronx, where she had lived most of her life. She was 89.

Dr. Yalow, a product of New York City schools and the daughter of parents who never finished high school, graduated magna cum laude from Hunter College in New York at the age of 19. Yet she struggled to be accepted for graduate studies.

Undeterred, she went on to carve out a renowned career in medical research, largely at a Bronx veterans hospital, and in the 1950s became a co-discoverer of an extremely sensitive way to measure insulin and other hormones in the blood.

The technique, called radioimmunoassay, invigorated the field of endocrinology, making possible major advances in diabetes research and in diagnosing and treating hormonal problems related to growth, thyroid function and fertility.

One use of the test is to prevent mental retardation in babies with underactive thyroid glands. No symptoms are present until a baby is more than 3 months old, too late to prevent brain damage. But a few drops of blood from a pinprick on the newborn's heel can be analyzed with radioimmunoassay to identify babies at risk.

The technique "brought a revolution in biological and medical research," the Karolinska Institute in Sweden said in awarding Dr. Yalow the Nobel Prize in Physiology or Medicine in 1977.

Dr. Yalow developed the technique with her longtime collaborator, Dr. Solomon A. Berson. Their work challenged what was then accepted wisdom about the immune system; skeptical medical journals initially refused to publish their findings.

Dr. Berson died in 1972, before Dr. Yalow was honored with the Nobel; the institute does not make awards posthumously. (Gerty Theresa Cori, an American born in Prague, was the first woman to be awarded a Nobel in medicine, in 1947, and eight more women have received that prize since Dr. Yalow did.)

"We are witnessing the birth of a new era of endocrinology," the Karolinska Institute said when the 1977 prize was awarded, "one that started with Yalow."

Rosalyn Sussman was born in the South Bronx on July 19, 1921. Her father, Simon Sussman, was a wholesaler of packaging materials who had moved from the Lower East Side of Manhattan to the Bronx; her mother, the former Clara Zipper, who was born in Germany, was a homemaker.

In an era when women were all but prohibited from science careers, Dr. Yalow knew from the time she was 8 years old that she wanted to be a scientist, she told interviewers. She loved the logic of science and its ability to explain the natural world, she said.

LAUREATE: Dr. Yalow was the second woman to earn a Nobel Prize in Medicine.

At Walton High School in the Bronx, she wrote, a "great" teacher had excited her interest in chemistry. (She was one of two Walton graduates, both women, to earn a Nobel in medicine, the other being Gertrude Elion, in 1988. Walton was closed in 2008 as a failing school.) Dr. Yalow's interests gravitated to physics after she read Eve Curie's 1937 biography of her mother, Marie Curie, a two-time Nobel laureate for her research on radioactivity.

Nuclear physics "was the most exciting field in the world," Dr. Yalow wrote in her official Nobel autobiography. "It seemed as if every major experiment brought a Nobel Prize."

She went on to Hunter College, becoming its first physics major. After she applied to Purdue University for a graduate assistantship to study physics, the university wrote back to her professor: "She is from New York. She is Jewish. She is a woman. If you can guarantee her a job afterward, we'll give her an assistantship."

No guarantee was possible, and the rejection hurt. "They told me that as a woman, I'd never get into graduate school in physics," she later said in an interview, "so they got me a job as a secretary at the College of Physicians and Surgeons and promised that, if I were a good girl, I would take courses there." The college is part of Columbia University.

World War II and the drafting of men into the military were creating academic opportunities for women; to her delight, Dr. Yalow was awarded a teaching assistantship at the College of Engineering at the University of Illinois. She tore up her steno books and headed to Champaign-Urbana, becoming the first woman to teach at the engineering school in 24 years.

There she faced pressure to prove herself. When she received an A-minus in one laboratory course, the chairman of the physics department said the grade confirmed that women could not excel at lab work; the slight fueled her determination.

She married a fellow graduate student, Aaron Yalow, in 1943. He died in 1992. Dr. Yalow received her doctorate in nuclear physics in 1945, and went to teach at Hunter College the following year. When she could not find a research position, she volunteered to work in a medical lab at Columbia University, where she was introduced to the new field of radiotherapy. She moved to the Bronx Veterans Administration Hospital (now the James J. Peters Veterans Affairs Medical Center) as a part-time researcher in 1947 and began working full time in 1950. That same year, she began her 22-year collaboration with Dr. Berson.

Dr. Berson was seen as the dominant partner. By virtue of his gender and medical degree, he had more contacts with journals and professional societies and in academia. Dr. Yalow was single-minded about her research, living near the hospital in a modest house for much of her professional life, never taking up hobbies and traveling only to lecture and attend conferences.

In their work on radioimmunoassay, Dr. Yalow and Dr. Berson used radioactive tracers to measure hormones that were otherwise difficult or impossible to detect because they occur in extremely low concentrations. They went on to use the test to measure concentrations of vitamins, viruses and other substances in the body. Today the test has been largely supplanted by a technique that does not use radioactivity.

Their early work met resistance. After discovering insulin antibodies, a finding fundamental to radioimmunoassay and one that challenged the accepted understanding of the immune system, scientific journals at first refused to publish their research. Few scientists believed antibodies could recognize a molecule as small as insulin. Dr. Yalow and Dr. Berson had to delete a reference to antibodies before The Journal of Clinical Investigation would accept their paper, and Dr. Yalow did not forget the incident; she included the original rejection letter as an exhibit in her Nobel lecture.

With Dr. Berson, Dr. Yalow made other discoveries. She determined that people with Type 2 diabetes produced more insulin than nondiabetics, providing early evidence that an inability to use insulin caused diabetes. Researchers in her lab at the Bronx hospital modified radioimmunoassay to detect other hormones, vitamin B12 and the hepatitis B virus. The latter adaptation allowed blood banks to screen donated blood for the virus.

Dr. Berson's death affected Dr. Yalow deeply; she named her lab in his honor so that his name would continue to appear on her published research.

She was elected to the National Academy of Sciences in 1975 and, the following year, received the Albert Lasker Medical Research Award, often a precursor to the Nobel. At her death she was senior medical investigator emeritus at the Bronx veterans medical center and the Solomon A. Berson distinguished professor-at-large at Mount Sinai School of Medicine in New York. She is survived by a son, a daughter and two grandchildren.

Five years after she received the Nobel, sharing the prize with two others for unrelated research, Dr. Yalow spoke to a group of schoolchildren about the challenges and opportunities of a life in science. "Initially, new ideas are rejected," she told the youngsters. "Later they become dogma, if you're right. And if you're really lucky you can publish your rejections as part of your Nobel presentation."

— *By Denise Gellene;*
Gina Kolata contributed reporting.

PAULINE BETZ ADDIE

A Tennis Champion Banished at Her Peak

AUG. 16, 1919 - MAY 31, 2011

Pauline Betz Addie, a dominant American tennis champion who at the height of her amateur career in the 1940s was abruptly barred from the sport because she had openly considered turning professional, died on May 31 in Potomac, Md. She was 91.

Betz Addie, who was groomed on the tennis courts of Los Angeles, was a five-time Grand Slam singles champion and the world's top-ranked woman when in April 1947 the United States Lawn Tennis Association notified her by cable — she was in Monte Carlo at the time while competing in Europe — that she was barred indefinitely from taking part in any further amateur matches.

Another American player, Sarah Palfrey Cooke, a multiple Grand Slam champion, was also suspended. The two were ruled ineligible for the 1947 French Open.

Betz, who was 27 at the time (and had not yet married and added her husband's name), had spoken openly about possibly leaving the amateur ranks and touring for pay with the likes of Jack Kramer and Gussie Moran. She and Cooke had discussed doing so together, and Cooke's husband, Elwood Cooke, had sent a letter to the tennis association's member clubs soliciting bookings. The letter, specifying fees the women would expect to receive, prompted the lawn tennis association to suspend them.

Betz had written to Cooke, who lived in Manhattan, asking how their plans for touring were coming, but she had not signed any professional contracts when the association made its ruling. Her defenders called the decision unjust and premature.

"She was ruled out as an amateur on the basis of intent," Kramer wrote (with Frank Deford) in his 1979 memoir "The Game: My 40 Years in Tennis." He likened the Betz suspension "to what the Olympic committee did to Jim Thorpe" when it took away Thorpe's Olympic titles because he had earlier played semiprofessional baseball.

"It was a crime," Kramer wrote.

After the ruling, Betz said, "I'm not going to sit in a corner and cry about this."

She then began an entertaining but historically insignificant stint on the fledgling professional tour circuit, abandoning her Grand Slam career to play for pay from 1947 to 1960. As a professional, earning $10,000 her first year, she went undefeated in a field far less challenging than the amateur ranks.

At the time of her suspension, she had been undefeated in her last 39 matches, earning the No. 1 ranking. She owned a half-dozen Grand Slam titles, five in singles, a lonely discipline in which she excelled by virtue of her athleticism and a competitive streak so fierce that she routinely thrashed her outclassed opponents without surrendering more than a couple of points. Her Grand Slam doubles crown came in the French Open's mixed doubles competition in 1946.

Her news media coverage was often gushing. In 1946 she made the cover of Time magazine. "Pauline is a trim 5 ft. 5; her hair is strawberry blonde, sun bleached and wiry," the accompanying article said. "Principally because of her green eyes she seems to have a ready-to-pounce, feline quality. A straightening of her shoulders is a characteristic mannerism — a squaring away that seems to symbolize in an otherwise relaxed girl a won't-be-beat spirit."

Betz Addie said her first wish was to be remembered as a good wife and parent. Her backup wish? To be remembered as one of the best of her era.

Though World War II curtailed Betz's ability to test herself on foreign surfaces, she won on the grass courts of Wimbledon in 1946 — the only year she competed there.

At home, however, she was a demon on all surfaces. After capturing the national indoor and clay titles in 1943, she prevailed on the grass at Forest Hills in Queens, where she fought her way to a record six consecutive finals from 1941 to 1946, winning four.

Betz's only defeats during that streak came in 1941 and 1945 against Cooke, Betz's stylistic opposite, who was superb hitting volleys. Betz referred to her as "a good friend and a thorn in my side." Cooke joined the professional circuit just ahead of Betz in 1947.

In 1949 Betz married Bob Addie, a sportswriter for The Washington Post, taking his surname. The next year, the player-turned-promoter Bobby Riggs persuaded her to join a co-ed barnstorming circuit featuring Pancho Segura as well as Kramer and Moran. Betz Addie and Moran (Gorgeous Gussie in the news media) became circuit rivals, Betz Addie wearing leopard print short-shorts to compete with Moran's famous lacy panties, which had caused an international stir at Wimbledon in 1949.

IN PEAK FORM: Betz during a 1946 Wimbledon match. At one point the world's top-ranked female player, she appeared on the cover of Time. A year later, she was abruptly barred from amateur matches.

In one match, Betz Addie outplayed Moran so thoroughly that Riggs asked her to be more merciful so that his floundering tour might appear genuinely competitive. She refused to lower her standards.

The tour was short-lived, but Betz continued to play professionally until 1960 while also teaching tennis. In 1955, she became the first woman to be named club professional at Bethesda's historic Edgemoor Tennis Club. The actor Spencer Tracy, a former boyfriend, was among her students.

Pauline May Betz was born on Aug. 16, 1919, in Dayton, Ohio, and raised in Los Angeles, where her tennis-playing mother taught physical education in the Watts section. Pauline bought her first tennis racket when she was 9, trading some of her father's pipe collection for it at a thrift shop; her father made her take on a paper route to pay him back.

Her quickness on her feet and her piercing backhand passing shot soon distinguished her as a potential star on the local public courts. In 1939 she attained her first national ranking in the top 10; she was 19. That same year she received a scholarship from Rollins College in Florida, where she played on the men's tennis team, filling the No. 4 spot behind No. 1 Kramer.

In college she was a gifted all-around athlete, whether playing table tennis, golf or pickup basketball games with men. After graduating in 1943, she climbed to the top of both the United States and international rankings.

Betz Addie and her husband, who died in 1982, had four sons and a daughter, all of whom survive her, as do five grandchildren and a great-grandson.

Motherhood did not diminish her on-court tenacity. In a 1959 exhibition, when she was five months pregnant with her fifth child, she defeated Althea Gibson, the first black woman to win a Grand Slam title. Betz Addie was inducted into the International Tennis Hall of Fame in 1965. In 1997, she marched in the United States Open parade of champions to help christen Arthur Ashe Stadium in Flushing Meadows in Queens.

Until 2003 she continued to compete at the club level, in part, she said, to "keep up" with her grandchildren. She also taught tennis at Sidwell Friends School and at clubs in the Washington area. She wrote two books, "Wings on My Tennis Shoes" and "Tennis for Teenagers."

Betz Addie said her first wish was to be remembered as a good wife and parent. Her backup wish? To be remembered as one of the best of her era. Kramer paid her that honor in his memoir, calling her the second-best female player he had ever seen, behind Helen Wills Moody. Betz Addie, he said, was "terribly underrated."

— *By Robin Finn*

ANDY ROBUSTELLI

In Football's Trenches, Lifting the Giants

DEC. 6, 1925 - MAY 31, 2011

Andy Robustelli, the Giants' Hall of Fame defensive end in their glory years of the late 1950s and early '60s, when shouts of "DEE-fense" rang from the stands at Yankee Stadium, died on May 31 in Stamford, Conn., his hometown. He was 85.

In the autumn of 1956, the Giants, one of the N.F.L.'s oldest franchises, finally vied with baseball's Yankees as a glamour attraction on the New York sports scene. The Giants' offense featured stars like Charlie Conerly, Frank Gifford, Kyle Rote, Alex Webster and Roosevelt Brown.

But it was the defensive alignment, featuring Robustelli, Roosevelt Grier, Dick Modzelewski and Jim Katcavage on the line, Sam Huff at middle linebacker, and a secondary led by Emlen Tunnell, that captured the fans' imagination. They evoked a celebrity aura, captured in the television documentary "The Violent World of Sam Huff."

"Never in the history of football had fans gone to a stadium to root for a 'DEE-fense,'" Gifford, a Hall of Fame halfback and receiver, recalled in his memoir, "The Whole Ten Yards."

Robustelli was a 19th-round draft pick of the Los Angeles Rams in 1951 out of tiny Arnold College in Milford, Conn., but he became a hard-hitting tackler, at 6 feet 1 inch and 230 pounds, and a superb pass-rusher with a keen sense of how an opponent's plays were developing.

He played in eight N.F.L. championship games, two with the Rams and six with the Giants after joining them in 1956. He was a first-team All-Pro six times, received the Maxwell Club's Bert Bell Award as the N.F.L.'s most outstanding player in 1962 and recovered 22 fumbles. He missed only one game in his 14 seasons, in the last three doubling as a Giants assistant. He was elected to the Pro Football Hall of Fame in 1971.

In 1974, Robustelli joined the Giants' front office as director of operations — essentially the general manager — and tried with little success to rebuild a losing team before leaving the post in 1978.

Robustelli, at right end, was part of a storied Giants defensive line that included Grier at right tackle, Modzelewski at left tackle and Katcavage at left end. They played together from 1956 to 1962, a remarkable stretch for a unit in football's trenches.

"We didn't want — we were afraid — to have substitutions, afraid they'd take our job away," Robustelli told Gerald Eskenazi, a reporter for The New York Times, in Eskenazi's book

"There Were Giants in Those Days."

"We just didn't want anybody else to have a shot at it, so we stayed in there all the time."

Tom Landry, the Giants' defensive coordinator in Robustelli's heyday, remembered Robustelli's devotion to the game. "He put more book time into his work than the others," Landry once said. "He thought all the time. Not just on the field, but in his room, at the dining table."

DEE-FENSE! From left, Robustelli, Roosevelt Grier, Dick Modzelewski and Jim Katcavage of the Giants.

Gifford said in a statement after Robustelli's death that "whereas Tom was the overall defensive coach, Andy basically ran the defensive line along with the linebackers."

"He was the leader in the clubhouse. He was quiet, but when Andy talked, everyone listened."

Andrew Richard Robustelli was born in Stamford on Dec. 6, 1925. His father, Lucien, was a barber; his mother, Katie, a seamstress. The young Robustelli played football, basketball and baseball at Stamford High School, served in the Navy during World War II, then played end on offense and defense at Arnold, a school with only a few hundred students. (It was later absorbed by the University of Bridgeport in Connecticut.)

As a rookie with the Rams, Robustelli had virtually no chance of beating out the star receivers Tom Fears and Crazy Legs Hirsch but won a job at defensive end for the Rams team that captured the 1951 N.F.L. championship.

When he was traded to the Giants in 1956, he became a key figure in a 4-3 alignment — four down linemen and three linebackers — installed by Landry.

The Giants defeated the Chicago Bears, 47-7, in the 1956 N.F.L. championship game on a frozen Yankee Stadium field, aided by sneakers from Robustelli's sporting goods store in Stamford. They won five division titles between 1958 and 1963 but lost in the championship game each time.

After retiring as a player at the end of the 1964 season, Robustelli expanded his business interests, opening a travel agency and a sports marketing business in Stamford. Ten years later, on his return to the Giants as director of operations, he inherited a team that had won only two games the previous season.

He soon hired Bill Arnsparger, the architect of the Miami Dolphins' defense, to replace Webster, the former Giants halfback, as head coach, but the Giants continued to founder. Their woes climaxed in November 1978 with "the fumble," a botched Giants handoff that was run into the end zone by the Philadelphia Eagles' Herm Edwards for a game-winning touchdown on the final play. John McVay, who had replaced Arnsparger two years earlier, was fired after that season, and Robustelli, who had been planning to leave, returned to his business interests after five losing seasons.

Robustelli is survived by six sons, three daughters, 29 grandchildren and 6 great-grandchildren. His wife, Jeanne, died in April 2011.

Long after his playing days ended, Robustelli reflected on his celebrated teammates, recalling a spirited rivalry between the offensive players and the defense. "I don't think the two ever got close," he told The Times in 1985.

As for the defense's mystique, Gifford wrote in his memoir how "everyone knew who Andy Robustelli was, and that he had a wife and three kids and lived in Connecticut," and how "Sam Huff even made the cover of Time magazine."

"If they made one of their famous goal-line stands, we'd hear about it for a week," Gifford remembered. "Or if they recovered a fumble, Sam might walk by me as I started onto the field and say, 'See if you can hold 'em for a while.' "

— *By Richard Goldstein*

HANS KEILSON

At 100, a Literary 'Genius' Reborn

DEC. 12, 1909 - MAY 31, 2011

HANS KEILSON, a German-born psychoanalyst who won literary fame at the very end of his long life when two of his long-forgotten works of fiction, set in Nazi-occupied Europe, were republished to great acclaim, died on May 31 in Hilversum, the Netherlands. He was 101.

Dr. Keilson, a physician by training, published his first novel at 23. That book, "Life Goes On," offered a dark picture of German political life between the wars, reflected in the troubles encountered by Max, a Jewish store owner modeled on Dr. Keilson's father, a textile merchant. It was banned by the Nazis in 1934.

Two years later Dr. Keilson emigrated to the Netherlands with his future wife, Gertrud Manz. He began a new novel, "The Death of the Adversary," about a young Jewish man's experiences in Germany as the Nazis gain a grip on power, but he put the manuscript aside after the German occupation of the Netherlands in 1940 forced him into hiding in Delft.

His experiences provided the material for the novella "Comedy in a Minor Key," about a Dutch couple who shelter an elderly Jew who dies of natural causes. After disposing of the body carelessly, they, too, must go into hiding.

The novella was published by a German-language Amsterdam press in 1947, the same year Anne Frank's diary was released. "The Death of the Adversary," which Dr. Keilson resumed writing after the war, came out in Germany in 1959, and a stilted English translation appeared in 1962. A brief notice in The New York Times described it as a "novel of suspense."

ONCE FORGOTTEN: Dr. Keilson's novels were rediscovered decades after they were first published.

Although the novel sold well and Time magazine named it one of the top 10 books of the year, along with works like Nabokov's "Pale Fire" and Katherine Anne Porter's "Ship of Fools," Dr. Keilson slipped into literary obscurity. He wrote no more fiction, he later said, because he believed that he no longer had an audience.

In 2007, Damion Searls, a literary translator, chanced upon "Comedy in a Minor Key" in an Austrian bookstore's sidewalk bargain bin and mounted a campaign to resurrect Dr. Keilson's works. In 2010, Farrar, Straus & Giroux reissued "The Death of the Adversary," which was translated to English by Ivo Jarosy in 1962. Mr. Searls's translation of "Comedy in a Minor Key" was also published in Britain by Hesperus Press.

The novelist Francine Prose, in The New York Times Book Review, declared both works masterpieces and their author, then 100, a genius. "Rarely have such harrowing narratives been related with such wry, off-kilter humor, and in so quiet a whisper," she wrote. "Read these books and join me in adding him to the list, which each of us must compose on our own, of the world's very greatest writers."

Hans Alex Keilson was born on Dec. 12, 1909, in Bad Freienwalde, a spa town near the Polish border. He studied medicine in Berlin, but because of Nazi racial laws he was unable to practice as a doctor. Instead he taught swimming and gymnastics at Jewish schools.

After his first novel was banned, his publisher, Samuel Fischer, told him to leave Germany as quickly as possible. Ms. Manz, his future wife, a graphologist, had also sensed impending disaster. After Dr. Keilson showed her a sample of Hitler's handwriting in 1935, she said, "He's going to set the world on fire."

In the Netherlands he established a pediatric practice but, out of caution, lived in a separate house from Ms. Manz, a Roman Catholic, on the same street. When their daughter was born in 1941, she said that the father was a German soldier.

Soon after the German occupation, Dr. Keilson was asked to join the Vrije Groepen Amsterdam, a resistance organization. For the rest of the war, supplied with a false Dutch passport, he traveled the country under the name Van den Linden, counseling Jewish children and teenagers separated from their parents and living underground.

This work motivated him to train as a psychoanalyst. He helped found the organization L'Ezrat Ha-Yeled (Children's Aid) to care for and treat Jewish orphans who had survived the Holocaust. In 1979 he completed his dissertation, "Sequential Traumatization in Children," a groundbreaking work on the effects of the war on orphaned and displaced Jewish children in the Netherlands.

Ms. Manz died in 1969. Dr. Keilson, who lived in Bussum, an Amsterdam suburb, is survived by his second wife, Marita Keilson-Lauritz, two daughters and three granddaughters.

Dr. Keilson brought his parents to the Netherlands in 1938, but his father, decorated with the Iron Cross for valor in World War I, hoped that his war record would protect him, and refused to go into hiding. The couple were rounded up and sent to Auschwitz, where they perished.

In his books Dr. Keilson handled heavy themes with a light hand. Hitler, the looming presence in "The Death of the Adversary," is never identified by name, only as "B" by the novel's young Jewish narrator. With artful indirection, Dr. Keilson delineated the psychology of dread, evasion, hatred and self-deception, and the complex relations between Jews and non-Jews in 1930s Germany.

In a different vein, but just as subtly, "Comedy in a Minor Key" found the humor and pathos in the almost accidental decency of ordinary people responding to morally horrific circumstances. The unexpected death of their boarder, a perfume salesman they know only as Nico, grieves Wim and Marie, the couple who hide him — but it's irksome, too.

"She had secretly imagined what it would be like on liberation day, the three of them arm in arm walking out of their house," the narrator writes of Marie. "It would give them a little sense of satisfaction, and everyone who makes a sacrifice needs a little sense of satisfaction. And then you'd feel that you, you personally, even if only just a little bit, had won the war."

In a wry coda, the narrator continues: "None of the three of them had any luck. But really, him least of all. Poor Nico!"

"There Stands My House," a memoir, was published in Germany in April, only weeks before his death. Dr. Keilson's first novel, in a translation by Mr. Searls, was to be published in 2012 by Farrar, Straus & Giroux.

Dr. Keilson, who insisted that his psychoanalytic work was more important than his fiction, reacted with surprise at the fuss over his books. "I'm not even a proper writer," he told The Observer of London in 2010.

But then he reconsidered. "Maybe I did manage to produce something which goes beyond the everyday," he said. "It's not unusual for works of literature to be rediscovered decades after they were written. But the odd thing with my situation is that I am still alive while that's happening."

— *By William Grimes*

news media, he became involved in the growing national debate on dying with dignity. In 1987 he visited the Netherlands, where he studied techniques that allowed Dutch physicians to assist in the suicides of terminally ill patients without interference from the legal authorities.

A year later, he returned to Michigan and began advertising in Detroit-area newspapers for a new medical practice in what he called "bioethics and obiatry," which would offer patients and their families "death counseling." He made reporters aware of his intentions, explaining that he did not charge for his services and bore all the expenses of euthanasia himself. He showed journalists the simple metal frame from which he suspended vials of drugs — the sedative thiopental and potassium chloride, which paralyzed the heart — that allowed patients to end their own lives.

He also talked about the "doctrine" he had developed to achieve two goals: ensuring the patient's comfort and protecting himself against criminal conviction. He required patients to express clearly a wish to die. Family physicians and mental health professionals were consulted. Patients were given at least a month to consider their decision and possibly change their minds. He videotaped interviews with patients, their families and their friends, and he videotaped the suicides, which he called medicides.

On June 4, 1990, Janet Adkins, an Oregon teacher who suffered from Alzheimer's disease, was the first patient to use Dr. Kevorkian's assistance. Mrs. Adkins's life ended on the bed inside Dr. Kevorkian's rusting 1968 Volkswagen van, which was parked in a campground near his home.

Immediately afterward he called the police, who arrested and briefly detained him. The next day Ron Adkins, Mrs. Adkins's husband, and two of his sons held a news conference in Portland and read the suicide note that Mrs. Adkins had prepared. In an interview with The New York Times that day, Dr. Kevorkian alerted the nation to his campaign.

"My ultimate aim is to make euthanasia a positive experience," he said. "I'm trying to knock the medical profession into accepting its responsibilities, and those responsibilities include assisting their patients with death."

By his account, he assisted in some 130 suicides over the next eight years. Patients from across the country traveled to the Detroit area to seek his help. Sometimes the procedure was done in homes, cars and campgrounds.

Prosecutors, jurists, the State Legislature, the Michigan health authorities and Gov. John Engler seemed helpless to stop him, though they spent years trying. In 1991 a state judge, Alice Gilbert, issued a permanent injunction barring Dr. Kevorkian from using his suicide machine. The same year, the state suspended his license to practice medicine. In 1993, Michigan approved a statute outlawing assisted suicide. The statute was declared unlawful by a state judge and the state Court of Appeals, but in 1994 the Michigan Supreme Court ruled that assisting in a suicide, while not specifically prohibited by statute, was a common-law felony and that there was no protected right to suicide assistance under the state Constitution.

None of the legal restrictions seemed to matter to Dr. Kevorkian. Several times he assisted in patient suicides just hours after being released from custody for helping in a previous one. After one arrest in 1993 he refused to post bond, and a day later he said he was on a hunger strike. During another arrest he fought with police officers and seemed to welcome the opportunity to be jailed.

He liked the attention. At the start of his third trial, on April 1, 1996, he showed up in court wearing Colonial-era clothing to show how antiquated he thought the charges were.

From May 1994 to June 1997, Dr. Kevorkian stood trial four times in the deaths of six patients. With the help of his young and flamboyant defense lawyer, Mr. Fieger, three of those trials ended in acquittals, and the fourth was declared a mistrial.

Mr. Fieger based his winning defense on the compassion and mercy that he said Dr. Kevorkian had shown his patients. Prosecutors felt differently. "He's basically thumbed his nose at law enforcement, in part because he feels he has public support," Richard Thompson, the prosecutor in Oakland County, Mich., told Time magazine in 1993.

But on March 26, 1999, after a trial that lasted less than two days, a Michigan jury found Dr. Kevorkian guilty of second-degree murder. That trial came six months after Dr. Kevorkian had videotaped himself injecting Thomas Youk, a patient suffering from amyotrophic lateral sclerosis (Lou Gehrig's disease), with the lethal drugs that caused Mr. Youk's death on Sept. 17, 1998.

Dr. Kevorkian sent the videotape to "60 Minutes," which broadcast it on Nov. 22. The tape showed Dr. Kevorkian going well beyond assisting a patient in causing his own death by performing the injection himself. The program portrayed him as a zealot with an agenda. "They must charge me; either they go or I go," he told Mike Wallace. "If they go, that means they'll never convict me in a court of law."

The broadcast prompted a national debate about medical ethics and media responsibility. It also served as prime evidence for a first-degree murder charge brought by the Oakland County prosecutor's office. In a departure from his previous trials, Dr. Kevorkian ignored Mr. Fieger's advice and defended himself — and not at all well. It was an act of arrogance he regretted, he said later.

"You had the audacity to go on national television, show the world what you did and dare the legal system to stop you," said Judge Jessica R. Cooper, who presided over the trial in Oakland County Circuit Court. "Well, sir, consider yourself stopped."

On June 1, 2007, Dr. Kevorkian was released from prison after he promised not to conduct another assisted suicide.

He was born Murad Kevorkian in Pontiac, Mich., on May 26, 1928, the second of three children and the only son born to Levon and Satenig Kevorkian, Armenian refugees. His father founded and owned a small excavation company.

Friends described the young Jack Kevorkian as an able student interested in art and music. He pursued a degree in engineering at the University of Michigan before switching to medicine and graduating in 1952.

He was the author of four books, including "Prescription: Medicide, the Goodness of Planned Death," published in 1991. He is survived by a sister; another sister died in 1994.

Weakened as he lay in the hospital, Dr. Kevorkian could not take advantage of the option that he had offered others and that he had wished for himself. "This is something I would want," Dr. Kevorkian once said.

"If he had enough strength to do something about it, he would have," Mr. Fieger said at a news conference in Southfield, Mich. "Had he been able to go home, Jack Kevorkian probably would not have allowed himself to go back to the hospital."

Dr. Kevorkian was a lover of classical music, and as his death drew near, according to a friend, nurses played recordings of Bach for him in his room.

— *By Keith Schneider*

HARRY BERNSTEIN

At 96, at Long Last, a Literary Sensation

MAY 30, 1910 - JUNE 3, 2011

Harry Bernstein, whose painfully eloquent memoir about growing up Jewish and poor in a northern English mill town earned him belated literary fame on its publication in 2007, when he was 96, died on June 3 in Brooklyn. He was 101.

In "The Invisible Wall: A Love Story That Broke Barriers," Mr. Bernstein described a childhood defined by grinding poverty and the unspoken divide separating Jews and Christians living on opposite sides of the same working-class street.

In spare, weighty prose, he evoked a long-vanished world of textile workers whose iron-soled clogs raised sparks on the cobblestones, of bicycle messengers delivering telegrams to families whose sons had been killed in the trenches of Flanders.

PERSISTENCE: Mr. Bernstein at work in 2007, the year his memoir was published.

With understated poignancy, he revisited the domestic dramas that made his family life an ordeal. His rage-filled, alcoholic father, a tailor, ruled the household like a vengeful god. His older sister, Lily, by falling in love with the son of a Christian shopkeeper, precipitated a crisis that his long-suffering mother saw in apocalyptic terms.

"I do not want to sit shiva for my daughter," she wrote to relatives in Chicago, referring to the Jewish period of mourning, as she begged for a steamship ticket for the imperiled young woman. "I do not want her to die."

The book was greeted with critical admiration, mingled with astonishment at the author's advanced age. But Mr. Bernstein was not finished.

"The first 25 years of my life are something I would rather forget, but the contrary has taken place," he told The Guardian of London in 2007. "The older I get the more alive those years have become."

A second installment of his memoirs, "The Dream," published in 2008, continued his life story, picking up the narrative with the family's move to Chicago in 1922 and describing Mr. Bernstein's struggles to become a writer.

His 67-year marriage to the former Ruby Umflat provided the material for his third volume of memoirs, "The Golden Willow: The Story of a Lifetime of Love," which was published in 2009.

Harry Louis Bernstein was born on May 30, 1910, in Stockport, now part of greater Manchester, where his parents had emigrated from Poland. His father, emotionally brutalized as a child and abandoned by his parents, tyrannized his timid wife and seven cowering children. When his daughter Lily won a scholarship to a prestigious grammar school, he dragged her by the hair to his tailor shop and put her to work, one of the more horrific episodes in "The Invisible Wall."

"I learned hatred from my father, but I learned love from my mother," Mr. Bernstein told The Chicago Sun-Times in 2008.

The family settled in the Humboldt Park neighborhood of Chicago, and Harry attended Lane Technical Preparatory School. After an instructor poured cold water on his dream of becoming an architect, he began writing.

"I was so confident I was going to do so well in the world," he told The Sun-Times. "I was writing for the school magazine, and I was a big shot."

After moving to New York, he published short stories in magazines like Story and Literary America and proletarian publications like The Anvil, but success eluded him.

Clifton Fadiman, the chief editor of Simon & Schuster, invited him to submit a novel, and Mr. Bernstein sent him "Hard Times and White Collars," about the working-class despair experienced by American executives during the Depression. It was rejected, but through Fadiman he found work as a script reader for Columbia Pictures.

In 1935 he met his future wife, an émigré from Poland, at a dance at Webster Hall in Manhattan organized by the League Against War and Fascism. The two soon married. His wife died in 2002; he is survived by their two children, one of whom he had been living with in Brooklyn Heights, as well as four grandchildren, three step-grandchildren and four step-great-grandchildren.

In the 1950s Mr. Bernstein tried to eke out a living as a freelance writer, selling work to The Daily News in New York, Popular Mechanics and Family Circle, but he ended up editing Home of

Tomorrow, a construction trade magazine, while his wife worked as a school secretary in Queens.

He continued to write fiction. "The Smile," his novel about the rise and fall of a fashion model, was published by West End Press in 1981 but sold poorly. Mr. Bernstein used to joke that he knew it sold at least one copy because a reader sent him a letter.

His wife's death left Mr. Bernstein bereft and unoccupied. "I was too much alone," he told The Star-Ledger of Newark. "My wife was dead. My friends were mostly gone. And so I found myself thinking about my past, and the people I knew and the place I grew up. I was looking for a home."

He sent the manuscript of "The Invisible Wall" to several New York publishers, who turned it down. It sat for a year in the unsolicited manuscript pile at Random House in Britain before an editor sent it along to Kate Elton, the publishing director at the Random House imprint Arrow, who called it "unputdownable." It was published in Britain by Hutchinson, another Random House imprint, and by Ballantine Books in the United States.

Mr. Bernstein had a large following in Italy, among other places. His next book, "What Happened to Rose," is to be published there in Italian by Edizioni Piemme in 2012.

— By William Grimes

Andrew Gold

A Soundtrack for the '70s

AUG. 2, 1951 - JUNE 3, 2011

Andrew Gold, who as a music wunderkind had a strong hand in shaping the Los Angeles-dominated pop-rock style of the 1970s, accompanying a bevy of stars in the studio and writing and recording hits like "Lonely Boy" and "Thank You for Being a Friend," died on June 3 at his home in Encino, Calif. He was 59.

His family said he had renal cancer and had died of heart failure.

A versatile musician — he played guitar, piano, bass and drums — Mr. Gold had barely finished high school when Linda Ronstadt enlisted him to play in her backup band, the Stone Poneys. Soon his instrumental and arranging work, as well as his voice, could be heard on her breakout 1974 album, "Heart Like a Wheel," in particular an admired guitar solo on "You're No Good," Ms. Ronstadt's hit version of the Clint Ballard Jr. tune.

He went on to become a much sought after studio musician, helping to define the seamless texture of recordings by James Taylor, Carly Simon, Maria Muldaur, Jackson Browne, Loudon Wainwright III and others.

After several years performing and recording with Ms. Ronstadt, Mr. Gold began a solo career that produced its first hit with "Lonely Boy." The song reached No. 7 on the Billboard singles chart in 1977 and led to other popular releases like "Never Let Her Slip Away," as well as four solo albums before the decade was over.

His "Thank You for Being a Friend," another mainstay of Top 40 radio, later became the theme song for the long-running NBC sitcom "The Golden Girls."

He also continued to collaborate with some of the biggest stars of the era, among them Art Garfunkel, Brian Wilson, Don Henley, Cher, Diana Ross and three former Beatles: John Lennon, Paul McCartney and Ringo Starr.